Jaroslava Hlaváčová (Ed.)

I0018757

ITAT 2017: Information Technologies – Applications and Theory

Proceedings of the 17th conference ITAT 2017

Martinské hole, Slovakia, September 22–26, 2017

ITAT 2017: Information Technologies – Applications and Theory
Proceedings of the 17th conference ITAT 2017
Martinské hole, Malá Fatra, Slovakia, September 22–26, 2017
Jaroslava Hlaváčová (Ed.)
Cover design: Róbert Novotný
Cover photo: Jiří Brožovský

Publisher: CreateSpace Independent Publishing Platform, 2017
ISBN 978-1974274741

Also published online by CEUR Workshop Proceedings vol. 1885
http://ceur-ws.org/Vol-1885/
ISSN 1613-0073

These proceedings contain papers from the conference ITAT 2017. All authors agreed to publish their papers in these proceedings. All papers were reviewed by at least two anonymous referees.

http://www.itat.cz/

Preface

The 17th annual conference ITAT took place in Hotel Martinské hole, Slovakia, at an altitude of 1223 m, from 22 to 26 September 2017.

ITAT, meaning Information Technologies — Applications and Theory, is a place where young researchers, doctoral students and their teachers meet every year to present their results from the various fields of computer science. They come mainly from the Czech and Slovak republic, but the conference is open to participants from other countries as well. In addition to the professional program, much time is devoted to informal discussions, and above all to the formation and maintenance of friendly relations between scientists from the both countries. The Slovak mountains make a perfect background for that. The 2017 conference consisted of the main track and 3 workshops:

- CIDM (Computational Intelligence and Data Mining)

- SloNLP (Slovenskočeský NLP workshop)

- W3-ChaT (WWW-Challenges and Trends)

All the 37 submitted papers were reviewed by two or more independent reviewers. The proceedings contain 34 scientific papers and abstracts of four invited talks:

Jiří Hana (Geneea): *Text Generation in Natural Languages*

Antoni Ligęza (AGH University of Science and Technology in Kraków, Poland): *Rules, Causality and Constraints. Model-Based Reasoning and Structural Knowledge Discovery*

Ostap Okhrin (Dresden University of Technology, Germany): *Estimations of the Hierarchical Archimedean Copula*

Lubomír Soukup (ÚTIA): *How Accurate Are Digital Maps?*

The conference was organized by Institute of Computer Science, The Faculty of Natural Sciences, P. J. Šafárik University, Košice, University of Žilina, Institute of Computer Science, The Academy of Sciences of the Czech Republic, Prague, The Faculty of Mathematics and Physics, Charles University, Prague Slovenská spoločnosť pre umelú inteligenciu (Slovak society for artificial intelligence). I would like to thank all organizers led by the conference spirit Peter Gurský, also to workshop organizers, program committee members, all anonymous referees, the invited speakers and authors of the submitted papers for contributing to the scientific program of ITAT 2017. Special thanks belong to our sponsor Profinit (http://www.profinit.eu/).

Jaroslava Hlaváčová
Charles University, Prague
Chair of the Program Committee

Contents

ITAT 2017   **1**

J. Hana: Generování textu v přirozeném jazyce 1

A. Ligęza: Rules, Causality and Constraints. Model-Based Reasoning and Structural Knowledge Discovery 2

O. Okhrin: Estimations of the Hierarchical Archimedean Copula 3

L. Soukup: Jak jsou přesné digitální mapy? 4

S. Cinková, A. Vernerová: Are Annotators'Word-Sense-Disambiguation Decisions Affected by Textual Entailment between Lexicon Glosses? 5

V. Kettnerová, M. Lopatková: Complex Predicates with Light Verbs in VALLEX: From Formal Model to Lexicographic Description 15

M. Linková, P. Gurský: Attributes Extraction from Product Descriptions on e-Shops 23

M. Lipovský, T. Vinař, B. Brejová: Approximate Abundance Histograms and Their Use for Genome Size Estimation 27

R. Pavel, P. Gurský: Focused Web Crawling of Relevant Pages on e-Shops 35

M. Plátek, F. Otto, F. Mráz: On h-Lexicalized Automata and h-Syntactic Analysis 40

R. Rabatin, B. Brejová, T. Vinař: Using Sequence Ensembles for Seeding Alignments of MinION Sequencing Data 48

Computational Intelligence and Data Mining — 5th International Workshop (CIDM 2017)   **55**

R. Brunetto, O. Trunda: Deep Heuristic-learning in the Rubik's Cube Domain: an Experimental Evaluation 57

P. Čížek, J. Faigl, J. Bayer: Enhancing Neural Based Obstacle Avoidance with CPG Controlled Hexapod Walking Robot 65

M. Danel, M. Skrbek: Humanoid Robot Control by Offline Actor-Critic Learning 71

J. Kalina, B. Peštová: Nonparametric Bootstrap Estimation for Implicitly Weighted Robust Regression 78

F. Knöll, V. Simko: Organizational Information improves Forecast Efficiency of Correction Techniques 86

M. Kopp, M. Nikl, M. Holeňa: Breaking CAPTCHAs with Convolutional Neural Networks . . 93

V. Kůrková: Bounds on Sparsity of One-Hidden-Layer Perceptron Networks 100

J. Motl, P. Kordík: Foreign Key Constraint Identification in Relational Databases 106

M. Navara, J. Šindelář: The Role of Information in the Two Envelope Problem 112

Z. Pitra, L. Bajer, J. Repický, M. Holeňa: Adaptive Doubly Trained Evolution Control for the
Covariance Matrix Adaptation Evolution Strategy 120
J. Puchýř, M. Holeňa: Random-Forest-Based Analysis of URL Paths 129
J. Repický, L. Bajer, Z. Pitra, M. Holeňa: Adaptive Generation-Based Evolution Control for
Gaussian Process Surrogate Models 136
T. Šabata, T. Borovička, M. Holeňa: K-best Viterbi Semi-supervized Active Learning in Se-
quence Labelling 144
M. Stepanovsky, A. Ibrova, Z. Buk, J. Veleminska: Estimation of Chronological Age from
Permanent Teeth Development 153
P. Vidnerová, R. Neruda: Evolution Strategies for Deep Neural Network Models Design . . 159
P. Vlašánek, I. Perfilieva: Inpainting Using F-Transform for Cartoon-Like Images 167

Slovenskočeský NLP workshop (SloNLP 2017)   **175**

T. Hercig, P. Krejzl, B. Hourová, J. Steinberger, L. Lenc: Detecting Stance in Czech News
Commentaries 176
T. Jelínek: FicTree: a Manually Annotated Treebank of Czech Fiction 181
L. Lenc, P. Král: Ensemble of Neural Networks for Multi-label Document Classification . . . 186
M. Novák: Coreference Resolution System Not Only for Czech 193
R. Rosa: MonoTrans: Statistical Machine Translation from Monolingual Data 201

"W3-ChaT" — WWW — Challenges and Trends (W3-ChaT 2017)   **209**

L. Grad-Gyenge: On the Optimal Setting of Spreading Activation Parameters to Calculate
Recommendations on the Knowledge Graph 210
B. Horváth, T. Horváth: Evaluating Data Sources for Crawling Events from the Web 218
J. Hradil: Identification and Origin of User Interfaces 223
M. Kopecky, M. Vomlelova, P. Vojtas: Repeatable Web Data Extraction and Interlinking . . . 228
T. Kliegr, J. Kuchař, S. Vojíř, V. Zeman: EasyMiner – Short History of Research and Current
Development 235
L. Peska: Multimodal Implicit Feedback for Recommender Systems 240

J. Hlaváčová (Ed.): ITAT 2017 Proceedings, p. 1
ISBN 978-1974274741, © 2017 J. Hana

ÎTAT

Generování textu v přirozeném jazyce

Jiří Hana[1]

Ústav formální a aplikované lingvistiky MFF UK, Malostranské nám. 2/25, 118 00 Praha 1
Jiri.Hana@mff.cuni.cz,
WWW home page: http://ufal.mff.cuni.cz/ hana/

Abstract: Přednáška představí problematiku generování textu na příkladu sportovních zpráv. Jde o společný projekt nakladatelství Economia a firmy Geneea. Vyvíjený systém vytváří novinové články popisující jednotlivá sportovní utkání. Články jsou generovány na základě strukturovaných dat o událostech na hřišti a dat v databázích, jakou je například znalostní báze Wikidata. V této fázi projektu jde pouze o fotbalové zápasy, ale v blízké budoucnosti bude systém rozšířen na další sporty a výhledově také na zprávy o počasí a zprávy z burzy.

Jiří Hana má zkušenosti jak z firemního, tak z univerzitního prostředí. Vystudoval informatiku na Matematicko-fyzikální fakultě UK a lingvistiku na Ohio State University. V USA strávil téměř 10 let. Mezi jeho zájmy patří morfologie, příklonky a jazyk cizinců. Je vý-zkumným pracovníkem na Ústavu formální a aplikované lingvistiky MFF UK a spoluzakladatelem společnosti Geneea Analytics, startupu vyvíjejícího systémy pro analýzu a generování textu.

J. Hlaváčová (Ed.): ITAT 2017 Proceedings, p. 2
ISBN 978-1974274741, © 2017 A. Ligęza

Rules, Causality and Constraints. Model-Based Reasoning and Structural Knowledge Discovery

Antoni Ligeza[1]

AGH University of Science and Technology in Kraków, Poland
ligeza@agh.edu.pl,
WWW home page: http://home.agh.edu.pl/ ligeza

Abstract: Data Mining techniques are widely applied to build models in the form of rules, decision tress or graphs. Some most successful techniques include algorithms for decision tree induction (with ID3, C4.5, C5.0 being the most prominent examples), frequent pattern mining (e.g. the Apriori algorithm for association rules mining) or Directed Acyclic Graphs for causal probabilistic modeling (the Bayesian Networks). In the domain of Fuzzy Sets there are approaches covering the experimental data (e.g. the Hao-Wang algorithm). Some more mathematically advanced tools incorporate Rough Sets Theory, Granular Sets, or approximation tools.

Such techniques, although useful in practice, are limited to discover the shallow knowledge only. They are based on efficient grouping techniques, relative frequency, or estimated probabilistic distributions. In general, they quite often answer the question "how does the system behave?" in terms of input-output relation, but unfortunately do not explain "why the systems behaves in a specific way" — with reference to it internal structure and components.

In contrast to widely explored popular Data Mining tools and techniques, the presentation is focused on investigating the phenomenon of causality and exploration of the paradigm of Model-Based Reasoning. An attempt is made to describe the idea of causal rules and functional dependencies on strictly logical background. The main focus is on modeling and discovering deep, causal knowledge, including the internal structure and components behavior of analyzed systems. Such a deep causal knowledge allows for different modes of Model-based Reasoning: deduction can be used to model expected system behavior, abduction can be used for analysis and diagnostic reasoning, and consistency-based reasoning can be used for structure discovery. As a tool we employ Constraint Programming. It seems that the presented approach can contribute to an interesting extension of the current Machine Learning capabilities.

Antoni Ligeza graduated from Faculty of Electrical Engineering, Automatics and Electronics (present: Faculty of Electrical Engineering, Automatics, Informatics and Electronics, EAIiE), AGH – University of Science and Technology in Cracow, Poland; received M.Sc. in electronics/automatic control in 1980. After completing Doctors Studies he received his Ph.D. degree in computer science (1983), and the habilitation (docent degree; polish Dr habilitowany) in 1994 in Computer Science/Artificial Intelligence, both from the EAIiE Faculty at AGH. In 2006 he received the professor title from the President of Poland. His main research concern Knowledge Engineering (Artificial Intelligence) including knowledge representation and inference methods, rule-based systems, automated plan generation, technical diagnostics, logics and systems science. Some most important original research results include development of backward plan generation model (1983), independent discovery of dual resolution method for automated inference (1991), the concepts of granular sets and relations (2000), granular attributive logic (2003) and diagnostic inference models in the form of logical AND/OR/NOT causal graphs (1995) and Potential Conflict Structures (1996). He was visiting professor at LAAS, Toulouse, France (1992, 1996), Universite de Nancy I, France (1994), University of Balearic Islands, Spain (1994, 1995, 2005), University of Girona, Spain (1996, 1997), and Universite de Caen, France (2004, 2005, 2007). He published (as author and co-author) more than 200 research papers, including recent monograph Logical Foundations for Rule-Based Systems", Springer, 2006. Member of IEEE Computer Society and ACM.

J. Hlaváčová (Ed.): ITAT 2017 Proceedings, p. 3
ISBN 978-1974274741, © 2017 O. Okhrin

ÎTAT

Estimations of the Hierarchical Archimedean Copula

Ostap Okhrin[1]

Dresden University of Technology, Germany
ostap.okhrin@tu-dresden.de,
WWW home page: https://tu-dresden.de/bu/verkehr/ivw/osv/die-professur/inhaber-in

Abstract: We discuss several estimators, of the hierarchical Archimedean copulas. In one, we propose the estimation of parametric hierarchical Archimedean copula while imposing an implicit penalty on its structure. Asymptotic properties of this sparse estimator are derived and issues relevant for the implementation of the estimation procedure are discussed. In the other method we propose the estimator, that uses cluster algorithm in order to obtain the structure and the parameters. Third method is based on the maximum likelihood technique. This talk is based on the several papers together with Y. Okhrin, W. Schmid, A. Ristig, A. Tetereva.

Ostap Okhrin (born 1984) studied mathematics (B.Sc. in 2004) and statistics (M.Sc. in 2005) at the Ivan Franko National University in Lviv, Ukraine. In 2008 he defended his PhD thesis at the Europa Universität Viadrina in Frankfurt (Oder) and was appointed as the Assistant Professor at the Humboldt-Universität zu Berlin. Prior his appointment at the TU Dresden he was an Associate Professor at the Humboldt-Universität zu Berlin (2014-2015). Since 2011 he made research stays at different international universities, f.e. SWUFE (Chengdu, China), Vienna University (Austria), Princeton University (USA), University of Chicago (USA), Michigan University (USA). Ostap Okhrin is in the editorial boards of four international Journals as well as author of articles in journals as Journal of the American Statistical Association, Journal of Econometrics, Econometric Theory, etc. He specialized in the multivariate distributions esp. copulas, their properties and applications in various fields from weather, over insurance to high-frequency data.

J. Hlaváčová (Ed.): ITAT 2017 Proceedings, p. 4
ISBN 978-1974274741, © 2017 L. Soukup

Jak jsou přesné digitální mapy?

Lubomír Soukup[1]

Ústav teorie informace a automatizace, AV ČR, Pod Vodárenskou věží 4, 182 08 Praha 8
soukup@utia.cas.cz,
WWW home page: http://www.utia.cas.cz/cs/people/soukup

Abstract: Na přednášce bude představena metodika tvorby digitálních map sestavených z různých datových zdrojů. Pozornost bude věnována polohové přesnosti digitálních map, která je významná zejména při porovnávání obsahu starých map se současnými mapami. Poukážeme přitom na souvislost se zpracováním digitálních obrazů i na specifika zpracování starých map a glóbu.

Lubomír Soukup absolvoval inženýrské studium na Stavební fakultě CVUT. Jeho studijním oborem byla geodezie a kartografie, specializace dálkový průzkum Země. Pracoval ve Výzkumném ústavu geodetickém, topografickém a kartografickém, potom na Stavební fakultě ČVUT v Praze a nakonec v Ústavu teorie informace a automatizace AV ČR, kde působí dodnes. Výzkumný zájem Lubomíra Soukupa se soustřeďuje na matematicko-statistické metody zpracování prostorových dat, zejména na geostatistické metody a bayesovský přístup. Tyto metody aplikuje na digitální obrazy a mapy. V současné době se zabývá především elastickou registrací (vlícová-ním) digitálních obrazů. V posledních letech se podílel na projektu *Výzkum možností pozemního InSAR pro určování deformací rizikových objektů a lokalit*, v jehož rámci vyvíjel algoritmy na zpracování dat z interferometrického radaru (InSAR). Výsledky tohoto projektu byly oceněny Cenou inovace roku 2016.

J. Hlaváčová (Ed.): ITAT 2017 Proceedings, pp. 5–14
ISBN 978-1974274741, © 2017 S. Cinková, A. Vernerová

Are Annotators' Word-Sense-Disambiguation Decisions Affected by Textual Entailment between Lexicon Glosses?

Silvie Cinková, Anna Vernerová

Charles University, Faculty of Mathematics and Physics
Institute of Formal and Applied Linguistics
Malostranské náměstí 25
118 00 Praha 1
Czech Republic
ufal.mff.cuni.cz
{cinkova,vernerova}@ufal.mff.cuni.cz

Abstract: We describe an annotation experiment combining topics from lexicography and Word Sense Disambiguation. It involves a lexicon (*Pattern Dictionary of English Verbs, PDEV*), an existing data set (*VPS-GradeUp*), and an unpublished data set (*RTE in PDEV Implicatures*). The aim of the experiment was twofold: a pilot annotation of Recognizing Textual Entailment (RTE) on PDEV implicatures (lexicon glosses) on the one hand, and, on the other hand, an analysis of the effect of Textual Entailment between lexicon glosses on annotators' Word-Sense-Disambiguation decisions, compared to other predictors, such as finiteness of the target verb, the explicit presence of its relevant arguments, and the semantic distance between corresponding syntactic arguments in two different patterns (dictionary senses).

1 Introduction

A substantial proportion of verbs are perceived as highly polysemous. Their senses are both difficult to determine when building a lexicon entry and to distinguish in context when performing Word Sense Disambiguation (WSD). To tackle the polysemy of verbs, diverse lexicon designs and annotation procedures have been deployed. One alternative way to classic verb senses (e.g. **to blush** - *to redden, as from embarrassment or shame*[1]) is *usage patterns* coined in the *Pattern Dictionary of English Verbs (PDEV)* [9], which will be explained in Section 2.2. Previous studies [3], [4] have shown that PDEV represents a valuable lexical resource for WSD, in that annotators reach good interannotator agreement despite the semantically fine-grained microstructure of PDEV. This paper focuses on cases challenging the interannotator agreement in WSD and considers the contribution of *textual entailment* (Section 2.3) to interannotator confusion.

We draw on a data set based on PDEV and annotated with graded decisions (cf. Section 2.4) to investigate features suspected of blurring distinctions between the patterns [1]. We have been preliminarily considering features related to language usage independently of the lexicon design, such as finiteness and argument opacity of the target

verb on the one hand, and those related to the lexicographical design of PDEV, such as semantic relations between implicatures within a lemma or denotative similarity of the verb arguments, on the other hand (see Section 3 for definitions and examples).

This paper focuses on a feature related to PDEV's design (see Section 2.3), namely on textual entailment between implicatures in pairs of patterns of the same lemma entry (henceforth *colempats*, see Section 3.1 for definition and more detail).

We pairwise compare all colempats, examining their scores in the graded decision annotation with respect to how much they compete to become the most appropriate pattern, as well as the scores of presence of textual entailment between their implicatures. To quantify the comparisons, we have introduced a measure of *rivalry* for each pair. The more the rivalry increases, the more appropriate both colempats are considered for a given KWIC[2] and the more similar their appropriateness scores are (see Section 3.2).

We confirm a significant positive association between rivalry in paired colempats and textual entailment between their implicatures.

2 Related Work

2.1 Word Sense Disambiguation

Word Sense Disambiguation (WSD)[18] is a traditional machine-learning task in NLP. It draws on the assumption that each word can be described by a set of word senses in a reference lexicon and hence each occurrence of a word in a given context can be assigned a word sense. Bulks of texts have been manually annotated with word senses to provide training data. Nevertheless, the extensive experience from many such projects has revealed that even humans themselves do not do particularly well interpreting word meaning in terms of lexicon senses, despite specialized lexicons designed entirely for this task: the English WordNet [8], PropBank [14], and OntoNotes

---

[1] http://www.dictionary.com/browse/blush

[2] *KWIC = key word in context: a corpus line containing a match to a particular corpus query*

1	*Pattern:* **Institution** *or* **Human abolishes Action** *or* **Rule** *or* **Privilege**
	Implicature: Institution *or* Human formally declares that Action = Punishment *or* Rule *or* Privilege is no longer legal or operative
	*Example: Then the Chancellor helped the industry by **abolishing** car tax in his Autumn Statement.*
2	*Pattern:* **Institution 1** *or* **Human abolishes Institution 2** *or* **Human_Role**
	Implicature: Institution 1 *or* Human formally puts an end to Institution 2 *or* Human_Role
	*Example: He also **abolished** duty-free shops, a move expected to earn the government K150,000,000 annually.*
3	*Pattern:* **Process abolishes State_of_Affairs**
	Implicature: Process brings State_of_Affairs to an end
	*Example: Masking the displays down **abolished** the effect of the differential perspective manipulations.*

Figure 1: PDEV entry with three patterns

Word Senses [12], to name but a few. Although the annotators, usually language experts, have neither comprehension problems nor are they unfamiliar with using lexicons, their interannotator agreement has been notoriously low. This in turn makes the training data unreliable as well as the evaluation of WSD systems harder.

Attempts have been made to increase the interannotator agreement by testing each entry on annotators while designing the lexicon [12], as well as word senses were clustered post hoc on the other hand (e.g. [17]), but even lexicographers have been skeptical about lexicons with hardwired word senses for NLP([13, 15]).

2.2 Pattern Dictionary of English Verbs (PDEV)

The reasoning behind PDEV is that a verb has no meaning in isolation; instead of word senses, it has a *meaning potential*, whose diverse components and their combinations are activated by different contexts. To capture the meaning potential of a verb, the PDEV lexicographer manually clusters random KWICs into a set of prototypical usage patterns, considering both their semantic and morphosyntactic similarity. Each PDEV *pattern* contains a *pattern definition* (a finite clause template where important syntactic slots are labeled with *semantic types*) and an *implicature* to explain or paraphrase its meaning, which also is a finite clause (Fig. 1). The PDEV implicature corresponds to *gloss* or *definition* in traditional dictionaries.

The *semantic types* (e.g. *Human, Institution, Rule, Process, State_of_Affairs*) are the most typical syntactic slot fillers, although the slots can also contain a set of collocates (a *lexical set*) and *semantic roles* complementary to semantic types. The semantic types come from an approximately 250-item shallow ontology associated with PDEV and drawing on the Brandeis Semantic Ontology (BSO), [19]. The notion of semantic types, lexical sets, and semantic roles (altogether dubbed *semlabels*) is, in this paper, particularly relevant for Section 3.5.

2.3 Recognizing Textual Entailment (RTE)

Recognizing Textual Entailment (RTE) is a computational-linguistic discipline coined by Dagan et al. [5]. The task of RTE is to determine, "given two text fragments, whether the meaning of one text can be inferred (entailed) from another text. More concretely, the applied notion of textual entailment is defined as a directional relationship between pairs of text expressions, denoted by T the entailing 'text' and by H the entailed 'hypothesis'. We say that T entails H if, typically, a human reading T would infer that H is most probably true". So, for instance, the text *Norway's most famous painting, 'The Scream' by Edvard Munch, was recovered yesterday, almost three months after it was stolen from an Oslo museum* entails the hypothesis *Edvard Munch painted 'The Scream'* [5].

2.4 Graded Decisions on Verb Usage Patterns: VPS-GradeUp

The VPS-GradeUp data set draws on Erk's experiments with paraphrases (USim)[7]. VPS-GradeUp consists of both graded-decision and classic-WSD annotation of 29 randomly selected PDEV lemmas: *seal, sail, distinguish, adjust, cancel, need, approve, conceive, act, pack, embrace, see, abolish, advance cure, plan, manage, execute, answer, bid, point, cultivate, praise, talk, urge, last, hire, prescribe,* and *murder*. Each lemma comes with 50 KWICs processed by three annotators[3] in parallel.

In the graded-decision part, the annotators judged each pattern for how well it described a given KWIC, on a Likert scale[4]. In the WSD part, each KWIC was assigned one best-matching pattern. The entire data set contains WSD judgments on 1,450 KWICs, corresponding to 11,400 graded decisions (50 sentences × 29 lemmas × sum of patterns). A more detailed description of VPS-GradeUp is given by Baisa et al.[1].

Fig. 2 shows a VPS-GradeUp sample of three KWICs of the verb *abolish* (see Fig. 1 to refer to the lexicon entry). Columns 1, 2, and 3 identify the pattern ID, lemma, and sentence ID, respectively. Columns 4-6 and 7-9 contain the graded and WSD decisions by the three annotators, respectively. Column 10 contains the annotated KWIC, which for Sentence 1 reads: *President Mitterrand said yesterday that the existence of two sovereign German states*

---

[3] linguists, professional but non-native English speakers

[4] Likert scale is a psychometric scale used in opinion surveys. It enables the respondents to scale their agreement/disagreement with a given opinion.

Pattern ID	Lemma	SentID	GD1 ▼	GD2 ▼	GD3 ▼	WSD1 ▼	WSD2 ▼	WSD3 ▼	KWIC
1	abolish	1.1	7	2	4	2	3	3	intersta
2	abolish	1.1	5	5	4	2	3	3	intersta
3	abolish	1.1	7	7	6	2	3	3	intersta
1	abolish	2.1	4	7	4	3	1	3	more fo
2	abolish	2.1	3	2	4	3	1	3	more fo
3	abolish	2.1	7	6	6	3	1	3	more fo
1	abolish	3.1	7	6	2	1	2	2	it is mis
2	abolish	3.1	5	7	7	1	2	2	it is mis
3	abolish	3.1	5	6	2	1	2	2	it is mis

Figure 2: A VPS-GradeUp annotation sample

could not be 'ABOLISHED at a stroke'. On the third table row, Pattern 3 was judged as maximally appropriate by Annotator 1 and 2; Annotator 3 gave one point less. In the WSD part, Annotator 1 voted for Pattern 2, while Annotators 2 and 3 preferred Pattern 3.

3　Important Concepts

3.1　Lempats and Colempats

To begin with, we introduce the concept of *lempats* and *colempats*. The lemma-pattern combination, as represented by Columns 1 and 2 in Fig. 2, is called *lempat*. All lempats sharing a common lemma are called *colempats*. That is, the table presents the colempats *abolish_1*, *abolish_2*, and *abolish_3* and their three annotator judgments on the sentences 1.1, 2.1, and 3.1. A pair of patterns, such as *abolish_3* and *cancel_1*, are also two lempats which we could compare, but they are not *co*lempats, because each belongs to a different lemma (*abolish* vs. *cancel*).

Fig.2, Columns 4-6, shows that, on Sentence 1.1, the annotators disagree in their WSD judgments (Annotator 2 and 3 voted for Pattern 3, but Annotator 1 preferred Pattern 2). This is probably caused by the fact that Annotators 1 and 2 had also regarded Pattern 2 as somewhat appropriate (Row 2). Interestingly, Annotator 1 even considered Pattern 1 maximally appropriate for the given KWIC, unlike the others, but eventually did neither vote for this pattern nor for Pattern 3. As with all manual annotations, human error cannot be a priori dismissed, but even the oddest judgments mostly turn out to come with a plausible explanation.

How do then the graded decisions map on the WSD judgments, if they do at all? To perform quantitative observations of how much two patterns compete in the WSD annotation, we needed a measure of *appropriateness* of a given pattern for a given KWIC across all annotators (see Section 3.2), along with yet another measure to tell which two patterns were the most serious competitors (*rivalry*, see Section 3.3).

Having a lempat, we need to measure its *appropriateness* for a given KWIC. To be able to examine the mapping between the graded-decisions and the WSD annotation, we observe *rivalry* within each possible pair of colempats for a given KWIC.

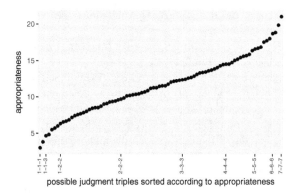

Figure 3: Shape of the appropriateness function

3.2　Appropriateness

The *appropriateness* of a pattern for a given KWIC line is based on the triple of graded annotation judgments, conflating their sum and standard deviation in this formula:

$$Appropriateness = \sum x - sd(x)/3.5$$

The function returns values ranging from 3 to 21. These are all possible sums of judgments by three annotators on 7-point Likert scales: as a minimum and maximum, a pattern can obtain 1 and 7 from each annotator, respectively. The 3.5 coefficient is roughly the maximum standard deviation (sd) possible with three judgments ranging from 1 to 7. Compared to mean or median, appropriateness discounts triples with higher dispersion. We made no effort to generalize this measure beyond the specific setup of this particular experiment with 7-point Likert scales and three annotators, and therefore the x value must be a natural number ranging from 1 to 7 and the sum must be the sum of exactly 3 such x.

Fig. 3 shows the shape of the curve. The x-axis contains all possible combinations of 1–7 triples with replacement, sorted in ascending order according to their corresponding appropriateness value. The curve is designed to reflect the opinion strength by steepness: the extreme positions indicate stronger opinions than central scale positions. Therefore the dispersion of the judgments affects appropriateness more strongly at both ends of the scale than around its center.

3.3　Rivalry

To compare the competition between PDEV pairs of patterns, we have introduced rivalry. Rivalry always concerns the appropriateness rates for a pair of patterns of one lemma (colempats), being computed for all pairs. Rivalry increases with the appropriateness of each colempat and with decreasing difference between the appropriateness values in the given colempat pair: the higher the rivalry, the more the two patterns compete for becoming selected as the best match in the WSD annotation. The rivalry function is simple:

$Rivalry = \max(appr_{pair}) - (\max(appr_{pair}) - \min(appr_{pair})) = \min(appr_{pair})$.

Under $appr_{pair}$ we understand the two computed appropriateness values of patterns in a colempat pair: $\max(appr)$ and $\min(appr)$. They represent the higher and the lower appropriateness, respectively. Hence, rivalry is defined as the difference between the higher appropriateness value and the difference between that and the lower appropriateness value, which boils down to the lower appropriateness. The idea behind rivalry is that, given the nature of the WSD annotation task, we are interested in colempats competing at the positive rather than at the negative end of the scale.

It is to be emphasized that rivalry is always computed *on a given KWIC*. Hence we cannot immediately tell e.g. the rivalry between *abandon_1* and *abandon_3* in general, but we get one rivalry value of this colempat pair for each of the 50 KWICs.

Measuring rivalry is interesting, even though we have not yet abstracted from individual KWICs; it enables us to identify cases of pattern overlap for further analysis of both the design of the patterns and of contextual features in the KWICs affected.

3.4 Corresponding Synslots

As Fig. 1 shows, the syntactic slot fillers of the target verb in the pattern definition are described by semantic labels (henceforth **semlabels**). Each syntactic slot (henceforth **synslot**) also has a syntactic function in the clause: *subject, object, adverbial*, or *complement*. When observing synslots across a pair of colempats, we check whether a synslot with a particular syntactic function (e.g. object) is present in both colempats in the pair. When this is the case, these two synslots are called *corresponding synslots*.

3.5 Semantic Distance between Corresponding Synslots

In a past experiment, we measured how the rivalry is impacted by the extent to which the sets of synslot fillers in a colempat pair are cognitively similar. We observed a statistically significant (yet weak) positive association. The synslot fillers were represented by the semlabels. To obtain their semantic similarity, we first built a corpus of pattern definitions and implicatures from the entire PDEV. Then we fed this corpus to a neural network, which created a vector representation for each word.[5] We defined

the mutual similarity of each two words by the cosine similarity of their vectors. For more details see [2].

3.6 Verb Finiteness

Finiteness is a morphosyntactic category associated with verbs. Virtually all verbs appear in finite as well as infinite forms when used in context. A finite verb form is such a verb form that expresses person and number. Languages differ in whether these categories are expressed morphologically (e.g. by affixes or stem vowel changes) or syntactically (obligatorily complemented with a noun/pronoun expressing these categories explicitly). Finite forms are typically all indicative and conditional forms, as well as some imperative forms, e.g. *reads, are reading, (they) read, čtu, čtěte, chtěl by, gehst, allons!*. Infinite forms are infinitives (*to read, to have read, to be heard, to have been heard*) and participles along with gerunds and supines (*reading, known, deleted, försvunnit*). The grammars of many languages know diverse other finite as well as infinite verb forms. Infinite forms typically allow more argument omissions than finite forms: *to go to town* vs. **went to town* (incorrect). This suggests that descriptions of events rendered by infinite verb forms may be more vague, and, in terms of annotation, more prone to match several different patterns/senses at the same time. Verb finiteness is easy to determine, and therefore it was only annotated by one annotator in our data set.

3.7 Argument Opacity

Argument opacity typically, but not necessarily, relates to verb finiteness. By argument opacity we mean how many arguments relevant for disambiguation of the target verb are either omitted in the context (e.g. subject in infinitive) or ambiguous or vague. Ambiguous and vague arguments are often arguments expressed by personal pronouns that refer to entities mentioned distantly from the target verb, sometimes even not directly, but by longer chains of pronouns (so-called *coreference* or *anaphora chains*), or arguments expressed by indefinite or negative pronouns. Some examples of opaque verb contexts follow:

The Greater London Council was ABOLISHED in 1986. (Who abolished it?)

The company's ability to adapt to new opportunities and capitalize on them depends on its capacity to share information and involve everyone in the organization in a systemwide search for ways to improve, ADJUST, adapt, and upgrade . (Who exactly adjusts what?)

---

[5] *text2vec* [22] – an implementation of the *word2vec* [16] neural network for R. The original task on which the neural network was trained was guessing context around each word. Its practical use draws on the so-called Distributional Hypothesis[10], according to which words with similar context distribution are more semantically related than those with dissimilar context distribution. The network creates a vector representation of each word, with the dimensions of each word vector being the other words. The similarity of two vectors reflects the distributional (and hence semantic) similarity of two words.

4 Textual Entailment Annotation

4.1 Annotation Procedure

Three annotators[6] obtained paired implicatures of colempats of each target verb and judged whether one entailed the other (specifying the direction), or whether the entailment is bidirectional or absent (cf. Section 2.3). The definition of entailment used here is based on the conception of *textual entailment* coined by Dagan et al. (cf. **RTE**, [6]). For the purposes of this paper, we collapsed the annotation into entailment presence-absence judgments.

4.2 Annotation Results

The three annotators processed 1,091 implicature pairs (both implicatures always belonged to the same lemma). The annotators were allowed to see the entire entry including example sentences, but they were told to focus on the implicatures. Their pairwise percentual agreement scores were 73.8, 74.6, and 83.3. Fleiss' kappa was moderate: 0.41. While RTE annotations usually reach 0.6 desired for semantic annotations, our worse result is understandable: the PDEV implicatures are much more abstract and hence more vague than regular text, since the arguments of the target verb are described by ontology labels. See an example of two pattern implicatures of the verb *seal*:

> *Human covers the surface of Artifact with Stuff.*
> *Human encloses Physical Object in an airtight Container.*

We merged the three annotations by taking the means of "yes" and "no" judgments replaced with 1 and 0, respectively. With this setup, the judgments could acquire only four values: 0, 0.33, 0.66, and 1. We treated them as values of a categorical ordinal variable.

Fig. 4 shows the annotation results for each lemma. To facilitate the reading, we displayed the judgments as the number of annotator votes in favor of entailment. The proportions are compared to the verb *see*, with its 192 colempat pairs. The annotator disagreement is represented by 1 and 2 votes. In terms of proportions within the given lemma, the most problematic verbs were the small[7] verbs *abolish*, *cancel*, *hire*, and *praise*, along with the large verbs *act*, *point*, and *talk*.

A typical colempat pair with full agreement on no implicature entailment is e.g. *act_10-12*. The example also includes the pattern definition for better understanding:

Pattern: *Phrasal verb.* Human *acts* Event *or* Human Role *or* Emotion *out.*
Implicature: Human *performs* Role, *not necessarily sincerely, or behaves as if feeling* Emotion.

---

[6]linguists familiar with PDEV as well as with RTE, professional but non-native English speakers

[7]i.e. with a small number of colempat pairs

Pattern: Idiom. Human *acts* POSDET age.
Implicature: *Human* behaves in a manner appropriate to their *age.*

Although both these events have something to do with behavior, we can neither normally assume that someone who acts their emotions out is necessarily behaving according to their age, nor the other way round. Thus we observe no implicature entailment relation between these two colempats.

A typical colempat pair with full agreement on implicature entailment is e.g. *act_1-9*. This example also illustrates that entailment does not require synonymy. The second implicature entails the first; that is, when an actor performs a character on theater, they are – normally – pursuing a motivated action by pretending to be a particular character for their audience.

Pattern: Human *or* Institution *or* Animal *or* Machine *acts*
Implicature: Human *or* Institution *or* Animal *or* Machine = Agent *performs a motivated* Action

Pattern: Human *acts* (Role) *(in* Performance*)*
Implicature: Human *plays* Role = Theatrical *(in* Performance*)*
However, the general nature of the implicatures makes the entailment annotation difficult. Below follows an example where one annotator voted against the entailment, the *act_1-11* pair. The *act_1* colempat is listed in the previous example. Here follows the *act_11* colempat:

Pattern: Phrasal verb. Human *acts up.*
Implicature: Human *behaves badly.* Human *is typically a naughty child..*

The annotators clearly disagree on whether bad behavior is normally perceived as a motivated action. They were instructed to focus only on the implicature. At the same time, they were allowed to see the entire entry. Most likely with this entry, two annotators were influenced by the very verb *act up*. The verb *act up* suggests a motivated action (e.g. start screaming to attract attention, this being perceived as bad manners in the given situation). The plain implicature leaves leeway for considering non-motivated actions (can very young infants act consiously?) or non-actions perceived as bad behavior (even a child can behave badly by *not* acting e.g. to someone's help).

The reasons for annotator disagreements are very diverse, including obvious annotation errors, and their ex post analysis is often subjective. We show a case from still the same verb, *act_1-12*. See *act_1* above again, *act_12* follows:

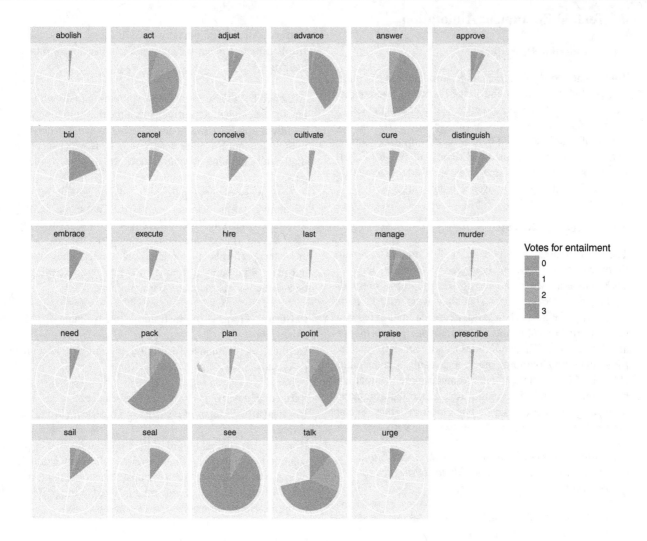

Figure 4: Proportional distribution of entailment judgments in individual lemmas, relating to the verb *see*, which has 190 possible colempat pairs.

Pattern: Phrasal verb. Machine *acts up.*
Implicature: Machine *fails to function correctly.*

Here, the pro-entailment decision by two annotators was most likely motivated by the fact that *act_1* specifies *Machine* as *Agent* and lets it perform a *motivated* action. Then, naturally, even malfunction can be a motivated action. The remaining annotator, on the other hand, did not accept malfunction as a motivated action.

Often the uncertainty lies in the interpretation of the semantic types. For instance, *hire_1-2* differ in the object of hiring. In the first colempat it is *Human* or *Institution*, whose services are obtained for payment. In the second colempat it is a *Physical Object*, which is used for an agreed period of time against payment. In real life, this corresponds to e.g. hiring a gardener to take care of a garden vs. hiring an apartment. Such two events naturally do not entail each other in any way. However, the general wording of implicatures allows one annotator to regard the

use of a *Physical Object* against payment as a service provided by a *Human* or *Institution*. Consider e.g. *Mary hires John to let her live in an apartment that belongs to him.*.

5   Association between Implicature Entailment and Rivalry

5.1   Linear Model with Rivalry Abstracted from Individual KWICs

While the textual entailment is observed between two colempat implicatures independently of their instances in corpus evidence, rivalry is always associated with both the given pair of colempats and the KWIC, with respect to which their appropriateness was judged (cf. Section 3.3). We had 50 rivalry scores for each colempat pair, since the VPS-GradeUp annotators were judging the appropriateness of each pattern for each of the 50 KWICs per lemma.

For each colempat pair we selected the KWIC on which their rivalry was highest.

To examine the association between the textual entailment between implicatures and rivalry between colempats, we built this linear regression model using the `lm()` function in base R [20].

```
Call:
lm(formula = abstr_rivalry ~ factor(numMeans),
data = all_entailment)

Residuals:
    Min       1Q    Median       3Q      Max
-0.17193 -0.02510 -0.01854  0.01936  0.38500

Coefficients:
             Estimate Std.Error t-value Pr(>|t|)
(Intercept) 0.167961  0.002754  60.984  < 2e-16 ***
numMeans0.3 0.041712  0.005380   7.753 2.05e-14 ***
numMeans0.6 0.084065  0.006107  13.765  < 2e-16 ***
numMeans1   0.155577  0.007134  21.806  < 2e-16 ***
---
Signif.
codes:
0 '***' 0.001 '**' 0.01 '*' 0.05 '.' 0.1 ' ' 1

Residual standard error: 0.06808 on 1087 degrees of
freedom
Multiple R-squared:  0.348,      Adjusted R-squared:
0.3462
F-statistic: 193.4 on 3 and 1087 DF,
p-value: < 2.2e-16
```

According to the Adjusted R-squared, it explains approximately 35% of the variance of rivalry. This means that entailment is quite a strong predictor. Apart from that, the individual coefficient values in the model nicely confirm our assumption that entailment causes rivalry increase: One vote for entailment (i.e. value 0.3) increases the rivalry coefficient by 0.04, two votes increase it by 0.08, and three votes increase it by 0.15. Their individual standard errors are one decimal point smaller than the coefficients themselves, which means that they would not overlap; that is, every single entailment vote matters. The model is highly significant, and so are all levels of the entailment values (p-value always much smaller than 0.05). This, along with the randomness of lemma selection, means that we can expect the results to be similar with other equally annotated verbs.

5.2 Linear Model with Rivalry on All KWICs

We ran the same experiment also without abstracting from the KWICs. The model is still highly significant, but extremely weak (explaining about 20% of the rivalry variation). This makes sense, since this time we also included observations with the same entailment conditions but lower rivalry. This way we introduced KWICs where the positive effect of entailment can have been overcome by the negative effect of other predictor values, which we have not included into the model.

```
Call:
lm(formula = rivalry ~ factor(entail_numMeans),
data = vyplyv)

Residuals:
    Min       1Q   Median      3Q      Max
-3.8233  -0.8442  -0.5540  0.2811  15.1558
```

```
Coefficients:
                   Estimate Std.Err t-value Pr(>|t|)
(Intercept)         3.55396 0.01149  309.38 <2e-16 ***
fctr(numMeans)0.3   1.20615 0.02244   53.74 <2e-16 ***
fctr(numMeans)0.6   1.12526 0.02547   44.17 <2e-16 ***
fctr(numMeans)1     3.26938 0.02976  109.84 <2e-16 ***
---
Signif.
codes:
0 '***' 0.001 '**' 0.01 '*' 0.05 '.' 0.1 ' ' 1

Residual standard error: 2.008 on 54534 degrees
of freedom
Multiple R-squared:  0.1985,
Adjusted R-squared:  0.1984
F-statistic:  4501 on 3 and 54534 DF,
p-value: < 2.2e-16
```

6 Discussion

We have observed a statistically significant positive effect of textual entailment of colempat implicatures on the rivalry between colempats in PDEV. It is evidently not the only cause of increasing rivalry, as shown by the weakness of the model, but has the strongest effect. The implicature is the part of patterns that corresponds to classic word senses in traditional lexicons. This suggests that the traditional conception of word senses as semantic definitions rather than usage definitions is very useful in sense distinction, whenever annotators agree. On the other hand, like with traditional word senses, the interannotator agreement is low. Like traditional word senses shaped as lexicon glosses/definitions, the implicatures are too abstract to bode well for interannotator agreement. The issue persists even when the annotation task is set up as an RTE task rather than recognizing synonymy and mutual exclusivity (according to which traditional WSD annotation decisions are taken)[8].

Apart from the textual entailment, we have been preliminarily examining other features suspect of increasing rivalry, such as the explicit presence/absence of relevant arguments (argument opacity, Section 3.7), semantic distance between labels used in corresponding syntactic positions within a colempat pair (based on text2vec [22]), and finiteness of the target verb in the KWICs (Section 3.6). A statistically significant linear model predicting rivalry finds all these predictors significant (Fig. 5).

However, the textual entailment turns out to be most effective rivalry increaser, raising each rivalry unit by 2.55 (to the extent we can believe averaged human judgments on implication). Interestingly, verb finiteness (promising more explicit contexts) does not help distinguish between patterns but in fact *increases* rivalry (i.e. blurs distinctions between colempats). Considering the argument opacity, opaque object is the most rivalry increasing predictor from the opacity family (coeff. 1.42). We have also been considering the factuality[9] of the events described by the tar-

---

[8]The RTE annotation task would possibly benefit from graded annotation by many annotators like word-similarity/relatedness experiments, e.g. [11].

[9][21]

```
Call:

lm(formula = rivalry ~ w2vec_hsdrff_Sum + z_finite + z_args.opaque
                + entail_mean, data = rival)
Residuals:
            Min       1Q      Median     3Q       Max
          -44 145   -0.7944  -0.4442   0.3024    161 824
Coefficients:
                   Estimate   Std. Err  t value   Pr(>|t|)
(Intercept)        385 483    0.04893   78 785    < 2e-16   ***
w2vec_hsdrff_Sum   -0.01200   0.00110   -10 908   < 2e-16   ***
z_finitey          0.34715    0.01713   20 264    < 2e-16   ***
z_args.opaquey     123 175    0.23520   5 237     1.64e-07  ***
z_args.opaqueobj   141 808    0.36389   3 897     9.75e-05  ***
z_args.opaquesubj  0.20601    0.02265   9 097     < 2e-16   ***
entail_mean        255 232    0.02152   118 592   < 2e-16   ***
---
Signif. codes:  0 '***' 0.001 '**' 0.01 '*' 0.05 '.' 0.1 ' ' 1
Residual standard error: 1.992 on 54531 degrees of freedom
Multiple R-squared:  0.2112, Adjusted R-squared:  0.2111
F-statistic:  2433 on 6 and 54531 DF,  p-value: < 2.2e-16
```

Figure 5: A linear model predicting rivalry from semantic distance, verb finiteness, argument opacity and textual entailment

get predicates (for which we have used verb finiteness here as a primitive proxy), but a pilot annotation has yielded poor interannotator agreement, making results based on such data even more speculative than those of textual entailment between colempat implicatures, so we have not included it in the model.

All the aforementioned predictors are apparently not general enough to beat the effects of individual lemmas: most lemmas are significant, have high coefficients, and increase the predictive power of the model in Fig. 6; cf. R-squared in both models: despite efforts to find universal linguistic features, each verb appears to remain a little universe in its own right.

7 Conclusion

We have confirmed that textual entailment between two colempat implicatures increases rivalry between these colempats. We also see that the more the annotators agree on the presence of entailment, the stronger its effect is: it grows with each annotator vote to even double when all three annotators agree, compared to two annotators.

8 Acknowledgements

This work was supported by the Czech Science Foundation Grant No. GA 15-20031S and by the LINDAT/CLARIN project No. LM2015071 of the MEYS CR.

References

[1] Vít Baisa, Silvie Cinková, Ema Krejčová, and Anna Vernerová. VPS-GradeUp: Graded Decisions on Usage Patterns. In *LREC 2016 Proceedings*, Portorož, Slovenia, May 2016.

[2] Silvie Cinková and Zdeněk Hlávka. Modeling Semantic Distance in the Pattern Dictionary of English Verbs. *Jazykovedný časopis*, to appear.

[3] Silvie Cinková, Martin Holub, Adam Rambousek, and Lenka Smejkalová. A database of semantic clusters of verb usages. In *Proceedings of the 8th International Conference on Language Resources and Evaluation (LREC 2012)*, pages 3176–3183, Istanbul, Turkey, 2012. European Language Resources Association.

[4] Silvie Cinkova, Ema Krejčová, Anna Vernerová, and Vít Baisa. Graded and Word-Sense-Disambiguation Decisions in Corpus Pattern Analysis: a Pilot Study. In Nicoletta Calzolari (Conference Chair), Khalid Choukri, Thierry Declerck, Marko Grobelnik, Bente Maegaard, Joseph Mariani, Asuncion Moreno, Jan Odijk, and Stelios Piperidis, editors, *Proceedings of the Tenth International Conference on Language Resources and Evaluation (LREC 2016)*, Paris, France, 2016. European Language Resources Association (ELRA).

[5] Ido Dagan, Bill Dolan, Bernardo Magnini, and Dan Roth. Recognizing textual entailment: Rational, evaluation and approaches. *Natural Language Engineering*, 15(4):i–xvii, 2009.

[6] Ido Dagan, Dan Roth, Mark Sammons, and Fabio Massimo Zanzotto. *Recognizing Textual Entailment: Models and Applications*. Synthesis Lectures on Human Language Technologies. Morgan & Claypool Publishers, 2013.

[7] Katrin Erk, Diana McCarthy, and Nicholas Gaylord. Investigations on Word Senses and Word Usages. In *Proceedings of the Joint Conference of the 47th Annual Meeting of the ACL and the 4th International Joint Conference on Natural Language Processing of the AFNLP*, pages 10–18, Suntec, Singapore, August 2009. Association for Computational Linguistics.

[8] C. Fellbaum, J. Grabowski, and S. Landes. Performance and confidence in a semantic annotation task. In *WordNet: An Electronic Lexical Database*, pages 217–238. Cambridge (Mass.): The MIT Press., Cambridge (Mass.), 1998. 00054.

[9] Patrick Hanks. *Pattern Dictionary of English Verbs*. http://pdev.org.uk/, UK, 2000.

[10] Zellig Harris. Distributional structure. *Word*, 23(10):146–162, 1954. 01136.

[11] Samer Hassan and Rada Mihalcea. Cross-lingual semantic relatedness using encyclopedic knowledge. In *In EMNLP 2009. Association for Computational Linguistics*, 2009. 00044.

[12] Eduard Hovy, Mitchell Marcus, Martha Palmer, Lance Ramshaw, and Ralph Weischedel. OntoNotes: the 90% solution. In *Proceedings of the Human Language Technology Conference of the NAACL, Companion Volume: Short Papers*, NAACL-Short '06, pages 57–60, Stroudsburg, PA, USA, 2006. Association for Computational Linguistics. 00346.

[13] Adam Kilgarriff. "I Don't Believe in Word Senses". *Computers and the Humanities*, 31(2):91–113, 1997.

[14] Karin Kipper, Anna Korhonen, Neville Ryant, and Martha Palmer. A large-scale classification of English verbs. *Language Resources and Evaluation*, 42(1):21–40, 2008. 00139.

[15] Ramesh Krishnamurthy and Diane Nicholls. Peeling an Onion: The Lexicographer's Experience of Manual Sense Tagging. *Computers and the Humanities*, 34:85–97, 2000. 00000.

[16] Tomas Mikolov, Wen tau Yih, and Geoffrey Zweig. Linguistic Regularities in Continuous Space Word Representations. In *HLT-NAACL*, pages 746–751. The Association for Computational Linguistics, 2013.

[17] Roberto Navigli. Meaningful Clustering of Senses Helps Boost Word Sense Disambiguation Performance. In *Proceedings of the 21st International Conference on Computational Linguistics and 44th Annual Meeting of the ACL*, pages 105–112, Sydney, Australia, 2006.

[18] Roberto Navigli. Word sense disambiguation: A survey. *ACM Comput. Surv.*, 41(2):10:1–10:69, February 2009. 00697.

[19] James Pustejovsky, Catherine Havasi, Jessica Littman, Anna Rumshisky, and Marc Verhagen. Towards a generative lexical resource: The Brandeis Semantic Ontology. In *Proceedings of the Fifth Language Resource and Evaluation Conference*, 2006.

[20] R Core Team. *R: A Language and Environment for Statistical Computing*. R Foundation for Statistical Computing, 2014.

[21] Roser Saurí and James Pustejovsky. Are You Sure That This Happened? Assessing the Factuality Degree of Events in Text. *Comput. Linguist.*, 38(2):261–299, June 2012. 00068.

[22] Dmitriy Selivanov. *text2vec: Modern Text Mining Framework for R*. R Foundation for Statistical Computing, 2016.

```
Call:


lm(formula = rivalry ~ w2vec_hsdrff_Sum + z_finite + z_args.opaque
+ entail_mean + lemmas, data = rival)
Residuals:
Min            1Q             Median      3Q          Max
-59 380        -0.7319        -0.1572     0.1800      159 160


Coefficients:
(Intercept)          73522017     0.1532486     47 976     < 2,00E-16    ***
w2vec_hsdrff_Sum     -0.0003296   0.0011026     -0.299     0.7650
z_finitey            0.1455412    0.0161223     9 027      < 2,00E-16    ***
z_args.opaquey       0.5009538    0.2156543     2 323      0.0202        *
z_args.opaqueobj     0.2547546    0.3372427     0.755      0.4500
z_args.opaquesubj    0.0532390    0.0217931     2 443      0.0146        *
entail_mean          1.8818343    0.0217515     86 515     < 2,00E-16    ***
lemmasact            -3.7824581   0.1512543     -25 007    < 2,00E-16    ***
lemmasadjust         -2.7990281   0.1619012     -17 288    < 2,00E-16    ***
lemmasadvance        -4.2765385   0.1515831     -28 213    < 2,00E-16    ***
lemmasanswer         -4.2405515   0.1508514     -28 111    < 2,00E-16    ***
lemmasapprove        -3.1989511   0.1621494     -19 728    < 2,00E-16    ***
lemmasbid            -3.9934306   0.1548404     -25 791    < 2,00E-16    ***
lemmascancel         -2.8219473   0.1621358     -17 405    < 2,00E-16    ***
lemmasconceive       -2.2675897   0.1583548     -14 320    < 2,00E-16    ***
lemmascultivate      -2.7869641   0.1816034     -15 346    < 2,00E-16    ***
lemmascure           -3.8352304   0.1688616     -22 712    < 2,00E-16    ***
lemmasdistinguish    -2.9855282   0.1580461     -18 890    < 2,00E-16    ***
lemmasembrace        -3.3944366   0.1624320     -20 898    < 2,00E-16    ***
lemmasexecute        -2.2898572   0.1686455     -13 578    < 2,00E-16    ***
lemmashire           -3.4752011   0.2089821     -16 629    < 2,00E-16    ***
lemmaslast           -1.2512805   0.2101987     -5 953     2.65e-09      ***
lemmasmanage         -2.9204488   0.1531206     -19 073    < 2,00E-16    ***
lemmasmurder         -3.5778433   0.2101611     -17 024    < 2,00E-16    ***
lemmasneed           0.2515703    0.1692646     1 486      0.1372
lemmaspack           -4.3029164   0.1501447     -28 658    < 2,00E-16    ***
lemmasplan           -1.7058389   0.1817877     -9 384     < 2,00E-16    ***
lemmaspoint          -3.2865632   0.1512721     -21 726    < 2,00E-16    ***
lemmaspraise         -0.2847921   0.2091486     -1 362     0.1733
lemmasprescribe      -0.2380621   0.2091980     -1 138     0.2551
lemmassail           -1.8942963   0.1567161     -12 087    < 2,00E-16    ***
lemmasseal           -3.8569221   0.1581722     -24 384    < 2,00E-16    ***
lemmassee            -4.3824168   0.1498710     -29 241    < 2,00E-16    ***
lemmastalk           -3.7339660   0.1502380     -24 854    < 2,00E-16    ***
lemmasurge           -0.8541827   0.1623112     -5 263     1.43e-07      ***
---
Signif. codes:  0 '***' 0.001 '**' 0.01 '*' 0.05 '.' 0.1 ' ' 1
Residual standard error: 1.809 on 54503 degrees of freedom
Multiple R-squared:  0.3497,     Adjusted R-squared:  0.3493
F-statistic: 862.2 on 34 and 54503 DF,  p-value: < 2.2e-16
```

Figure 6: Linear model enriched with lemmas as predictors

J. Hlaváčová (Ed.): ITAT 2017 Proceedings, pp. 15–22
ISBN 978-1974274741, © 2017 V. Kettnerová, M. Lopatková

Complex Predicates with Light Verbs in VALLEX:
From Formal Model to Lexicographic Description

Václava Kettnerová and Markéta Lopatková

Charles University, Faculty of Mathematics and Physics, Prague, Czech Republic
{kettnerova,lopatkova}@ufal.mff.cuni.cz

Abstract: Natural languages are typically characterized by a large area where grammar and lexicon overlap. Complex predicates with light verbs represent a typical language phenomenon at the lexicon-grammar interface. Their theoretically adequate representation thus requires a close interplay between the lexicon and the grammar. In this paper, we introduce a formal model for the lexicographic description of Czech complex predicates of the given type. The central type of Czech complex predicates are composed of light verbs and predicative nouns. We demonstrate that although their syntactic structure formation is highly complex, it still exhibits enough regularity to be captured by formal rules.

1 Motivation

Complex predicates with light verbs (CPs) consist of two syntactic units, a light verb (LV) and a predicative noun (PN) (or, sporadically, a predicative adjective or adverb); this verb-noun pair forms a single predicative unit, as for example *dát radu* 'give advice', *dostat rozkaz* 'get an order', *mít radost* 'be happy' (lit. have joy), or *uzavřít dohodu* 'make an agreement'. Due to their complex characteristics, CPs proven to be challenging for syntactic theories as well as for natural language processing tasks.

Complex predicates with light verbs are characterized by a discrepancy in their syntax and semantics [1]: whereas the meaning of a CP is primarily expressed by the predicative noun, forming thus the semantic core of the CP, it is the semantically impoverished light verb which serves as the syntactic center of a sentence. We can exemplify this discrepancy on the CP *uzavřít dohodu* 'make an agreement', as used in (1). This CP is semantically characterized by three participants, namely 'Party_1' (*Francie* 'France'), 'Party_2' (*Německo* 'Germany'), and 'Obligation' (*neútočení* 'non-aggression'), all these participants are provided by the predicative noun *dohoda* 'agreement'. However, two of these participants – 'Party_1' and 'Party_2' – are expressed in the surface structure of the sentence not as nominal but as verbal modifications, namely as the subject and as the indirect object, while only the participant 'Obligation' is expressed as a nominal modification, namely as its attribute, see (1). The syntactic structure of the given

sentence is thus formed by valency complementations of both the light verb and the predicative noun. In contrast, the sentence with the predicative verb *uzavřít* 'close; turn off', see e.g. (2), is characterized by two participants, 'Agent' and 'Affected_object', being evoked by the verb, they are expressed on the surface as valency complementations of the given verb.

(1) *Francie*$_{Sb-verb}$ *uzavřela s Německem*$_{InObj-verb}$ *dohodu*$_{Obj-verb}$ *o neútočení*$_{Atr-noun}$.
'France made an agreement with Germany on non-aggression.'

(2) *Hasiči*$_{Sb-verb}$ *uzavřeli přívod*$_{Obj-verb}$ *plynu*.
'Firemen turned off the gas main.'

Although the contribution of light verbs and predicative nouns to the syntactic structure formation of CPs has been put under scrutiny within various theoretical frameworks – see e.g. argument merger formulated within the Government Binding theory [2], argument fusion [3] and argument composition within the Lexical-Functional Grammar [4], and the study by Alonso Ramos drawing on the Meaning ↔ Text Theory [5] – many of its aspects still remain unclear.

Czech, as an inflectional language encoding syntactic relations by morphological cases, provides a great opportunity to study the distribution of valency complementations in syntactic structures of CPs since morphological forms of valency complementations serve as valuable clues for determining whether a certain valency complementation belongs to the light verb or to the predicative noun. However, none of the works focused on Czech CPs provides an explicit description of the syntactic structure formation of CPs, see esp. [6, 7].

In this paper, we summarize our theoretical results described earlier and relate the proposed model with an extensive data annotation, see esp. [8, 9, 10]. We focus on the deep and surface structure of CPs, mainly with respect to the contribution of valency complementations to the syntactic structure of CPs made by the light verb and by the predicative noun and with respect to the role of coreference between the complementations in these structures (Section 3). On the basis of our theoretical findings, we propose an economic and linguistically informed formal model of CPs consisting of a grammatical part (Section 3) and a lexical part (Section 4). Finally, grounded on extensive data annotation, we introduce an overall typology of CPs based on their coreferential characteristics and provide basic statistics for Czech CPs (Section 5).

2   VALLEX and FGD Framework

The proposed representation of CPs is elaborated within the Functional Generative Description (FGD), a stratificational and dependency-oriented theoretical linguistic framework [11]. One of the core concepts of FGD is that of valency [12]: at the layer of linguistically structured meaning (also the deep syntactic layer), it is the valency that provides the structure of a dependency tree. The valency theory of FGD has been applied in several valency lexicons, esp. PDT-Vallex[1] [13] and VALLEX[2] [14], and verified on extensive corpus data, esp. within the Prague Dependency Treebank (PDT)[3]. VALLEX, being the most elaborated lexicon of Czech verbs, forms a solid basis for the lexical component of FGD.

For the purpose of representation of language phenomena bridging between the grammar and the lexicon (e.g., diatheses and reciprocity), VALLEX is divided into a *lexical part* (i.e., the data component) and a *grammatical part* (i.e., the grammar component) [15, 16]. This division proves to be useful also for the representation of CPs.

Data component. The central organizing concept of the lexical part of VALLEX is the concept of *lexeme*. The lexeme associates a set of lexical forms, representing the verb in an utterance, with a set of *lexical units*, corresponding to their individual senses.

The data component consists of an inventory of lexical units of verbs with their respective valency frames underlying their deep syntactic structures. Each valency frame is modeled as a sequence of frame slots corresponding to valency complementations of a verb labeled by (rather coarse-grained) deep syntactic roles such as 'Actor' (ACT), 'Patient' (PAT), 'Addressee' (ADDR), 'Effect' (EFF), 'Direction', 'Location', 'Manner', etc. Further, the information on obligatoriness ('?' in front of a role label indicates its optionality in this text) and on possible morphological forms (here in subscript) is specified for each valency complementation. Each lexical unit can be further described by additional syntactic and syntactic-semantic information, e.g., on reciprocity, diatheses (as e.g. passivization), syntactico-semantic class etc.

For the lexicographic representation of CPs, the VALLEX lexicon was extended to cover also predicative nouns. In addition, the respective lexical units

representing light verbs and predicative nouns were enriched with attributes that allow a user to derive valency structures of the whole CPs – these attributes are thoroughly described in Section 4.

Grammar component. The grammar component represents a part of the overall grammar of Czech, it stores formal rules directly related to the valency structure of verbs. This component serves for an economic description of systematic changes in the valency structure of verbs associated with various syntactic phenomena, esp. with passivization and reciprocity. It also comprises rules allowing for the derivation of deep and surface syntactic structures of CPs. These rules are presented in Section 3.

3   Grammar Component: Formation of Deep and Surface Syntactic Structures of CPs

3.1   Deep Syntactic Structure

The deep syntactic structure of CPs is formed by both valency complementations from the valency frame of the light verb and complementations from the frame of the predicative noun.

Predicative nouns. The valency frame of a predicative noun describes the usage of the noun in nominal structures. Individual valency complementations are semantically saturated – they correspond to individual semantic participants characterizing a situation denoted by the noun, as can be exemplified on the predicative noun $dohoda_{PN}$ 'agreement', see its valency frame and example illustrating its nominal structure in (3) and the correspondence between its valency complementations and its semantic participants in (4):

(3) $dohoda_{PN}$ 'agreement':
$ACT_{2,pos}\ ADDR_{s+7}\ PAT_{na+6,o+6,inf,aby,zda,že,cont}$
$dohoda\ Francie_{Party\_1,ACT(2)}$
$s\ Německem_{Party\_2,ADDR(s+7)}\ o\ neútočení_{Obligation,PAT(o+6)}$
'the agreement of France with Germany on non-aggression'

(4)
ACT	$\Leftrightarrow$	Party_1
ADDR	$\Leftrightarrow$	Party_2
PAT	$\Leftrightarrow$	Obligation

Light verbs. The deep structure of a light verb is formed by its valency frame, with one position (labeled CPHR) reserved for a predicative noun. A single light verb may be characterized by different deep syntactic structures, i.e., described by different valency frames which combine with different predicative nouns, see e.g. the light verb $uzavřít_{LV}$ in (5) and (7).

---

[1]http://lindat.mff.cuni.cz/services/PDT-Vallex/
[2]http://ufal.mff.cuni.cz/vallex/3.0/
[3]http://ufal.mff.cuni.cz/pdt3.0

Light verbs, being (to some extent) semantically bleached, do not evoke any semantic participants. As a result, their valency complementations are characterized primarily as semantically underspecified deep syntactic positions, see schemes provided in (6) and (8) (compare also with [5]).

(5) $uzavřít_{LV}$ 'make'
     ACT_1 $ADDR_{s+7}$ $CPHR_4$

(6)
ACT	$\Leftrightarrow$	$\emptyset$
ADDR	$\Leftrightarrow$	$\emptyset$
CPHR	$\Leftrightarrow$	PN

(This LV combines, e.g., with the PNs *dohoda* 'agreement' and *sázka* 'bet'.)

(7) $uzavřít_{LV}$ 'end, conclude':
     ACT_1 $CPHR_4$

(8)
| ACT | $\Leftrightarrow$ | $\emptyset$ |
| CPHR | $\Leftrightarrow$ | PN |

(This LV combines, e.g., with the PNs *debata* 'discussion' and *vyšetřování* 'inquiry'.)

The only exception when a light verb contributes its semantic participant is represented by CPs with causative LVs. The causative LVs are seen as initiating the event denoted by the predicative noun selecting the given verb. These verbs thus contribute the 'Instigator' participant (and the nouns their respective semantic participants). For example, the LV $uzavřít_{LV}$ 'close' that is instantiated, e.g., in the CP $uzavřít$ $přístup$ 'close an access' represents the causative LV, with the 'Instigator' mapped onto its ACT, see the valency frame of this verb (9) and the scheme of the mapping of semantic participants and valency complementations (10):

(9) $uzavřít_{LV}$ 'close':
     ACT_1 $CPHR_4$ $?BEN_3$

(10)
ACT	$\Leftrightarrow$	Instigator
CPHR	$\Leftrightarrow$	PN
BEN	$\Leftrightarrow$	$\emptyset$

(This LV combines, e.g., with the PN *přístup* 'access'.)

Within CPs, *semantically underspecified* valency complementations of LVs *acquire semantic capacity via coreference* with valency complementations of the predicative nouns with which they form CPs. These coreferential relations between valency complementations of LVs and complementations of PNs thus characterize the deep syntactic structure of individual CPs.

Complex predicates with light verbs. The deep syntactic structure of a CP is formed via an interplay between the valency frames of the respective LV and PN that form the given CP. A crucial role in the formation of the deep syntactic structure of a CP plays (i) the number of semantic participants involved in a situation denoted by the CP, and (ii) coreferential relations between the valency complementations of the LV and the PN [8]. The deep syntactic structure of a CP thus consists of:

- all *nominal valency complementations*, as they (directly) correspond to semantic participants;

- all *verbal valency complementations*, as their semantic saturation is acquired in one of the following ways:
  – the CPHR valency position, as it is reserved for the predicative noun;
  – the verbal valency complementation corresponding to the 'Instigator' participant (if present);
  – other verbal valency complementations, as they corefer with individual nominal valency complementations.

Let us exemplify the deep structure formation on the example of the CP $uzavřít$ $dohodu$ 'make an agreement'. The predicative noun $dohoda_{PN}$ 'agreement' is characterized by three semantic participants corresponding to three valency complementations of this noun, as indicated in (3) and (4). The light verb $uzavřít_{LV}$ 'make' is characterized by the valency frame provided in (5). The CPHR position of the light verb is filled with the PN *dohoda* 'agreement', the remaining valency complementations ACT and ADDR of the light verb enter into coreference with the ACT and ADDR of the given predicative noun, respectively (thus they obtain their semantic capacity from the given nominal complementations), see scheme (11), the sentence below and the deep dependency tree of the given CP in Figure 1:

(11) $uzavřít$ $dohodu$ 'make an agreement':[4]
ACT_{LV}	$\leftrightarrow$	ACT_{PN}	$\Leftrightarrow$	Party_1
$ADDR_{LV}$	$\leftrightarrow$	$ADDR_{PN}$	$\Leftrightarrow$	Party_2
		PAT_{PN}	$\Leftrightarrow$	Obligation
$CPHR_{LV}$			$\Leftrightarrow$	$dohoda_{PN}$

$Francie_{Party\_1}$ $uzavřela$ s $Německem_{Party\_2}$ $dohodu_{PN}$ o $neútočení_{Obligation}$.
'France made an agreement with Germany on non-aggression.'

In many cases, a predicative noun can select different light verbs (and thus create different CPs), and so makes it possible to embed the expressed event "into different general semantic scenarios and thus to perspectivize it from the point of view of different participants" [8]. For example, the predicative noun $rozkaz_{PN}$

---

[4]In the schemes, correspondence between semantic participants and valency complementations is marked with $\Leftrightarrow$ whereas $\leftrightarrow$ is reserved for coreference relations.

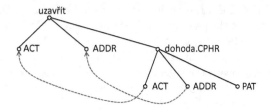

Figure 1: The deep dependency structure of the CP *uzavřít dohodu* 'make an agreement' .

selects either the light verb *dát*$_{LV}$ 'to give', or the light verb *dostat*$_{LV}$ 'to get'. This noun evokes three semantic participants, namely 'Speaker', 'Recipient', and 'Information'. When it selects the light verb *dát*$_{LV}$ 'to give', the situation expressed by this noun is viewed from the perspective of the 'Speaker' as it occupies the prominent subject position given by the ACT of the light verb, see example (12), while selecting the light verb *dostat*$_{LV}$ 'to get', the situation is perspectivized from the 'Recipient', see example (13).

(12) *Generál*$_{Speaker,ACT-LV}$ *dal rozkaz*
      vojákům$_{Recipient,ADDR-LV}$ *k ústupu*$_{Information,PAT-PN}$.
      'The general gave soldiers the order to retreat.'

(13) *Vojáci*$_{Recipient,ACT-LV}$ *dostali od generála*$_{Speaker,ORIG-LV}$
      rozkaz k ústupu$_{Information,PAT-PN}$.
      'Soldiers got the order to retreat by the general.'

3.2 Surface Syntactic Structure

The theoretical analysis supported by the extensive empirical data annotation has revealed that with CPs in Czech, each semantic participant is typically expressed in the surface sentence just once.[5] Despite the fact that semantic participants are contributed to CPs – with the exception of the verbal 'Instigator' – by predicative nouns, Czech CPs have a strong tendency to express these participants in the surface structure as verbal modifications, see as well [7]. Namely, those participants characterizing a CP that are referred to by both valency complementations of the PN as well as (via coreference) complementations of the LV are primarily expressed on the surface as the verbal modifications. On the other hand, those participants that are mapped only onto valency complementations of the PN are realized as the nominal modifications.

As a result, the rules governing the formation of the surface syntactic structure of Czech CPs can be summarized as follows:

- As *verbal modifications*, all valency complementations from the *valency frame of the light verb* are primarily expressed in the surface structure, namely:[6]
  (i) the valency complementation filled by the predicative noun (the CPHR functor): it is obligatorily expressed in the surface structure as a verbal modification;
  (ii) the valency complementation corresponding to 'Instigator' (if present): it can be expressed in the surface structure only as a verbal modification;
  (iii) other verbal valency complementations: they are primarily expressed in the surface structure as verbal modifications, too.

- As *nominal modifications*:
  (iv) those valency complementations from the *valency frame of the predicative noun* that are not in coreference with verbal ones are primarily expressed in the surface structure.[7]

For instance, within the CP *uzavřít dohodu* 'make an agreement', the following valency complementations are expressed in the surface structure: all the valency complementations of the LV *uzavřít* 'to make' (see its valency frame in (5)) are expressed as verbal modifications on the surface, namely: CPHR reserved for the predicative noun *dohoda* 'agreement' (principle (i)) in the direct object position, the verbal ACT and ADDR in the subject position and the indirect object position, respectively (principle (iii)) (these valency complementations refer to the 'Party_1' and 'Party_2' via coreference with the ACT and ADDR of the PN , see scheme (11)). From the valency complementations of the PN *dohoda* 'agreement' (the valency frame in (3)), only PAT (referring to 'Obligation', not being in coreference with any verbal complementation) is expressed on the surface as a nominal modification (principle (iv)); the remaining ACT and ADDR complementations of this noun (being in coreference with the verbal ACT and ADDR) are subject to systemic ellipsis; see the example sentence below and its surface dependency tree in Figure 2:

Francie$_{Party\_1,ACT-LV}$ *uzavřela s Německem*$_{Party\_2,ADDR-LV}$
dohodu$_{PN,CPHR-LV}$ *o neútočení*$_{Obligation,PAT-PN}$.

---

[5]The only exception is represented by the semantic participant mapped onto the nominal ACT: under certain conditions, this participant can be expressed twice, both as a verbal and as a nominal modification (e.g., *Vrchní komisař*$_{Agens,ACT(1)-LV}$ *již své*$_{Agens,ACT(pos)-PN}$ *vyšetřování*$_{PN}$ *zločinu*$_{Incident,PAT(2)-PN}$ *uzavřel*$_{LV}$. 'The chief inspector has already concluded his investigation of the crime.').

[6]We disregard the cases of valency complementations unexpressed on the surface due to their optionality, actual ellipsis, generalization etc.

[7]In some cases, a nominal valency complementation coreferring with a verbal one may be alternatively expressed in the surface structure as a nominal modification, see e.g.
(a) *S Německem*$_{Party\_2,ACT-LV}$ *Francie*$_{Party\_1,ACT-LV}$ *uzavřela dohodu*$_{PN,CPHR-LV}$. vs.
(b) *Francie*$_{Party\_1,ACT-LV}$ *uzavřela dohodu*$_{PN,CPHR-LV}$ *s Německem*$_{Party\_2,ACT-PN}$,
with the 'Party_2' participant (*s Německem*) preferably analyzed as a verbal (in (a)) or a nominal (in (b)) modification.

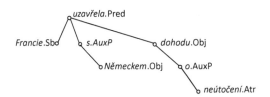

Figure 2: The surface dependency structure of the sentence *Francie uzavřela s Německem dohodu o neútočení.* 'France made an agreement with Germany on non-aggression.' (simplified)

'France made an agreement with Germany on non-aggression.'

4 Data Component: Interlinking Lexical Units

As was shown above, the deep and surface syntactic structures of CPs are formed as a combination of valency structures of respective predicative nouns and light verbs, with respect to the coreference between their individual valency complementations. The process of both the deep and surface structure formation is regular enough to be described on the rule basis. These rules operate on the information provided by the data component of the lexicon.

In the data component of the VALLEX lexicon, individual lexical units of verbs and predicative nouns are described. In addition to the core valency information in a form of valency frames, these lexical units carry three special attributes linking the respective pairs of lexical units of the PN and LV allowing for the derivation of both deep and surface syntactic structures of the whole complex predicate, namely attributes lvc, map and instig.

Attribute lvc. Respective lexical units of LVs and PNs that form CPs are linked by the attribute lvc, the value of which is a list of references to respective lexical units. This attribute is attached to lexical units of predicative nouns and (for user's convenience) to lexical units of light verbs as well. Figure 3 illustrates three lexical units for the LV *uzavřít*_{LV} 'make; end, conclude; close, terminate' (see also (5), (7) and (9)).

If a LV forms syntactic structures with different PNs characterized by different coreferential relations more instances of the attribute lvc (indexed with numbers) are assigned to the relevant lexical unit.

Attribute map. The information on the coreference between valency complementations of LVs and complementations of PNs is provided in the attribute map. This attribute is attached to PNs (as it is the PN that

selects an appropriate LV). The value of the map attribute is a list of pairs of coreferring complementations. Figure 4 illustrates three lexical units for three PNs, namely, *dohoda*_{PN} 'agreement' (see also (3)), *vyšetřování*_{PN} 'investigation', and *přístup*_{PN} 'access'.

Each PN can be assigned more than one attribute map reflecting different coreference relations; in such cases, the map attributes are co-indexed with the relevant lvc attributes to allow for the correct formation of the CPs structures.

Attribute instig. The information on the mapping of the 'Instigator' onto a valency complementation of relevant LVs is recorded in the attribute instig attached to the verbal valency frame, see lexical unit 3 in Figure 3.

If a LV forms syntactic structures with different PNs characterized by different coreferential relations, the instig attribute is co-indexed with the respective lvc attribute, containing the list of references to PNs that select the LV with the 'Instigator'.

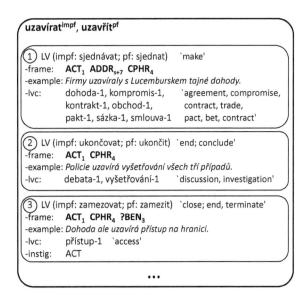

Figure 3: Three lexical units for the LV *uzavřít*, which are instantiated, e.g., in the CPs *uzavřít dohodu* 'make an agreement', *uzavřít vyšetřování* 'close an investigation', and *uzavřít přístup* 'close an access', respectively (simplified).

5 Corpus Data Analysis

The following Tables 1 and 2 summarize the corpus analysis of Czech CPs formed by 129 verb lemmas from the VALLEX lexicon (those LVs were selected that have at least one valency frame with the CPHR functor in the PDT corpus, see Section 2). The CPs were extracted from the Czech National Corpus,

dohoda

(1) ujednání; domluva   `agreement'
-frame: $\textbf{ACT}_{2,pos}$ $\textbf{ADDR}_{s+7}$ $\textbf{PAT}_{na+6,o+6,inf,aby,zda,\check{z}e,cont}$
-example: *dohoda Francie s Německem o neútočení*
-lvc: uzavírat/uzavřít-1, vypovídat/vypovědět-5
-map: $\text{ACT}_{PN}\text{-ACT}_{LV}$ & $\text{ADDR}_{PN}\text{-ADDR}_{LV}$

      •••

vyšetřování

(1) objasňování; prozkoumávání   'investigation'
-frame: $\textbf{ACT}_{2,pos}$ $\textbf{PAT}_{2,pos}$
-example: *vyšetřování všech odhalených případů zpronevěry*
-lvc: uzavírat/uzavřít-2, vést-5
-map: $\text{ACT}_{PN}\text{-ACT}_{LV}$

      •••

přístup

(1) možnost někam vstoupit; přistoupení   'access'
-frame: $\textbf{ACT}_1$ $\textbf{DIR3}_{do+2,k+3,na+4}$
-example: *přístup na hranici; přístup na trh práce*
-lvc: otvírat/otevírat/otevřít-1, uzavírat/uzavřít-3
-map: $\text{ACT}_{PN}\text{-BEN}_{LV}$

      •••

Figure 4: Three lexical units for the PNs *dohoda* 'agreement', *vyšetřování* 'investigation', and *přístup* 'access', respectively (simplified).

SYN2010, by the Word Sketch Engine [17] allowing to identify for each verb lemma its nominal collocates expressed as its direct object (function has_obj4). From the obtained list of collocations, only those nominal collocates were indicated by human annotators that represent PNs (560 noun lemmas in total). As a key criterion for identifying CPs, the coreference between the ACT of the noun and some of valency complementations of the LV has been adopted [18]. This criterion was satisfied by 1,025 collocations, which represent the most frequent and semantically salient CPs of the selected light verbs.

The identified CPs were further annotated with respect to the coreference between valency complementations of the LV and PN and with respect to the mapping of 'Instigator' (where it was relevant), see esp. [10]. Tables 1 and 2 summarize results of the annotation process. Table 1 contains those CPs the light verbs of which behave unambiguously with respect to the causative feature, i.e., they are either non-causative (∅ in the 'Instig' column), or causative. With the CPs with causative light verbs, the Instigator was mapped either onto verbal ACT, or onto verbal ORIG. In the annotation, 12 types of coreferential relation between verbal and nominal valency complementations were identified; the most frequent was represented by the coreference between ACT of the light verb and ACT of the predicative noun (506 CPs, i.e. almost 50 % of all analyzed CPs).

In the annotation, a specific type of CPs characterized by an ambiguous character with respect to the

causativity of LVs was found (122 cases, i.e. almost 12% of CPs). These CPs are formed by PNs characterized by the semantic participants 'Experiencer' and 'Stimulus'. Two situations occur with these CPs. First, the valency complementation of a PN corresponding to 'Stimulus' enters in coreference with ACT of the LV with which the given PN forms the CP (as exemplified in (14), Figure 5); in this case, the LV behaves as non-causative verb. Second, the given complementation of a PN is not in coreference with any verbal complementation; in this case, the LV contributes the 'Instigator' to the CP (example (15), Figure 6). For example, with the CP *vyvolat protest*, the semantic participant 'Stimulus' given by the PN $protest_{PN}$ 'protest' mapped onto PAT of the noun either enters in coreference with the ACT of the LV $vyvolat_{LV}$ 'to raise', see example (14), or remains without coreference, see example (15).

(14) $Stavba_{Stimulus,ACT-LV}$ *dálnice*   *vyvolala*
      u $obyvatel_{Experiencer,LOC-LV}$ $protesty_{PN,CPHR-LV}$.
      'The construction of the motorway has prompted protests of the inhabitants.'

(15) $Stavba_{Instigator,ACT-LV}$ *dálnice*   *vyvolala*
      u $obyvatel_{Experiencer,LOC-LV}$ $protesty_{PN,CPHR-LV}$ *proti*
      $postupu_{Stimulus,PAT-PN}$ *radních.*
      'The construction of the motorway has prompted protests of the inhabitants against the decision of councillors.'

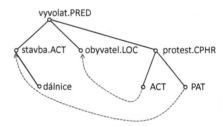

Figure 5: The deep dependency structure of the non-causative example (14) (simplified).

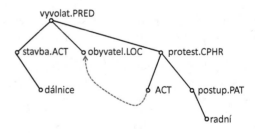

Figure 6: The deep dependency structure of the causative example (15) (simplified).

Table 1: Unambiguous Czech CPs identified in the corpus data, sorted according to causativity of LVs and types of coreference between verbal and nominal valency complementations.

'Instig'	coreference			#	%	examples
∅	$ACT_{PN}- ACT_{LV}$			506	49.4	*mít chuť, vést život, uzavřít debatu, uzavřít vyšetřování*
	$ACT_{PN}- ACT_{LV}$	&	$ADDR_{PN}- ADDR_{LV}$	120	11.7	*dát rozkaz, poskytnout rozhovor, uzavřít dohodu, uzavřít sázku*
	$ACT_{PN}- ACT_{LV}$	&	$PAT_{PN}- ADDR_{LV}$	93	9.1	*navázat vztah*
	$ACT_{PN}- ORIG_{LV}$	&	$ADDR_{PN}- ACT_{LV}$	28	2.7	*dostat nabídku, získat informace*
	$ACT_{PN}- ORIG_{LV}$	&	$PAT_{PN}- ACT_{LV}$	22	2.1	*dostat ránu, dostat pokutu*
	$ACT_{PN}- ACT_{LV}$	&	$PAT_{PN}- DIR3_{LV}$	28	2.7	*obracet pozornost, položit důraz*
	$ACT_{PN}- ACT_{LV}$	&	$PAT_{PN}- LOC_{LV}$	22	2.1	*najít inspiraci, najít potěšení*
	$ACT_{PN}- LOC_{LV}$	&	$PAT_{PN}- ACT_{LV}$	22	2.1	*najít odezvu, nalézt pochopení*
ACT_{LV}	$ACT_{PN}- ADDR_{LV}$			53	5.2	*dát naději, vynést slávu, vzít odvahu*
	$ACT_{PN}- LOC_{LV}$			26	2.5	*probouzet podezíravost, vzbudit zdání*
	$ACT_{PN}- BEN_{LV}$			8	0.8	*zvednout náladu, otevřít přístup, uzavřít přístup*
$ORIG_{LV}$	$ACT_{PN}- ACT_{LV}$			18	1.8	*dostat příležitost, získat výhodu*

Table 2: Ambiguous Czech CPs identified in the corpus data, sorted according to causativity of LVs and types of coreference between verbal and nominal valency complementations.

without 'Instigator' coreference			with 'Instigator' 'Instig'	coreference	#	%	examples
$ACT_{PN}- LOC_{LV}$	&	$PAT_{PN}- ACT_{LV}$	ACT_{LV}	$ACT_{PN}- LOC_{LV}$	92	9.0	*vyvolat protest, budit důvěru*
$ACT_{PN}- ADDR_{LV}$	&	$PAT_{PN}- ACT_{LV}$	ACT_{LV}	$ACT_{PN}- ADDR_{LV}$	23	2.2	*přinést radost, činit obtíž*
$ACT_{PN}- LOC_{LV}$	&	$ORIG_{PN}- ACT_{LV}$	ACT_{LV}	$ACT_{PN}- LOC_{LV}$	3	0.3	*vzbudit pocit*
$ACT_{PN}- LOC_{LV}$	&	$ADDR_{PN}- ACT_{LV}$	ACT_{LV}	$ACT_{PN}- LOC_{LV}$	4	0.4	*vyvolat podezření*

6 Conclusion

In this paper, we have summarized results of our analysis of Czech complex predicates with light verbs. We have described its lexicographic model based on a close cooperation of the lexical and grammar component. Although our proposal is primarily designed for the Valency Lexicon of Czech verbs VALLEX, we suppose that its main tenets can be easily adopted by other lexical resources as well. Finally, we have introduced the annotation of a large collection of linguistic data which will be integrated in the VALLEX lexicon soon.

Acknowledgements

The work on this project has been supported by the grant of the *Czech Science Foundation* (project GA15-09979S) and partially by the LINDAT/CLARIN project of the *Ministry of Education, Youth and Sports of the Czech Republic* (project LM2015071).

This work has been using language resources distributed by the LINDAT/CLARIN project of the *Ministry of Education, Youth and Sports of the Czech Republic* (project LM2015071).

References

[1] Algeo, J.: Having a look at the expanded predicate. In Aarts, B., Meyer, C.F., eds.: The Verb in Contemporary English: Theory and Description. Cambridge University Press, Cambridge (1995) 203–217

[2] Grimshaw, J., Mester, A.: Light verbs and θ-marking. Linguistic inquiry **19** (1988) 205–232

[3] Butt, M.: The light verb jungle: Still hacking away. In Amberber, M., Baker, B., Harvey, M., eds.: Complex Predicates in Cross-Linguistic Perspective. Cambridge University Press, Cambridge (2010) 48–78

[4] Hinrichs, E., Kathol, A., Nakazawa, T.: Complex Predicates in Nonderivational Syntax. Syntax and Semantics 30. Academic Press, San Diego (1998)

[5] Alonso Ramos, M.: Towards the synthesis of support verb constructions: Distribution of syntactic actants between the verb and the noun. In Wanner, L., Mel'čuk, I.A., eds.: Selected Lexical and Grammatical Issues in the Meaning-Text Theory. John Benjamins Publishing Company, Amsterdam, Philadelphia (2007) 97–137

[6] Radimský, J.: Verbo-nominální predikát s kategoriálním slovesem. Editio Universitatis Bohemiae Meridionalis, České Budějovice (2010)

[7] Macháčková, E.: Constructions with verbs and abstract nouns in Czech (analytical predicates). In Čmejrková, S., Štícha, F., eds.: The Syntax of Sentence and Text: A Festschrift for František Daneš. Volume 42 of Linguistic and Literary Studies in Eastern Europe. John Benjamins Publishing Company, Amsterdam, Philadelphia (1994) 365–374

[8] Kettnerová, V., Lopatková, M.: At the lexicon-grammar interface: The case of complex predicates in the functional generative description. In Hajičová, E., Nivre, J., eds.: Proceedings of Depling 2015, Uppsala, Sweden, Uppsala University (2015) 191–200

[9] Kettnerová, V.: Syntaktická struktura komplexních predikátů. Slovo a slovesnost (2017) (in print).

[10] Kettnerová, V., Lopatková, M.: Ke koreferenci u komplexních predikátů s kategoriálním slovesem. Korpus – gramatika – axiologie (2017) (submitted).

[11] Sgall, P., Hajičová, E., Panevová, J.: The Meaning of the Sentence in Its Semantic and Pragmatic Aspects. Reidel, Dordrecht (1986)

[12] Panevová, J.: Valency Frames and the Meaning of the Sentence. In Luelsdorff, P.A., ed.: The Prague School of Structural and Functional Linguistics. John Benjamins Publishing Company, Amsterdam/Philadelphia (1994) 223–243

[13] Urešová, Z.: Valence sloves v Pražském závislostním korpusu. Ústav formální a aplikované lingvistiky, Praha (2011)

[14] Lopatková, M., Kettnerová, V., Bejček, E., Vernerová, A., Žabokrtský, Z.: Valenční slovník českých sloves VALLEX. Karolinum, Praha (2016)

[15] Kettnerová, V., Lopatková, M., Bejček, E.: The Syntax-Semantics Interface of Czech Verbs in the Valency Lexicon. In: Proceedings of the XV EURALEX International Congress, Oslo, University of Oslo (2012) 434–443

[16] Lopatková, M., Kettnerová, V.: Alternations: From Lexicon to Grammar And Back Again. In Hajičová, E., Boguslavsky, I., eds.: Proceedings of the Workshop on Grammar and Lexicon: Interactions and Interfaces (GramLex), Ōsaka, Japan, ICCL, The COLING 2016 Organizing Committee (2016) 18–27

[17] Kilgarriff, A., Baisa, V., Bušta, J., Jakubíček, M., Kovář, V., Michelfeit, J., Rychlý, P., Suchomel, V.: The sketch engine: ten years on. Lexicography ASIALEX 1 (2014) 7–36

[18] Kettnerová, V., Lopatková, M., Bejček, E., Vernerová, A., Podobová, M.: Corpus based identification of czech light verbs. In Gajdošová, K., Žáková, A., eds.: Proceedings of the Seventh International Conference Slovko 2013; Natural Language Processing, Corpus Linguistics, E-learning, Lüdenscheid, Germany, Slovak National Corpus, L'. Štúr Institute of Linguistics, Slovak Academy of Sciences, RAM-Verlag (2013) 118–128

J. Hlaváčová (Ed.): ITAT 2017 Proceedings, pp. 23–26

Attributes Extraction from Product Descriptions on e-Shops

Michaela Linková, Peter Gurský

Institute of Computer Science

Faculty of Science, P.J.Šafárik University in Košice

Jesenná 5, 040 01 Košice, Slovakia

michaela.linkova@student.upjs.sk, peter.gursky@upjs.sk

Abstract. Some e-shops present product attributes in structured form, but many others use the textual description only. Attributes of products are essential in automated product deduplication. We suggest methods for automated extraction of attributes and their values from product descriptions to a structural form. The structural data extracted from other e-shops are used as background knowledge.

1 Introduction

Nowadays there is an increasing interest in effective process of extracting information from big amount of data. The problem of searching and obtaining relevant information is handled by several areas of computer science. Project Kapsa [1] deals with extraction and unification of information from web pages, focusing on products on e-shops. The aim of the project is the creation and management of a collection of products which are offered by e-shops. Crucial part of processing the e-shops' data is a deduplication of products, i.e. the decision if any two products extracted from different e-shops are the same. To increase the precision of the deduplication, structured data about the products (product properties and their values) are essential.

Although some e-shops present attributes of products in table from, many other e-shops provide a textual description only. The descriptions usually contain values of many product properties and are written in natural language.

This work-in-progress paper presents our current methods of automatic extraction of product attributes with their values from product descriptions. Products have attributes of 3 main types: String, number with unit and Boolean. Each type is presented individually in natural language. Therefore we propose unique extraction method for each attribute type.

2 State of the Art

To extract product attribute/property with its value from a text description, we need to recognize that the attribute and/or its value are mentioned in the text. Named-entity recognition (NER) is a close research area to our problem. NER is the information extraction task of identifying and classifying mentions of people, organizations, locations and other named entities within text. Approaches to NER are surveyed in [3]. The dominant technique for addressing the NER problem is supervised learning. A usual NER method consists of tagging words of a test corpus when they are annotated as entities in the (rather big) training corpus. A semi-supervised techniques decrease amount of manual annotation needed to train a classifier. Typically, the sentences in Wikipedia articles are considered annotated, because they contain context links to other Wikipedia pages in sentences. The titles of such pages are then considered to be the names of the entities and their URLs become the identifiers. The common learning constellation for supervised and semi-supervised techniques is the processing of annotated texts. Majority of learning models process entity names as well as surrounding words. Many learning approaches have been used to handle NER: Hidden Markov Models [4], decision trees [5], Support Vector Machines [6], Conditional Random Fields [7].

Another approach, similar to NER, is terminology / entity / term extraction. The goal of terminology extraction is to automatically extract relevant terms from text, typically based on a vocabulary of domain-relevant (possibly multi-word) terms. Typical approach is to extract term candidates using linguistic processors and filter them using statistical and/or machine learning methods. The C-value/NC-value method [8] can be an example. To handle multi-word terms, the methods usually use n-grams, that is, the combination of n words appearing in the corpus.

3 Background Knowledge

Unlike general named entity recognition, as a part of natural language processing, we can profit from knowledge of product domain and drastically reduce the number of possible entities to search in product description. The product domain can be determined from the product web presentation, since it is usually presented on specific position on every product detail page of the e-shop.

The second advantage is the structured and annotated data of product domain in background knowledge. These data are extracted from the e-shops with structured attribute presentation in form of tables. Therefore, we can use the dictionary of the attribute names in different languages (English, Slovak ...) and variations (synonyms, abbreviations) for each attribute of a given product domain. Similarly, we can use various forms of units' names (e.g. kg, kilograms, kilos, kilogramov, kíl ...). Our background database contains also unit conversions between convertible units (e.g. grams vs. kg). Finally, the attribute types and the list of extracted values of each attribute and product domain is stored in the background knowledge.

The annotation of attributes in Kapsa [1] is a semiautomatic process driven by administrator in web GUI. Input for the annotation is a list of attribute names and values in String form for each product extracted from e-shop web pages, possibly with some additional tags. The annotation produces a set of rules that determines product domain, attribute identification (including attribute deduplication), attribute type, value and unit extraction, etc. If the product domain or attribute is already annotated for other e-shop, annotator usually just plays the role of the validator of an automatic annotation.

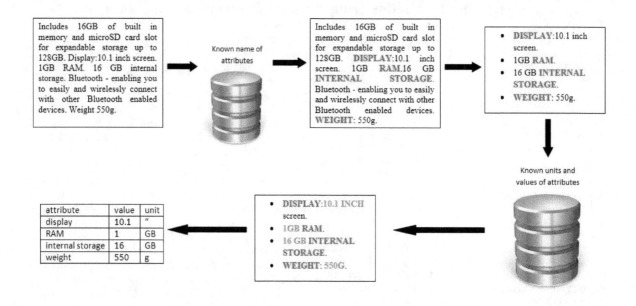

Figure 1: Extraction of attributes having number type

4 Extraction Methods

Our analysis of products' descriptions showed that attributes and their values are presented differently for Boolean, String and number types in natural language. Since we have the type information for each attribute we are searching for in background knowledge, we can utilize extraction method for each type. All of the presented methods are still works in progress and represent the baseline methods for the future work. Some of possible modifications, we believe that they can improve the quality of methods, are proposed at the ends of the following sections as well as in the experiments section.

4.1 Extraction of Boolean Attributes

Our method for extraction of Boolean attributes suggests, that the presence of the attribute name in product description induce that the value of the product's attribute is 'true'. The method searches every variation of the attribute name (languages and synonyms) that is present in background knowledge. If the attribute name is matched, the attribute with value 'true' is sent to output result.

Since quite a lot of the attributes were misspelled or inflected in our test data, we have replaced the exact search of the attribute names by fuzzyfied search using Levenshtein (editing) distance. The threshold for the positive result was set to 75% match of the attribute name. The method uses fuzzyfied search, only if the exact match is not found.

We believe that improvement of our method can be achieved by stemming or lemmatization of the attribute names and words of the product description to cover inflections as an equivalent to exact match. Another improvement can be to include common misspelled attribute names to background knowledge. However it

requires an administrator intervention and converts our automatic method to the semiautomatic.

Our method does not recognize sentences as positive or negative. So the sentence *The mobile phone does not have thermosensor,* induces the result that the product has Boolean attribute thermosensor with value 'true'. The approaches known from sentiment analysis can be incorporated to cover this problem.

4.2 Extraction of Numeric Attributes

Attributes of number type have their values composed of a number and a unit (12 g, 15 cm, 42 '', 2 pieces...). Our method is composed of 4 main steps. First, the method searches for attribute names like the method extracting the Boolean attribute names. Next, all the variants of the attribute unit and the variants of units convertible to this unit are searched in the sentence, where the attribute name was found. The only exception is the unit *pieces*, because it is not common in natural language sentences (e.g. *2 shelfs* instead of *2 pieces of shelves*). In our method the search of the units requires an exact match. If both the attribute name and the unit was found, then, in the third step, the numbers are searched in the sentence using regular expression "([0-9]+)(\\ )*(\\.)*(\\,)*([0-9]*)". If the sentence contains more numbers, the closest number to the attribute name is selected in the 4th step.

The extraction method can be extended to cover word variants of the numbers (i.e. one, two, twenty-three...), but it requires new dictionary for each language. Stemming and lemmatization can be also used for unit search (in Slovak language there are 3 variants for singular and plural forms of units e.g. kilogram, kilogramy, kilogramov).

4.3 Extraction of String Attributes

String attributes are the most sensitive type to the size of background knowledge. The specialty of this type is that

Table 1. Precision, recall and F-score for English descriptions

Domain	numeric			Boolean			String		
	P	**R**	**F**	**P**	**R**	**F**	**P**	**R**	**F**
tablet	100	97.47	98.7	100	100	100	100	50	66.67
refrigerator	100	100	100	100	100	100	100	100	100
average	100	98.8	99.4	100	100	100	100	85.71	92.31

Table 2. Precision, recall and F-score for Slovak descriptions

Domain	numeric			Boolean			String		
	P	**R**	**F**	**P**	**R**	**F**	**P**	**R**	**F**
tablet	87.5	20.59	33.34	100	78.95	88.24	100	70	82.35
refrigerator	100	50	66.67	80	88.88	84.21	80	70.59	75
average	96.15	35.71	52.08	92	82.14	89.79	86.36	70.37	77.55

the attribute values are often self-explanatory and the attribute name isn't necessary. For example, in the sentence *"This Candy GC41472D1S Washing Machine with stylish Silver finish looks great in any home."* three String attributes can be found: producer (Candy), product name (*Candy GC41472D1S*) and color (*Silver*). If the washing machine was already extracted from another e-shop in structural form, all the String values are present in the background data and can be used to identify the attributes.

Extraction method for String attributes firstly searches for attribute names as well as the previous methods do. If the attribute name is found, values of the same attribute extracted from all products of the same domain are searched in the same sentence. If the value is found the attribute-value pair is sent to the result. String attributes of the product domain, which were not found in the first step, are searched only by their known values. Since each value corresponds to some attribute in the background knowledge, it is easy to send attribute-value pair to the result. The implemented method does not use the fuzzyfied search of the attribute values in product descriptions.

Similarly to the attribute names search, the attribute value search could by extended with stemming and lemmatization to cover inflections as an equivalent to exact match.

5   Experiments

To verify the methods, we created test data containing the real e-shops product descriptions of 2 domains: fridges and tablets. We have selected 20 products from each domain. 10 descriptions were in English and 10 were in Slovak. We have manually selected attributes and their values that appeared in the descriptions and typed them into the test table. Each product description was an input for our extraction methods and the results were compared to the manually selected ones.

Tablet descriptions contained 4 Boolean attributes, 1 String attribute and 5 Number attributes. Fridge descriptions contained 4 Boolean attributes, 4 String attributes and 9 number attributes.

The background knowledge was created by extraction of structured data from 2 e-shops with table representation of attributes. Data contained 142 tablets and 41 fridges[1]. All attributes found in test data descriptions were present in background knowledge.

The results of our tests are summed up in tables 1 and 2 separately for English and Slovak descriptions.

5.1   Results for Numeric Attributes

Method for attributes of numeric type correctly found 98.8% of all attribute name and value pairs in English descriptions, but only 35.71% of pairs in Slovak description. Such a low recall in our test is caused by various reasons. We have analyzed the results and identified the following problems:

- the absence of synonymic names of given attribute in the background dictionary,

- the absence of the synonymic unit of the attribute value,

- presence of a shortcut, instead of full form of attribute name, or missing words of the full multi-words terms,

- missing attribute name (just the value and units were present in the description),

- different order of words in multi-word name of attribute, and

- other words inserted into multi-word name of attribute.

The first three problems are caused by a small dictionary. After adding more e-shops to the background knowledge, it should become a less important problem. Different e-shops can use different terminology and unit abbreviations, which expands the background knowledge dictionary.

Sentence *"V chladničke je možné uchovávať 225 l potravín v 4 sklenených poličkách"* (en. It is possible to store 225 l of groceries on 4 glass shelves) mentions the

---

[1] Dataset is available at:
http://kapsa.sk/2017-itat-dataset.zip

volume of the refrigerator and the number of shelves in the refrigerator, but because the full names of the attributes are not present in the sentence, the method for numeric types did not find these product properties in the sentence. A definite solution for the missing attribute name problem would probably not be easy. One approach can be to use attribute values' units. If the unit found in the description, is used by only one known attribute of the product domain, the value and unit can be assigned to the attribute.

The last two reasons deal with multi-word names. The solution to the problem can be to search each word of the term separately. If each word of multi-word term was found in the same sentence, then we can declare the match. It is possible that automatic morphological analysis of the sentence can improve this approach, because it can reveal the connections between words and reduce false matches of such method.

The precision of the method is decreased by fuzzy matches, when the editing distance of 75% was too generous and matched the words with different meaning. We can improve the precision using stemming or lemmatization instead of fuzzy matching with editing distance. Another improvement can be achieved by accepting fuzzy matched words only if they are not present in classic dictionary of the language, i.e. they are probably misspelled.

5.2 Results for Boolean Attributes

The method for Boolean type of attribute was the most successful in finding attributes. Using this method, all the required attributes were found in the English descriptions and 82.14% of the attributes in the Slovak descriptions. The reason for not finding attributes in our tests within Slovak descriptions was similar to the synonymic variations mentioned in the previous method. Concretely, the term in our dictionary had fewer words, because some words were split into two words. Since we do fuzzy comparisons word-by-word, it made the match less than 75%.

For example, the sentence *Už žiadna námraza, Technológia No Frost zabraňuje vzniku námrazy a udržiava konštantnú teplotu v celej chladničke,* (en. No more frost cover, the technology No Frost prevent frost creation and keeps constant temperature throughout the fridge) didn't match with our two-word term *Technológia NoFrost*. The solution would be to add *Technológia No Frost* to the directory.

Since we used Levenshtein distance to search for a name, the method found two attributes in two descriptions that were not there. These were the Auto Defrost and NoFrost attributes.

5.3 Results for String Attributes

The method for attributes of String type is special, because it does not need the attribute name. It causes the ambiguity of the attribute assignment.

For example, in the sentence *Farba kombinovanej chladničky Goddness je biela.*(en. The color of the Goddness fridge is white.), the value *biela* (en. *white*) is appropriate for attributes color and color of the front of the refrigerator.

The second problem is again the small dictionary, this time, the dictionary of known attribute values. For example, in sentence *Pri hrúbke len 6,1 mm je vôbec najtenší iPad zároveň aj najschopnejší* (en. Having the depth only 6.1 mm, it is the thinnest iPad as well as the most capable.), the method did not found attribute "product name", since *iPad* value is not in the value dictionary. Again, to remove the problem of the absence of an attribute value, it is sufficient to increase the set of attribute values in the dictionary.

The precision was decreased by false fuzzy match of the attribute value with different word. Again, we can improve the precision using stemming or lemmatization instead of fuzzy matching with editing distance.

6   Conclusions

This work-in-progress paper presents our base-line algorithms for automatic attribute-value pairs extraction from product descriptions on e-shops. We divided attributes to 3 main types: Boolean, String and numeric. Boolean attributes are matched, if the name is found in the description. String attributes are search by match with pair attribute name and its value or by value only. Numeric attributes require three things to find: attribute name, number and unit.

We have probed our methods against real world data, analyzed the results and proposed the improvements that would be incorporated in our methods in the future.

This work was supported by the Agency of the Slovak Ministry of Education for the Structural Funds of the EU, under project CeZIS, ITMS: 26220220158

References

[1] Project Kapsa, web page: http://kapsa.sk/
[2] J. NothMan at al.: Learning multilingual named entity recognition from Wikipedia. Artificial Intelligence 194 (2013) 151–175
[3] D. Nadeau, S. Sekine, A survey of named entity recognition and classification, Lingvisticae Investigationes 30 (2007) 3–26
[4] D. M. Bikel et al.: Nymble: a High-Performance Learning Name-finder. In ANLP-97, Washington, D.C., pp. 194 – 201, 1997.
[5] J. Cowie: Description of the CRL/NMSU System Used for MUC-6. In Proceedings of the Sixth Message Understanding Conference, Morgan Kaufmann, 1995
[6] J. M. Castillo et al.: Named Entity Recognition Using Support Vector Machine for Filipino Text Documents. International Journal of Future Computer and Communication, Vol. 2, No. 5, October 2013
[7] J. Lafferty, A. McCallum, F. Pereira: Conditional Random Fields: Probabilistic models for segmenting and labeling sequence data. In proceedings of ICML, pages 282–289., 2001
[8] K. Frantzi, S. Ananiadou, J. Tsujii: The C-value/NC-value Method of Automatic Recognition of Multi-word Terms. In proceedings of ECDL, pp. 585-604. ISBN 3-540-65101-2, 1998

J. Hlaváčová (Ed.): ITAT 2017 Proceedings, pp. 27–34
ISBN 978-1974274741, © 2017 M. Lipovský, T. Vinař, B. Brejová

Approximate Abundance Histograms and Their Use for Genome Size Estimation

Mário Lipovský, Tomáš Vinař, Broňa Brejová

Faculty of Mathematics, Physics, and Informatics,
Comenius University, Mlynská dolina, 842 48 Bratislava, Slovakia

Abstract: DNA sequencing data is typically a large collection of short strings called reads. We can summarize such data by computing a histogram of the number of occurrences of substrings of a fixed length. Such histograms can be used for example to estimate the size of a genome. In this paper, we study a recent tool, Kmerlight, which computes approximate histograms. We discover an approximation bias, and we propose a new, unbiased version of Kmerlight. We also model the distribution of approximation errors and support our theoretical model by experimental data. Finally, we use another tool, CovEst, to compute genome size estimates from approximate histograms. Our results show that although CovEst was designed to work with exact histograms, it can be used with their approximate versions, which can be produced in a much smaller memory.

1 Introduction

A genome is a collection of DNA molecules storing genetic information in a cell. It can be represented as a set of long strings over the alphabet $\Sigma = \{A, C, G, T\}$ (each string corresponding to one chromosome). In a DNA sequencing experiment, many reads are produced from a genome. These reads are short substrings obtained from random locations of the genome, potentially with some sequencing errors. For a genome to be analyzed, the DNA sequence of individual chromosomes must be first assembled from the reads, but the process of genome assembly is computationally demanding and error-prone.

However, it is possible to estimate the genome size and some other characteristics without the need of genome assembly [2, 9, 5, 8]. These estimates are computed from a summary statistic of reads called the k-mer abundance histogram. A k-mer is a substring of length exactly k and the histogram summarizes the number of occurrences of individual k-mers in the input set of reads.

Most of the histogram computing methods count the occurrences of each k-mer in the input data using hash tables or suffix arrays [6, 4, 3]. Consequently, their memory usage increases at least linearly with the number of processed distinct k-mers. To reduce the memory requirements, k-mer abundance histograms can be computed approximately. One of the newest such algorithms, Kmerlight [8], combines the techniques of sampling and hashing to maintain a sketch of k-mers and from the contents of the sketch computes an estimate of the histogram.

The approximate histograms were already used as an input for genome size estimation [8], however the impact of the approximation errors on the accuracy of the resulting estimates was not evaluated. In this paper, we study the character of errors of the Kmerlight's histograms and their influence on the subsequent genome size estimation.

We start with an empirical study of the approximation errors of Kmerlight algorithm, and we discover that Kmerlight produces systematically biased estimates of some histograms. We explain the source of the bias and propose an unbiased modification of Kmerlight. Next we model the distribution of Kmerlight's errors with the normal distribution, and we propose a formula that describes Kmerlight's variance. We then experimentally test our theoretical model and explore its limitations.

Finally, we use CovEst software [2] to estimate the sizes of simulated genomes from approximate histograms produced by Kmerlight. We describe how different properties of the input influence the accuracy of the estimates, and we compare the estimates based on exact histograms to the estimates based on approximate histograms.

2 Errors in Kmerlight's Approximate Abundance Histograms

A k-mer is a substring of length exactly k. A read of length r thus contains $r - k + 1$ k-mers. If a k-mer occurs i times among all input reads, we say its abundance is i. In this paper, we use the value $k = 21$ as in previous works [9, 2].

Definition 1. *The k-mer abundance histogram is a sequence $f = f_1, f_2, \ldots f_m$, where f_i is the number of k-mers that occur in the input set exactly i times, and m is the maximum observed abundance.*

Counting the abundance of each individual k-mer appearing in a large input file requires large memory. As we are only interested in the histogram, the problem of k-mer counting can be avoided, allowing us to estimate the histogram more efficiently. We can reduce the amount of required memory from dozens of gigabytes to hundreds of megabytes, allowing these computations to be performed on a personal computer rather than on a cluster.

We will consider streaming algorithms, which in general process a sequence of items (in our context k-mers) in a single pass using only a limited amount of memory and time. These algorithms maintain an approximate summary, or a *sketch*, of the previously viewed k-mers and with each new k-mer the sketch is updated. When all the k-mers are processed, the sketch can be analyzed to provide the estimate of the k-mer abundance histogram.

In 2002, Bar-Yossef et al. presented three algorithms for estimating the number of distinct elements in a stream ($F_0 = \sum_{i=1}^{m} f_i$) with theoretical guarantees [1]. In 2014, Melsted and Halldórsson [5] implemented and extended Algorithm 2 from the aforementioned paper [1] and used it for k-mer counting. Their algorithm KmerStream can also estimate f_1, the number of k-mers with abundance one.

KmerStream was further improved by Sivadasan et al. in 2016 [8], and their software Kmerlight estimates the whole histogram ($f_1, \ldots, f_m$). As we focus on Kmerlight in our work, we will describe it in detail.

2.1 Kmerlight

Kmerlight maintains a sketch of processed k-mers. Its output are estimates $\hat{F}_0, \hat{f}_1, \ldots, \hat{f}_m$ obtained from the final content of the sketch. The scheme uses parameters W, r, u and two hash functions $g : \Sigma^k \to \{0, \ldots, 2^W - 1\}$ and $h : \Sigma^k \to \{0, \ldots, r-1\} \times \{0, \ldots, u-1\}$. In the analysis, we will assume that g and h hash each string from Σ^k uniformly and independently over their range of values.

The sketch consists of W levels. Each level w has a hash table with r counters $T_w[0], \ldots, T_w[r-1]$. Each counter stores its value $T_w[c].v$ (the abundance of a particular k-mer) and an auxiliary information $T_w[c].p \in \{0, \ldots, u-1\}$.

To process an input k-mer x we first select its level w as the number of trailing zeroes in the binary representation of $g(x)$. As a result, the probability of selecting level w is $1/2^w$. Next, using has function h, the k-mer is hashed into a pair (c, j) and processed as follows:

- If counter $T_w[c]$ is empty, its value is increased to 1 and j is stored as an auxiliary information $T_w[c].p$.

- If $T_w[c]$ is not empty, and $T_w[c].p$ equals j, the counter value $T_w[c].v$ is incremented.

- Finally, if $T_w[c].p \neq j$, the counter is marked as dirty. Dirty counters are not modified by future updates.

Note that all occurrences of the same k-mer will be stored in the same counter at the same level. The value of this counter should correspond to the abundance of this k-mer. Since two or more different k-mers may hash into the same counter, collisions may occur. The auxiliary information helps to detect some of these collisions.

Estimator of F_0. Since on average $F_0/2^w$ distinct k-mers are hashed into level w, the probability that a counter at this level remains empty is approximately $p = (1 - \frac{1}{r})^{F_0/2^w}$. In this estimate and in all subsequent analyses, we assume that the number of distinct k-mers at level w is exactly $F_0/2^w$, although in fact it is a binomial random variable with this number as the mean.

The expected number of empty counters at level w is thus $r \cdot p$. Let us denote the number of observed empty

counters at level w as $t_0^{(w)}$. Using the assumption $t_0^{(w)} \approx r \cdot p$ we can derive the estimator of F_0:

$$\hat{F}_0 = 2^w \cdot \frac{\ln(t_0^{(w)}/r)}{\ln\left(1 - \frac{1}{r}\right)}. \tag{1}$$

To estimate the number of distinct k-mers F_0 using this formula, we choose level $w = w^*$, so that the number of empty counters $t_0^{(w)}$ at this level is closest to $r/2$. It has been shown that selecting this level provides a bounded error of $\hat{F}_0$ with a guaranteed probability [1].

Estimator of f_i. The expected number of distinct k-mers with abundance i hashed to level w is $f_i/2^w$. When a k-mer is hashed into level w, the probability that it is stored in a collision-free counter is $(1 - \frac{1}{r})^{F_0/2^w - 1}$, which is the probability that no other k-mer from level w will get hashed into the same counter. Thus we can estimate the number of collision-free counters with value i as

$$f_i/2^w \cdot \left(1 - \frac{1}{r}\right)^{F_0/2^w - 1} \tag{2}$$

If we denote the number of observed collision-free counters with value i as $t_i^{(w)}$, we can derive the estimator of f_i:

$$\hat{f}_i = t_i^{(w)} \cdot 2^w \cdot \left(1 - \frac{1}{r}\right)^{1 - F_0/2^w} \tag{3}$$

To estimate f_i, the algorithm selects level $w = w_i^*$ so that it maximizes $t_i^{(w)}$ – the number of observed collision-free counters with value i.

Undetected collisions. The value $t_i^{(w)}$ is based on the number of non-dirty counters with value i, but these include both true positives (collision-free counters) and false positives (counters with undetected collisions). The expected number of false positive at one level is at most r/u, where $0, \ldots u-1$ is the range of auxiliary information [8]. Parameter u can be set to make false positives negligible; thus we will assume that all collisions are being detected.

Median amplification. To decrease the variance of the estimates and to use of multiprocessing, t independent instances of Kmerlight's sketch are run concurrently. Estimate $\hat{F}_0$ is selected as the median of $\hat{F}_0^{(1)}, \ldots, \hat{F}_0^{(t)}$, and final estimates of f_i are also the medians of t instances.

Accuracy and complexity. Parameters r, u ant t provide a trade-off between the memory and accuracy. Assuming that $W = \Theta(\log F_0)$, the algorithm uses $O(t \cdot r \cdot \log(F_0))$ memory words, and processing of one k-mer requires $O(t)$ time. The authors have shown that the algorithm computes estimates $\hat{F}_0$ and $\hat{f}_i$ for sufficiently large f_i ($f_i \geq F_0/\lambda$) with a bounded relative error $(1 - \varepsilon)F_0 \leq \hat{F}_0 \leq (1 + \varepsilon)F_0$, $(1 - \varepsilon)f_i \leq \hat{f}_i \leq (1 + \varepsilon)f_i$ with probability at least $1 - \delta$, when the parameters are set as follows: $t = O(\log(\lambda/\delta))$, $r = O(\frac{\lambda}{\varepsilon^2})$ and $u = O(\frac{\lambda F_0}{\varepsilon^2})$. Due to loose

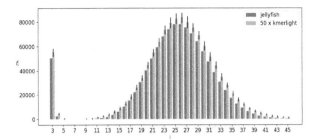

Figure 1: The exact values f_i produced by Jellyfish (blue) and approximate values $\hat{f}_i$ produced by Kmerlight averaged from 50 trials (orange). The error bars express the standard deviation of $\hat{f}_i$. Columns for $i = 1, 2$ are omitted, having values approximately $10^7, 10^6$ respectively.

constants, these asymptotic estimates cannot be used to set parameters for obtaining desirable error bounds. The accuracy of the algorithm was tested experimentally with arbitrary parameters $W = 64, t = 7, r \in \{2^{16}, 2^{18}\}, u = 2^{13}$.

2.2 Empirical Study of Approximation Errors

To study the character of approximation errors, we start with several observations on generated data. We have first generated a genome: a random sequence $g_1 \ldots g_L$ consisting of L characters A, C, G, T, each with probability $1/4$. Next we have generated $c \cdot L/\ell$ reads of length $\ell = 100$, where c is a parameter describing the depth of coverage of the genome by reads. For each read, we have uniformly selected a random starting position $s \in \{1, \ldots, L - \ell + 1\}$. The read then consists of characters $g_s g_{s+1} \ldots g_{s+\ell-1}$. Finally we have simulated sequencing errors by modifying each base randomly with probability e. Our initial experiment has used a single data set with parameters $L = 10^6$, $c = 50$, and $e = 0.02$.

For this data set, Figure 1 shows the exact k-mer abundance histogram ($k = 21$) produced by Jellyfish [4] and the means and standard deviations of the estimates $\hat{f}_i$ from 50 Kmerlight runs on the same input. Kmerlight was run with parameters $W = 64, t = 7, r = 2^{15}, u = 2^{13}$.

Perhaps the most striking feature of this histogram is that Kmerlight systematically overestimates values of f_i. In Section 2.3, we clarify the source of this bias and present an unbiased estimator.

Kmerlight guarantees precise estimates of those values of f_i that are close to F_0. Unfortunately, in sequencing data, sequencing errors often create many unique k-mers, and thus we have f_1 close to F_0, while the remaining f_i are much smaller. In the extreme case of very low values of f_i, the probability that at least one k-mer with abundance i becomes stored in a collision-free counter at any level approaches to zero. If no k-mer survives the collisions ($t_i^{(w)} = 0$) then $\hat{f}_i = 0$. In our experiment, Kmerlight produced zero estimates for $f_i < 500$.

Figure 1 shows that the absolute error $(\hat{f}_i - f_i)$ and variance of $\hat{f}_i$ decrease with decreasing f_i. However, relative

errors $(\hat{f}_i - f_i)/f_i$ and their variance increase with decreasing f_i (data not shown). Kmerlight guarantees bounded errors for high values of f_i, but a theoretical quantitative analysis of the error distribution was not presented in the previous work [8]. We provide a quantitative estimate of the variance in Section 2.4.

2.3 Kmerlight Approximation Bias and Unbiased Version

As we will explain in this section, the bias of Kmerlight estimates towards higher values is caused by its selection of level w_i^* used to calculate $\hat{f}_i$. Level w_i^* is chosen to maximize $t_i^{(w)}$ – the number of collision-free counters with value i at level w. We believe that the authors hoped to minimize the variance of the estimator $\hat{f}_i$ by including as many k-mers in the estimate as possible.

Analytical w^+. To understand which levels w_i^* are selected by Kmerlight, we will analytically find the level w_i^+ that maximizes $E(t_i^{(w)})$ – the expected number of collision-free counters with value i.

As shown in equation (2), $E(t_i^{(w)}) = f_i/2^w \cdot \left(1 - \frac{1}{r}\right)^{F_0/2^w - 1}$. The value of w_i^+ at which $E(t_i^{(w)})$ is maximized can be obtained from inequalities $E(t_i^{(w_i^+ - 1)}) \leq E(t_i^{(w_i^+)}) \leq E(t_i^{(w_i^+ + 1)})$. By manipulating the inequalities we get

$$\frac{1}{4} \leq \left(1 - \frac{1}{r}\right)^{F_0/2^{w_i^+}} \leq \frac{1}{2}, \qquad (4)$$

and finally, we can calculate w_i^+:

$$\lg F_0 + \lg\lg \frac{r}{r-1} - 1 \leq w_i^+ \leq \lg F_0 + \lg\lg \frac{r}{r-1}.$$

Symbol lg denotes the binary logarithm. Note these inequalities have at most two integer solutions.

The choice of level w_i^+ does not depend on values of i or f_i, but only on F_0 and r. Since $w_1^+ = w_2^+ = \cdots = w_m^+$, from now on we will refer to this level simply by w^+. This level also maximizes the expected number of all non-empty collision-free counters $E(t^{(w)})$, where $t^{(w)} = \sum_{i=1}^{m} t_i^{(w)}$.

Explanation of bias. The number of collision-free counters at levels $w^+ - 1$ and $w^+ + 1$ is typically similar to the number of collision-free counters at level w^+. There are two times more k-mers hashed into level $w^+ - 1$ than into w^+, but also more collisions happen at $w^+ - 1$. These two effects partially cancel each other and maintain similar values of $E(t^{(w)})$ for $w = w^+ - 1, w^+, w^+ + 1$. As a result, any of these levels can hold the maximal $t^{(w)}$ and become chosen by Kmerlight as its w_i^*. This typically leads to values of $t_i^{(w_i^*)}$ higher than the expected value $E(t_i^{(w)})$ for fixed level $w = w_i^*$. To obtain $\hat{f}_i$, value $t_i^{(w_i^*)}$ is multiplied by

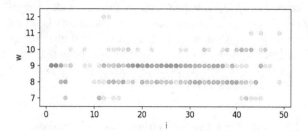

Figure 2: Each column shows up to seven levels w_i^* that were selected by one of $t = 7$ instances of Kmerlight in the experiment from Section 2.2. If a level was chosen by more instances, its circle is darker. Note that if no counters hold value i in the whole sketch, Kmerlight's instance does not choose any level.

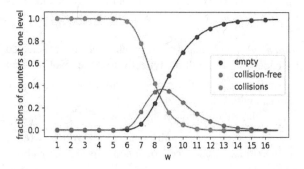

Figure 3: Values p_e, p_{cf}, p_c represent the theoretical fractions of empty, collision-free and collided counters at each level respectively. To make the values comparable to the results from Section 2.2, we set $F_0 = 1.2 \times 10^7, r = 2^{15}$.

$2^{w_i^*} \cdot \left(1 - \frac{1}{r}\right)^{1 - F_0/2^{w_i^*}}$. Thus biased $t_i^{(w_i^*)}$ also leads to biased estimator $\hat{f}_i$.

To illustrate this, Figure 2 shows values w_i^* for different f_i extracted from one Kmerlight run. The analytical level $w^+ = 9$ is selected most frequently, but Kmerlight often chooses level 8 or 10 to maximize $t_i^{(w)}$. Note that for $3 \leq i \leq 15$ and $i \geq 40$, the values of f_i are low, and thus $t_i^{(w)}$ have a high relative variance. The maximal $t_i^{(w)}$ can thus be reached at levels more distant from $w^+ = 9$.

In order to further demonstrate the similarity of $E(t^{(w)})$ at the levels close to w^+, Figure 3 displays the theoretical fractions of empty, collided, and non-empty collision-free counters at different levels of the sketch. Focusing on a single level w, let us denote as p_{cf} the probability that a single counter is non-empty and collision-free, p_e the probability that this counter is empty, and p_c the probability that it holds a collision. The number of distinct k-mers hashed into one counter (X) follows a binomial distribution, $X \sim \text{Bin}(F_0/2^w, 1/r)$, and we can use this distribution to compute $p_{cf} = P[X = 1]$, $p_e = P[X = 0]$, and $p_c = P[X > 1]$. Note that the expected number of non-empty collision-free counters at one level is $E(t^{(w)}) = r \cdot p_{cf}$.

The presented settings incidentally represent an un-

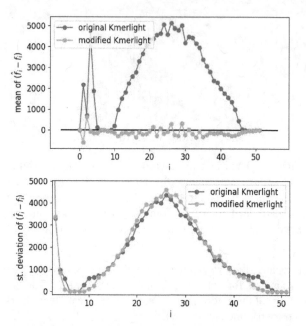

Figure 4: Mean (top) and standard deviation (bottom) of estimate errors ($\hat{f}_i - f_i$) produced by the original (blue) and modified (orange) Kmerlight in 300 trials.

favorable situation for Kmerlight, because $E(t^{(8)}) \approx E(t^{(9)})$. If there was a greater difference between $E(t^{(w^+)})$, $E(t^{(w^+-1)})$ and $E(t^{(w^++1)})$, Kmerlight would choose the level w^+ much more often than the other levels and so it would have a smaller chance of choosing $t_i^{(w_i^*)} > E(t^{(w^+)})$.

Removing bias from estimates of f_i. Our observation suggests a simple modification to remove the bias from estimates of f_i. In particular, we will use the level w^+ that maximizes the expected number of collision-free counters $E(t^{(w)})$, instead of the level w_i^* that maximizes the observed number of collision-free counters $t_i^{(w)}$.

The modified Kmerlight creates sketches and estimates F_0 in the same way as the original algorithm. Then using $\hat{F}_0$ and r, it calculates w^+, as discussed above. Finally, values of f_i are estimated from the observed counts of collision-free counters at level w^+ by equation (3).

Note that we do not prove analytically that this estimator is unbiased. Simplifications in our analysis may cause some small biases in the estimator, but we demonstrate experimentally that the estimator works well on our generated data. In Figure 4, we compare the original and modified Kmerlight in 300 trials of both versions on the same data as in Section 2.2. While the original Kmerlight overestimates f_i significantly, the modified Kmerlight achieves $E(\hat{f}_i) \approx f_i$, without much change in the variance.

2.4 Evaluation of Approximation Variance

In this section, we estimate the variance of $\hat{f}_i$. We will consider estimates obtained at a fixed level w (for example

$w = w^+$). Recall that $E(t_i^{(w)}) = f_i/2^w \cdot (1 - 1/r)^{F_0/2^w - 1}$. We will consider $t_i^{(w)}$ to follow a binomial distribution $Bin(f_i, p_s)$, where $p_s = 1/2^w \cdot (1 - 1/r)^{F_0/2^w - 1}$. This simplification corresponds to a simple sampling process in which we sample each of f_i k-mers with probability p_s, and we discard each k-mer with probability $1 - p_s$. Note that this approach assumes that each k-mer remains collision free independently of others, which is not the case.

Since a random variable following $Bin(n, p)$ has variance of $np(1 - p)$, $Var(t_i^{(w)}) = f_i \cdot p_s \cdot (1 - p_s)$. The estimate of f_i is obtained as t_i/p_s, so

$$Var(\hat{f}_i) = Var\left(\frac{t_i}{p_s}\right) = \frac{1}{p_s^2} \cdot Var(t_i) = \frac{f_i \cdot (1 - p_s)}{p_s} \quad (5)$$

Effect of medians. Kmerlight chooses the estimate $\hat{f}_i$ as a median of estimates of t independent sketches: $\hat{f}_i = \mathrm{med}(\hat{f}_i^{(1)}, \ldots \hat{f}_i^{(t)})$. For a continuous random variable with a density function $f(x)$ and mean $\bar{x}$, its sample median from a sample of size n is asymptotically[1] normal:

$$\mathrm{med}(x) \sim N\left(\bar{x}, \frac{1}{4nf(\bar{x})^2}\right). \quad (6)$$

As the binomial distribution of $t_i^{(w)}$ is a discrete distribution, we will approximate $Bin(f_i, p_s)$ with $N(\mu = f_i p_s, \sigma^2 = f_i p_s(1 - p_s))$. The density function of normal distribution in its mean μ is $\frac{1}{\sqrt{2\pi\sigma^2}}$.

Using approximations (5), (6), variance of $\hat{f}_i$ selected as a median of t instances can be derived as follows:

$$Var(\hat{f}_i) \approx \frac{2\pi}{4t}Var(\hat{f}_i^{(l)}) = \frac{\pi}{2t}\frac{f_i \cdot (1 - p_s)}{p_s}. \quad (7)$$

Experiments. We ran the modified Kmerlight in 300 trials on the data presented in Section 2.2. Figure 5 shows histograms of values of $\hat{f}_i$ for selected[2] values of i. We compare these histograms with two normal distributions. The best normal fit is a Gaussian with its mean and standard deviation obtained from the observed values of $\hat{f}_i$. The plotted theoretical prediction uses the exact value of f_i as its mean and the variance is calculated according to equation (7) using the exact values of f_i and F_0.

The quality of normal approximation largely depends on the true value of f_i. According to our approximation, the expected number of counters with value i at level w^+ is $E(t_i) = f_i \cdot p_s$. For this dataset, $w^+ = 9$, and thus the sampling probability p_s is approximately $1/2^9 \cdot \frac{1}{2} \approx 1/1000$ when we use the upper bound from equation (4).

For the lowest values of f_i (i.e. f_6, f_{10}), we have $E(t_i) < 1$. So typically no k-mers survive the collisions at level

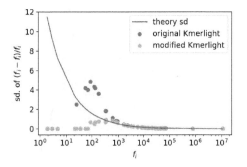

Figure 6: The blue and orange points show the standard deviation of relative error $(\hat{f}_i - f_i)/f_i$ of estimates $\hat{f}_i$ computed by the original and modified Kmerlight respectively in 300 runs on dataset from Section 2.2. The green line represents the approximation of standard deviation calculated using equation (7).

w^+, and thus $t_i = 0$ and $\hat{f}_i = 0$. Due to the use of medians, at least one k-mer must survive in at least four instances to produce $t_i > 1$. As a result, we obtain $\hat{f}_i = 0$ in all trials even for $f_{10} = 140$. Since the estimates $\hat{f}_i$ are always zero, our estimates of variances for these f_i are very imprecise.

If the value f_i is such that $E(t_i)$ is around 1 (i.e. f_{13}, f_{16}), a very small number of k-mers hash into collision-free counters at level w_i^* or w^+. Therefore the estimator $\hat{f}_i$ can reach only a limited set of discrete values ($\hat{f}_i = 0$ if no k-mer survives collisions, $\hat{f}_i = 1/p_s \approx 1000$ if one k-mer is in collision-free counter, $\hat{f}_i = 2/p_s \approx 2000$ if two k-mers survive, ...), as it can be seen in Figure 5. The approximation with normal distribution is not precise for these values f_i, since the distribution of $\hat{f}_i$ is clearly discrete.

Finally, for higher f_i, where $E(t_i) \gg 1$, the estimator $\hat{f}_i$ takes on various values, and the approximation with normal distribution seems reasonable, as it can be seen from the bottom row of Figure 5.

We have also applied Kolmogorov-Smirnov tests to test the normality of $\hat{f}_i$. These tests reject normality for $f_i < 20,000$ with our dataset of 300 trials at the significance level of 5%. Overall, we conclude that for sufficiently high values of f_i the distribution of $\hat{f}_i$ can be approximated by Gaussian with variance calculated by (7).

Finally we present the comparison of Kmerlight's variance and its theoretical prediction in Figure 6. In this experiment, our estimate of the standard deviation of Kmerlight's estimates has error less than 5% even for lower f_i with values around $1000 \approx 1/p_s$, where the normal approximation was still inadequate. The experiment further suggests that an accurate estimate of variance for the lowest values of $f_i < 100$ would be zero.

Figure 6 also reveals a difference in variances between the original and modified Kmerlight's estimates for $f_i \in (100, 1000)$. The original Kmerlight searches for a level w that maximizes $t_i^{(w)}$ so even if only one k-mer with abundance i survives the collisions at any level of the sketch, Kmerlight will use it to estimate $\hat{f}_i$. We did not include

---

[1]Even for a sample of only 7 observations drawn from the normal distribution, the relative error of this approximation is only about 6% [7].

[2]To select values $i = 6, 10, 13, 16, 32, 23$, we have sorted the values f_i and selected each eighth value. We have also included f_1, f_2, since they differ from other f_i by orders of magnitude.

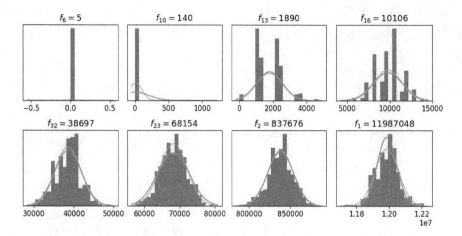

Figure 5: Empirical probability densities (blue histograms), the best normal fits (orange lines) and theoretical estimates (green) of distributions of $\hat{f}_i$ for multiple abundances. Histograms come from 300 runs of modified Kmerlight. Horizontal axes display the values of estimates $\hat{f}_i$.

this effect into the variance estimation, hence the estimates for these f_i are not precise for the original Kmerlight.

2.5 Choice of Kmerlight's Parameters

Sivadasan et al [8] provide theoretical bounds on Kmerlight's approximation errors, but they do not provide methods for setting parameters in practical scenarios. In this section, we show how to set the parameters in order to achieve relative error bounded by ε with probability $1 - \delta$, under the assumption that $\hat{f}_i$ is distributed according to the normal approximation derived in the previous section.

We first derive a two-sided prediction interval of $\hat{f}_i$. Let $u\left(\frac{\alpha}{2}\right)$ be the critical value of the normal distribution for significance level $\frac{\alpha}{2}$. By standardization we get $(\hat{f}_i - f_i)/\sigma \,\dot{\sim}\, N(0,1)$, and so we have

$$P\left[-u\left(\frac{\alpha}{2}\right) \leq \frac{\hat{f}_i - f_i}{\sigma} \leq u\left(\frac{\alpha}{2}\right)\right] \approx 1 - \alpha.$$

If we set $\varepsilon = u\left(\frac{\alpha}{2}\right)\sigma/f_i$, we obtain the bounds for $\hat{f}_i$:

$$P\left[(1 - \varepsilon)f_i \leq \hat{f}_i \leq (1 + \varepsilon)f_i\right] \approx 1 - \alpha.$$

To achieve bounded error with probability at least $1 - \delta$ simultaneously for m different values of i, we set $\alpha = \frac{\delta}{m}$ following the Bonferroni correction.

Standard deviation σ can be calculated by the equation (7) using F_0, f_i, r, t. Note that σ depends logarithmically on F_0 and thus a rough estimate of F_0 is sufficient. We restrict the bounded precision only for sufficiently large f_i by setting $f_i = F_0/\lambda$ ($\lambda = 1000$ for example). The estimates of larger f_i will be even more precise. Finally, by using $\varepsilon = u\left(\frac{\alpha}{2}\right)\sigma/f_i$, we can calculate error bound ε for a given probability δ and parameters r, t, λ. This allows us to efficiently explore various values of r, and t and their influence on approximation errors. For example, we can find parameters which minimize the approximation error for a fixed memory limit.

3 Genome Size Estimation

One motivation for computing k-mer abundance histograms from sequencing data is to obtain genome size estimates. Here we use CovEst software [2] developed in our group to compare the accuracy of genome size estimates produced from the exact and approximate histograms.

We use data generated as described in Section 2.2, but we vary parameters L (genome size), c (genome coverage by reads), e (sequencing error rate). For each set of genome parameters (c, e, L) we have generated 50 data sets. Then we computed the exact histogram using Jellyfish software [4] and two approximate histograms using the original and the modified version of Kmerlight. Finally we ran CovEst on these three histograms using the model without repeats, and we collected three estimates of coverage $\hat{c}_j, \hat{c}_{ok}, \hat{c}_{mk}$. In all experimental results, we focus on the estimates of coverage $\hat{c}$. By dividing the sum of lengths of all reads by $\hat{c}$, we can obtain estimates of genome size $\hat{L}$.

In the first experiment (top row of Figure 7) we investigate the effect of increasing sequencing error rates on the accuracy of coverage estimates. On exact histograms, CovEst produces unbiased estimates of coverage with their variance increasing with error rate. Estimates based on approximate histograms are clearly less accurate but still achieve a relatively good precision.

Mean errors are consistently lower for modified Kmerlight than the errors of the original Kmerlight. Pair Student's t-tests reject hypotheses $mean(\hat{c}_{ok} - \hat{c}_{mk}) = 0$ for three of four presented datasets, with exception of the dataset with $e = 0.05$ where the p-value is 0.3. Thus we conclude that the estimates based on modified Kmerlight's histograms are significantly better than the estimates based on original Kmerlight's histograms. With modified Kmerlight, CovEst produces estimates with all errors bounded by 0.4%, 1%, 4%, 15% for sequencing error rates of $0, 0.01, 0.05, 0.1$ respectively, and we consider these estimates sufficiently accurate.

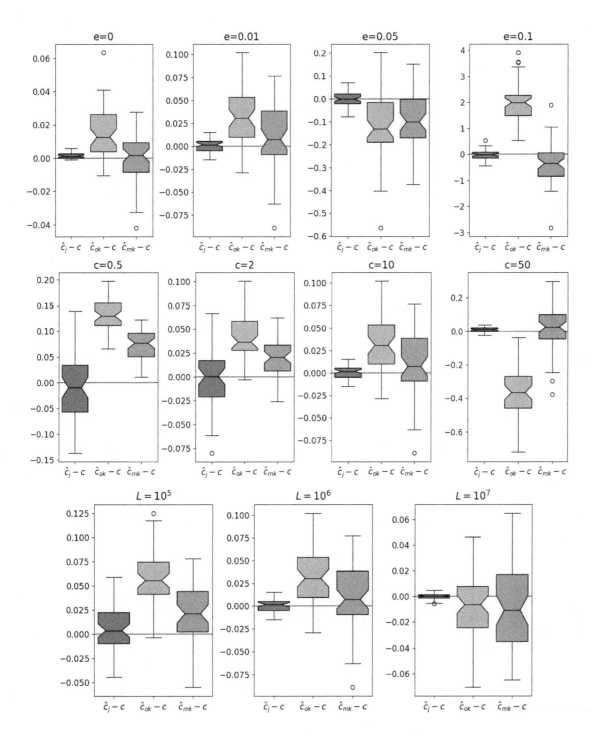

Figure 7: Distributions of coverage estimate errors $\hat{c} - c$ for different parameters. Each boxplot represents 50 estimates of the coverage on different generated genomes. Blue, orange and green boxes describe the estimate errors with Jellyfish, original Kmerlight and modified Kmerlight used to compute the k-mer abundance histogram. Note that vertical axes use different scales since the values span across multiple orders of magnitude in different datasets. As the default parameters, we use $L = 10^6$, $c = 10$ and $e = 0.01$. In each experiment, we altered the value of one parameter, keeping the other two fixed. Top row: different error rates, middle row: different coverage values, bottom row: different genome sizes.

In the second experiment (middle row of Figure 7), we study the accuracy for different genome coverage values. All CovEst estimates $\hat{c}_j$ in our experiment range in $30\%, 6\%, 0.3\%, < 0.1\%$ intervals around the true coverage for coverages of 0.5, 2, 10 and 50. The variance of $\hat{c}_j$ is comparable to variance of $\hat{c}_{ok}, \hat{c}_{mk}$ for two lower coverages, but with increasing coverage, estimates based on approximate histograms become less accurate. However, since the maximal errors reach values of only 0.3, which is less than 1% of the true coverage $c = 50$, we also consider these estimates as useful. Modified Kmerlight significantly outperforms the original Kmerlight on all four presented datasets (verified by t-tests).

Finally, with increasing genome size (bottom row of Figure 7), CovEst's estimates become more precise on the exact histograms, and estimates on approximated histograms maintain a roughly constant precision for the examined genome sizes. As the coverage estimate errors are bounded by 1% for all datasets, we also consider the approximate histograms sufficiently accurate for the genome size estimation. Modified Kmerlight reaches smaller mean error on the two smaller genomes than the original Kmerlight.

4 Conclusion

In this paper, we have studied the character of approximation errors in the k-mer approximation histograms produced by Kmerlight [8]. We have discovered that Kmerlight's estimates of $\hat{f}_i$ are biased towards higher values and provided a new estimate without this bias. We have demonstrated that for sufficiently large values of f_i, the distribution of estimates can be well approximated by a normal distribution. This approximation can be used to tune the parameters of the method.

We have also demonstrated that approximate histograms produced by Kmerlight are sufficiently accurate to produce reasonable estimates of genome size, and that for most settings our modified version of Kmerlight leads to more accurate genome size estimation than the original Kmerlight. An important avenue for further research is to compare the accuracy CovEst results on real sequencing data.

The use of approximate histograms allows significant reduction in memory; for example for genome size $L = 10^8$, coverage $c = 50$ and error rate $e = 0.1$ ($F_0 = 3.6 \cdot 10^9$), Kmerlight can produce an approximate histogram in only 83MB of memory, whereas Jellyfish needs 34Gb.

Note that our modified Kmerlight uses only one of 64 Kmerlight's levels to compute estimates for all f_i, so it naively seems that we could maintain only this level and reduce the memory consumption by a factor of 64. However, our version still uses the full 64 levels to compute $\hat{F}_0$, which is needed to find the desired level w^+. We could try to estimate $\hat{F}_0$ separately, particularly, if two passes over the data are allowed. For example, we could roughly guess F_0 from the size of sequencing data and use fewer levels. It might be also sufficient to estimate F_0 with smaller hash tables. We did not inquire deeper into this topic, but we believe that by such techniques the memory consumption could be further decreased by a significant factor.

Also note that the k-mer abundance histogram and many algorithms used for its computation can be generalized to a histogram of any input items. Thus the applicability of this topic goes beyond the field of bioinformatics.

Acknowledgments. This research was funded by VEGA grants 1/0684/16 (BB) and 1/0719/14 (TV), and a grant from the Slovak Research and Development Agency APVV-14-0253.

References

[1] Z. Bar-Yossef, T.S. Jayram, R. Kumar, D. Sivakumar, and L. Trevisan. Counting distinct elements in a data stream. In *International Workshop on Randomization and Approximation Techniques (RANDOM)*, pages 1–10. Springer, 2002.

[2] M. Hozza, T. Vinař, and B. Brejová. How Big is That Genome? Estimating Genome Size and Coverage from k-mer Abundance Spectra. In *String Processing and Information Retrieval (SPIRE)*, pages 199–209. Springer, 2015.

[3] S. Kurtz, A. Narechania, J. C. Stein, and D. Ware. A new method to compute k-mer frequencies and its application to annotate large repetitive plant genomes. *BMC Genomics*, 9(1):517, 2008.

[4] G. Marçais and C. Kingsford. A fast, lock-free approach for efficient parallel counting of occurrences of k-mers. *Bioinformatics*, 27(6):764, 2011.

[5] P. Melsted and B. V. Halldórsson. Kmerstream: streaming algorithms for k-mer abundance estimation. *Bioinformatics*, 30(24):3541–3547, 2014.

[6] P. Melsted and J. Pritchard. Efficient counting of k-mers in DNA sequences using a bloom filter. *BMC Bioinformatics*, 12(1):333, 2011.

[7] P. R. Rider. Variance of the median of small samples from several special populations. *Journal of the American Statistical Association*, 55(289):148–150, 1960.

[8] N. Sivadasan, R. Srinivasan, and K. Goyal. Kmerlight: fast and accurate k-mer abundance estimation. *CoRR*, abs/1609.05626, 2016.

[9] D. Williams, W. L. Trimble, M. Shilts, F. Meyer, and H. Ochman. Rapid quantification of sequence repeats to resolve the size, structure and contents of bacterial genomes. *BMC Genomics*, 14(1):537, 2013.

J. Hlaváčová (Ed.): ITAT 2017 Proceedings, pp. 35–39
ISBN 978-1974274741, © 2017 R. Pavel, P. Gurský

Focused Web Crawling of Relevant Pages on e-Shops

Rudolf Pavel, Peter Gurský

Institute of Computer Science
Faculty of Science, P.J.Šafárik University in Košice
Jesenná 5, 040 01 Košice, Slovakia
rudolf.pavel@student.upjs.sk, peter.gursky@upjs.sk

Abstract: E-shop data extraction requires all detail pages of products to be crawled. To maintain extracted data actual, the crawling needs to be periodical. E-shops contain many irrelevant pages such as ads, basket or contact information that are good to avoid during a crawling process. This paper presents a focused web crawling method based on an analysis of a previous initial crawling that eliminates irrelevant paths from the following crawls of the e-shop. The method preserves the ability to collect all products of all product domains, even the new ones.

1 Introduction

Focused crawling is a common way to search and collect data relevant to user's needs on the web. The scope of project Kapsa [1] is to retrieve information about e-shop products by crawling and extracting, and presenting them in unified form, which simplifies user's choice of preferred product. This paper focuses on the beginning of the process, i.e. crawling and extracting products data from e-shops.

Crawling all objects (HTML files, images, scripts, CSS files …) from e-shop portal generates quite extensive data traffic. Polite crawling handles this issue by download speed restriction. Polite crawling of even small complete e-shop can easily take more than one hour.

The aim of our crawling is not retrieving all pages of the e-shop, just the pages that contain detail data about products. Any other downloaded page increases crawling time and e-shop's traffic.

To extract the most detailed information about a product on e-shop, the crawler needs to navigate itself to product's detail. Detail page usually contains product name, price, photos, product properties, product description, customer reviews, etc. Useful property of detail pages is, that they usually have uniform design, different from any other page on e-shop. Thus the identification of a detail page can be done by few simple rules applicable for every product on e-shop: presence of an element on special position of the HTML source (product name, price tag, product image, etc.) and/or special URL form. These rules can be easily created by administrator together with data extraction rules in annotation web browser extension Exago [2]. We believe that automatic content based detection of detail page is also possible, but we didn't focus on it.

Product prices are changing in time, some products can be removed form an e-shop, new products can be added and sometimes a completely new product domain can be inserted to an e-shop portfolio. To keep data about offered products actual, crawling of e-shops needs to be periodical.

The naïve approach to decrease the amount of pages of periodical crawling, would be to remember URLs of all detail pages of an e-shop and download them the next time. This approach decreases the amount of downloaded pages drastically. On the other hand, new products and product domains would not be detected, which is undesirable.

To retrieve all offered products and product domains, the crawling method must fetch also webpages containing lists of products as well as webpages that lead to them. We call these pages, together with detail pages, the *relevant pages*. All other pages and objects are irrelevant and we want to avoid downloading them.

Navigation through relevant pages can be configured by a set of manually created rules too. This approach is typical for most web scrappers. Manual creation of such navigation rules is usually not an easy task, if we want all relevant pages to be downloaded.

In this paper we present our automatic approach to crawl all relevant pages based on analysis of initial complete crawl of an e-shop. Following crawlings of the e-shop navigates on every relevant page excluding irrelevant pages, until e-shop design is changed. The changed design is easily detected, because the original extraction rules cease to function. In this case, crawler can switch to classic crawling approach and inform administrator that the extraction rules need to be changed.

2 Related Work

Focused crawling systems are usually designed to collect web pages with a certain topic. Such crawlers guess the relevance of the page based on anchor texts and PageRank and prioritize the URLs to crawl like in [4,7]. These crawlers do not care about site map.

Methods based on context graphs [12], learning automata [8] and Hidden Markov Models (HMM) [5,6] analyzes downloaded pages with classifiers and set the priority of all URLs found on them uniformly, based on score of the page. The classifiers give high rates to the pages that are similar to pages that leaded to desired goals. The position of the links on the page is not considered.

The method in [9] analyzes the relevance of parts of downloaded pages separately using their HTML structure position and prefers the URLs found in relevant parts of the pages.

Periodical crawling research is mainly focused on estimation of frequency of repeatable crawls to maintain up-to-date data [10].

The combined task of downloading and extracting data from web pages is called Web scrapping. There are a lot of web scrappers on the market. We haven't found any web scrapper, which cooperates with optimized crawling as the one, presented in this paper.

3 Initial Crawling and Its Analysis

Project Kapsa uses a modification of open source web crawler Crawler4j [3]. It's a multithreaded crawler written in Java. If there is a need to simulate clicks and/or scrolling

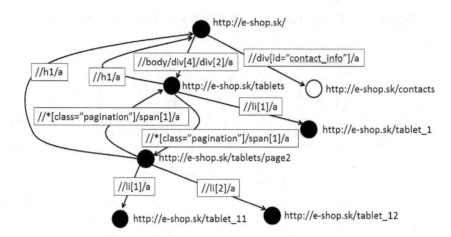

Figure 1: Initial crawling graph of a fictive e-shop http://e-shop.sk. Black vertexes represent relevant pages, white vertex represents a sample of irrelevant pages. Elements on pages containing links to other pages are represented as outgoing edges, labeled with XPath localization of the elements, heading to those pages.

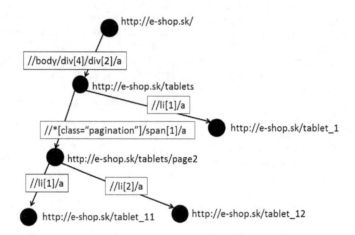

Figure 2: DAG with relevant pages and relevant XPaths extracted from the graph in Figure 1 in bottom-up analysis.

actions on the web page (page content is changed by JavaScript calls), Selenium-WebDriver is used.

Crawling is configured by wrapper – the result of annotation process in web browser extension Exago [2]. Wrapper consists of the following data:

- *seed_URL*, which is the starting page of the crawling process, usually the home page,
- detail page identification rules, and
- product data extraction rules.

The detail page identification rules are a combination of XPaths or/and regular expressions. XPath can localize an element or elements on a web page and regular expression can locate special substrings of the element content. Regular expressions are also applicable to URL. Each rule can be set to be mandatory (the rule must match) or forbidden (the rule may not match).

Initial crawling starts on *seed_URL* and navigates to every object of the same domain recursively. Unlike the standard crawling, we do not store downloaded pages. Every page is checked to be detail page. Detail pages are

sent to Extractor module that extracts all product details and stores them to storage. If the page is not a detail page, the crawler analyzes the page source to extract all links together with their XPath position on the page. It is important to note, that every URL is downloaded only once, even if it is present on many pages.

It is usual that there are links to other products on detail pages, typically they are recommended using collaborative filtering ("people that bought this also bought:" section). Our method does not analyze source of detail pages for new URL links on them. There are two main reasons for that:

- All products on a common e-shop are accessible from some product list page, i.e. a page containing list of links to subset of products. It is highly unlikely that there would be some product on e-shop accessible only from other product detail page.
- The navigation graph would contain more edges with no positive effect. With some effort a situation can be found, when we can eliminate a download of some product list page, because all products on it are

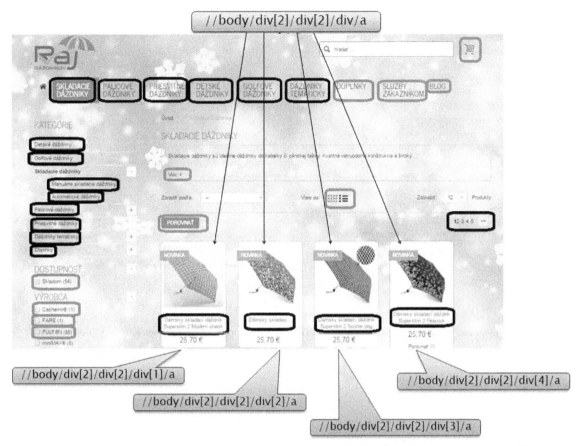

Figure 3: XPaths and their generalized XPath of elements representing list of products on www.rajdazdnikov.sk

accessible from other detail pages, but this can be only temporary status. If a new product would be added, it could be missed out in the next crawl.

The results of the initial crawling are extracted products and a directed graph of the e-shop links. Edges are labeled by XPaths that leads to HTML elements where the link was found. Detail pages have no outgoing edges – thus they are leafs of the graph.

3.1 Bottom-up Analysis: Creation of DAG with Relevant Pages and Relevant Links

When the whole e-shop is crawled and all products are extracted, the analysis of collected crawling data prepares the next optimized crawling, which usually takes place a few days later.

Bottom-up analysis creates a reduced graph that contains only vertexes with relevant pages. This graph is always a directed acyclic graph (DAG).

The analysis follows edges of the initial crawling graph in opposite direction.

- Initial step: every detail page vertex is added to a result graph.
- Iteration step: Let B be a set of all vertexes added in the previous step. Let A be a set of all vertexes, not present in a result graph, which have an outgoing edge to any vertex in B. Add set A and edges from A to B to the result graph.

- The iteration stops, if DAG contains seed_URL or no vertexes were added in the previous step, i.e. set A was empty.

Since we do not add all outgoing edges of vertexes in set A, just the ones that lead to vertexes in B, no cycle can be present in the result graph.

Unfortunately, this graph is not necessary connected. We need a connected graph to reach every detail page by navigation from seed_URL. Therefore, in the final step:

- Let M be a set of all vertexes in DAG with no incoming edges. Add all edges and vertexes on the shortest paths in from seed_URL to every vertex in M in original graph to result DAG.

3.2 Generalization of Relevant XPaths on Relevant Pages

During the initial crawling, each visited web page, except the detail pages, is processed to localize URL links in the HTML source. For every element containing URL, the pair of URL and XPath localizing the element in HTML is stored. Bottom-up analysis divides pages and XPaths to relevant and irrelevant. Fig. 3. shows a print screen of e-shop www.rajdazdnikov.sk. Links to relevant pages are encircled by light gray oval and irrelevant ones by a dark gray oval. When crawling, we want to follow every relevant link and no irrelevant links.

If we look at the elements of relevant links, we can see that some of them have very similar XPaths. This is, because they are presented to user in repeating structures, typically in lists. On Fig. 3 we can see four XPaths of elements with links heading to detail pages of umbrellas. The XPaths differ only in numbers in the last brackets. When we remove the brackets with the numbers, the resulting single generalized XPath localizes all four elements. This generalized XPath will localize all products on any page of the same HTML template, even if it contains less or more products.

Input for the algorithm that extracts generalized XPaths, is a list of XPath-URL pairs of relevant links found on the page. First, the pairs are divided to clusters of pairs, which differ only in one number between brackets on the same position. This is done by iterative partial clustering based on the longest common prefix. Finally, in each cluster, the different numbers and surrounding brackets of XPaths are removed resulting in a single generalized XPath for the cluster.

3.3 Top-Down Analysis: Creation of Generalized XPaths Graph

Having the algorithm that computes a list of generalized XPaths, we can run the algorithm on each relevant page of the DAG except the detail pages. The result is the modified DAG that has all edge labels replaced by generalized versions of the previous XPaths.

There is an important observation that pages accessible by the same generalized XPath, are all detail pages, or they all have (almost) equal set of generalized XPaths on them. This is because the objects accessible from the same list structure are logically of the same type (typically, they are all products, or all of them are product domains with list of products).

Sometimes, children of the same parent in the DAG do not have exactly the same set of generalized XPaths. Usually, some of the generalized XPaths are common, and some of them are missing on few of them. Pagination of the list is usually the reason. Some product domains are large and require paginated list of products and some are so small, that all products can fit into one page, therefore pagination links list and its generalized XPath are missing.

If there are only two pagination pages in product domain, there is only one XPath in its own cluster of similar XPaths and no generalization inside the cluster is possible. In this case the XPath has an extra pair of brackets with a number in it, when compared to corresponding generalized XPath in page's siblings in DAG. The more specific XPath (with extra brackets) can be replaced by more general one from its siblings.

Many times, the parent in DAG has equal (sub)set of generalized XPaths as some of its children, typically they are all lists of products.

The analysis of DAG goes from the root of DAG that is the seed_URL (usually the home page of the e-shop) using breadth-first traverse. In every vertex, we obtain the pairs of generalized XPaths and clusters of vertexes reachable by them. Vertexes in each cluster have computed their own generalized XPaths. The generalized XPaths of vertexes in cluster are unified with each other and possibly with parent vertex, if they have at least half of generalized XPath unifiable.

Next, a hash of the set of its generalized XPaths is computed and stored in each vertex. If the vertex corresponds to detail page, the hash's value is set to 0.

Finally, the generalized crawling graph is created. This is done by unification of the vertexes having the same hash. This graph has usually at least one edge heading to the same vertex.

Consider the DAG on Figure 2. The analysis starts with seed_URL http://e-shop.sk. Since it has only one outgoing edge, no generalization is possible, and the analysis goeas to vertex http://e-shop.sk/tables. This vertex has two outgoing edges, but not unifiable, so it has two pairs of generalized XPaths and set of vertexes reachable by them: {</li[1]/a,   {http://e-shop.sk/tablet_1}>}   and {<//*[class="pagination"]/span[1]/a,   {http://e-shop.sk/ tablets/page2}>}. The first pair has detail page in the cluster, so the analysis continues with the second pair. Vertex http://e-shop.sk/tablets/page2 has only one pair of generalized XPath and set of vertexes reachable by it: {<//**li**/a,   {http://e-shop.sk/tablet_11,   http://e-shop.sk/ tablet_12}>}. Then we try to unify this pair with pairs in parent vertex, which is successful resulting in pairs for both vertexes: {<//**li**/a,   {http://e-shop.sk/tablet_1,   http://e-shop.sk/tablet_11,   http://e-shop.sk/tablet_12}>}   and {<//*[class="pagination"]/span[1]/a,   {http://e-shop.sk/ tablets/page2}>}. Finally each vertex computes hash of its generalized XPaths. The clusters in pairs are replaced by the hash of their representatives which creates the edges of the final generalized crawling graph as depicted in Fig. 4.

The final generalized crawling graph is stored as a configuration for the next focused crawlings of the e-shop.

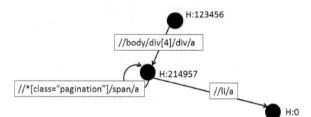

Figure 4: Generalized XPaths graph obtained from the graph in Fig. 2.

3.4 Crawling with Generalized Crawling Graph

Having the generalized crawling graph, the traversal trough the e-shop uses it as a finite-state automaton. Crawling starts at start state of the automaton and the seed_URL. On each downloaded page, all generalized XPaths of the outgoing edges are computed. Found URLs are scheduled to be downloaded together with the state on the end of the corresponding edge.

4   Conclusions

We have tested our approach on two e-shops so far: peazenkyshop.sk and rajdazdnikov.sk. The results of our experiments are in the table below:

Table 1. Number of all pages vs. number of pages downloaded by crawling with generalized crawling graph

e-shop	#products	#pages	#downloaded
penazenkyshop.sk	512	2730	1966
rajdazdnikov.sk	265	303	290

We can see that number of downloaded pages decreased to 72% resp. 96% in our tests. The tests showed that focused crawling is faster than initial crawling and the same set of detail pages was downloaded, which is our goal.

We showed that our automatic creation of crawling strategy is sufficient to eliminate irrelevant pages and download all detail pages.

This work was supported by the Agency of the Slovak Ministry of Education for the Structural Funds of the EU, under project CeZIS, ITMS: 26220220158

References

[1] Project Kapsa web page: http://kapsa.sk/

[2] P. Gurský, M. Vereščák, *Extrakcia štruktúrovaných objektov z webových portálov na pár klikov*, WIKT & DaZ, ISBN 978-80-227-4619-9, pp.225-228, 2016

[3] Crawer4j: Open source web crawler for Java, available on: https://github.com/yasserg/crawler4j

[4] Y. Uemura, T. Itokawa, T. Kitasuka, M. Aritsugi: An Effectively Focused Crawling System. Innovations in Intell. Machines – 2, SCI 376, Springer, pp. 61–76., 2012

[5] H. Liu, J. Janssen, E. Milios: Using HMM to learn user browsing patterns for focused Web crawling. Data & Knowledge Engineering 59, Elsevier, pp. 270–291, 2006

[6] S. Batsakis, E.G.M. Petrakis, E. Milios: Improving the performance of focused web crawlers. Data & Knowledge Engineering 68, Elsevier, pp. 1001-1013, 2009

[7] M.M.G. Farag, S. Lee, E.A. Fox: Focused crawler for events. International Journal on Digital Libraries, DOI 10.1007/s00799-016-0207-1, pp 1–17, 2017

[8] J.A. Torkestani: An adaptive focused Web crawling algorithm based on learning automata. Applied Intelligence, Volume 37, Issue 4, pp 586–601, 2012

[9] A. Patel, N. Schmidt: Application of structured document parsing to focused web crawling. Computer Standards & Interfaces 33, Elsevier, DOI 10.1016/j.csi.2010.08.002, pp. 325–331, 2011

[10] K. S. Kim, K. Y. Kim, K. H. Lee, T. K. Kim, W. S. Cho: Design and Implementation of Web Crawler Based on Dynamic Web Collection Cycle. Computer Standards & Interfaces, Volume 33, Issue 3, pp. 325-331, 2011

[11] G. Gouriten, S. Maniu, P. Senellart: Scalable, Generic, and Adaptive Systems for Focused Crawling. Proceedings of the 25th ACM conference on Hypertext and social media, ISBN: 978-1-4503-2954-5, pp. 35-45, 2014

[12] M. Diligenti, F. Coetzee, S. Lawrence, C. Giles, M. Gori: Focused crawling using context graphs. Proceedings of VLDB, pp. 527–534., 2000

J. Hlaváčová (Ed.): ITAT 2017 Proceedings, pp. 40–47
ISBN 978-1974274741, © 2017 M. Plátek, F. Otto, F. Mráz

On h-Lexicalized Automata and h-Syntactic Analysis

Martin Plátek[1], F. Otto[2], and F. Mráz[1] *

[1] Charles University, Department of Computer Science
Malostranské nám. 25, 118 00 PRAHA 1, Czech Republic
martin.platek@mff.cuni.cz, frantisek.mraz@mff.cuni.cz
[2] Fachbereich Elektrotechnik/Informatik, Universität Kassel
D-34109 Kassel, Germany
otto@theory.informatik.uni-kassel.de

Abstract: Following some previous studies on list automata and restarting automata, we introduce a generalized and refined model – the *h-lexicalized restarting list automaton* (LxRLAW). We argue that this model is useful for expressing transparent variants of lexicalized syntactic analysis, and analysis by reduction in computational linguistics. We present several subclasses of LxRLAW and provide some variants and some extensions of the Chomsky hierarchy, including the variant for the lexicalized syntactic analysis. We compare the input languages, which are the languages traditionally considered in automata theory, to the so-called *basic* and *h-proper languages*. The basic and h-proper languages allow stressing the transparency of h-lexicalized restarting automata for a superclass of the context-free languages by the so-called complete correctness preserving property. Such a type of transparency cannot be achieved for the whole class of context-free languages by traditional input languages. The transparency of h-lexicalized restarting automata is illustrated by two types of hierarchies which separate the classes of infinite and the classes of finite languages by the same tools.

1 Introduction

Chomsky introduced his well-known hierarchy of grammars to formulate the phrase-structure (immediate constituents) syntax of natural languages. However, the syntax of most European languages (including English) is often considered as a lexicalized syntax. In other words, the categories of Chomsky are bound to immediate constituents (phrases), while by lexicalized syntax they are bound to individual word-forms. In order to give a general theoretical basis for lexicalized syntax that is comparable to the Chomsky hierarchy, we follow some previous studies of list and restarting automata (see [1, 4, 5, 13]) and introduce a generalized and refined model that formalizes lexicalization in a natural way – the *h-lexicalized restarting list automaton with a look-ahead window* (LxRLAW). We argue that, through the use of restarting operations

and basic and h-proper languages, this new model is better suited for modeling (i) lexicalized syntactic analysis (h-syntactic analysis) and specially (ii) (lexicalized) analysis by reduction of natural languages (compare [6, 7]).

Analysis by reduction is a technique for deciding the correctness of a sentence. It is based on a stepwise simplification by reductions preserving the (in)correctness of the sentence until a short sentence is obtained for which it is easy to decide its correctness. Restarting automata were introduced as an automata model for analysis by reduction. While modeling analysis by reduction, restarting automata are forced to use very transparent types of computations. Nevertheless, they still can recognize a proper superset of the class of context-free languages (CFL). The first observation, which supports our argumentation, is that LxRLAW allow characterizations of the Chomsky hierarchy for classes of languages and for h-syntactic analysis as well.

An LxRLAW M is a device with a finite state control and a read/write window of a fixed size. This window can move in both directions along a tape (that is, a list of items) containing a word delimited by sentinels. The LxRLAW-automaton M uses an input alphabet and a working alphabet that contains the input alphabet. Lexicalization of M is given through a morphism which binds the individual symbols from the working alphabet to symbols from the input alphabet. M can decide (in general non-deterministically) to rewrite the contents of its window: it may delete some items from the list (moving its window in one or the other direction), insert some items into the list, and/or replace some items. In addition, M can perform a *restart operation* which causes M to place its window at the left end of the tape, so that the first symbol it contains is the left border marker, and to reenter its initial state.

In the technical part we adjust some known results to results on several subclasses of LxRLAW that are obtained by restricting its set of operations to certain subsets, and we also provide some variants and extensions of the Chomsky hierarchy of languages. E.g., an LxRLAI uses an input alphabet only.

We recall and newly introduce some constraints that are suitable for restarting automata, and we outline ways for new combinations of constraints, and more transparent computations.

---

*The first and the third author were partially supported by the Czech Science Foundation under the project 15-04960S.

Section 2 contains the basic definitions. The characterizations of the Chomsky hierarchy by certain types of LxRLAW is provided in Section 3.

In Section 4 we introduce RLWW-automata as a restricted type of LxRLAW and give several new constraints for them. By the basic and h-proper languages we show the transparency of h-lexicalized restarting automata through the so-called complete correctness preserving property. Using the new constraints and the basic and h-proper languages, we are able to separate classes of finite languages in a similar way as the classes of infinite languages and establish in this way new hierarchies, which can create a suitable tool for the classification of syntactic phenomena for computational linguistics. The paper concludes with Section 5.

2 Definitions

In what follows, we use $\subset$ to denote the proper subset relation. Further, we will sometimes use regular expressions instead of the corresponding regular languages. Finally, throughout the paper λ will denote the empty word and $\mathbb{N}_+$ will denote the set of all positive integers.

An *h-lexicalized two-way restarting list automaton*, LxRLAW for short, is a one-tape machine $M = (Q, \Sigma, \Gamma, \mathmaç, \$, q_0, k, \delta, h)$, where Q is the finite set of states, Σ is the finite input alphabet, Γ is the finite working alphabet containing Σ, the symbols $\mathmaç, \$ \notin \Gamma$ are the markers for the left and right border of the work space, respectively, $h : \Gamma \cup \{\mathmaç, \$\} \to \Sigma \cup \{\mathmaç, \$\}$ is a mapping creating a (letter) morphism from $\mathmaç\Gamma^*\$$ to $\mathmaç\Sigma^*\$$ such that, for each $a \in \Sigma \cup \{\mathmaç, \$\}$, $h(a) = a$; $q_0 \in Q$ is the initial state, $k \geq 1$ is the size of the *read/write window*, and

$$\delta : Q \times \mathscr{PC}^{\leq k} \to$$
$$\mathscr{P}((Q \times (\{\mathsf{MVR}, \mathsf{MVL}\} \cup \{\mathsf{W}(v), \mathsf{SR}(v), \mathsf{SL}(v), \mathsf{I}(v)\}))$$
$$\cup \{\mathsf{Restart}, \mathsf{Accept}, \mathsf{Reject}\})$$

is the *transition relation*. Here $\mathscr{P}(S)$ denotes the powerset of a set S,

$$\mathscr{PC}^{\leq k} := (\mathmaç \cdot \Gamma^{k-1}) \cup \Gamma^k \cup (\Gamma^{\leq k-1} \cdot \$) \cup (\mathmaç \cdot \Gamma^{\leq k-2} \cdot \$),$$

is the set of *possible contents* of the read/write window of M, and $v \in \mathscr{PC}^{\leq n}$, where $n \in \mathbb{N}$.

According to the transition relation, if M is in state q and sees the string u in its read/write window, it can perform nine different steps, where $q' \in Q$:

1. A *move-right step* $(q, u) \longrightarrow (q', \mathsf{MVR})$ assumes that $(q', \mathsf{MVR}) \in \delta(q, u)$ and $u \neq \$$. It causes M to shift the read/write window one position to the right and to enter state q'.

2. A *move-left step* $(q, u) \longrightarrow (q', \mathsf{MVL})$ assumes that $(q', \mathsf{MVL}) \in \delta(q, u)$ and $u \notin \mathmaç \cdot \Gamma^* \cdot \{\lambda, \$\}$. It causes M to shift the read/write window one position to the left and to enter state q'.

3. A *rewrite step* $(q, u) \longrightarrow (q', \mathsf{W}(v))$ assumes that $(q', \mathsf{W}(v)) \in \delta(q, u)$, $|v| = |u|$, and the sentinels are at the same positions in u and v (if at all). It causes M to replace the contents u of the read/write window by the string v, and to enter state q'. The head does not change its position.

4. An *S-right step* $(q, u) \longrightarrow (q', \mathsf{SR}(v))$ assumes that $(q', \mathsf{SR}(v)) \in \delta(q, u)$, v is shorter than u, containing all sentinels in u. It causes M to replace u by v and to enter state q'; the new position of the head is on the first item of v (the contents of the window is thus 'completed' from the right; the positional distance to the right sentinel decreases).

5. An *S-left step* $(q, u) \longrightarrow (q', \mathsf{SL}(v))$ assumes that $(q', \mathsf{SL}(v)) \in \delta(q, u)$, v is shorter than u, containing all sentinels in u. It causes M to replace u by v, to enter state q', and to shift the head position by $|u| - |v|$ items to the left – but to the left sentinel $\mathmaç$ at most (the contents of the window is 'completed' from the left; the distance to the left sentinel decreases if the head position was not already at $\mathmaç$).

6. An *insert step* $(q, u) \longrightarrow (q', \mathsf{I}(v))$ assumes that $(q', \mathsf{I}(v)) \in \delta(q, u)$, u is a proper subsequence of v (keeping the obvious sentinel constraints). It causes M to replace u by v (by inserting the relevant items), and to enter state q'. The head position is shifted by $|v| - |u|$ to the right (the distance to the left sentinel increases).

7. A *restart step* $(q, u) \longrightarrow \mathsf{Restart}$ assumes that $\mathsf{Restart} \in \delta(q, u)$. It causes M to place its read/write window onto the left end of the tape, so that the first symbol it sees is the left border marker $\mathmaç$, and to reenter the initial state q_0.

8. An *accept step* $(q, u) \longrightarrow \mathsf{Accept}$ assumes that $\mathsf{Accept} \in \delta(q, u)$. It causes M to halt and accept.

9. A *reject step* $(q, u) \longrightarrow \mathsf{Reject}$ assumes that $\mathsf{Reject} \in \delta(q, u)$. It causes M to halt and reject.

A *configuration* of M is a string $\alpha q \beta$ where $q \in Q$, and either $\alpha = \lambda$ and $\beta \in \{\mathmaç\} \cdot \Gamma^* \cdot \{\$\}$ or $\alpha \in \{\mathmaç\} \cdot \Gamma^*$ and $\beta \in \Gamma^* \cdot \{\$\}$; here q represents the current state, $\alpha\beta$ is the current contents of the tape, and it is understood that the head scans the first k symbols of β or all of β when $|\beta| < k$. A *restarting configuration* is of the form $q_0\mathmaç w\$$, where $w \in \Gamma^*$; if $w \in \Sigma^*$, then $q_0\mathmaç w\$$ is an *initial configuration*. We see that any initial configuration is also a restarting configuration. Any restart transfers M into a restarting configuration.

In general, the automaton M is *non-deterministic*, that is, there can be two or more steps (instructions) with the same left-hand side (q, u), and thus, there can be more than one computation for an input word. If this is not the case, the automaton is *deterministic*.

A *computation* of M is a sequence $C = C_0, C_1, \ldots, C_j$ of configurations, where C_0 is an initial configuration and C_{i+1} is obtained by a step of M from C_i, for all $0 \le i < j$.

An *input word* $w \in \Sigma^*$ *is accepted by M*, if there is a computation which starts with the initial configuration $q_0 \mathrm{c} w\$ $ and ends by executing an Accept instruction. By $L(M)$ we denote the language consisting of all input words accepted by M; we say that M *accepts the input language* $L(M)$.

A *basic (or characteristic, or working) word* $w \in \Gamma^*$ *is accepted by M*, if there is a computation which starts with the restarting configuration $q_0 \mathrm{c} w\$ $ and ends by executing an Accept instruction. By $L_C(M)$ we denote the language consisting of all basic words accepted by M; we say that M *accepts the basic (characteristic) language* $L_C(M)$.

Further, we take $L_{\mathrm{hP}}(M) = \{ h(w) \in \Sigma^* \mid w \in L_C(M) \}$, and we say that M *recognizes (accepts) the h-proper language* $L_{\mathrm{hP}}(M)$.

Finally, we take $L_A(M) = \{ (h(w), w) \mid w \in L_C(M) \}$ and we say that M *determines the h-syntactic analysis* $L_A(M)$.

We say that, for $x \in \Sigma^*$, $L_A(M, x) = \{ (x, y) \mid y \in L_C(M), h(y) = x \}$ is the *h-syntactic analysis* for x by M. We see that $L_A(M, x)$ is non-empty only for $x \in L_{\mathrm{hP}}(M)$.

In the following we only consider finite computations of LxRLAW-automata, which finish either by an accept or by a reject operation.

An LxRLAI M is an LxRLAW for which the input alphabet and the working alphabet are equal.

Fact 1. (Equality of Languages for LxRLAI-automata). *For each* LxRLAI*-automaton* M, $L(M) = L_C(M) = L_{\mathrm{hP}}(M)$.

– **Cycles, tails:** Any finite computation of an LxRLAW-automaton M consists of certain phases. Each phase starts in a restarting configuration. In a phase called a *cycle*, the window moves along the tape performing non-restarting operations until a Restart operation is performed and thus a new restarting configuration is reached. If after a restart configuration no further restart operation is performed, any finite computation necessarily finishes in a halting configuration – such a phase is called a *tail*.

– **Cycle-rewritings:** We use the notation $q_0 \mathrm{c} u\$ \vdash_M^c q_0 \mathrm{c} v\$ $ to denote a cycle of M that begins with the restarting configuration $q_0 \mathrm{c} u\$ $ and ends with the restarting configuration $q_0 \mathrm{c} v\$ $. Through this relation we define the relation of *cycle-rewriting* by M. We write $u \Rightarrow_M^c v$ iff $q_0 \mathrm{c} u\$ \vdash_M^c q_0 \mathrm{c} v\$ $ holds. The relation $u \Rightarrow_M^{c^*} v$ is the reflexive and transitive closure of $u \Rightarrow_M^c v$.

We point out that the cycle-rewriting is a very important feature of LxRLAW.

– **Reductions:** If $u \Rightarrow_M^c v$ is a cycle-rewriting by M such that $|u| > |v|$, then $u \Rightarrow_M^c v$ is called a *reduction* by M.

2.1 Further Refinements on LxRLAW

Here we introduce some constrained types of rewriting steps which assume $q, q' \in Q$ and $u \in \mathscr{PC}^{\le k}$.

A *delete-right step* $(q, u) \to (q', \mathrm{DR}(v))$ is an S-right step $(q, u) \to (q', \mathrm{SR}(v))$ such that v is a proper subsequence of u, containing all the sentinels from u (if any).

A *delete-left step* $(q, u) \to (q', \mathrm{DL}(v))$ is an S-left step $(q, u) \to (q', \mathrm{SL}(v))$ such that v is a proper sub-sequence of u, containing all the sentinels from u (if any).

A *contextual-left step* $(q, u) \to (q', \mathrm{CL}(v))$ is an S-left step $(q, u) \to (q', \mathrm{SL}(v))$, where $u = v_1 u_1 v_2 u_2 v_3$ and $v = v_1 v_2 v_3$ for some v_1, u_1, v_2, u_2, v_3, such that v contains all the sentinels from u (if any).

A *contextual-right step* $(q, u) \to (q', \mathrm{CR}(v))$ is an S-right-step $(q, u) \to (q', \mathrm{SR}(v))$, where $u = v_1 v_2 v_3$ and $v = v_1 v_3$ for some v_1, v_2, v_3, such that v contains all the sentinels from u (if any).

Note that the contextual-right step is not symmetrical to the contextual-left step. We will use this fact in Section 4.

The set $OG = \{\mathrm{MVL}, \mathrm{MVR}, \mathrm{W}, \mathrm{SL}, \mathrm{SR}, \mathrm{DL}, \mathrm{DR}, \mathrm{CL}, \mathrm{CR}, \mathrm{I}, \mathrm{Restart}\}$ represents the set of types of steps, which can be used for characterizations of subclasses of LxRLAW. This set does not contain the symbols Accept and Reject, corresponding to halting steps, as they are used for all LxRLAW-automata. Let $\mathsf{T} \subseteq OG$. We denote by T-automata the subset of LxRLAW-automata which only use transition steps from the set $\mathsf{T} \cup \{\mathrm{Accept}, \mathrm{Reject}\}$. For example, $\{\mathrm{MVR}, \mathrm{W}\}$-automata only use move-right steps, W-steps, Accept steps, and Reject steps.

Notations. For brevity, the prefix det- will be used to denote the property of being deterministic. For any class $\mathscr{A}$ of automata, $\mathscr{L}(\mathscr{A})$ will denote the class of input languages that are recognized by automata from $\mathscr{A}$, $\mathscr{L}_C(\mathscr{A})$ will denote the class of basic languages that are recognized by automata from $\mathscr{A}$, and $\mathscr{L}_{\mathrm{hP}}(\mathscr{A})$ will denote the class of h-proper languages that are recognized by automata from $\mathscr{A}$. Moreover, $\mathscr{L}_A(\mathscr{A})$ will denote the class of h-syntactic analyses that are determined by automata from $\mathscr{A}$. Let us note that we use the more simple notation $\mathscr{L}_P(\mathscr{A})$ in [15] and other papers in a different sense than the denotation $\mathscr{L}_{\mathrm{hP}}(\mathscr{A})$ here.

For a natural number $k \ge 1$, $\mathscr{L}(k\text{-}\mathscr{A})$ ($\mathscr{L}_C(k\text{-}\mathscr{A})$ or $\mathscr{L}_{\mathrm{hP}}(k\text{-}\mathscr{A})$) will denote the class of input (basic or h-proper) languages that are recognized by those automata from $\mathscr{A}$ that use a read/write window of size k.

– **Monotonicity of Rewritings.** We introduce various notions of *monotonicity* as important types of constraints for computations of LxRLAW-automata.

Let M be an LxRLAW-automaton, and let $C = C_k, C_{k+1}, \ldots, C_j$ be a sequence of configurations of M, where C_{i+1} is obtained by a single transition step of M from C_i, $k \le i < j$. We say that C is a *sub-computation* of M.

Let $RW \subseteq \{\mathrm{W}, \mathrm{SR}, \mathrm{SL}, \mathrm{DR}, \mathrm{DL}, \mathrm{CR}, \mathrm{CL}, \mathrm{I}\}$. Then we denote by $\mathrm{W}(C, RW)$ the maximal (scattered) sub-sequence of C, which contains those configurations from C that correspond to RW-steps (that is, those configurations in which a transition step of one of the types from the set RW is applied). We say that $\mathrm{W}(C, RW)$ is the *working sequence* of C determined by RW.

Let C be a sub-computation of an LxRLAW-automaton M, and let $C_w = \mathfrak{c}\alpha q\beta\$$ be a configuration from C. Then $|\beta\$|$ is the *right distance* of C_w, which is denoted by $D_r(C_w)$, and $|\mathfrak{c}\alpha|$ is the *left distance* of C_w, which is denoted by $D_l(C_w)$.

We say that a working sequence $\mathrm{W}(C, RW) = (C_1, C_2, \ldots, C_n)$ is RW-monotone (or RW-*right-monotone*) if $D_r(C_1) \geq D_r(C_2) \geq \ldots \geq D_r(C_n)$.

A sub-computation C of M is RW-monotone if $\mathrm{W}(C, RW)$ is RW-monotone. If we write (right-)monotone, we actually mean $\{\mathsf{W}, \mathsf{SR}, \mathsf{SL}, \mathsf{DR}, \mathsf{DL}, \mathsf{CR}, \mathsf{CL}, \mathsf{I}\}$-right-monotone, that is, monotonicity with respect to any type of (allowed) rewriting and inserting for the corresponding type of automaton. By completely(-right-)monotone, we actually mean monotone with respect to each configuration of the computation.

For each of the prefixes $\mathsf{X} \subset [RW, \lambda, \mathrm{completely}]$ we say that M is X-*monotone* if each of its (sub)computations is X-monotone.

Fact 2. *Let M be an $\{\mathsf{MVR}, \mathsf{SR}, \mathsf{SL}, \mathsf{W}, \mathsf{I}\}$-automaton. Then M is completely-monotone.*

Remark on PDA. It is not hard to see that a 1-$\{\mathsf{MVR}, \mathsf{SR}, \mathsf{SL}, \mathsf{W}, \mathsf{I}\}$-automaton is a type of normalized pushdown automaton. The top of the pushdown is represented by the position of the head, and the content of the pushdown is represented by the part of the tape between the left sentinel and the position of the head. In fact, in a very similar way the pushdown automaton was introduced by Chomsky. A k-$\{\mathsf{MVR}, \mathsf{SR}, \mathsf{SL}, \mathsf{W}, \mathsf{I}\}$-automaton can be interpreted as a pushdown automaton with a k-lookahead, and with a limited look under the top of the pushdown at the same time. (det-)PDAs can be simulated even by (det-)1-$\{\mathsf{MVR}, \mathsf{SL}, \mathsf{W}\}$-automata. In the following, we will consider the automata which fulfill the condition of completely-right-monotonicity for pushdown automata (PDA).

3 Characterizations of the Chomsky Hierarchy

We transform and enhance some results from [1, 5] concerning input languages to basic and h-proper languages.

det-$\{\mathsf{MVR}\}$- and $\{\mathsf{MVR}\}$-automata work like deterministic and nondeterministic finite-state automata, respectively. The only difference is that such automata can accept or reject without visiting all symbols of an input word. Nevertheless, these automata can be simulated by deterministic and nondeterministic finite-state automata, respectively, which instead of an Accept-step enter a special accepting state in which they scan the rest of the input word. Since the regular languages are closed under homomorphisms, we have the following proposition.

Proposition 3. *For $\mathscr{X} \in \{\mathscr{L}, \mathscr{L}_\mathrm{C}, \mathscr{L}_{\mathrm{hP}}\}$, the classes $\mathscr{X}(1\text{-det-}\{\mathsf{MVR}\})$ and $\mathscr{X}(1\text{-}\{\mathsf{MVR}\})$ coincide with the class REG of regular languages.*

Observe that for LxRLAW-automata with window size 1, the operation SR coincides with the operations DR and CR, and that the operation SL coincides with the operations DL and CL, and that in this situation all these operations just delete the symbol currently inside the window.

Proposition 4. *For $\mathscr{X} \in \{\mathscr{L}, \mathscr{L}_\mathrm{C}, \mathscr{L}_{\mathrm{hP}}\}$:*
$$\mathscr{X}(\{\mathsf{MVR}, \mathsf{CL}, \mathsf{W}\}) \subseteq \mathrm{CFL},$$
where CFL is the class of context-free languages.

Proof. Any $\{\mathsf{MVR}, \mathsf{CL}, \mathsf{W}\}$-automaton $M = (Q, \Sigma, \Gamma, \mathfrak{c}, \$, q_0, k, \delta, h)$ can be simulated by a pushdown automaton (PDA) P which stores the current content of the window of M in its control unit (as a state). On an input word w, P first tries to read the first k symbols of w and to store them within its control unit. If w is of length less than k, then P accepts or rejects w upon encountering the right sentinel $\$$. Otherwise, P continues while preserving the following invariant: the contents of the pushdown store of P equals the part the tape of M to the left of its current position, the contents of the window of M and its state are both stored in the control unit of P, and the rest of the tape of M to the right of its window is the unread part of the input of P.

Hence, P accepts exactly $L(M)$ by entering an accepting state and reading the rest of its input whenever M performs an Accept-step. If we include all working symbols of M into the input alphabet of P, we obtain a PDA P' such that $L(P') = L_\mathrm{C}(M)$, thus the basic language of M is context-free. As CFL is closed under homomorphisms, also the h-proper language of M is context-free, too. $\square$

Proposition 5. *For $\mathscr{X} \in \{\mathscr{L}, \mathscr{L}_\mathrm{C}, \mathscr{L}_{\mathrm{hP}}\}$, the class $\mathscr{X}(1\text{-}\{\mathsf{MVR}, \mathsf{CL}, \mathsf{W}\})$ coincides with the class CFL of context-free languages.*

Proof. According to Proposition 4, each language accepted by a 1-$\{\mathsf{MVR}, \mathsf{CL}, \mathsf{W}\}$-automaton as an input language or as a basic language is context-free. It remains to proof the opposite inclusion. Let L be a context-free language. Clearly, the empty language and the language $\{\lambda\}$ can be accepted by a 1-$\{\mathsf{MVR}, \mathsf{CL}, \mathsf{W}\}$-automaton.

W.l.o.g. we can suppose that $L \setminus \{\lambda\}$ is generated by a context-free grammar $G = (\Pi, \Sigma, S, P_G)$ in Chomsky normal form. We can construct a PDA P accepting the language $L \setminus \{\lambda\}$ by empty store. For each nonempty word $w \in L$, the PDA P can guess and simulate a rightmost derivation of w according to G in reverse order. That is, P will perform a bottom-up analysis of w which uses a shift-operation that moves the next input symbol onto the pushdown and reductions according to the rewrite rules from P_G. The reduction according to a rule of the form $X \to x$, for $X \in \Pi$, $x \in \Sigma$, consists of popping x from the top of the pushdown and pushing X onto the pushdown. The reduction according to a rule of the form $X \to YZ$, where X, Y, Z are nonterminals of G, consists of popping YZ (in reversed order) from the pushdown and pushing X onto the pushdown.

The empty word λ can be immediately accepted or rejected by a 1-$\{MVR, CL, W\}$-automaton M when $\lambda \in L$ or $\lambda \notin L$, respectively. For each nonempty word $w \in \Sigma^*$, each computation of P on w can be simulated by M in such a way that the top of the pushdown will be in the window of M. The rest of the contents of the pushdown of P will be stored on the part of the tape of M to the left of the position of its window.

A shift-operation of P can be simulated by a MVR-step. The reduction according to a rule of the form $X \to x$, for $X \in \Pi$, $x \in \Sigma$, will be simulated by the W-step which rewrites x in the window of M by X. The reduction according to a rule of the form $X \to YZ$, where $X, Y, Z \in \Pi$, will be simulated by the CL-step which deletes the tape cell containing Z and a W-step which rewrites the symbol Y in the window of M by X. As P accepts when the pushdown contains the single symbol S, M will perform an Accept-step, when the only symbol on its tape is the initial nonterminal S. Clearly, $L(M) = L(P)$. Additionally, M can check that after each MVR-step the symbol which appears within its window is either the sentinel \$ or a terminal from Σ. In this way it is ensured that M does not accept any word containing a working symbol, hence $L_C(M) = L_{hP}(M) = L$. $\square$

It is easy to see that a linear-bounded automaton working on a tape containing an input word delimited by sentinels directly corresponds to a 1-$\{MVR, MVL, W\}$-automaton. We can also see that a $\{MVR, MVL, W\}$-automaton can be simulated by a 1-$\{MVR, MVL, W\}$-automaton. Recall that the class CSL is closed under non-erasing homomorphisms. Therefore, we have the following statement.

Proposition 6. *For $\mathscr{X} \in \{\mathscr{L}, \mathscr{L}_C, \mathscr{L}_{hP}\}$, the class $\mathscr{X}(\{MVR, MVL, W\})$ coincides with the class* CSL *of context-sensitive languages.*

By adding the ability to insert cells within the working tape to the operations MVR, MVL and W, we can easily simulate an arbitrary Turing machine. Hence we have the following proposition.

Proposition 7. *For $\mathscr{X} \in \{\mathscr{L}, \mathscr{L}_C, \mathscr{L}_{hP}\}$, the class $\mathscr{X}((\text{det-})\{MVR, MVL, W, I\})$ coincides with the class* RE *of recursively enumerable languages.*

From the previous results we obtain the following variant of the Chomsky hierarchy for the classes of the h-syntactic analysis which follows from the corresponding hierarchies for the classes of h-proper and basic languages.

Corollary 1. *We have the following hierarchy:*
$$\mathscr{L}_A(\{MVR\}) \subset \mathscr{L}_A(\{MVR, CL, W\}),$$

$$\mathscr{L}_A(\{MVR, CL, W\}) \subset \mathscr{L}_A(\{MVR, MVL, W\}),$$
$$\mathscr{L}_A(\{MVR, MVL, W\}) \subset \mathscr{L}_A(\{MVR, MVL, W, I\}).$$

In a similar way we can obtain the deterministic variants of the Chomsky hierarchy.

4   RLWW-Automata with New Constraints

Here we formulate the h-lexicalized two-way restarting automaton in weak accepting (cyclic) form, and some of its subclasses. By considering basic and h-proper languages, this new type of automaton is close to the method of analysis by reduction (see [6]), its computations are transparent, and it reflects well the structure of its basic and h-proper languages.

An *h-lexicalized two-way restarting automaton in weak accepting form* (originally called *cyclic form*) M, an *hRLWW-automaton* for short, is a $\{MVR, MVL, SL, SR, Restart\}$-automaton, which uses an SL-step or SR-step exactly once in each cycle (only one of them), and directly accepts only words that fit into its window.

An hRLWW-automaton is called an hRLW-*automaton* if its working alphabet coincides with its input alphabet. Note that in this situation, each restarting configuration is necessarily an initial configuration.

An hRLW-automaton is called an hRL-*automaton* if each of its rewrite steps is a DL- or DR-step.

An hRL-automaton is called an hRLC-*automaton* if each of its rewrite steps is a CL- or CR-step.

An hRLWW-automaton is called an hRLWWC-*automaton* if each of its rewrite steps is a CL-step or CR-step.

An hRLWW-automaton is called an hRRWW-*automaton* if it does not use any MVL-steps. Analogously, we obtain hRRW-*automata*, hRR-*automata*, and hRRC-*automata*.

We see that for hRLWW-automata, all cycle-rewritings are reductions. We also have the following simple facts, which illustrate the transparency of computations of hRLWW-automata due their basic and h-proper languages.

Fact 8. (Complete Correctness Preserving Property).
Let M be a deterministic hRLWW-*automaton, let $C = C_0, C_1, \cdots, C_n$ be a computation of M, and let ¢u_i\$ be the tape contents of the configuration C_i, $0 \le i \le n$. If $u_i \in L_C(M)$ for some i, then $u_j \in L_C(M)$ for all $j = 0, 1, \ldots, n$.*

Fact 9. (Complete Error Preserving Property).
Let M be a deterministic hRLWW-*automaton, let $C = C_0, C_1, \cdots, C_n$ be a computation of M, and let ¢u_i\$ be the tape contents of the configuration C_i, $0 \le i \le n$. If $u_i \notin L_C(M)$ for some i, then $u_j \notin L_C(M)$ for all $j = 0, 1, \ldots, n$.*

Fact 10. (Prefix Correctness Preserving Property).
Let M be an hRLWW-*automaton, let $C = C_0, C_1, \cdots, C_n$ be a computation of M, and let ¢u_i\$ be the tape contents of the configuration C_i, $0 \le i \le n$. If $u_i \in L_C(M)$ for some i, then $u_j \in L_C(M)$ for all $j \le i$.*

Fact 11. (Suffix Error Preserving Property).
Let M be an hRLWW-*automaton, let* $C = C_0, C_1, \cdots, C_n$ *be a computation of M, and let* $\mathfrak{c}u_i\$$ *be the tape contents of the configuration* C_i, $0 \leq i \leq n$. *If* $u_i \notin L_C(M)$ *for some i, then* $u_j \notin L_C(M)$ *for all* $j \geq i$.

Corollary 2. (Equality of Languages for hRLW-automata).
For each hRLW-*automaton M,* $L(M) = L_C(M) = L_{hP}(M)$.

From the last corollary above, the Complete Error and Complete Correctness Preserving Properties for deterministic hRLW-automata, and the Suffix Error Preserving Property and the Prefix Correctness Preserving Property for hRLW-automata follow for their input, basic, and h-proper languages.

4.1 On Regular Languages and Correctness Preserving Computations

Proposition 12. *The class* REG *is characterized by basic and h-proper languages of deterministic* hRLWW-*automata which use only the operations* MVR, ĊR, Restart, *and which use the operation* CR *only when the window is at the position just to the right of the left sentinel. We denote such automata by* det-Rg2.

Proof. We outline only the main ideas of the proof. First we show that any basic language and h-proper language of a det-Rg2 is regular. Let M_k be a k-det-Rg2-automaton. It is not hard to see that M_k can be simulated by a finite automaton A_{k+1} with a stack of size $k+1$ stored within its finite control, and therefore $L_C(M_k) = L(A_{k+1})$, and $L_{hP}(M_k) = L_{hP}(A_{k+1})$. Since the regular languages are closed under homomorphisms, $L_{hP}(A_{k+1})$ is a regular language, too.

On the other hand, we can see from the pumping lemma for regular languages that any regular language $L \subseteq \Sigma^*$ can be accepted by a det-Rg2-automaton with working (and input) alphabet Σ. □

Remark. Since det-Rg2-automata are deterministic hRLWW-automata, we see that they are completely correctness preserving for their basic languages.

4.2 Monotonicity and h-Proper Languages

As an hRRWWC-automaton is an hRRWW-automaton which uses only CL-operations instead of SL-operations and CR-operations instead of SR-operations, we can prove the following theorem in a similar way as it was done for a stronger version of hRRWW-automata in the technical report [15].

Theorem 13. $\mathsf{CFL} = \mathscr{L}_{hP}(\text{det-mon-hRLWWC})$.

Proof. The proof is based mainly on ideas from [15]. Here it is transformed for hRLWW-automata with the constraint of the weak accepting form.

If $M = (Q, \Sigma, \Gamma, \mathfrak{c}, \$, q_0, k, \delta, h)$ is a right-monotone hRLWW-automaton, then its characteristic language $L_C(M)$ is context-free [14]. As $L_{hP}(M) = h(L_C(M))$, and as CFL is closed under morphisms, it follows that $L_{hP}(M)$ is also context-free.

Conversely, assume that $L \subseteq \Sigma^*$ is a context-free language. Without loss of generality we may assume that L does not contain the empty word. Thus, there exists a context-free grammar $G = (N, \Sigma, S, P)$ for L which is in *Greibach normal form*, that is, each rule of P has the form $A \to a\alpha$ for some string $\alpha \in N^*$ and some letter $a \in \Sigma$. For the following construction we assume that the rules of G are numbered from 1 to m.

From G we construct a new grammar $G' := (N, \Delta, S, P')$, where $\Delta := \{ (\nabla_i, a) \mid 1 \leq i \leq m$ and the i-th rule of G has the form $A \to a\alpha \}$ is a set of new terminal symbols that are in one-to-one correspondence to the rules of G, and

$$P' := \{A \to (\nabla_i, a)\alpha \mid A \to a\alpha \text{ is the } i\text{-th rule of } G, 1 \leq i \leq m\}.$$

Obviously, a word $\omega \in \Delta^*$ belongs to $L(G')$ if and only if ω has the form $\omega = (\nabla_{i_1}, a_1)(\nabla_{i_2}, a_2) \cdots (\nabla_{i_n}, a_n)$ for some integer $n > 0$, where $a_1, a_2, \ldots, a_n \in \Sigma$, $i_1, i_2, \ldots, i_n \in \{1, 2, \ldots, m\}$, and the sequence of these indices describes a (left-most) derivation of $w := a_1 a_2 \cdots a_n$ from S in G. Let us take $h((\nabla_i, a)) = a$ for all $(\nabla_i, a) \in \Delta$. Then it follows that $h(L(G')) = L(G) = L$. From ω this derivation can be reconstructed deterministically. In fact, the language $L(G')$ is deterministic context-free. Hence, there exists a deterministic right-monotone hRRC-automaton M for this language (see [4]). By interpreting the symbols of Δ as auxiliary symbols, we obtain a deterministic right-monotone hRRWWC-automaton M' such that $h(L_C(M')) = L_{hP}(M') = h(L(M)) = h(L(G')) = L$. Observe that the input language $L(M')$ of M' is actually empty. □

Remark. By means of h-lexicalized restarting automata, the above construction corresponds to the linguistic effort to obtain a set of categories (auxiliary symbols) that ensures the correctness preserving property for the respective analysis by reduction. Note that in its reductions, the automaton M' above only uses delete operations (in a special way). This is highly reminiscent of the basic (elementary) analysis by reduction learned in (Czech) basic schools.

4.3 Hierarchies

In this subsection we will show similar results for finite and infinite classes of basic and h-proper languages and for classes of h-syntactic analysis given by certain subclasses of hRLWW-automata. At first we introduce some useful notions.

For a (sub)class X of hRLWW-automata, by fin(i)-X we denote the subclass of X-automata which can perform at most i reductions, and by fin-X we denote the union of fin(i)-X over all natural numbers i.

By $L_C(M, i)$ we denote the subset of $L_C(M)$ containing all words accepted by at most i reductions. We take $L_{hP}(M, i) = h(L_C(M, i))$.

Proposition 14. *Let $i \geq 0$, and let M be an hRLWW-automaton. Then there is a fin(i)-hRLWW-automaton M_1 such that $L_C(M, i) = L_C(M_1)$, and if $u \Rightarrow_{M_1} v$, then $u \Rightarrow_M v$. If M is deterministic, then M_1 is deterministic as well.*

Proof. The basic idea of the construction of M_1 is to add to the finite control of M the counter of possible cycles on the starting word by M. While simulating the first cycle of M, M_1 already simulates the next up to $i - 1$ cycles of M rejecting all words which are not acceptable with at most i cycles by M. □

We can see that a similar proposition can also be shown for hRRWW-automata.

For a positive integer k, let the prefix de(k)- denote hRLWW-automata which delete at most k symbols in each reduction.

The next proposition lays the foundation to the desired hierarchies. In order to show the next proposition we consider the following sequence of languages for $k \geq 1$: $Lrg_k = \{ (a^k)^i \mid i \geq 1 \}$.

Proposition 15. $\mathscr{L}_{hP}(k\text{-de}(k)\text{-det-fin}(1)\text{-Rg2}) \setminus \mathscr{L}_{hP}((k-1)\text{-hRLWW}) \neq \emptyset$, *for all $k \geq 2$.*

Proof. We outline the basic ideas only. We can construct a k-det-Rg2-automaton MR_k such that $L_C(MR_k) = L_{hP}(MR_k) = Lrg_k$. For MR_k a window of the size k suffices, because MR_k can first move its window to the right of the left sentinel. If it sees a^k, then it performs a CR-step which deletes a^k. Next, if the window contains only the right sentinel, the automaton accepts, otherwise it restarts.

From Proposition 14 we can see that there is a k-det-Rg2-automaton MR'_k such that $L_C(MR'_k) = L_{hP}(MR'_k) = L_{hP}(MR_k, 1)$.

On the other hand, there is no $(k-1)$-hRLWW-automaton accepting $L_{hP}(MR'_k)$ as its h-proper language. For a contradiction, let us suppose that $L_{hP}(M) = L_{hP}(MR'_k)$ for a $(k-1)$-hRLWW-automaton M. Then M accepts a word $w \in L_C(M)$ such that $h(w) = a^k \in L_{hP}(MR_k, 1)$. In an accepting computation on w, automaton M must perform at least one reduction, but it can delete at most $(k-1)$ symbols by which it obtains a word w' of length between 1 and $k-1$, hence $h(w') \notin L_{hP}(MR'_k)$ – a contradiction to $L_{hP}(M) = L_{hP}(MR'_k)$. □

Corollary 3. *For all types $X \in \{$det-Rg2, hRR, hRRC, hRRW, hRRWWC, hRRWW, hRL, hRLC, hRLW, hRLWWC, hRLWW$\}$, all prefixes $pr_1 \in \{\lambda, fin\}$, all prefixes $pref_X \in \{\lambda, \text{mon}, \text{det}, \text{det-mon}\}$, and all $k \geq 2$, the following holds:*
$\mathscr{L}_{hP}(k\text{-}pr_1\text{-}pref_X\text{-}X) \subset \mathscr{L}_{hP}((k+1)\text{-}pr_1\text{-}pref_X\text{-}X)$ *and*
$\mathscr{L}_{hP}(\text{de}(k)\text{-}pr_1\text{-}pref_X\text{-}X) \subset \mathscr{L}_{hP}(\text{de}(k+1)\text{-}pr_1\text{-}pref_X\text{-}X)$.

Remark. The next theorem enables us to classify finite linguistic observations in a similar way as infinite formal languages. It refines a part of the Chomsky hierarchy and gives a useful tool for classifications of several syntactic phenomena of natural languages. In order to show the next theorem we consider the following sequences of languages for $k \geq 1$: $Lcf_{k+1} = \{ a^i b^{i \cdot k} \mid i \geq 1 \}$ and $Lcs_{k+1} = \{ a^i b^i c^{i \cdot k}, a^{i+1} b^i c^{i \cdot k} \mid i \geq 1 \}$.

Theorem 16. *For $X = $ hRLWWC, and $k \geq 2$ the following holds:*

(1) $\mathscr{L}_{hP}(k\text{-det-Rg2}) \subset \mathscr{L}_{hP}(k\text{-det-mon-}X) \subset \mathscr{L}_{hP}(k\text{-det-}X)$,

(2) $\mathscr{L}_A(k\text{-det-Rg2}) \subset \mathscr{L}_A(k\text{-det-mon-}X) \subset \mathscr{L}_A(k\text{-det-}X)$,

(3) $\mathscr{L}_{hP}(k\text{-det-fin-Rg2}) \subset \mathscr{L}_{hP}(k\text{-det-fin-mon-}X) \subset \mathscr{L}_{hP}(k\text{-det-fin-}X)$,

(4) $\mathscr{L}_A(k\text{-det-fin-Rg2}) \subset \mathscr{L}_A(k\text{-det-fin-mon-}X) \subset \mathscr{L}_A(k\text{-det-fin-}X)$.

Proof. We outline the main ideas of the proof. For $k \geq 2$ and $X = $ hRLWWC, the following inclusions follow from definitions:

(1) $\mathscr{L}_{hP}(k\text{-det-Rg2}) \subseteq \mathscr{L}_{hP}(k\text{-det-mon-}X) \subseteq \mathscr{L}_{hP}(k\text{-det-}X)$,

(2) $\mathscr{L}_A(k\text{-det-Rg2}) \subseteq \mathscr{L}_A(k\text{-det-mon-}X) \subseteq \mathscr{L}_A(k\text{-det-}X)$,

(3) $\mathscr{L}_{hP}(k\text{-det-fin-Rg2}) \subseteq \mathscr{L}_{hP}(k\text{-det-fin-mon-}X) \subseteq \mathscr{L}_{hP}(k\text{-det-fin-}X)$,

(4) $\mathscr{L}_A(k\text{-det-fin-Rg2}) \subseteq \mathscr{L}_A(k\text{-det-fin-mon-}X) \subseteq \mathscr{L}_A(k\text{-det-fin-}X)$.

It remains to show that all these inclusions are proper. We use the sequence of context-free languages Lcf_k to show the first proper inclusion in all four propositions.

For any natural number $k \geq 2$, it is not hard to construct a k-det-mon-hRLC-automaton Mcf_k such that $L_C(Mcf_k) = L_{hP}(Mcf_k) = Lcf_k$. By applying Proposition 14 for $i = k$, we can construct a k-det-mon-fin(k)-hRLC-automaton Mcf'_k such that $L_C(Mcf'_k) = L_{hP}(Mcf'_k) = L_{hP}(Mcf_k, k)$.

For a contradiction, let us suppose that there is an k-det-Rg2-automaton M_k such that $L_{hP}(M_k) = L_{hP}(Mcf_k, k)$. Let us consider the word $a^{k+1} b^{(k+1)(k-1)} \in L_{hP}(Mcf'_k)$. As this word is longer than k, M_k must use at least one cycle to accept a word w such that $h(w) = a^{k+1} b^{(k+1)(k-1)}$. Since any k-det-Rg2-automaton can delete only some of the first k symbols we have a contradiction to the complete correctness preserving property of M_k. Thus, the first inclusion is proper for all four propositions of the theorem.

Using languages Lcs_k we can show the second inclusion to be proper in all four propositions. Let $k \geq 2$ be an integer. It is easy to construct a k-det-hRLC-automaton Mcs_k such that $L_C(Mcs_k) = L_{hP}(Mcs_k) = Lcs_k$. By applying Proposition 14 for $i = k$, we can construct a k-det-fin(k)-hRLC-automaton Mcs'_k such that $L_C(Mcs'_k) = L_{hP}(Mcs'_k) = L_{hP}(Mcs_k, k)$.

In order to derive a contradiction, let us assume that there is a k-mon-det-hRLWWC-automaton M_k such that

$L_{hP}(M_k) = L_{hP}(Mcs_k, k)$. Let us consider the word $a^{k+1}b^{k+1}c^{(k+1)(k-1)} \in L_{hP}(Mcs'_k)$. As this word is longer than $2k$, M_k must use at least two cycles to accept a word w such that $h(w) = a^{k+1}b^{k+1}c^{(k+1)(k-1)}$. Because of the correctness preserving property M_k must reduce w into a word w_1 such that $h(w_1) = a^{k+1}b^k c^{k\cdot(k-1)}$, and then it must reduce w_1 to a word w_2 such that $h(w_2) = a^k b^k c^{k\cdot(k-1)}$. But these two reductions violate the condition of monotonicity – a contradiction to the monotonicity constraint of M_k. Hence, the second inclusion is proper in all four propositions of the theorem. □

5 Conclusion

We have introduced the h-lexicalized restarting list automaton (LxRLAW), which yields a formal environment that is useful for expressing the lexicalized syntax in computational linguistics. We presented a basic variant of the Chomsky hierarchy of LxRLAW-automata, which can be interpreted as a hierarchy of classes of input, basic, and h-proper languages, and a hierarchy of h-syntactic analyses as well.

In the main part of the paper we have concentrated on h-lexicalized (deterministic) hRLWW-automata fulfilling the constraint of weak accepting form. We have stressed the transparency of computations of these automata for their basic and h-proper languages due to the complete correctness preserving property. We believe that the automata having the complete correctness preserving property constitute a meaningful class of automata and that they cover a significant class of languages, including the class CFL.

The newly added property of weak accepting form is particularly important for computational linguistic, since it allows to use finite observations (languages) for classifications of classes of infinite and finite languages as well, as we have shown in Section 4.3.

hRLWW-automata can be considered as a refined analytical counterpart to generative Marcus contextual grammars (see e.g. [8]) and Novotny's pure grammars (see e.g. [12]). Contextual and pure grammars work with the (complete) generative correctness preserving property. We have applied many useful techniques for the formalization of syntactic analysis of Czech sentences from Ladislav Nebeský (see e.g. [11]).

We plan in the close future to show a transfer from the complete correctness preserving monotone hRRWW-automaton to the complete correctness preserving monotone LxRLAW-automaton without any restart, which in fact works like a push-down automaton. Such an automaton computes in linear time. It is also possible to obtain similar hierarchies for this type of automata as for the hRRWW-automata from Section 4.3.

We also plan to study some relaxations of the complete correctness preserving property.

References

[1] Michal P. Chytil, Martin Plátek, Jörg Vogel: A note on the Chomsky hierarchy. *Bulletin of the EATCS* 27: 23–30 (1985)

[2] Petr Jančar, František Mráz, Martin Plátek, Jörg Vogel: Restarting automata. In: Horst Reichel (ed.): FCT'95, Proc., pages 283–292, LNCS 965, Springer, Berlin (1995)

[3] Petr Jančar, František Mráz, Martin Plátek: Forgetting Automata and Context-Free Languages. Acta Informatica 33: 409–420 (1996)

[4] Petr Jančar, František Mráz, Martin Plátek, Jörg Vogel: On monotonic automata with a restart operation. *J. Autom. Lang. Comb.* 4: 287–311 (1999)

[5] Petr Jančar, Martin Plátek, Jörg Vogel: Generalized linear list automata. ITAT 2004, Univerzita P. J. Šafárika v Košiciach, 2005, p. 97–105, ISBN 80-7097-589-X (2005)

[6] Markéta Lopatková, Martin Plátek, Vladislav Kuboň: Modeling syntax of free word-order languages: Dependency analysis by reduction. In: Václav Matoušek, Pavel Mautner, Tomáš Pavelka (eds.), TSD 2005, Proceedings, pages 140–147, LNCS 3658, Springer, Berlin (2005)

[7] Markéta Lopatková, Martin Plátek, Petr Sgall: Towards a formal model for functional generative description: Analysis by reduction and restarting automata. *Prague Bull. Math. Linguistics* 87: 7–26 (2007)

[8] Solomon Marcus: Contextual grammars and natural languages. Handbook of Formal Languages, pages 215–235, Springer, Berlin (1997)

[9] František Mráz: Lookahead hierarchies of restarting automata. *J. Autom. Lang. Comb.* 6: 493–506 (2001)

[10] František Mráz, Friedrich Otto, Martin Plátek: The degree of word-expansion of lexicalized RRWW-automata – A new measure for the degree of nondeterminism of (context-free) languages. *Theoretical Computer Science* 410: 3530–3538 (2009)

[11] Ladislav Nebeský: On One Formalization of Sentence Analysis. Slovo a slovesnost, 104–107, (1962)

[12] Miroslav Novotný: With Algebra from Language to Grammar and back (in Czech: S algebrou od jazyka ke gramatice a zpět). Academia, Praha (1988)

[13] Friedrich Otto: Restarting automata and their relations to the Chomsky hierarchy. In: Zoltan Esik, Zoltan Fülöp (eds.): Developments in Language Theory, Proceedings of DLT'2003, pages 55–74, LNCS 2710, Springer, Berlin (2003)

[14] Martin Plátek: Two-way restarting automata and j-monotonicity. In: LLeszek Pacholski, Peter Ružička (eds.): SOFSEM'01, Proc., pages 316–325, LNCS 2234, Springer, Berlin (2001)

[15] Martin Plátek, Friedrich Otto, František Mráz: On h-Lexicalized Restarting List Automata, Technical report, www.theory.informatik.uni-kassel.de/projekte/RL2016v6.4.pdf, Kassel (2017)

J. Hlaváčová (Ed.): ITAT 2017 Proceedings, pp. 48–54
ISBN 978-1974274741, © 2017 R. Rabatin, B. Brejová, T. Vinař

Using Sequence Ensembles for Seeding Alignments of MinION Sequencing Data

Rastislav Rabatin, Broňa Brejová, and Tomáš Vinař

Faculty of Mathematics, Physics and Informatics, Comenius University,
Mlynská dolina, 842 48 Bratislava, Slovakia

Abstract: Sequence similarity search is in bioinformatics often solved by seed-and-extend heuristics: we first locate short exact matches (hits) by hashing or other efficient indexing techniques and then extend these hits to longer sequence alignments. Such approaches are effective at finding very similar sequences, but they quickly loose sensitivity when trying to locate weaker similarities.

In this paper, we develop seeding strategies for data from MinION DNA sequencer. This recent technology produces sequencing reads which are prone to high error rates of up to 30%. Since most of these errors are insertions or deletions, it is difficult to adapt seed-and-extend algorithms to this type of data. We propose to represent each read by an ensemble of sequences sampled from a probabilistic model, instead of a single sequence. Using this extended representation, we were able to design a seeding strategy with 99.9% sensitivity and very low false positive rate. Our technique can be used to locate the part of the genome corresponding to a particular read, or even to find overlaps between pairs of reads.

1 Introduction and Background

Sequence alignment is one of the basic problems in bioinformatics. The goal is to find regions of sequence similarity between two sequences (usually DNA sequences or proteins) or between a query sequence and a large sequence database. Although the highest scoring alignment can be found by a simple dynamic programming algorithm (Smith and Waterman, 1981), its quadratic running time is too slow for large databases. Most sequence alignment tools therefore follow the seed-and-extend paradigm, well-known from BLAST (Altschul et al., 1990). The first step is to build an index of one of the sequences, and then use it to efficiently identify short substrings that occur in both sequences. Each such short exact match, called *hit*, forms a *seed* of a potential alignment. In the extension phase, sequences surrounding each hit are inspected, and the hit is extended to a full alignment, or discarded, if no high scoring alignment can be found. The *sensitivity* of such an approach depends largely on how likely it is for a real alignment to contain a hit. Without the hit, the extension phase is never triggered, and the alignment cannot be identified. On the other hand, the *running time* depends mainly on how many false hits will trigger unnecessary extensions.

The original BLAST (Altschul et al., 1990) used 11 consecutive matches as a seed. Consecutive matches of a fixed length are very easy to index by standard hashing techniques. Several other more complex seeding strategies are used in modern alignment tools (Brown, 2008).

In this work, we consider read mapping, which is a specific alignment task, where the query sequence is a read produced by a DNA sequencing machine, and the database consists of the known reference genome of the same or very closely related organism to the one we are sequencing. The goal is to find the region of the reference genome from which a particular sequencing read was obtained. This task is relatively simple for DNA sequencing technologies with low error rates, because we are looking for almost exact matches between the reads and the reference genome; the goal is to map a large number of reads as quickly as possible. However, in this paper we consider reads produced by MinION sequencer (Ip et al., 2015), which can have up to 30% error rate, and thus pose a challenge for read mappers. The main advantages of the MinION sequencing device are its small size and portability, and its ability to sequence very long reads (reads as long as 100 kbp were reported).

In this paper, we explore the use of simple seeding strategies for mapping MinION reads to the reference sequence. Instead of a single read sequence as a query, we propose to use an ensemble of sequences sampled from a hidden Markov model used for base calling. With such an ensemble of sequences representing alternative predictions of the true read sequence, we were able to achieve very high sensitivity and a very small number of false hits using a relatively simple alignment seeding strategy.

To sequence DNA, MinION uses measurements of electric current as a single-stranded fragment of DNA passes through a nanopore. The electric current depends mostly on the context of k bases of DNA passing through the pore at the time of the measurement. As the DNA fragment moves through the pore, this context changes and measurements change accordingly.

The raw measurements are processed by MinKnow software from Oxford Nanopore. MinKnow first splits raw measurements into *events*, where each event would ideally correspond to a single-base shift of the DNA through the pore. Each event is characterized by the mean and the variance of the corresponding raw measurements. This sequence of events is then uploaded to a cloud-based service Metrichor for base calling.

The exact details of the algorithms behind MinKnow and Metrichor are not disclosed by Oxford Nanopore.

However, the whole process is naturally modelled by a hidden Markov model (HMM) (Durbin et al., 1998, Chapter 3) with hidden states corresponding to k-mers of the underlying DNA sequence and observations representing the mean value of the current in each event. In fact, data provided by Oxford Nanopore include parameters of such a model. Open-source base caller Nanocall based on this idea was recently implemented by David et al. (2016), with accuracy similar to Metrichor. To decode a sequence of observations, Nanocall uses the standard Viterbi algorithm (Viterbi, 1967) for finding the most probable state path. Another open-source base caller DeepNano is based on recurrent neural networks (Boža et al., 2016).

Base calls produced by the Viterbi algorithm contain many errors (David et al., 2016; Boža et al., 2016); a typical error rate would be around 30%, dominated mostly by insertions and deletions. Currently, two general-purpose aligners are used in the community to map MinION reads: BWA-MEM (Li and Durbin, 2010), and LAST (Kielbasa et al., 2011). Both of these tools follow the seed-and-extend paradigm, but they use variable seed lengths, indexed with FM-index (Ferragina and Manzini, 2000) or suffix arrays (Manber and Myers, 1993). By extending seeds to the point of only a few occurrences, one can avoid most costly false positives. The adjustments for MinION reads in case of BWA-MEM and LAST include lowering the minimum length of a seed to be considered as a valid hit, and changes that make the extension phase less stringent. GraphMap tool (Sovic et al., 2016), specifically targeting MinION data, uses seeds allowing insertions and deletions in the context of a complex multi-step algorithm that goes well beyond a simple seed-and-extend framework.

All of these tools consider Metrichor base calls, equivalent to the most probable state path in the HMM, as the query sequence. Our approach to the challenges imposed by MinION reads is to use an ensemble of sub-optimal sequences instead of a single DNA sequence. To this end, we have implemented a sampling algorithm that can generate samples from the posterior distribution of state paths in an HMM given the sequence of observations (see, e.g. Cawley and Pachter (2003)). We adapt common seeding strategies to such ensembles of sequences and show that on real data we can find a seed that is easy to index, 99.9% sensitive, and yields only a small number of false positives that would trigger extension phase unnecessarily.

Sampling of suboptimal MinION base calls was also considered by Szalay and Golovchenko (2015). They use sampling from the base calling HMM to arrive at the correct consensus sequence for an alignment of multiple reads. Due to the nature of errors in MinION reads and availability of a reasonable probabilistic model, we consider sampling strategies to be a promising alternative in many applications of MinION.

2 HMM for Sampling MinION Base Calls

Both Oxford Nanopore Metrichor base caller and recently released open-source base caller Nanocall (David et al., 2016) use hidden Markov models. Briefly, each hidden state of the HMM represents one k-mer passing through the pore, and the emission of the state is the value of the electric current. Actual measurements of the current provided by the device with high sampling rate are segmented by the MinKnow software into discrete *events*, each corresponding to the shift of the DNA sequence through the pore by a single base. The base callers then use the HMM to obtain the sequence of hidden states given the sequence of events from the MinION read.

Definition of the model. Our HMM follows the same general idea. The set of states of our HMM is composed of all 4^k possible k-mers (we denote state for a k-mer x by S_x) and the starting state S_0. Different versions of MinION use different values of k; in our experiments we have used a data set with $k = 5$, while the newer chemistry uses $k = 6$.

Emission of state S_x is represented as a continuous random variable. The probability of observing a measurement e for a k-mer x is given as

$$\Pr(e \mid x) \sim \mathcal{N}(scale \cdot \mu_x + shift, \sigma_x \cdot var), \qquad (1)$$

where $\mathcal{N}(\mu, \sigma)$ is the normal distribution with mean μ and standard deviation σ. Parameters μ_x, σ_x (specific for each version of the chemistry and each k-mer x), and *scale*, *shift*, *var* (scaling parameters specific for each read) are provided by Oxford Nanopore and can be obtained from the FAST5 file containing each read. Starting state S_0 is silent.

Under ideal conditions, each event corresponds to a shift by a single base in the DNA sequence. This corresponds to four outgoing transitions from each state S_x to state S_y, where x and y overlap by exactly $k - 1$ bases (i.e., S_{AACTG} has transitions to states S_{ACTGA}, S_{ACTGC}, S_{ACTGG}, and S_{ACTGT}). This organization closely resembles de Bruijn graphs commonly used in sequence assembly (Pevzner et al., 2001). All four transitions have an equal probability. From the starting state S_0, we have a transition to each possible S_x with equal probability $1/4^k$.

Segmentation of raw measurements into events is known to be error prone. In particular, two events with similar measurements can be fused together, or a single event can be split artificially into multiple events. Thus the assumption that each event corresponds to a single-nucleotide shift is unrealistic. To account for this fact, we have introduced additional transitions to our model.

First, we have added a self-transition (so called *split transition*) to each state, which models splitting of a single true event into multiple predicted events. Second, we have also added so called *skip transitions* between all pairs of states S_x and S_y, which correspond to shifts of the k-mer by up to k bases instead of one.

The transition probabilities for split and skip transitions are not provided by MinION. We have estimated these parameters directly from the data, as outlined in Section 3. Alternatively, we could employ a more elaborate error model for Oxford Nanopore event segmentation process.

Inference in the model. A traditional way of decoding HMMs is by finding the most probable sequence of states by the Viterbi algorithm (Viterbi, 1967), which is the approach taken both by Metrichor and Nanocall. The resulting sequence of states (which is, in fact, a sequence of k-mers corresponding to individual events) can be translated into the DNA sequence. In most cases, the neighbouring k-mers in the sequence should be shifted by one, and thus each state in the sequence introduces one additional base of the DNA sequence. However, split and skip transitions may introduce between 0 and k bases for each event. In these cases, the result is not necessarily unique: for example state sequence $S_{ACTCTC}S_{CTCTCA}$ could correspond to one of the sequences ACTCTCA, ACTCTCTCA, ACTCTCTCTCA, or even ACTCTCCTCTCA. We have decided to adopt the shortest possible interpretation, as is done in Nanocall.

Since the base calls produced by the Viterbi algorithm contain many errors, we have decided to explore the use of an ensemble of alternative sequences instead of a single base call sequence. To this end, we have implemented the stochastic traceback algorithm (see, e.g. Cawley and Pachter (2003)) to generate samples from the posterior distribution of state paths given the sequence of observations.

Briefly, for a given sequence of observations $e_1 e_2 \ldots e_n$, the algorithm starts by computing *forward probabilities*, where $F(i,s)$ is the probability of generating first i observations $e_1 e_2 \ldots e_i$, and ending in state s (Rabiner, 1989). The last state s_n of the path is sampled proportionally to the probabilities $F(n, s_n)$. When state s_n is fixed, we can sample state s_{n-1} proportionally to $F(n-1, s_{n-1}) \cdot t_{s_{n-1}, s_n}$, where $t_{s, s'}$ is the transition probability from state s to state s'. This can be continued, until we sample the complete path $s_1 \ldots s_n$. The running time of the algorithm is $O(nm^2)$, where n is the length of the sequence and m is the number of states. Forward probabilities need to be computed only once if multiple samples are required for the same read.

Figure 1 illustrates typical differences between individual samples. Note that the samples are almost identical in some regions, but these high-confidence regions are interspersed by regions with very high uncertainty. This is a typical pattern for MinION data.

3 Experiments

Our goal is to consider various seeding strategies for seed-and-extend algorithms. As discussed in Section 1, a typical seed-and-extend algorithm first uses an index structure to locate hits between the query sequence and the target. For example, the most basic BLAST strategy looks for exact matches of length 11 (Altschul et al., 1990). It then tries to extend each cluster of hits to a full alignment. The extension phase usually involves dynamic programming and is therefore time consuming.

The seed-and-extend algorithms cannot locate alignments that do not contain a hit of the seed between the query and the target sequence. We call these alignments *false negatives*. Note that even a single hit is often sufficient to locate the whole alignment, depending on the particular extension strategy. On the other hand, spurious hits between random locations can also trigger extension. We call such spurious hits *false positives*. Unsuccessful extension of spurious hits often dominates the running time of the alignment algorithm, and consequently, we need to minimize the number of false positives.

In this section, we concentrate on the evaluation of a trade-off between false positives and false negatives for a variety of seeding strategies. We start from simple strategies, e.g. k consecutive exact matches between the reference sequence and the Viterbi base call, and we also propose several novel seeding strategies using the sampling framework and multiple hit requirement that greatly improve the trade-off.

Data preprocessing and model training. To evaluate seeding strategies, we use a data set composed of real sequencing reads from the model bacteria *E. coli* (strain MG1655) with accession number ERR968968 produced by the Cold Spring Harbor Laboratory by using MinION sequencer with SQK-MAP005 kit. For simplicity, we have only considered template reads (complement reads from the reverse strand use different model parameters).

Some of the MinION reads are of very low quality and consequently it is impossible to map them to the reference sequence even with the most sensitive tools available. To filter out these low quality reads, we have mapped Metrichor base calls to the reference genome by BWA-MEM (Li and Durbin, 2010) with `-x ont2d` parameters optimized for mapping Oxford Nanopore reads. The reads that did not map to the reference at all were discarded. We also discarded reads where Metrichor predicted skips in the event sequence longer than two. From the original 27,073 reads, we were left with 25,162 reads.

From these reads, we have randomly selected a training set (693 reads) and a testing set (307 reads). The training set was used to estimate the transition probabilities in our HMM. In particular, we set the probability of each transition to be proportional to the number of times the transition was observed in the training data set. We added pseudocount of 1 to avoid zero transition probabilities for rare transitions.

Preparing testing data. For each sequence in the testing set, we have produced a Viterbi base call and 250 samples from the posterior distribution as outlined in Section 2. Figure 2 shows comparison of sequence identities of individual base calls to the reference genome. Note that our Viterbi base calls are not too different from Metrichor base

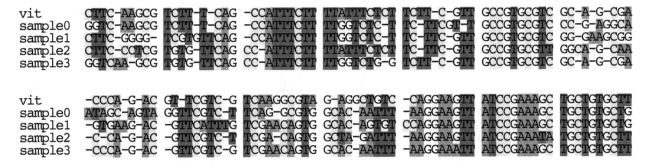

Figure 1: **Example of base calling samples from a MinION read.** The first line corresponds to the Viterbi base call, other lines correspond to four samples from the posterior distribution defined by the HMM. Base calls were aligned according to events in the sequence of observations.

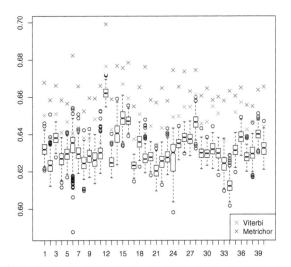

Figure 2: **Comparison of sequence identity to the reference genome for Metrichor base calls, our Viterbi base calls, and posterior samples for 40 randomly selected reads.** All sequences were aligned to the reference by BWA-MEM. Sequence identity of Metrichor, Viterbi, and a box plot distribution of sequence identities of 250 samples are shown on the y-axis.

calls; slight decrease in the quality of calls is expected due to simplicity of the model we have used (the decrease in the sequence identity is similar to that observed by David et al. (2016)). Sampled sequences have in general lower sequence identity than the Viterbi base call, as can be expected, since they correspond to sub-optimal paths through the model. However, the difference from the Viterbi base call identities is not very high.

Experimental setup and evaluation. To evaluate application of various seeding strategies in MinION data, we have split the reads into *windows*, each corresponding to 500 events. These windows represent our query sequences. For each window we have an alignment of all samples and

the Viterbi base call. This alignment was based on event boundaries: we have padded all sequences generated for one event in individual samples by gap symbols so that they have the same length (see also Figure 1).

The Viterbi base call sequence from each window was aligned to the reference genome by LAST software (Kielbasa et al., 2011) with parameters -q 1 -a 1 -b 1 -T 1. We have kept only those windows that aligned to a unique place in the genome, and the alignment covered the entire length of the window. After this step, we were left with 3192 windows out of 4948. A randomly chosen subset of 143 windows was used as a validation set for exploring various seeding strategies, and the remaining 3049 windows were used for final testing. The region of the reference covered by the alignment to the window is considered to be the only true alignment of the window to the reference sequence.

When testing a seeding strategy, we locate hits of a particular seed in both the query window and the reference sequence. We represent each hit by the coordinates of the left endpoints of the hit in the query window and in the reference. The seed hit is considered to be *valid*, if the endpoint in the reference is within the region covered by the alignment of this particular window and on the correct strand of DNA. The entire window of a read is considered to be a *true positive (TP)*, if it contains at least one valid hit; we assume that the extension algorithm would be able to recover the alignment within this window starting from this hit. The *sensitivity (Sn)* of the seeding strategy is the number of true positives divided by the total number of windows.

Many seed hits are invalid, and they contribute to the false positive rate. Often we see clusters of hits with very similar coordinates in both reference and the query window. Presumably the extension algorithm would be called only once for each such cluster. Therefore, we compute the number of *false positives* by greedily selecting one hit from each cluster so that each hit in the cluster differs in both coordinates by at most 10 from the selected hit.

Simple seeding strategies. The simplest seeding strategy is to consider k consecutive exact matches as a hit. The traditional approach would create an index of all k-mers in the reference genome and then scan all k-mers in the query windows. Each cluster of matching k-mers would trigger the extension phase.

For example, if we consider the Viterbi base calls and use 13 exact consecutive matches as a seed, we will be able to map 98.8% windows to the correct region of the reference (see Fig. 3), but we will also incur a substantial number of false positives (more than 240,000 or about 80 per each query window).

Our strategy of using sampling instead of Viterbi base calls works as follows. In the basic version of our approach (see $t = 1$ in Fig. 3), we consider k-mers from n different samples from the given window. Each k-mer can potentially form the seed triggering the extension phase of the alignment. To match the sensitivity of the Viterbi base calls for $k = 13$, we need only $n = 3$ samples. One advantage of our approach is that we can increase the sensitivity by increasing the number of samples n. For example with 8 samples we reach 99.9% sensitivity and with 14 samples 100% sensitivity. The cost for this very high sensitivity is a high false positive rate; even with 3 samples we have about $2.6\times$ more false positives than the Viterbi.

To improve the false positive rate, we use a simple pre-filtering step: at each position in the window we consider only those k-mers that appear in at least t different samples. Assuming that the true sequence has a high posterior probability in the model, we expect that it will occur in many samples, whereas most other variants would occur rarely and thus be filtered out. Indeed, for $t = 4$ we can reach the sensitivity of the Viterbi algorithm with about 20% reduction in the false positive rate, using $n = 25$ samples. Performance for other values of n and t can be found in Figure 3.

Multiple seed hits to trigger extension. We have also considered a more complex seeding strategy, where we first find matching 10-mers, and then we join them into *chains* of length 3. This technique has previously proved to be very effective for regular alignment tasks (Altschul et al., 1997).

Matching 10-mers in the chain are required to have increasing coordinates in both the read and the reference sequence, and the distance between starts of adjacent matching k-mers in the chain must be at least 10 and at most 50 in both sequences. However, the distances of the two 10-mer matches in the two sequences may differ, accommodating insertions and deletions in the intervening regions. The entire chain is then again represented by its leftmost point in both the read and the reference for the purpose of determining if it is valid.

As we see in Figure 4, this seeding strategy is too stringent for the Viterbi base calls, achieving only 71.3% sensitivity. On the other hand, false positives are extremely rare, totaling only 136 in all 3049 windows.

When using samples, different 10-mer matches in the chain may come from different samples. The chaining of weaker hits helps to accommodate regions with high uncertainty present in the MinION data. Some settings of our strategy can achieve the same sensitivity as the Viterbi algorithm with even lower false positives, but more importantly, by considering more samples, we can increase sensitivity while keeping the false positives quite low (Figure 4). For example, for $t = 2$ and $n = 43$ our strategy can reach 99.9% sensitivity with only 6407 false positives.

4   Conclusions and Future Work

In this paper, we have examined the problem of mapping MinION reads to the reference sequence. The error rate of MinION is high, with many insertions and deletions. Consequently the standard alignment techniques do not achieve sufficient mapping sensitivity.

Instead of representing the read by a single base called sequence, we have proposed to use an ensemble of sequences generated from the posterior distribution defined by the HMM capturing the properties of the MinION sequencing. We have adapted the standard k-mer based techniques for alignment seeding to ensembles of sequences and identified a seed (three 10-mer hits spaced by at most 50 bases) that achieved 99.9% sensitivity with an extremely small number of false positives. With such a low false positive rate, we could investigate more precise (and slower) algorithms for the extension phase as the next step towards sensitive alignment of MinION reads.

An obvious extension of our approach would be to consider spaced seeds (Ma et al., 2002). Our experiments suggest that a typical MinION read consists of short regions of high-confidence sequence (often under 15 bases) interspersed with regions of high uncertainty with many insertions and deletions. The spaced seeds would have to target mainly the high-confidence regions; however, these regions seem to be too short to admit complex seeds of any significant weight. One possibility would be to build a probabilistic model capturing high-confidence and high-uncertainty regions and transitions between them, and attempt to design optimized spaced seeds, for example by techniques suggested by Brejova et al. (2004).

Another option would be to use seeds that also allow indels at do not care positions. These types of seeds were successfully used by Sovic et al. (2016) for MinION read mapping, but the overall algorithm was much more complicated than a simple seed-and-extend. Moreover, these types of seeds are much more difficult to index than continuous or spaced seeds and we believe, that our sampling approach together with multiple chained seed hits provides an elegant answer to the problem.

In this work, we have only considered template reads from MinION. However, MinION attempts to read both strands of the same DNA molecule and these two readouts can be combined in postprocessing to a single sequence

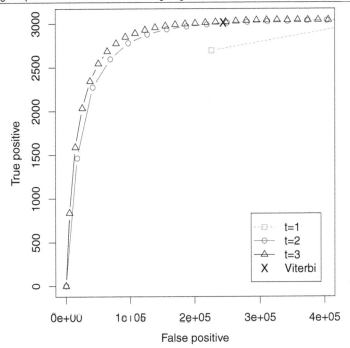

Method	Sn	FP
Viterbi	0.988	243796
$t=1, n=2$	0.974	433890
$t=1, n=3$	0.990	625782
$t=1, n=8$	0.999	1456049
$t=2, n=7$	0.963	156472
$t=2, n=11$	0.990	280912
$t=2, n=26$	0.999	727678
$t=3, n=12$	0.960	122830
$t=3, n=18$	0.988	216743
$t=3, n=38$	0.999	529692
$t=4, n=17$	0.957	110197
$t=4, n=25$	0.989	192648
$t=4, n=53$	0.999	488198
$t=5, n=22$	0.956	103666
$t=5, n=34$	0.988	196604
$t=5, n=72$	0.999	497944

Figure 3: **Performance of our approach compared to the Viterbi base calls for seeding with a single 13-mer.** The x-axis of the plot is the total number of false positives on the whole testing set; the y-axis is the number of true positives out of 3049 windows in total. Performance of the Viterbi base calls is shown by the black X. Three lines show our approach for different values of threshold t for filtering k-mers. Each point on the line represents performance for a particular number of samples $n = 1, 2, \ldots$. The table shows sensitivity and the number of false positives for selected values of n and t. In particular for each t, we show the smallest value of n achieving sensitivity at least 95%, the sensitivity of the Viterbi algorithm, and sensitivity at least 99.9%.

called 2D read. Since 2D reads are much more accurate (typical error rate is about 15%), most researchers use only 2D reads in further analysis. Accurate 1D read mapping would allow researchers to consider all data; usually there is about $4 - 5\times$ more 1D reads than 2D reads (Ip et al., 2015). Moreover, recent application of MinION to monitoring disease outbreaks (Quick et al., 2016) require that reads are analyzed on-the-fly as they are produced, and at this stage 2D reads are not available.

In this paper, we have evaluated seeding strategies for mapping reads to the reference genome. In future work, we would like to investigate the seed-and-extend approaches for read-to-read alignment. With our sampling approach, we would not need to commit to a single interpretation of either of the sequences, potentially increasing the sensitivity of detecting overlaps between reads in a given data set. Sensitive read-to-read alignment is essential for *de novo* genome assembly.

Acknowledgements. This research was funded by APVV grant APVV-14-0253 and VEGA grants 1/0719/14 (TV) and 1/0684/16 (BB).

References

Altschul, S. F., Gish, W., Miller, W., Myers, E. W., and Lipman, D. J. (1990). Basic local alignment search tool. *Journal of Molecular Biology*, 215(3):403–410.

Altschul, S. F., Madden, T. L., Schaffer, A. A., Zhang, J., Zhang, Z., Miller, W., and Lipman, D. J. (1997). Gapped BLAST and PSI-BLAST: a new generation of protein database search programs. *Nucleic Acids Research*, 25(17):3389–3392.

Boža, V., Brejová, B., and Vinař, T. (2016). Deep-Nano: Deep recurrent neural networks for base calling in MinION nanopore reads. Technical Report arXiv:1603.09195, arXiv.org.

Brejova, B., Brown, D. G., and Vinar, T. (2004). Optimal spaced seeds for homologous coding regions. *Journal of Bioinformatics and Computational Biology*, 1(4):595–610.

Brown, D. G. (2008). A survey of seeding for sequence alignment. In *Bioinformatics algorithms: techniques and applications*, pages 126–152. John Wiley & Sons, Inc.

Cawley, S. L. and Pachter, L. (2003). HMM sampling and applications to gene finding and alternative splicing. *Bioinformatics*, 19(S2):ii36–41.

David, M., Dursi, L. J., Yao, D., Boutros, P. C., and Simpson, J. T. (2016). Nanocall: An open source basecaller

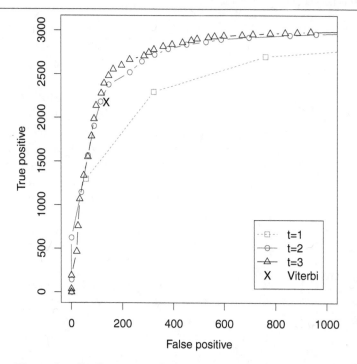

Method	Sn	FP
Viterbi	0.713	136
$t=1, n=2$	0.752	323
$t=1, n=5$	0.967	2412
$t=1, n=13$	0.999	18249
$t=2, n=7$	0.715	114
$t=2, n=15$	0.950	588
$t=2, n=43$	0.999	6407
$t=3, n=13$	0.747	117
$t=3, n=26$	0.952	495
$t=3, n=80$	0.999	6180
$t=4, n=18$	0.714	89
$t=4, n=39$	0.950	517
$t=4, n=139$	0.999	8877
$t=5, n=24$	0.721	139
$t=5, n=51$	0.954	483
$t=5, n=165$	0.999	7003

Figure 4: **Performance of our approach compared to the Viterbi base calls for seeding with a chain of three 10-mers,** each in distance at most 50 from the previous one. The plot and the table have the same form as in Figure 3.

for Oxford Nanopore sequencing data. Technical Report bioRxiv:046086, Cold Spring Harbor Laboratory.

Durbin, R., Eddy, S. R., Krogh, A., and Mitchison, G. (1998). *Biological Sequence Analysis: Probabilistic Models of Proteins and Nucleic Acids.* Cambridge University Press.

Ferragina, P. and Manzini, G. (2000). Opportunistic data structures with applications. In *Foundations of Computer Science (FOCS)*, pages 390–398. IEEE.

Ip, C. L. C., Loose, M., Tyson, J. R., de Cesare, M., Brown, B. L., Jain, M., Leggett, R. M., Eccles, D. A., Zalunin, V., Urban, J. M., Piazza, P., Bowden, R. J., Paten, B., Mwaigwisya, S., Batty, E. M., Simpson, J. T., Snutch, T. P., Birney, E., Buck, D., Goodwin, S., Jansen, H. J., O'Grady, J., and Olsen, H. E. (2015). MinION Analysis and Reference Consortium: Phase 1 data release and analysis. *F1000Research*, 4:1075.

Kielbasa, S. M., Wan, R., Sato, K., Horton, P., and Frith, M. C. (2011). Adaptive seeds tame genomic sequence comparison. *Genome Research*, 21(3):487–493.

Li, H. and Durbin, R. (2010). Fast and accurate long-read alignment with Burrows-Wheeler transform. *Bioinformatics*, 26(5):589–595.

Ma, B., Tromp, J., and Li, M. (2002). PatternHunter: faster and more sensitive homology search. *Bioinformatics*, 18(3):440–445.

Manber, U. and Myers, G. (1993). Suffix arrays: a new method for on-line string searches. *SIAM Journal on Computing*, 22(5):935–948.

Pevzner, P. A., Tang, H., and Waterman, M. S. (2001). An Eulerian path approach to DNA fragment assembly. *Proceedings of the National Academy of Sciences of the USA*, 98(17):9748–9753.

Quick, J. et al. (2016). Real-time, portable genome sequencing for Ebola surveillance. *Nature*, 530(7589):228–232.

Rabiner, L. R. (1989). A tutorial on hidden Markov models and selected applications in speech recognition. *Proceedings of the IEEE*, 77(2):257–286.

Smith, T. F. and Waterman, M. S. (1981). Identification of common molecular subsequences. *Journal of Molecular Biology*, 147(1):195–197.

Sovic, I., Sikic, M., Wilm, A., Fenlon, S. N., Chen, S., and Nagarajan, N. (2016). Fast and sensitive mapping of nanopore sequencing reads with GraphMap. *Nature Communications*, 7:11307.

Szalay, T. and Golovchenko, J. A. (2015). De novo sequencing and variant calling with nanopores using PoreSeq. *Nature Biotechnology*, 33(10):1087–1091.

Viterbi, A. J. (1967). Error bounds for convolutional codes and an asymptotically optimum decoding algorithm. *IEEE Transactions on Information Theory*, 13(2):260–269.

Computational Intelligence and Data Mining — 5th International Workshop (CIDM 2017)

As a part of the conference ITAT 2017, the 5th international workshop "Computational Intelligence and Data Mining" has been organized. It is aimed at participants with research interests in any of these related areas, especially at PhD students and postdocs. Interested participants were invited to submit a paper in English of up to 8 double-column pages, prepared according to the instructions at the ITAT 2017 web pages.

As this workshop started, 4 years ago, it had only 7 regular submissions. However, the interest in the computational intelligence and data mining workshops has been gradueally increasing since that time. This year, we have 2 invited talks by internationally renowned esxperts, and 17 regular papers had been submitted to the workshop, among which 16 have been accepted for oral presentations and for inclusion in these proceedings.

A key factor influencing the overall quality of a workshop and of the final versions of the submitted papers is the workshop's program committee. The 5th international workshop "Computational Intelligence and Data Mining" is grateful to the 27 reviewers from 10 countries who read the submitted papers, and have provided competent, and in most cases very detailed, feedback to their authors. Most of them have a great international reputation witnessed by hundreds of WOS citations.

Workshop Program Committee

Dirk Arnold, University of Dalhousie
Jose Luis Balcazar, Technical university of Catalonia, Barcelona
Petr Berka, University of Economics, Prague
Hans Engler, University of Georgetown
Jan Faigl, Czech Technical University, Prague
Pitoyo Hartono, University of Chukyo
Martin Holeňa, Czech Academy of Sciences, Prague
Ján Hric, Charles University, Prague
Jan Kalina, Czech Academy of Sciences, Prague
Jiří Kléma, Czech Technical University, Prague
Pavel Kordík, Czech Technical University, Prague
Tomas Krilavičius, Vytautas Magnus University, Kaunas
Věra Kurková, Czech Academy of Sciences, Prague
Stéphane Lallich, University of Lyon

J. Hlaváčová (Ed.): ITAT 2017 Proceedings, pp. 57–64
ISBN 978-1974274741, © 2017 R. Brunetto, O. Trunda

Deep Heuristic-learning in the Rubik's Cube Domain:
an Experimental Evaluation

Robert Brunetto and Otakar Trunda

Charles University in Prague, Faculty of Mathematics and Physics
Malostranské náměstí 25, Praha, Czech Republic
robert@brunetto.cz otakar.trunda@mff.cuni.cz

Abstract: Recent successes of neural networks in solving combinatorial problems and games like Go, Poker and others inspire further attempts to use deep learning approaches in discrete domains. In the field of automated planning, the most popular approach is informed forward search driven by a heuristic function which estimates the quality of encountered states. Designing a powerful and easily-computable heuristics however is still a challenging problem on many domains.

In this paper, we use machine learning to construct such heuristic automatically. We train a neural network to predict a minimal number of moves required to solve a given instance of Rubik's cube. We then use the trained network as a heuristic distance estimator with a standard forward-search algorithm and compare the results with other heuristics. Our experiments show that the learning approach is competitive with state-of-the-art and might be the best choice in some use-case scenarios.

1 Introduction

Neural networks (NNs) have already proven to be able to cope with noisy and unstructured data like hand-written texts, images, sounds, classification of real-world objects based on incomplete description, and many others.

Recently, they also succeeded in several purely combinatorial domains like the game of Go. Nowadays, the program AlphaGo [15] that utilizes a deep neural net can beat top-class human players which was impossible just two years ago. No other approach is currently known to be able to play Go on such level. NNs are also a key component of the best Poker engine DeepStack [12] and several attempts have been made to use them for solving instances of Travelling Salesman Problem and other combinatorial problems [2].

In planning, the machine learning approaches are already being used in several ways, for example to select the best search algorithm, preprocess the problem or to promote searching of promising areas. See *International Planning Competition - Learning Track* [1] for more details.

Some attention has also been dedicated to heuristic learning, where the task is to automatically induce a heuristic function from training samples using a machine learning model. Models typically used in this area are very simple (like a decision tree or a shallow NN) and are not fine-tuned for the specific problem. In most cases, the are only used as a black box.

With recent rapid development of deep learning models, many new possibilities are now available in this area. Learning algorithms now exist for efficient training of deep feed-forward networks and also many other types of NNs have been developed and successfully used. For example, there are Deep Recurrent Networks like *LSTM*, Deep Convolutional Networks, Neural Turing Machines and others [2]. Using the CUDA framework, it is now possible to train such networks much faster on specialized graphic cards.

In this paper, we try to utilize some of such more complex models to learn an efficient heuristic function for solving the Rubik's cube puzzle. We work with the standard 3x3x3 cube, but our approach is in principle applicable to larger cubes as well.

1.1 Motivation

Our main motivation is to correct the error that heuristics make when estimating the distance. Admissible heuristics are often quite accurate near a goal state, but on states that are far from any goal state they significantly underestimate the real value [8]. The network should be able to find out in which situations such underestimation occurs and correct it appropriately.

Assuming that a set of admissible heuristics will be used as features, the network will play the role of a judge deciding which heuristics are trustworthy and which are not (in various circumstances).

Unlike in similar papers on heuristics learning, we include a simplified description of the state among the input features. Existing approaches only learn the goal-distance of the state using a few precomputed features that don't contain state description but mostly only heuristic estimates. We believe, that state description is important so that the network could distinguish between different types of states. Identifying types of states is crucial for the network to find out in which kinds of states the given heuristics underestimate and by how much.

---

2 Background

2.1 Rubik's Cube

The famous puzzle - Rubik's cube may serve as an example of a planning problem. The task is to find a sequence of actions leading form given initial state to specified goal state.

From a search perspective, the number of unique states of the standard 3x3x3 cube is $8! * 3^8 * 12! * 2^{12} * \frac{1}{12}$ which is about $4 * 10^{19}$. Every state can be solved optimally in at most 26 quarter-moves. There is a single goal state and the branching factor is 12 when using a symmetry breaking representation. We consider a model using quarter-moves meaning that it is allowed to rotate layers only by $90°$. The half-move representation allows sides to be rotated by $180°$ in a single move.

To be able to describe some other properties of the cube, we first need to define a few additional notions. The 3x3x3 cube consists of 27 little cubes which we call *cubies*. Some faces of these cubies are colored, or more precisely they carry colored stickers. In the goal state, all faces of the large cube contains only stickers of the same color.

If we disassembled the cube, we would get 8 corner-cubies, each of which carrying 3 colored stickers, 12 edge-cubies, each with 2 stickers on them and 6 central-cubies each having 1 sticker.

A cube of any size can easily be solved suboptimally using a simple algorithm that runs in time $\mathcal{O}(n^2)$, where n is the size of the cube. Finding optimal solutions seems to be much harder, although the complexity class of this task has long been unknown. It has only recently been proven that solving Rubik's cube optimally is indeed NP-hard [4, 5].

Current state-of-the-art approaches for finding optimal or near-optimal solutions often utilize forward state space search using a pattern database as a heuristic [11, 16]. Pattern databases (PDBs) are precomputed solutions to smaller problems which are created from the original by abstracting-away some of its features. For example, if we only consider the 8 corner cubies of a standard 3x3x3 cube, we will get a 2x2x2 cube which is much easier to solve. The whole state space of this smaller problem may be enumerated, solved optimally for each state and stored in a database. For each state of the standard cube, we can then *project* it on the pattern by ignoring everything except the corners, look-up this state in the database and use its evaluation as a lower bound on the length of the plan. The set of features that we consider in the smaller problem is called *pattern* and features that are not included in the pattern are ignored.

A single pattern never contains all cubies. Using it as a heuristic leads to a state where all cubies contained in the pattern are correctly placed but others are not. In such states, the heuristic value is 0 and the algorithm has a hard time finding the goal state since it has no further guidance. For efficient searching it is necessary to combine several PDBs with different patterns or to combine PDB with other types of heuristics. There are many ways of combining the heuristics, from simple ones, like taking maximum, to more complex ones like *additive PDBs* or *cost partitioning* [10].

2.2 Heuristic Learning

The task of heuristic learning is to automatically create a heuristic function for given problem based on some training data. The learning is typically done a priory, where the training data are provided before the search. Heuristic can also be learned on-the-fly, where previous attempts to solve the problem serve as training data to learn future search strategy [7].

Several attempts have been made to utilize NNs for the heuristic learning task [1, 2, 14, 3, 17]. In the typical setting, a set of *features* is computed for every state in the training set as well as the optimal distance-to-go to the nearest goal state, and the network is then used to learn a mapping from features to distance estimate. After the learning process is finished, the network is used as a heuristic distance estimator together with an informed forward search algorithm like A* or IDA*.

Heuristics that are learned in this way provide no guarantees on admissibility. The goal of learning is so that the heuristic would be close to the real value but not necessarily always admissible - i.e. smaller than the real distance-to-go. Since search with an inadmissible heuristic doesn't typically guarantee finding optimal solutions, this approach is only suitable in cases where close-to-optimal solutions are sufficient. It is however possible to guarantee optimality even with an inadmissible heuristic by modifying the search strategy [9].

From the complexity perspective, the task of heuristic learning in general is hard. It is known that the task of finding optimal solutions to some planning problems like generalized 15-puzzle, Sokoban, and many more is NP-hard or even harder. It is also known that with an accurate-enough heuristic, the search time may be polynomial. Namely, if $\forall x : (h^*(x) - h(x)) \in \mathcal{O}(\log(h^*(x)))$ where x are states, h is heuristic and h^* is the real goal distance, then the search time is polynomial [13, p. 99]. It is therefore obvious that such heuristic cannot be computed in polynomial time unless some complexity classes collapse. The learned heuristic will probably not be able to solve large problems optimally in polynomial time but it may still outperform classic human-designed heuristics.

2.3 Notation

In the rest of the text, we use the following notation:

- S is the set of all states of the Rubik's cube
- $g \in S$ is the goal state
- $h^* : S \mapsto \mathbb{N}^0$ is goal-distance of states

- $F = (f_1, f_2, \ldots, f_n)$ is the set of real-valued features of states, where $\forall i : f_i : S \mapsto \mathbb{R}$

- $h_{NN} : F(S) \mapsto \mathbb{R}$ is the function that the neural network will approximate, where $F(S) = \{(f_1(s), f_2(s), \ldots, f_n(s)) \mid s \in S\}$

h_{NN} will then be used as a heuristic. When referring to this heuristic's value, we will write $h_{NN}(s)$ instead of $h_{NN}(f_1(s), f_2(s), \ldots, f_n(s))$. The goal of the learning is that $h_{NN}(s)$ is close to $h^*(s)$ for all states.

3 Getting the Training Data

There is a big issue of obtaining the training data. It is problematic to compute the real goal distances for a large number of training states due to enormous time complexity of such task. We have tried another way of generating training samples using backward search and random walks. This way we don't get exact goal-distances, but the obtained values should be close enough to them for most states.

3.1 Generating Samples by Random Walks

This approach works as follows:

1. Run a breadth-first search (BFS) from the goal state, store every visited state together with its goal-distance for as long as the memory suffices.

2. From the BFS frontier select K states at random.

3. From each of these K states, run a short random walk.

4. Among the states visited by random walks, select the desired number of states as a training set.

For the states visited by BFS, we know the exact goal distance. We have been able to generate 10^7 states which consumed about 5.5 GB of memory. This set contained all states with goal distance of 5 or lower and some states with goal distance of 6.

Random walks start from the BFS frontier and have length of 19. Random walk is forbidden to re-visit a state that it has visited previously, but two different random walks may intersect. The estimated goal distance of a node is then calculated as goal distance of the initial state of the random walk + the length of the random walk before it encountered the given state.

True goal distance of the state, where the random walk starts is known since it lies in the BFS frontier. For the other states that the random walk encounters, we only have an estimate of the goal distance. We believe, that for most states the estimate will be reasonably close to the real value, especially for states closer to the goal (i.e. closer to the BFS frontier) but the values are in general over-estimated.

Length of the random walks was set to 19 so that they could visit states that are as far as 25 from the goal state.

(The BFS expands nodes to depth 6 and then a random walk goes for another 19 steps). The maximum distance to the goal of every state is 26, but the number of states that actually require 26 steps is very low so we ignore them in the training process.

If two random walks intersect, we recompute the goal distances of their states such that the triangle inequality holds. I.e. if some state is visited by a shorter walk, all its neighbours are informed of this shorter path and are recomputed if necessary. Then the information is passed on to their neighbours, their neighbours' neighbours etc. Experiments however show, that such intersections rarely happen.

A small number of random walks returns back to the set of states visited by BFS. Such random walks we discard from further use.

We generated a total of 100 000 samples evenly distributed in the state space.

3.2 Generating Samples Using an Optimal Solver

Our experiments showed that the random walks approach is not efficient enough. It introduces a significant noise into the training set which increases the training error of the network.

The noise is caused by the fact that a random walk of length k leads to a state whose real goal distance is typically smaller than k and cannot be exactly determined. Our experiments showed that the random walk over-estimates the goal distance by approximately 20%. The target value associated with the sample is in this case a random variable with mean of roughly $0.8 * k$ and a non-zero variance. It is impossible for the network to predict the noise caused by this variance which significantly increases the training error.

To counter this problem, we used an optimal solver to generate training samples with exact target values. We used the *Cube Explorer 5.13* software available on http://kociemba.org/cube.htm. The solver is quite fast on most inputs - it can optimally solve samples that are as far as 15 from the goal within a few seconds. There are however no guarantees on the runtime and some samples may require much more time to solve. For example, the super-flip position, which is among the hardest takes more than 30 minutes to solve optimally with *Cube Explorer*.

We generated over 100 000 cube configurations by very long random walks from goal state. We then used the solver to find optimal solutions for each of these configurations. From the resulting optimal paths, we selected the training samples. We selected 3-4 configurations from every optimal path.

This way we generated a total of 345 396 training samples. Each of the samples is associated with a true goal distance. Generating the samples took about 48 wall-clock hours on 40 computers with 8 cores each. That gives about 15 000 CPU hours.

4 Feature Selection

We use a total of 22 features for every state. Some of the features are computed by PDB heuristics, some by other simpler heuristics and some of them describe the state directly.

We use 8 PDB heuristics with different patterns. The first pattern contains all 8 corner cubies and each of the other 7 patterns is composed by a set of 6 edge cubies. Every pattern contains different set of edge cubies and every edge cubie is included in some pattern.

All databases together contain about 150 million entries, take about 450 MB of memory and creating them took about 15 CPU hours.

Another five features are provided by simpler heuristics. These heuristics only count number of stickers that violate some conditions. They don't take into account cubies, i.e. they pretend that we can "unstick" some colored stickers from the cube and then stick them some place else. Heuristics count the number of such unstick-stick operations necessary to get the goal state of the cube. Heuristics work as follows:

- *errors*: Number of stickers that are not on the correct face. This number is then divided by 12 so that the resulting heuristic is admissible. (It is possible to move 12 stickers in a single move.)

- *distance*: The same as previous but stickers that need to go to the opposite face count as two because they require at least two moves to be placed correctly. The number is then also divided in order to be admissible.

- *pairs-different*: The total number of neighbouring pairs of stickers that are not in correct place. Neighbouring pair consists of two stickers on the same face that are next to each other (i.e. touching by an edge). Among all neighbouring pairs, we count those in which the two stickers have different colors. The number is then again normalized so that the estimate is admissible.

- *face-different*: The same as before but we consider every two stickers that are on the same face as a *pair* even if they are not next to each other.

- *face-error*: This only considers one specific face and counts how well it is completed.

The mentioned heuristics may look very similar but they actually work differently. For example, if we use the heuristics *pairs-different* and *face-different* to search for a solution of 8x8x8 cube, we get a very different kinds of states. Figures 1 and 2 show two states where the two heuristics got stuck respectively. The *pairs-different* heuristic (figure 1) created a number of connected components of the same color on each face, while *face-different* (figure 2) maximized the total number of colored stickers that are together on each face but it didn't create any coherent patterns.

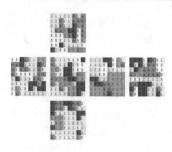

Figure 1: State found by the *pairDifferent* heuristic with coherent regions of the same color.

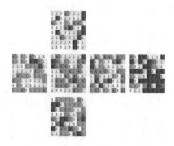

Figure 2: State found by the *faceDifferent* heuristic with much fewer coherent regions.

The rest of the features we use describe the state directly by specifying relations between cubies' current positions and their goal positions.

There are three types of cubies as described in 2.1: *centres, vertices* and *edges*. The central cubies never change their relative positions so we don't use them in this phase. For the other two types, we count every possible relation between positions of two cubies in the cube.

For example: two corner cubies may be in four different relative positions:

1. they are in the same place (i.e. they are both the same cubie)

2. they are on the same edge but not the same cubie

3. they are in the same face but not on the same edge

4. they are not in the same face (i.e. opposite corners of the cube)

In the given state, we determine the target position of every corner-cubie and then compute relation between the cubie's current position and it's target position. We then count the number of cubies that are in relations 1, 2, 3 and 4 respectively and use these numbers as features. For example, if we get numbers (8, 0, 0, 0), it means that in the given state, all corners are already in their respective correct positions.

We do the same for edge-cubies. Edges might be in 5 different relative positions, so this gives us another 5 features. (The number of edges that are in relation of $1, \ldots, 5$ with their target positions.)

These features are not based on heuristics or estimating goal-distance. Instead they provide a description of the state. All these features combined should provide enough information such that the network recognizes types of states in which given heuristics underestimate the real goal-distance and will be able to correct the estimate.

5 Network Design and Training

The network consists of 6 layers in total. The input layer contains 22 neurons that reads the 22 features we use. All features are real numbers within range $[0, 20]$. The four hidden layers contain 40, 36, 36 and 10 neurons respectively and all of them are feed-forward layers with *tanh* as their activation function. The output layer contains 1 neuron that computes the response of the network using linear activation. The response should be roughly within $[0, 25]$ since in all training samples the target value was inside this interval.

The architecture and layers' sizes were designed according to "best practices" for the networks with similar number of inputs. We tried several other architectures (a cascade network, different numbers of hidden layers) but this one achieved best results.

To create and train the network, we used *Matlab Neural Network Toolkit*. We trained the network on a computer with processor *Intel Core i7 920 (4x 2.66 GHz + Hyper-Threading), 12 GB RAM*, graphic card *Nvidia GeForce 210* that supports CUDA. The training took about 5 hours.

Other training parameters like *batch-size*, *learning rate* and so on were kept on the default values suggested for this kind of network by the framework.

5.1 Training Results

We only present training results obtained by the exact sample-generation strategy using the optimal solver. The strategy using random walks also works but leads to larger training error.

The accuracy of fit is depicted in figure 3. Histogram shows number of samples that are within a specified distance from their respective targets. Ideally, all samples should be in the column marked 0. We see that the network's answers are slightly biased since most samples lie in the column 1. This means that the network underestimates the true value.

Figure 4 shows more precisely the distribution of training error. The horizontal axis enumerates intervals and the height of columns represents the percentage of samples whose training error (in absolute value) lies within the specified interval. We can see that for more than 60% of samples, the error of estimation was less than 2. The mean absolute error was 1.94 with median of 1.22. The mean square error on the test set was 4.8 and median square error was 1.48. With the random walk sample-generation strategy the network only achieved mean square error of 8.9.

The training results show that for most samples the network was able to reasonably estimate their goal-distance

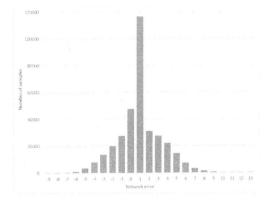

Figure 3: Histogram of accuracy of fit.

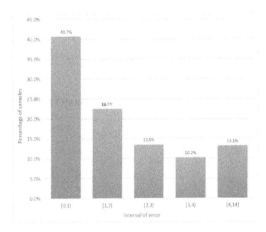

Figure 4: Distribution of training error of samples

but there is a few samples where the error is quite high. There is almost no difference between performance on training set and test set which suggests that the network is not over-fitted and should be able to generalize well.

Figure 5 shows a more thorough analysis of the network's performance. On the bottom axes, there are error of the network and the target value (which is the goal-distance of the sample). Height of the column represents the number of samples that falls into the respective category.

We can see that on samples that are close to the goal, the network is very accurate, has almost zero variance and low bias. On samples that are further from goal the network's answers became inaccurate. The variance increases and there is a slight bias towards under-estimating the real value.

6 Experiments

We used the trained network as a heuristic with IDA* algorithm on several randomly generated Rubik's cube instances. We compared the performance with other heuristics. *Iterative Deepening A* (IDA*)* is an algorithm similar to A* with the difference, that breadth-first search strategy is replaced by several cost-limited depth-first search runs.

We run each heuristic on all 320 problems with time limit of 5 minutes for each search instance. Experiments took about 115 CPU hours and run on 20 computers.

We measured several criteria:

- time required to solve the instance (capped at 300 seconds)

- number of expanded nodes during the search

- length of solution found

- minimal heuristic value of states that the algorithm encountered during the search

The heuristics $h_{max(simple)}$ and $h_{max(PDB)}$ are admissible. The sum of PDBs is not guaranteed to be admissible in this case and neither is the response of NN. The sumation-based heuristics are more greedy and might be at least able to find sub-optimal solutions quickly.

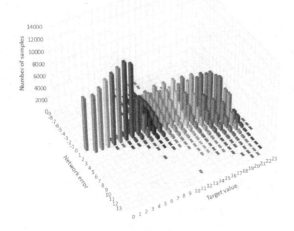

Figure 5: Distribution of training error with respect to target value.

The cost is computed in the same manner as with A* - using a heuristic estimator, and the limit successively increases until a solution is found. The algorithm provides the same guarantees as A* while requiring significantly less memory and slightly more time.

6.1 Experimental Setting

We generated 320 random instances of Rubik's cube and tried to solve them by IDA* with several heuristics. We generated samples by random walks starting in the goal state. We label the instances by length of the random walk that was used. Instances that were created by short random walks are easier because the instance is closer to the goal state. We generate instances by random walks of lengths 10, 14, 18, 22, 26, 30, 34 and 38. We run 40 walks of each length to get 320 instances in total.

In the experimental evaluation, we used six heuristics:

1. maximum of the five simple heuristics that we used as features (those that count stickers), denoted $h_{max(simple)}$

2. sum of these five heuristics, denoted $h_{sum(simple)}$

3. maximum of the eight PDB heuristics mentioned earlier, denoted $h_{max(PDB)}$

4. sum of these eight heuristics, denoted $h_{sum(PDB)}$

5. neural network as it was trained, denoted h_{NN}

6. neural network with a post-processing, denoted h_{NN+}

In the post-processing, we simply take maximum of the result of the network and the PDB heuristic, i.e. $h_{NN+} = \max(h_{NN}, h_{max(PDB)})$. Since the $h_{max(PDB)}$ is admissible, it makes no sense to estimate a value that is lower than $h_{max(PDB)}$. Furthermore, the network already has access to PDB estimates because it takes them as its input features.

6.2 Results

A table with detailed results can be downloaded at this link.

We present the results grouped by the length of random walk that was used to generate the problem instance. We call this the *difficulty of the instance*. The longer walk was used, the further from goal the instance is and therefore requires a longer sequence of actions to solve.

The number of solved instances by specific algorithms is shown in figure 6. We can see that with increasing difficulty of the problem the number of solved instances drops rapidly. This is mostly due to relatively strict time limit of 5 minutes for solving each instance.

We can also see that *NN* and *NN+* heuristics solved the largest number of problems in most categories. In total, h_{NN} solved 130 problems, h_{NN+} 129 problems and $h_{max(PDB)}$ 126 problems. $h_{sum(PDB)}$ achieved much worse results and *Simple heuristics* scored the worst.

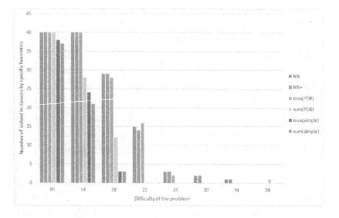

Figure 6: Number of problems solved by specific algorithms.

Figure 7 shows average number of expanded nodes of algorithms. Results are grouped by problem difficulty and only solved instances are considered. *Simple heuristics* have the largest number of expanded nodes (on problems that they have been able to solve) because they are the least informed ones.

PDBs have systematically higher number of expansion than both versions of neural networks. This suggests that both h_{NN} and h_{NN+} are more informed than $h_{max(PDB)}$. The effect is partially caused by the fact that evaluating h_{NN} is much slower than $h_{max(PDB)}$ and therefore the network is able to expand less nodes withing given time limit.

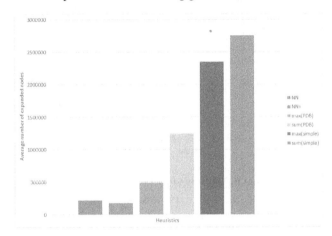

Figure 7: Expanded nodes of solved instances for specific algorithms.

Figure 8 analyzes run-times of individual heuristics. Problems are divided into categories according to how much time it took to solve them. The horizontal axis represents those categories as time intervals and height of columns shows how many problems fall into such category.

We can see that both networks as well as PDBs have been able to solve significant number of problems in time lesser than 1 second (for each problem). The run-time of h_{NN}, h_{NN+} and $h_{max(PDB)}$ are comparable. The time-performance of the other three heuristics is much worse.

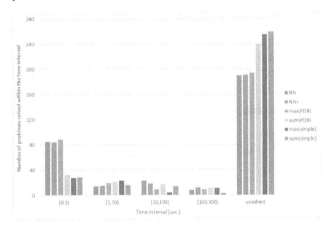

Figure 8: Histogram of run-time demands of problems.

Figure 9 shows average length of solution found by spe-

cific heuristics. Only solved instances are considered. The figure shows that *simple heuristics* found best solutions on average in categories 14 and 18. This is however caused by the fact that *simple heuristics* were only able to solve small problems that have shorter solutions and unsuccessful attempts are not considered in the average.

$h_{sum(PBD)}$ exhibits the worst average quality of solutions, but it has been able to solve the largest problem. This is caused by the fact that $h_{sum(PBD)}$ is the most greedy of all heuristics used. $h_{max(PBD)}$ has been able to find solutions with better average quality than both versions of the network. This is not surprising, since PDBs solved very similar set of problems as the NNs did and $h_{max(PBD)}$ is admissible so it guarantees finding optimal solutions. On average, NN found solutions that are 8.75% longer than optimal solutions found by PDBs. (Measured on instances that were solved by both h_{NN} and $h_{max(PDB)}$.

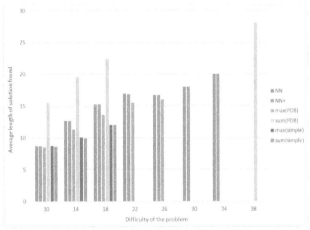

Figure 9: Average length of solution of solved instances for specific algorithms.

In figure 10 we can see the average of minimal heuristic value of states encountered during the search. Only unsolved instances are considered, because on solved problems the minimal heuristic value is always 0. We can see some interesting results here. $h_{sum(PDB)}$ was able to find states very close to the goal on most unsolved problems. It exhibits the lowest overall values even though the heuristic is very greedy and over-estimates the true value significantly.

On average, h_{NN} found states with better heuristic values than h_{NN+}. This is counter-intuitive as h_{NN+} is more informed. The result is most likely caused by the fact that h_{NN} under-estimated the true value of some states during the search, so it only "thought" it found close-to-goal states but it wasn't really the case. h_{NN+} is less prone to such under-estimating.

7 Conclusion

We trained and experimentally tested a neural network to estimate goal distances of Rubik's cube problems.

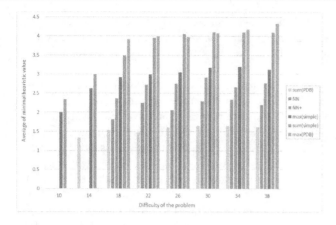

Figure 10: Average of minimal heuristic value found on unsolved problems.

The network is competitive with state-of-the-art pattern databases.

Our experiments show that PDBs are very fast and reasonably accurate while the network's evaluation is much slower because it involves computing the input features. Network therefore has lower search-speed in terms of nodes expanded per second. The NN heuristic, however, compensates this by being more informed than PDBs and can solve slightly larger number of problems withing given time limit.

On unsolved task the network seems to be able to find states that are closer to goal than $h_{max(PDB)}$. PDBs on the other hand guarantee optimality of solutions which the network does not.

We believe that the network represents an interesting and viable way of combining several heuristics together and for some use-case scenarios it may be the best choice. An ideal use-case scenario for NN is situation where we solve many problems from the same domain, there is enough time to prepare for the search (to train the network) and optimal solutions are not strictly required.

As a future work, we would like to find a balance between accuracy and speed of the network. By using a small set of suitable features, it should be possible to train network that is accurate and it's evaluation is still fast.

Acknowledgement

This research was supported by SVV project number 260 453.

References

[1] Shahab Jabbari Arfaee, Sandra Zilles, and Robert C. Holte. Bootstrap learning of heuristic functions. In Ariel Felner and Nathan R. Sturtevant, editors, *Proceedings of the Third Annual Symposium on Combinatorial Search, SOCS 2010*. AAAI Press, 2010.

[2] Irwan Bello, Hieu Pham, Quoc V. Le, Mohammad Norouzi, and Samy Bengio. Neural Combinatorial Optimization with Reinforcement Learning. In *Proceedings of the Fifth International Conference on Learning Representations*, 2017.

[3] Hung-Che Chen and Jyh-Da Wei. Using neural networks for evaluation in heuristic search algorithm. In *Proceedings of the Twenty-Sixth AAAI Conference on Artificial Intelligence*, 2011.

[4] E. D. Demaine, S. Eisenstat, and M. Rudoy. Solving the Rubik's Cube Optimally is NP-complete. *ArXiv e-prints*, June 2017.

[5] Erik D. Demaine et al. Algorithms for solving rubik's cubes. In Camil Demetrescu and Magnús M. Halldórsson, editors, *Proceedings of Algorithms – ESA 2011: 19th Annual European Symposium*, pages 689–700. Springer Berlin Heidelberg, 2011.

[6] Dieter Fox and Carla P. Gomes, editors. *Proceedings of the Twenty-Third AAAI Conference on Artificial Intelligence, AAAI 2008, Chicago, Illinois, USA, July 13-17, 2008*. AAAI Press, 2008.

[7] Youssef Hamadi, Eric Monfroy, and Frédéric Saubion. *Autonomous search*. Springer-Verlag, 2012.

[8] Malte Helmert and Robert Mattmüller. Accuracy of admissible heuristic functions in selected planning domains. In Fox and Gomes [6], pages 938–943.

[9] Erez Karpas and Carmel Domshlak. Optimal search with inadmissible heuristics. In *Proceedings of International Conference on Automated Planning and Scheduling*, 2012.

[10] Thomas Keller, Florian Pommerening, Jendrik Seipp, Florian Geißer, and Robert Mattmüller. State-dependent cost partitionings for cartesian abstractions in classical planning. In *Proceedings of the 25th International Joint Conference on Artificial Intelligence (IJCAI 2016)*, 2016.

[11] Richard E. Korf. Finding optimal solutions to rubik's cube using pattern databases. In *Proceedings of the Fourteenth National Conference on Artificial Intelligence and Ninth Conference on Innovative Applications of Artificial Intelligence, AAAI'97/IAAI'97*, pages 700–705. AAAI Press, 1997.

[12] Matej Moravčík et al. DeepStack: Expert-level artificial intelligence in heads-up no-limit poker. *Science*, 356(6337):508–513, 2017.

[13] Stuart J. Russell and Peter Norvig. *Artificial Intelligence: A Modern Approach*. Prentice Hall, 3 edition, 2010.

[14] Mehdi Samadi, Ariel Felner, and Jonathan Schaeffer. Learning from multiple heuristics. In Fox and Gomes [6], pages 357–362.

[15] D. Silver, A. Huang, et al. Mastering the game of Go with deep neural networks and tree search. *Nature*, 529(7587):484–489, 2016.

[16] Nathan R. Sturtevant, Ariel Felner, and Malte Helmert. Exploiting the rubik's cube 12-edge PDB by combining partial pattern databases and bloom filters. In Stefan Edelkamp and Roman Barták, editors, *Proceedings of the Seventh Annual Symposium on Combinatorial Search, SOCS 2014*. AAAI Press, 2014.

[17] Jordan Thayer, Austin Dionne, and Wheeler Ruml. Learning inadmissible heuristics during search. In *Proceedings of International Conference on Automated Planning and Scheduling*, 2011.

J. Hlaváčová (Ed.): ITAT 2017 Proceedings, pp. 65–70
ISBN 978-1974274741, © 2017 P. Čížek, J. Faigl, J. Bayer

Enhancing Neural Based Obstacle Avoidance with CPG Controlled Hexapod Walking Robot

Petr Čížek, Jan Faigl, and Jan Bayer

Czech Technical University in Prague, Faculty of Electrical Engineering, Technická 2, 166 27 Prague, Czech Republic
{cizekpe6|faiglj|bayerja1}@fel.cvut.cz

Abstract: Avoiding collisions with obstacles and intercepting objects based on the visual perception is a vital survival ability of any animal. In this work, we propose an extension of the biologically based collision avoidance approach to the detection of intercepting objects using the Lobula Giant Movement Detector (LGMD) connected directly to the locomotion control unit based on the Central Pattern Generator (CPG) of a hexapod walking robot. The proposed extension uses Recurrent Neural Network (RNN) to map the output of the LGMD on the input of the CPG to enhance collision avoiding behavior of the robot in cluttered environments. The presented results of the experimental verification of the proposed system with a real mobile hexapod crawling robot support the feasibility of the presented approach in collision avoidance scenarios.

1 Introduction

Avoiding collisions with obstacles and intercepting objects is a vital survival ability for any animal. For a mobile robot moving from one place to another, the contact with a fixed or moving object may have fatal consequences. Therefore, it is desirable to study the problem of collision avoidance and derive new and computationally efficient ways to trigger collision avoiding behavior.

In this work, we concern a problem of biologically inspired motion control and collision avoidance with a legged walking robot equipped with a forward looking camera only. We propose to utilize a Central Pattern Generator (CPG) approach [1] for robot locomotion control and the vision-based collision avoidance approach using the Lobula Giant Movement Detector (LGMD) [2] which are both combined in the proposed controller based on Recurrent Neural Network (RNN).

The proposed solution builds on our previous results published in [3] in which only a simple mapping function is utilized for transforming the output of the LGMD neural network directly to the locomotion control parameters of the CPG controller [1]. Such a solution works well in laboratory conditions, but, unfortunately, it is error-prone in the cluttered environment. It is mainly because of the way how the LGMD neural network processes the visual data and due to a simple mapping function. The LGMD reacts on the lateral movement of vertical edges in the image regardless their depth in the scene. In a cluttered environment, this results that the output is heavily influenced by a lot of stimuli from the distinctive edges in a far distance

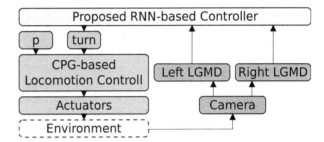

Figure 1: Overview of the proposed control system structure. Different colors discriminate the individual functional parts of the architecture.

from the robot. Moreover the mapping function translates the output of the LGMD directly to the locomotion control parameters. Hence, the reaction of the robot is based solely on the current observation of the environment which results in situations when the robot hits an obstacle from the side that has successfully avoided earlier but it is already out of the field of view. Therefore, we propose to enhance the collision avoiding behavior of the robot by incorporating a memory mechanism by means of the RNN.

The overall structure of the proposed system is depicted in Fig. 1. Regarding to the previous approaches, here, we would like to emphasize a practical verification of the proposed method on a real walking robot as the specific nature of the legged locomotion makes the problem more difficult in comparison to the wheeled [4, 5] or flying [6] robots. The main difference originates in abrupt motions of the camera induced by the locomotion of the robot which negatively influences the output of the collision avoiding visual pathway.

The reminder of the paper is organized as follows. The most related approaches on the neural-based collision avoidance using vision are summarized in Section 2. Section 3 describes the individual building blocks of the proposed control architecture. Evaluation results and their discussion are detailed in Section 4. Concluding remarks and suggestions for future work are dedicated to Section 5.

2 Related Work

The problem of collision avoidance has been studied ever since the mobile robots appeared. Hence, there is a lot of different approaches using different sensors and different processing techniques. In this work, we are focused on vision-based neural obstacle avoidance methods and the most related approaches are described in the rest of this section.

Direct mapping of the visual perception on the robot control command using a feed-forward neural network has been already utilized in several methods. The problem of road following using neural networks, which dates back to 90s, can be considered as a special case of the collision avoidance problem [7]. However, such approaches cannot be considered as biologically-based because of artificial nature of the examined roads.

In [2], the Lobula Giant Movement Detector (LGMD) neural network has been introduced in robotics to imitate the way how insects avoid collisions with an intercepting object [8]. The approach has been widely adopted for its simplicity and relatively good performance with wheeled [2, 4, 5] and flying [6] robots. However, these approaches experimentally verify the collision avoidance with a real robot either in a closed arena where it is necessary to avoid collisions with walls or in a scenario where a static robot is supposed to detect an intercepting object. Moreover, the walls of the arena or the obstacles were homogeneously distributed or coated with a high contrast artificial pattern which significantly improves the behavior of the LGMD. In our approach, we focus on the deployment of the LGMD in heavily cluttered unstructured environment, and thus evaluate the approach in more realistic scenarios.

An experimental study on the prediction of evasive steering maneuvers in urban traffic scenarios has been recently published in [9]. In this approach, the performance of the LGMD is improved by introducing so-called "danger zones" which are the image areas that will most likely indicate the incoming threat.

Another approach presented in [10] compares the performance of the LGMD and Directional Selective Neurons (DSN) in the ability to avoid collisions. Both of them are to be found in the visual pathways of insects. The reported results show that the LGMD can be trained using evolutionary techniques to outperform the DSN in the collision recognition ability.

Regarding our target scenario, the most relevant approach to the proposed solution has been presented in [11]. The authors use a biologically-inspired collision avoidance approach based on the extraction of nearness information from the image depth estimation to detect obstacles and avoid collisions. The whole system allows a simulated hexapod robot to navigate cluttered environment while actively avoiding obstacles. However, the approach uses a direct feed-forward approach for the motion control and it has not been deployed in a real-world scenario.

The herein proposed control mechanism utilizes a Recurrent Neural Network (RNN) that has been already utilized in collision avoiding scenarios using odor sensors on whiskers [12] or a set of infrared rangefinders [13]. A vision-based collision avoidance for an UAV based on the

RNN has been recently presented in [14] which trains the UAV to avoid collisions during autonomous indoor flight. This work served as the inspiration for our neural-based autonomous agent.

3 Proposed Solution

Three basic functional parts can be identified within the proposed collision avoiding system. They are depicted in three different colors in Fig. 1. The first part is the locomotion control unit based on the chaotic oscillator [15] depicted in an orange color whose purpose is to control the walking pattern and to solve the kinematics. It allows to change the type of the motion gait based on the pre-set parameter p and steer the robot motion according to the input signal *turn* defining the turning radius. The second part is the visual pathway depicted in a green color which utilizes the LGMD neural network for avoiding approaching objects and triggering escape behavior. The main idea of the proposed approach is to use the LGMD outputs for setting the hexapod control parameters, in particular, the turning radius *turn* of the robot. In this work, we are proposing to use the RNN-based approach for the translation of the LGMD output to the *turn* parameter which is dedicated to the last part depicted in a yellow color. Each part is discussed in more detail in the following sections.

3.1 CPG-Based Locomotion Control

The locomotion control is based on our previous work presented in [1]. It utilizes only one chaotic CPG [15] consisting of two interconnected neurons with a control input computed solely based on the input period p. The CPG stabilizes a periodic orbit of p from the chaotic oscillation, so the output is a discrete periodic signal. The period $p \in \{4, 6, 8, 12\}$ directly determines the resulting walking pattern (motion gait): tripod, ripple, tetrapod, and wave, respectively [16].

Afterwards, the output of the chaotic oscillator is shaped and post-processed in order to obtain a signal usable for a trajectory generator and to determine the phase of individual legs, i.e., whether the leg is swinging or supporting the body. Afterwards, the output of the chaotic oscillator is thresholded and a triangle wave alternating between -1 and 1 is produced, where the upslope (swing phase) is a constant and the downslope (support phase) depends on the period p. Based on the leg coordination rules [17], individual delays are applied to the triangular wave per each leg to produce the rhythmic pattern for each leg.

The result of the post-processing module is fed into a trajectory generator, which determines the position of foot-tips according to the input signal along with the parameter *turn*, which is given by the RNN-based controller. The *turn* parameter is equal to the distance (in millimeters) from the robot center to the turning center on a line perpendicular to the heading of the robot connecting the

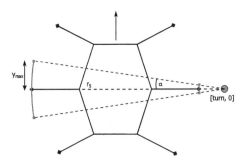

Figure 2: Trajectory generation - the turning point denoted as the small red disk is given by *turn* parameter. α is computed as the maximum angle given the turning radius and the maximum step size y_{max}.

default positions of the middle legs. Based on the *turn* parameter and the triangular wave, the trajectory generator uniquely determines the foot-tip positions of each leg on the constructed arcs which are limited by the angle α. The value of α is computed from the distance of the furthest leg from the pivotal point established by *turn* and the maximum step size y_{max}. The idea of the trajectory generator is visualized in Fig. 2. The output of the trajectory generator is transformed into the joint space using the inverse kinematics module and then performed by the robot actuators. Notice, the speed of the robot forward motion is determined by the period p, while the robot angular velocity is controlled by the *turn* parameter, which is adjusted by the RNN-based controller from the LGMD output.

3.2 LGMD Neural Network

The LGMD [2] is a neural network found in the visual pathways of insects, such as locusts [8], which responds selectively to objects approaching the animal on a collision course. It is composed of four groups of cells: *Photoreceptive*, *Excitatory*, *Inhibitory*, and *Summation* arranged in three layers; and two individual cells: *Feed-forward inhibitory* and *Lobula Giant Movement Detector*. The structure of the network is visualized in Fig. 3.

The *Photoreceptive layer* processes the sensory input from the camera. Its output is the difference between two successive grayscale camera frames and it is computed as

$$P_f(x,y) = L_f(x,y) - L_{f-1}(x,y), \qquad (1)$$

where L_f is the current frame, L_{f-1} is the previous frame and (x,y) are the pixel coordinates. In principle, the *Photoreceptive layer* implements a contrast enhancement and forms the input to the following two groups of neurons – the *Inhibition layer* and *Excitatory layer*.

The response of the *Inhibition layer* is computed as

$$I_f(x,y) = \sum_{i=-n}^{n} \sum_{j=-n}^{n} P_{f-1}(x+i,y+j)w_I(i,j), \qquad (2)$$

$$(i \neq j, \text{ if } i = 0),$$

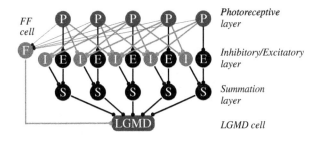

Figure 3: LGMD neural network model

where w_I are the inhibition weights set as

$$w_I = \begin{bmatrix} 0.06 & 0.12 & 0.25 & 0.12 & 0.06 \\ 0.12 & 0.06 & 0.12 & 0.06 & 0.12 \\ 0.25 & 0.12 & 0 & 0.12 & 0.25 \\ 0.12 & 0.06 & 0.12 & 0.06 & 0.12 \\ 0.06 & 0.12 & 0.25 & 0.12 & 0.06 \end{bmatrix}. \qquad (3)$$

The *Inhibition layer* is essentially smoothing the *Photoreceptive layer* output values and filtering those caused by noise or camera imperfections. The inhibition weights w_I are selected experimentally with respect to the LGMD description in [2] which uses 3×3 matrix of inhibition weights, but on an image with a much lower resolution.

The *Excitatory layer* is used to time delay the output of *Photoreceptive layer* and it is calculated as

$$E = |P_f(x,y)|. \qquad (4)$$

The response of the *Summation layer* is computed as

$$S_f(x,y) = E(x,y) - |I_f(x,y)| W_I, \qquad (5)$$

where $W_I = 0.4$ is the global inhibition weight. Let S'_f be a matrix for which each value exceeding the threshold T_r is passed and any lower value is set to 0

$$S'_f(x,y) = \begin{cases} S_f(x,y) & \text{if } S_f(x,y) \geq T_r \\ 0 & \text{otherwise} \end{cases}. \qquad (6)$$

Then, an excitation of the *LGMD cell* is computed as

$$U_f = \sum_{x=1}^{k} \sum_{y=1}^{l} |S'_f(x,y)| \qquad (7)$$

and finally, the *LGMD cell* output is

$$u_f = (1 + e^{-U_f n_{cell}^{-1}})^{-1}, \qquad (8)$$

where n_{cell} is the total number of cells (the number of pixels). Note, the output of u_f is in the interval $u_f \in [0.5, 1]$.

Typically, the LGMD neural network contains *Feed-forward cell* which is not utilized in the proposed scheme based on the results of the experimental evaluation. The purpose of the *Feed-forward cell* is to suppress the output of the *LGMD cell* in a case of fast camera movements.

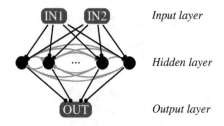

Figure 4: LSTM recurrent neural network model

However, due to the specific nature of the legged loco-motion, this feature is undesirable as it makes the LGMD network less sensitive.

In our setup, two LGMD neural networks are utilized in parallel to distinguish the direction of the interception, and thus be able to steer the robot in the opposite direction to achieve the desired obstacle avoiding behavior. The input image from a single camera is split into left and right parts with the overlapping center part. Each of the LGMDs provide the output which we denote u_f^{left} and u_f^{right} for the left and the right LGMD respectively.

3.3 RNN-Based Controller

In our previous work [3], we utilized a direct mapping function between the LGMDs output tuple and the *turn* parameter of the CPG. The particular mapping function was designed as

$$\Phi(e) = \begin{cases} 100/2e & \text{for } |e| \geq 0.2 \\ 10000 \cdot \text{sgn}(e) & \text{for } |e| < 0.2 \end{cases}, \quad (9)$$

where error e is calculated as the difference of the LGMD outputs $e = u_f^{left} - u_f^{right}$.

However, the direct mapping function failed in the collision avoidance in cluttered environment. Therefore, we developed an RNN-based controller that takes the left and right LGMD outputs on its input and provides an estimate of the *turn* parameter on its output.

In the proposed controller, we utilized the Recurrent Neural Network (RNN) based on the Long Short Term Memory (LSTM) [18] with two inputs, one hidden layer, and one output that estimate the error e which is then used with the mapping function given by (9). The Backpropagation Through Time (BPTT) [19] is utilized for the RNN training, which unrolls the network over the time resulting in a feed-forward neural network. As there are only two real number inputs to the network, it is unnecessary to use sliding window approaches to the learning as it is possible to feed the data to the network in a full length. The structure of the LSTM neural network is visualized in Fig. 4.

The main idea is to connect the RNN directly to the outputs of the left and right LGMDs and let the neural network estimate the parameter e which is then translated by (9) to the *turn* parameter of the CPG-based locomotion controller.

4 Experimental Evaluation

The experimental verification of the proposed neural-based controller is focused on the ability of the hexapod walking robot to avoid collisions with the obstacles on its path. We are emphasizing the practical verification with a real walking robot to thoroughly test the proposed solution and provide insights on the achieved performance.

The experimental evaluation has been considered with the hexapod walking robot visualized in Fig. 5a. The robot has six legs attached to the trunk that hosts the sensors. In particular, the Logitech C920 camera with the field of view $78°$ to provide the LGMD with the visual input has been utilized. The image data fed into the LGMD neural network has been subsampled to the resolution of 176×144 pixels and divided into two parts overlapping in 10% of the image area.

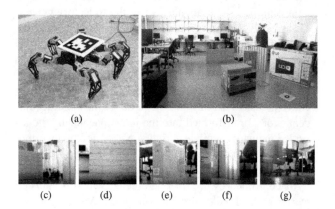

(a)   (b)

(c)   (d)   (e)   (f)   (g)

Figure 5: (a) The hexapod walking robot, (b) the laboratory test environment, and (c-g) typical images captured by the robot

The robot has operated in an arena surrounded by obstacles, which are formed by tables, chairs and boxes (see Fig. 5b). The robot movement has been tracked by a visual localization system which tracks the AprilTag [20] pattern attached to the robot, which allows to capture the real trajectory the robot was traversing. Typical images captured by the robot during traversing the arena are visualized in Fig. 5c-g. As the LGMD reacts strongly on the lateral movement of vertical edges in the image, it is much harder to avoid obstacles in the cluttered environment where the edges are distributed non-homogeneously in contrast to experiments performed in [2, 4, 6].

4.1 RNN Training Process

The LSTM neural network [18] has been trained using the BPTT technique [19]. The training process has been performed as follows. First, 10 sample trajectories have been collected by manually guiding the robot through the environment while avoiding the obstacles. The outputs of both the LGMDs have been recorded and the parameter *turn* has been adjusted manually, from which the corresponding error parameter e has been computed. The sampled trajectories contain altogether 22530 sample points. Next, the neural network has been trained with these 10 trajectories in 1000 iterations.

The herein utilized RNN has 2 inputs, 16 hidden states, and 1 output. The 16 hidden states have been selected as a compromise between the complexity of the RNN and the behavior observed during the experimental verification. As one of the problems of the former solution is the behavior of the robot when it successfully initiate the obstacle avoidance but it then hits it from the side, we selected 16 hidden states as the memory buffer to provide sufficient capacity for the robot to traverse 0.4 m given its dimensions, speed and camera frame rate.

The sigmoid function has been used as the activation function of the RNN

$$f(x) = \frac{1}{1 + e^{-x}}. \tag{10}$$

As the LGMD outputs are in the range $u_f \in [0.5, 1]$ and the error function $e \in [-0.5, 0.5]$, the RNN has been trained to estimate the value of $e + 0.5$ which is feasible for the sigmoid function with the range of $f(x) \in [0, 1]$.

4.2 Experimental Results

Altogether, 20 trials have been performed in the laboratory arena to verify the ability of the robot to avoid collisions. The robot has been directed to intercept different obstacles and its behavior has been observed. The algorithm failed only in 3 trials while the previous approach based on the direct control proposed in [3] is unable to operate in such a heavily cluttered environment at all. The first failed trial is specific by a direct collision with a low-textured wooden barrier (see Fig. 5d), hence the LGMDs failed to detect an approaching object. The second and third failures fall into the category of sideway interception when the robot successfully starts to avoid the obstacle but the robot hits it later from a side.

Fig. 6 shows three typical trajectories crawled by the hexapod robot in the laboratory arena. The trajectory is overlaid with the perpendicular arrows that characterize the direction and magnitude of the error e that is used for the robot steering which correspond to the direction in which the neural-based controller is sensing an obstacle. Besides, the corresponding plot of the LGMD outputs and the comparison of the control output provided by the proposed neural-based controller e_{rnn} and the direct control method e_{direct} is visualized in Fig. 7.

Further, we let the robot to continuously crawl the area and avoid obstacles. The robot has crawled the distance of approx. 140 m while colliding only 8 times.

4.3 Discussion

The presented results indicate that the proposed neural-based locomotion controller with the collision avoidance feedback provided by the LGMD neural network and the RNN-based controller is feasible. Moreover, the utilization of the RNN considerably improves the collision avoiding behavior in comparison to the direct control mechanism presented in [3]. The difference between the control principles can be best observed in Fig. 7a. It can be seen that the RNN filters oscillations in the error e which would disable the robot from avoiding the collision in a case of the direct control.

On the other hand, it is not particularly clear what is the RNN-based controller reacting to, as the dependency of the output on the distance to the closest obstacle has not been confirmed. This can be observed in Fig. 6c and the corresponding plot of the error function in Fig. 7c where the controller starts to oscillate after successfully avoiding the first obstacle. Other experimental trials have shown that these oscillations do not affect the collision avoiding behavior; however, it is unclear how and why they are produced by the neural controller.

The results indicate that the RNN calculates a weighted average of the LGMD outputs over a short period. However, further analysis of the behavior of the controller is necessary to reliably evaluate its properties.

Last but not least, the proposed controller performs only a collision avoiding behavior and does not guide the robot to any particular goal. Thus, we consider an extension of the proposed method to incorporate a higher level goal following to the architecture of the neural-based controller as a future work.

5 Conclusion

In this paper, we propose an extension of the biologically based collision avoidance approach with a Recurrent Neural Network to enhance the collision avoiding behavior of a hexapod walking robot. The proposed extension allows the robot to operate in heavily cluttered environments. The herein presented experimental results indicate feasibility of the controller which failed to avoid collision in only 3 out of 20 performed trials. The experimental results raised questions about the cause of the observed oscillations that deserve future investigation. Besides, we aim to improve the proposed biologically-based architecture to follow a specific target location, and thus developed biologically inspired autonomous navigation.

Acknowledgments – This work was supported by the Czech Science Foundation (GAČR) under research project No. 15-09600Y. The support of the Grant Agency of the CTU in Prague under grant No. SGS16/235/OHK3/3T/13 to Petr Čížek is also gratefully acknowledged.

References

[1] P. Milička, P. Čížek, and J. Faigl, "On chaotic oscillator-based central pattern generator for motion control of hexapod walking robot," in *Informačné Technológie - Aplikácie*

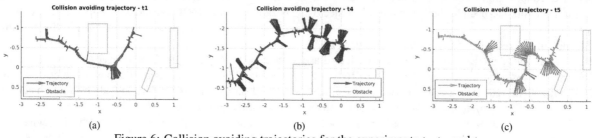

Figure 6: Collision avoiding trajectories for the experiments t_1, t_4, and t_5

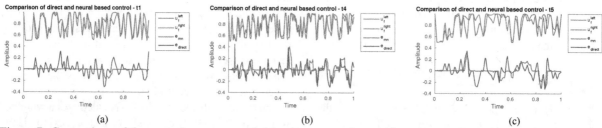

Figure 7: Comparison of the control output provided by the proposed neural-based controller e_{rnn} and the direct method e_{direct} for the experiments t_1, t_4, and t_5

a Teória (ITAT), CEUR Workshop Proceedings, vol. 1649, 2016, pp. 131–137.

[2] M. Blanchard, F. Rind, and P. F. M. J. Verschure, "Collision avoidance using a model of the locust LGMD neuron," *Robotics and Autonomous Systems (RAS)*, vol. 30, no. 1-2, pp. 17–38, 2000.

[3] P. Čížek, P. Milička, and J. Faigl, "Neural based obstacle avoidance with CPG controlled hexapod walking robot," in *IEEE International Joint Conference on Neural Networks (IJCNN)*, 2017, pp. 650–656.

[4] S. Yue and F. C. Rind, "Collision detection in complex dynamic scenes using an LGMD-based visual neural network with feature enhancement," *IEEE Transactions on Neural Networks*, vol. 17, no. 3, pp. 705–716, 2006.

[5] Q. Fu, S. Yue, and C. Hu, "Bio-inspired collision detector with enhanced selectivity for ground robotic vision system," in *British Machine Vision Conference*, 2016.

[6] S. B. i Badia, P. Pyk, and P. F. M. J. Verschure, "A biologically based flight control system for a blimp-based UAV," in *IEEE International Conference on Robotics and Automation (ICRA)*, 2005, pp. 3053–3059.

[7] D. A. Pomerleau, *Neural network perception for mobile robot guidance.* Springer Science and Business Media, 2012, vol. 239.

[8] D. M. Wilson, "The central nervous control of flight in a locust," *Journal of Experimental Biology*, vol. 38, no. 47, pp. 471–490, 1961.

[9] M. Hartbauer, "Simplified bionic solutions: a simple bio-inspired vehicle collision detection system," *Bioinspiration and Biomimetics*, vol. 12, no. 2, p. 026007, 2017.

[10] S. Yue and F. C. Rind, "Redundant neural vision systems – competing for collision recognition roles," *IEEE Transactions on Autonomous Mental Development*, vol. 5, no. 2, pp. 173–186, 2013.

[11] H. G. Meyer, O. J. N. Bertrand, J. Paskarbeit, J. P. Lindemann, A. Schneider, and M. Egelhaaf, *A Bio-Inspired Model for Visual Collision Avoidance on a Hexapod Walking Robot*, 2016, pp. 167–178.

[12] J. Kodjabachian and J. A. Meyer, "Evolution and development of neural controllers for locomotion, gradient-following, and obstacle-avoidance in artificial insects," *IEEE Transactions on Neural Networks*, vol. 9, no. 5, pp. 796–812, 1998.

[13] B.-Q. Huang, G.-Y. Cao, and M. Guo, "Reinforcement learning neural network to the problem of autonomous mobile robot obstacle avoidance," in *International Conference on Machine Learning and Cybernetics*, vol. 1, 2005, pp. 85–89.

[14] K. Kelchtermans and T. Tuytelaars, "How hard is it to cross the room? - training (recurrent) neural networks to steer a UAV," *CoRR*, vol. abs/1702.07600, 2017.

[15] S. Steingrube, M. Timme, F. Wörgötter, and P. Manoonpong, "Self-organized adaptation of a simple neural circuit enables complex robot behaviour," *Nature Physics*, vol. 6, no. 3, pp. 224–230, 2010.

[16] N. Porcino, "Hexapod gait control by a neural network," in *IEEE International Joint Conference on Neural Networks (IJCNN)*, 1990, pp. 189–194.

[17] D. M. Wilson, "Insect walking," *Annual Review of Entomology*, vol. 11, no. 1, pp. 103–122, 1966.

[18] S. Hochreiter and J. Schmidhuber, "Long short-term memory," *Neural Computation*, vol. 9, no. 8, pp. 1735–1780, 1997.

[19] I. Sutskever, "Training recurrent neural networks," Ph.D. dissertation, University of Toronto, 2013.

[20] E. Olson, "AprilTag: A Robust and Flexible Visual Fiducial System," in *IEEE International Conference on Robotics and Automation (ICRA)*, 2011, pp. 3400–3407.

J. Hlaváčová (Ed.): ITAT 2017 Proceedings, pp. 71–77
ISBN 978-1974274741, © 2017 M. Danel, M. Skrbek

Humanoid Robot Control by Offline Actor-Critic Learning

Marek Danel, Miroslav Skrbek

Faculty of Information Technology
Czech Technical University
Prague, Czech Republic
danelmar@fit.cvut.cz, skrbek@fit.cvut.cz

Abstract: In this paper, we present our results on application of reinforcement learning on full body control of a humanoid robot. The task we try to learn is achieving vertical position of robot's torso from an initial position of laying flat on the ground. Our experimental setup includes an instance of the NAO robot in the Webots simulation environment. We use an actor-critic neural agent. As this is a work in progress, we only train offline from a sample of random movements. We present a series of experiments on a simplified task and a final evaluation on the humanoid robot control task that shows improvement over random policy.

Keywords: reinforcement learning, humanoid robot, actor-critic, offline learning, neural networks

1 Introduction

Nowadays, there are humanoid robot bodies available with high degree of movement freedom. They are also equipped with sensors, which provide large amount of input from robot's environment in multiple modes as well as input from robot's own body. This immense amount of input data and freedom of actions poses a challenge of fully exploiting robot's potential.

In real-world environment, any movement is subject to unpredictable deviations. When performing fixed sequences of movements, a robot will end up in a very different final position every time due to cumulating inaccuracies of every step in the sequence. Therefore, many subtle and significant changes to originally planned sequence need to be made continuously to compensate for stochasticity of the real-world environment. A feasible control policy needs to translate sensory readings to appropriate action in every time step.

Complexity of such policy makes it very time consuming to engineer using model-based methods. Also, it is impossible to predict all situations a robot can encounter in real-world. Ability to learn by reinforcement from the environment is necessary for true autonomy. Therefore, we aim to deploy and adapt reinforcement learning algorithms to humanoid robotics.

Deploying reinforcement learning algorithms to a humanoid robot is a difficult task as the dimensionality of state and action space is high. Robot NAO, which we use in our experiments, has 25 degrees of freedom. The robot should learn to control its body by directly applying torque to its actuators. This means that all the dynamics of its body are responsibility of the learning algorithm. As we have shown in our previous work [1], deploying the Deep Deterministic Policy Gradient Algorithm (DDPG) [2] yields very little results out of the box.

In this work, we evaluate applicability of actor-critic agents to humanoid body control. We focus on testing the capability of actor-critic method to infer the correct action from available experience. We first compare multiple common perceptron optimization methods to get best possible results on a simplified task. Then, we use the findings from simplified task to set up an experiment with the robot in a simulated environment, where we show an improvement over random policy baseline.

2 Background

In the field of Reinforcement Learning (RL), we model agent in its environment as a Markov Decision Process (MDP). MDP consists of state space S, action space A, transition dynamics given by probability density $P(s_{t+1}|s_t, a_t)$, and a reward function $R(s, a)$. By small letters s and a we denote state and action respectively and subscript them with t and $t+1$ whenever the distinction between subsequent time steps is necessary. In every time step, agent observes the state of the MDP, picks an action according to its policy π and receives a reward determined by the reward function. The policy π is defined as probability of taking an action given the state agent has observed $\pi = P(a|s)$. Alternatively, policy can be constrained to a deterministic form. Then, it is simply a function of state that returns action to be performed $a_t = \pi(s_t)$. In our work, we use only the deterministic form of a policy.

We assume full observability of the environment. Under this assumption, the *state* and its *observation* are equal. They are often used interchangeably and in the rest of the paper we use both these terms.

The neural actor-critic algorithms are model free approaches that learn a policy by function approximation. The function approximation is used to evaluate utility (or value) of actions in given state expressed as a single real value. This evaluation function is called action value function and it is always denoted by $Q(s, a)$. When the utility of actions is known, it is possible to pick the most useful one. Another commonly used term is a state value function $V(s)$, which evaluates utility of a state. The relationship between the action value function and the state value function is:

$$V(s) = max_a Q(s,a) \qquad (1)$$

2.1 Actor-Critic Agent and How it Learns

The DDPG algorithm utilizes an actor-critic neural network architecture. The actor network implements the deterministic policy. The critic approximates the action value function $Q(s,a)$, and the actor network is trained to maximize the value of actions it outputs with respect to the action value function the critic approximates. The mathematical formulation of the actor is therefore $argmax_a Q(s,a)$.

The critic network is trained to minimize the error of action value prediction. An action is valuable for the immediate reward received upon taking it and also for all the rewards received in future for which taking that specific action was critical. Most often, the value of an action is defined as exponentially weighted sum of future rewards:

$$Q(s_t, a_t) = \sum_{i=t}^{\infty} \gamma^i r_{t+i} \qquad (2)$$

where $\gamma \in (0,1)$ is a discount factor that controls preference of close or distant outcomes. The action value of this form can be interpreted as an expected discounted cumulative reward or as an expected discounted return.

An optimal policy picks the most valuable action in each state. For such a policy, the Bellman Equation holds:

$$Q(s_t, a_t) = r_t + \gamma Q(s_{t+1}, a_{t+1}) \qquad (3)$$

We take this relationship as an objective function for training critic network. The approximation error Y_t in a time step t can be obtained by a simple modification:

$$Y_t = Q(s_t, a_t) - (r_t + \gamma Q(s_{t+1}, a_{t+1})) \qquad (4)$$

Since calculation of the error includes the approximated function $Q(s,a)$ itself, the training bootstraps from $Q(s,a) = 0$, or a random distribution of values close to zero.

3 Related Work

The most inspiration we draw from the DDPG [2] algorithm by DeepMind, which was our starting point. This algorithm was already applied to control of robotic arms with 7 degrees of freedom by Gu et al. [3].

Our previous work we tried to apply the DDPG algorithm to the humanoid robot control task, which has shown little success [1]. We continue this work by exploring deeper possible causes of failure. A major one is most likely the regression accuracy. The mean error of the critic network was around 0.7. Considering sample

standard deviation of reward values of around 0.62 this is likely to seriously hurt the learning process while combined with Bellman style propagation of discounted long-term rewards.

The most closely related work to ours is probably an example of learning a humanoid robot to stand up from sitting on a chair by Iida et al. [4]. They also control directly joint torques and use an actor-critic architecture, but with radial basis networks and Temporal Difference critic updates. This means that their critic network approximates the state value function. Its update rule is stated in equation 5.

$$\nabla V(s_t) = r_t + \gamma V(s_{t+1}) - V(s_t) \qquad (5)$$

Unlike Sun and Roos [5] or Tutsoy et al. [6], we do not use animation primitives or inverse kinematics to lower dimensionality of the task. We want to impose no restrictions to the freedom of movements created by learning algorithm. This makes the problem much more challenging and the solution more useful if we are successful. We also do not want to rely on prior knowledge of body dynamics like inverse kinematics. Relying on the model of the specific device makes the method bound to it and makes the solution on the accuracy of the mathematical model. On the other hand, a model-free Reinforcement Learning method has potential to find perfectly working behaviors even for a damaged device with altered dynamics.

Beside the method we explore, there are Evolution Strategies (ES) and Policy Gradient (PG) methods that have also been successful in optimizing policies with continuous state and actions. Our method itself could be called a to PG method as it improves the policy by following its estimated gradient. However, it does so in quite an unusual way compared to classic PG algorithms, as it derives the gradient from a learned action-value $Q(s,a)$ function. Therefore, it is also a Q-Learning approach. The PG and ES methods are all competitive with the DDPG algorithm we started with and they deserve careful evaluation of applicability to NAO too.

Policy Gradient methods use a stochastic policy to generate a batch of randomized trajectories, then propagate discounted returns to all recorded actions and update the policy parameters in the ascent direction of likelihood of greater returns. The Trust Region Policy Optimization algorithm (TRPO) [7], a state of the art PG algorithm, uses Fisher information matrix for parameter scaling independency [8] and Kullback–Leibler divergence to normalize the magnitude of gradient ascent steps.

Salimans et al. [9] achieve comparable results to TRPO in MuJoCo physics simulator locomotion environments. Their approach is an Evolution Strategy, that represents the population by a factored gaussian distribution over weights of the neural network, which implements the policy. As black box optimization methods, Evolution Strategies work only with parameters perturbations and sampled values of the objective function, which is the result of an episode. The lack of per-transition evaluation of the decisions made by the policy is the main difference from PG methods [8]. It also makes them generally less sample efficient. However, they are more suitable for parallelization [9].

4 Approach

In following experiments, we use actor-critic neural network architecture with offline learning from fixed sample of random trajectories. We focus on testing the capability of actor-critic method to infer the correct action from available experience. A sample of trajectories generated by random policy should be enough to infer first few moves from the initial state. A random policy is a policy that samples random actions uniformly over the action space. Having the trajectories pre-generated also speeds up our experiments.

We train without propagating long-term effects by bootstrapping critic with the Bellman equation, as it could be an undesirable source of variance. Therefore, the critic in this case implements a straightforward regression of rewards from state and action pairs, which should be sufficient for tasks in this paper. We implement both networks as multilayer perceptrons with one hidden layer. We compare results of stochastic gradient descend, ADAM optimizer [10] and LBFGS optimizers and some hyperparameters to find a setup that yields stable results.

The expected outcome is a policy that makes a *reliable* partial progress towards moving the robot to the upright posture. The fixed sample of random movements makes it unlikely to accomplish the whole task, as the samples of state and action are concentrated around the starting point and will be missing further along the unknown optimal trajectory.

4.1 Artificial Task

We start parameter exploration with a simpler artificial task to lower computational costs, and make it possible to perform more exhaustive search. More benefits of evaluating on an artificial task include elimination of noise and availability of known optimal policy.

The artificial task is defined as follows:

- *state* - real vector $s \in \mathbb{R}^d$. Represents agents position in a d-dimensional space. Dimensionality d is a parameter of the task.

- *action* - a real vector $a \in \mathbb{R}^d$ of values in range $\in [-1, 1]$. Represents a direction and distance in which the agent wants to move.

- *transition* - $s_{t+1} = s_t + a_t$.

- *reward function* - $r(s, a) = ||s|| - ||s + a||$.

An episode ends when $\exists c \in s; c > 3$, which is considered a failure. The agent has breached the boundary of allowed space. As a successful completion of the task is considered when the agent gets to the zero-position closer than a threshold value: $||s|| < 0.001$.

4.2 Getting up Task

The goal is to achieve a vertical posture of robot's torso. We measure how much a posture is vertical by readings from accelerometer located in torso. In a vertical posture, the acceleration on Z axis of the accelerometer is approximately -9.8 ms^{-2} which equals gravitational acceleration of the earth. To complete this task the robot does not need to stand on its feet necessarily. Any stable sitting posture is enough. The reward function $r(s_t, s_{t+1})$ is defined for every transition from state s_t to state s_{t+1} as the difference of the vertical acceleration (See equation 6). We denote an acceleration measured on axis Z in state s_t as $AccelZ(s_t)$.

$$r(s_t, s_{t+1}) = -(AccelZ(s_{t+1}) - AccelZ(s_t)) \qquad (6)$$

The location of accelerometer in robot's body is shown at the figure 2.

A specific characteristic of this task is no implicit division to episodes. The robot can make some progress towards the goal. Whenever it makes a wrong move, it will fall back to the initial position or some state along the way. This effect of gravity exposes the agent to new states and it is desirable to let the agent go on trying to learn independence of initial position.

We suppose that this nature of the task makes it unfavorable for propagation of discounted return by bootstrapping critic with Bellman equation. After a few rewarding actions, the robot will be in partially upright position, where any imprecise movement can cause fall. While exploring such states with random policy, there will be a strong imbalance between subsequent actions that bring more progress and rewards, and actions that cause the whole progress to be lost. Bootstrapping too early, before the subsequent correct actions have been sampled, will cause incorrect inference of long-term action utility. Therefore, we have decided to train only the immediate reward signal prediction with the critic network.

4.3 Experimental Setup

All experiments take place in Webots simulator with single instance of robot NAO. Figure 1 shows a block diagram of the whole experimental setup for robotic task. Observation of the environment includes:

- 25 joint angles that are to be reached and maintained by servomotors.

- 25 actual measured joint angles

- 3 real values of gyroscope

- 3 real values of accelerometer

- 8 feet force sensors readings

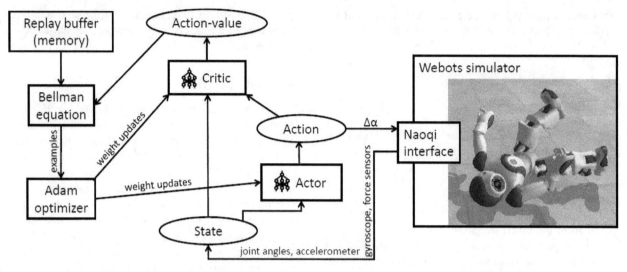

Figure 1: Block diagram of experimental setup. Boxes denote software components, ellipses denote data.

Figure 2: Location of accelerometer in robot's body and its coordinate system.

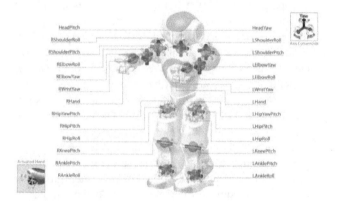

Figure 3: Joints with their degrees of freedom marked.

Some more sensory data are supported but are not available in the Webots simulator (e.g. joint absolute current values). Image from two cameras is also available, but we do not use this input yet.

In this environment, the policy controls directly the torque applied to all 25 actuators in 13 joints. An illustration of robot's joints and their degrees of freedom presented on the figure 3. The action vector $a \in (-1,1)^{25}$ specifies the fraction of maximum torque to be used in positive or negative direction.

The implementation of action in this form for NAO was not straightforward as NAO's API has a built-in feedback control mechanism that maintains specified angles of robot's joints. The API allows to set new posture to be maintained and a torque limit. To simulate direct torque control, we set the torque limit for every joint and compute the change in the maintained angle of i-th joint $\Delta\alpha_i$ by following relationship:

$$\Delta\alpha_i = \omega_{max,i} * a_i * \Delta t \qquad (7)$$

Where the $\omega_{max,i}$ is the maximum rotation velocity of the i-th joint (with full torque) and Δt is a duration of the action. This way we make sure that a joint is being moved with the specified force during the whole interval Δt and reaches its destination angle right at the end of the action time frame.

4.4 Performance Metrics

There are several ways to measure how successful the learned policy is. The more important of all metrics is observation by a human expert. Only human expert is able to tell whether what the robot is doing makes sense. However, it is impossible to evaluate many trained models this way as the time of human expert is precious. Therefore, numerical measures are necessary to compare policies with each other to select a few suitable for evaluating further.

A simple sum of collected rewards is not very informative metric for this task. Recall, that the reward function returns the difference in accelerometer readings between subsequent states. Then, the sum of collected rewards up to timestep t is equal to accelerometer reading in time

Table 1: Action errors achieved with different optimizer combinations

algorithm	critic optimizer	actor optimizer	mean action error mean	mean action error sd	mean maximum action error	maximum action error sd
optimal policy			0.000		0.000	
actor-critic	lbfgs	sgd	0.073	0.2250	0.263	0.3524
actor-critic	lbfgs	adam	0.096	0.1001	0.337	0.2335
actor-critic	adam	sgd	0.134	0.2181	0.381	0.3890
actor-critic	lbfgs	lbfgs	0.188	0.1571	0.532	0.2282
actor-critic	adam	adam	0.199	0.2073	0.558	0.4048
actor-critic	adam	lbfgs	0.272	0.2175	0.648	0.3215
random policy			0.886	0.04277	1.494	0.2632
worst possible policy			1.670	0.01607	2.000	

step t plus the accelerometer reading in the initial state. Suppose there are two policies π_1 and π_2. The policy π_1 reliably achieves half of rewards that lead to target states and falls 10 times during the testing episode. The policy π_2 reliably achieves half of rewards that lead to target states and falls 100 times during the testing episode. Then policy π_1 is obviously better and it is likely to end up with higher score than π_2. However, it is certainly not guaranteed as the final posture of both policies is random variable.

The maximum cumulative reward is also not very informative measure. More precisely, by maximum cumulative reward we mean the highest sum of rewards collected up to some time step of a testing episode. See equation 8 for formal specification.

$$max_t(\sum_{i=0}^{t} r(s_i,a_i)) \qquad (8)$$

This metric does not capture well the stability of learning. Poorly trained models that result in very variable policies can lead the robot near to the target posture occasionally without really learning anything. Therefore, we expect high variance of measurements of this metric.

The metric we consider most informative for the getting up task is mean cumulative reward over all time steps of the test episode. We define the mean cumulative reward as:

$$\frac{\sum_{t=0}^{n}(\sum_{i=0}^{t} r(s_i,a_i))}{n} \qquad (9)$$

is number of time steps where n is number of time steps of test episode. In other words, this metric is an average verticality of robot's posture weighted by time spent in that posture. This metric is favorable to policies that can make progress and also can maintain it or recover quickly after fall.

5 Results

5.1 Artificial Task

A first experiment is presented in Table 1. We have compared different optimization methods of actor and critic

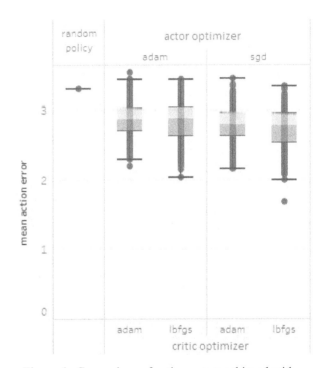

Figure 4: Comparison of action errors achieved with different optimizers for critic and actor respectively for artificial task in 10 dimensions. Random policy as a baseline.

networks for artificial task of 1 dimension. The presented measures are mean and maximum action error during testing episode. All results are averaged over 40 training attempts. The error of an action is computed as a magnitude of difference from known optimal action. For critic and actor 4 hidden units were sufficient for this task. Adding more does not improve performance. The compared optimization methods are ADAM, Limited memory Broyden–Fletcher–Goldfarb–Shanno (lbfgs) and stochastic gradient descend with annealed learning rate.

We include optimal policy, random policy and worst possible policy for comparison. Optimal policy can be easily derived from the artificial task definition. The worst

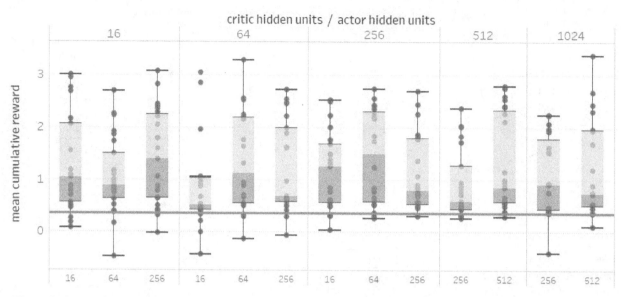

Figure 5: Comparison of results achieved with different critic and actor hidden layer sizes. The red line marks average performance of random policy.

policy can be derived from the same way as the optimal policy and it is the exact opposite of it. The worst policy computes the worst action available in each state. Random policy samples actions uniformly over the action space.

We can see that all configurations produce policies strongly biased towards the optimal policy. In further experiments, we use the top two configurations.

Figure 4 shows the same comparison with artificial task in 10 dimensions. The number of hidden units we needed for these results was 160 for critic and 80 for actor. Adding more hidden units brought only little improvement for considerable computation time cost. Also, number of random action samples was increased from 4000 to 12000. Results on 10-dimensional artificial task also show improvement over random policy. However, the bias towards the optimal policy is significantly weaker compared to 1 dimension. Therefore, we expect even smaller difference between random policy and learned policy for the robot control task.

5.2 Getting up Task

Figure 5 show comparison of results achieved with different number of units in one hidden layer of critic and actor networks. For every configuration, we show mean cumulative reward over testing episode of 20 trained models. This is a very early experiment, so we start from small neural networks to save computation time. All configurations achieved average score much higher than random movements policy. However, the variance between policies trained with the same configuration is high and there can be found policies that perform worse than random. For the best configuration of actor of size 64 and critic of size 256 the improvement over random policy can be confirmed by two sample t-test (p-value: 0.00026).

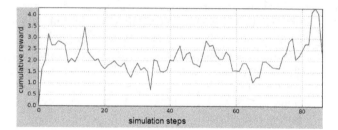

Figure 6: Cumulative reward per simulation step during an example testing episode.

An example of progress made by a trained policy during a testing episode is shown in the Figure 6. This policy achieved mean cumulative reward score of 2.17. The robot made a quick progress in getting off the ground and then was able to maintain it with oscillations. The posture usually reached with the well-trained policy is shown in Figure 7. The robot was able to support its weight with arms and push itself from the ground a bit. Since the first few moves seem to be learned well, it looks reasonable to gather another batch of experience by performing random actions after those few successful steps. An exploration schedule like this would almost certainly end up in a local optimum. Nevertheless, it would be an interesting result in this environment we suspect to be very noisy.

6 Conclusion

We have shown a partial progress in learning humanoid robot control by actor-critic approach. The improvement over random movements policy is clear but rather small. Experiments with artificial task of varying dimensionality show strong performance decrease in higher dimensions despite more data provided. Results show, that more

Figure 7: A reliably reached posture along the path to getting up from the ground.

precise hyperparameter search could bring some improvement of unknown magnitude. Therefore, feasibility of offline actor-critic learning for humanoid robot body control remains an open question.

Acknowledgment

This research has been supported by CTU grant SGS17/213/OHK3/3T/18. Computational resources were provided by the CESNET LM2015042 and the CERIT Scientific Cloud LM2015085, provided under the programme "Projects of Large Research, Development, and Innovations Infrastructures"

References

[1] M. Danel, "Reinforcement learning for humanoid robot control," in *POSTER*, May 2017.

[2] T. P. Lillicrap, J. J. Hunt, A. Pritzel, N. Heess, T. Erez, Y. Tassa, D. Silver, and D. Wierstra, "Continuous control with deep reinforcement learning," *CoRR*, vol. abs/1509.02971, 2015. [Online]. Available: http://arxiv.org/abs/1509.02971

[3] S. Gu, E. Holly, T. P. Lillicrap, and S. Levine, "Deep reinforcement learning for robotic manipulation," *CoRR*, vol. abs/1610.00633, 2016. [Online]. Available: http://arxiv.org/abs/1610.00633

[4] S. Iida, S. Kato, K. Kuwayama, T. Kunitachi, M. Kanoh, and H. Itoh, "Humanoid robot control based on reinforcement learning," in *Micro-Nanomechatronics and Human Science, 2004 and The Fourth Symposium Micro-Nanomechatronics for Information-Based Society, 2004.*, Oct 2004, pp. 353–358.

[5] Z. Sun and N. Roos, "An energy efficient dynamic gait for a nao robot," in *2014 IEEE International Conference on Autonomous Robot Systems and Competitions (ICARSC)*, May 2014, pp. 267–272.

[6] O. Tutsoy, D. E. Barkana, and S. Colak, "Learning to balance an nao robot using reinforcement learning with symbolic inverse kinematic," *Transactions of the Institute of Measurement and Control*, vol. 0, no. 0, p. 0142331216645176, 0. [Online]. Available: http://dx.doi.org/10.1177/0142331216645176

[7] J. Schulman, S. Levine, P. Moritz, M. I. Jordan, and P. Abbeel, "Trust region policy optimization," *CoRR*, vol. abs/1502.05477, 2015. [Online]. Available: http://arxiv.org/abs/1502.05477

[8] F. Stulp and O. Sigaud, "Policy improvement: Between black-box optimization and episodic reinforcement learning," 2013.

[9] T. Salimans, J. Ho, X. Chen, and I. Sutskever, "Evolution Strategies as a Scalable Alternative to Reinforcement Learning," *ArXiv e-prints*, Mar. 2017.

[10] D. P. Kingma and J. Ba, "Adam: A method for stochastic optimization," *CoRR*, vol. abs/1412.6980, 2014. [Online]. Available: http://arxiv.org/abs/1412.6980

J. Hlaváčová (Ed.): ITAT 2017 Proceedings, pp. 78–85
ISBN 978-1974274741, © 2017 J. Kalina, B. Peštová

Nonparametric Bootstrap Estimation for Implicitly Weighted Robust Regression

Jan Kalina, and Barbora Peštová

Institute of Computer Science CAS, Prague, Czech Republic
kalina@cs.cas.cz

Abstract: Implicitly weighted robust regression estimators for linear and nonlinear regression models include linear and nonlinear versions of the least trimmed squares and least weighted squares. After recalling known facts about these estimators, a nonparametric bootstrap procedure is proposed in this paper for estimates of their variances. These bootstrap estimates are elaborated for both the linear and nonlinear model. Practical contributions include several examples investigating the performance of the nonlinear least weighted squares estimator and comparing it with the classical least squares also by means of the variance estimates. Another theoretical novelty is a proposal of a two-stage version of the nonlinear least weighted squares estimator with adaptive (data-dependent) weights.

1 Introduction

Regression methodology has the aim to model (describe, estimate) a continuous variable (response) depending on one or more independent variables (regressors), which may be continuous and/or discrete. Such modelling finds applications in an enormously wide spectrum of applications and allows to predict values of an important variable, which is considered to play the role of the response, for particular values of regressors.

Standard estimation methods in various linear and nonlinear regression models are known to be too vulnerable (sensitive) to the presence of outlying measurements (outliers), which occur in real data for various reasons, e.g. measurement errors, different conditions or violations of assumptions of the model under consideration.

Therefore, numerous robust regression methods have been proposed since the development of robust statistical estimation in 1960s as diagnostic tools for classical methods. Some of them can be understood as reliable self-standing procedures tailor-made to suppress the effect of data contamination by various kinds of outliers [20, 6, 2, 13]. In the course of time, the breakdown point has become one of crucial measures of robustness, which can be interpreted as a high resistance (insensitivity) against outlying measurements in the data and one of crucial measures of robustness of statistical estimators. The finite-sample breakdown point is defined as the minimal fraction of data that can drive an estimator beyond all bounds when set to arbitrary values [13].

While M-estimators represent the most widely used robust statistical methods, they have been criticized for their low breakdown point in linear regression. Thus, other methods with a high value of the breakdown point (asymptotically up to $1/2$) are desirable, which are commonly denoted as highly robust.

This paper is devoted to the question of estimating the variance of highly robust implicitly weighted estimators in linear and nonlinear models, which has not been investigated in literature. After recalling the least weighted squares estimator in Section 2, a bootstrap estimate of its variance is described and illustrated in Section 3. The methodology is further generalized to nonlinear regression in Section 4, where also a two-stage version of the nonlinear least weighted squares estimator is proposed and investigated. Three examples comparing the performance of standard and robust methods in the nonlinear model are presented in a separate Section 5 and conclusions are summarized in Section 6.

2 Least Weighted Squares

This section recalls the least weighted squares estimator, which is one of promising tools estimating parameters of the standard linear regression model

$$Y_i = \beta_0 + \beta_1 X_{i1} + \cdots + \beta_p X_{ip} + e_i, \quad i = 1, \ldots, n. \quad (1)$$

Here, $Y = (Y_1, \ldots, Y_n)^T$ denotes a continuous response, $(X_{1j}, \ldots, X_{nj})^T$ is the j-th regressor for $j = 1, \ldots, p$ and $e_1, \ldots, e_n$ are random errors of the model. The least squares estimator b_{LS} of $\beta = (\beta_0, \ldots, \beta_p)^T$ is well known to be highly vulnerable to the presence of outlying measurements in the data [13]. Therefore, numerous robust regression methods have been proposed as alternatives to the least squares.

The least weighted squares (LWS) estimator of β in the model (1) represents one of available robust estimators, which was proposed in [25]. It is based on implicit weighting of individual observations, down-weighting less reliable observations, which might be potential outliers with a high influence on the results. Thus, if suitable weights are used, it may reach a high breakdown point [12].

The weights are assigned to individual observations after an (implicitly given) permutation, which is determined only during the computation of the estimator. For a given estimate $b = (b_0, b_1, \ldots, b_p)^T \in \mathbb{R}^p$ of β, let a residual be defined as

$$u_i(b) = Y_i - b_0 - b_1 X_{i1} - \cdots - b_p X_{ip}, \quad i = 1, \ldots, n. \quad (2)$$

Squared residuals will be considered in ascending order

$$u^2_{(1)}(b) \leq u^2_{(2)}(b) \leq \cdots \leq u^2_{(n)}(b). \tag{3}$$

The LWS estimator of β denoted as b_{LWS} is defined as

$$\arg\min \sum_{i=1}^{n} w_i u^2_{(i)}(b) \tag{4}$$

over $b \in \mathbb{R}^p$ for specified (given) magnitudes of nonnegative weights $w_1, w_2, \ldots, w_n$. We need to note that the knowledge of these magnitudes is crucial for the estimator to be properly defined (i.e. avoiding a circular definition) as (3) are fixed as well allowing to assign the weights directly to be non-increasing with respect to residuals (cf. [25, 24, 23]). An adaptation of the approximate algorithm of [20] may be used for computing the LWS algorithm.

Concerning the choice of weights, a general recommendation can be given to require the sequence $w_1, \ldots, w_n$ non-increasing with $\sum_{i=1}^{n} w_i = 1$. Some choices (from the simplest to the most complicated) include

- Linearly decreasing weights

$$w_i^{LD} = \frac{2(n-i+1)}{n(n+1)}, \quad i = 1, \ldots, n. \tag{5}$$

- Linearly decreasing weights for a true level of contamination $\varepsilon \cdot 100\,\%$. Let us assume $\varepsilon \in [0, 1/2)$ and $h = \lceil \varepsilon n \rceil$, where

$$\lceil x \rceil = \min\{n \in \mathbb{N}; \ n \geq x\}. \tag{6}$$

The weights equal

$$w_i = \begin{cases} (h-i+1)/h, & i \leq h, \\ 0, & i > h. \end{cases} \tag{7}$$

- Data-dependent adaptive weights of [6]. With such weights, the LWS estimator attains a 100 % asymptotic efficiency of the least squares under Gaussian errors.

Weights according to (7) as well as the adaptive weights of [6] ensure a high breakdown point of the LWS estimator, which cannot be said about weights (5).

The least trimmed squares (LTS) estimator (e.g. [18]) denoted as b_{LTS} represents a special case of the LWS with weights equal either to zero or one. The LTS estimator depends on the value of the trimming constant h, requiring

$$w_{h+1} = \cdots = w_n = 0 \quad \text{and} \quad n/2 < h < n. \tag{8}$$

The advantages of the LWS compared to the LTS include sub-sample robustness, more delicate approach for dealing with moderately outlying values, robustness to heteroscedasticity [23], the possibility to derive diagnostic tools and to define a corresponding robust correlation coefficient or estimator of σ^2 [16, 17].

3 Nonparametric Bootstrap for the LWS

In this section, a new estimate of the variance for the least trimmed squares and least weighted squares estimators is proposed in Section 3.1. The proposal enables a systematic comparison of their estimation performances. An illustration on a real data set is presented in Section 3.2.

3.1 Bootstrap Variance Estimation for the LWS Estimator

The aim of this section is to apply resampling (bootstrap) techniques to estimate $\mathrm{var}\, b_{LTS}$ and $\mathrm{var}\, b_{LWS}$. The resulting bootstrap estimates are conceptually simple and can be computed for real data in a straightforward (although rather computationally demanding) way.

Let us first recall basic principles of bootstrap estimation (bootstrapping), which has found a big popularity in various statistical tasks. In general, bootstrap estimation exploits resampling with replacement. Incorporating the basic principles of bootstrapping, one may develop a great variety of resampling techniques that provide us with new possibilities of analyzing data. The range of bootstrap methods is rather large, including residual bootstrap, nonparametric bootstrap, semiparametric bootstrap, Bayesian bootstrap etc. Also the terminology is not used in a unique way. Unfortunately, not much can be said about properties of bootstrap estimates on a general level. Interesting comparisons of bootstrap procedures in a regression setup (but for the total least squares) were presented in [19], where some bootstrap approaches are valid but some are proven not to be consistent and thus not suitable.

In the specific task of estimating variability of regression estimators, the bootstrapping approach is very suitable. While the seminal work [3] described bootstrap estimation from a philosophical perspective, practical approaches to bootstrapping in linear regression were proposed by subsequent papers [9] or [8]. Other theoretical results were derived in [10, 11].

In this paper, we focus our attention to nonparametric bootstrap. However, a residual bootstrap may be a suitable alternative as well.

Under (1), we recall that

$$\mathrm{var}\, b_{LS} = \sigma^2 (X^T X)^{-1}. \tag{9}$$

An explicit formula for $\mathrm{var}\, b_{LWS}$ could be derived as analogy to [24]. Such result however remains impossible to be directly computed for real data, as it depends on

- Unknown magnitudes of $e_1, \ldots, e_n$,
- The asymptotic value of $(X^T X)/n$, which can be however hardly evaluated for a fixed sample size.

Such approach is also complicated because of the necessity to express the weights by means of a weight function and there is also a more restrictive assumption of normally distributed errors. Therefore, we take resort to a bootstrap estimate of var b_{LWS}. Its computation is described by Algorithm 1, where the final estimate has the form of a bootstrap covariance matrix in step 5. An analogous procedure can be used for estimating var b_{LTS}.

Algorithm 1 Nonparametric bootstrap for the LWS in linear regression.

Input: Data rows $(X_{i1}, \ldots, X_{ip}, Y_i)$, $i = 1, \ldots, n$
Output: Empirical covariance matrix computed from individual estimates of $\hat{\gamma}_{LWS}$
1: Compute the least weighted squares estimator $\hat{\beta}_{LWS}$ of β in model (1)
2: **for** $r = 1$ to R **do** // repeat in order to obtain the empirical distribution
3:   Generate n new bootstrap data rows

$$(_{(r)}X_{j1}^*, \ldots, _{(r)}X_{jp}^*, _{(r)}Y_j^*), \quad j = 1, \ldots, n, \quad (10)$$

   by sampling with replacement from the original set of data rows $(X_{i1}, \ldots, X_{ip}, Y_i)$, $i = 1, \ldots, n$
4:   Consider a linear regression model in the form

$$_{(r)}Y_j^* = _{(r)}\gamma_0 + _{(r)}\gamma_{1\,(r)}X_{j1}^* + \cdots + _{(r)}\gamma_{p\,(r)}X_{jp}^* + _{(r)}v_j \quad (11)$$

   with $j = 1, \ldots, n$ and random errors $v_1, \ldots, v_n$
5:   Estimate $_{(r)}\gamma = (_{(r)}\gamma_0, _{(r)}\gamma_1, \ldots, _{(r)}\gamma_p)^T$ in (11) by the LWS
6:   Store the estimate from the previous step as $_{(r)}\hat{\gamma}_{LWS}$
7: **end for**
8: Compute the empirical covariance matrix from values $_{(r)}\hat{\gamma}_{LWS}$, $r = 1, \ldots, R$

3.2 Example: Linear Model for Investment Data

The aim of the following example is to compare variance estimates of the LWS estimator with variances of other regression estimators. An investment data set that considers a regression of $n = 22$ yearly values of real gross private domestic investments in the USA in 10^9 USD against the GDP is used. We consider a linear model

$$Y_i = \beta_0 + \beta_1 X_i + e_i, \quad i = 1, \ldots, n, \quad (12)$$

while the same data set was previously analyzed (considering another model) in [17].

The computations were performed in R software for the least squares, Huber's M-estimator (see [13]), LTS and LWS. Table 1 presents estimates of the intercept b_0 and slope b_1 together with packages of R software, which were used for the computation. The bootstrap procedure of Section 3.1 was used to find the covariance matrix of various robust regression estimators and the results are also presented in Table 1. There, the standard deviation of all estimates is denoted as s_0 for the intercept and s_1 for the slope.

For the least squares, the bootstrap estimates are very close to the exact result (9). The number of bootstrap repetitions within Algorithm 1 is chosen as 10000, which is

Estimator	b_0 (s_0)	b_1 (s_1)	R package
Least squares	−582 (108.9)	0.239 (0.016)	base
Huber's M-estimator	−576 (135.0)	0.238 (0.020)	MASS
LTS ($h = 13$)	−252 (742.0)	0.185 (0.106)	robustbase
LWS (weights [6])	−465 (207.2)	0.221 (0.031)	own code

Table 1: Results of the example with investment data of Section 3.2. The classical and robust estimates of parameters β_0 and β_1 (without brackets) are accompanied by nonparametric bootstrap estimates of their standard deviation (underneath in brackets) denoted as s_0 and s_1, which were evaluated by the bootstrap procedure of Section 3.1.

sufficient for the asymptotics. Actually, we compared results obtained for 100 bootstrap samples and the results were very close. This is in accordance with our experience and a small number of bootstrap samples indeed seems to be sufficient if a single constant is estimated rather than the whole empirical distribution.

The smallest variance is obtained with the least squares estimator. Huber's M-estimator attains only a slightly higher variance. The loss of the LTS is remarkable. However, we point out at the closeness of the LWS result (computed with weights [6]) to the least squares or Huber's M-estimator compared to the very crude LTS result. Both the LTS and LWS are highly robust, but their performance for this data set without severe outliers reveals a great difference between them in terms of efficiency. The LWS cannot be the winner and must stay behind the least squares, but its retardation is only mild and its superiority against the LTS shows that the LWS (perceived as a generalization of the LTS) eliminates the main disadvantage of the LTS, namely its low efficiency for non-contaminated samples [7].

To the best of our knowledge, the superiority of the LWS compared to the LTS in terms of efficiency has never been presented in the literature. Our result indicates a possibly strong argument in favor of the efficiency of the LWS, at least for a single data set, while no theoretical result on the relative efficiency of LWS compared to LWS is available. Our result is empirical, which is obtained for a rather simplistic data set with only a single regressor, was obtained as an application of the nonparametric bootstrap estimation of the robust regression estimates proposed in Section 3.1.

4 Nonparametric Bootstrap in Robust Nonlinear Regression

In this section, the standard nonlinear regression model is recalled in Section 4.1 and the nonlinear least weighted squares estimator in Section 4.2. A two-stage version of the nonlinear least weighted squares is proposed in Section 4.3 as an extension of the methodology of Section 3.1. In addition, a two-stage version of the nonlinear least weighted squares estimator is proposed and theoretically investigated.

4.1 Nonlinear Regression Model

Let us consider the nonlinear regression model

$$Y_i = f(\beta_1 X_{i1} + \cdots + \beta_p X_{ip}) + e_i, \quad i = 1, \ldots, n, \quad (13)$$

where f is a given continuous nonlinear function, $Y = (Y_1, \ldots, Y_n)^T$ is a continuous response and $(X_{1j}, \ldots, X_{nj})^T$ is the j th regressor for $j = 1, \ldots, p$. By $e_1, \ldots, e_n$ we denote the model's random errors. The classical estimator, which is the nonlinear least squares (NLS) estimator of β, is vulnerable to the presence of outliers in the data.

The nonlinear least trimmed squares (NLTS) estimator represents a natural extension of the LTS estimator to the nonlinear model (13). The breakdown point of the NLTS was derived already in [22], other properties were later investigated in [5]. The estimator may achieve a high robustness, if of course a suitable value of h is used reflecting the true contamination level in the data. An approximate algorithm may be obtained as an extension of the algorithm of [20]; however, it requires a tedious implementation and we are not aware of any implementation of NLTS in statistical software.

4.2 Nonlinear Least Weighted Squares

This section recalls the definition of the nonlinear least weighted squares (NLWS) estimator, which was proposed as our extension of the LWS estimator from the linear regression to the nonlinear model [14] and at the same time a weighted analogy of the NLTS estimator. So far, theoretical properties of the NLWS have not been derived and there is also no evidence in examples showing the robustness and efficiency of the estimator.

In the model (13), let

$$u_i(b) = Y_i - f(b_1 X_{i1} - \cdots - b_p X_{ip}), \quad i = 1, \ldots, n, \quad (14)$$

denote a residual corresponding to the i-th observation for a given estimator $b = (b_1, \ldots, b_p)^T \in \mathbb{R}^p$ of regression parameters $\beta = (\beta_1, \ldots, \beta_p)^T$. Let us now assume the magnitudes $w_1, w_2, \ldots, w_n$ of nonnegative weights to be given. The NLWS estimator of the parameters in the model (1) is defined as

$$\arg \min \sum_{i=1}^{n} w_i u_{(i)}^2(b), \quad (15)$$

where the argument of the minimum is computed over all possible values of $b = (b_1, \ldots, b_p)^T$ and the residuals are arranged as in (3).

The choice of weights has a determining influence on properties of the NLWS estimator. If it is allowed to have zero weights for the most outlying observations, then the estimator can be conjectured to be highly robust, which follows directly from the assignment of implicit weights to the observations in (15). Again, weights (7) (but not (5)) ensure a high breakdown point. The NLWS estimator with such weights is highly robust from the same reasons as the LWS estimator in the linear regression. The main reason for the robustness of the NLWS estimator is the construction of the estimator itself, just like for the LWS estimator in the linear regression.

An approximate algorithm for the optimization task (23) can be obtained as a straightforward adaptation of the LTS algorithm for the linear regression (cf. [20, 14]); nevertheless, its properties in this context have not been investigated. Empirical investigations will be performed on real data sets in Section 5.

4.3 Two-stage NLWS

In this section, a version of the NLWS estimator is proposed, which constructs data-dependent adaptive weights. The estimator has a two-stage structure and is inspired by a two-stage LWS estimator of [6].

Čížek [6] proved his two-stage estimator with quantile-based adaptive weights in the linear model to possess a high breakdown point and at the same time a 100 % asymptotic efficiency of the least squares under Gaussian errors. Further, he evaluated its relative efficiency to be high (over 85 %) compared to maximum likelihood estimators in a numerical study under various distributional models for samples of several tens of observations.

We propose a two-stage estimator denoted as 2S-NLWS which can be described as an improved version of the NLWS estimator which contains a construction of data-dependent adaptive weights. The model (13) is considered. The computation of the 2S-NLWS starts with an initial highly robust estimator $\hat{\beta}^0$ of β and proceeds to proposing values of the weights based on comparing the empirical distribution function of squared residuals with its theoretical counterpart assuming normality.

In the first stage, it is crucial to choose a suitable initial estimator, because it influences the properties of the resulting 2S-NLWS estimator. Therefore, it is recommendable to use a consistent estimator which is highly robust, i.e. NLTS with h between (say) $n/2$ and $3n/4$ or NLWS with weights (7). Residuals of the initial fit will be denoted as $u_1^0, \ldots, u_n^0$. We will need the notation $\left(G_n^0\right)^{-1}$ for the empirical quantile function computed from these residuals, F_χ^{-1} for the quantile function of χ_1^2 distribution and

$$b_n = \min\left\{ \frac{m}{n}; \ u_{(m)}^2 > 0 \right\}. \quad (16)$$

In the second stage, the weights for the 2S-NLWS estimator are constructed. They are defined by means of a weight function $\tilde{w}(t)$ for $t \in [0,1]$, where

$$\tilde{w}(t) = \frac{F_\chi^{-1}(\max\{t, b_n\})}{(G_n^0)^{-1}(\max\{t, b_n\})}. \qquad (17)$$

In other words, weights for a fixed number of observations n are given as

$$\tilde{w}(t) = \frac{F_\chi^{-1}(t)}{(G_n^0)^{-1}(t)} \quad \text{for} \quad t \in \left\{\frac{1}{2n}, \frac{3}{2n}, \ldots, \frac{2n-1}{2n}\right\}. \qquad (18)$$

The computation of the 2S-NLWS estimator is straightforward. In a non-contaminated model, the 2S-NLWS estimator can be easily proven to have a full efficiency of the least squares, just like in the linear case [6].

Theorem 1. *Random vectors $X_1, \ldots, X_n$ are assumed to be independent identically distributed. Let $e_1, \ldots, e_n$ be independent identically distributed, independent on $X_1, \ldots, X_n$ and fulfilling $e_i \sim N(0, \sigma^2)$ for each i. Let the initial estimator $\hat{\beta}^0$ be consistent with a corresponding consistent estimator of σ^2. Then it holds*

$$\tilde{w}(t) \xrightarrow{P} \sigma^2 \quad \text{for each } t \in (0,1), \qquad (19)$$

where $\xrightarrow{P}$ denotes the convergence in probability.

Proof. Analogy of [6]. □

Corollary 1. *Under the assumptions of Theorem 1, the 2S-NLWS estimator $\hat{\beta}_{2S-NLWS}$ fulfils*

$$\hat{\beta}_{2S-NLWS} \xrightarrow{P} \beta. \qquad (20)$$

Concerning other properties of the 2S-NLWS estimator, the breakdown point seems to require much more effort to be derived. Nevertheless, it remains clear that robustness properties of the 2S-NLWS are strongly influenced by those of the initial estimator.

5 Examples on Robust Estimation in Nonlinear Regression

This section presents three examples investigating the performance of various estimators in the nonlinear regression, especially focused on the soundness of the proposed methodology of Section 4. An example illustrating the performance of the NLWS estimator in both non-contaminated and contaminated data is presented in Section 5.1. The next example in Section 5.2 investigates the tightness of an approximate algorithm for computing the NLWS estimator. The final example presented in Section 5.3 exploits the nonparametric bootstrap estimation of the variance of various estimators in the nonlinear regression model.

Estimator	b_1	b_2
Original data set		
NLS	190.8	0.060
NLTS ($h = 18$)	191.6	0.061
NLWS (weights [6])	191.4	0.061
Contaminated data set		
NLS	193.9	0.067
NLTS ($h = 18$)	191.8	0.060
NLWS (weights [6])	191.6	0.061

Table 2: Results of example with real data of Section 5.1. Classical and robust estimators of β_1 and β_2 in the nonlinear regression model are computed in the original as well as contaminated version of the data set.

5.1 Example: Puromycin Data

This example has the aim to compare the performance of classical and robust estimators in the nonlinear model. This will be performed on a real data set without apparent outliers. To show the sensitivity of the NLS and on the other hand the robustness (resistance) of the NLTS and NLWS, the computations are repeated on a modified version of this data set, which contains one outlier.

A standard data set called Puromycin with $n = 23$ observations, which is available in the package `datasets` of R software, is considered. The reaction velocity (rate) Y is explained as a response of the substrate concentration X in the nonlinear regression model

$$Y_i = \frac{\beta_1 X_i}{\beta_2 + X_i} + e_i, \quad i = 1, \ldots, n, \qquad (21)$$

where the aim is to estimate regression parameters β_1 and β_2.

The results of the least squares and NLWS estimators are shown in Table 2. The NLWS estimator turns out to perform reliably on a data set contaminated by outlying measurements as well as on data without such contamination. In addition, we verified the constant $R = 10000$ in Algorithm 1 to be more than sufficient in the nonlinear regression model and a moderate sample size.

Further, we also consider a contaminated data set, obtained by modifying the value of the observation in the Puromycin data set. Particularly, the substrate concentration (i.e. the regressor) of the first observation was modified from 0.02 to 0.05 to become the only outlier in the data set. This reveals the influence of a (local) change of one observation on the results and reveals the true advantage of the robust estimators. Robust estimates namely remain almost unchanged, while the contamination is revealed on the NLS estimator. In other words, the NLS starts to differ from the robust estimators, while all estimates were much more similar for the original data set.

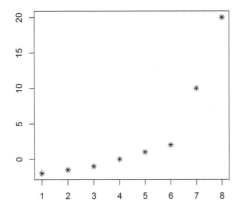

Figure 1: Data in the example of Section 5.2.

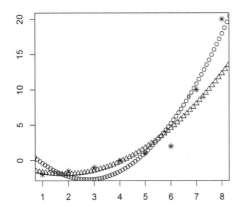

Figure 2: Results of the example of Section 5.2. The NLS (circles) and NLWS (triangles) in the example of Section 5.2.

5.2 Example: Simulated Data

The performance of the NLWS estimator will be now illustrated and investigated on a numerical example with simulated data. The data set consisting of 8 data points is shown in Figure 1. The nonlinear regression model is used in the form

$$Y_i = \beta_0 + \beta_1 (X_i - \beta_2)^2 + e_i, \quad i = 1, \dots, n, \quad (22)$$

where $Y_1, \dots, Y_n$ are values of the response, $X_1, \dots, X_n$ values of the only regressor, β_0, β_1 and β_2 are regression parameters and $e_1, \dots, e_n$ are random errors. Figure 2 shows fitted values corresponding to the NLS fit and also the

| | Loss function | | |
Estimator	(23)	(24)	(25)
NLS	23.44	2.47	1.21
NLTS ($h = 5$)	46.06	1.93	1.11
NLWS (weights (5))	70.94	6.82	0.67

Table 3: Results of the example with simulated data of Section 5.2. Values of various loss functions computed for the NLS, NLTS and NLWS estimators.

NLWS fit with the linearly decreasing weights. The NLS fit has the tendency to fit well also influential data points. The robust fit better explains a subset of data points, while it considers data points corresponding to larger values of the regressor to be outliers.

Table 3 gives values of loss functions

$$\sum_{i=1}^{n} u_i^2(b), \quad (23)$$

$$\sum_{i=1}^{h} u_{(i)}^2(b) \quad (24)$$

and

$$\sum_{i=1}^{n} w_i u_{(i)}^2(b) \quad (25)$$

corresponding to the NLS, NLTS and NLWS, respectively. These are evaluated for all of the three estimates.

The NLS estimator minimizes (23) as expected and thus can be expected to yield also a rather small value of (25). The NLWS estimator has a much larger value of (23) compared to the NLS fit. However, the algorithm used for computing the NLWS has found even a much smaller value of (25) than the NLS. On the whole, the results of Table 3 thus give a clear evidence in favor of the reliability of the algorithm for computing the NLWS estimator.

5.3 Example: Nonlinear Model for Investment Data

The bootstrap based variance estimation procedure described in Section 3.1 can be also utilized in the context of nonlinear regression models. The following example incorporates such an approach in order to compare the variances of the NLS, NLTS, and NLWS estimators.

The validity of the nonparametric bootstrap in linear regression model (i.e., Algorithm 3.1) is, however, going to be verified only via a simulation study. Theoretical justification of the nonparametric bootstrap procedure needs to be provided by a formal proof with properly stated assumptions. In general, bootstrapping should be used with caution, because the nonparametric bootstrap algorithm does not always provide a consistent estimate.

The same data set is used as in Section 3.2. This time, a nonlinear regression model

$$Y_i = \beta_1 (X_i - \bar{X})^2 + \beta_2 X_i + \beta_3 + e_i, \quad i = 1, \dots, n, \quad (26)$$

is considered, where the centering of the regressor using its mean $\bar{X}$ is done for the sake of numerical stability.

Three robust estimators are computed together with bootstrap estimates of their variances. The results are shown in Table 4. The conclusions are analogous to those of the example in Section 3.2, namely the NLTS estimator loses its efficiency very much compared to the NLS. The NLS remains to be the most efficient, i.e. retains the smallest variance for the data set which does not contain severe outliers. Still, the NLWS loses relatively little compared to the NLS while it is able to outperform the NLTS

Estimator	β_1 (s_1)	β_2 (s_2)	β_3 (s_3)
NLS	$3.7 \cdot 10^{-5}$	0.22	98
	$(3.4 \cdot 10^{-5})$	(0.07)	(74)
NLTS ($h = 13$)	$4.1 \cdot 10^{-5}$	0.25	112
	$(1.8 \cdot 10^{-4})$	(0.36)	(381)
NLWS (weights (5))	$4.0 \cdot 10^{-5}$	0.25	107
	$(6.7 \cdot 10^{-5})$	(0.13)	(140)

Table 4: Results of the example of Section 5.3. The classical and robust estimates of parameters $\beta_1, \beta_2, \beta_3$ computed for (26) are shown without brackets and accompanied by bootstrap estimates of their standard deviation denoted as s_1, s_2 and s_3 shown in brackets.

strongly. Thus, we can say that the NLWS estimator is able to combine the robustness with efficiency reasonably well, in comparison to the non-efficient (but much more renowned) NLTS estimator.

6 Conclusions

This paper investigates robust estimator for the linear and nonlinear regression methods and nonparametric bootstrap approaches to estimating its variance. Implicitly weighted estimators are considered, which include the least trimmed squares and least weighted squares (in linear and nonlinear versions).

After recalling the state of the art on implicitly weighted robust estimation in Section 2, a bootstrap method for estimating the variance of the LWS estimator is proposed in Section 3. A numerical example shows the LWS to have a much smaller variance compared to the more popular LTS estimator, which reveals another strong argument in favor of the LWS estimator and questions whether the LTS estimator deserves to be the most common highly robust regression estimator.

Considerations for the linear regression are further generalized to nonlinear regression. Thus, the main contribution can be found in Section 4 on the NLWS estimation, which has not been much investigated in the references so far. Our work is devoted to a bootstrap estimate suitable for estimating the variance of the NLWS estimator. In addition, a new version of the estimator is proposed, which computes data-dependent adaptive weights. Their construction allows to define the 2S-NLWS, which is improved compared to the basic NLWS in terms of efficiency.

Several examples reveal the suitability of the idea of the NLWS for modelling a nonlinear trend in the data. It also follows from the set of examples that an approximate algorithm, which is available for the NLWS, turns out to be reliable. The examples also give a warning that the NLWS estimator behaves in a rather intricate way and the estimator is much more complex compared to linear regression.

We also computed nonparametric bootstrap estimate of the variance of nonlinear estimators. These empirical results allow us to conclude that there seems a major advantage of the NLWS compared to the NLTS, although the NLS remains to be recommendable for data without severe outliers. The NLWS seems to be close to a reasonable combination of the efficiency (for normal regression errors) with high robustness (for models with contamination), which represents a dream of robust statisticians since the dawn of robust statistical inference.

The examples investigated in this paper lead us also to formulating the following disadvantages of robust estimators in nonlinear regression:

- They require various tuning constants with a difficult interpretation;
- Various robust methods yield rather different results;
- Computational intensity;
- Robustness only with respect to outliers but not to a misspecification of the model.

Important limitations of the robust nonlinear estimation include a non-robustness to small modifications of the nonlinear function f in the model (see [2]). Robust nonlinear estimators also require rather tedious proofs of their properties.

Some of the properties of robust estimators valid in the linear regression are not valid in the nonlinear model at all. As an example let us mention diagnostic tools, which can be derived for robust estimators in linear regression, but would be rather controversial in the nonlinear model [15]. The results on simulated data in Section 5.2 reveal that the residuals are far from homoscedasticity, even if the assumption of homoscedastic disturbances in the regression model is fulfilled. Thus, we find residuals to be unsuitable for making conclusions about the disturbances (random errors). While tests from the linear regression are no longer valid for the NLWS estimator, we do not recommend to use residuals even for a subjective diagnostics concerning the disturbances.

We intend to apply the robust regression methods of this paper within a future research in the area of metalearning, which aims at comparing the suitability of various machine learning methods for different data. Robustifying metalearning for regression methods is however not only a matter of using robust regression methods, but the process of metalearning itself suffers from instability [21] and a robust analogy of the whole process of metalearning is highly desirable to be performed in a complex and systematic way.

Acknowledgments

The project was supported by the project 17-01251S "Metalearning for extracting rules with numerical consequents" of the Czech Science Foundation.

References

[1] Agresti, A.: Analysis of ordinal categorical data. 2nd edn., Wiley, New York, 2010

[2] Baldauf, M., Silva, J.M.C.S.: On the use of robust regression in econometrics. Economic Letters **114** (2012) 124–127

[3] Bickel, P.J., Freedman, D.A.: Some asymptotic theory for the bootstrap. Annals of Statistics **9** (1981) 1196–1217

[4] Brazdil, P., Giraud-Carrier, C., Soares, C., Vilalta, E.: Metalearning: Applications to data mining. Springer, Berlin, 2009

[5] Čížek, P.: Least trimmed squares in nonlinear regression under dependence. Journal of Statistical Planning and Inference **136** (2006) 3967–3988

[6] Čížek, P.: Semiparametrically weighted robust estimation of regression models. Computational Statistics & Data Analysis, **55** (2011) 774–788

[7] Čížek, P.: Reweighted least trimmed squares: An alternative to one-step estimators. Test **22** (2013) 514–533

[8] Efron, B., Tibshirani, R.J.: An introduction to the bootstrap. Chapman & Hall/CRC, Boca Raton, 1994

[9] Freedman, D.A., Peters, S.C.: Bootstrapping a regression equation: Some empirical results. Journal of the American Statistical Association **79** (1984) 97–106

[10] Godfrey, L.: Bootstrap tests for regression models. Palgrave Macmillan, London, 2009

[11] Hall, P., DiCiccio, T.J., Romano, J.P.: On smoothing and the bootstrap. Annals of Statistics **17** (1989) 692–704

[12] Jurczyk, T.: Ridge least weighted squares. Acta Universitatis Carolinae Mathematica et Physica **52** (2011) 15–26

[13] Jurečková, J., Sen, P.K., Picek, J.: Methodology in robust and nonparametric statistics. CRC Press, Boca Raton, 2012

[14] Kalina, J.: Some robust estimation tools for multivariate models. Proceedings International Days of Statistics and Economics MSED 2015, Melandrium, Slaný, 2015, 713–722.

[15] Kalina, J.: On robust information extraction from high-dimensional data. Serbian Journal of Management **9** (2014) 131–144

[16] Kalina, J.: Implicitly weighted methods in robust image analysis. Journal of Mathematical Imaging and Vision **44** (2012) 449–462

[17] Kalina, J.: Least weighted squares in econometric applications. Journal of Applied Mathematics, Statistics and Informatics **5** (2009) 115–125

[18] Mount, D.M., Netanyahu, N.S., Piatko, C.D., Silverman, R., Wu, A.Y.: On the least trimmed squares estimator. Algorithmica **69** (2014) 148–183

[19] Pešta, M.: Total least squares and bootstrapping with application in calibration. Statistics: A Journal of Theoretical and Applied Statistics **47** (2013) 966–991

[20] Rousseeuw, P.J., van Driessen, K.: Computing LTS regression for large data sets. Data Mining and Knowledge Discovery **12** (2006) 29–45

[21] Smith-Miles, K., Baatar, D., Wreford, B., Lewis, R.: Towards objective measures of algorithm performance across instance space. Computers and Operations Research **45** (2014) 12–24

[22] Stromberg A.J., Ruppert, D.: Breakdown in nonlinear regression. Journal of the American Statistical Association **87** (1992) 991–997

[23] Víšek J.Á.: Consistency of the least weighted squares under heteroscedasticity. Kybernetika **47** (2011) 179–206

[24] Víšek J.Á.: The least trimmed squares, Part III: Asymptotic normality. Kybernetika **42** (2006) 203–224

[25] Víšek J.Á.: Regression with high breakdown point. In Antoch J., Dohnal G. (Eds.): Proceedings of ROBUST 2000, Summer School of JČMF, JČMF and Czech Statistical Society, Prague, 2001, 324–356.

J. Hlaváčová (Ed.): ITAT 2017 Proceedings, pp. 86–92
ISBN 978-1974274741, © 2017 F. Knöll, V. Simko

Organizational Information improves Forecast Efficiency of Correction Techniques

Florian Knöll[1] and Viliam Simko[2]

[1] Karlsruhe Institute of Technology (KIT),
Fritz-Erler-Straße 23, 76133 Karlsruhe, Germany
knoell@kit.edu

[2] FZI Research Center for Information Technology at the Karlsruhe Institute of Technology,
Haid-und-Neu-Str. 10-14, 76131 Karlsruhe, Germany
simko@fzi.de

Abstract: Financial services within corporations have an essential need for accurate forecasts. In corporations, experts typically generate judgmental cash flow forecasts in a decentralized fashion and provide data that is important in corporate risk management. But the accuracy of these forecasts is most likely reduced by biases of the organizational structure. As for the importance of cash flow forecasts, usually correction techniques are applied with statistical methods based on historical data. In most cases the organizational biases are not included into the correction techniques. This paper argues that disregarding the organizational information actually decreases forecast efficiency. Forecast efficiency provides statistical information for the amount of structure within forecasts and errors. In case of aggregated cash flows in accounting, the forecasts highly depend on return margins. The empirical results in this paper show that debiasing with forecasts correction based on organizational information can improve forecast efficiency by 56 % to a statistical approach. The reduction of inefficient pattern show statistics arguing for forecast correction that rely on organizational biases (standard deviation of error 0.20) instead of basic statistical approaches that harm forecast efficiency (standard deviation of error 0.28).

1 Introduction

Corporations with global operations typically generate forecasts for cash flow items on a regular basis (e.g., monthly or quarterly), at different organizational levels, business divisions, and countries. These forecasts are often generated in a decentralized fashion by the subsidiaries, where the subsidiaries send thousands of item-level forecasts and revisions to corporate headquarters. These forecasts are then consolidated and used in crucial tasks of the corporate finance department (such as in [14] or even to access with cash flow forecasts the company's stock market value [13]).

The tasks in corporate departments strongly depend on the quality of the forecasts, as they provide the data base for the financial planning operations and subsequent management activities. For instance, due to forecast inaccuracies, the corporate hedging to reduce foreign exchange risks will result in increased costs or uncovered currency risks.

1.1 The Problem of Judgmental Forecasts

Usually, cash flow forecasts result from the judgment of human experts [24] and are revised several months or quarters after the initial forecast until the date of the actual realization finalizes the sequence of forecasts. The initial forecast and the sequence of adjusted forecasts is referred to as *forecasting process*, while the sequence of adjustments in revisions is usually coined as *revisioning process* or simply *revisioning*. When judgmental forecasting takes place, the forecasts can be prone to individual biases and latent human factors that entail forecasting processes in many ways [16, 18]. Additionally, the organizational structures and dependencies of the environment can change the forecaster's expectation, resulting in *organizational biases* that result in forecast inaccuracies [6].

1.2 Correction Techniques and Organizational Biases

Improving biased forecasts is possible with forecast correction techniques that analyze and change the human prediction with statistical models [12]. For instance, [15] found dependencies of timing and magnitude of cash flow revisions. Their results state that cash flow forecast processes are more accurate when they show a high revision at a late state of the process compared to a high revision at the early stage.

However, current forecast correction techniques often employ solely statistical methods – leaving out the organizational biases for approaches of forecast improvement. In corporate finance, several important key performance indicators (KPI) exist that aggregate many figures. An example of such key figure is *Earnings Before Interest, Taxes, Depreciation, and Amortization* (EBITDA) margin, which can be used as one of the primary proxies for a company's current operating profitability [19]. When humans try to achieve personal objectives (e.g., bonus payments by financial incentives) predefined targets that rely on these figures, for instance percentage return margins, these organizational biases can alter forecasts and their adjustments in a revisioning process [11].

In addition, in the realm of cash flows, several business functions might influence the realization volume of cash flows. The looming failure to meet earnings targets (which might reduce manager's bonus payments) is an incentive to hold-back invoices received within term of credit. Alternatively, managers can trigger invoices issued earlier or might change payment terms in order to align annual cash results with targets. Conversely, if earning targets have been met already, there might be an incentive to delay the issuing of invoices until the next year to increase the probability of meeting next year's targets. In particular, the papers of [4], [7], and [5] show that realizations are often shifted according to earnings management policies. When the volumes are shifted, the forecast errors can be expected to exhibit a systematic bias.

1.3 Efficiency Theory

Biases often translate to observable patterns in forecasting processes and one measurement to analyze the systematic behavior of revisioning is the *efficiency theory*. The theory in market finance [10] and forecasting [22] suggest that processes are efficient if they describe a random walk. The theory states that non-random walks promote inefficient forecasting since correlations among revisions with revisions or errors are expected to show statistical insufficiency that has the potential to anticipate future adjustments or errors. The application of this theory provides evidence that correlations exist in many cases [2, 17, 1, 9, 8].

1.4 Our Contribution

This paper argues that efficiency provides a statistical tool to evaluate different correction approaches. The analysis of efficiency figures can provide insights for the differences of model predictions. The analyses for accounting cash flows contribute to the current research as they show that including organizational information into correction models is key for further improvements in correction techniques. When the empirical outcomes of these organizational models are compared to purely statistical model approaches they show that both models reduce the error, but the disregard of organizational information in the purely statistical approach does crucially harm the forecast efficiency. Moreover, this insight is also applicable to other domains, where exploratory data analysis and forecast correction play an important role in time series forecasting.

1.5 Structure of the Paper

The remainder of the paper is structured as follows. The data description in Section 3 is followed by the notation that is introduced in Section 4. Section 5 describes the design for the empirical analysis and the concept of forecast efficiency in detail. Section 6 presents the results and interpretation of the analysis. In Section 7 discusses the implications of this work for future improvements in forecast correction.

2 Related Work

Organizational biases can result in forecast inaccuracies as pointed out by Daniel et al. [6] but does not correct them in any way. He identified "dividend thresholds" as a organizational bias, which alters the forecasts.

In the paper [21], the authors analyzed short time series within the year and used a Bayesian method to account for sub-seasonal information for the seasonal based correction. In contrast to their setting, our forecast series are even shorter (5 reference points instead of 12), the application of linear regression models (instead of Bayesian models), and we account for one single information in our paper focuses a margin target at the end of year (instead of the whole sub-annual pattern).

Regarding seasonality, Yelland [27] concludes that a simple stable seasonal pattern model can perform surprisingly well, if it uses "theory-free" descriptions of booking processes. His findings are in resonance to the theme that simple empirically-based models do frequently better than complex ones.

The authors of [3] promote that in marketing and finance simple models sometimes predict more accurately than complex models. The authors argue that "the benefits of simplicity are often overlooked because the importance of the bias component of prediction error is inflated, and the variance component of prediction error (based on oversensitivity to different samples) is neglected." Reasoned by their study, we correct the forecasts with a simple linear regression model.

3 Empirical Cash Flow Data

The data stems from a record of cash flow forecasts and realizations provided by a multinational sample corporation. With over 100,000 employees, the company generates annual revenues in the billion Euro range. The corporation is headquartered in Germany, but has worldwide more than 300 separate legal entities. The subsidiaries are grouped into four distinct divisions (D1 – D4), based on their business portfolios.

Each subsidiary operates officially independently of the corporation, while there are some organizational dependencies. First, based on the set of local plans, the corporation re-adjusts the planning to an overall view, and sets the target requirements for local operations for being rated as a "successful" subsidiary. Second, in the corporation the fiscal year ends in December and the subsidiaries that meet targets is assumed to be most pronounced at the end of the year. Third, as the subsidiaries operate independently, they have their own financial information system, a heterogeneous payment structure (e.g., incentivization bonuses) and have to ensure liquidity for their operations (e.g., with earnings management processes). Fourth, each subsidiary that is participating in the forecasting process – mostly large-volume entities – enters its expectations on future cash flow in a digital, corporate-based forecasting system.

Financial risk management is centralized, with the local subsidiaries reporting cash flows to the corporation's central finance department, where these serve as the basis for further actions in corporate finance. Therefore, the corporate finance department receives cash flow forecasts (*forecasts*) generated by the subsidiaries worldwide, denominated in foreign currencies. After the realization date, the corporation receives in every month the cash flow figures for realizations (*actuals*). The data available cover itemtypes of invoices issued (*II*) and invoices received (*IR*) from the corporate IT system. In order to evaluate possible strategies and provide further information for KPI figures such as percentage return ratio the forecasts and actuals are aggregated for the corporate risk management. As a proxy for the percentage return margin within a fiscal year, the entity's *ratio* of aggregated revenues (II) and expenses (IR) is calculated.

The aggregated data set used in the analysis for this paper covers forecasts and actual for the entity's ratios. Delivered by the subsidiaries on a quarterly basis, the forecasts cover intervals with horizons of up to 15 months (five quarters). The dataset for actual invoices ranges from January 2008 to December 2013 with the corresponding forecasts covering the actuals' period.

In total, actuals and forecasts are available for the 67 largest subsidiaries resulting in 25 different currencies for the dataset. Actuals grouped by division, subsidiary, currency and item-type result in 72 actual time series. Overall, the dataset consists of 3,087 monthly invoice actuals, with five associated forecasts each. The underlying raw dataset of non-aggregated forecasts cover 102.360 items. Table 1 gives a brief summary of the dataset.

4   Notation and Forecasting Process

The notation presented in this section is commonly used in current literature on [22].

Denoting the actual of cash flow margin ratio as $_0R$, the lead time $t > 0$ of a forecast $_tR$ for $_0R$ refers to a quarter of the year until the actual date ($t = 0$). Figure 1 visualizes the temporal structure of an example forecasting process in five steps for an actual $_0R$. The initial forecast ratio $_5R$ is delivered with a lead time of five periods and is revised four times until the last one–period–ahead forecast $_1R$ is generated.

Since ratios are specific for an entity, for reasons of comparability, this work focuses on normalized ratios (Def. 1). Therefore, the notation $_tR$ refers to the normalized ratio instead of the entity specific ratio ($_tR := _tR^{(E)}$).

Definition 1 (Normalized ratio). *Normalized ratio is obtained by subtracting the minimum ratio within an entity from R and dividing by the difference of its maximum and minimum ratio. The values are always between zero and one per entity.*

$$_tR_{y=Y,m=M}^{(E)} = \frac{_tR_{y=Y,m=M}^{entity=E} - min(\bigcup R)}{max(\bigcup R) - min(\bigcup R)}$$

while:

$$\bigcup R = \{_tR_{date}^{entity} : entity = E \wedge date < (Y,M)\}$$

Definition 2 (Target ratio). *The suggested annual return target (*target ratio*) that an entity has to reach at the end of the year $y = Y$ is defined as:*

$$T(_0R_{y=Y})$$

As targets are unknown (to us), but business development measured with EBITDA figures seem rather stable over the years, the target ratio in $y = Y$ is estimated by averaging the December actual ratios of the three preceding years ($_0R_{y=Y-j,m=12}$, for $j \in \{1,2,3\}$).

Definition 3 (Revision). *The revision for ratios describes the adjustment from the second to last forecast before the actual. It is formally defined as;*

$$_{12}R = _1R - _2R$$

This paper uses the last revision because generally the latest judgmental forecast incorporates the most information and is the most accurate [20].

Definition 4 (Difference from target). *The difference from target is defined as:*

$$TargetDiff = T(_0R) - _1R$$

Definition 5 (Error). *Finally, the* error *is defined as:*

$$_tE = _0R - _tR$$

Table 2 gives a brief overview of the defined metrics.

5   Research Design

Improving forecast accuracy is an important goal, where usually correction techniques such as linear regressions are applied in the literature for analysis and correction of biases. These statistical forecast correction techniques build models that usually employ information of basic features based on historical data. An example of such a basic statistic model can be found in Def 6. Here, the forecast error $_1E$ is regressed using basic variables such as regression intercept, ratio $_1R$, and revision $_{12}R$. Theoretically valid, this model optimizes the error based on the human forecaster's prediction and revisioning behavior. But, this paper argues that correction approaches should incorporate important organizational information too. As noted before, reaching predefined target KPIs is an important strategic goal. The difference to the percentage return margin target is symbolized with *TargetDiff* and measures the distance to the organizational prerequisites. To overcome this organizational bias, the information of *TargetDiff* is integrated into the regression model as shown in Def 7.

Table 1: The summary of the analyzed cash flow data.

Divisions	Subsidiaries	Currencies	Time Series	Actuals	Forecasts
D1	10	7	11	618	3090
D2	13	8	15	608	3040
D3	6	4	7	420	2100
D4	38	20	39	1441	7205
All	67	25	72	3087	15435

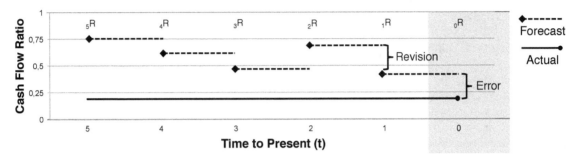

Figure 1: Temporal structure of margin ratio forecasts $_tR$ ($t > 0$) with the corresponding actual margin ratio $_0R$.

Table 2: Notation used in the analyses.

Notation	Metric
$_tR$	Forecast Ratio (normalized)
$TargetDiff$	Difference from target
$_0R$	Actual Ratio (normalized)
$_{12}R$	Revision
$T(_0R)$	Target
$_tE$	Error

Definition 6 (Basic statistic model M_{Basic}).

$$_1E \sim \beta_0 + \beta_1(_1R) + \beta_2(_{12}R)$$

Definition 7 (Organizational model M_{Orga}).

$$_1E \sim \beta_0 + \beta_1(_1R) + \beta_2(_{12}R) + \beta_3(TargetDiff)$$

Typically, correction techniques evaluate their results with some error metric, such as error (deviation), absolute error, percentage error, absolute percentage error, and so on. Slightly different use cases can favor a specific error measure as most of them have known flaws that suit one case but not the other ones. The research presented in this paper tries to be independent of those restrictions that make comparison of scientific results difficult and hinders reproducibility. Therefore, the comparison of both models is evaluated in an error-metric-independent way.

Based on the efficiency theory [22], proposed tests for the structure in terms of correlations amongst revisions and between revisions and errors. Forecast processes that show no correlation structures (with significant p-values)

are considered as *weak-form efficient*. Otherwise, existing structures hint to information that could be incorporated into revisions because revisions are predictable. With $t \in \mathbb{R}_0^+$ denoting the lead-time to the realization of an actual (at $t = 0$), Nordhaus suggests testing for weak-form efficiency using the Propositions (P1) and (P2).

Proposition 1 (P1). *Forecast error at t is independent of all revisions up to $(t+1)$.*

Proposition 2 (P2). *Forecast revision at t is independent of all revisions up to $(t+1)$.*

Combining the argumentation for organizational debiasing and efficiency, the authors propose the following hypotheses:

Hypothesis 1. *Does forecast correction that incorporates organizational information (that organizationally biases forecasts) improve forecast efficiency?*

Hypothesis 2. *How does efficiency for organizational correction differ from basic statistical approaches?*

These hypotheses are evaluated based on the two regression models. Both models are trained for each month of the year independently to consider the seasonality in the business data. Therefore, the data is split into 12 subsets that are accessed to train one specific model for each month (resulting in 24 models). To show the benefit of the organizational information empirically, the model prediction needs to add the original forecast $_1R$ to derive a new model prediction. These model predictions will then be compared to the original forecasts ($M_\varnothing$ symbolizes the expert forecast) and with each other in terms of forecast efficiency. The baseline for comparison is the original forecast based on $M_\varnothing$, which will be evaluated first. For reasons of clarity, the model forecast substitutes the original forecast, which leads to three possible forecast processes "$_5R$, $_4R$, $_3R$, $_2R$, $_1R(M_{\{\varnothing,Orga,Basic\}})$, $_0R$" with changed revision and error measures for $_{12}R$ and $_1E$ depending on the selected model. Logically, the evaluation focuses on these changed measurements only. Additionally, the indication for error quantiles and statistics for efficiency are provided.

6 Empirical Analysis

This section presents the empirical results. These consist of correlation analysis for efficiency, with a revision and error analysis, followed by the analysis of the underlying statistics. For the correlation analysis the experiments use the R programming language [23] and the libraries `corrplot` [25] and `knitr` [26].

As noted before, the forecast efficiency is an important goal of forecasting processes. The forecast efficiency of the resulting prediction of the models M_{Orga} and M_{Basic} are compared to each other and the baseline $M_\varnothing$. The baseline of forecast efficiency for $M_\varnothing$ is shown in Figure 2. It should be noted that in the figures, we hide irrelevant cells (marked using "x" sign) and we show all and only the cells relevant for the efficiency analysis as proposed in [22].

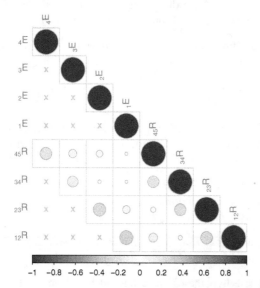

Figure 2: Shows correlation of revisions with errors and revisions of experts, without any correction (baseline model $M_\varnothing$).

The comparison of models $M_\varnothing - M_{Basic}$ and $M_{Basic} - M_{Orga}$ (difference in correlation) are depicted in Figure 3 and Figure 4 respectively.

The Figure 3 shows that the basic statistical model increases efficiency (marked in blue) compared to the baseline by $(_{12}R,_1E) = 92\%$ and $(_{23}R,_1E) = 70\%$. But, all the other dependencies have decreased efficiency (marked

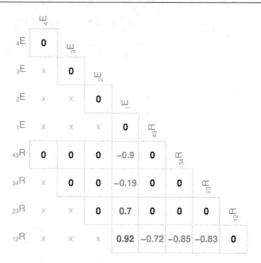

Figure 3: Shows percentage improvement in correlation of a basic statistical model M_{Basic} over the baseline model $M_\varnothing$ (positive numbers exemplify the improvement).

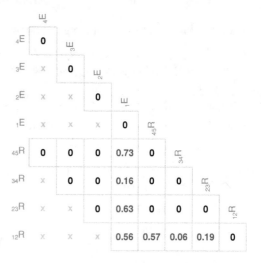

Figure 4: Shows percentage improvement in correlation of our organizational model M_{Orga} over the baseline model M_{Basic} (positive numbers exemplify the improvement).

in red). Comparison between the basic statistical model and the organizational model in Figure 4 shows an additional increase of efficiency relative to M_{Basic} by 56% for the final forecast. More remakable, the whole forecasting process is more efficient (see $(_{12}R,_{23}R)$, $(_{12}R,_{34}R)$ and $(_{12}R,_{45}R)$) stating that the organizational debiasing approach is superior to the basic statistical approaches.

The Figure 5 shows important information for the error quantiles of the forecasts. This figure also provides additional support for the performance of M_{Orga} through the $_1E$ measure. The organizational model outperforms the statistical model especially for the 1. quartile ($\Delta = 0.072$), median ($\Delta = 0.017$), and 3. quartile ($\Delta = 0.120$). Only for minimum, maximum, and for mean error ($\Delta = 0.002$) the statistical model seems beneficial.

The results for $Cor(_{12}R,_1E)$ are not significant after cor-

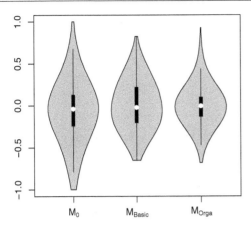

Figure 5: Quantiles of error $_1E$ of the expert and the statistically / organizationally corrected forecasts.

rection due to the high efficiency, but the details are shown in Table 3. The Spearman covariance for the approaches states that revisions and error have a lower joint variability. The organizational model has a positive covariance, while the statistical model has a negative covariance with a higher magnitude. Also, the table shows that organizational model increases standard deviation for the revision, but it reduces for the error. It is arguable with these numbers that the organizational model's revision focuses with meaningful revisions on the reduction of the error, while the statistical model's revision focuses on changing the error with minor corrections. This enables future approaches to detect other, currently unknown biases to be identified and removed.

Overall, the results state several advantages of the organizational model in comparison to the statistical model. First, in the sense of Nordhaus the organizational debiasing model improves forecast efficiency for $Cor(_{12}R, _1E)$, supporting Hypothesis 1. Second, the error distribution is narrowed, especially for the 1st and 3rd Quartile. Third, the advantage of bias reduction instead of error optimization. The second and third finding support Hypothesis 2.

7   Conclusions and Outlook

Empirical analyses on forecast efficiency or on cash flow biases might be a very interesting paper topic for the specific research communities and therefore easy to find. However, linking these settings to forecast correction techniques that account for organizational biases in a predictive model have not been explored in the forecast community so far.

This research addresses two research gaps: (1) Linking organizational information to forecast correction techniques and evaluating the result independently from a specific error metric. The results show that organizational information is beneficial to forecast efficiency. (2) Analyses of correction models that compare basic statistical approaches to organizational approaches have been left unattended.

This study contributes with the conclusion that the different results for corrective models may be inherent to each approach.

Relevance for the Data Mining Community

For the data mining community the paper might change the understanding of the link between exploratory data analysis and forecast correction. Exploring data can actually show the way how to correct forecasts in a model-independent way. We would like to stress that the results of this paper were not achieved with a neural network, a random forest, or a complex machine learning algorithm. Instead, the results are achieved with a simple linear regression models.

The importance of exploratory data analysis is strengthened as data understanding additionally allows a differentiation between biases with pattern and errors.

The most important result of this study is probably the statement that a basic statistical model "just" tries to optimize the selected component (e.g. the error), while an organizational model tries to reduce the bias itself. As a result of the organizational model enables the possibility to identify further unknown biases and correct these biases with a second model. Understanding the error components is important. When a forecaster distinguishes the signal from the noise, the error should decrease by the way or making predictions more confident. Therefore, even if no error decrease is achieved with one organizational debiasing model, a patch of models for the most important organizational biases will definitely increase the accuracy.

Managerial Implications

From the perspective of a manager and forecast researcher it is important to understand in which way business-related factors may affect forecasts and indirectly correction models. In the case of cash flow forecasts in a corporate setting one important factors is the percentage margin target, as these might provide incentivization to alter forecasts and actuals of cash flows. The underlying value of this information is stated in terms of forecast efficiency. The analysis showed that efficiency increases.

Based on this research, application of the presented approach would be interesting also for forecasting in other domains. The efficiency theory could provide an alternative approach to understand the value of specific information within forecast correction (compared to other measures such as entropy or information gain).

Outlook

It might be reasonable to recommend in the forecasting community that future approaches shall not minimize the error component, by changing forecasts and revisions marginally. Instead, maximization or at least the change of forecasts and revisions in an acceptable big magnitude that

Approach	Covariance($_{12}R,_1E$)	Std.Dev.($_{12}R$)	Std.Dev.($_1E$)
$M_\varnothing$ (Baseline)	-246092.58	0.24	0.34
M_{Orga} (Organizational)	8968.19	0.28	0.20
M_{Basic} (Statistical)	-20360.87	0.21	0.28

Table 3: Table shows metric details for Spearman correlation values of the revision and the error in ratio of the expert and the organizationally / statistically corrected forecasts.

result in marginally errors is recommended. A high revision will determine how long the forecast result is aligned to the bias pattern. Based on the results, the understanding of forecasts and best applied correction techniques is obtained on the way.

References

[1] Masahiro Ashiya. Testing the Rationality of Forecast Revisions Made by the IMF and the OECD. *Journal of Forecasting*, 25(1):25–36, 2006.

[2] D. A. Bessler and J. A. Brandt. An Analysis of Forecasts of Livestock Prices. *Journal of Economic Behavior & Organization*, 18(2):249–263, 1992.

[3] Henry Brighton and Gerd Gigerenzer. The Bias Bias. *Journal of Business Research*, 68(8):1772–1784, 2015.

[4] David Burgstahler and Ilia Dichev. Earnings Management to Avoid Earnings Decreases and Losses. *Journal of Accounting and Economics*, 24(1):99–126, 1997.

[5] David Burgstahler and Michael Eames. Management of Earnings and Analysts' Forecasts to Achieve Zero and Small Positive Earnings Surprises. *Journal of Business Finance & Accounting*, 33(5–6):633–652, 2006.

[6] N. D. Daniel, D. J. Denis, and L. Naveen. Do Firms Manage Earnings to Meet Dividend Thresholds? *Journal of Accounting and Economics*, 45(1):2–26, 2008.

[7] Francois Degeorge, Jayendu Patel, and Richard Zeckhauser. Earnings Management to Exceed Thresholds. *Journal of Business*, 72(1):1–33, 1999.

[8] Bruno Deschamps and Christos Ioannidis. Can Rational Stubbornness Explain Forecast Biases? *Journal of Economic Behavior & Organization*, 92:141–151, 2013.

[9] Jonas Dovern and Johannes Weisser. Accuracy, Unbiasedness and Efficiency of Professional Macroeconomic Forecasts: An Empirical Comparison for the G7. *International Journal of Forecasting*, 27(2):452–465, 2011.

[10] E. F. Fama. Efficient Capital Markets: A Review of Theory and Empirical Work. *The Journal of Finance*, 25(2):383–417, 1970.

[11] F. Guidry, A. J. Leone, and S. Rock. Earnings-Based Bonus Plans and Earnings Management by Business-Unit Managers. *Journal of Accounting and Economics*, 26(1):113–142, 1999.

[12] Jiawei Han, Jian Pei, and Micheline Kamber. *Data Mining: Concepts and Techniques*. Elsevier, 2011.

[13] S. N. Kaplan and R. S. Ruback. The Valuation of Cash Flow Forecasts: An Empirical Analysis. *The Journal of Finance*, 50(4):1059–1093, 1995.

[14] C. S. Kim, D. C. Mauer, and A. E. Sherman. The Determinants of Corporate Liquidity: Theory and Evidence. *Jour. of Financial and Quant. Analysis*, 33(3):335–359, 1998.

[15] Florian Knöll, Verena Dorner, and Thomas Setzer. Relating Cash Flow Forecast Errors to Revision Patterns. In *Proc. of MKWI*, pages 1217–1228. MKWI - Prescriptive Analytics in IS, Universitätsverlag Ilmenau, 2016.

[16] Michael Lawrence, Paul Goodwin, Marcus O'Connor, and Dilek Önkal. Judgmental Forecasting: A Review of Progress Over the Last 25 Years. *International Journal of Forecasting*, 22:493–618, 2006.

[17] Michael Lawrence and Marcus O'Connor. Sales Forecasting Updates: How Good are They in Practice? *International Journal of Forecasting*, 16(3):369–382, 2000.

[18] J. Leitner and U. Leopold-Wildburger. Experiments on Forecasting Behavior with Several Sources of Information– A Review of the Literature. *European Journal of Operational Research*, 213(3):459–469, 2011.

[19] B. Marr. *Key Performance Indicators (KPI): The 75 Measures Every Manager Needs to Know*. Pearson UK, 2012.

[20] S. K. McNees. The Role of Judgment in Macroeconomic Forecasting Accuracy. *International Journal of Forecasting*, 6(3):287–299, 1990.

[21] M. Mendoza and E. de Alba. Forecasting an accumulated series based on partial accumulation ii: A new bayesian method for short series with stable seasonal patterns. *International Journal of Forecasting*, 22(4):781–798, 2006.

[22] W. D. Nordhaus. Forecasting Efficiency: Concepts and Applications. *The Review of Economics and Statistics*, 69(4):667–674, 1987.

[23] R Core Team. *R: A Language and Environment for Statistical Computing*. Vienna, Austria: R Foundation for Statistical Computing., 2013.

[24] N. R. Sanders and K. B. Manrodt. The Efficacy of Using Judgmental Versus Quantitative Forecasting Methods in Practice. *Omega*, 31(6):511–522, 2003.

[25] Taiyun Wei and Viliam Simko. *corrplot: Visualization of a Correlation Matrix*, 2016. R package version 0.77.

[26] Yihui Xie. *knitr: A Comprehensive Tool for Reproducible Research in R*. Chapman and Hall/CRC, 2014. ISBN 978-1466561595.

[27] P. M. Yelland. Stable Seasonal Pattern Models for Forecast Revision: A Comparative Study. *International Journal of Forecasting*, 22(4):799–818, 2006.

J. Hlaváčová (Ed.): ITAT 2017 Proceedings, pp. 93–99
ISBN 978-1974274741, © 2017 M. Kopp, M. Nikl, M. Holeňa

Breaking CAPTCHAs with Convolutional Neural Networks

Martin Kopp[1,2], Matěj Nikl[1], and Martin Holeňa[1,3]

[1] Faculty of Information Technology, Czech Technical University in Prague
Thákurova 9, 160 00 Prague
[2] Cisco Systems, Cognitive Research Team in Prague
[3] Institute of Computer Science, Academy of Sciences of the Czech Republic
Pod Vodárenskou věží 2, 182 07 Prague

Abstract: This paper studies reverse Turing tests to distinguish humans and computers, called CAPTCHA. Contrary to classical Turing tests, in this case the judge is not a human but a computer. The main purpose of such tests is securing user logins against the dictionary or brute force password guessing, avoiding automated usage of various services, preventing bots from spamming on forums and many others.

Typical approaches to solving text-based CAPTCHA automatically are based on a scheme specific pipeline containing hand-designed pre-processing, denoising, segmentation, post processing and optical character recognition. Only the last part, optical character recognition, is usually based on some machine learning algorithm. We present an approach using neural networks and a simple clustering algorithm that consists of only two steps, character localisation and recognition. We tested our approach on 11 different schemes selected to present very diverse security features. We experimentally show that using convolutional neural networks is superior to multi-layered perceptrons.

Keywords: CAPTCHA, convolutional neural networks, network security, optical character recognition

1 Introduction

The acronym CAPTCHA[1] stands for Completely Automated Public Turing test to tell Computers and Humans Apart, and was coined in 2003 by von Ahn et al [20]. The fundamental idea is to use hard AI problems easily solved by most human, but unfeasible for current computer programs. Captcha is widely used to distinguish the human users from computer bots and automated scripts. Nowadays, it is an established security mechanism to prevent automated posting on the internet forums, voting in online polls, downloading files in large amounts and many other abusive usage of web services.

There are many available captcha schemes ranging from classical text-based over image-based to many unusual custom designed solutions, e.g. [3, 4]. Because most of the older schemes have already been proven vulnerable to attacks and thus found unsafe [7, 19] new schemes are being invented. Despite that trend, there are still many places where the classical text-based schemes are used as the main or at least as a fallback solution. For example, Google uses the text-based schemes when you fail in their newer image-based ones.

This paper is focused on automatic character recognition from multiple text-based CAPTCHA schemes using artificial neural networks (ANNs) and clustering. The ultimate goal is to take a captcha challenge as an input while outputting transcription of the text presented in the challenge. Contrary to the most prior art, our approach is general and can solve multiple schemes without modification of any part of the algorithm.

The experimental part compares the performance of the shallow (only one hidden layer) and deep (multiple hidden layers) ANNs and shows the benefits of using a convolutional neural networks (CNNs) multi-layered perceptrons (MLP).

The rest of this paper is organised as follows. The related work is briefly reviewed in the next section. Section 3 surveys the current captcha solutions. Section 4 presents our approach to breaking captcha challenges. The experimental evaluation is summarised in Section 5 followed by the conclusion.

2 Related Work

Most papers about breaking captcha heavily focus on one particular scheme. As an example may serve [11] with preprocessing, text-alignment and everything else fitted for the scheme reCapthca 2011. To our knowledge, the most general approach was presented in [7]. This approach is based on an effective selection of the best segmentation cuts and presenting them to *k*-nn classifier. It was tested on many up-to-date text-based schemes with better results than specialized solutions.

The most recent approaches use neural networks [19]. The results are still not that impressive as the previous approaches, but the neural-net-based approaches improve very quickly. Our work is based on CNN, being motivated by their success in pattern recognition, e.g. [6, 14].

The Microsoft researcher Chellapilla who intensively studied human interaction proofs stated that, depending on the cost of the attack, automated scripts should not be more successful than 1 in 10 000 attempts, while human success rate should approach 90% [10]. It is generally considered a too ambitious goal, after the publication of [8] showing

---

[1]The acronym captcha will be written in lowercase for better readability.

the human success rate in completing captcha challenges and [9] showing that random guesses can be successful. Consequently, a captcha is considered compromised when the attacker success rate surpasses 1%.

3   Captcha Schemes Survey

This section surveys the currently available captcha schemes and challenges they present.

3.1   Text-Based

The first ever use of captcha was in 1997 by the software company Alta-Vista, which sought a way to prevent automated submissions to their search-engine. It was a simple text-based test which was sufficient for that time, but it was quickly proven ineffective when the computer character recognition success rates improved. The most commonly used techniques to prevent automatic recognition can be divided into two groups called anti-recognition features and anti-segmentation features.

The anti-recognition features such as different sizes and fonts of characters or rotation was a straightforward first step to the more sophisticated captcha schemes. All those features are well accepted by humans, as we learn several shapes of letters since childhood, e.g. handwritten alphabet, small letters, capitals. The effective way of reducing the classifier accuracy is a distortion. Distortion is a technique in which ripples and warp are added to the image. But excessive distortion can make it very difficult even for humans and thus the usage of this feature slowly vanishes being replaced by anti-segmentation features.

The anti-segmentation features are not designed to complicate a single character recognition but instead they try to make the automated segmentation of the captcha image unmanageable. The first two features used for this purpose were added noise and confusing background. But it showed up that both of them are bigger obstacle for humans than for computers and therefore, they where replace by occlusion lines, an example can be seen in Figure 1. The most recent anti-segmentation feature is called negative kerning. It means that the neighbouring characters are moved so close to each other that they can eventually overlap. It showed up that humans are still able to read the overlapping text with only a small error rate, but for computers it is almost impossible to find a right segmentation.

Figure 1: Older Google reCaptcha with the occlusion line.

3.2   Audio-Based

From the beginning, the adoption of captcha schemes was problematic. Users were annoyed with captchas that were hard to solve and had to try multiple times. The people affected the most were those with visual impairments or various reading disorders such as dyslexia. Soon, an alternative emerged in the form of audio captchas. Instead of displaying images, a voice reading letters and digits is played. In order to remain effective and secure, the captcha has to be resistant to automated sound analysis. For this purpose various background noise and sound distortion are added. Generally, this scheme is now a standard alternative option on major websites that use captcha.

3.3   Image-Based

Currently, the most prominent design is image-based captcha. A series of images showing various objects is presented to the user and the task is to select the images with a topic given by a keyword or by an example image. For example the user is shown a series of images of various landscapes and is asked to select those with trees, like in Figure 2. This type of captcha has gained huge popularity especially on touchscreen devices, where tapping the screen is preferable over typing. In the case of Google reCaptcha there are nine images from which the $4-6$ are the correct answer. In order to successfully complete the challenge a user is allowed to have one wrong answer.

Figure 2: Current Google reCaptcha with image recognition challenge.

Relatively new but fast spreading type of image captcha combines the pattern recognition task presented above with object localisation. Also the number of squares was increased from 9 to 16.

3.4   Other Types

In parallel with the image-based captcha developed by Google and other big players, many alternative schemes appeared. They are different variations of text-based schemes hidden in video instead of distorted image, some simple logical games or puzzles. As an example of an easy to solve logical game we selected the naughts and crosses, Figure 3. All of those got recently dominated by Google's noCaptcha button. It uses browser cookies, user profiles and history to track users behaviour and distinguish real users from bots.

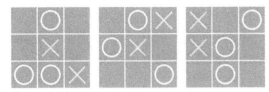

Figure 3: A naughts and crosses game used as a captcha.

4   Our Approach

Our algorithm has two main stages localisation and recognition. The localisation can be further divided into heat map generation and clustering. Consequently, our algorithm consist of three steps:

1. Create a heat map using a sliding window with an ANN, that classifies whether there is a character in the center or not.

2. Use the k-means algorithm to determine the most probable locations of characters from the heat map.

3. Recognize the characters using another specifically trained ANN.

4.1   Heatmap Generation

We decided to use the sliding window technique to localize characters within a CAPTCHA image. This approach is well known in the context of object localization [16]. A sliding window is a rectangular region of fixed width and height that *slides* across an image. Each of those windows serve as an input for a feed-forward ANN with a single output neuron. Its output values are the probability of its input image having a character in the center. Figure 4 shows an example of such heat map. To enable a character localization even at the very edge of an image one can expand each input image with black pixels.

Figure 4: Example of a heat map for a challenge generated by scheme s16.

4.2   Clustering

When a heat map is complete, all points with value greater than 0.5 are added to the list of points to be clustered. As this is still work in progress we simplified the situation by knowing the number of characters within the image in advance and therefore, knowing the correct number of clusters k, we decided to use k-means clustering to determine windows with characters close to their center. But almost an arbitrary clustering algorithm can be used, preferably some, that can determine the correct number of clusters.

The k centroids are initialized uniformly from left to right, vertically in the middle, as this provides a good initial estimation. Figure 5 illustrates the whole idea.

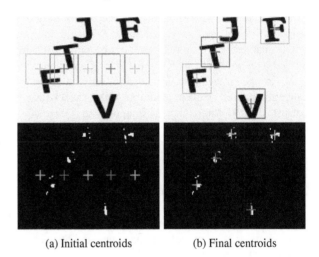

(a) Initial centroids   (b) Final centroids

Figure 5: Heatmap clustering on random character locations

4.3   Recognition

Assuming that the character localization part worked well, windows containing characters are now ready to be recognized. This task is known to be easy for computers to solve; in fact, they are even better than humans [10].

Again, a feed-forward ANN is used. This time with an output layer consisting of 36 neurons to estimate the probability distribution over classes: numbers 0–9 and uppercase letters A–Z. Finally, a CAPTCHA transcription is created by writing the recognized characters in the ascending order of their x-axis coordinates.

5 Experimental Evaluation

This section describes the selection of a captcha suite and generation of the labelled database, followed by a detailed description of the artificial neural networks used in our experiments. The last part of this section presents results of the experiments.

5.1 Experimental Set up

Training an ANN usually requires a lot of training examples (in the order of millions in the case of a very deep CNN). It is advised to have at least multiple times the number of all parameters in the network [13]. Manually downloading, cropping and labelling such high number of examples is infeasible. Therefore, we tested three captcha providers with obtainable source code to be able to generate large enough datasets: Secureimage PHP Captcha [5], capchas.net [2] and BotDetect captcha [1]. We selected the last one as it provides the most variable set of schemes.

BotDetect CAPTCHA is a paid, up-to-date service used by many government institutions and companies all around the world [1]. They offer a free licence with an access to obfuscated source codes. We selected 11 very diverse schemes out of available 60, see Figure 6 for example of images, and generated 100.000 images cropped to one character for each scheme. The cropping is done to 32x32 pixel windows, which is the size of a sliding window. Cropped images are then used for training of the localization as well as the recognition ANN. The testing set consist of 1000 whole captcha images with 5 characters each.

Schemes display various security features such as random lines and other objects occluding the characters, jagged or translucent character edges and global warp. The scheme s10 - *Circles* stands out with its colour inverting randomly placed circles. This property could make it harder to recognize than others, because the solver needs to account for random parts of characters and their background switching colours.

5.2 Artificial Neural Networks

The perceptron with single hidden layer (SLP), the perceptron with three hidden layers (MLP) and the convolutional neural networks were tested in the localization and recognition. In all ANNs, rectified linear units were used as activation functions.

First experiment tested the influence of the number of hidden neurons of a SLP. The number of hidden neurons used for the localization network was $lns=\{15,30,60,90\}$ and the number of neurons for the recognition network was $rns=\{30,60,120,180,250\}$. The results depicted in Figure 7 show the recognition rate for 1000 whole captcha images (all characters have to be correctly recognized) on the scheme s10. The scheme s10 was selected because we consider it the most difficult one.

(a) Snow (s04)   (b) Stitch (s08)

(c) Circles (s10)   (d) Mass (s14)

(e) BlackOverlap (s16)   (f) Overlap2 (s18)

(g) FingerPrints (s25)   (h) ThinWavyLetters (s30)

(i) Chalkboard (s31)   (j) Spiderweb (s41)

(k) MeltingHeat2 (s52)

Figure 6: Schemes generated by the BotDetect captcha

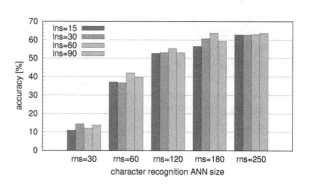

Figure 7: Comparison of SLP recognition rate on the scheme s10, depending on the number of neuron use by the localization network (lns) and the recognition network (rns).

The next experiments was the same but the MLP with three hidden layers was used instead of SLP. Results, depicted in Figure 8, suggest that adding more hidden layers does not improve accuracy of the localization neither of the recognition. Therefore, the rest experiments were done using SLP as it can be trained faster.

Both CNNs architectures resemble the LeNet-5 presented in [17] for handwritten digits recognition. The localization CNN consists of two convolutional layers with six and sixteen 5x5 kernels, each of them followed by the

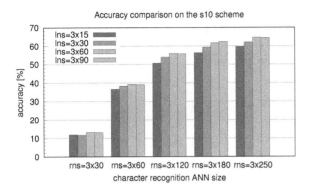

Figure 8: Comparison of MLP recognition rate on the scheme s10, depending on the number of neuron use by the localization network (lns) and the recognition network (rns).

Table 1: Results of the statistical test of Friedman [12] and the correction for simultaneous hypotheses testing by Holm [15] and Shaffer [18]. The rejection thresholds are computed for the family-wise significance level $p = 0.05$ for a single scheme.

Algorithms	p	Holm	Shaffer
SLP+SLP vs. CNN+CNN	7.257e-7	0.0083	0.0083
SLP+SLP vs. SLP+CNN	1.456e-4	0.01	0.0166
CNN+SLP vs. CNN+CNN	5.242e-4	0.0125	0.0166
CNN+SLP vs. SLP+CNN	0.020	0.0166	0.0166
SLP+SLP vs. CNN+SLP	0.137	0.025	0.025
SLP+CNN vs. CNN+CNN	0.247	0.05	0.05

2x2 max pooling layers, and finally, the last layer of the network is a fully connected output layer.

The recognition CNN contains an additional fully-connected layer with 120 neurons right before the output layer as illustrated in Figure 9.

5.3 Results

After choosing the right architectures, we followed by testing the accuracy of captcha transcription on each scheme separately where both training and testing sets were generated by the same scheme. All images in the test set contained 5 characters and only the successful transcription of all of them was accepted as a correct answer. The results, depicted in Figure 10, show appealing performance of all tested configurations. In the most cases it doesn't matter if the localization network was a SLP or a CNN, but the CNN clearly outperforms the SLP in the role of a recognition network. This observation is also confirmed by the statistical test of Friedman [12] with corrections for simultaneous hypothesis testing by Holm[15] and Shaffer [18], see Table 1.

A subsequent experiment tested the accuracy of captcha transcription when training and testing sets consist of im-

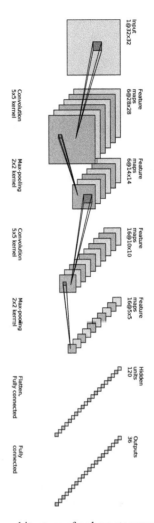

Figure 9: The architecture of a character recognition CNN.

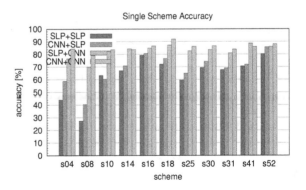

Figure 10: The accuracy of captcha image transcription separately for each scheme.

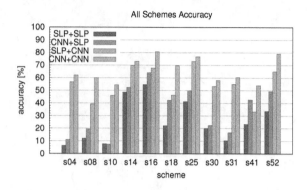

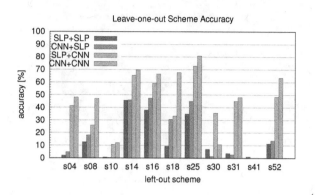

Figure 11: The accuracy of captcha image transcription when example images generated by all schemes were available in the training and test sets.

Figure 12: The accuracy of captcha image transcription in leave-one-scheme-out scenario.

ages generated by all schemes. Both training and testing set contained examples generated by all schemes. The results are depicted in Figure 11. In this experiment the CNN outperformed the SLP not only in the recognition but even in the localization accuracy. The most visible difference is on schemes s08, s18, s41. Overall performance is again compared by the statistical test with results summarized in Table 2. All accuracies are lower than in the previous experiment, as the data set complexity grown (data were generated by multiple schemes), but the number of training examples remained the same.

Table 2: Results of the statistical test of Friedman [12] and the correction for simultaneous hypotheses testing by Holm [15] and Shaffer [18]. The rejection thresholds are computed for the family-wise significance level $p = 0.05$ for all schemes.

Algorithms	p	Holm	Shaffer
SLP+SLP vs. CNN+CNN	1.259e-7	0.0083	0.0083
CNN+SLP vs. CNN+CNN	2.799e-4	0.01	0.0166
SLP+SLP vs. SLP+CNN	9.569e-4	0.0125	0.0166
SLP+CNN vs. CNN+CNN	0.047	0.0166	0.0166
SLP+SLP vs. CNN+SLP	0.098	0.025	0.025
CNN+SLP vs. SLP+CNN	0.098	0.05	0.05

The last experiment tested the accuracy of captcha transcription in leave-one-scheme-out scenario. The training set contained images generated by only 10 schemes and the images used for testing were all generated by the last yet unseen scheme. Trying to recognize characters from images generated by an unknown scheme is a challenging task, furthermore the schemes were selected to differ form each other as much as possible. The results are depicted in Figure 12. All configurations using a perceptron as the recognition classifier fail in all except the most simple schemes, e.g. s12 and s16. The combination of two CNNs is the best in all cases, with only exception being the scheme s30, where the combination of the localization

perceptron and the recognition CNN is the best. Overall, the accuracy may seem relatively low, especially for schemes s10, s30, s31 and s41, but lets recall that recognition rate of 1% is already considered enough to compromise the scheme. The failure of CNNS on scheme s41 is understandable as the spiderweb background confuses the convolutional kernels learned on other schemes.

This is the most important experiment showing the ability to solve yet unseen captcha .The ranking of all algorithms is summarized in Table 3 and the statical tests in Table 4.

Table 3: Average Rankings of the algorithms

Algorithm	Ranking
CNN+CNN	1.27
SLP+CNN	2.00
CNN+SLP	3.27
SLP+SLP	3.45

Table 4: Results of the statistical test of Friedman [12] and the correction for simultaneous hypotheses testing by Holm [15] and Shaffer [18]. The rejection thresholds are computed for the family-wise significance level $p = 0.05$ for the leave-one-scheme-out scenario.

Algorithms	p	Holm	Shaffer
SLP+SLP vs. CNN+CNN	7.386e-5	0.0083	0.0083
CNN+SLP vs. CNN+CNN	2.799e-4	0.01	0.0166
SLP+SLP vs. SLP+CNN	0.008	0.0125	0.0166
CNN+SLP vs. SLP+CNN	0.020	0.0166	0.0166
SLP+CNN vs. CNN+CNN	0.186	0.025	0.025
SLP+SLP vs. CNN+SLP	0.741	0.05	0.05

The above experiments show that most of current schemes can be compromised using two convolutional networks or a localization perceptron and a recognition CNN.

6   Conclusion

In this paper, we presented a novel captcha recognition approach, which can fully replace the state-of-the art scheme specific pipelines. Our approach not only consists of less steps, but it is also more general as it can be applied to a wide variety of captcha schemes without modification. We were able to compromise 10 out of 11 using two CNNs or a localization perceptron and a recognition CNN without previously seeing any example image generated by that particular scheme. Furthermore, we were able to break all 11 captcha schemes using a CNN for the localization as well as for the recognition, with the accuracy higher than 50% when we included example images of each character generated by the particular scheme into the training set. Lets recall that 1% recognition rate is enough for a scheme to be considered compromised.

We experimentally compared the ability of SLP, MLP and CNN to transcribe characters from captcha images. According to our experiments, CNNs performs much better in both localization and recognition.

Acknowledgement

The research reported in this paper has been supported by the Czech Science Foundation (GAČR) grant 17-01251 and student grant SGS17/210/OHK3/3T/18.

References

[1] Botdetect captcha generator [online], 2017. www.captcha.com [Cited 2017-06-01].

[2] Free captcha-service [online], 2017. www.captchas.net [Cited 2017-06-01].

[3] Metal captcha, 2017. www.heavygifts.com/metalcaptcha [Cited 2017-06-01].

[4] Resisty captcha, 2017. www.wordpress.org/plugins/resisty [Cited 2017-06-01].

[5] Secureimage php captcha [online], 2017. www.phpcaptcha.org [Cited 2017-06-01].

[6] Jimmy Ba, Volodymyr Mnih, and Koray Kavukcuoglu. Multiple object recognition with visual attention. In *International Conference on Learning Representations*, 2015.

[7] Elie Bursztein, Jonathan Aigrain, Angelika Moscicki, and John C Mitchell. The end is nigh: Generic solving of text-based captchas. In *8th USENIX Workshop on Offensive Technologies (WOOT 14)*, 2014.

[8] Elie Bursztein, Steven Bethard, Celine Fabry, John C Mitchell, and Dan Jurafsky. How good are humans at solving captchas? a large scale evaluation. In *2010 IEEE Symposium on Security and Privacy*, pages 399–413. IEEE, 2010.

[9] Elie Bursztein, Matthieu Martin, and John Mitchell. Text-based captcha strengths and weaknesses. In *Proceedings of the 18th ACM conference on Computer and communications security*, pages 125–138. ACM, 2011.

[10] Kumar Chellapilla, Kevin Larson, Patrice Simard, and Mary Czerwinski. Designing human friendly human interaction proofs (hips). In *Proceedings of the SIGCHI conference on Human factors in computing systems*, pages 711–720. ACM, 2005.

[11] Claudia Cruz-Perez, Oleg Starostenko, Fernando Uceda-Ponga, Vicente Alarcon-Aquino, and Leobardo Reyes-Cabrera. Breaking recaptchas with unpredictable collapse: heuristic character segmentation and recognition. In *Pattern Recognition*, pages 155–165. Springer, 2012.

[12] Milton Friedman. The use of ranks to avoid the assumption of normality implicit in the analysis of variance. *Journal of the american statistical association*, 32(200):675–701, 1937.

[13] Ian Goodfellow, Yoshua Bengio, and Aaron Courville. *Deep Learning*. MIT Press, 2016. http://www.deeplearningbook.org.

[14] Ian Goodfellow, Yaroslav Bulatov, Julian Ibarz, Sacha Arnoud, and Vinay Shet. Multi-digit number recognition from street view imagery using deep convolutional neural networks. In *International Conference on Learning Representations*, 2014.

[15] Sture Holm. A simple sequentially rejective multiple test procedure. *Scandinavian journal of statistics*, pages 65–70, 1979.

[16] CH. Lampert, MB. Blaschko, and T. Hofmann. Beyond sliding windows: Object localization by efficient subwindow search. In *CVPR 2008*, pages 1–8, Los Alamitos, CA, USA, 2008. Max-Planck-Gesellschaft, IEEE Computer Society.

[17] Yann LeCun, Léon Bottou, Yoshua Bengio, and Patrick Haffner. Gradient-based learning applied to document recognition. *Proceedings of the IEEE*, 86(11):2278–2324, 1998.

[18] Juliet Popper Shaffer. Multiple hypothesis testing. *Annual review of psychology*, 46(1):561–584, 1995.

[19] F. Stark, C. Hazırbaş, R. Triebel, and D. Cremers. Captcha recognition with active deep learning. In *GCPR Workshop on New Challenges in Neural Computation*, 2015.

[20] Luis Von Ahn, Manuel Blum, Nicholas J Hopper, and John Langford. Captcha: Using hard ai problems for security. In *Advances in Cryptology—EUROCRYPT 2003*, pages 294–311. Springer, 2003.

J. Hlaváčová (Ed.): ITAT 2017 Proceedings, pp. 100–105
ISBN 978-1974274741, © 2017 V. Kůrková

Bounds on Sparsity of One-Hidden-Layer Perceptron Networks

Věra Kůrková

Institute of Computer Science, Czech Academy of Sciences
vera@cs.cas.cz,
WWW home page: http://www.cs.cas.cz/~vera

Abstract: Limitations of one-hidden-layer (shallow) perceptron networks to sparsely represent multivariable functions is investigated. A concrete class of functions is described whose computation by shallow perceptron networks requires either large number of units or is unstable due to large output weights. The class is constructed using pseudo-noise sequences which have many features of random sequences but can be generated using special polynomials. Connections with the central paradox of coding theory are discussed.

1 Introduction

To identify and explain efficient network designs, it is necessary to develop a theoretical understanding to the influence of a proper choice of network architecture and type of units on reducing network complexity. Bengio and LeCun [5], who recently revived the interest in deep networks, conjectured that "most functions that can be represented compactly by deep architectures cannot be represented by a compact shallow architecture". On the other hand, a recent empirical study demonstrated that shallow networks can learn some functions previously learned by deep ones using the same numbers of parameters as the original deep networks [1].

It is well-known that shallow networks with merely one hidden layer of computational units of many common types can approximate within any accuracy any reasonable function on a compact domain and also can exactly compute any function on a finite domain [9, 22]. All these universality type results are proven assuming that numbers of network units are potentially infinite or, in the case of finite domains, are at least as large as sizes of the domains. However, in practical applications, various constraints on numbers and sizes of network parameters limit feasibility of implementations.

Whereas many upper bounds on numbers of units in shallow networks which are sufficient for a given accuracy of function approximation are known (see, e.g, the survey article [10] and references therein), fewer lower bounds are available. Some bounds hold merely for types of computational units that are not commonly used (see, e.g., [20, 19]). Proofs of lower bounds are generally much more difficult than derivation of upper ones.

Characterization of tasks which can be computed by considerably sparser deep networks than shallow ones requires proving lower bounds on complexity of shallow networks which are larger than upper bounds on complexity of deep ones. An important step towards this goal is exploration of functions which cannot be computed or approximated by shallow networks satisfying various sparsity constraints.

Investigation of sparsity of artificial neural networks has a biological motivation. A number of studies confirmed that only a small fraction of neurons have a high rate of firing at any time (sparse activity) and that each neuron is connected to only a limited number of other neurons (sparse connectivity) [17]. The most simple measure of sparse connectivity between hidden units and network outputs is the number of non zero output weights. This number is in some literature called "l_0-pseudo-norm". However, it is neither a norm nor a pseudo-norm. Its minimization is a not convex problem and its solution is NP-hard [23]. Thus instead of "l_0-pseudo-norm", l_1 and l_2-norms have been used as measures of network sparsity as they can be implemented as stabilizers in weight-decay regularization techniques (see, e.g., [8] and references therein). Also in online dictionary learning, l_1-norms were used as stabilizers [21, 7].

Bengio et al. [4] suggested that a cause of large model complexities of shallow networks might be in the "amount of variations" of functions to be computed. In [14], we presented some examples showing that sparsity of shallow networks computing the same input-output functions strongly depends on types of their units. We proposed to use as a measure of sparsity variational norms tailored to dictionaries of computational units. These norms were used as tools in nonlinear approximation theory. We showed that variational norms can be employed to obtain lower bounds on sparsity measured by l_1-norms. For many dictionaries of computational units, we derived lower bounds on these norms using a probabilistic argument based on the Chernoff Bound [14, 15]. The bounds hold for almost all functions representing binary classifiers on sufficiently large finite domains. In [13] we complemented these probabilistic results by a concrete construction of binary classifiers with large variational norms with respect to signum perceptrons.

In this paper, we investigate sparsity of shallow networks computing real-valued functions on finite rectangular domains. Such domains can be 2-dimensional (e.g., pixels of photographs) or high-dimensional (e.g., digitized high-dimensional cubes), but typically they are quite large. We describe a construction of a class of functions on such domains based on matrices with orthogonal rows. Estimating variational norms of these functions from bellow, we obtain lower bounds on l_1-norms of shallow networks with signum perceptrons. We show that these networks must have either large numbers of hidden units or some of their output weights must be large. Both are not desirable as large output weights ma lead to non stability of computation. We illustrate our general construction by a concrete class of circulant matrices generated by pseudo-noise sequences. We discuss the effect of pseudo-randomness on network complexity.

The paper is organized as follows. Section 2 contains basic concepts on shallow networks and dictionaries of computational units. In Section 3, sparsity is investigated in terms of l_1-norm and norms tailored to computational units. In Section 4, a concrete construction of classes of functions with large variational norms based on orthogonal matrices is described. In Section 5, the general results are illustrated by a concrete example of matrices obtained from pseudo-noise sequences. Section 6 is a brief discussion.

2 Preliminaries

One-hidden-layer networks with single linear outputs (*shallow networks*) compute input-output functions from sets of the form

$$\mathrm{span}_n\, G := \left\{ \sum_{i=1}^{n} w_i g_i \,|\, w_i \in \mathbb{R}, g_i \in G \right\},$$

where G, called a *dictionary*, is a set of functions computable by a given type of units, the coefficients w_i are called output weights, and n is the number of hidden units. This number is the simplest measure of *model complexity*.

In this paper, we focus on representations of functions on finite domains $X \subset \mathbb{R}^d$. We denote by

$$\mathscr{F}(X) := \{f \,|\, f : X \to \mathbb{R}\}$$

the *set of all real-valued functions on* X. On $\mathscr{F}(X)$ we have the Euclidean inner product defined as

$$\langle f, g \rangle := \sum_{u \in X} f(u)g(u)$$

and the Euclidean norm

$$\|f\| := \sqrt{\langle f, f \rangle}.$$

We investigate networks with units from the dictionary of *signum perceptrons*

$$P_d(X) := \{\mathrm{sgn}(v \cdot . + b) : X \to \{-1, 1\} \,|\, v \in \mathbb{R}^d, b \in \mathbb{R}\}$$

where $\mathrm{sgn}(t) := -1$ for $t < 0$ and $\mathrm{sign}(t) := 1$ for $t \geq 0$. Note that from the point of view of model complexity, there is only a minor difference between networks with

signum perceptrons and those with Heaviside perceptrons as

$$\mathrm{sgn}(t) = 2\vartheta(t) - 1$$

and

$$\vartheta(t) := \frac{\mathrm{sgn}(t) + 1}{2},$$

where $\vartheta(t) = 0$ for $t < 0$ and $\vartheta(t) = 1$ for $t \geq 0$. An advantage of signum perceptrons is that all units from the dictionary $P_d(X)$ have the same size of norms equal to $\sqrt{\mathrm{card}\, X}$.

3 Measures of Sparsity

The most simple measure of sparse connectivity between the hidden layer and the network output is the number of non-zero output weights. In some literature, the number of non-zero coefficients among w_i's in an input-output function

$$f = \sum_{i=1}^{n} w_i g_i \tag{1}$$

from $\mathrm{span}\, G$ is called an "l_0-*pseudo-norm*" in quotation marks and denoted $\|w\|_0$. However, it is neither a norm nor a pseudo-norm. The quantity $\|w\|_0$ is always an integer and thus $\|\cdot\|_0$ does not satisfy the homogeneity property of a norm ($\|\lambda x\| = |\lambda| \|x\|$ for all λ). Moreover, the "unit ball" $\{w \in \mathbb{R}^n \,|\, \|w\|_0 \leq 1\}$ is non convex and unbounded.

Minimization of the "l_0-pseudo-norm" of the vector of output weights is a difficult non convex optimization task. Instead of "l_0", l_1-*norm* defined as

$$\|w\|_1 = \sum_{i=1}^{n} |w_i|$$

and l_2-*norm* defined as

$$\|w\|_2 = \sqrt{\sum_{i=1}^{n} w_i^2}$$

of output weight vectors $w = (w_1, \ldots, w_n)$ have been used in weight-decay regularization [8]. These norms can be implemented as stabilizers modifying error functionals which are minimized during learning. A network with a large l_1 or l_2-norm of its output-weight vector must have either a large number of units or some output weights must be large. Both of these properties are not desirable as they imply a large model complexity or non stability of computation caused by large output weights.

Many dictionaries of computational units are over-complete and thus the representation (1) as a linear combination of units from the dictionary need not be unique. For a finite dictionary G, the minimum of the l_1-norms of output-weight vectors of shallow networks with units from G computing f is equal to a norm tailored to the dictionary G. This norm, called G-*variation*, has been used as a tool for estimation of rates of approximation of functions by networks with increasing "l_0-pseudo-norms". G-variation is defined for a bounded subset G of a normed linear space $(\mathscr{X}, \|.\|)$ as

$$\|f\|_G := \inf\left\{c \in \mathbb{R}_+ \mid \frac{f}{c} \in \mathrm{cl}_{\mathscr{X}}\, \mathrm{conv}\,(G \cup -G)\right\},$$

where $-G := \{-g \mid g \in G\}$, $\mathrm{cl}_{\mathscr{X}}$ denotes the closure with respect to the topology induced by the norm $\|\cdot\|_{\mathscr{X}}$, and conv is the convex hull. Variation with respect to the dictionary of Heaviside perceptrons (called *variation with respect to half-spaces*) was introduced by Barron [2] and we extended it to general sets in [11].

As G-variation is a norm, it can be made arbitrarily large by multiplying a function by a scalar. Also in theoretical analysis of approximation capabilities of shallow networks, it has to be taken into account that the approximation error $\|f - \mathrm{span}_n G\|$ in any norm $\|.\|$ can be made arbitrarily large by multiplying f by a scalar. Indeed, for every $c > 0$,

$$\|cf - \mathrm{span}_n G\| = c\|f - \mathrm{span}_n G\|.$$

Thus, both G-variation and errors in approximation by $\mathrm{span}_n G$ have to be studied either for sets of normalized functions or for sets of functions of a given fixed norm.

G-variation is related to l_1-sparsity, it can be used for estimating its lower bounds. The proof of the next proposition follows easily from the definition.

Proposition 1. *Let G be a finite subset of $(\mathscr{X}, \|.\|)$ with $\mathrm{card}\, G = k$. Then, for every $f \in \mathscr{X}$*

$$\|f\|_G = \min\left\{\sum_{i=1}^{k}|w_i| \,\Big|\, f = \sum_{i=1}^{k} w_i g_i,\, w_i \in \mathbb{R},\, g_i \in G\right\}.$$

Another important property of G-variation is its role in estimates of rates of approximation by networks with small "l_0-pseudo-norms". This follows from the Maurey-Jones-Barron Theorem [3]. Here we state its reformulation from [11, 16, 12] in terms of G-variation merely for finite dimensional Hilbert space $(\mathscr{F}(X), \|.\|)$ with the Euclidean norm. By G^o is denoted the set of normalized elements of G, i.e., $G^o = \{\frac{g}{\|g\|} \mid g \in G\}$.

Theorem 2. *Let $X \subset \mathbb{R}^d$ be finite, G be a finite subset of $\mathscr{F}(X)$, $s_G = \max_{g \in G}\|g\|$, and $f \in \mathscr{F}(X)$. Then for every n,*

$$\|f - \mathrm{span}_n G\| \leq \frac{\|f\|_{G^o}}{\sqrt{n}} \leq \frac{s_G\|f\|_G}{\sqrt{n}}.$$

Theorem 2 together with Proposition 1 imply that for any function that can be l_1-sparsely represented by a shallow network with units from a dictionary G and for any n, there exists an input-output function f_n of a network with n units such that $f_n = \sum_{i=1}^{n} w_i g_i$ (and so $\|w\|_0 \leq n$) such that

$$\|f - f_n\| \leq \frac{s_G\|f\|_G}{\sqrt{n}}.$$

Lower bounds on variational norms can be obtained by geometrical arguments. The following theorem from [16] shows that functions which are "nearly orthogonal" to all elements of a dictionary G have large G-variations.

Theorem 3. *Let $(\mathscr{X}, \|.\|_{\mathscr{X}})$ be a Hilbert space and G its bounded subset. Then for every $f \in \mathscr{X} \setminus G^{\perp}$,*

$$\|f\|_G \geq \frac{\|f\|^2}{\sup_{g \in G}|g \cdot f|}.$$

4 Constructive Lower Bounds on Variational Norms

In this section, we derive lower bounds on l_1-sparsity of shallow signum perceptron networks from lower bounds of variational norms with respect to signum perceptrons.

Theorem 3 implies that functions which are nearly orthogonal to all elements of a dictionary have large variations. The inner product

$$\langle f, g \rangle = \sum_{x \in X} f(x)g(x)$$

of any two functions f, g on a finite domain X is invariant under reordering of the points in X.

To estimate inner products of functions with signum perceptrons on sets of points in general positions is quite difficult, so we focus on functions on square domains

$$X = \{x_1, \ldots, x_n\} \times \{y_1, \ldots, y_n\} \subset \mathbb{R}^d$$

formed by points in grid-like positions. For example, pixels of pictures in $\mathbb{R}^d$ as well as digitized high-dimensional cubes can form such square domains. Functions on square domains can be represented by square matrices. For a function f on $X = \{x_1, \ldots, x_n\} \times \{y_1, \ldots, y_n\}$ we denote by $M(f)$ the $n \times n$ matrix defined as

$$M(f)_{i,j} = f(x_i, y_j).$$

On the other hand, an $n \times n$ matrix M induces a function f_M on X such that

$$f_M(x_i, y_j) = M_{i,j}.$$

We prove a lower bound on variation with respect to signum perceptrons for functions on square domains represented by matrices with orthogonal rows. To obtain these bounds from Theorem 3, we have to estimate inner products of these functions with signum perceptrons. We derive estimates of these inner products using the following two lemmas. The first one is from [13] and the second one follows from the Cauchy-Schwartz Inequality.

Lemma 1. *Let $d = d_1 + d_2$, $\{x_i \mid i = 1, \ldots, n\} \subset \mathbb{R}^{d_1}$, $\{y_j \mid j = 1, \ldots, n\} \subset \mathbb{R}^{d_2}$, and $X = \{x_1, \ldots, x_n\} \times \{y_1, \ldots, y_n\} \subset \mathbb{R}^d$. Then for every $g \in P_d(X)$ there exists a* *reordering of rows and columns of the $n \times n$ matrix $M(g)$ such that in the reordered matrix each row and each column starts with a (possibly empty) initial segment of -1's followed by a (possibly empty) segment of $+1$'s.*

Lemma 2. *Let M be an $n \times n$ matrix with orthogonal rows, $v_1, \ldots, v_n$ be its row vectors, $a = max_{i=1,\ldots,n}\|v_i\|$. Then for any subset I of the set of indices of rows and any subset J of the set of indices of columns of the matrix M,*

$$\left| \sum_{i \in I} \sum_{j \in J} M_{i,j} \right| \leq a\sqrt{\text{card}\,I\,\text{card}\,J}.$$

The following theorem gives a lower bound on variation with respect to signum perceptrons for functions induced by matrices with orthogonal rows.

Theorem 4. *Let M be an $n \times n$ matrix with orthogonal rows, $v_1, \ldots, v_n$ be its row vectors, $a = max_{i=1,\ldots,n}\|v_i\|$, $d = d_1 + d_2$, $\{x_i \mid i = 1, \ldots, n\} \subset \mathbb{R}^{d_1}$, $\{y_j \mid j = 1, \ldots, m\} \subset \mathbb{R}^{d_2}$, $X = [x_i \mid i = 1, \ldots, n] \times [y_j \mid j - 1, \ldots, n] \subset \mathbb{R}^d$, and $f_M : X \to \mathbb{R}$ be defined as $f_M(x_i, y_j) = M_{i,j}$. Then*

$$\|f_M\|_{P_d(X)} \geq \frac{a}{\lceil \log_2 n \rceil}.$$

Sketch of the proof.
For each signum perceptron $g \in P_d(X)$, we permute both matrices: the one induced by g and the one with orthogonal rows. To estimate the inner product of the permuted matrices, we apply Lemmas 1 and 2 to a partition of both matrices into submatrices. The submatrices of permuted $M(g)$ have all entries either equal to $+1$ or all entries equal to -1. The permuted matrix M has orthogonal rows and thus we can estimate from above the sums of entries of its submatrices with the same rows and columns as submatrices of $M(g)$. The partition is constructed by iterating at most $\lceil \log_2 n \rceil$-times the same decomposition. By Theorem 3,

$$\|f_M\|_{P_d(X)} \geq \frac{\|f_M\|^2}{\sup_{g \in P_d(X)}\langle f_M, g \rangle} \geq \frac{a}{\lceil \log_2 n \rceil}.$$

$\square$

Theorem 4 shows that shallow perceptron networks computing functions generated by orthogonal $n \times n$ matrices must have l_1-norms bounded from bellow by $\frac{a}{\lceil \log_2 n \rceil}$.

All signum perceptrons on a domain X with $\text{card}\,X = n \times n$ have norms equal to n. The largest lower bound implied by Theorem 4 for functions induced by $n \times n$ matrices with orthogonal rows, which have norms equal to n, is achieved for matrices where all rows have the same norms equal to $\sqrt{n}$. Such functions have variations with respect to signum perceptrons at least

$$\frac{\sqrt{n}}{\lceil \log_2 n \rceil}.$$

In particular, when the domain is the $2d$-dimensional Boolean cube $\{0,1\}^{2d} = \in^d \times \{0,1\}^d$, then the lower bound is

$$\frac{2^{d/2}}{d}.$$

So the lower bounds grows with d exponentially.

5 Computation of Functions Induced by Pseudo-Noise Sequences by Shallow Perceptron Networks

In this section, we apply our general results to a class of circulant matrices with rows formed by shifted segments of pseudo-noise sequences. These sequences are deterministic but exhibit some properties of random sequences.

An infinite sequence $a_0, a_1, \ldots, a_i, \ldots$ of elements of $\{0,1\}$ is called *k-th order linear recurring sequence* if for some $h_0, \ldots, h_k \in \{0,1\}$

$$u_i - \sum_{j=1}^{k} u_{i-j} h_{k-j} \quad \text{mod } 2$$

for all $i \geq k$. It is called *k-th order pseudo-noise (PN) sequence* (or *pseudo-random sequence*) if it is k-th order linear recurring sequence with minimal period $2^k - 1$. PN-sequences are generated by *primitive polynomials*. A polynomial

$$h(x) = \sum_{j=0}^{m} h_j x^j$$

is called *primitive polynomial of degree m* when the smallest integer n for which $h(x)$ divides $x^n + 1$ is $n = 2^m - 1$.

PN sequences have many useful applications because some of their properties mimic those of random sequences. A *run* is a string of consecutive 1's or a string of consecutive 0's. In any segment of length $2^k - 1$ of a k-th order PN-sequence, one-half of the runs have length 1, one quarter have length 2, one-eighth have length 3, and so on. In particular, there is one run of length k of 1's, one run of length $k-1$ of 0's. Thus every segment of length $2^k - 1$ contains $2^{k/2}$ ones and $2^{k/2} - 1$ zeros [18, p.410].

An important property of PN-sequences is their low autocorrelation. The *autocorrelation* of a sequence $a_0, a_1, \ldots, a_i, \ldots$ of elements of $\{0,1\}$ with period $2^k - 1$ is defined as

$$\rho(t) = \frac{1}{2^k - 1} \sum_{j=0}^{2^k - 1} -1^{a_j + a_{j+t}}. \tag{2}$$

For every PN-sequence and for every $t = 1, \ldots, 2^k - 2$,

$$\rho(t) = -\frac{1}{2^k - 1} \tag{3}$$

[18, p. 411].

Let $\tau : \{0,1\} \to \{-1,1\}$ be defined as

$$\tau(x) = -1^x$$

(i.e., $\tau(0) = 1$ and $\tau(1) = -1$). We say that a $2^k \times 2^k$ matrix $L_k(\alpha)$ *is induced by a k-th order PN-sequence* $\alpha = (a_0, a_1, \ldots, a_i, \ldots)$ when for all $i = 1, \ldots, 2^k$, $L_{i,1} = 1$, for all $j = 1, \ldots, 2^k$, $L_{1,j} = 1$, and for all $i = 2, \ldots, 2^k$ and $j = 2, \ldots, 2^k$

$$L_k(\alpha)_{i,j} = \tau(A_{i-1,j-1})$$

where A is the $(2^k - 1) \times (2^k - 1)$ circulant matrix with rows formed by shifted segments of length $2^k - 1$ of the sequence α. The next proposition following from the equations (2) and (3) shows that for any PN-sequence α the matrix $L_k(\alpha)$ has orthogonal rows.

Proposition 5. *Let* k *be a positive integer,* $\alpha = (a_0, a_1, \ldots, a_i, \ldots)$ *be a k-th order PN-sequence, and* $L_k(\alpha)$ *be the* $2^k \times 2^k$ *matrix induced by* α. *Then all pairs of rows of* $L_k(\alpha)$ *are orthogonal.*

Applying Theorem 4 to the $2^k \times 2^k$ matrice $L_k(\alpha)$ induced by a k-th order PN-sequence α we obtain a lower bound of the form $\frac{2^{k/2}}{k}$ on variation with respect to signum perceptrons of the function induced by the matrix $L_k(\alpha)$. So in any shallow perceptron network computing this function, the number of units or sizes of some output weights depend on k exponentially.

6   Discussion

We investigated limitations of shallow perceptron networks to sparsely represent real-valued functions. We considered sparsity measured by the l_1-norm which has been used in weight-decay regularization techniques [8] and in online dictionary learning [7]. We proved lower bounds on l_1-norms of output weight vectors of shallow signum perceptron networks computing functions on square domains induced by matrices with orthogonal rows. We illustrated our general results by an example of a class of matrices constructed using pseudo-noise sequences. These deterministic sequences mimic some properties of random sequences. We showed that shallow perceptron networks, which compute functions constructed using these sequences, must have either large numbers of hidden units or some of their output weights must be large.

There is an interesting analogy with the central paradox of coding theory. This paradox is expressed in the title of the article "Any code of which we cannot think is good" [6]. It was proven there that any code which is truly random (in the sense that there is no concise way to generate the code) is good (it meets the Gilbert-Varshamov bound on distance versus redundancy). However despite sophisticated constructions for codes derived over the years, no one has succeeded in finding a constructive procedure that yields such good codes. Similarly, computation of "any function of which we cannot think" (truly random) by shallow perceptron networks might be untractable. Our results show that computation of functions exhibiting some randomness properties by shallow perceptron networks is

difficult in the sense that it requires networks of large complexities. Such functions can be constructed using deterministic algorithms and have many applications. Properties of pseudo-noise sequences were exploited for constructions of codes, interplanetary satellite picture transmission, precision measurements, acoustics, radar camouflage, and light diffusers. These sequences permit designs of surfaces that scatter incoming signals very broadly making reflected energy "invisible" or "inaudible".

Acknowledgments. This work was partially supported by the Czech Grant Agency grant GA 15-18108S and institutional support of the Institute of Computer Science RVO 67985807.

References

[1] L. J. Ba and R. Caruana. Do deep networks really need to be deep? In Z. Ghahrani and et al., editors, *Advances in Neural Information Processing Systems*, volume 27, pages 1–9, 2014.

[2] A. R. Barron. Neural net approximation. In K. S. Narendra, editor, *Proc. 7th Yale Workshop on Adaptive and Learning Systems*, pages 69–72. Yale University Press, 1992.

[3] A. R. Barron. Universal approximation bounds for superpositions of a sigmoidal function. *IEEE Trans. on Information Theory*, 39:930–945, 1993.

[4] Y. Bengio, O. Delalleau, and N. Le Roux. The curse of highly variable functions for local kernel machines. In *Advances in Neural Information Processing Systems*, volume 18, pages 107–114. MIT Press, 2006.

[5] Y. Bengio and Y. LeCun. Scaling learning algorithms towards AI. In L. Bottou, O. Chapelle, D. DeCoste, and J. Weston, editors, *Large-Scale Kernel Machines*. MIT Press, 2007.

[6] J. T. Coffey and R. M. Goodman. Any code of which we cannot think is good. *IEEE Transactions on Information Theory*, 36:1453 – 1461, 1990.

[7] D. L. Donoho. For most large undetermined systems of linear equation the minimal l_1-norm is also the sparsest. *Communications in Pure and Applied Mathematics*, 59:797–829, 2006.

[8] T. L. Fine. *Feedforward Neural Network Methodology*. Springer, Berlin Heidelberg, 1999.

[9] Y. Ito. Finite mapping by neural networks and truth functions. *Mathematical Scientist*, 17:69–77, 1992.

[10] P. C. Kainen, V. Kůrková, and M. Sanguineti. Dependence of computational models on input dimension: Tractability of approximation and optimization tasks. *IEEE Transactions on Information Theory*, 58:1203–1214, 2012.

[11] V. Kůrková. Dimension-independent rates of approximation by neural networks. In K. Warwick and M. Kárný, editors, *Computer-Intensive Methods in Control and Signal Processing. The Curse of Dimensionality*, pages 261–270. Birkhäuser, Boston, MA, 1997.

[12] V. Kůrková. Complexity estimates based on integral transforms induced by computational units. *Neural Networks*, 33:160–167, 2012.

[13] V. Kůrková. Constructive lower bounds on model complexity of shallow perceptron networks. *Neural Computing and Applications*, DOI 10.1007/s00521-017-2965-0, 2017.

[14] V. Kůrková and M. Sanguineti. Model complexities of shallow networks representing highly varying functions. *Neurocomputing*, 171:598–604, 2016.

[15] V. Kůrková and M. Sanguineti. Probabilistic lower bounds for approximation by shallow perceptron networks. *Neural Networks*, 91:34–41, 2017.

[16] V. Kůrková, P. Savický, and K. Hlaváčková. Representations and rates of approximation of real-valued Boolean functions by neural networks. *Neural Networks*, 11:651–659, 1998.

[17] S. B. Laughlin and T. J. Sejnowski. Communication in neural networks. *Science*, 301:1870–1874, 2003.

[18] F. MacWilliams and N. A. Sloane. *The Theory of Error-Correcting Codes*. North Holland Publishing Co., 1977.

[19] V. E. Maiorov and R. Meir. On the near optimality of the stochastic approximation of smooth functions by neural networks. *Advances in Computational Mathematics*, 13:79–103, 2000.

[20] V. E. Maiorov and A. Pinkus. Lower bounds for approximation by MLP neural networks. *Neurocomputing*, 25:81–91, 1999.

[21] J. Mairal, F. Bach, J. Ponce, and G. Sapiro. Online learning for matrix factorization and sparse coding. *Journal of Machine Learning Research*, 11:19–60, 2010.

[22] A. Pinkus. Approximation theory of the MLP model in neural networks. *Acta Numerica*, 8:143–195, 1999.

[23] A. M. Tillmann. On the computational intractability of exact and approximate dictionary learning. *IEEE Signal Processing Letters*, 22:45–49, 2015.

J. Hlaváčová (Ed.): ITAT 2017 Proceedings, pp. 106–111
ISBN 978-1974274741, © 2017 J. Motl, P. Kordík

Foreign Key Constraint Identification in Relational Databases

Jan Motl, Pavel Kordík

Czech Technical University in Prague,
Thákurova 9, 160 00 Praha 6, Czech Republic,
jan.motl@fit.cvut.cz, pavel.kordik@fit.cvut.cz

Abstract: For relational learning, it is important to know the relationships between the tables. In relational databases, the relationships can be described with foreign key constraints. However, the foreign keys may not be explicitly specified. In this article, we present how to automatically and quickly identify primary & foreign key constraints from metadata about the data. Our method was evaluated on 72 databases and has F-measure of 0.87 for foreign key constraint identification. The proposed method significantly outperforms in runtime related methods reported in the literature and is database vendor agnostic.

1 Introduction

Whenever we want to build a predictive model on relational data, we have to be able to connect individual tables together [3]. In *Structured Query Language* (SQL) databases, the *relationships* (connections) between the tables can be defined with *foreign key* (FK) constraints. However, FK constraints are not always available. This can happen, for example, whenever we work with legacy databases or data sources, like *comma separated value* (CSV) files.

Identification of relationships from database belongs to *reverse engineering* from databases [14] and can be done manually or by means of handcrafted rules [2, 3, 7, 17]. Manual FK constraint discovery is very time-consuming for complex databases [11]. And handcrafted systems may overfit to small collections of databases, used for the training. Therefore we use machine learning techniques for this task and evaluate them on a collection of 72 databases.

Unfortunately, FK constraint identification is difficult. If we have n columns in a database, then there can be n^2 FK constraints, as each column can reference any column in the database, including itself[1]. Hence, there is n^2 candidate FK constraints.

Example 1. *If we have a medium-sized database with 100 tables, each with 100 columns, then we have to consider 10^8 candidate FK constraints.*

We can evaluate probability p that a single candidate FK constraint is a FK constraint with a classifier (e.g. logistic regression) in a constant time. Hence, if we assumed that the probability $p_{i,j}$, which denotes a probability that a column i references column j, is independent of all other candidate FK constraints in the database, the computational complexity of FK constraint identification would be $O(n^2)$. However, the probabilities do not appear to be independent.

Example 2. *If we had two columns A, B and we had known that $p_{A,B} = 0.9$ and $p_{B,A} = 0.8$ then under assumption of independence it would be reasonable to predict that column A references column B and also that column B references column A. However, directed cyclic references[2] do not generally appear in the databases as it would make updates inconveniently difficult [10]. Hence, our example database most likely contains only one FK constraint with A referencing B.*

If we accepted that the FK constraints are not independent of each other, we could generate each possible combination of FK constraints and calculate the probability that the candidate combination of FK constraints is the true combination of FK constraints. The computational complexity of such algorithm is $O(2^{n^2})$. Clearly, a practical algorithm must take simplifying assumptions to scale to complex databases.

The applications of the FK constraint discovery, besides relational learning, include *data quality* assessment [1] and *database refactoring* [11].

The paper is structured as follows: first, we describe related work, then we describe our method, then we describe our experiments and their results, discuss the results and provide a conclusion.

2 Related Work

Li et al. [8] formulated a related problem, attribute correspondence identification, as a classification problem.

Rostin et al. [16] formulate FK constraint identification as a classification problem.

Meurice et al. [11] compared different data sources for the FK constraint identification: database schema, Hibernate XML files, JPA Java code and SQL code. Based on their analysis, the database schema data source has four times higher recall than any other data source. In this article, we focus solely on the database schema data source. Furthermore, they introduce 4 rules for filtering the candidate FK constraints: the "likeliness" of the candidate FK constraint must be above a threshold, the FK constraints cannot be bidirectional, the column(s) of the selected FK

---

[1]We have not observed any instance of a column referencing itself. Nevertheless, SQL standard does not forbid it.

[2]However, undirected cyclic references are commonly used, for example, to model hierarchies.

constraints can be used only once and there can be only a single (undirected) path from FK constraints between any two tables.

Chen et al. [3] describe how to significantly accelerate FK constraint identification by pruning unpromising candidates at multiple levels. We inspire from them and use multi-level architecture as well. Furthermore, they introduce 4 rules for filtering the candidate FK constraints: explore FK constraints only between the tables selected by the user, only a single FK constraint can exist between two tables, directed cycles from FK constraints are forbidden and there can be only a single (undirected) path from FK constraints between any two tables. We inspire from Meurice's and Chen's articles and reformulate their rules as *integer linear programming* (ILP) problem.

3   Method

To make the relationship identification fast, a predictive model was trained only on the metadata about the data, which are accessible with *Java Database Connectivity* (JDBC) API. This approach has the following properties:

1. It is fast and scalable.
2. It is database vendor agnostic.
3. It is not affected by the data quality.

The problem of relationship identification was decomposed into two subproblems: identification of *primary keys* (PKs) and identification of FK constraints (Figure 1). The reasoning behind this decomposition is that identification of PKs is a relatively easy task. And knowledge of PKs simplifies identification of FK constraints because FK constraints frequently reference PKs[3].

The identification of the PKs is performed in two stages: scoring and optimization. During the scoring phase, a probability that an attribute is a part of a PK (a PK can be *compound* — composed of multiple attributes) is predicted with a classifier. The probability estimates are then passed into the optimization stage, which delivers a binary prediction.

The same approach is taken for FK constraint identification. During the scoring phase, a probability that a candidate FK constraint is a FK constraint is estimated with a classifier. The probabilities are then passed into an optimizer, which returns the most likely FK constraints.

3.1   Primary Key Scoring

All metadata that are exposed by JDBC[4] about attributes (as obtained with *getColumns* method) and tables (as obtained with *getTables*) were collected and considered as features for classification. For brevity, we describe and justify only features used by the final model.

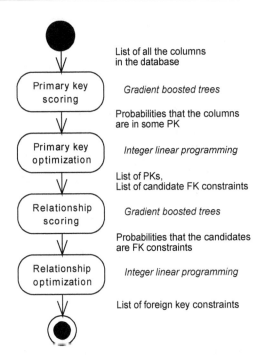

Figure 1: The algorithm decomposition.

Data types like *integer* or *char* are generally more likely to be PKs than, for example, *double* or *text*. To promote portability of the trained model, we do not use database data types but JDBC data types, which have the advantage that they are the same regardless of the database vendor.

Since some databases offer only a single data type for numerical attributes, we also note whether numerical attributes can contain **decimals**, as PKs are unlikely to contain decimal numbers.

Doppelgänger is an attribute, which has a name similar to another attribute in the same table. For example, *atom_id1* is a doppelgänger to *atom_id2*. Doppelgängers frequently share properties, i.e. either both of them are in the PK or neither of them is in the PK.

Ordinal position defines the position of the attribute in the table. PKs are frequently at the beginning of the tables.

String distance between the column and table names are helpful for identification of PKs and FKs. Opinions on the best measure for PK and FK constraint identification vary. For example, [16] uses exact match while [3] uses Jaro-Winkler distance. After testing all string measures available in *stringdist* package [9], we found that Levenshtein distance delivers the best discriminative power on the tested databases.

Keywords like *id* or *pk* frequently mark PKs. The presence of the keywords is analyzed after the attribute/table name tokenization, which works with camel case and snake case notation.

JDBC also provides attributes that leak information about the presence of the PK, like *isNullable*, *isAutoIncrement* and *isGeneratedColumn*. Since it is unreasonable to

---

[3]A FK may reference any attribute that is unique, not only PKs. Nevertheless, all FKs in the analyzed databases reference PKs.

[4]See docs.oracle.com for the documentation.

assume that these metadata would be set correctly after importing data from CSV files, they were excluded from the model.

For comparison to features extracted from the data (and not metadata), two additional features were extracted: whether the attribute contains nulls (*containsNull*) and whether the attribute contains unique values (*isUnique*). These features are generally expensive to calculate [3]. Nevertheless, some databases, like PostgreSQL, automatically generate these statistics for each attribute in the database and provide a vendor-specific access to these statistics.

3.2 Primary Key Optimization

Since each table in a well-designed database should contain a PK, a single most likely PK is identified for each table in the database. If the single most likely PK attribute in a table is a doppelgänger, all its doppelgängers in the table are declared to be part of the PK as well, creating a compound key. The described optimization can be solved with an ILP solver, which we use mostly because foreign key optimization (section 3.4) is using ILP formulation as well.

3.3 Foreign Key Scoring

Features for FK constraints are a combination of features calculated for individual attributes from section 3.1 (prefixed with *fk* and *pk* respectively) with features unique for the FK constraints. The description of the unique features follows.

Data types between FK and PK attributes should match. Nevertheless, SQL permits FK constraints between *char* and *varchar* data types.

Data lengths between FK and PK attributes should match. Nevertheless, SQL explicitly permits FK constraints between attributes of different character lengths as defined in the SQL-92 specification, section 8.2.

String distance between FK column name and PK table name should be small because FK column names frequently embed a part of the PK table name. Similarly, FK column name should be similar to PK column name because FK column names frequently embed a part of the PK column name. On the other end, FK column name should generally differ from FK table name as they are not directly related.

Furthermore, to be able to compare metadata-based features to data-based features, we tested whether all non-null values in the FK are present in the PK (*satisfiesFKConstraint*). This is generally an expensive feature to calculate [3]. Nevertheless, some databases, like PostgreSQL, automatically calculate histograms for each attribute in the background and offer a vendor specific interface to access the histograms. And based on the range of the histograms many candidate FK constraints can be pruned. More advanced data-based features (e.g. similarity of the FK and PK distributions) were not explored as the focus of the article is on the metadata-based features.

3.4 Foreign Key Optimization

The optimization can be formulated as an integer linear optimization problem on a directed graph $G = (V, E)$, where V is the set of attributes in the database and E is the set of candidate FK constraints. The p_{ij} is the estimated probability that the candidate FK constraint referencing FK i to PK j is a FK constraint. The probabilities are estimated with a classification model trained on features described in section 3.3. Compound FKs are modeled as multiple FK constraints (one FK constraint for each attribute). We define variable x_{ij}:

$$x_{ij} = \begin{cases} 1 & \text{if the candidate FK constraint is a FK constraint} \\ 0 & \text{otherwise} \end{cases}$$

(1)

The optimization problem is then:

$$\max_X \sum_{[i,j] \in E} x_{ij} - 2 \sum_{[i,j] \in E} x_{ij}(1 - p_{ij}) \quad (2a)$$

s.t.

$$\sum_{j \in V} x_{ij} \leq 1, \qquad \forall i, \quad (2b)$$

$$\sum_{i \in S, j \in S, [i,j] \in E} x_{ij} \leq |S| - 1, \quad \forall S \subseteq V, |S| \geq 1, \quad (2c)$$

$$x_{i_1 j_1} - x_{i_2 j_2} = 0, \qquad \forall P, F \subseteq V, i \in F, j \in P, |P| \geq 2, \quad (2d)$$

$$x_{i_1 j} - x_{i_2 j} = 0, \qquad \forall D \subseteq V, i \in D, j \in V, \quad (2e)$$

$$x_{ij} \in \{0, 1\}, \qquad \forall i \in V, j \in V. \quad (2f)$$

The objective function defines all FK constraint candidates x_{ij} with $p_{ij} > 0.5$ as FK constraints if it does not violate any of the following constraints.

Unity constraint 2b enforces that a FK can reference only a single PK. While a single FK can in theory reference multiple different PKs, no such occurrence appeared in the analyzed databases.

Acyclicity constraint 2c ensures that the graph is (directionally) acyclic. However, this formulation of acyclicity requires an exponential number of constraints. To deal with that, we generate acyclicity constraints lazily [15]. Acyclicity constraint is desirable because if p_{ij} is high, p_{ji} is generally high as well (particularly for $i = j$). But directed cycles (even over intermediate tables) do not appear in the analyzed databases.

Completeness constraint 2d says that if a PK is compound, then either all or neither attribute of the PK P is referenced from the FK table by attributes F. Completeness constraint ensures that compound FKs are syntactically correct.

Doppelgänger constraint 2e says that if attributes are doppelgängers to each other, then either all or neither attribute from the doppelgänger set D reference the (same) PK attribute.

Constraint 2f defines the problem as an integer programming problem.

It should be noted that if constraints 2d and 2e are removed, we get an optimization problem similar to the identification of minimum spanning tree in a graph [6]. Hence, the FKs can be efficiently optimized with Dijkstra algorithm with a modified termination condition (the algorithm terminates once the objective function starts to increase).

4 Results

Following paragraphs describe an empirical comparison of 5 classifies on 3 different sets of features from 72 databases.

4.1 Data

We used all 72 relational databases from relational repository [12]. The databases range from classical relational benchmarking databases (like *TPC-C* or *TPC-H*) to real-world databases used in challenges (e.g. from PKDD in 1999 or from Predictive Toxicology Challenge in 2000). The collection of the databases contains in total 1343 PKs, 1283 FK constraints, 6129 attributes and 788 tables. That means that on average approximately 1 of 5 attributes is part of a PK. The count of all *possible relationships* is 1,232,392 (in theory, a FK can reference any attribute in the database, including itself). That means that on average approximately 1 of 960 tested relationships are FK constraints.

4.2 Algorithm

Following classification algorithms were tested on the problem: decision tree, gradient boosted trees, naive Bayes, neural network and logistic regression as implemented in RapidMiner 7.5. Since the best results were obtained with gradient boosted trees, the reported results are for gradient boosted trees.

4.3 Measure

For evaluation of the classification models, AUC and F-measure [5] were used. Classification accuracy was omitted due to a significant class imbalance in FK identification task. AUC evaluates the ability of the model to rank. Hence, AUC is used to evaluate the quality of scoring. On the other end, F-measure is suitable for the evaluation of the quality of thresholding. Hence, F-measure is used to evaluate the quality of the optimization.

4.4 Validation

To measure the generalization of the models to new unobserved databases, *batch cross-validation* over databases [16, section 4.3] was performed. Since 72 databases were analyzed, it means that each model was trained and evaluated 72 times. The batch cross-validation has the advantage, in comparison to 10-fold cross-validation, that the samples from a single database are either all in the training set or all in the testing set. Hence, if the samples from a single database are more similar to each other than to samples from other databases, we may expect that batch cross-validation will deliver a less optimistically biased estimate of the model accuracy on new unobserved databases than 10-fold cross-validation.

4.5 Feature Importance

Generally, it is desirable to minimize the count of utilized features to make the model easier to understand and deploy. Table 1 depicts feature importance for PK identification as reported by gradient boosted trees for features that remained after backward selection.

Table 1: Feature importance for primary key identification for different feature sets. Higher weight means higher importance.

Feature	All	Meta	Ordinal	Data
ordinalPosition	3279	1970	2581	-
isDoppelgänger	142	99	-	-
isDecimal	80	81	-	-
containsNull	18	-	-	239
levenshteinToTable	15	124	-	-
dataType	14	71	-	-
isUnique	9	-	-	780
containsKeyword	7	21	-	-
AUC	**0.985**	0.970	0.934	0.784

The single most important feature for PK identification is the position of the attribute in the table. This is not so surprising because all non-compound PKs in the analyzed databases (with the exception of *Hepatitis* database) were the first attribute in the table. Indeed, if we always predicted that the first attribute in a table is a PK, we get F-measure equal to 0.934 ± 0.007.

Table 2 lists feature importance for FK constraint identification. Interestingly, the knowledge whether the FK constraint is satisfiable is the least important feature from the selected features.

4.6 Optimization Contribution

The PK optimization improves F-measure of PK identification from 0.845 ± 0.069 to 0.875 ± 0.057. While FK optimization improves F-measure of FK constraint identification from 0.743 ± 0.020 to 0.870 ± 0.022.

Table 2: Feature importance for foreign key constraint identification. Higher weight means higher importance.

Feature	All	Meta	Data
levenshteinFkColToPkTab	298.1	301.2	-
levenshteinFkColToFkTab	245.8	246.0	-
fk_isDoppelgänger	210.6	210.4	-
levenshteinFkColToPkCol	182.2	182.2	-
fk_containsKeyword	160.2	160.3	-
dataLengthAgree	92.2	92.2	-
pk_isDoppelgänger	60.3	60.3	-
fk_isPrimaryKey	57.8	57.8	-
fk_ordinalPosition	48.4	48.2	-
dataTypeAgree	10.3	10.2	-
satisfiesFKConstraint	1.6	-	382
AUC	**0.990**	0.988	0.934

4.7 Runtime & Scalability

The time required to score all 72 databases is 55 seconds in total, where 95% of the runtime is due to the fact that JDBC collects metadata about the attributes for each table individually, causing many round trips between the algorithm and the database server. When we replaced JDBC calls with a single query to *information_schema*, which provides all the data at the database level, the total runtime decreased to 5 seconds.

Furthermore, the algorithm was tested on our university database with 909 tables. The runtime was 18 minutes, due to the quadratic growth of candidate FK constraints with the count of attributes in the database [3]. To keep the memory requirements manageable, FK candidates were scored on the fly and only the top n FK candidates with the highest probability were kept in a heap for FK optimization.

5 Discussion

Table 3 depicts a comparison of our approach to different approaches in the literature. Since the implementations of the referenced approaches are not available, we take and report the measurements for the biggest common denominator of the evaluated databases — the TPC-H database. The approaches differ in the utilized features (e.g. Kruse et al. utilize SQL scripts, while our approach does not) and objectives (e.g. Chen et al. aim to maximize precision at the expense of recall). The results of our method for all 72 databases are available for download at https://github.com/janmotl/linkifier.

Empirical comparison of our metadata-based approach to other metadata-based approaches is in Table 4. Oracle Data Modeler [13] estimates FK constraints based on the knowledge of PKs (it is assumed that a FK must reference a PK), equality of column names between the FK and the PK and equality of the data types between the FK and the PK. SchemaCrawler [4] is using an extended version of

these three filters. SchemaCrawler assumes that a FK must reference either a PK or a column with a unique constraint. The column names must equal but differences in the presence/absence of *id* keyword and differences between singular and plural forms are ignored, improving the recall. And datatypes must equal including their length (except of *varchar* datatype), improving the precission.

5.1 Limitations

The metadata-based identification of PK and FK constraints is limited by the quality of the metadata. For example, if all the columns in the database had non-informative names and all the columns were typed as *text*, the accuracy of the predictions would suffer.

But even if the metadata are of hight quality, our metadata-base approach is not able to reliably reconstruct a hierarchy of subclasses. The problem is illustrated in Figure 2. Based on the table and PK names, we can correctly infer that *Person* and *Vendor* are subclasses of *BusinessEntity*. However, our metadata-based method has no means how to infer that *Customer* and *Employee* are subclasses of *Person* and not directly of *BusinessEntity*.

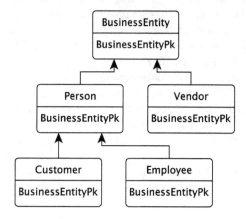

Figure 2: Example entity diagram with a hierarchy of subclasses.

Both these limitations can be addressed by extending the metadata-based approach by appropriate data-based features. For example, whenever a subclass can reference multiple superclasses, the superclass with the lowest row count, which still satisfies the FK constraint, should be selected.

6 Conclusions

We described a method for foreign key constraint identification, which does not put any assumptions on the schema normalization, data quality, availability of vendor specific metadata or human interaction. The code for primary & foreign key constraint identification was designed to be database vendor agnostic and was successfully tested against Microsoft SQL Server, MySQL, PostgreSQL and Oracle. The code with a graphical user interface is

Table 3: Literature review of different approaches to foreign key constraint identification on TPC-H 1GB database. Unknown values are represented with a question mark.

Reference	Features	Objective	Precision	Recall	F-measure	Runtime [s]
Zhang et al. [17]	Data	F-measure	**1.00**	**1.00**	**1.00**	501
Chen et al. [3]	Data, Metadata	Precision	**1.00**	**1.00**	**1.00**	14
Rostin et al. [16]	Data, Metadata	F-measure	?	?	0.95	450
Our	Metadata	F-measure	0.77	0.77	0.77	**1**

Table 4: Empirical evaluation of metadata-based approaches to foreign key constraint identification on 72 databases together.

Implementation	F-measure	Runtime [s]
Oracle Data Modeler	0.06	**2.07**
SchemaCrawler	0.17	4.65
Our	**0.87**	5.14

published at GitHub (https://github.com/janmotl/linkifier) under BSD license. The runtime is dominated by the connection lag to the server and if the requirement on the code portability is lifted, we are able to predict primary & foreign key constraints for all 72 tested databases in 5 seconds.

7 Acknowledgments

We would like to thank Aleš Fišer, Jan Kukačka, Jiří Kukačka, Manuel Muñoz and Batal Thibaut for their help. We furthermore thank the anonymous reviewers, their comments helped to improve this paper. This research was partially supported by the Grant Agency of the Czech Technical University in Prague, grant No. SGS17/210/OHK3/3T/18.

References

[1] Ziawasch Abedjan, Lukasz Golab, and Felix Naumann. Profiling relational data: a survey. *VLDB J.*, 24(4):557–581, 2015.

[2] John G. Bennett, Perry A. Gee, and Charles E. Gayraud. System and Methods Including Automatic Linking of Tables for Improved Relational Database Modeling with Interface, 1997.

[3] Zhimin Chen, Vivek Narasayya, and Surajit Chaudhuri. Fast Foreign-Key Detection in Microsoft SQL Server Power-Pivot for Excel. *VLDB Endow.*, 7(13):1417–1428, 2014.

[4] Sualeh Fatehi. SchemaCrawler, 2017.

[5] Tom Fawcett. An introduction to ROC analysis. *Pattern Recognit. Lett.*, 27(8):861–874, jun 2006.

[6] Dorit S. Hochbaum. Integer Programming and Combinatorial Optimization. *IEOR269 notes*, 2010.

[7] Sebastian Kruse, Thorsten Papenbrock, Hazar Harmouch, and Felix Naumann. Data Anamnesis: Admitting Raw Data into an Organization. *IEEE Data Eng. Bull.*, pages 8–20, 2016.

[8] Wen Syan Li and Chris Clifton. SEMINT: a tool for identifying attribute correspondences in heterogeneous databases using neural networks. *Data Knowl. Eng.*, 33(1):49–84, 2000.

[9] Nick Logan. Package stringdist. Technical report, CRAN, 2016.

[10] Victor Markowitz. Safe referential integrity and null constraint structures in relational databases. *Inf. Syst.*, 19(4):359–378, jun 1994.

[11] Loup Meurice, Fco Javier Bermúdez Ruiz, Jens H. Weber, and Anthony Cleve. Establishing referential integrity in legacy information systems - Reality bites! *Proc. - 30th Int. Conf. Softw. Maint. Evol. ICSME 2014*, pages 461–465, 2014.

[12] Jan Motl and Oliver Schulte. The CTU Prague Relational Learning Repository, 2015.

[13] Oracle. Oracle SQL Developer Data Modeler, 2017.

[14] Lurdes Pedro de Jesus and Pedro Sousa. Selection of Reverse Engineering Methods for Relational Databases. *Proc. Third Eur. Conf. Softw. Maint.*, pages 194–197, 1998.

[15] Ulrich Pferschy and Rostislav Staněk. Generating subtour elimination constraints for the TSP from pure integer solutions. *Cent. Eur. J. Oper. Res.*, pages 1–30, 2016.

[16] Alexandra Rostin, Oliver Albrecht, Jana Bauckmann, Felix Naumann, and Ulf Leser. A machine learning approach to foreign key discovery. *12th Int. Work. Web Databases (WebDB), Provid. Rhode Isl.*, (WebDB):1–6, 2009.

[17] Meihui Zhang, Marios Hadjieleftheriou, Beng Chin Ooi, Cecilia M. Procopiuc, and Divesh Srivastava. On multi-column foreign key discovery. *Proc. VLDB Endow.*, 3(1-2):805–814, 2010.

J. Hlaváčová (Ed.): ITAT 2017 Proceedings, pp. 112–119
ISBN 978-1974274741, © 2017 M. Navara, J. Šindelář

The Role of Information in the Two Envelope Problem

Mirko Navara, Jiří Šindelář

Center for Machine Perception, Department of Cybernetics,
Faculty of Electrical Engineering, Czech Technical University in Prague,
Technická 2, 166 27 Prague, Czech Republic,
navara@cmp.felk.cvut.cz, sindeji3@fel.cvut.cz,
WWW home page: http://cmp.felk.cvut.cz/~navara/

Abstract: We offer a new view on the two envelope problem (also called the exchange paradox). We describe it as a zero-sum game of two players, having only partial information. We first explain a standard situation and show that the mean gain—when defined—is really zero. However, there are even more paradoxical situations in which the information obtained by the players supports the exchange of envelopes. We explain that this does not lead to a contradiction and we demonstrate it also by computer simulation. The reason for this paradox is that the mean gain does not exist and that the players have different information, supporting their contradictory decisions.

1 Formulation of the Problem

The *two envelope problem* (also called the *exchange paradox*) is a famous logical puzzle demonstrating a paradox in logic and probability. We adopt its formulation from [14], expressed here as a game of two players:

> There are two indistinguishable envelopes, each containing money, one contains twice as much as the other. Player A picks one envelope of his choice; player B receives the second envelope. They can keep the money contained in their envelopes or switch the envelopes (if both agree on it). Should they switch?

There is an easy answer:

Argument 1. *The situation is symmetric. Thus there is no reason for (or against) switching.*

However, there are other interpretations suggesting something else:

Argument 2. *The situation is symmetric. Thus the probability of having the envelope with the higher or lower amount is 1/2. If the envelope of player A contains the amount a, then the other envelope contains 2a (and the exchange results in a gain of a) or a/2 (and the exchange results in a loss of a/2). In average, the mean gain is*

$$\frac{1}{2}a - \frac{1}{2}\frac{a}{2} = \frac{a}{4},$$

thus switching is always recommended.

Another point of view is the following:

Argument 3. *The smaller amount is x, the bigger is 2x. They are assigned randomly (with probabilities 1/2) to players A and B. The mean values for both players are*

$$\frac{1}{2}x - \frac{1}{2}2x = \frac{3}{2}x$$

and there is no reason for (or against) switching.

We presented several arguments; each of them seems correct, but their conclusions are contradictory.

Surprisingly, the debate about this paradox is still not finished (cf. [3]).

> "Currently, there is no consensus on a demonstration, since most people generally reject each other's demonstrations." [5]

One reason is that many authors merely defended their solution (mostly correct), cf. [6, 13]. However, to resolve the paradox, it is necessary to explain the errors in the contradicting arguments.[1] The topic was studied not only by mathematicians and logicians but also by philosophers (e.g., [4, 11]). For some of them, a sufficient explanation is that *a* in Argument 2 denotes different amounts; the smaller one in the first case and the bigger one in the second case [4, 13]. However, this is not forbidden, this is just what a random variable means. Thus a more advanced analysis is needed.

The paradox has more variants (cf. [11]). The method of choice of the amounts was not specified. (This is usual in such puzzles. They rarely start with a precise definition of a random experiment generating the data. Instead of that, it was said that two amounts are given, one of them twice greater than the other.) Here we assume that they were drawn as realizations of some random variable with a given distribution (known or unknown to players). Nevertheless, the formulation of the problem does not specify this at all, and some authors (e.g. [9]) consider this amount as given (without any randomness); such formulation excludes a probabilistic analysis. Thus we do not consider it here. Besides, it is not specified whether we first draw the (realization of) random variable X (the smaller amount) or the contents of the envelope given to player A, described

---

[1] We experienced this misunderstanding also during the reviewing process of this paper: "Argument 3 is correct, so there is no paradox." However, what is wrong on Argument 2?

by random variable A. It is natural to assume that the binary choice of envelopes is made with equal probabilities and independently of all other random events (or parameters) of the experiment. Here we apply the probabilistic approach to the problem in its original form: We first draw a positive amount x from some distribution. We put this amount into one envelope and $2x$ into the other envelope. Both envelopes have probability $1/2$ to be chosen by player A. The remaining envelope is given to player B.

It is also not specified whether the players know the amounts in their envelopes. This knowledge is useless if the distribution is unknown. On the other hand, knowing the distribution, the amounts bring useful information for the decision. We suppose that the players know the distribution from which x was drawn. We discuss this case in detail. Some of its consequences seem to determine the strategy also without looking inside the envelope, but—as we shall show—this need not correspond to conclusions made in the former case.

We present an explanation of the paradox (based on [12]) using results of probability and information theory. The standard explanation of the exchange paradox (following [7]) is presented in Section 2 and demonstrated by an example in Section 3. As a new contribution, we modify this example to two even more surprising and counterintuitive versions of the paradox, which we explain in detail in Sections 4 and 5. In Section 6, we verify the results by a computer simulation.

2 Exchange Paradox: First Level

We introduce a third member of the experiment, the banker C, who controls the game and puts (his) money in the envelopes. We assume that the smaller amount, x, was chosen by a realization of a random variable X. (The larger amount in the second envelope is $2x$.) The distribution of random variable X is known to the banker and also to the players. For simplicity, we assume that the distribution is discrete and the amounts are positive. Then we do an independent random experiment (e.g., tossing a coin) with two equally probable results, expressed by a random variable U, whose possible values are 0 and 1 and expectation $EU = 1/2$. If $U = 0$, player A receives the smaller amount, x; if $U = 1$, player A receives the bigger amount, $2x$. He does not know x, only the contents of his envelope, specified by realization a of random variable A,

$$A = \begin{cases} x & \text{if } X = x \text{ and } U = 0, \\ 2x & \text{if } X = x \text{ and } U = 1, \end{cases}$$
$$A = (1+U)X.$$

Player B receives the other envelope and knows only its contents, specified by realization b of random variable B,

$$B = \begin{cases} x & \text{if } X = x \text{ and } U = 1, \\ 2x & \text{if } X = x \text{ and } U = 0, \end{cases}$$
$$B = (2-U)X.$$

If the players exchange the envelopes, the gain of A is $G = B - A$. For player B, G is the loss and $-G$ is the gain.

Random variables X and U are independent. If X has an expectation EX, then

$$EA = (1+EU)EX = \frac{3}{2}EX,$$
$$EB = (2-EU)EX = \frac{3}{2}EX,$$
$$EG = EB - EA = 0.$$

This is in accordance with Arguments 1 and 3. It remains to find an error in Argument 2.

As U, X are independent,

$$P(U=0|X=x) = P(U=0) = \frac{1}{2},$$
$$P(U=1|X=x) = P(U=1) = \frac{1}{2}$$

for all x. However, this does not apply to conditional probabilities $P(U=0|A=a), P(U=1|A=a)$ because U, A are dependent:

$$P(U=0|A=a) = \frac{P(U=0, A=a)}{P(A=a)}$$
$$= \frac{P(U=0, X=a)}{P(A=a)} = \frac{P(X=a)}{2P(A=a)},$$
$$P(U=1|A=a) = \frac{P(U=1, A=a)}{P(A=a)}$$
$$= \frac{P(U=1, X=\frac{a}{2})}{P(A=a)} = \frac{P(X=\frac{a}{2})}{2P(A=a)},$$

where

$$P(A=a) = P(U=0, A=a) + P(U=1, A=a)$$
$$= P(U=0, X=a) + P(U=1, X=\frac{a}{2})$$
$$= \frac{1}{2}\left(P(X=a) + P(X=\frac{a}{2})\right).$$

Notice that $P(U=0|A=a)$ is the conditional probability of gain and $P(U=1|A=a)$ is the conditional probability of loss given $A=a$. Their ratio is

$$\frac{P(X=a)}{P(X=\frac{a}{2})}.$$

As there is no uniform distribution on an infinite countable set (a fact ignored even in [10]), $P(X=a), P(X=\frac{a}{2})$ cannot be equal for all a. Typically, the conditional probability of gain, $P(U=0|A=a)$, is higher for "small" values of a and smaller for "high" values, although the notions "small" and "high" are relative. In any case, these probabilities converge to 0 when a goes to infinity, hence there must be values "sufficiently large" so that $P(X = a) < P(X = \frac{a}{2})$ and the conditional probability of gain $P(U = 0 | A = a) < \frac{1}{2}$. This can also lead to an effective strategy based on random switching [9, 10].

Given $A = a$, switching brings a gain with conditional probability distribution

$$P(G = g | A = a) = \frac{P(G = g, A = a)}{P(A = a)},$$

where

$$P(G = g, A = a) = \begin{cases} P(U = 0, X = a) & \text{if } g = a, \\ P(U = 1, X = \frac{a}{2}) & \text{if } g = -\frac{a}{2}, \\ 0 & \text{otherwise.} \end{cases}$$

$$= \begin{cases} \frac{1}{2} P(X = a) & \text{if } g = a, \\ \frac{1}{2} P(X = \frac{a}{2}) & \text{if } g = -\frac{a}{2}, \\ 0 & \text{otherwise.} \end{cases}$$

We obtain

$$P(G = g | A = a) = \begin{cases} \dfrac{P(X = a)}{P(X = a) + P(X = \frac{a}{2})} & \text{if } g = a, \\[3mm] \dfrac{P(X = \frac{a}{2})}{P(X = a) + P(X = \frac{a}{2})} & \text{if } g = -\frac{a}{2}, \\[3mm] 0 & \text{otherwise.} \end{cases}$$

The conditional expectation of the gain is always defined and it is

$$E(G | A = a) = \frac{a P(X = a) - \frac{a}{2} P(X = \frac{a}{2})}{P(X = a) + P(X = \frac{a}{2})}. \tag{1}$$

These values may differ from 0.

The (unconditional) distribution of the gain is

$$P(G = g) = \begin{cases} \frac{1}{2} P(X = g) & \text{if } g > 0, \\ \frac{1}{2} P(X = -g) & \text{if } g < 0, \\ 0 & \text{otherwise} \end{cases}$$

and its expectation is

$$EG = \sum_g g P(G = g) \tag{2}$$

$$= \frac{1}{2} \left(\sum_{g > 0} g P(X = g) + \sum_{g < 0} g P(X = -g) \right) \tag{3}$$

$$= \frac{1}{2} \left(\sum_{g > 0} g P(X = g) - \sum_{h > 0} h P(X = h) \right) = 0$$

(after substitution $g := -h$), provided that the sum (2) is absolutely convergent. In this case

$$EG = \sum_a P(A = a) E(G | A = a) \tag{4}$$

$$= \sum_a \frac{1}{2} \left(a P(X = a) - \frac{a}{2} P(X = \frac{a}{2}) \right)$$

$$= \frac{1}{2} \left(\sum_a a P(X = a) - \sum_b b P(X = b) \right) = 0$$

(after substitution $a := 2b$). This explains the error in Argument 2 provided that the expectation of G is defined.

Remark 1. There is another arrangement suggested in [8, 11]: First, the amount a in the envelope of player A is drawn from some distribution. Then the random variable U (as before) decides whether the second envelope will contain $2a$ or $\frac{a}{2}$. In this arrangement, random variables U and A are independent and Argument 2 is valid. Arguments 1 and 3 fail because of an intervention of the banker; it is him who puts additional money in the second envelope, so that the total amount may be $3a$ or $\frac{3}{2}a$. This is not a zero-sum game, and it is not symmetric.

3 Example of the First Level of Paradox

Let T be a random variable with geometrical distribution with quotient $q \in (0, 1)$:

$$P(T = t) = \frac{q^t}{1 - q}, \qquad t \in \{0, 1, 2, \ldots\}.$$

Let $X = 2^T$, thus X attains values $1, 2, 4, 8, \ldots$ with probabilities

$$P(X = 2^t) = \frac{q^t}{1 - q}, \qquad t \in \{0, 1, 2, \ldots\}.$$

In this arrangement, a player can deduce the contents of both envelopes only if he holds 1. For any other value, both cases are possible—switching may bring a gain or a loss.

Suppose that the expectation of X exists; this happens iff $q < \frac{1}{2}$. Then

$$EX = \sum_{t=0}^{\infty} 2^t \frac{q^t}{1 - q} = \frac{1}{(1 - q)(1 - 2q)}.$$

The joint distribution of U and A is given (for $a = 2^s$, $s \in \{0, 1, 2 \ldots\}$) by

$$P(U = 0, A = a) = P(U = 0, X = a) = \frac{q^s}{1 - q},$$

$$P(U = 1, A = a) = P(U = 1, X = \frac{a}{2}) = \begin{cases} \dfrac{q^{s-1}}{1 - q} & \text{if } s \geq 1, \\[3mm] 0 & \text{if } s = 0. \end{cases}$$

For $q = 0.25$, it is shown in Fig. 1.

If player A has $a = 2^s$, the conditional probability of his gain by switching is

$$P(U = 0 | A = 2^s) = \frac{P(X = a)}{P(X = a) + P(X = \frac{a}{2})} = \frac{q}{q + 1} \tag{5}$$

for all $s \in \{1, 2, \ldots\}$ (and 1 for $s = 0$). As $q < 1/2$, this probability is less than $1/3$. The conditional expectation

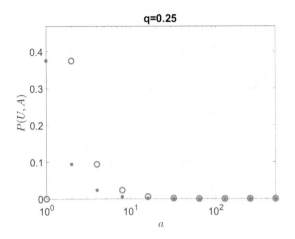

Figure 1: Joint distribution of U and A for $q = 0.25$. Values a of A are on the horizontal axis; blue dots denote $P(U = 0, A = a)$, orange circles $P(U = 1, A = a)$.

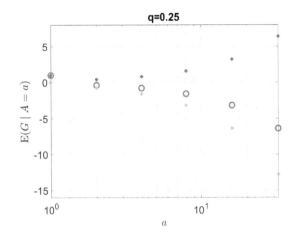

Figure 2: Conditional expectation of gain given $A = a$ for $q = 0.25$ (orange circles). It is a mixture (=convex combination) of the cases $U = 0$ (blue dots) and $U = 1$ (yellow dots).

of his gain is

$$
\begin{aligned}
\mathrm{E}(G|A = 2^s) &= \frac{2^s P(T = s) - 2^{s-1} P(T = s - 1)}{P(T = s) + P(T = s - 1)} \\
&= \begin{cases} 2^{s-1} \cdot \dfrac{2q - 1}{q + 1} & \text{if } s \in \{1, 2, \dots\}, \\ 1 & \text{if } s = 0. \end{cases}
\end{aligned} \tag{6}
$$

For $q = 0.25$, it is shown in Fig. 2. The contributions of conditional expectations $\mathrm{E}(G|A = a)$ to the unconditional expected gain $\mathrm{E}G$ are $\mathrm{E}(G|A = a) \cdot P(A = a)$, see Fig. 3. The conditional expectation is positive only for $s = 0$ (i.e., $a = 1$), negative otherwise. This determines the right strategy of switching: Switch only if you hold 1. The two players never both agree on switching the envelopes because at most one of them holds 1.

If player A does not know the contents of his envelope, he may use only its distribution

$$
P(A = 2^s) = \begin{cases} \dfrac{1}{2}\left(\dfrac{q^s}{1-q} + \dfrac{q^{s-1}}{1-q}\right) & \text{if } s \in \{1, 2, \dots\}, \\ \dfrac{1}{2}\dfrac{1}{1-q} & \text{if } s = 0, \\ 0 & \text{otherwise}, \end{cases}
$$

$$
= \begin{cases} \dfrac{1}{2} q^{s-1} \dfrac{q+1}{1-q} & \text{if } s \in \{1, 2, \dots\}, \\ \dfrac{1}{2}\dfrac{1}{1-q} & \text{if } s = 0, \\ 0 & \text{otherwise}. \end{cases}
$$

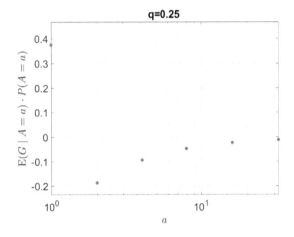

Figure 3: The contributions of conditional expectations of gain given $A = a$ to the unconditional expected gain for $q = 0.25$.

The unconditional expectation of the gain is

$$
\begin{aligned}
\mathrm{E}G &= \sum_{s=0}^{\infty} P(A = 2^s)\,\mathrm{E}(G|A = 2^s) \\
&= \frac{1}{2}\left(\frac{1}{1-q} + \sum_{s=1}^{\infty}(2q)^{s-1}\frac{2q-1}{1-q}\right) \\
&= \frac{1}{2}\left(\frac{1}{1-q} + \frac{1}{1-2q}\cdot\frac{2q-1}{1-q}\right) = 0,
\end{aligned} \tag{7}
$$

in accordance with our arguments.

4 Exchange Paradox: Second Level

In Section 2, we presented a standard explanation of the exchange paradox. It is based on the assumption that the amount in the envelopes has an expectation. This can fail even for some common distributions. (This fact is ignored, e.g., in [9].) We discovered that this leads to a more advanced paradox. We have found out that Nalebuff [8] proposed the same example, and similar ones can be found in [2]. However, Nalebuff only noticed that both players might be convinced that switching brings gain to them and that the above arguments are not applicable if the expectation does not exist. It seems that no detailed analysis was published since, and this is what we do here.

Let us consider the situation from Section 3 if $q > \frac{1}{2}$. Then the expectation EX does not exist. (The respective sum of a geometric series with quotient $2q > 1$ is $+\infty$.) For $q = 0.75$, the joint distribution of U and A is shown in Fig. 4.

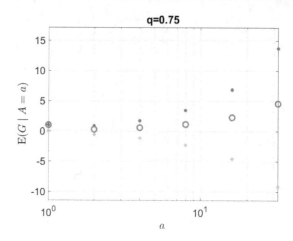

Figure 5: Conditional expectation of gain given $A = a$ for $q = 0.75$ (orange circles). It is a mixture of the cases $U = 0$ (blue dots) and $U = 1$ (yellow dots).

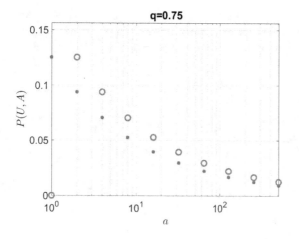

Figure 4: Joint distribution of U and A for $q = 0.75$. Values a of A are on the horizontal axis; blue dots denote $P(U = 0, A = a)$, orange circles $P(U = 1, A = a)$.

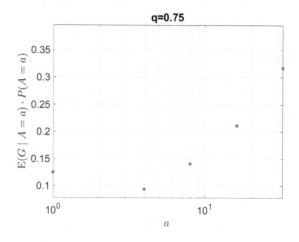

Figure 6: The contributions of conditional expectations of gain given $A = a$ to the unconditional expected gain for $q = 0.75$.

The expectation of the gain, EG, does not exist because the sum (2) is not absolutely convergent; it is a difference of two infinite sums in (3).

Still formula (6) for the conditional expectation of the gain is valid,

$$E(G|A = 2^s) = \begin{cases} 2^{s-1} \cdot \dfrac{2q-1}{q+1} & \text{if } s \in \{1, 2, \ldots\}, \\ 1 & \text{if } s = 0. \end{cases}$$

Thus $E(G|A = 2^s) > 0$ for all $s \in \{1, 2, \ldots\}$. For $q = 0.75$, see Fig. 5. (Notice that formula (5) for the conditional probability of gain $P(U = 0|A = 2^s)$ for $s \neq 0$ still holds and gives a constant value from the interval $(\frac{1}{3}, \frac{1}{2})$.) Player A has a strong argument for switching the envelopes, independently of the amount in his envelope. (Thus he may "rationally" decide for switching without looking inside the envelope.) Such distributions are called *paradoxical* in [2].

The same argument applies to player B. Although he holds a different amount in his envelope, he also prefers switching. We have again a paradox, now supported by a

probabilistic analysis. The only thing which does not work as in Section 3 is formula (7) for unconditional gain; the sum is not absolutely convergent. However, the unconditional gain is not needed for decision if the conditional one is always positive. How can we now defend Argument 1?

First of all, we refuse the possibility (considered in [2, 4, 6]) that players A and B will change the envelopes there and back forever. After one exchange and looking inside, they would know the contents of both envelopes and decide deterministically with full information. One of the players has the larger amount (and he knows that), so he would not agree to switch again.

If the players know only the amount in the envelope they received first, they have *different information*, and this is the key difference.

Example 1. *Suppose that A has 4 and B has 8. Then*

A knows that B can have 2 or 8, while B knows that A can have 4 or 16. Using Argument 2, A might expect that switching brings him a mean gain of 1. Using the model described in this section (formula (5) remains valid), he knows that his chance of gain is lower,

$$\frac{q}{q+1} \in \left(\frac{1}{3}, \frac{1}{2}\right).$$

For q = 0.75, this chance is $3/7 \doteq 0.43$, still sufficient to give a positive conditional mean gain of

$$\frac{8q+2}{q+1} - 4 = \frac{4}{7}.$$

Player B may apply the same arguments, leading to twice higher estimates of his gain.

Example 2. *Suppose now that A has 4 and B has 2. Then A knows that B can have 2 or 8, while B knows that A can have 1 or 4. From the point of view of player A, the situation is the same as in Ex. 1. Player B may apply the same arguments, leading to twice lower estimates of his gain, still supporting the decision to switch.*

In Exs. 1 and 2, we saw that probabilistic analysis suggests switching to both players. This apparently brings a gain to only one of them, but their arguments overestimate their chances. This explains why they may have contradictory views on the effect of the switching of envelopes (both thinking that the other envelope is "better").

To understand this paradox better, imagine the reverse game: Suppose that the players see the contents of the other player's envelope (and not of their own). Then the same reasoning (based on the information received) would support keeping the envelopes (and no switching). This shows that it is the *different incomplete information* which supports their paradoxical behavior. (The role of incomplete information and other arrangements of the experiment are discussed in [11] for the "first level" of the paradox.)

This situation is not so counterintuitive. Imagine for instance a poker game where two players hold a poker in their hands. They both evaluate their chances of winning as very high, although it is clear that only one is in the winning position. In the reverse game, where they see the cards of the opponent (and not their own), each player would estimate the chances of his opponent as very high, and he would surrender.

The two envelope problem in this setting possesses the same feature: the partial information given to players is overly optimistic. Thus looking inside the envelopes is not so helpful as it seems. Therefore, if rational players do not look inside any of the envelopes, the latter argument makes their choice ambivalent, and they would accept Argument 1. Even if they look in the envelopes, they will not accept Argument 2, knowing (from the above analysis of the model) that its prediction is biased and too optimistic.

5 Exchange Paradox: Third Level

Another modification of the example of Section 3 with $q = 1/2$ is also of particular interest. The joint distribution of U and A is shown in Fig. 7. Formula (5) for the conditional

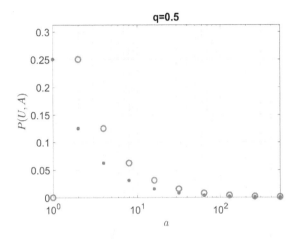

Figure 7: Joint distribution of U and A for $q = 0.5$. Values a of A are on the horizontal axis; blue dots denote $P(U = 0, A = a)$, orange circles $P(U = 1, A = a)$.

probability of gain gives $P(U = 0|A = 2^s) = 1/3$ if $s \neq 0$. The loss is twice more probable but twice smaller. Thus the conditional expectation of the gain simplifies to

$$E(G|A = 2^s) = \begin{cases} 0 & \text{if } s \in \{1, 2, \ldots\}, \\ 1 & \text{if } s = 0, \end{cases}$$

see Fig. 8 for the conditional expectations and Fig. 9 for their contributions to the unconditional expectation EG.

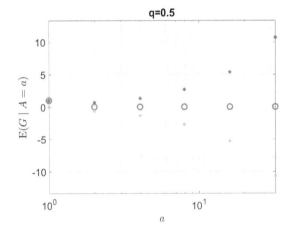

Figure 8: Conditional expectation of gain given $A = a$ for $q = 0.5$ (orange circles). It is a mixture of the cases $U = 0$ (blue dots) and $U = 1$ (yellow dots).

It seems that player A (as well as B) may only gain by

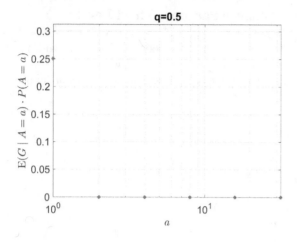

Figure 9: The contributions of conditional expectations of gain given $A = a$ to the unconditional expected gain for $q = 0.5$.

switching (if he holds 1), in all other cases the risk of loss is compensated by the same expected gain. In the sum in (7), only the first summand is nonzero, and it is positive. So the sum exists and evaluates to

$$\frac{1}{2}\frac{1}{1-q} > 0.$$

The arguments from Section 4 are applicable. Moreover, switching is supported by a computation which results in a positive unconditional gain (of a player not looking in his envelope). However, this argument is wrong. As in Section 4, the expectation of the gain, EG, does not exist because the sum (2), as a difference of two infinite sums in (3), is not absolutely convergent. Formula (7) uses only one possible arrangement of the summands, leading to an invalid conclusion. If player B applies the same argument, he uses another arrangement of the summands and gets a positive expected gain for himself, loss for A. Thus the sum (2) does not exist and the discussion from Section 4 fully applies, despite the seemingly trivial (wrong) sum (7).

6 Simulations

To verify the results, we also used computer simulations. We computed the average gain from 1000 samples and repeated this 5000 times. The results were displayed as histograms of the averages, see Figs. 10, 11, 12 for quotients $q = 0.25, 0.5, 0.75$, respectively. For $q = 0.75$, the linear scale could not be used for the horizontal axis. The semilogarithmic scale would not allow negative values. Therefore, we used the 31st root as a compromise which combines non-linearity similar to the logarithm and possibility of displaying negative values.

As expected, the histograms show relatively frequent occurrences of averages with high absolute value in cases

of $q = 0.5, 0.75$, where the expectation does not exist. The values are distributed approximately symmetrical with respect to zero, verifying that no envelope appears "better" and Argument 2 does not apply in practice, as predicted by the theoretical analysis in previous sections.

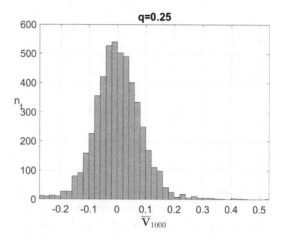

Figure 10: Histogram of average gains of 1000 samples for $q = 0.25$.

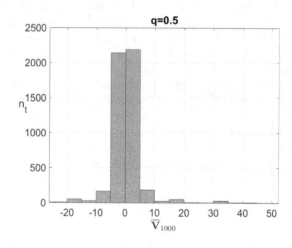

Figure 11: Histogram of average gains of 1000 samples for $q = 0.5$.

7 Conclusions

We explained the two envelope paradox in its classical form, as well as in two advanced instances in which the players find rather convincing (and still insufficient) probabilistic arguments for switching the envelopes. The latter is our novel contribution to the discussion of the paradox. We confirmed the following conclusion

"a perfectly rational player would simply recognize that his subjective probabilities provide a

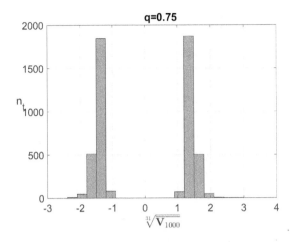

Figure 12: Histogram of average gains of 1000 samples for $q = 0.75$. The values on the horizontal axis are mapped by the 31st root.

misleading account using Bayesian decision theory and would therefore ignore those results" [1]

also in the case of nonexisting expectation, which was not considered in the cited source.

This topic has consequences in psychology, but it is also important in economics because it explains behavior at a market which is seemingly well-motivated, but in fact wrong. Besides, this paradox can be a good example and motivation for the study of statistics and information theory.

Acknowledgments. The first author was supported by the Ministry of Education of the Czech Republic under Project RVO13000.

References

[1] Bliss, E.: A Concise Resolution to the Two Envelope Paradox. 2012, arXiv:1202.4669

[2] Broome, J.: The Two-envelope Paradox. *Analysis* 55 (1995): 6–11 doi:10.1093/analys/55.1.6

[3] Cover, T.M.: Pick the largest number. In: Cover, T, Gopinath, B., *Open Problems in Communication and Computation*. Springer-Verlag, 1987

[4] Falk, R.: The Unrelenting Exchange Paradox. *Teaching Statistics* 30 (2008), 86–88 doi:10.1111/j.1467-9639.2008.00318.x

[5] Gerville-Réache, L.: Why do we change whatever amount we found in the first envelope: the Wikipedia "two envelopes problem" commented. University of Bordeaux - IMB UMR 52-51, 2014, arXiv:1402.3311

[6] Green, L.: The Two Envelope Paradox. 2012, http://www.aplusclick.com/pdf/LeslieGreenTwoEnvelopes.pdf, 2017-06-03

[7] Jackson, F., Menzies, P., Oppy, G.: The two envelope "paradox", *Analysis* 54 (1994) 43-45.

[8] Nalebuff, B.: Puzzles: The Other Person's Envelope is Always Greener. *Journal of Economic Perspectives* 3 (1988): 171–81 doi:10.1257/jep.3.1.171

[9] Martinian, E.: The Two Envelope Problem. https://web.archive.org/web/20071114230748/http://www.mit.edu/~emin/writings/envelopes.html, 2017-06-03, archive version of an original from 2007-11-14

[10] McDonnell, M. D., Abbott, D.: Randomized switching in the two-envelope problem. *Proceedings of the Royal Society A* 465 (2111): 3309–3322 doi:10.1098/rspa.2009.0312

[11] Priest, G., Restall, G.: Envelopes and Indifference, In: *Dialogues, Logics and Other Strange Things*, College Publications, 2007, 135–140

[12] Šindelář, J.: Two Envelopes Problem. Preprint of Bachelor Thesis, CTU, Prague, 2017-05-04

[13] Schwitzgebe, E., Dever, J.: The Two Envelope Paradox and Using Variables Within the Expectation Formula, *Sorites* (2008) 135–140

[14] Two envelopes problem. Wikipedia, 2017-05-10, https://en.wikipedia.org/wiki/Two_envelopes_problem

J. Hlaváčová (Ed.): ITAT 2017 Proceedings, pp. 120–128
ISBN 978-1974274741, © 2017 Z. Pitra, L. Bajer, J. Repický, M. Holeňa

Adaptive Doubly Trained Evolution Control
for the Covariance Matrix Adaptation Evolution Strategy

Zbyněk Pitra[1,2,3], Lukáš Bajer[3,4], Jakub Repický[3,4], and Martin Holeňa[3]

[1] National Institute of Mental Health
Topolová 748, 250 67 Klecany, Czech Republic
z.pitra@gmail.com

[2] Faculty of Nuclear Sciences and Physical Engineering, Czech Technical University in Prague
Břehová 7, 115 19 Prague 1, Czech Republic

[3] Institute of Computer Science, Academy of Sciences of the Czech Republic
Pod Vodárenskou věží 2, 182 07 Prague 8, Czech Republic
bajeluk@gmail.com, j.repicky@gmail.com, holena@cs.cas.cz

[4] Faculty of Mathematics and Physics, Charles University in Prague
Malostranské nám. 25, 118 00 Prague 1, Czech Republic

Abstract: An area of increasingly frequent applications of evolutionary optimization to real-world problems is continuous black-box optimization. However, evaluating real-world black-box fitness functions is sometimes very time-consuming or expensive, which interferes with the need of evolutionary algorithms for many fitness evaluations. Therefore, surrogate regression models replacing the original expensive fitness in some of the evaluated points have been in use since the early 2000s. The Doubly Trained Surrogate Covariance Matrix Adaptation Evolution Strategy (DTS-CMA-ES) represents a surrogate-assisted version of the state-of-the-art algorithm for continuous black-box optimization CMA-ES. The DTS-CMA-ES saves expensive function evaluations through using a surrogate model. However, the model inaccuracy on some functions can slow-down the algorithm convergence. This paper investigates an extension of DTS-CMA-ES which controls the usage of the model according to the model's error. Results of testing an adaptive and the original version of DTS-CMA-ES on the set of noiseless benchmarks are reported.

1 Introduction

Evolutionary algorithms have become very successful in continuous black-box optimization. That is, in optimization where no mathematical expression of the optimized function is available, neither an explicit nor implicit one, and it is necessary to empirically evaluate the fitness functions through series of measurements or simulations.

Considering real-world applications, the evaluation of a black-box function can be very time-consuming or expensive. Taking into account this property, the optimization method should evaluate as small amount of points as possible and still reach the target distance to the function optimal value.

The *Covariance Matrix Adaptation Evolution Strategy* (CMA-ES) [4] is considered to be the state-of-the-art optimization algorithm for continuous black-box optimization. On the other hand, the CMA-ES can consume many

evaluations to find the optimum of the expensive fitness function. This property resulted in the development of several surrogate-assisted versions of the CMA-ES (an overview can be found in [11]), where a part of evaluations is performed by a regression surrogate model instead of the original fitness function.

The *local meta-model CMA-ES* (lmm-CMA-ES), proposed in [7] and later improved in [1], builds a quadratic regression model for each point using a set of points already evaluated by the fitness function. The convergence of the algorithm is speeded-up by using a control of changes in population ranking after the fraction of the offspring is evaluated by the original fitness.

A different surrogate-assisted approach, utilizing an ordinal SVM to estimate the ranking of the fitness function values, called ^{s}*ACM-ES, has been introduced in [8] and later improved in BIPOP-^{s}*ACM-ES-k [9] to be more robust against premature convergence to local optima. The parameters of the SVM surrogate model are themselves optimized using the CMA-ES algorithm.

In 2016, the *Doubly Trained Surrogate CMA-ES* (DTS-CMA-ES) algorithm, using the ability of Gaussian processes to provide the distribution of predicted points, was introduced in [10]. The algorithm employs uncertainty criteria to choose the most promising points to be evaluated by the original fitness.

Results obtained with the three above-mentioned surrogate-assisted algorithms on noiseless functions [11] suggest that on some fitness functions (e. g., *attractive sector* function) the surrogate model happens to suffer from a loss of accuracy. Whereas the first of these algorithms controls the number of points evaluated by the original fitness function to prevent the model from misleading the search, the DTS-CMA-ES has the amount of evaluated points fixed. Therefore, some control of the amount of points evaluated by the original fitness in each generation could speed-up the DTS-CMA-ES convergence.

This paper extends the original DTS-CMA-ES with an online adaptation of the number of the points evaluated by the original fitness. This extended version of DTS-

---

Algorithm 1 DTS-CMA-ES [10]

Input: λ (population-size), y_{target} (target value),
    f (original fitness function), α (ratio of original-
    evaluated points), $\mathcal{C}$ (uncertainty criterion)

1: $\sigma, \mathbf{m}, \mathbf{C} \leftarrow$ CMA-ES initialize
2: $\mathcal{A} \leftarrow \varnothing$ {*archive initialization*}
3: **while** minimal y_k from $\mathcal{A} > y_{\text{target}}$ **do**
4:   $\{\mathbf{x}_k\}_{k=1}^{\lambda} \sim \mathcal{N}\left(\mathbf{m}, \sigma^2 \mathbf{C}\right)$ {*CMA-ES sampling*}
5:   $f_{\mathcal{M}1} \leftarrow$ trainModel$(\mathcal{A}, \sigma, \mathbf{m}, \mathbf{C})$ {*model training*}
6:   $(\hat{\mathbf{y}}, \mathbf{s}^2) \leftarrow f_{\mathcal{M}1}([\mathbf{x}_1, \ldots, \mathbf{x}_\lambda])$ {*model evaluation*}
7:   $\mathbf{X}_{\text{orig}} \leftarrow$ select $\lceil \alpha\lambda \rceil$ best points accord. to $\mathcal{C}(\hat{\mathbf{y}}, \mathbf{s}^2)$
8:   $\mathbf{y}_{\text{orig}} \leftarrow f(\mathbf{X}_{\text{orig}})$ {*original fitness evaluation*}
9:   $\mathcal{A} = \mathcal{A} \cup \{(\mathbf{X}_{\text{orig}}, \mathbf{y}_{\text{orig}})\}$ {*archive update*}
10:   $f_{\mathcal{M}2} \leftarrow$ trainModel$(\mathcal{A}, \sigma, \mathbf{m}, \mathbf{C})$ {*model retrain*}
11:   $\mathbf{y} \leftarrow f_{\mathcal{M}2}([\mathbf{x}_1, \ldots, \mathbf{x}_\lambda])$ {*2nd model prediction*}
12:   $(\mathbf{y})_k \leftarrow y_{\text{orig},i}$ for all original-evaluated $y_{\text{orig},i} \in \mathbf{y}_{\text{orig}}$
13:   $\sigma, \mathbf{m}, \mathbf{C} \leftarrow$ CMA-ES update
14: **end while**
15: $\mathbf{x}_{\text{res}} \leftarrow \mathbf{x}_k$ from $\mathcal{A}$ where y_k is minimal

Output: $\mathbf{x}_{\text{res}}$ (point with minimal y)

Algorithm 2 Adaptive DTS-CMA-ES

Input: λ (population-size), y_{target} (target value),
    f (original fitness function), β (update rate),
    α^0, $\alpha_{\min}$, $\alpha_{\max}$ (initial, minimal, and maximal ratio
    of original-evaluated points), $\mathcal{C}$ (uncertainty criterion),
    $\mathcal{E}^{(0)}$, $\mathcal{E}_{\min}$, $\mathcal{E}_{\max}$ (initial, minimal, and maximal error)

1: $\sigma, \mathbf{m}, \mathbf{C}, g \leftarrow$ CMA-ES initialize
2: $\mathcal{A} \leftarrow \varnothing$ {*archive initialization*}
3: **while** minimal y_k from $\mathcal{A} > y_{\text{target}}$ **do**
4:   $\{\mathbf{x}_k\}_{k=1}^{\lambda} \sim \mathcal{N}\left(\mathbf{m}, \sigma^2 \mathbf{C}\right)$ {*CMA-ES sampling*}
5:   $f_{\mathcal{M}1} \leftarrow$ trainModel$(\mathcal{A}, \sigma, \mathbf{m}, \mathbf{C})$ {*model training*}
6:   $(\hat{\mathbf{y}}, \mathbf{s}^2) \leftarrow f_{\mathcal{M}1}([\mathbf{x}_1, \ldots, \mathbf{x}_\lambda])$ {*model evaluation*}
7:   $\mathbf{X}_{\text{orig}} \leftarrow$ select $\lceil \alpha\lambda \rceil$ best points accord. to $\mathcal{C}(\hat{\mathbf{y}}, \mathbf{s}^2)$
8:   $\mathbf{y}_{\text{orig}} \leftarrow f(\mathbf{X}_{\text{orig}})$ {*fitness evaluation*}
9:   $\mathcal{A} = \mathcal{A} \cup \{(\mathbf{X}_{\text{orig}}, \mathbf{y}_{\text{orig}})\}$ {*archive update*}
10:   $f_{\mathcal{M}2} \leftarrow$ trainModel$(\mathcal{A}, \sigma, \mathbf{m}, \mathbf{C})$ {*model retrain*}
11:   $\mathbf{y} \leftarrow f_{\mathcal{M}2}([\mathbf{x}_1, \ldots, \mathbf{x}_\lambda])$ {*2nd model prediction*}
12:   $(\mathbf{y})_k \leftarrow y_{\text{orig},i}$ for all original-evaluated $y_{\text{orig},i} \in \mathbf{y}_{\text{orig}}$
13:   $\mathcal{E}^{\text{RDE}} \leftarrow \text{RDE}_\mu(\hat{\mathbf{y}}, \mathbf{y})$ {*model's error estimation*}
14:   $\mathcal{E}^{(g)} \leftarrow (1-\beta)\mathcal{E}^{(g-1)} + \beta\mathcal{E}^{\text{RDE}}$ {*exponen. smooth*}
15:   $\alpha \leftarrow$ update using linear transfer function in Eq.(2)
16:   $\sigma, \mathbf{m}, \mathbf{C}, g \leftarrow$ CMA-ES update
17: **end while**
18: $\mathbf{x}_{\text{res}} \leftarrow \mathbf{x}_k$ from $\mathcal{A}$ where y_k is minimal

Output: $\mathbf{x}_{\text{res}}$ (point with minimal y)

CMA-ES is compared with the original version as well as with the other two above mentioned surrogate models on the noiseless part of the *Comparing-Continuous-Optimisers (COCO) platform* [5, 6] in the expensive scenario and compares it to the original CMA-ES, lmm-CMA-ES, $^s*$ACM-ES, and original DTS-CMA-ES. Section 2 describes the original DTS-CMA-ES in more detail. Section 3 defines the adaptivity employed to improve the original DTS. Section 4 contains the experimental part. Section 5 summarizes the results and concludes the paper.

2   Doubly Trained Surrogate CMA-ES

The DTS-CMA-ES, introduced in [10], is outlined in Algorithm 1. The algorithm utilizes the ability of GP to estimate the whole probability distribution of fitness to select individuals out of the current population using some uncertainty criterion. The selected individuals are subsequently reevaluated with the original fitness and incorporated into the set of points utilized for retraining the GP model. The CMA-ES strategy parameters (σ, $\mathbf{m}$, $\mathbf{C}$, etc.) are calculated using the original CMA-ES algorithm.

3   Adaptivity for the DTS-CMA-ES

In this section, we propose a simple adaptation mechanism for the DTS-CMA-ES. In DTS-CMA-ES, the number of points evaluated by the original fitness function in one generation is controlled by the ratio α. The higher values of α, the more points are evaluated by the original fitness. As a consequence, more training points are available for the surrogate model around the current CMA-ES mean $\mathbf{m}$. In addition, the CMA-ES is less misled by a smaller amount

of points evaluated by the model. On the other hand, the lower values of α imply less evaluations by the original fitness and possibly a faster convergence of the algorithm. The ratio α can be controlled according to the surrogate model precision. Taking into account that the CMA-ES is dependent only on the ordering of the μ best individuals from the current population, we suggest to use the Ranking Difference Error described in the following paragraph.

The *Ranking Difference Error* (RDE$_\mu$), is a normalized version of the error measure used by Kern in [7]. It is the sum of differences of rankings of the μ best points in the population of size λ, normalized by the maximal possible such error for the respective μ, λ ($\rho(i)$ and $\hat{\rho}(i)$ are the ranks of the i-th element in vectors $\mathbf{y}$ and $\hat{\mathbf{y}}$ respectively, where $\mathbf{y}$'s ranking is expected to be more precise)

$$\text{RDE}_\mu(\hat{\mathbf{y}}, \mathbf{y}) = \frac{\sum_{i:\rho(i)\leq\mu} |\hat{\rho}(i) - \rho(i)|}{\max_{\pi \in \text{Permutations of } (1,\ldots,\lambda)} \sum_{i:\pi(i)\leq\mu} |i - \pi(i)|}.$$

(1)

The adaptive DTS-CMA-ES (aDTS-CMA-ES), depicted in Algorithm 2, differs from the original DTS-CMA-ES in several additional steps (lines 13–15) processed after the surrogate model $f_{\mathcal{M}2}$ is retrained using the new original-evaluated points from the current generation (line 10). First, the quality of the model is estimated using the RDE$_\mu(\hat{\mathbf{y}}, \mathbf{y})$ measured between the first model's prediction $\hat{\mathbf{y}}$ and the vector $\mathbf{y}$ which is composed of the available original fitness values (from $\mathbf{y}_{\text{orig}}$) and the retrained model's predictions for the points which are not original-evaluated. Due to noisy observation of the model's error

$\mathcal{E}^{RDE}$, we have employed exponential smoothing of the measured error using the update rate β (line 14). As the next step (line 15), α is calculated via linear transfer function of $\mathcal{E}^{(g)}$

$$\alpha = \begin{cases} \alpha_{min} & \mathcal{E}^{(g)} \leq \mathcal{E}_{min} \\ \alpha_{min} + \frac{\mathcal{E}^{(g)} - \mathcal{E}_{min}}{\mathcal{E}_{max} - \mathcal{E}_{min}} (\alpha_{max} - \alpha_{min}) & \mathcal{E}^{(g)} \in (\mathcal{E}_{min}, \mathcal{E}_{max}) , \\ \alpha_{max} & \mathcal{E}^{(g)} \geq \mathcal{E}_{max} \end{cases} \tag{2}$$

where $\mathcal{E}_{min}$ and $\mathcal{E}_{max}$ are lower and upper bounds for saturation to the values of α_{min} and α_{max} respectively.

Having analyzed the RDE_μ error measures on the COCO/BBOB testbed, we observed that the measured RDE error $\mathcal{E}^{(g)}$ depends on the ratio α and the dimension D:

$$\mathcal{E}_{min} = f_{min}^{\mathcal{E}}(\alpha, D), \quad \mathcal{E}_{max} = f_{max}^{\mathcal{E}}(\alpha, D). \tag{3}$$

Especially dependence on α is not surprising: from the definition of RDE_μ follows that the more reevaluated points, the higher number of summands in nominator of (1) and hence the higher RDE_μ value. Due to mutual dependence of the parameters $\mathcal{E}$ and α, the calculation of α in each generation is performed in a cycle until convergence of α:

(1) calculate error thresholds $\mathcal{E}_{min}$, $\mathcal{E}_{max}$ using the last used ratio α – either from the previous iteration, or from the previous generation (see equation (3))

(2) calculate new ratio α using newly calculated $\mathcal{E}_{min}$, $\mathcal{E}_{max}$ (see equation (2))

In our implementation, the functions $f_{min}^{\mathcal{E}}$ and $f_{min}^{\mathcal{E}}$ are results of multiple linear regression – see section 4.1 for the details of these linear models. The remaining parts of the algorithm are similar to the original DTS-CMA-ES.

4   Experimental Evaluation

In this section, we compared the performances of the aDTS-CMA-ES to the original DTS-CMA-ES [10], the CMA-ES [4], and two other surrogate-assisted versions of the CMA-ES, the lmm-CMA-ES [1, 7] and the ^{s*}ACM-ES [9], on the noiseless part of the COCO/BBOB framework [5, 6].

4.1   Experimental Setup

The considered algorithms were evaluated using the 24 noiseless COCO/BBOB single-objective benchmarks [5, 6] in dimensions $D = 2, 3, 5$ and 10 on 15 different instances per function. The functions were divided into three groups according to the difficulty of their modeling with a GP model, where two groups were used for tuning aDTS-CMA-ES parameters and the remaining group was utilized to test the results of that tuning. The method of dividing the functions into those groups will be described below in connection with the aDTS-CMA-ES settings. The experiment stopping criteria were reaching either the maximum budget of 250 function evaluations per dimension (FE/D), or reaching the target distance from the function optimum $\Delta f_T = 10^{-8}$. The following paragraphs summarize the parameters of the compared algorithms.

The original CMA-ES was tested in its IPOP-CMA-ES version (Matlab code v. 3.61) with the following settings: the number of restarts = 4, IncPopSize = 2, $\sigma_{start} = \frac{8}{3}$, $\lambda = 4 + \lfloor 3 \log D \rfloor$. The remaining settings were left default.

The lmm-CMA-ES was employed in its improved version published in [1]. The results have been downloaded from the COCO/BBOB results data archive [1] in its GECCO 2013 settings.

We have used the bi-population version of the ^{s*}ACM-ES, the BIPOP-^{s*}ACM-ES-k [9]. Similarly to the lmm-CMA-ES, the algorithm results have also been downloaded from the COCO/BBOB results data archive[2].

The original DTS-CMA-ES was tested using the overall best settings from [10]: the prediction variance of Gaussian process model as the uncertainty criterion, the population size $\lambda = 8 + \lfloor 6 \log D \rfloor$, and the ratio of points evaluated by the original fitness $\alpha = 0.05$. The results of the DTS-CMA-ES are slightly different from previously published results [10, 11] due to a correction of a bug in the original version which was affecting the selection of points to be evaluated by the original fitness using an uncertainty criterion.

The aDTS-CMA-ES was tested with multiple settings of parameters. First, the linear regression models of lower and upper bounds for the error measure $\mathcal{E}_{min}$, $\mathcal{E}_{max}$ were identified via measuring RDE_μ on datasets from DTS-CMA-ES runs on the COCO/BBOB benchmarks.

As a first step, we figured out six BBOB functions which are the *easiest* (E) and six which are the *hardest* (H) to regress by our Gaussian process model based on the RDE_μ measured on 1250 *independent testsets* per function in each dimension: 10 sets of λ points in each of 25 equidistantly selected generations from the DTS-CMA-ES runs on the first 5 instances, see Table 1 for these sets of functions and their respective errors. The functions which were not identified as E or H form the *test* function set.

Using the same 25 DTS-CMA-ES "snapshots" on each of 5 instances, we calculated medians (Q_2) and the third quartiles (Q_3) of *measured* RDE_μ on populations from both groups of functions (E) and (H), where we used five different proportions of original-evaluated points $\alpha = \{0.04, 0.25, 0.5, 0.75, 1.00\}$ which were available for retrained models and thus also for measuring models' errors $\mathcal{E}^{(g)}$. These quartiles were regressed by multiple linear regression models using stepwise regression from a full quadratic model of the ratio α and dimension D or its logarithm $\log(D)$ (decision whether to use $\log(D)$ or D

---

[1] http://coco.gforge.inria.fr/data-archive/2013/lmm-CMA-ES_auger_noiseless.tgz

[2] http://coco.gforge.inria.fr/data-archive/2013/BIPOP-saACM-k_loshchilov_noiseless.tgz

was according to the RMSE of the final stepwise models); the stepwise regression was removing terms with the highest p-value > 0.05. The coefficients $\mathcal{E}_{\min}^{Q2}$ and $\mathcal{E}_{\min}^{Q3}$ of the lower thresholds were estimated on the data from (E) and the coefficients $\mathcal{E}_{\max}^{Q2}$ and $\mathcal{E}_{\max}^{Q3}$ of the higher thresholds on the data from (H), which resulted in the following models:

$$
\begin{aligned}
\mathcal{E}_{\min}^{Q2}(\alpha, D) &= (1 \quad \log(D) \quad \alpha \quad \alpha\log(D) \quad \alpha^2) \cdot b_1 \\
\mathcal{E}_{\min}^{Q3}(\alpha, D) &= (1 \quad D \quad \alpha \quad \alpha D \quad \alpha^2) \cdot b_2 \\
\mathcal{E}_{\max}^{Q2}(\alpha, D) &= (1 \quad D \quad \alpha \quad \alpha D \quad \alpha^2) \cdot b_3 \\
\mathcal{E}_{\max}^{Q3}(\alpha, D) &= (1 \quad \log(D) \quad \alpha \quad \alpha\log(D) \quad \alpha^2) \cdot b_4
\end{aligned}
$$

where

$$
b_1 = \begin{pmatrix} 0.11 \\ -0.0092 \\ -0.13 \\ 0.044 \\ 0.14 \end{pmatrix} \quad
b_2 = \begin{pmatrix} 0.17 \\ -0.00067 \\ -0.095 \\ 0.0087 \\ 0.15 \end{pmatrix} \quad
b_3 = \begin{pmatrix} 0.18 \\ -0.0027 \\ 0.44 \\ 0.0032 \\ -0.14 \end{pmatrix} \quad
b_4 = \begin{pmatrix} 0.35 \\ -0.047 \\ 0.44 \\ 0.044 \\ -0.19 \end{pmatrix}.
$$

For the remaining investigations, three different values of exponential smoothing update rate were used for comparison $\beta = \{0.3, 0.4, 0.5\}$. The minimal and maximal values of α were set to $\alpha_{\min} = 0.04$ and $\alpha_{\max} = 1.0$ because lower α values than 0.04 would yield to less than one original-evaluated point per generation, and the aDTS-CMA-ES has to be able to spend the whole populations for the original evaluations in order to work well on functions where GP model is poor (e. g., on f_6 *Attractive sector*). The initial error and original ratio values were set to $\mathcal{E}^{(0)} = 0.05$ and $\alpha^0 = 0.05$. The rest of aDTS-CMA-ES parameters were left the same as in the original DTS-CMA-ES settings.

4.2 Results

The results in Figures 1, 2, and 3 and in Table 3 show the effect of adaptivity implemented in the DTS-CMA-ES. The graphs in Figures 1, 2 and 3 depict the scaled logarithm $\Delta_f^{\log}$ of the median Δ_f^{med} of minimal distances from the function optimum over runs on 15 independent instances as a function of FE/D. The scaled logarithms of Δ_f^{med} are calculated as

$$
\Delta_f^{\log} = \frac{\log \Delta_f^{\mathrm{med}} - \Delta_f^{\mathrm{MIN}}}{\Delta_f^{\mathrm{MAX}} - \Delta_f^{\mathrm{MIN}}} \log_{10}\left(1/10^{-8}\right) + \log_{10} 10^{-8}
$$

where Δ_f^{MIN} (Δ_f^{MAX}) is the minimum (maximum) $\log \Delta_f^{\mathrm{med}}$ found among all the compared algorithms for the particular function f and dimension D between 0 and 250 FE/D. Such scaling enables the aggregation of $\Delta_f^{\log}$ graphs across arbitrary number of functions and dimensions (see Figure 3). The values are scaled to the $[-8, 0]$ interval, where -8 corresponds to the minimal and 0 to the maximal distance. This visualization has a better ability to distinguish the differences in the convergence of tested algorithms

more than the default visualization used by the COCO/B-BOB platform and that is why it was used in this article.

We have tested the statistical significance of differences in algorithms' performance on 12 COCO/BBOB *test* functions in 10D for separately two evaluation budgets using the Iman and Davenport's improvement of the Friedman test [2]. Let #FE$_T$ be the smallest number of function evaluations on which at least one algorithm reached the target, i. e., satisfied $\Delta_f^{\mathrm{med}} \leq \Delta f_T$, or #FE$_T$ = 250D if no algorithm reached the target within 250D evaluations. The algorithms are ranked on each COCO/BBOB *test* function with respect to Δ_f^{med} at a given budget of function evaluations. The null hypothesis of equal performance of all algorithms is rejected at a higher function evaluation budget #FEs = #FE$_T$ ($p < 10^{-3}$), as well as at a lower budget #FEs = $\frac{\text{#FE}_T}{3}$ ($p < 10^{-3}$).

We test pairwise differences in performance utilizing the post-hoc Friedman test [3] with the Bergmann-Hommel correction controlling the family-wise error in cases when the null hypothesis of equal algorithms' performance was rejected. To illustrate algorithms' differences, the numbers of *test* functions at which one algorithm achieved a higher rank than the other are reported in Table 3. The table also contains the pairwise statistical significances.

We have compared the performances of aDTS-CMA-ES using twelve settings differing in $\mathcal{E}_{\min}$, $\mathcal{E}_{\max}$, and β. Table 2 illustrates the counts of the 1st ranks of the compared settings according to the lowest achieved Δ_f^{med} for 25, 50, 100, and 200 FE/D respectively. The counts are summed across the testing sets of benchmark functions in each individual dimension.

Although the algorithm is rather robust to exact setting of smoothing update rate, we have found that the lower the β, the better the performance is usually observed (see Table 2), and thus the following experiments use the rate $\beta = 0.3$.

When comparing the convergence rate, the performance of aDTS-CMA-ES with $\mathcal{E}_{\min}^{Q2}$ is noticeable lower especially on Rosenbrock's functions (f_8, f_9) and Different powers f_{14} where the RDE$_\mu$ error often exceeds the lower error threshold even if a lower number of original-evaluated points would be sufficient for higher speedup of the CMA-ES. The adaptive control, on the other hand, helps especially on the Attractive sector f_6, which has the optimum in a point without continues derivatives and is therefore hard-to-regress by GPs, or on Shaffers' functions f_{17}, f_{18} where the aDTS-CMA-ES is probably able to adapt to multimodal neighbourhood around function's optimum and performs best of all the compared algorithms. Within the budget of 250 FE/D, the aDTS-CMA-ES (especially with $\mathcal{E}_{\min}^{Q2}$) is also able to find one of the best fitness value on regularly multimodal Rastrigin functions f_3, f_4 or f_{15} where the GP model apparently does not prevent the original CMA-ES from exploiting the global structure of a function.

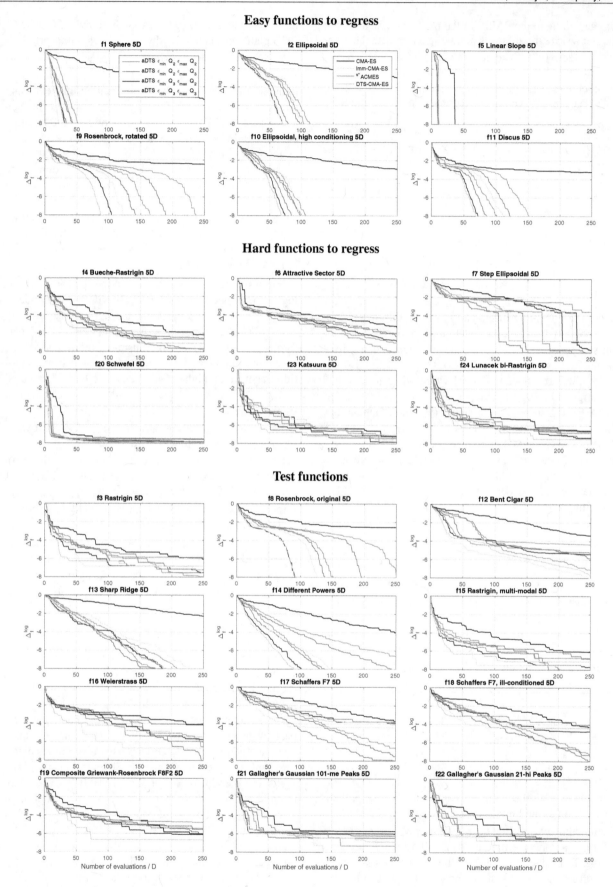

Figure 1: Algorithm comparison on 24 COCO/BBOB noiseless functions in 5D. $\varepsilon_{\min}$, $\varepsilon_{\max}$: minimal and maximal error, $Q2$, $Q3$: median and third quartile.

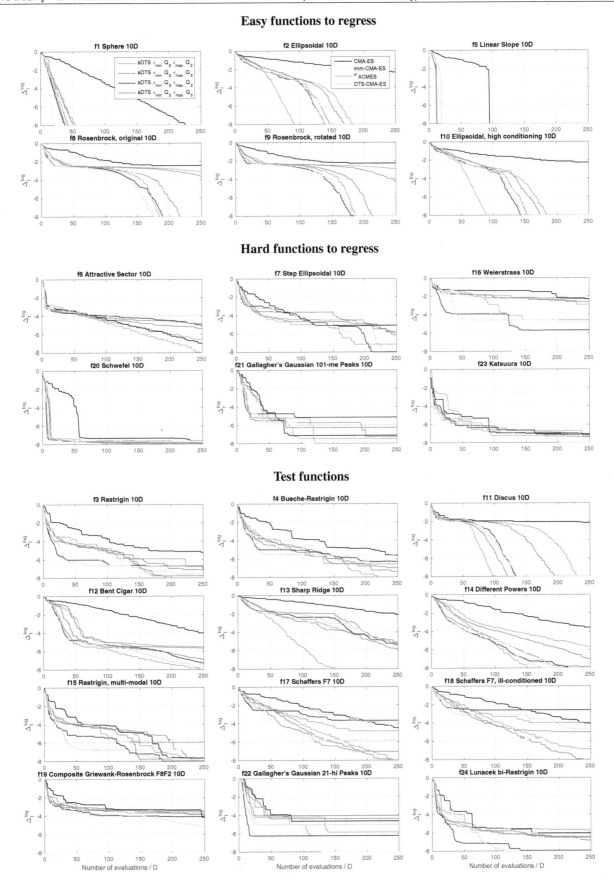

Figure 2: Algorithm comparison on 24 COCO/BBOB noiseless functions in 10D. ε_{min}, ε_{max}: minimal and maximal error, $Q2$, $Q3$: median and third quartile.

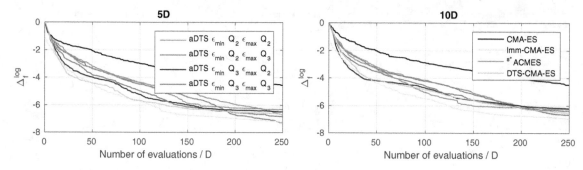

Figure 3: Algorithm comparison using averaged $\Delta_f^{\log}$ values on 12 *test* functions from the COCO/BBOB testbed in $5D$ and $10D$. $\varepsilon_{\min}$, $\varepsilon_{\max}$: minimal and maximal error, $Q2$, $Q3$: median and third quartile.

Table 1: The *easiest* (1.–6.) and the *hardest* (19.–24.) to regress six COCO/BBOB functions by the Gaussian process used in the DTS-CMA-ES (columns f) according to the corresponding medians of RDE_μ error measured in 25 generations from 5 instances on independent testsets of size $\lambda = 8 + \lfloor 6\log D \rfloor$ using $\mu = \lambda/2$.

	2D		3D		5D		10D		20D	
	f	RDE_μ	f	RDE_μ	f	RDE_μ	f	RDE_μ	f	RDE_μ
1.	5	0.00	5	0.00	5	0.00	5	0.04	5	0.04
2.	1	0.08	1	0.11	1	0.16	1	0.18	1	0.08
3.	2	0.10	2	0.13	10	0.18	10	0.26	24	0.18
4.	10	0.10	10	0.14	2	0.21	8	0.27	15	0.19
5.	11	0.10	9	0.16	11	0.23	2	0.27	19	0.20
6.	8	0.14	8	0.18	9	0.24	9	0.29	3	0.21
19.	18	0.46	23	0.43	24	0.41	21	0.40	18	0.38
20.	20	0.52	15	0.43	4	0.44	16	0.41	23	0.47
21.	24	0.53	24	0.49	23	0.45	23	0.47	6	0.48
22.	6	0.54	20	0.51	6	0.51	6	0.50	21	0.51
23.	7	0.54	6	0.52	20	0.54	20	0.54	20	0.52
24.	19	0.54	7	0.54	7	0.56	7	0.57	7	0.56

Table 2: Counts of the 1st ranks from 12 benchmark *test* functions from the BBOB/COCO testbed according to the lowest achieved Δ_f^{med} for different FE/$D = \{25, 50, 100, 200\}$ and dimensions $D = \{2, 3, 5, 10\}$. Ties of the 1st ranks are counted for all respective algorithms. The ties often occure when $\Delta f_T = 10^{-8}$ is reached (mostly on f_1 and f_5).

FE/D	2D				3D				5D				10D				Σ			
	25	50	100	200	25	50	100	200	25	50	100	200	25	50	100	200	25	50	100	200
$\varepsilon_{\min}^{Q2}, \varepsilon_{\max}^{Q2}, \beta = 0.3$	1	0	0	2	1	2	2	3	0	0	0	0	0	0	0	1	2	2	2	6
$\varepsilon_{\min}^{Q2}, \varepsilon_{\max}^{Q2}, \beta = 0.4$	0	0	0	2	1	0	0	3	0	0	0	0	0	0	0	0	1	0	0	5
$\varepsilon_{\min}^{Q2}, \varepsilon_{\max}^{Q2}, \beta = 0.5$	2	0	0	3	0	0	0	3	0	0	0	0	0	0	0	1	2	0	0	7
$\varepsilon_{\min}^{Q2}, \varepsilon_{\max}^{Q3}, \beta = 0.3$	2	0	1	4	1	0	0	3	0	0	2	2	0	0	0	2	3	0	3	11
$\varepsilon_{\min}^{Q2}, \varepsilon_{\max}^{Q3}, \beta = 0.4$	0	0	1	4	0	0	0	4	0	1	2	3	0	0	3	4	0	1	6	15
$\varepsilon_{\min}^{Q2}, \varepsilon_{\max}^{Q3}, \beta = 0.5$	1	0	0	3	0	0	0	4	0	0	0	3	0	0	0	1	1	0	0	11
$\varepsilon_{\min}^{Q3}, \varepsilon_{\max}^{Q2}, \beta = 0.3$	1	0	3	4	4	5	5	5	5	3	3	5	7	6	3	4	17	14	14	18
$\varepsilon_{\min}^{Q3}, \varepsilon_{\max}^{Q2}, \beta = 0.4$	1	4	1	4	1	0	1	4	5	4	0	4	1	2	3	2	8	10	5	14
$\varepsilon_{\min}^{Q3}, \varepsilon_{\max}^{Q2}, \beta = 0.5$	1	3	1	5	0	2	2	3	1	0	1	2	3	0	0	1	5	5	4	11
$\varepsilon_{\min}^{Q3}, \varepsilon_{\max}^{Q3}, \beta = 0.3$	0	2	2	4	1	3	3	3	0	3	3	4	0	1	2	1	1	9	10	12
$\varepsilon_{\min}^{Q3}, \varepsilon_{\max}^{Q3}, \beta = 0.4$	0	2	3	4	3	0	3	4	1	1	0	4	0	2	0	1	4	5	6	13
$\varepsilon_{\min}^{Q3}, \varepsilon_{\max}^{Q3}, \beta = 0.5$	3	1	2	3	0	0	1	3	0	0	1	2	1	1	1	2	4	2	5	10

Table 3: A pairwise comparison of the algorithms on 12 *test* functions in 10D over the COCO/BBOB for different evaluation budgets. The number of wins of i-th algorithm against j-th algorithm over all benchmark functions is given in i-th row and j-th column. The asterisk marks the row algorithm being significantly better than the column algorithm according to the Friedman post-hoc test with the Bergmann-Hommel correction at family-wise significance level $\alpha = 0.05$.

10D	$\mathcal{E}^{Q2}_{min}, \mathcal{E}^{Q2}_{max}$		$\mathcal{E}^{Q2}_{min}, \mathcal{E}^{Q3}_{max}$		$\mathcal{E}^{Q3}_{min}, \mathcal{E}^{Q2}_{max}$		$\mathcal{E}^{Q3}_{min}, \mathcal{E}^{Q3}_{max}$		CMA-ES		lmm-CMA-ES		^{s*}ACM-ES		DTS-CMA-ES	
#FEs/#FE$_T$	$\frac{1}{3}$	1	$\frac{1}{3}$	1	$\frac{1}{3}$	1	$\frac{1}{3}$	1	$\frac{1}{3}$	1	$\frac{1}{3}$	1	$\frac{1}{3}$	1	$\frac{1}{3}$	1
$\mathcal{E}^{Q2}_{min}, \mathcal{E}^{Q2}_{max}$	—	—	6	5	4	6	4	8	12	11	2	5	6	8	3	7
$\mathcal{E}^{Q2}_{min}, \mathcal{E}^{Q3}_{max}$	6	7	—	—	3	5	5	6	11	10	2	6	7	7	2	5
$\mathcal{E}^{Q3}_{min}, \mathcal{E}^{Q2}_{max}$	8	6	9	7	—	—	7	7	12*	9	4	5	8	5	3	2
$\mathcal{E}^{Q3}_{min}, \mathcal{E}^{Q3}_{max}$	8	4	7	6	5	5	—	—	11*	10	4	6	9	7	4	4
CMA-ES	0	1	1	2	0	3	1	2	—	—	1	1	2	4	0	1
lmm-CMA-ES	10	7	10	6	8	7	8	6	11*	11	—	—	10	6	7	5
^{s*}ACM-ES	6	4	5	5	4	7	3	5	10	8	2	6	—	—	3	7
DTS-CMA-ES	9	5	10	7	9	10	8	8	12*	11*	5	7	9	5	—	—

5 Conclusions & Future work

In this paper, we have presented a work-in-progress on adaptive version of the surrogate-assisted optimization algorithm DTS-CMA-ES. The online adjustment of the ratio between the original- and model-evaluated points according to the error of the surrogate model is investigated. The new adaptive version of the algorithm employs RDE$_\mu$ between the fitness of current population predicted using the first-trained model and the retrained model.

Results of parameter tunning show that lower values of the exponential smoothing rate β provide better results. On the other hand, different combinations of slower and more rapid update behaviours bring better CMA-ES speedup for different kinds of functions, and choice of this parameter could depend on the experimenter's domain knowledge. We found that the adaptive approach speeds up the CMA-ES more than three other surrogate CMA-ES algorithms, namely DTS-CMA-ES, ^{s*}ACM-ES, and lmm-CMA-ES, on several functions after roughly 150 FE/D.

The adaptivity of the DTS-CMA-ES is still, to a certain extent, work in progress. A future perspective of improving aDTS-CMA-ES is to additionally investigate different types and properties of adaptive control of the number of points evaluated by the original fitness in each generation. Another conceivable direction of future research can be found in online switching between different types of surrogate models suitable for the aDTS-CMA-ES.

Acknowledgements

The reported research was supported by the Czech Science Foundation grant No. 17-01251, by the Grant Agency of the Czech Technical University in Prague with its grant No. SGS17/193/OHK4/3T/14, and by the project Nr. LO1611 with a financial support from the MEYS under the NPU I program. Further, access to computing and storage facilities owned by parties and projects contributing to the National Grid Infrastructure MetaCentrum, provided under the programme "Projects of Large Infrastructure for Research, Development, and Innovations" (LM2010005), is greatly appreciated.

References

[1] A. Auger, D. Brockhoff, and N. Hansen. Benchmarking the local metamodel CMA-ES on the noiseless BBOB'2013 test bed. In *Proceedings of the GECCO '13 Companion*, 2013.

[2] J. Demšar. Statistical comparisons of classifiers over multiple data sets. *Journal of Machine Learning Research*, 7:1–30, 2006.

[3] S. García and F. Herrera. An extension on "statistical comparisons of classifiers over multiple data sets" for all pairwise comparisons. *Journal of Machine Learning Research*, 9:2677–2694, 2008.

[4] N. Hansen. The CMA Evolution Strategy: A Comparing Review. In *Towards a New Evolutionary Computation*, number 192, pages 75–102. Springer, 2006.

[5] N. Hansen, A. Auger, S. Finck, and R. Ros. Real-parameter black-box optimization benchmarking 2012: Experimental setup. Technical report, INRIA, 2012.

[6] N. Hansen, S. Finck, R. Ros, and A. Auger. Real-parameter black-box optimization benchmarking 2009: Noiseless functions definitions. Technical Report RR-6829, INRIA, 2009. Updated February 2010.

[7] S. Kern, N. Hansen, and P. Koumoutsakos. Local Meta-models for Optimization Using Evolution Strategies. In *PPSN IX Proceedings*, volume 4193 of *Lecture Notes in Computer Science*, pages 939–948. Springer, 2006.

[8] I. Loshchilov, M. Schoenauer, and M. Sebag. Self-adaptive surrogate-assisted covariance matrix adaptation evolution strategy. In *Proceedings of the GECCO '12*, pages 321–328. ACM, 2012.

[9] I. Loshchilov, M. Schoenauer, and M. Sebag. BI-population CMA-ES Algorithms with Surrogate Models and Line Searches. In *Proceedings of the GECCO '13 Companion*, pages 1177–1184. ACM Press, 2013.

[10] Z. Pitra, L. Bajer, and M. Holeňa. Doubly trained evolution control for the Surrogate CMA-ES. In *PPSN XIV Proceedings*, pages 59–68. Springer, 2016.

[11] Z. Pitra, L. Bajer, J. Repický, and M. Holeňa. Overview of surrogate-model versions of covariance matrix adaptation evolution strategy. In *Proceedings of the GECCO '17 Companion*. ACM, 2017.

J. Hlaváčová (Ed.): ITAT 2017 Proceedings, pp. 129–135
ISBN 978-1974274741, © 2017 J. Puchýř, M. Holeňa

Random-Forest-Based Analysis of URL Paths

Jakub Puchýř, Martin Holeňa

Czech Technical University, puchyjak@fit.cvut.cz
Czech Academy of Sciences, Prague, martin@cs.cas.cz

Abstract: One of the key sources of spreading malware are malicious web sites – either tricking user to install malware imitating legitimate software or, in the case of various exploit kits, initiating malware installation even without any user action. The most common technique against such web sites is blacklisting. However, it provides little to no information about new sites never seen before. Therefore, there has been important research into predicting malicious web sites based on their features. This work-in-progress paper presents a light-weight prediction method using solely lexical features of the site URL and classification by random forests. To this end, three possibilities of feature extraction have been elaborated and investigated on real-world data sets with respect to precision and recall. The obtained results indicate that there is nearly never a significant difference betrweeen the considered methods, and that in spite of the limitation to the lexical features of the site URL, they have an impressive performance in terms of area under the precision-recall curve for the path parts of URLs.

Keywords: malicious URLs detection, classification, random forest

1 Introduction

Protecting devices from malicious software is a never ending fight. There are multiple ways how malware can infect an end point device but the most common way how malware can spread itself is via malicious web sites – either tricking user to install it by imitating legitimate software or, in the case of various exploits kits, install itself without any user action or knowledge. An ideal defence against such a threat would be to block any malicious site before it can even serve its content. The most common technique, which is widely used in practice, is blacklisting. While such technique is extremely fast (just searching for the URL within the list), it provides only limited protection, since no blacklist is perfectly up-to-date [6]. In particular blacklisting provide us with little to none additional information about new, never before seen sites.

Aware of this problem security researchers have proposed various systems to protect users. We can basically divide these approaches into two groups based on information they are using. The first one is considering the content of the web site. Provos et al. [5] proposed a solution based on the position of iframes and the existence of obfuscated javascript to detect malicious landing-pages. This approach is usually more reliable because it provides

all necessary informations. On the other hand, it is clearly slower since it must process more data and it is potentially dangerous since it needs to actually access the content. Zhang et al. [8] proposed method to detect phishing sites based on the TF-IDF of the whole document.

The other approach is to consider only the URL itself and information related to it, such as DNS and whois records. To this end, multiple approaches have been proposed, such as classification based on bag-of-word representation of the URL by Ma et al.[3], [4] or characters n-grams representation used by Verma et al. [7] to detect phishing sites. Both of these studies show that systems based on lexical and host based features can have very low percentage of misclassified samples; unfortunately, the studies do not differentiate between benign site classified as a malicious one and vice versa. In real-word scenarios, however, the misclassification of benign site is much more severe. Motivated by these studies, we focus on fast and light-weight classification of the URL, where we use only lexical based features of the URL and where we are trying to minimize the number of misclassified benign sites, i.e. to maximize specificity, even at the expense of a higher number of misclassified samples, ie.e, at the expense of lower accuracy. The goal of our approach is to provide classification method which would be fast and keep the number of falsely classified URLs as low as blacklisting, yet would still be able to generalize and thus be ideal as a pre-filtering method for some slower, more precise methods.

In the previously mentioned papers we can see that there are multiple different algorithms which reach very similar results, thus we decided to do the very opposite. We use only one algorithm – random forest in our case – and compare its result on different types of features generated from the same set of the URLs. To demonstrate this approach we have used a large number of URLs, labelled by a paticular antivirus software, to build our classification system. Using this data, we show that classification models based only the on the lexical parts of URL can still reach a high precision and that a different representation might be more suitable for different parts of the URL.

The following two sections recall in turn several methods for extracting features from the URL, and our algorithm of choice – random forests. After that, we describe three variants of the proposed method. These variants are experimentally compared in Section 5, after which the paper concludes.

2 Feature Extraction

Uniform Resource Locators (URLs) are the global addresses of resources on World Wide Web and they are the primary means by which users browse through the Internet. They are human-readable text strings with the structure depicted in a figure 1. The "host" is arguably the most important part of the URL. One of the main ideas, why classification based on the lexical structure of a URL might work, is that malicious URLs tend to look different. The benign URLs, especially the host parts, are mostly short and easy to remember in comparison to malicious ones.

In this section, we provide an overview of the problem and a discussion of the features used for URL classification.

Figure 1: Example of URL and its components.

2.1 Problem Overview

A site with unsolicited content may belong to several categories such as spam, phishing, drive-by exploits, etc., but for our purpose we treat all of these categories as one, since the ultimate decision is always the same - whether to allow access to a given site, or not. We go by medical terminology which is commonly used in cyber security. Labelling a sample as a *positive* means labelling it as a malicious URL and *negative* means benign one.

We classify sites based only on the lexical structure of URLs without considering any additional information such as reputation or content. While these informations might improve accuracy, we exclude them for several reasons. First, we focus on light-weight and fast classification, thus downloading a content is out of our scope for its slowness. Second, accessing the content of a page before getting known whether it is malicious is potentially dangerous, since you might get infected before blocking the site. The reason for not using reputation or host-based information is more a technical issue since such information is fairly hard to get and the information itself might not be up to date. That is especially unsuitable in case of malicious domains, since some of them tend to exist only for few days or even hours. Nevertheless we show in Section 5 that classifying web sites using only the lexical features of the URLs can still be sufficient for a high precision.

2.2 Features Pertaining to a URL

From the point of view of classification, the most important parts are host, port, path, and query. We do not consider the fragment part since it is basically non-existent in malicious URLs and we do not use the scheme part either. One might argue, that using a secure protocol (such as https) is a strong indicator for a benign site. That is true – almost all tested malicious URL do not use secure layer. Unfortunately a lot of benign URLs, especially not very known ones, do not use it either, thus we decided to not use scheme based features to avoid skewed results.

Since our goal is to design light-weight and fast classification system, we can not afford to use complicated representation. We combine a few real-valued, hand selected features such as length of the entire URL and its parts, the number of subdomains, number of non-alphanumeric characters in a path, etc., with several text representation techniques.

1. The Bag-of-words (BoW) representation, where each part of the URL is represented as a bag of its words. While this representation is quick to compute, it suffers from two major drawbacks. The feature space is extremely large (theoretically unbounded) and the word ordering is lost which is especially troublesome in our case since we do not use any additional information but the URL. Therefore, we slightly modify the BoW to keep some additional information such as top and second level domains and last words in a path, since that is usually a file extension for a downloaded file. While models using this representation might reach high precision, they have one major drawback. Some of the malicious URLs tend to generate their domain names in a pseudo-random way, that is they generate many names which differ in a few characters, yet they still look very similar. This is the case where BoW absolutely fails as it has no way how to detect these changes.

2. To overcome this we use following technique. Character N-grams is a representation where each consecutive N characters are considered a feature. While this representation does not preserve the word ordering either, it bounds the size of feature space by $O(\Sigma^N)$ where Σ is the size of the alphabet, and to a certain extent improves BoW inability to generalize over long, pseudo-random generated words.

   While inspecting the structure of URLs, we noticed that some of the malicious URLs differ only in a few characters. Moreover, these random characters are always on the same position, thus we use a generalization of character N-grams.

3. Character N-grams with k don't care symbols is a generalization of N-grams representation, where each N-gram is transformed into a set of $\binom{N}{k}$-grams with k don't care symbols. For example, 4-grams *ITAT* and *ICAT* are transformed into following set of 4-grams with one don't care symbol: *?TAT, I?AT, IT?T, ITA?, ?CAT, IC?T, ICA?* , where "?" marks a position of the don't care symbol.

This representation is as fast to compute as the previous ones and reduces the size of the feature space even more – to $O\left(\binom{N}{k}\Sigma^{N-k}\right)$. Moreover it has the best ability to generalize as we show in the results in Section 5.

3   Random Forests

We chose random forests as our classification algorithm for several reasons. It provides us with a probabilistic output, it is capable of handling a huge number of features, which is especially important in our case, and it handles naturally problems with multiple classes.

A random forest is an ensemble of randomly trained decision trees and it is characterized by multiple parameters such as the forest size T, the maximum depth D for each tree in the forest, the training objective function.

Each split node i, i.e, inner node of the tree, is associated with a binary split function

$$h(\boldsymbol{v},\boldsymbol{\Phi}_i) \in \{True, False\},$$

where $\boldsymbol{v} = (x_1, x_2, \ldots, x_d) \in \mathbb{R}^d$ denotes the feature vector and $\boldsymbol{\Phi}_i$ is the optimal parameter of the i-th split node. The data arriving at the split node i are sent to its left or right child depending on the result of the value returned by the corresponding split function.

3.1   Training

The training process is typically repeated independently for each tree in a forest. During training, the optimal parameter of the split node needs to be computed for every split node in a tree. To this end, we have chosen to maximize an information gain objective function:

$$\boldsymbol{\Phi}_i^* = arg\ max_{\boldsymbol{\Phi}_i} I_i$$

where I_i is the information gain of the i-th split node, defined as:

$$I_i = H(S_i) - \sum_{j \in \{L,R\}} \frac{|S_i^j|}{|S_i|} H(S_i^j)$$

with j indexing the two child nodes. H is the (Shannon) entropy of a set S of training points:

$$H(S) = - \sum_{c \in C} p(c) \log p(c),$$

where $p(c)$ is the empirical probability based on S of the class $c \in C$.

3.2   Testing

During testing, each test point $\boldsymbol{v}$ is pushed through all trees in a forest T until it reaches a corresponding leaf. The tree predictions are combined through averaging:

$$p(c \mid v) = \frac{1}{T} \sum_{t \in T} p_t(c|v).$$

4   Proposed Approach and Its Variants

We focus on designing fast and light-weight system for URL classification, which uses only a minimal amount of available information about the given site. With such a small amount of information, it is hardly possible to reach 100% accuracy of classification. Aware of this problem, we suggest our classification system to be used as a pre-filter for some method using a broader spectrum of features. Hence, our goal is to design a system with extremely low number of false positives, thus reaching high precision. Since we design our system as a pre-filter, any false-positive result is a final one whereas false-negative results might be adjusted by some of the later methods. Therefore, we decided to prioritize precision over accuracy.

We describe two slightly different systems which differ only in the last step - the way how the final classification is produced. The feature extraction is common to both systems and it is executed in the way described in Section 2.2.

The first, common approach for building such a system is to simply train a classifier (random forest in our case) on the gathered data and set the threshold high enough to minimize the number of false positives. We propose another solution that is based on the fact that each part of the URL (i.e. host, path, or query) has a different lexical structure and wording. Therefore, we train specialized models for each part of the URL separately and the final model is a team of these. The final classification is done via a voting of all models, where the URL is classified as malicious if at least one of the models classified it so. An advantage of using separate models for each part is that it reduces the dimensionality and overall size of the model. That is especially case for the host part, since there are usually multiple URLs that differ only in the path or query part. Thanks to this, we can afford to either train more complex models or to retrain them more frequently, and thus indirectly increase accuracy of our models.

5   Experimental Evaluation

In this section we describe experiments that were performed to test and compare the proposed methods. We evaluated the methods with two performance measures. Both of them measure the performance of a whole family of classifiers corresponding to some finite set Θ of decision thresholds. The first one is an area under the precision-recall curve, where precision and recall corresponding to a threshold Θ are defined the standard way, i.e.

$$precision = \frac{tp(\Theta)}{tp(\Theta) + fp(\Theta)}$$
$$recall = \frac{tp(\Theta)}{tp(\Theta) + fn(\Theta)}$$

where $tp(\theta), fp(\theta), tn(\theta)$, and $fn(\theta)$ denote the number of true positives, false positives, true negatives and

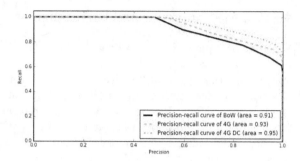

Figure 2: Precision-recall curve for host based features.

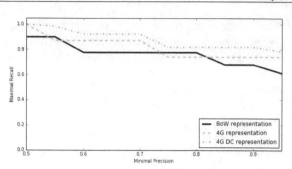

Figure 3: Rho function for host based features.

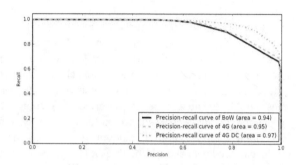

Figure 4: f-recall curve for path based features.

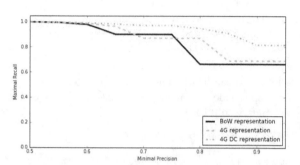

Figure 5: Rho function for path based features.

Table 1: Size of the small datasets and size of feature space

TLD	URLs	BoW	4G	4GDC	TLD	URLs	BoW	4G	4GDC
com	180381	323785	164395	197993	eu	1845	10863	2058	24086
ru	38281	115616	37059	112531	ua	1732	9970	1832	22460
net	26140	91532	26319	109033	in	1676	9872	1791	23592
com.br	10687	31055	10595	40173	ro	1480	7811	1592	17095
org	10469	51784	11139	80083	biz	1361	8801	1598	21942
info	6036	33933	6788	60505	cc	1151	7063	1255	19328
de	5791	28068	6148	44288	us	1090	6462	1212	16487
it	4939	20732	5081	34099	me	1034	5935	1144	16098
lt	3688	12085	3746	25337	com.au	955	6383	1066	14857
co.uk	2290	12804	2437	24812					

false negatives for the classifier corresponding to the threshold θ.

The second one the maximal recall among classifiers from the considered family that have precision above fixed limit:

$$\rho(l) = \max\left\{ \frac{tp(\theta)}{tp(\theta)+fn(\theta)} \Big| \theta \in \Theta, \frac{tp(\theta)}{tp(\theta)+fp(\theta)} \geq l \right\}$$

We evaluated each of the proposed feature generation techniques in the following way. For each method we used a separate balanced dataset which contained the same set of labelled URLs and then trained the several random forests with different number of trees T and maximum depth D. We always used 80% of data for training and 20% for testing. For the N-grams representations we chose to use 4-grams and 4-grams with 1 don't care symbol which

we shorten as 4G and 4GDC respectively in the following sections.

Table 2: Number of URLs in each dataset and dimensionality of the corresponding feature space for each of the considered feature extraction methods.

Data	URLs	BoW	4G	4GDC
Host	508074	452 950	977 754	223 281
Path	2732415	3 559 094	5 264 007	1 875 289

5.1 Employed Data

We used the set of labelled URLs provided by one of the antivirus companies, which were collected over the period of one month.

We didn't explicitly extract URLs related to one type of threat (such as URLs related to malicious/phishing campaigns) and thus the URLs structures are partially unrelated. It is because URLs of different malicious campaigns differs from each other even though they are labelled the same – as a malicious. For example URLs related to a phishing campaign targeting facebook will have similar structure but they will be different from URLs connected to C&C servers of some particular botnet.

To test all suggested methods, we generated multiple datasets from it. Namely we created several small datasets from host parts of the URLs to test statistical significance of our methods, where each dataset contains only URLs with the same top-level domains (such as '.com') or country-code second-level domains (such as 'co.uk').

The number of URLs in each dataset and the dimensionality of the corresponding feature space for each of the considered feature extraction methods are in table 1.

Next, we used datasets for host and path URL-parts and for each considered method of feature extraction. Table 2 contains the number of URLs in each dataset and the dimensionality of the corresponding feature space for each of the considered feature extraction methods.

5.2 Main Results

The comparison of the three considered feature extraction methods for the area under the precision-recall curve and for the maximal recall of classifiers with precision above 0.8 is for 4 different combinations of the forest size and tree depth summarized in Tables 6 and 7, respectively. The considered family of classifiers was constructed using the 20 thresholds 0.05, 0.1,...,1. For each of those 4 combinations, the hypotheses that all three methods lead to the same area under the precision-recall curve and to the same maximal recall of classifiers with precision above 0.8 were tested with the Friedman test [1]. The results of their testing are given in Tables 3 and 4, respectively.

Table 3: Friedman test for a maximal recall function for different values of T and D. The exact values are shown in each column for T and D respectively.

values of T D	10 200	10 50	50 200	50 50
χ^2 statistic	2.9500	2	0.1100	8.3200
p-value	0.2300	0.3700	0.9500	0.0160

Table 4: Friedman test for an area under precision recall curve for different values of T and D. The exact values are shown in each column for T and D respectively.

values of T D	10 200	10 50	50 200	50 50
χ^2 statistic	1.2600	2.2100	1.3700	0.3200
p-value	0.5300	0.3300	0.5000	0.8500

The test rejected only the hypothesis of the same maximal recall for a single considered combination tree depth

50 + forest size 50. For that combination, we performed the posthoc test of equal mean ranks with respect to the maximal recall for the 3 possible pairs of the compared methods [1]. The results of that posthoc test are presented in Table 5.

Table 5: Post hoc test for maximum recall function for random forest with $T = 50$ and $D = 50$.

	4G-4GDC	4G-BoW	4GDC-BoW
Statistic	2.1089	2.7578	0.6489
p-value	0.0175	0.0029	0.2582

They imply that the hypothesis of equal mean ranks with respect to the maximal recall is on the significance level 0.05 rejected for the pairs of methods 4G–4GDC and 4G–BoW, but not for the pair 4GDC–BoW. This implication is valid for several kinds of corrections with respect to the simultaneous testing of all three pairwise hypotheses, e.g., the correction according to Holm, the correction according to Shaffer, and the most general correction according to Bergmann and Hommel [2].

In addition, we compared the considered feature extraction methods on the host and path part of URLs. For comparability of results, we chose the same random forest parameters as before. Namely we used the number of trees $T = 20$ and maximum depth $D = 100$.

For classification using only the host part of the URLs, the results show, that the techniques rank from the best as follows: 4-grams with one don't care symbol, 4-grams, BoW. All methods are able to reach a high precision, but it can be seen that BoW generalize poorly on features based on the host part only. It is not surprising, since all of the URL in the dataset were unique from each other, thus BoW could reliably detect only URLs for which at least some subdomains of the URL were shared by the training and testing part of the dataset.

When we used only path parts of URLs, the results were similar. Surprisingly, the BoW representation performed almost as well as 4-grams while 4-grams with don't care symbol significantly improved recall for high thresholds. Although we expected this results with representation using don't care symbols, we can not explain why 4-grams have not outperformed BoW.

6   Conclusion

This work-in-progress paper is a small contribution to research into predicting malicious web sites. It presented a light-weight approach using solely lexical features of the site URL and classification by random forests. Three methods for the extraction of such URL features have been considered and experimentally validated on real-world data. The data included on the one hand smaller datasets containing the host parts of URLs from 19 mutually unrelated (mostly top-level) domains, on the other

Table 6: Comparison of the area under the precision-recall curve between the considered feature extraction methods for particular combinations of random forest parameters T and D. The comparison is based on the datasets from the 19 domains listed in Table 1, each value shows how frequently the method in the row yielded a higher area under the precision-recall curve than the column method.

>	4G	4GDC	BoW
4G	-	7	8
4GDC	12	-	9
BoW	11	10	-

(a) $T = 10$ and $D = 200$

>	4G	4GDC	BoW
4G	-	7	7
4GDC	12	-	8
BoW	11	11	-

(b) $T = 10$ and $D = 50$

>	4G	4GDC	BoW
4G	-	10	8
4GDC	9	-	7
BoW	11	12	-

(c) $T = 50$ and $D = 200$

>	4G	4GDC	BoW
4G	-	9	11
4GDC	10	-	10
BoW	8	9	-

(d) $T = 50$ and $D = 50$

hand one large dataset containing the host parts and one large dataset containing the path parts of URLs from a mixture of many top-level domains. All dataset were specific for each considered feature extraction method. The considered methods were compared with respect to the area under the precision-recall curve and with respect to the maximal recall of classifiers with precision above 0.8. The smaller datasets with the host parts of URLs alowed for testing differences between the methods. No significant differences between the methods have been found with respect to the area under the precision-recall curve, whereas with respect to the maximal recall of classifiers with given precision, significant differences were only for one combination of the forest size and tree depth, and only between 4-grams and 4-grams with one don't care symbol, and 4-grams and the bag-of-words representation. Finally, the results obtained on the large datasets show that in spite of the restriction to lexical features, all three methods achieve quite impressive area under the precision-recall curve for the path parts of URLs.

Acknowledgement

The research reported in this paper has been supported by the Czech Science Foundation (GAČR) grant 17-01251.

References

[1] J. Demšar. Statistical comparisons of classifiers over multiple data sets. *Journal of Machine Learning Research*, 7:1–30, 2006.

[2] S. Garcia and F. Herrera. An extension on Statistical Comparisons of Classifiers over Multiple Data Sets for all pairwise comparisons. *Journal of Machine Learning Research*, 9:2677–2694, 2008.

[3] Justin Ma, Lawrence K. Saul, Stefan Savage, and Geoffrey M. Voelker. Beyond blacklists: Learning to detect malicious web sites from suspicious urls. In *Proceedings of the 15th ACM SIGKDD International Conference on Knowledge Discovery and Data Mining*, KDD '09, pages 1245–1254, New York, NY, USA, 2009. ACM.

[4] Justin Ma, Lawrence K. Saul, Stefan Savage, and Geoffrey M. Voelker. Identifying suspicious urls: An application of large-scale online learning. In *Proceedings of the 26th Annual International Conference on Machine Learning*, ICML '09, pages 681–688, New York, NY, USA, 2009. ACM.

Table 7: Comparison of the maximal recall of classifiers with precision above 0.8 between the considered feature extraction methods for particular combinations of T and D. The comparison is based on datasets from the 19 domains listed in Table 1, each value shows how frequently the method in the row yielded a higher maximal recall of classifiers with precision above 0.8 than the column method.

>	4G	4GDC	BoW
4G	-	9	6
4GDC	10	-	7
BoW	13	12	-

(a) $T = 10$ and $D = 200$

>	4G	4GDC	BoW
4G	-	11	6
4GDC	8	-	6
BoW	13	11	-

(b) $T = 10$ and $D = 50$

>	4G	4GDC	BoW
4G	-	9	9
4GDC	10	-	9
BoW	10	10	-

(c) $T = 50$ and $D = 200$

>	4G	4GDC	BoW
4G	-	5	4
4GDC	14	-	8
BoW	15	11	-

(d) $T = 50$ and $D = 50$

[5] Niels Provos, Panayiotis Mavrommatis, Moheeb Abu Rajab, and Fabian Monrose. All your iframes point to us. In *Proceedings of the 17th Conference on Security Symposium*, SS'08, pages 1–15, Berkeley, CA, USA, 2008. USENIX Association.

[6] Sushant Sinha, Michael Bailey, and Farnam Jahanian. *Shades of Grey: On the effectiveness of reputation-based blacklists*, pages 57–64. 2008.

[7] Rakesh Verma and Avisha Das. What's in a url: Fast feature extraction and malicious url detection. In *Proceedings of the 3rd ACM on International Workshop on Security And Privacy Analytics*, IWSPA '17, pages 55–63, New York, NY, USA, 2017. ACM.

[8] Yue Zhang, Jason I. Hong, and Lorrie F. Cranor. Cantina: A content-based approach to detecting phishing web sites. In *Proceedings of the 16th International Conference on World Wide Web*, WWW '07, pages 639–648, New York, NY, USA, 2007. ACM.

J. Hlaváčová (Ed.): ITAT 2017 Proceedings, pp. 136–143
ISBN 978-1974274741, © 2017 J. Repický, L. Bajer, Z. Pitra, M. Holeňa

Adaptive Generation-Based Evolution Control
for Gaussian Process Surrogate Models

Jakub Repický[1,2], Lukáš Bajer[1,2], Zbyněk Pitra[2,3,4], and Martin Holeňa[2]

[1] Faculty of Mathematics and Physics, Charles University in Prague
Malostranské nám. 25, 118 00 Prague 1, Czech Republic
[2] Institute of Computer Science, Czech Academy of Sciences
Pod Vodárenskou věží 2, 182 07 Prague 8, Czech Republic
[3] Faculty of Nuclear Sciences and Physical Engineering, Czech Technical University in Prague
Břehová 7, 115 19 Prague 1, Czech Republic
[4] National Institute of Mental Health
Topolová 748, 250 67 Klecany, Czech Republic
{repicky,bajer,pitra,martin}@cs.cas.cz

Abstract: The interest in accelerating black-box optimizers has resulted in several surrogate model-assisted version of the Covariance Matrix Adaptation Evolution Strategy, a state-of-the-art continuous black-box optimizer. The version called Surrogate CMA-ES uses Gaussian processes or random forests surrogate models with a generation-based evolution control. This paper presents an adaptive improvement for S-CMA-ES, in which the number of generations using the surrogate model before retraining is adjusted depending on the performance of the last instance of the surrogate. Three algorithms that differ in the measure of the surrogate model's performance are evaluated on the COCO/BBOB framework. The results show a minor improvement on S-CMA-ES with constant model lifelengths, especially when larger lifelengths are considered.

1 Introduction

The problem of optimization of real-valued functions without a known mathematical expression, arising in many engineering tasks, is referred to as continuous black-box optimization. Evolutionary strategies, a class of randomized population-based algorithms inspired by natural evolution, are a popular choice for continuous black-box optimization. Especially the Covariance Matrix Adaptation Evolution Strategy (CMA-ES) [6] is considered the state-of-the-art continuous black-box optimizer of the several past decades. Since values of a black-box function can only be obtained empirically and at considerable costs in practice, the number of function evaluations needed to obtain a desired function value is a key criterion for evaluating black-box optimizers.

The technique of surrogate modelling aims at saving function evaluations by building a surrogate model of the fitness and using that for a portion of function evaluations conducted in the course of the evolutionary search. Several surrogate model-assisted versions of the CMA-ES have been developed (see [11] for a recent comparison of some of the most notable algorithms). Surrogate CMA-ES (S-CMA-ES) [2] utilizes random forests- or Gaussian

processes-based surrogate models, which possess an inherent capability to quantify uncertainty of the prediction.

In order to control surrogate model's error, S-CMA-ES uses the surrogate model for a given number of generations g_m before a new instance of the model is trained on a population evaluated with the fitness, which is a strategy called generation-based evolution control [9]. In [2], two model lifelengths, in particular $g_m \in \{1,5\}$, have been benchmarked on the COCO/BBOB framework. In many cases, the higher lifelength outperformed the lower one in earlier phases of the optimization, but the reverse order was observed towards later phases of the optimization. In this paper, we propose an adaptive version of the S-CMA-ES(A-S-CMA-ES), in which an adequate number of model-evaluated generations is estimated as a function of previous model's error. We restrict our attention to Gaussian processes, since they outperformed random forest-based surrogates [2]. We consider three different surrogate error measures and compare all of them on the COCO/BBOB framework.

The remainder of this paper is organized as follows. Section 2 outlines basic concepts of S-CMA-ES. The proposed adaptive improvement is described in Section 3. Experimental setup is given in Section 4. Experimental results are reported in Section 6. Section 7 concludes the paper.

2 Surrogate CMA-ES

The CMA-ES operates on a population of λ candidate solutions sampled from a multivariate normal distribution:

$$\mathbf{x}_k \sim \mathcal{N}(\mathbf{m}, \sigma^2 \mathbf{C}) \quad k = 1, \ldots, \lambda, \qquad (1)$$

where $\mathcal{N}$ is the normal distribution function; $\mathbf{m}$ and $\mathbf{C}$ are the mean and the covariance matrix of the estimated search distribution, respectively; and the σ is the overall search step size. The candidate solutions are ranked according to their fitness values:

$$y_k = f(\mathbf{x}_k) \quad k = 1, \ldots, \lambda. \qquad (2)$$

Upon a (weighted) selection of $\mu < \lambda$ highest ranked points, the mean and the covariance matrix of the multivariate normal distribution are adapted according to a procedure that takes as input, among other variables, a cumulation of the past search steps [5]. The S-CMA-ES modifies the CMA-ES by replacing its sampling (1) and fitness-evaluation (2) steps with a procedure depicted in Algorithm 1.

Algorithm 1 Surrogate part of S-CMA-ES

Input: g (generation)
    g_m (number of model-evaluated generations)
    $\sigma, \lambda, \mathbf{m}, \mathbf{C}$ (CMA-ES internal variables)
    r (maximal distance between $\mathbf{m}$ and a training point)
    n_{req} (minimal number of points for training)
    n_{max} (maximal number of points for training)
    $\mathscr{A}$ (archive), $f_{\mathscr{M}}$ (model), f (fitness)
1:   $\mathbf{x}_k \sim \mathcal{N}(\mathbf{m}, \sigma^2 \mathbf{C})$ $k = 1, \ldots, \lambda$ {sampling}
2:   **if** g is original-fitness-evaluated **then**
3:      $y_k \leftarrow f(\mathbf{x}_k)$ $k = 1, \ldots, \lambda$ {fitness evaluation}
4:      $\mathscr{A} \leftarrow \mathscr{A} \cup \{(\mathbf{x}_k, y_k)\}_{k=1}^{\lambda}$
5:      $(\mathbf{X}_{\text{tr}}, \mathbf{y}_{\text{tr}}) \leftarrow$ choose n_{tr} training points within the Mahalanobis distance r from $\mathscr{A}$, assuring that $n_{\text{req}} \leq n_{\text{tr}} \leq n_{\text{max}}$
6:      $f_{\mathscr{M}} \leftarrow$ train_model$(\mathbf{X}_{\text{tr}}, \mathbf{y}_{\text{tr}})$
7:      mark $(g+1)$ as model-evaluated
8:   **else**
9:      $\hat{y}_k \leftarrow f_{\mathscr{M}}(\mathbf{x}_k)$ {model evaluation}
10:     **if** g_m model generations have passed **then**
11:        mark $(g+1)$ as original-fitness-evaluated
12:     **end if**
13: **end if**
Output: $f_{\mathscr{M}}, \mathscr{A}, (y_k)_{k=1}^{\lambda}$

Depending on the generation number g, the procedure evaluates all candidate solutions either with the real fitness or with the model. In each case, the sampling of the estimated multivariate normal distribution is unchanged (step 1).

If the population is original-fitness-evaluated (step 3), the new evaluations are saved in an archive of known solutions (step 4). Afterwards, a new model is trained on a set of points within the Mahalanobis distance r from the current CMA-ES distribution $\mathcal{N}(\mathbf{m}, \sigma\mathbf{C})$ (step 5).

In model-evaluated generations, the fitness values of the whole population of candidate solutions are estimated by the model (step 9).

2.1 Gaussian Processes

A Gaussian process (GP) is a collection of random variables $(f(\mathbf{x}))_{\mathbf{x} \in \mathbb{R}^D}$, such that any finite subcollection $\mathbf{f} = (f(\mathbf{x}_1), \ldots, f(\mathbf{x}_N))$ has an N-dimensional normal distribution. A Gaussian process is defined by a mean function $\mu(\mathbf{x})$ (often assumed to be zero) and a covariance function $k(\mathbf{x}, \mathbf{x}; \theta)$, where θ is a vector of parameters of k, hence

hyperparameters of the Gaussian process. Given a set of training data $X = \{\mathbf{x}_1, \ldots, \mathbf{x}_N\}$, the covariance matrix of a GP prior is $\mathbf{K}_N + \sigma_n^2 \mathbf{I}_N$, where $\mathbf{K}_N$ is a $N \times N$ matrix given by $\{\mathbf{K}_N\}_{i,j} = k(\mathbf{x}_i, \mathbf{x}_j; \theta)$ for all $i, j = 1, \ldots, N$; σ_n^2 is the variance of an additive, i. i. d. noise and $\mathbf{I}_N$ is a $N \times N$ identity matrix. Given a new point $\mathbf{x}_* \notin X$, Gaussian process regression is derived by conditioning the joint normal distribution of $(f(\mathbf{x}_1), \ldots, f(\mathbf{x}_N), f(\mathbf{x}_*))$ on the prior, which yields a univariate Gaussian (see [12] for more details). The hyperparameters θ of a GP regression model are estimated using the maximum likelihood estimation method.

3 Adaptive Evolution Control for Surrogate CMA-ES

The generation-based evolution strategy optimizes the fitness function and the surrogate model thereof in certain proportion. On problem areas that can be approximated well, a surrogate-assisted optimization might benefit from frequent utilization of the model, while on areas that are hard for the surrogate to approximate, frequent utilization of the model might degenerate the performance due to the model's inaccuracy.

The proposed evolution control adapts the lifelength of a new model depending on the previous model's error measured on the current generation.

Consider a generation g that is marked as original-fitness-evaluated, and a newly-trained surrogate model $f_{\mathscr{M}}$. If $f_{\mathscr{M}}$ is the first surrogate trained so far, put $g_m = 1$. Otherwise, an error ε of a previous surrogate model $f_{\mathscr{M}}^{\text{last}}$ is estimated on the newly evaluated population $(\mathbf{x}_1^{(g+1)}, \ldots, \mathbf{x}_{\lambda}^{(g+1)})$ (Algorithm 2). The error ε is then mapped into a number of consecutive generations $g_m, g_m \in [0, g_m^{\text{max}}]$, for which the surrogate $f_{\mathscr{M}}$ will be used (Algorithm 3).

We consider three different model error measures. As the CMA-ES depends primarily on the ranking of candidate solutions, the first two proposed error measures, *Kendall correlation coefficient* and *Rank difference* are based on ranking. The third one, *Kullback-Leibler divergence* a. k. a. *information gain*, measures a difference between a multivariate normal distribution estimated from the fitness values $\mathbf{y}$ and a multivariate normal distribution estimated for the predicted values $\hat{\mathbf{y}}$.

Kendall rank correlation coefficient Kendall rank correlation coefficient τ measures similarity between two different orderings of the same set. Let $\mathbf{y} = (f(\mathbf{x}_1), \ldots, f(\mathbf{x}_{\lambda}))$ and $\hat{\mathbf{y}} = (f_{\mathscr{M}}^{\text{last}}(\mathbf{x}_1), \ldots, f_{\mathscr{M}}^{\text{last}}(\mathbf{x}_{\lambda}))$ be the sequences of the fitness values and the predicted values of a population $\mathbf{x}_1, \ldots, \mathbf{x}_{\lambda}$, respectively. A pair of indices (i, j), such that $i \neq j, i, j \in \{1, \ldots, \lambda\}$, is said to be concordant, if both $y_i < y_j$ and $\hat{y}_i < \hat{y}_j$ or if both $y_i > y_j$ and $\hat{y}_i > \hat{y}_j$. A discordant pair $(i, j), i \neq j, i, j \in \{1, \ldots, \lambda\}$ is one fulfilling that both $y_i < y_j$ and $\hat{y}_i > \hat{y}_j$ or both $y_i > y_j$ and $\hat{y}_i < \hat{y}_j$. Let n_c and d_c denote the number of concordant and discordant

---

Algorithm 2 Model error estimation

Input: error_type (one of {"Kendall", "Rank-Difference", "Kullback-Leibler"})

   g (CMA-ES generation number)

   $\mathbf{x}_1^{(g+1)},\ldots,\mathbf{x}_\lambda^{(g+1)}$ (a newly sampled population)

   $\mathbf{y},\hat{\mathbf{y}}$ (fitness values and model predictions in generation g)

   $\mathbf{c}_{\mathrm{cma}} = (c_c, c_1, c_\mu, c_\sigma, d_\sigma)$ (CMA-ES constants)

   $\mathbf{v}_{\mathrm{cma}}^{(g)} = (\mathbf{m}^{(g)}, \mathbf{C}^{(g)}, \mathbf{p}_\sigma^{(g)}, \mathbf{p}_c^{(g)}, \sigma^{(g)})$ (CMA-ES variables at generation g)

   $\varepsilon_{\max}$ (maximal error so far)

1: **if** error_type = "Kendall" **then**
2:    $\tau \leftarrow$ Kendall rank correlation coefficient between $\mathbf{y}$ and $\hat{\mathbf{y}}$
3:    $\varepsilon \leftarrow \frac{1}{2}(1-\tau)$
4: **else if** error_type = "Rank-Difference" **then**
5:    $\varepsilon \leftarrow \varepsilon_{\mathrm{RD}}^\mu(\hat{\mathbf{y}},\mathbf{y})$
6: **else if** error_type = "Kullback-Leibler" **then**
7:    $(\mathbf{m}^{(g+1)}, \mathbf{C}^{(g+1)}, \sigma^{(g+1)}) \leftarrow$
      cma_update$((\mathbf{x}_1^{(g+1)},\ldots,\mathbf{x}_\lambda^{(g+1)}),\mathbf{y},\mathbf{c}_{\mathrm{cma}},\mathbf{v}_{\mathrm{cma}}^{(g)})$
8:    $(\mathbf{m}_{\mathcal{M}}^{(g+1)}, \mathbf{C}_{\mathcal{M}}^{(g+1)}, \sigma^{(g+1)}) \leftarrow$
      cma_update$((\mathbf{x}_1^{(g+1)},\ldots,\mathbf{x}_\lambda^{(g+1)}),\hat{\mathbf{y}},\mathbf{c}_{\mathrm{cma}},\mathbf{v}_{\mathrm{cma}}^{(g)})$
9:    $\varepsilon \leftarrow D_{\mathrm{KL}}(\mathcal{N}(\mathbf{m}_{\mathcal{M}}^{(g+1)}, \sigma_{\mathcal{M}}^{(g+1)}\mathbf{C}_{\mathcal{M}}^{(g+1)}) \|$
      $\mathcal{N}(\mathbf{m}^{(g+1)}, \sigma^{(g+1)}\mathbf{C}^{(g+1)}))$
10:    **if** $\varepsilon > \varepsilon_{\max}$ **then**
11:       $\varepsilon_{\max} \leftarrow \varepsilon$
12:    **end if**
13:    $\varepsilon \leftarrow \frac{\varepsilon}{\varepsilon_{\max}}$ {normalize in proportion to the historical maximum}
14: **end if**

Output: $\varepsilon \in [0,1]$

---

pairs of indices from $\{1,\ldots,\lambda\}$, respectively. The Kendall correlation coefficient τ between vectors $\mathbf{y}$ and $\hat{\mathbf{y}}$ is defined as:

$$\tau = \frac{2}{\lambda(\lambda-1)}(n_c - n_d).$$

In the corresponding branch of Algorithm 2, the value τ is decreasingly scaled into interval $[0,1]$.

Ranking difference error The ranking difference error is a normalized version of a measure used in [10]. Given $r_1(i)$ the rank of the i-th element of $\hat{\mathbf{y}}$ and $r_2(i)$ the rank of the i-th element of $\mathbf{y}$, the ranking difference error is the sum of element-wise differences between r_1 and r_2 taking into account only the μ best-ranked points from $\hat{\mathbf{y}}$:

$$\varepsilon_{\mathrm{RD}}^\mu(\hat{\mathbf{y}},\mathbf{y}) = \frac{\sum_{i:r_1(i)\leq\mu}|r_2(i)-r_1(i)|}{\max_{\pi\in S_\lambda}\sum_{i:\pi(i)\leq\mu}|i-\pi(i)|},$$

where S_λ is the group of all permutations of set $\{1,\ldots,\lambda\}$.

Kullback-Leibler divergence Kullback-Leibler divergence from a continuous random variable Q with probability

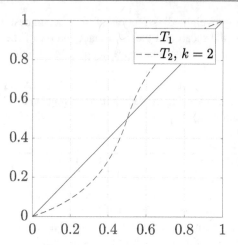

Figure 1: Model error transfer functions

density function q to a continuous random variable P with probability density function p is defined as:

$$D_{\mathrm{KL}}(P\|Q) = \int_{-\infty}^{\infty} p(x) \log \frac{p(x)}{q(x)}\, dx.$$

For two multivariate normal distributions $\mathcal{N}_1(\mu_1,\Sigma_1)$ and $\mathcal{N}_2(\mu_2,\Sigma_2)$ with the same dimension k, the Kullback-Leibler divergence from $\mathcal{N}_2$ to $\mathcal{N}_1$ is:

$$D_{\mathrm{KL}}(\mathcal{N}_1\|\mathcal{N}_2) = \frac{1}{2}\left(\mathrm{tr}(\Sigma_2^{-1}\Sigma_1) + \ln\left(\frac{|\Sigma_2|}{|\Sigma_1|}\right) + \right.$$
$$\left. (\mu_2-\mu_1)^T\Sigma_2^{-1}(\mu_2-\mu_1) - k \right).$$

The algorithm of model error estimation (Algorithm 2) in generation g computes Kullback-Leibler divergence from a CMA-estimated multivariate normal distribution $\mathcal{N}(\mathbf{m}^{(g+1)}, \mathbf{C}^{(g+1)})$ w.r.t. fitness values $\mathbf{y}$ to a CMA-estimated multivariate normal distribution $\mathcal{N}(\mathbf{m}_{\mathcal{M}}^{(g+1)}, \mathbf{C}_{\mathcal{M}}^{(g+1)})$ w.r.t. predicted values $\hat{\mathbf{y}}$. Procedure cma_update in steps 7 and 8 refers to one iteration of the CMA-ES from the point when a new population has been sampled. The result is normalized by the historical maximum (step 13).

Adjusting the number of model generations The number of consecutive model generations g_m is updated by Algorithm 3. The history of surrogate model errors ε is exponentially smoothed with a rate r_u (step 1). The error is truncated at a threshold ε_T so that resulting $g_m = g_m^{\max}$ for all values $\varepsilon \geq \varepsilon_T$ (step 3). We consider two different transfer functions $T_1, T_2 : [0,1] \to [0,1]$ (plotted in Figure 1) that scale the error into the admissible interval $[0, g_m^{\max}]$:

$$T_1(x) = x \qquad (3)$$

$$T_2(x;k) = \frac{(x-\frac{1}{2})(1+\frac{1}{k})}{|2(x-\frac{1}{2})|+\frac{1}{k}} + \frac{1}{2}, k > 0. \qquad (4)$$

Algorithm 3 Updating the number of model generations

Input: ε (estimation of surrogate model error, $\varepsilon \in [0,1]$)
  $\varepsilon_T \in [0,1]$ (a threshold at which the error is truncated to 1)
  $\gamma: [0,1] \rightarrow [0,1]$ (transfer function)
  r_u (error update rate)
  ε_{last} (model error from the previous iteration)
  g_m^{max} (upper bound for admissible number of model generations)

1: $\varepsilon \leftarrow (1 - r_u)\varepsilon_{last} + r_u\varepsilon$ {exponential smoothing}
2: $\varepsilon_{last} \leftarrow \varepsilon$
3: $\varepsilon \leftarrow \frac{1}{\varepsilon_T} \min\{\varepsilon, \varepsilon_T\}$ {truncation to 1}
4: $g_m \leftarrow \text{round}(\gamma(1-\varepsilon)g_m^{max})$ {scaling into the admissible interval}

Output: g_m – updated number of model-evaluated generations

Both functions are defined on $[0,1]$, moreover, $T_i(0) = 0$ and $T_i(1) = 1$ for $i = 1,2$. Transfer function T_2 is a simple sigmoid function defined to be slightly less sensitive near the edges than in the middle. More control can thus be achieved in the regions of low and high error values. The parameter k determines the steepness of the sigmoid curve.

4 Experimental Setup

The proposed adaptive generation-based evolution control for the S-CMA-ES with three different surrogate model error measures is evaluated on the noiseless testbed of the COCO/BBOB (Comparing Continuous Optimizers / Black-Box Optimization Benchmarking) framework [7,8] and compared with the S-CMA-ES and CMA-ES.

Each function is defined everywhere on $\mathbb{R}^D$ and has its optimum in $[-5,5]^D$ for all dimensionalities $D \geq 2$. For every function and every dimensionality, 15 trials of the optimizer are run on independent instances, which differ in linear transformations of the x-space or shifts of the f-space. In our experiments, instances recommended for BBOB 2015 workshop, i.e., $\{1,\ldots,5,41,\ldots 50\}$, were used. Each trial is terminated when the f_{opt} is reached within a small tolerance $\Delta f_t = 10^{-8}$ or when a given budget of function evaluations, 250D in our case, is used up. Experiments were run for dimensionalities 2, 3, 5, 10 and 20. The algorithms' settings are summarized in the following subsections.

4.1 CMA-ES

The CMA-ES results in BBOB format were downloaded from the BBOB 2010 workshop archive [1]. The CMA-ES used in those experiments was in version 3.40.beta and utilized a restart strategy (known as IPOP-CMA-ES), where the population size is increased by factor IncPopSize after

[1] http://coco.gforge.inria.fr/data-archive/bbob/2010/

Table 1: Discretization of the A-S-CMA-ES parameters.

Parameter	Discretization
γ	T_1 (3), T_2 (4)
ε_T	$0.5, 0.9$
g_m	$5, 10, 20$
r_u	$0.2, 0.5, 0.8$

each restart [1]. The default parameter values employed in the CMA-ES are $\lambda = 4 + \lfloor 3\log D \rfloor$, $\mu = \lfloor \frac{\lambda}{2} \rfloor$, $\sigma_{start} = \frac{8}{3}$, IncPopSize = 2.

4.2 S-CMA-ES

The S-CMA-ES was tested with two numbers of model-evaluated generations, $g_m = 1$ (further denoted as "GP-1") and $g_m = 5$ ("GP-5"). All other S-CMA-ES settings were left as described in [2]. In particular, the Mahalanobis distance was $r = 8$, the starting values (θ, l) of the Matérn covariance function $k_{Matérn}^{\nu=3/2}$ were $(0.5, 2)$ and the starting value of the GP noise parameter σ_n^2 was 0.01. If not mentioned otherwise, the corresponding settings of adaptive versions of the S-CMA-ES are as just stated.

In order to find the most promising settings for each considered surrogate error measure, a full factorial experiment was conducted on one half of the noiseless testbed, namely on functions f_i for $i \in \{2,3,6,8,12,13,15,17,18,21,23,24\}$. The discretization of continuous parameters $(\gamma, \varepsilon_T, g_m^{max}, r_u)$ is reported in Table 1. All possible combinations of the parameters were ranked on the 12 selected functions according to the lowest achieved Δf^{med} (see Section 6) for different numbers of function evaluations #FEs/$D = 25, 50, 125, 250$. The best settings were chosen according to the highest sum of 1-st rank counts. Ties were resolved according to the lowest sum of ranks. All of the best settings included maximum model-evaluated generations $g_m^{max} = 5$. The remaining of the winning values are summarized in the following paragraphs.

Kendall correlation coefficient (ADA-Kendall) Transfer function $\gamma = T_2$, error threshold $\varepsilon_T = 0.5$ and update rate $r_u = 0.2$.

Ranking difference error (ADA-RD) The same, except transfer function was $\gamma = T_1$.

Kullback-Leibler divergence (ADA-KL) Transfer function $\gamma = T_2$, error threshold $\varepsilon_T = 0.9$ and update rate $r_u = 0.5$.

5 CPU Timing

In order to assess computational costs other than the number of function evaluations, we calculate CPU timing per

Table 2: The time in seconds per function evaluation for the Adaptive S-CMA-ES.

Algorithm	2D	3D	5D	10D	20D
ADA-KL	0.38	0.26	0.34	0.69	3.36
ADA-Kendall	0.47	0.45	0.61	1.29	6.27
ADA-RD	0.57	0.60	0.71	1.63	7.90

function evaluation for each algorithm and each dimensionality. Each experiment was divided into jobs by dimensionalities, functions and instances. All jobs were run in a single thread on the Czech national grid MetaCentrum. The average time per function evaluation for each algorithm and each tested dimensionality is summarized in Table 2.

6   Results

We test the difference in algorithms' convergence for significance on the whole noiseless testbed with the non-parametric Friedman test [3]. The algorithms are ranked on each BBOB function with respect to medians of log-scaled minimal distance Δf from the function optimum, denoted as Δf^{med}, at a fixed budget of function evaluations.

To account for different optimization scenarios, the test is conducted separately for all considered dimensionalities of the input space and two function evaluation budgets, a higher and a lower one. Let #FE$_t$ be the smallest number of function evaluations at which at least one algorithm reached the target, i. e., satisfied $\Delta f^{\mathrm{med}} \leq \Delta f_t$, or #FE$_t$ = 250D if the target has not been reached. We set the higher budget for the tests to #FE$_t$ and the lower budget to $\frac{\text{#FE}_t}{3}$.

Mean ranks from the Friedman test are given in Table 3. The critical value for the Friedman test is 2.29.

The mean ranks differ significantly for all tested scenarios except for both tested numbers of function evaluations in 2D and the higher tested number of function evaluations in 3D. Starting from 5D upwards, the lowest mean rank is achieved either by ADA-Kendall or ADA-RD at both tested #FEs.

In order to show pairwise differences, we perform a pairwise $N \times N$ comparison of the algorithms' average ranks by the post-hoc Friedman test with the Bergmann-Hommel correction of the family-wise error [4] in cases when the null hypothesis of equal algorithms' performance was rejected. To better illustrate algorithms differences, we also count the number of benchmark functions at which one algorithm achieved a higher rank than the other. The pairwise score and the statistical significance of the pairwise mean rank differences are reported in Table 4. In the post-hoc test, ADA-Kendall significantly outperforms both the CMA-ES and GP-5 in 10D and 20D. It also significantly outperforms GP-1 in 10D at the higher tested #FEs.

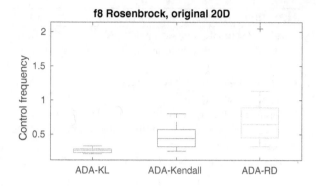

Figure 2: Average control frequency (the ratio of the number of total original-fitness-evaluated generations to the number of total model-evaluated generations) in A-S-CMA-ES measured in 15 trials of each algorithm on f_8 in 20D.

For illustration, the average control frequency given by the ratio of the number of total original-fitness-evaluated generations to the number of total model-evaluated generations within one trial, for data from 15 trials on f_8 (Rosenbrock's function) in 20D is given in Figure 2. The algorithm ADA-KL led to generally lower control frequencies than its competitors, which might explain its slightly inferior performance. Similar results were observed for the remaining functions and dimensionalities.

The cases when ADA-Kendall and ADA-RD are able to switch between more exploitation-oriented and more data-gathering-oriented behaviour can be studied on the results from COCO's postprocessing. GP-5 outperforms both GP-1 and the CMA-ES on the lower and middle parts of the empirical distribution functions (ECDFs) basically for all dimensionalities (Figure 3). On the other hand, GP-1 outperforms GP-5 especially in later phases of the search (Figure 3).

The ability of ADA-Kendall and ADA-RD to switch to a less-exploitation mode when appropriate is eminent on the ECDFs plots in 20D, especially on the moderate and the all-function groups (top right and bottom right on Figure 3), with exception of the well structured multimodal group (middle right), when they fail in the middle part and the weakly structured multimodal group (bottom left), when they fail towards the end of the search.

7   Conclusion

In this paper, we implemented several modifications of the Surrogate CMA-ES (S-CMA-ES), an algorithm using generation-based evolution control in connection with GPs. We considered three measures of surrogate model error according to which an adequate number of upcoming model-evaluated generations could be estimated online. Three resulting algorithms were compared on the COCO/BBOB framework with the S-CMA-ES parametrized by two different numbers of consecutive model-evaluated

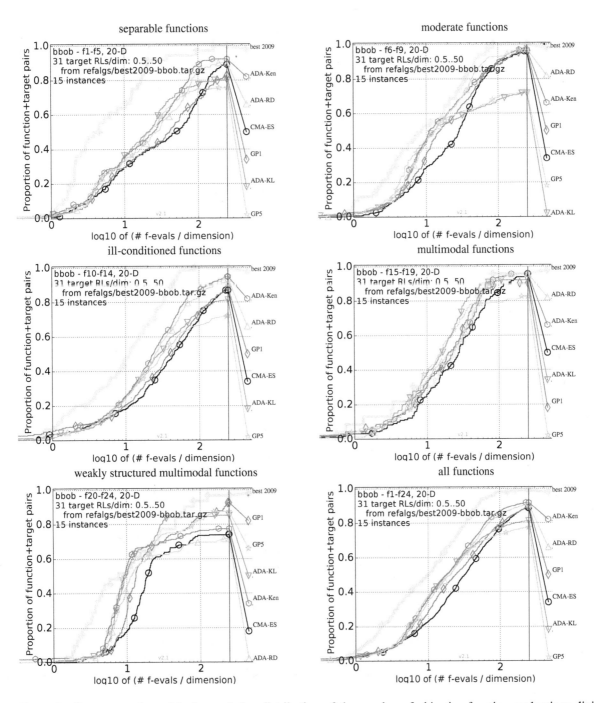

Figure 3: Bootstrapped empirical cumulative distribution of the number of objective function evaluations divided by dimension (FEvals/DIM) for all functions and subgroups in 20-D. The targets are chosen from $10^{[-8..2]}$ such that the best algorithm from BBOB 2009 just not reached them within a given budget of $k \times$ DIM, with 31 different values of k chosen equidistant in logscale within the interval $\{0.5, \ldots, 50\}$. The "best 2009" line corresponds to the best aRT observed during BBOB 2009 for each selected target.

Table 3: Mean ranks of the CMA-ES, the S-CMA-ES and all A-S-CMA-ES versions over the BBOB and the Iman-Davenport variant of the Friedman test for the 10 considered combinations of dimensionalities and evaluation budgets. The lowest value is highlighted in bold. Statistically significant results at the significance level $\alpha = 0.05$ are marked by an asterisk.

Dim	2D		3D		5D		10D		20D	
$^{\#FEs}/_{\#FE_t}$	$\frac{1}{3}$	1	$\frac{1}{3}$	1	$\frac{1}{3}$	1	$\frac{1}{3}$	1	$\frac{1}{3}$	1
CMA-ES	4.04	4.25	4.25	3.96	4.38	3.58	4.67	3.83	4.58	4.42
GP-1	3.38	3.94	4.21	3.62	3.92	4.02	3.69	3.92	3.54	3.27
GP-5	3.54	3.12	**2.83**	4.08	3.81	4.35	4.25	4.42	4.23	4.52
ADA-KL	3.23	**2.85**	3.29	3.44	3.69	3.73	3.60	4.04	3.15	3.65
ADA-Ken	3.98	3.46	3.25	**2.90**	2.90	2.96	**2.27**	**2.40**	**2.33**	**2.23**
ADA-RD	**2.83**	3.38	3.17	3.00	**2.31**	**2.35**	2.52	2.40	3.17	2.92
F_F	1.48	1.89	2.52*	1.67	4.47*	4.13*	7.82*	6.50*	5.35*	6.62*

generations. Since the work on the adaptive extension is still in progress, the presented results summarize the performance of all compared algorithms on the whole BBOB framework or its function groups. We found two error measures, the Kendall rank correlation and the rank difference error, that significantly outperformed the S-CMA-ES used with a higher number of model-evaluated generations, especially in higher dimensionalities of the input space. However, both of these algorithms provided only a minor improvement of the S-CMA-ES used with a lower number of model-evaluated generations and in some tested scenarios fell behind both tested settings of the S-CMA-ES. An area for further research is the adjustment of other surrogate model parameters beside the control frequency, such as the number of the training points or the radius of the area from which they are selected.

8   Acknowledgments

The research reported in this paper has been supported by the Czech Science Foundation (GAČR) grant 17-01251.

Access to computing and storage facilities owned by parties and projects contributing to the National Grid Infrastructure MetaCentrum, provided under the programme "Projects of Large Research, Development, and Innovations Infrastructures" (CESNET LM2015042), is greatly appreciated.

References

[1] A. Auger and N. Hansen. A restart CMA evolution strategy with increasing population size. In *2005 IEEE Congress on Evolutionary Computation*. IEEE, 2005.

[2] L. Bajer, Z. Pitra, and M. Holeňa. Benchmarking Gaussian processes and random forests surrogate models on the BBOB noiseless testbed. In *Proceedings of the Companion Publication of the 2015 on Genetic and Evolutionary Computation Conference - GECCO Companion '15*. Association for Computing Machinery (ACM), 2015.

[3] J. Demšar. Statistical comparisons of classifiers over multiple data sets. *J. Mach. Learn. Res.*, 7:1–30, December 2006.

[4] S. García and F. Herrera. An extension on "statistical comparisons of classifiers over multiple data sets" for all pairwise comparisons. *J. Mach. Learn. Res.*, 9:2677–2694, 2008.

[5] N. Hansen. The CMA evolution strategy: A tutorial. *CoRR*, abs/1604.00772, 2016.

[6] N. Hansen, A. Auger, R. Ros, S. Finck, and P. Pošík. Comparing results of 31 algorithms from the Black-box Optimization Benchmarking BBOB-2009. In *Proceedings of the 12th annual conference comp on Genetic and evolutionary computation - GECCO '10*, pages 1689–1696, New York, NY, USA, 2010. ACM.

[7] N. Hansen, S. Finck, R. Ros, and A. Auger. Real-parameter Black-Box Optimization Benchmarking 2009: Noiseless functions definitions. Technical report, INRIA, 2009, updated 2010.

[8] N. Hansen, S. Finck, R. Ros, and A. Auger. Real-parameter Black-Box Optimization Benchmarking 2012: Experimental setup. Technical report, INRIA, 2012.

[9] Y. Jin and B. Sendhoff. Fitness approximation in evolutionary computation–A survey. In *Proceedings of the Genetic and Evolutionary Computation Conference*, GECCO '02, pages 1105–1112, San Francisco, CA, USA, 2002. Morgan Kaufmann Publishers Inc.

[10] S. Kern, N. Hansen, and P. Koumoutsakos. *Local Metamodels for Optimization Using Evolution Strategies*, pages 939–948. Springer Berlin Heidelberg, Berlin, Heidelberg, 2006.

[11] Z. Pitra, L. Bajer, J. Repický, and M. Holeňa. Overview of surrogate-model versions of covariance matrix adaptation evolution strategy. In *Proceedings of the Genetic and Evolutionary Computation Conference 2017, Berlin, Germany, July 15–19, 2017 (GECCO '17)*. ACM, July 2017. To appear.

[12] C. E. Rassmusen and C. K. I. Williams. *Gaussian processes for machine learning*. Adaptive computation and machine learning series. MIT Press, 2006.

Table 4: A pairwise comparison of the algorithms in 2D, 3D, 5D, 10D and 20D over the BBOB for 2 different evaluation budgets. The comparison is based on medians over runs on 15 instances for each of all the 24 functions. The number of wins of i-th algorithm against j-th algorithm over all benchmark functions is given in i-th row and j-th column. The asterisk marks the row algorithm achieving a significantly lower value of the objective function than the column algorithm according to the Friedman post-hoc test with the Bergmann-Hommel correction at family-wise significance level $\alpha = 0.05$.

2D	CMA-ES		GP-1		GP-5		ADA-KL		ADA-Ken		ADA-RD	
#FEs/#FE$_t$	1/3	1	1/3	1	1/3	1	1/3	1	1/3	1	1/3	1
CMA-ES	—	—	8	8	11	8	10	7	11	10	7	9
GP-1	16	16	—	—	12	9	13	8	13	9	9	6
GP-5	13	16	12	15	—	—	11	10	14	13	9	14
ADA-KL	14	17	11	15	13	13	—	—	16	14	12	15
ADA-Ken	13	14	11	15	10	10	8	9	—	—	7	11
ADA-RD	17	15	15	17	15	9	12	9	17	12	—	—

3D	CMA-ES		GP-1		GP-5		ADA-KL		ADA-Ken		ADA-RD	
#FEs/#FE$_t$	1/3	1	1/3	1	1/3	1	1/3	1	1/3	1	1/3	1
CMA-ES	—	—	11	9	7	13	8	10	9	9	7	8
GP-1	13	15	—	—	7	14	7	11	6	8	10	9
GP-5	17	11	17	10	—	—	15	9	13	6	14	9
ADA-KL	16	14	17	13	9	15	—	—	13	11	10	9
ADA-Ken	15	15	18	16	11	17	11	13	—	—	11	12
ADA-RD	17	16	14	15	10	14	14	15	13	10	—	—

5D	CMA-ES		GP-1		GP-5		ADA-KL		ADA-Ken		ADA-RD	
#FEs/#FE$_t$	1/3	1	1/3	1	1/3	1	1/3	1	1/3	1	1/3	1
CMA-ES	—	—	8	12	11	14	11	14	7	10	2	8
GP-1	16	12	—	—	11	12	11	12	9	7	3	4
GP-5	13	10	13	12	—	—	10	6	9	5	8	7
ADA-KL	13	10	13	11	14	18	—	—	7	10	8	5
ADA-Ken	17	14	15	17	15	19	17	14	—	—	10	9
ADA-RD	22*	16	21*	20*	16*	17*	16	19	14	14	—	—

10D	CMA-ES		GP-1		GP-5		ADA-KL		ADA-Ken		ADA-RD	
#FEs/#FE$_t$	1/3	1	1/3	1	1/3	1	1/3	1	1/3	1	1/3	1
CMA-ES	—	—	7	12	13	14	10	14	1	8	1	4
GP-1	17	12	—	—	15	15	14	14	4	5	5	4
GP-5	11	10	9	9	—	—	8	11	6	4	8	5
ADA-KL	14	10	10	10	16	13	—	—	8	5	9	8
ADA-Ken	23*	16*	20	19*	18*	20*	16	19*	—	—	13	12
ADA-RD	23*	20*	19	20*	16*	19*	15	15*	11	12	—	—

20D	CMA-ES		GP-1		GP-5		ADA-KL		ADA-Ken		ADA-RD	
#FEs/#FE$_t$	1/3	1	1/3	1	1/3	1	1/3	1	1/3	1	1/3	1
CMA-ES	—	—	7	5	11	12	9	13	4	3	3	5
GP-1	17	19	—	—	14	17	12	16	7	6	9	8
GP-5	13	12	10	7	—	—	4	5	6	5	10	6
ADA-KL	15	11	12	8	20	19	—	—	9	8	13	10
ADA-Ken	20*	21*	17	18	18*	19*	15	16	—	—	17	17
ADA-RD	21	19*	15	16	14	18*	11	14	7	7	—	—

J. Hlaváčová (Ed.): ITAT 2017 Proceedings, pp. 144–152
ISBN 978-1974274741, © 2017 T. Šabata, T. Borovička, M. Holeňa

K-best Viterbi Semi-supervized Active Learning in Sequence Labelling

Tomáš Šabata[1], Tomáš Borovička[1], and Martin Holeňa[2]

[1] Faculty of Information Technology,
Czech Technical University in Prague,
Prague, The Czech Repubic
[2] Institute of Computer Science,
Czech Academy of Sciences,
Prague, The Czech Republic

Abstract: In application domains where there exists a large amount of unlabelled data but obtaining labels is expensive, active learning is a useful way to select which data should be labelled. In addition to its traditional successful use in classification and regression tasks, active learning has been also applied to sequence labelling. According to the standard active learning approach, sequences for which the labelling would be the most informative should be labelled. However, labelling the entire sequence may be inefficient as for some its parts, the labels can be predicted using a model. Labelling such parts brings only a little new information. Therefore in this paper, we investigate a sequence labelling approach in which in the sequence selected for labelling, the labels of most tokens are predicted by a model and only tokens that the model can not predict with sufficient confidence are labelled. Those tokens are identified using the k-best Viterbi algorithm.

1 Introduction

Hidden Markov models (HMMs) and conditional random fields (CRFs) are very popular models in sequence labelling tasks such as handwriting recognition, speech recognition, DNA analysis, video analysis, information extraction or natural language processing (NLP). They achieve good results if a high quality and fully annotated dataset is available. Unfortunately, in these tasks, obtaining labels for data may be expensive. The annotation cost is a motivation for using active learning. Active learning usually begins with a small labelled set $\mathcal{L}$ and in each iteration, the most informative instance of an unlabeled set $\mathcal{U}$ is chosen, annotated by an oracle and added to the set $\mathcal{L}$. The model is retrained using the extended set $\mathcal{L}$ and the whole process repeats till a stopping criterion is met. This approach is valuable in tasks where unlabeled data are easily available but obtaining their labels is expensive. In this case, it aims at achieving higher accuracy with minimal cost.

Nevertheless, labelling long sequences can be troublesome, in particular for a human annotator who is prone to create labels of lower quality. To address the problem, we can combine active learning with semi-supervised learning. Semi-supervised active learning in sequence labelling means that a model labels those parts of a sequence that

are easy to predict and let the annotator to focus only on parts of sequences that are the most uncertain.

In this paper, we propose a semi-supervised active learning approach that uses the k-best Viterbi algorithm to detect candidates for manual labelling. The proposed approach was experimentally evaluated on an NLP task, part-of-speech tagging.

In the second section, we provide an overview of related work in active and semi-supervised learning. The third section recalls some basics of hidden Markov models that are necessary for understanding of the proposed approach which is introduced in the fourth section. An experiment description, its result and analysis are given in the fifth section. The paper is concluded by a discussion of the results and possible future work.

2 Related work

While active learning has been studied for classification and regression tasks [1], less attention has been given to the task of sequence labelling. Despite this, the most of the algorithms developed for the task of classification can also be adapted for the task of sequence labelling [2].

Active learning can be applied in three different scenarios: *pool-based sampling*, *stream-based selective sampling* and *membership query synthesis*. The most commonly used scenario is pool-based sampling originaly proposed in [3]. It has been studied for many real-world problem domains with sequence labelling included. For example, speech recognition [4], information retrieval [5] or named entitiy recognition [6]. The main idea of pool-based active learning is using a *query strategy framework* to find the most informative sample (sequence) from the unlabeled set (pool) of samples. This selected sample is annotated and added to the labelled set. The model is retrained, and the whole process repeats. The second scenario, stream-based selective sampling, is also possible to use in sequence labeling [7] but it is used less commonly. The difference against pool-based sampling is that samples are coming in a stream and the framework decides to annotate the sample or to discard it. The discarded samples are never later used in training. The main idea of the third scenario, membership query synthesis, is that a learner can query any unlabeled instance, usually generated de novo.

Active learning can use one of six different query strategy frameworks [1]. The most commonly used frameworks are *Uncertainty Sampling* [8] and *Querry-by-Committee* [9]. Uncertainty Sampling selects sample in which the model is least confident. Query-by-Committee maintains a committee of predictors, and the sample on which the predictors disagree most regarding their predictions is considered to be the most informative. Other query strategies applicable to sequences are *Expected Gradient Length, Information Density, Fisher Information* and *Future Error Reduction* [2]. The *Future Error Reduction* framework is not commonly used due to its high computational complexity.

Semi-supervised learning methods were developed with the same motivation of a partly unlabeled dataset. *Self-Training* is a commonly used technique where the predictor is firstly trained on a small labelled dataset and then used to annotate data. The most confident labels are added to the training set, and the predictor is retrained. Self-training has found application in several tasks of natural language processing [10, 11, 12]. Another technique, *Co-training*, is a multi-learner algorithm where learners have independent, complementary features of the dataset and produce labelled examples separately [13]. Semi-supervized learning was also applied to sequence modelling tasks [14, 15].

In tasks where a large amount of labelled data is required (for example, NLP tasks), the semi-supervised learning does not perform well due to the propagation of many tagging errors through the learning dataset. The problem of the data pollution was partially solved in [16], where a human was put into training loop to correct labelled examples. However, correction of labelled data can be time-consuming and is similar to labelling the data from scratch. To address the problem, a semi-supervised active learning which does not need any human inspection was proposed in [17]. The approach uses active learning to find the most informative sequences. The model labels the most informative sequences and uses a marginal probability of each sequence token to decide if the prediction is confident. The method contains two parameters, a delay of running semi-supervised approach and a confidence threshold. A proper setting of parameters is necessary to achieve the desired results.

Inspired by the semi-supervised method in [17], we proposed a method that does not need the confidence threshold parameter due to using the k-best Viterbi paths.

3 Preliminaries

In the paper, we focus on a task of part of speech tagging. For the simplicity, our approach is shown by means of HMM but can be extended to CRF as well. In this section, the principles of an HMM will be recalled.

3.1 Hidden Markov Models

With each HMM, a random process indexed by time is connected, which is assumed to be in exactly one of a set of N distinct states at any time. At regularly spaced discrete times, the system changes its state according to probabilities of transitions between states. The time steps associated with time changes are denoted $t = 1, 2, 3, \dots$. The actual state at a time step t is denoted q_t.

The process itself is assumed to be a first-order Markov chain which is described as a matrix of transition probabilities $A = \{a_{ij}\}$, defined

$$a_{ij} = P(q_t = y_j | q_{t-1} = y_i), \quad 1 \le i, j \le N. \quad (1)$$

A simple observable Markov chain is too restrictive to describe the reality. However, it can be extended. Denoting Y the variable recording the states of the Markov chain, an HMM is obtained through completing Y with a random variable X. In the context of that HMM, X is called 'observable variable' or 'output variable', whereas Y is called 'hidden variable'. The hidden variable Y takes values in the set $\{y_1, y_2, ..., y_N\}$ and the observable variable X takes values in a set $\{x_1, x_2, ..., x_M\}$.

We assume to have an observation sequence $O = o_1 o_2 ... o_T$ and a state sequence $Q = q_1 q_2 ... q_T$ which corresponds to the observation sequence. HMM can be characterised using three probability distributions:

1. A state transition probability distribution $A = \{a_{i,j}\}$.

2. A probability distribution of observable variables, $B = \{b_i(x_k)\}$, where $b_i(x_k)$ is the probability of o_t assuming the value x_k if q_t is in the state y_i and it is defined

$$b_i(k) = P(o_t = x_k | q_t = y_i). \quad (2)$$

3. An initial state distribution $\pi = \{\pi_i\}$ is defined by

$$\pi_i = P(q_1 = y_i).$$

With these three elements, HMM is fully defined and denoted $\theta = (A, B, \pi)$.

The parameters of an HMM can be learned either in a semi-supervised way with the Baum-Welch algorithm [18] or in a fully-supervised way with the maximum-likelihood estimation (MLE). In the fully-supervised way, values of both observable and hidden variables are known.

In the MLE, we assume a training set $D = \{(o^1, q^1), ..., (o^n, q^n)\}$ of a size n whose elements are independent. The MLE consists in taking those parameters θ^* that maximize the probability of the training set:

$$\theta^* = \text{argmax}_\theta P(D|\theta). \quad (3)$$

Due to (1) and (2), the probability in (3) turns to:

$$P(D|\theta) = \prod_{i,j} a_{i,j}^{T_{i,j}} \prod_{i,k} [b_i(k)]^{E_i(k)}, \sum_j a_{i,j} = 1, \sum_k b_i(k) = 1$$

where $T_{i,j}$ stands for number of transitions from state y_i to state y_j in the training set and $E_i(k)$ stands for number of emissions of value x_j in state y_i. Then, parameters A and B can be obtained by following formulas:

$$a_{i,j} = \frac{T_{i,j} + r_{i,j}}{\sum_{j'}(T_{i,j'} + r_{i,j'})} \text{ and } b_i(k) = \frac{E_i(k) + r_i(k)}{\sum_{k'}(E_i(k) + r_i(k'))}, \tag{4}$$

where $r_{i,j}$ and $r_i(k)$ are our prior beliefs. The prior beliefs are used in the case of an insufficiently large dataset, where the estimate would lead to zero probabilities of events which never occurred in D.

To simplify the notation, we define variables α and β as follows:

$$\alpha_t(i) = p(o_1, ..., o_t, q_t = y_i | \theta), \tag{5}$$
$$\beta_t(i) = p(o_t + 1, ..., o_T, q_t = y_i | \theta). \tag{6}$$

These variables are computed using the following *forward-backward* algorithm [18]:

$$\alpha_1(i) = \pi_i b_i(o_1),$$
$$\alpha_{t+1}(i) = \left(\sum_{j=1}^N \alpha_t(j) a_{j,i}\right) b_i(o_{t+1}),$$

respectively,

$$\beta_T(i) = 1,$$
$$\beta_t(i) = \sum_{j=1}^N a_{i,j} b_j(o_{t+1}) \beta_{t+1}(j).$$

3.2 Marginal probability

Once, the model is learned, it can be used for the prediction of a sequence of hiddden states given an observable sequence. In the task of finding the most likely states sequence, it is possible to find the sequence that maximises the expected number of correctly assigned states. From (5) follows that the *marginal probability* of being in a specific state i at a particular time t is:

$$\gamma_t(i) = \frac{\alpha_t(i)\beta_t(i)}{\sum_{j=1}^n \alpha_t(j)\beta_t(j)} \tag{7}$$

Then, maximising the expected number of correctly assigned states can be achieved through applying $q_t = \arg\max_{y_i \in Y} \gamma_t(y_i)$ to the whole sequence. However, the approach can find a sequence with very low or even zero probability in case the sequence is not feasible.

3.3 Viterbi algrithm

Viterbi algorithm is a dynamic programming algorithm that finds the most likely state sequence as a whole by maximising of $P(Q,O|\theta)$. It gradually counts the maximal probability of the state chain from its beginning till the state in time t with the state q_t being y_i represented by

a variable $\delta_t(i) = \max_{q_1,...,q_{t-1}} P(q_1, ..., q_t = y_i, o_1, ..., o_t)$. The algorithm is initialized as follows:

$$\delta_1(i) = \pi_i b_i(o_1), \tag{8}$$

and for each $2 \le t \le T$ and each y_i from Y, the algorithm calculates the variable $\delta_t(i)$:

$$\delta_t(i) = (max_{1 \le j \le N} \delta_{t-1}(y_j) a_{i,j}) b_i(o_t). \tag{9}$$

In each time t and for each node i, the algorithm stores the link to one of all predecessor nodes with which it forms the best path. These links are stored in the additional two-dimensional array $\psi_t(i)$, where:

$$\psi_1(i) = 0,$$
$$\psi_t(i) = \arg\max_{1 \le j \le N} \delta_{t-1}(j) a_{ji}.$$

The probability of the most probable sequence can be found by $\max_{1 \ leqi \le N} \delta_T(i)$ and the most probable state path $Q^* = (q_1^*, q_2^*, ..., q_T^*)$ can be found by backtracking:

$$q_T^* = \arg\max_{1 \le i \le N} \delta_T(i),$$
$$q_t^* = \psi_{t+1}(q_{t+1}^*).$$

The Viterbi algorithm has a similar structure as the forward-backward algorithm, and both have complexity $\mathcal{O}(N^2 T)$.

4 Proposed approach

Our proposed approach is an adaptation of the semi-supervised active learning method (*SeSAL*), originally proposed in [17]. Both SeSAL and our adaptation are based on a standard fully-supervized active learning algorithm (*FuSAL*). The concept of FuSAL algorithm is decribed by pseudocode in Algorithm 1.

An *utility function* $\phi_M(x)$ represents an informativness of the sample x given the model M. In the algorithm, any utility function can be used to find the most informative sequence [2].

In the SeSAL, the most informative instance is annotated by a model M and only the tokens whose predicted labels have a confidence smaller than a given threshold are given to a human annotator (oracle). Finding the optimal threshold value is an optimisation task minimising the dataset pollution and the number of queried labels. If the threshold is too high, a human annotates labels in which the model is well confident. On the other hand, if the threshold is too low, the algorithm accepts incorrectly labelled tokens which may result in a polluted training set.

In the SeSAL, they use a parameter called *delay* that represents a number of iterations of the FuSAL before the algorithm is switched to SeSAL. This helps to avoid producing errors comming from incorrect labels comming from an insufficiently converged model.

Algorithm 1 FuSAL algorithm

Given:
  $\mathcal{L}$: set of labeled examples
  $\mathcal{U}$: set of unlabeled examples
  ϕ_M: utility function

Algorithm:
1: **while** stopping criterion is not met **do**
2:   learn model M from $\mathcal{L}$
3:   for all $x_i \in \mathcal{U}{:}u_{x_i} \leftarrow \phi_M(x_i)$
4:   select $x^* = \arg\max_{x_i} u_{x_i}$
5:   query an oracle for labels y of x^*
6:   remove x^* from $\mathcal{U}$
7:   insert $<x^*,y>$ into $\mathcal{L}$
8: **end while**

In our approach, the confidence of labels is replaced by calculating the k best Viterbi paths to find tokens where predictions of the model differ in the k most likely sequences. The number of paths affects the behaviour of the algorithm, however, we assume this parameter to be less data dependent than confidence threshold. We call the approach *k-best Viterbi SeSAL*. The pseudocode of it is described in Algorithm (2).

Algorithm 2 k-best Viterbi SeSAL algorithm

Given:
  $\mathcal{L}$: set of labeled examples
  $\mathcal{U}$: set of unlabeled examples
  ϕ_M: utility function
  k: number of paths

Algorithm:
1: **while** stopping criterion is not met **do**
2:   learn model M from $\mathcal{L}$
3:   for all $x_i \in \mathcal{U}{:}u_{x_i} \leftarrow \phi_M(x_i)$
4:   select $x^* = \arg\max_{x_i} u_{x_i}$
5:   find the k best Viterbi paths $\{v_1,...,v_k\}$
6:   **for** t in length(x^*) **do**
7:     **if** $v_i(t)$ for all $i = 1,...,k$ are equal **then**
8:       label $x^*(t)$ with $y(t) = v_1(t)$
9:     **else**
10:       query an oracle for a label $y(t)$ of $x^*(t)$
11:     **end if**
12:   **end for**
13:   remove x^* from $\mathcal{U}$
14:   insert $<x^*,y>$ into $\mathcal{L}$
15: **end while**

The proposed approach uses the approach from the FuSAL active learning framework to find the most informative instance (lines 2-4). Then, the semi-supervised learning is applied in order to label the instance. The algorithm computes the k best Viterbi sequences that are used to detect not likely labels (line 5).

The Viterbi algorithm described in section 3.3 provides only one best sequence. To produce k best sequences it is not enough to store only one best label per node. The simplest way how to modify Viterbi algorithm is to store up to k best predecessors that can form k best sequences. Unfortunately, with this modification, the algorithm has the computational complexity of $\mathcal{O}(kTN^2)$. This computational overload can be lowered by the iterative Viterbi A* algorithm which has the complexity of $\mathcal{O}(T + kT)$ in the best case and $\mathcal{O}(TN^2 + kTN)$ in the worst case [19].

With the k-best Viterbi paths found, the algorithm loops trough the decoding (lines 6-12). The label is accepted only if all sequences produced it. Otherwise, a human annotator (oracle) is called to label the instance.

5 Experiment and results

In this section, we describe an experiment used for the evaluation of the proposed method. The method is evaluated on an NLP task called part-of-speech tagging (POS). The input to the POS is a set of meaningful sentences. The output is a set of tag sequences, one tag for each word. Word classes (noun, verb, adjective, etc.) or their derivates are the most often used tagsets. The number of tags is not limited.

POS is a difficult task for two reasons. First, the number of possible words in the text can be very high, and it may contain words that occur rarely. Second, some words can have assigned several tags, and to find the correct tag, the context of the sentence is needed. CRFs can take a wide context into account and thus is the most commonly used in the POS. However, though it is impossible to take a wide context into account in HMM, it is a sufficiently good performing model for our experiment.

In our experiment, we used data from the Natural language toolkit [20], which provides data for many NLP tasks such as POS, chunking, entity recognition, information extraction, etc. A few statistics for the employed benchmark datasets are provided in Table 1. Each dataset contains its proper tagset and a simplified tagset with 12 tags representing ten basic word classes, a dot and the rest.

Table 1: Benchmark datasets.

Dataset	#sentences	#words	#tags
Brown	57340	56057	472
CoNLL2000	10948	21589	44
Treebank	3914	12408	46

In order to compare the datasets, HMMs were trained using supervised learning on the full dataset with all labels available. Accuracy and the F_1 score measures were used for the performance comparison. The performance was measured for both the original tagset (Acc 1 and F-score 1) and the simplified tagset (Acc 2 and F-score 2). The data was randomly split into training and testing sets in a 7:3 ratio. The performance of the supervised learning is shown in Table 2. Due to the results in the table, we consider

HMM to be sufficiently well performing in the experiment. The worse F-score in the case of Brown dataset with all tags is caused an approximately ten times higher number of possible hidden values.

Table 2: Prediction performance learned on the full dataset. Training and testing data were randomly split in a 7:3 ratio. Acc 1 and F-score 1 represent results based on all tags, whereas, Acc 2 and F-score represent results based on simplified tags.

Dataset	Acc 1	Acc 2	F-score 1	F-score 2
Brown	.9421	.9572	.4520	.9245
Conll2000	.9508	.9546	.9080	.9408
Treebank	.9189	.9307	.8205	.9291

5.1 Experimental setup

For most of the experiments we used the following settings. In the base model, HMM, tags were considered to be hidden state values and words were considered to be observable variable values. The parameters of the model were estimated using MLE. To handle words that have not occurred in the training set, we added uniformly distributed pseudo-counts to both matrices A and B. Prior beliefs were set to be uniformly distributed, therefore, each word has the probability of $1/|words|$.

In order to simulate a standard situation in active learning, the original dataset was randomly split into training and testing sets in a 7:3 ratio and then, the training set was randomly split into labelled and unlabeled sets in a 3:7 ratio.

In each iteration of the experiment, the most informative instance was selected, annotated and put into the labelled training set. As most informative were considered instances maximizing the employed one of the following four uncertainty measures:

- least confidence

$$\phi_{LC}(x) = 1 - P(y_1^*|x; \theta),$$

- margin

$$\phi_M(x) = -(P(y_1^*|x; \theta) - P(y_2^*|x; \theta)),$$

- total token entropy

$$\phi_{TE}(x) = -\sum_{t=1}^{T}\sum_{n=1}^{N} P(y_t = n|x; \theta)\log P(y_t = n|x; \theta),$$

- k-best sequences entropy

$$\phi_{SE}(x) = -\sum_{\hat{y} \in V} P(\hat{y}|x; \theta)\log P(\hat{y}|x; \theta),$$

where V is set of k-best Viterbi sequences and y_k^* is the k-th most probable sequence of labels. The behaviour of different uncertainty measures is investigated in the experiment in Section 5.2.

After finding them most informative sequence, semi-supervised learning was applied. The sequence was labelled according to Algorithm 2. The algorithm has one parameter, the number of k best sequences. The effect of the parameter on the performance of the proposed approach is described in the experiment in Section 5.3.

5.2 Uncertainty measure

At first, we study effects of uncertainty measures on the proposed method. The measures were evaluated on the TreeBank dataset with 30% labeled instances. The parameter k was set to 100.

The experiment has shown that the computational complexity of the k-best sequence entropy measure and the margin measure is too high for practical usage due to the calculation of the k best Viterbi paths (two best Viterbi paths respectively) for each unlabeled instance. Moreover, active learning that uses as a measure the k-best sequences entropy had a tendency to choose short sentences. In that case, active learning had a lower accuracy than the random sampling method.

The computational complexity of least confident and total token entropy measures were reasonable even for datasets with a big number of unlabeled samples. The performance comparison is shown in Figures 1 and 2. According to the experiment results, FuSAL with the least confident measure achieved higher accuracy after 50 iterations. However, the total token entropy measure achieved the certain level of accuracy in less queried tokens which can be preferable for some tasks.

Taking into account the computational complexity of the methods, the least confidence measure is used in the rest of the experiment.

5.3 Parameter settings

In semi-supervised learning, a well performing model is crucial to produce good quality labels. In SeSAL algorithm, the parameter delay controls how many iterations of FuSAL algorithm is used before semi-supervised approach is applied. The goal of this experiment was an analysis of the relationship between the parameter delay and the parameter k. Since the proposed method does not use the delay parameter, it has been simulated using datasets with a different number of labelled samples. The experiment was evaluated on the biggest dataset, Brown, with three initial settings a) 10% of labelled samples, b) 30% of labelled samples, c) 60% of labelled samples.

It has been shown that the value of the parameter k is highly correlated with the number of labelled samples in the dataset. In the dataset with 10% of labelled samples, the high value of the parameter k has shown to be crucial

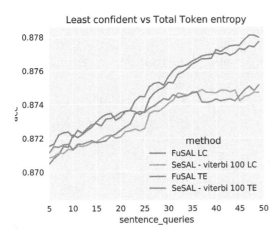

Figure 1: Comparison of the least confident measure (LC) and the total token entropy measure (TE) for different numbers of queries in connection with FuSAL and Viterbi SeSAL.

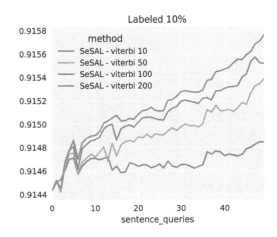

Figure 3: An accuracy regarding a number of queried sentences where 10% of the training set is labeled

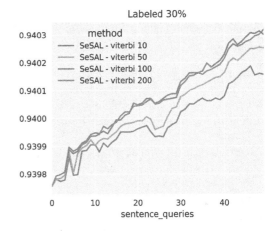

Figure 4: An accuracy regarding a number of queried sentences where 30% of the training set is labeled

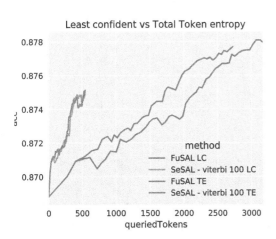

Figure 2: Comparison of the least confident measure (LC) and the total token entropy measure (TE) for different numbers of queries in connection with FuSAL and Viterbi SeSAL.

to reduce the number of errors propagated to the training dataset (Figure 3). With increasing number of labelled samples, a high value of the parameter k becomes less effective. In Figure 4 the difference between parameter k=100 and k=200 almost vanished. Moreover, regarding the number of queried labels, the settings k=100 becomes more efficient (Figure (5)). The same trend was also observed in the case where 60% of instances were labelled.

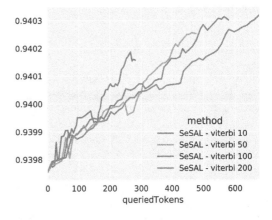

Figure 5: An accuracy regarding a number of queried tokens where 30% of the training set is labeled

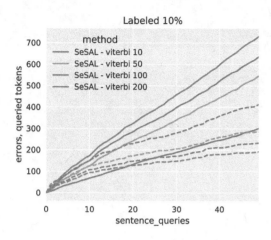

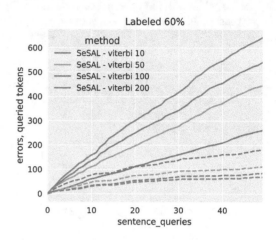

Figure 6: A number of queried tokens (solid line) and errors (dashed line) regarding a number of sentences where 10% of the training set is labeled.

Figure 7: A number of queried tokens (solid line) and errors (dashed line) regarding a number of sentences where 60% of the training set is labeled.

5.4 Number of queried tokens and errors propagation

The parameter k affects the number of queried tokens and the number of errors propagated to the learning set. The optimal setting of the parameter minimises both. The experiment in this section analyses the relationship between tokens and errors.

One should consider the number od labelled samples in setting of the parameter k. In the case of less labelled samples, the parameter k should be set to a higher number to avoid production of errors (Figure 6). After several iterations, when the base model is more accurate, higher values of parameter k become less effective (Figure 7).

However, even with an almost labelled dataset and the settings k = 200 we were not able to avoid errors in labelling. From all 2402 annotated tokens, 57 were annotated wrongly. We consider the complicated control of an acceptable error rate as one of the biggest disadvantages of the proposed method.

5.5 Comparison with other methods

To evaluate the performance of the proposed method in comparison with other methods an accuracy was measured regarding the number of queried sentences and the number of queried tokens. Furthermore, the number of errors propagated to the learning set was measured. All experiments were evaluated on the Brown dataset with the simplified tagset.

The SeSAL with uncertainty threshold and the proposed method can be compared only if the parameters are set such that the methods produce an approximately same number of errors. In the experiment, confidence threshold was set to 0.48 and parameter of the number of paths k was set to 100.

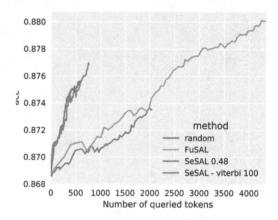

Figure 8: Achieved accuracy over the number of queried tokens.

As expected, the FuSAL method achieved the highest accuracy because all labels were annotated manually, thus correctly. In the number of queried tokens, Viterbi SeSAL achieved bigger accuracy in more queried tokens (Figure 8). The explanation can be seen in Figure 9 where the number of errors and the number of queried tokens was measured. In the given settings, the number of errors propagated to the learning set was lower in Viterbi SeSAL at the expense of the number of queried tokens. Although, after several iterations, the error rate of the proposed method has been lower than in the SeSAL method.

6 Conclusion and future work

We proposed a semi-supervised active learning method that is easy to setup for the sequence labelling and is suf-

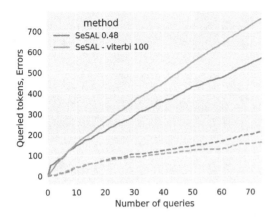

Figure 9: The number of queried tokens (solid line) and the number of errors (dashed line) over the number of queries.

ficiently well performing in comparison with the semi-supervised active learning method that use an uncertainty threshold and a marginal probability. The proposed method uses k best Viterbi paths to find the tokens in which the model is not sufficiently confident.

The number of errors, the number of queried tokens and the computational complexity are controlled by the parameter k. In order to reduce the number of errors propagated to the labelling set, the parameter k should be set as high as it is reasonable in terms of the computational time. The computational complexity of k-best Viterbi path algorithm can be partially reduced using iterative Viterbi A* algorithm. In addition to a high computation complexity, a complicated control of the number of propagated errors is disadvantage of the proposed method.

An area for further research is the exploration of Co-training in combination with the Query-by-Committee active learning framework where both approaches consider several different views of the data. Furthermore, the semi-supervised active learning method that can be applied to both probabilistic and deterministic sequential models should be more studied to find a general solution for them.

Acknowledgements

The reported research was supported by the CTU grant nr. SGS17/210/OHK3/3T/18 and by the Czech Science Foundation grant nr. 17-01251.

References

[1] Burr Settles. Active learning literature survey. *University of Wisconsin, Madison*, 52(55-66):11, 2010.

[2] Burr Settles and Mark Craven. An analysis of active learning strategies for sequence labeling tasks. In *Proceedings of the conference on empirical methods in natural language processing*, pages 1070–1079. Association for Computational Linguistics, 2008.

[3] David D Lewis and William A Gale. A sequential algorithm for training text classifiers. In *Proceedings of the 17th annual international ACM SIGIR conference on Research and development in information retrieval*, pages 3–12. Springer-Verlag New York, Inc., 1994.

[4] Gokhan Tur, Dilek Hakkani-Tür, and Robert E Schapire. Combining active and semi-supervised learning for spoken language understanding. *Speech Communication*, 45(2):171–186, 2005.

[5] Cynthia A Thompson, Mary Elaine Califf, and Raymond J Mooney. Active learning for natural language parsing and information extraction. In *ICML*, pages 406–414, 1999.

[6] Lin Yao, Chengjie Sun, Shaofeng Li, Xiaolong Wang, and Xuan Wang. Crf-based active learning for chinese named entity recognition. In *Systems, Man and Cybernetics, 2009. SMC 2009. IEEE International Conference on*, pages 1557–1561. IEEE, 2009.

[7] Ido Dagan and Sean P Engelson. Committee-based sampling for training probabilistic classifiers. In *Proceedings of the Twelfth International Conference on Machine Learning*, pages 150–157. The Morgan Kaufmann series in machine learning,(San Francisco, CA, USA), 1995.

[8] David D Lewis and Jason Catlett. Heterogeneous uncertainty sampling for supervised learning. In *Proceedings of the eleventh international conference on machine learning*, pages 148–156, 1994.

[9] H Sebastian Seung, Manfred Opper, and Haim Sompolinsky. Query by committee. In *Proceedings of the fifth annual workshop on Computational learning theory*, pages 287–294. ACM, 1992.

[10] David Yarowsky. Unsupervised word sense disambiguation rivaling supervised methods. In *Proceedings of the 33rd annual meeting on Association for Computational Linguistics*, pages 189–196. Association for Computational Linguistics, 1995.

[11] Ellen Riloff, Janyce Wiebe, and Theresa Wilson. Learning subjective nouns using extraction pattern bootstrapping. In *Proceedings of the seventh conference on Natural language learning at HLT-NAACL 2003-Volume 4*, pages 25–32. Association for Computational Linguistics, 2003.

[12] Chuck Rosenberg, Martial Hebert, and Henry Schneiderman. Semi-supervised self-training of object detection models. 2005.

[13] Avrim Blum and Tom Mitchell. Combining labeled and unlabeled data with co-training. In *Proceedings of the eleventh annual conference on Computational learning theory*, pages 92–100. ACM, 1998.

[14] Andrew M. Dai and Quoc V. Le. Semi-supervised sequence learning. *CoRR*, abs/1511.01432, 2015.

[15] Shi Zhong. Semi-supervised sequence classification with hmms. *International Journal of Pattern Recognition and Artificial Intelligence*, 19(02):165–182, 2005.

[16] David Pierce and Claire Cardie. Limitations of co-training for natural language learning from large datasets. In *Proceedings of the 2001 Conference on Empirical Methods in Natural Language Processing*, pages 1–9, 2001.

[17] Katrin Tomanek and Udo Hahn. Semi-supervised act-
     ive learning for sequence labeling. In *Proceedings of
     the Joint Conference of the 47th Annual Meeting of the
     ACL and the 4th International Joint Conference on Natural
     Language Processing of the AFNLP: Volume 2-Volume 2*,
     pages 1039–1047. Association for Computational Linguist-
     ics, 2009.

[18] Lawrence R Rabiner. A tutorial on hidden markov models
     and selected applications in speech recognition. *Proceed-
     ings of the IEEE*, 77(2):257–286, 1989.

[19] Zhiheng Huang, Yi Chang, Bo Long, Jean-Francois
     Crespo, Anlei Dong, Sathiya Keerthi, and Su-Lin Wu. It-
     erative viterbi a* algorithm for k-best sequential decoding.
     In *Proceedings of the 50th Annual Meeting of the Associ-
     ation for Computational Linguistics: Long Papers-Volume
     1*, pages 611–619. Association for Computational Linguist-
     ics, 2012.

[20] Steven Bird, Ewan Klein, and Edward Loper. *Natural Lan-
     guage Processing with Python*. O'Reilly Media, 2009.

J. Hlaváčová (Ed.): ITAT 2017 Proceedings, pp. 153–158
ISBN 978-1974274741, © 2017 M. Stepanovsky, A. Ibrova, Z. Buk, J. Veleminska

Estimation of Chronological Age from Permanent Teeth Development

Michal Stepanovsky[1], Alexandra Ibrova[2], Zdenek Buk[1], and Jana Veleminska[2]

[1] Faculty of Information Technology, Czech Technical University in Prague,
Thakurova 9, 160 00 Prague, Czech Republic
[2] Department of Anthropology and Human Genetics, Faculty of Science, Charles University,
Vinicna 7, 128 43 Prague, Czech Republic

Abstract: This paper compares traditional averages-based model with other various age estimation models in the range from the simplest to the advanced ones, and introduces novel Tabular Constrained Multiple-linear Regression (TCMLR) model. This TCMLR model has similar complexity as traditional averages-based model (it can by evaluated manually), but improves the mean absolute error in average about 0.30 years (approx. 3.6 months) for males, and 0.18 years (approx. 2.2 months) for females, respectively. For all models, the chronological age of an individual is estimated from mineralization stages of dentition. This study was based on a sample of 976 orthopantomographs taken of 662 boys and 314 girls of Czech nationality aged between 2.7 and 20.5 years.

1 Introduction

For age estimation of children and adolescents one of the most stable markers for age estimation is the development of dentition. There are various limitations for age estimation from dental remains, for review see [1, 2]. There are various methods for calculating the age of an individual from mineralization stages of dentition (e.g.[3–5]) which are traditional, easy to use and provide a decent level of accuracy. A number of authors developed modifications of these methods in order to increase the accuracy, adjust the tables for specific populations or to develop a more complex approach (e.g. [6–8]). The goal of this paper is to investigate the question if sophisticated methods provide an improvement of results at such level that they are worth engaging in forensic practice.

2 Material and Methods

The study sample consists of 662 boys and 314 girls of Czech nationality with the age distribution as shown by histograms in the Figure 1.

Development of each tooth was divided into 14 sub-stages, and each stage was assigned a numerical value ranging from 1 to 14 [3]. "Initial cusp formation" was denoted as stage 1, the "Coalescence of cusps" as stage 2 and so forth until the last stage "Apical closure complete" as stage 14. Stage 0 was used when no data was available. Table 1 summarizes tooth development stages.

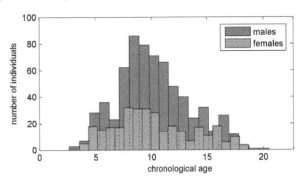

Figure 1: Age distribution histograms

Table 1: Tooth development stages

Meaning	Coding	
	single-rooted teeth	multi-rooted teeth
Initial cusp formation	1	1
Coalescence of cusps	2	2
Cusp outline complete	3	3
Crown $\frac{1}{2}$ complete	4	4
Crown $\frac{3}{4}$ complete	5	5
Crown complete	6	6
Initial root formation	7	7
Initial cleft formation	–	8
Root length $\frac{1}{4}$	8	9
Root length $\frac{1}{2}$	9	10
Root length $\frac{3}{4}$	10	11
Root length complete	11	12
Appex $\frac{1}{2}$ closed	12	13
Apical closure complete	13	14

Figure 2 illustrates development stages for single-rooted and multi-rooted teeth, as well as, the position of single-rooted and multi-rooted teeth in maxilla and mandible.

The correlation matrix is visualized in Figure 3 for males and in Figure 4 for females, respectively. The first row/column represents chronological age, the subsequent 16 rows/columns represent left and right teeth coming from mandible; and next subsequent 16 rows/columns represent left and right teeth coming from maxilla. The ordering of teeth is as follows: I1, I2, C, P1, P2, M1, M2 and M3. The minimum value in correlation matrix is 0.32 for males, and 0.61 for females. The correlation coefficient between chronological age and development stages of various teeth range from 0.71 to 0.93 for males,

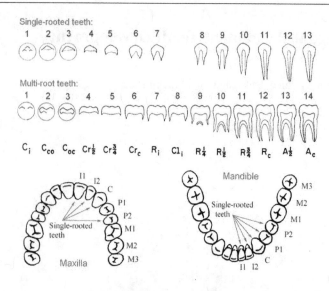

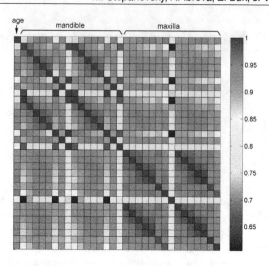

Figure 4: Correlation matrix for females

Figure 2: Tooth development stages and the position of single-rooted and multi-rooted teeth

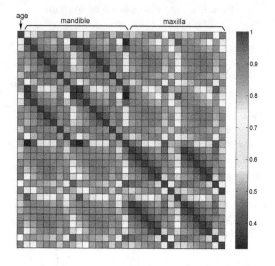

Figure 3: Correlation matrix for males

and from 0.82 to 0.95 for females. From these matrices, we can observe strong correlation between corresponding left and right teeth for both mandible and maxilla, and tendency of higher correlation between neighboring teeth.

In the rest of the paper the subscript 'd' stands for mandible, 'x' for maxilla, 'Sin' for sinistra and 'Dx' for dexter. The correlation coefficient between development stage to the chronological age for the most correlated teeth for males is as follows: $P2_{x,Dx} : 0.93$, $P2_{x,Sin} : 0.93$, $M2_{x,Dx} : 0.92$, $M2_{x,Sin} : 0.92$, $M2_{d,Dx} : 0.92$, $P1_{x,Dx} : 0.92$, $P1_{x,Sin} : 0.92$, $M2_{d,Sin} : 0.92$, $P2_{d,Sin} : 0.89$, $P1_{d,Dx} : 0.89$, $P2_{d,Dx} : 0.89$ and $P1_{d,Sin} : 0.89$. Similarly, for females: $M2_{x,Dx} : 0.95$, $P2_{x,Dx} : 0.95$, $P2_{x,Sin} : 0.95$, $P1_{x,Dx} : 0.95$, $P1_{x,Sin} : 0.95$, $P1_{d,Dx} : 0.95$, $P1_{d,Sin} : 0.95$, $C_{x,Sin} : 0.94$, $C_{x,Dx} : 0.94$, $P2_{d,Sin} : 0.94$, $M2_{x,Sin} : 0.94$ and $P2_{d,Dx} : 0.94$.

2.1 Investigated Methods without Transformation of Input Data

Here we describe investigated methods, which directly use tooth development stages as an input.

Model #1: Multiple linear regression model (MLR) [13] is based on a method that approximates dental age by a linear equation. In this model the collinear attributes were removed, and attribute selection using the Akaike information metric was used to remove attributes with the smallest standardized coefficient if this improves the final model.

Model #2: The Support Vector Machine (SVM) regression can be used to avoid difficulties of using linear functions in the high dimensional feature space. The nonlinear transformation that maps observations to a high-dimensional space is usually referenced as a kernel. For our analysis, a polynomial kernel with exponent set to 2.0 was used, and the value of ε was set to 0.04.

Model #3: Multilayer perceptron (MLP) is a feedforward artificial neural network that consists of multiple layers of nodes with each layer connected to the next one [13]. In our analysis, a single hidden layer network was used, consisting of 16 nodes in the input layer (corresponding to the individual teeth), 8 neurons in the hidden layer and 1 neuron in the output layer. Backpropagation is used as the learning algorithm. Neurons in the hidden layer are all sigmoid, and the output neuron is an unthresholded linear unit.

Model #4: Radial Basis Function neural network (RBF) has similar topology to the previous MLP, but each node in the hidden layer is a normalized Gaussian radial basis function. It uses the k-means clustering algorithm to provide the basis functions. The minimum standard deviation for the clusters was set to 0.1 and the number of clusters was set to 20 for the merged dataset, 20 for males and 10 for females.

Model #5: Radial Basis Function neural network with BFGS method (RBF-BFGS) is similar to model #4. It is trained in a fully supervised manner by WEKA's Optimization class by minimizing squared error with the BFGS (Broyden–Fletcher–Goldfarb–Shanno) method.

Model #6: K-nearest neighbors (KNN) is a simple algorithm that stores all available data and estimates the output value of new observations based on a similarity measure. The brute force search algorithm is used to find the 10 nearest neighbors and Manhattan distance is used to measure the distance.

Model #7: KStar is, similarly to KNN, an instance-based classifier which differs in using an entropy-based distance function. The distance function reflects the complexity of transforming an instance into another one. Using entropic distance as a metric has a number of benefits including handling of real valued attributes and missing values.

Model #8: Regression tree (RepTree in Weka) is a non-parametric supervised learning method which builds regression model in the form of a tree structure.

Model #9: M5P Tree is similar to the previous regression tree model #8. The main difference is that leaves do not provide a piecewise constant function (one specific value at each leaf) but rather various MLR models as discussed above (see model #1) reflecting tooth age estimation capabilities in various age ranges.

2.2 Investigated Methods with Transformation of Input Data

The tooth development stage represents an ordinal categorical variable with a nonlinear monotonic relationship to the dental age of an individual. Therefore, we also examined the possibility of replacing tooth development stages by the representative median (or average) age before creating the model. The median (or average) age was computed from all individuals of representative population who have the same mineralization stage for the same tooth type. This potentially eliminates the nonlinear relationship and transforms the tooth development stage into a ratio-scaled continuous variable. Models using this transformation are referred as "tabular".

Model #10: Tabular model based on age averages, e.g. [3, 12], is a widely-used classical method of age estimation in forensic practice because of its simplicity. The model uses tables containing the average age of all individuals from a representative population who have an equally developed specific tooth type. These tables can be found e.g. in Smith [12]. Age estimation of unknown individual is realized by estimating the developmental stage of each available tooth from an X-ray image, looking up the age for each estimated stage in the tables and computing the average value of age. This means that each tooth has the same contribution/weight for the final age estimation.

Model #11: Tabular model based on age medians could be considered as an alternative to model #10, where the only difference is that medians are used instead of age averages.

Model #12: Tabular constrained multiple linear regression model (TCMLR) is similar to MLR (model #1) but uses the transformation of input data as described above and only non-negative coefficients. For this model, we compare two versions – version A and version B. In the version A, the collinear attributes were removed and a greedy method was used for the attribute selection using the Akaike information metric. Moreover, the teeth producing negative coefficients in the created model were simply not included. This guarantees the ordering of the model outputs with respect of increasing tooth development stages – i.e. higher development stage results in higher estimated age. In the version B, we use the algorithm implemented in Matlab by lsqnonneg, which is a function designed to solve non-negative least-squares problem and it is based on algorithm described in [16].

Other models, namely **Model #13 – #20**, use the transformation of input data into median age as described above and are based on their non-tabular counterparts, e.g. tabular SVM is based on SVM, etc. Model #13 is realized in two versions – polynomial kernel with exponent equal to 1.0 and 2.0.

Data processing and analysis were performed using software tools Matlab [24] and Weka [25]. The mean absolute error and root mean squared error for all presented models (#1 – #20) was estimated by using 5-fold cross-validation, where the models are completely build upon the training set and no information from the testing set is involved during the training phase. Hyperparameters of used models were tuned on the training set only.

3 Comparison of Considered Models

A comparison of the considered models by using 5-fold cross-validation for males and females is shown in Table 2, where MAE means mean absolute error and RMS means root mean squared error. All presented models produce the estimated age of an individual as an output. The table is ordered in four categories from the simplest models at the top (dental age can be easily estimated) to the most complex models at the bottom (almost impossible to evaluate the model without computer). The comparison shows that the conventional model based on age averages (#10) fails in terms of age estimation accuracy. Significantly better results provide the Tabular multiple linear regression model (#12), M5P tree model (#9), tabular M5P tree model (#20) and tabular Support Vector Machine with first-order polynomial kernel (#13), which has similar complexity as baseline model #10 (all models are user-friendly). The mean absolute error for all these models is under 0.7 years and root mean squared error is about 0.9 years. The model #9

Table 2: Comparison of considered models

	Males MAE /RMS	Females MAE / RMS	
Tab. age avg. (#10)	0.96 / 1.20	0.83 / 0.91	☺
Tab. age med. (#11)	0.95 / 1.25	0.83 / 0.89	☺
MLR (#1)	0.76 / 1.02	0.78 / 1.08	☺
Tab. MLR, v.A (#12)	0.66 / 0.86	0.65 / 0.86	☺
Tab. MLR, v.B (#12)	0.69 / 0.90	0.64 / 0.84	☺
M5P tree (#9)	0.69 / 0.92	0.70 / 0.91	☺
Tab. M5P tree (#20)	0.65 / 0.86	0.65 / 0.89	☺
TSVM, exp=1 (#13)	0.65 / 0.86	0.64 / 0.85	☺
Reg. tree (#16)	0.85 / 1.22	0.82 / 1.11	😐
Tab. reg. tree (#19)	0.80 / 1.10	0.79 / 1.02	😐
SVM (#2)	0.70 / 0.94	0.71 / 0.95	☹
TSVM, exp=2 (#13)	0.73 / 0.96	0.83 / 1.05	☹
MLP (#3)	0.91 / 1.16	0.84 / 1.08	☹
Tab. MLP (#14)	0.76 / 0.98	0.80 / 1.04	☹
RBF (#4)	0.74 / 0.99	0.80 / 1.02	😫
Tab. RBF (#15)	0.76 / 0.99	0.77 / 1.00	😫
RBF-BFGS (#5)	0.65 / 0.86	0.67 / 0.88	😫
TRBF-BFGS (#16)	0.63 / 0.83	0.67 / 0.88	😫
KNN (#6)	0.64 / 0.85	0.66 / 0.87	😫
Tab. KNN (#17)	0.63 / 0.84	0.65 / 0.84	😫
KStar (#7)	0.65 / 0.85	0.69 / 0.88	😫
Tab. KStar (#18)	0.63 / 0.86	0.66 / 0.87	😫

☺ = very easy to evaluate manually; 😐 = easy to evaluate; ☹ = the model size or procedure can be confusing; 😫 = the model is hard or almost imposible to evaluate without computer.

estimates the age directly from the teeth development stages (tree model is built upon this information), whereas the models #12, #13 (with first-order polynomial kernel) and #20 in the first step replace each tooth development stage by median age. This eliminates the nonlinearity between development stage and chronological age and allows for great reduction of the generated M5P tree in the model #20, which in fact collapses (after pruning) into just one leaf. Therefore, the model #20 has become principally equivalent to model#12. This indicates that in this case it is fully sufficient to build only one tabular multiple linear regression model for the whole age range of the studied population. Slightly better accuracy provide RBF neural network with BFGS (#5), tabular RBF neural network with BFGS (#16), Tabular Support Vector Machine (#13), K-nearest neighbors (#6), tabular K-nearest neighbors (#17), KStar (#7) and tabular KStar model (#18). Nevertheless, these models are almost impossible to evaluate without help of computer and models #6, #17, #7 and #18 include entire data set of all 976 orthopantomographs (data set is integral part of these models).

In the Figure 5 and Figure 6 is illustrated the model performance of tabular multiple linear regression model, version A – Model #12. This model provide acceptable accuracy while being user-friendly. Comparing to the

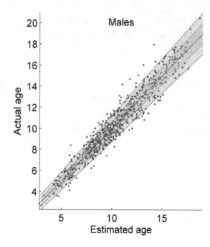

Figure 5: The model performance of tabular MLR model for males, version A (Model #12)

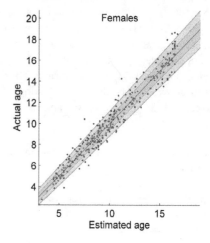

Figure 6: The model performance of tabular MLR model for females, version A (Model #12)

traditional age estimation model #10, the mean squared error is reduced about 0.3 years for males, and 0.18 years for females, respetively.

4 Description of Selected Model

We have chosen TCMLR model with non-negative coefficients (model #12, version A) as the best candidate for application in forensic praxis. This model is easy to use and provides sufficient age estimation accuracy. Tabular M5P tree model #20 provides almost identical results because in this case M5P tree has degraded into just one leaf, and thus it is similar to model #12. TSVM model with exp=1.0 provides slightly better performance. However, negative coefficients appearing in this TSVM model cause undesirable side effects — the more the corresponding tooth is developed, the more the estimated age is decreased. This can be in contrast with expected behavior of the dental age estimation model in praxis.

Table 3: Median age table for males, mandible

Tooth devel.	I1	I2	C	P1	P2	M1	M2	M3
1	–	–	–	–	–	–	–	8.9
2	–	–	–	–	3.9	–	–	9.3
3	–	–	–	3.6	4.6	–	4.9	9.9
4	–	–	3.9	4.3	4.9	–	5.3	10.5
5	2.6	3.6	4.6	5.2	5.8	–	6.1	11.5
6	3.4	4.4	5.5	5.9	6.4	2.8	6.9	12
7	4.2	4.9	6.1	6.7	7.7	3.5	7.9	13.4
8	4.8	5.6	7.2	7.9	8.6	4.2	8.8	14.7
9	5.6	6.4	8.3	9	9.8	5	9.8	15.4
10	6.7	7.5	9.5	10.2	10.7	5.9	11.1	16.6
11	7.9	8.7	10.7	11.3	12.1	7.4	12.1	17.8
12	9	9.8	12.3	13.1	14.3	8.5	13.9	19.2
13	11.3	11.8	15.2	15.7	16.3	10	15.4	20.7
14	x	x	x	x	x	12.4	16.9	22.2

Table 5: Median age table for females, mandible

Tooth devel.	I1	I2	C	P1	P2	M1	M2	M3
1	–	–	–	–	–	–	3.9	8.8
2	–	–	–	–	–	–	4.4	9.5
3	–	–	–	–	4.6	–	4.8	9.8
4	–	–	3.8	4.6	5	–	5.3	10.3
5	–	3	4.5	5	5.9	–	6.3	11.5
6	2.7	4.2	5.1	5.9	6.8	2.9	6.9	12.8
7	4.1	4.7	6.3	7	7.7	–	7.9	13.8
8	4.6	5.5	7.4	8.1	8.7	3.9	8.7	14.3
9	5.6	6.9	8.6	9.4	10.1	4.6	9.5	15.1
10	7.2	8.3	10	10.7	11.7	5.8	10.7	16.1
11	8.6	10	11.9	12.5	13.2	7.3	12.2	17.5
12	10.6	12.1	14.2	14.8	15.2	8.8	14	(18.7)
13	14.2	15.4	16.3	16.4	16.7	10.6	15.4	(20.4)
14	x	x	x	x	x	14.2	16.8	(22.2)

Table 4: Median age table for males, maxilla

Tooth devel.	I1	I2	C	P1	P2	M1	M2	M3
1	–	–	–	–	–	–	–	8.3
2	–	–	–	–	4.6	–	4.9	9.2
3	–	3.8	–	–	4.9	–	4.9	9.8
4	–	–	4.2	4.9	5.6	3.6	5.5	10.5
5	4.2	4.7	5.2	5.9	6.3	3.9	6.3	11.5
6	5.1	5.6	6	7	7.5	4.2	7.3	12.6
7	5.7	6.2	7	7.8	8.3	4.9	8.2	13.1
8	6.4	7.1	8	8.8	9.3	5.7	9.2	14.3
9	7.6	8.1	8.9	9.9	10.4	6.3	10.2	15.8
10	8.6	9.1	10.3	10.9	11.7	7.4	11.3	16.3
11	9.8	10.2	11.3	12.3	12.7	8.8	12.3	17.1
12	10.3	11	13.2	14.1	14.4	10	13.4	17.8
13	12.2	13.2	15.7	16.3	16.5	9.8	14.7	(18.5)
14	x	x	x	(18.7)	x	12.2	16.6	(19.2)

Table 6: Median age table for females, maxilla

Tooth devel.	I1	I2	C	P1	P2	M1	M2	M3
1	–	–	–	–	–	–	4.3	–
2	–	–	–	–	–	1.8	4.8	8.8
3	–	–	–	–	4.9	–	5.3	9.5
4	–	–	4.4	5.1	5.3	–	5.4	10.4
5	4	4.6	5.1	6	6.2	3.1	6.2	11.5
6	4.5	5.1	6.2	7	7.3	4.2	7.1	12.2
7	5.2	6.2	7	7.9	8.2	4.6	8.2	13.7
8	6.3	7	8	8.8	9.2	5.2	9	14.6
9	7.4	8.2	9.1	10.1	10.5	6.1	10.2	15.6
10	8.7	9.4	10.6	11.4	11.8	7.5	11.2	16.4
11	10.4	11.1	12.3	12.6	12.8	9.1	12.2	17.9
12	12.5	13.1	14.3	14.5	14.8	10.7	13.2	19.6
13	15.4	15.6	16.2	16.3	16.4	12.7	15	(21.3)
14	x	x	x	(18.3)	x	15.5	16.7	(23.4)

Comparing to a tradional averages-based model (#10), TCMLR model follows the similar procedure, however instead of computing the average from partial age estimations corresponding to each individual tooth (this corresponds to multiplying by constant $k_i = 1/16 = 0.0625$ for all i=1, 2, ...,16), it uses multiple-linear equation with non-negative coefficients (1) or (2) to estimate dental age of individual.

$$Age_{males} = 0.08M1_d + 0.17M2_d + 0.13M3_d + 0.33P2_x + \\ + 0.21M2_x + 0.20M3_x - 1.04, \quad (1)$$

$$Age_{females} = 0.24P1_d + 0.16M2_d + 0.13I1_x + 0.18C_x + \\ + 0.11P1_x + 0.09M1_x + 0.15M2_x - 0.53, \quad (2)$$

where the average value between sinister and dexter was used for calculation. For instance $M1_d = (M1_{d,Sin} + M1_{d,Dx})/2$. The value of corresponding median age in dependency of tooth development stage can be found in Tab. 3, Tab. 4, Tab. 5 and Tab. 6. These tables are obtained from our study sample and weighted smoothing was used to capture the relationship between tooth development and median age. Values in the brackets were computed by the extrapolation of the existing data.

4.1 Rules for Replacing Missing Values

In the case when all required teeth by equation (1) or (2) are not available – $M1_d, M2_d, M3_d, P2_x, M2_x, M3_x$ for males and $P1_d, M2_d, I1_x, C_x, P1_x, M1_x, M2_x$ for females, the transformation as described in Sec. 2.2 allows for simple rules for replacing missing values. In that case, the missing value can be simply estimated as an average from available data (corresponding median age from all available teeth).

5 Conclusion

In this paper, we compared various age estimation models. The main aim was to explore whether popular data mining methods provide significantly better results over the traditional method based on age averages. The results show that most of the complex data mining methods included in this study (they can be evaluated only by using computer) can improve the mean absolute error in average about 0.32 years (approx. 3.8 months) for males, and 0.18 years (approx. 2.2 months) for females, comparing to traditional model used in forensic praxis. However, the similar accuracy provide simple linear models, for instance, TCMLR model has lower accuracy only about 0.03 years (11 days) for males. Moreover, the simplicity of TCMLR model is a great benefit for real application in forensic praxis. Results of this paper also indicate that instead of using tooth development stages as ordinal categorical variable it is better to replace them by ratio-scaled continuous variable (median age) before creating the model. This eliminates nonlinear input-output relationships and allows for achieving higher model accuracy by using simple linear models. Moreover, this transformation helps to introduce simple rules for replacing missing values – no need to estimate development stage of missing tooth, but the average of median ages corresponding to available teeth can be used.

6 Acknowledgements

The research was supported by the Charles University Grant Agency, research grant GAUK No. 526216 and by Institucionalni podpora na rozvoj vyzkumne org. RVO13000.

References

[1] Cunha E, Baccino E, Martrille L, et al (2009) The problem of aging human remains and living individuals: A review. Forensic Sci Int 193:1–13.

[2] Franklin D (2010) Forensic age estimation in human skeletal remains: Current concepts and future directions. Leg Med 12:1–7.

[3] Moorrees CFA, Fanning EA, Hunt EE (1963) Age variation of formation stages for ten permanent teeth. J Dent Res 42:1490–1502.

[4] Demirjian A, Goldstein H, Tanner JM (1973) A new system of dental age assessment. Hum Biol an Int Rec Res 45:211–227.

[5] Nolla CM (1960) The development of the permanent teeth. J Dent Child 27:254–266.

[6] Teivens A, Mörnstad H (2001) A comparison between dental maturity rate in the Swedish and korean populations using a modified Demirjian method. J Forensic Odontostomatol 19:21–35.

[7] Blenkin MRB, Evans W (2010) Age estimation from the teeth using a modified demirjian system. J Forensic Sci 55:1504–1508. doi: 10.1111/j.1556-4029.2010.01491.x

[8] Harris EF (2011) Dental age: The effects of estimating different events during mineralization. Dent Anthropol 24:59–63.

[9] Corsini MM, Schmitt A, Bruzek J (2005) Aging process variability on the human skeleton: Artificial network as an appropriate tool for age at death assessment. Forensic Sci Int 148:163–167. doi: 10.1016/j.forsciint.2004.05.008

[10] Buk Z, Kordik P, Bruzek J, et al (2012) The age at death assessment in a multi-ethnic sample of pelvic bones using nature-inspired data mining methods. Forensic Sci Int 220:294.e1-294.e9. doi: 10.1016/j.forsciint.2012.02.019

[11] Velemínská J, Pilný A, Čepek M, et al (2013) Dental age estimation and different predictive ability of various tooth types in the Czech population: data mining methods. Anthropol Anzeiger 70:331–345.

[12] Smith BH (1991) Standards of human tooth formation and dental age assessment. In: Kelley MA, Larsen CS (eds) Adv. Dent. Anthropol. Wiley-Liss, New York, pp 143–168

[13] Witten IH, Frank E, Hall MA (2011) Data Mining: Practical Machine Learning Tools and Techniques (Third Edition). Morgan Kaufmann Publishers Inc., San Francisco

[14] Hastie T, Tibshirani R, Friedman J (2009) The Elements of Statistical Learning: Data Mining, Inference, and Prediction, Second Edition. Springer-Verlag New York

[15] Manikandan S (2011) Measures of central tendency: Median and mode. J Pharmacol Pharmacother 2:214–215. doi: 10.4103/0976-500X.83300

[16] Lawson, C.L. and R.J. Hanson, Solving Least Squares Problems, Prentice-Hall, 1974, Chapter 23, p. 161.

[17] P. E. Gill, W. Murray and M. H. Wright, Practical Optimization, Academic, London, 1981.

[18] Rasmus Bro, Sijmen De Jong: A fast non-negativity-constrained least squares algorithm. Journal of chemometrics, VOL. 11, 393–401 (1997)

[19] S.K. Shevade, S.S. Keerthi, C. Bhattacharyya, K.R.K. Murthy: Improvements to the SMO Algorithm for SVM Regression. In: IEEE Transactions on Neural Networks, 1999.

[20] Frank E (2014) Fully supervised training of Gaussian radial basis function networks in WEKA.

[21] Cleary JG, Trigg LE (1995) K*: An Instance-based Learner Using an Entropic Distance Measure. In: Proc. 12th Int. Conf. Mach. Learn. pp 108–114

[22] Quinlan RJ (1992) Learning with Continuous Classes. In: 5th Aust. Jt. Conf. Artif. Intell. pp 343–348

[23] Wang Y, Witten HI (1997) Induction of model trees for predicting continuous classes. In: Proceeding 9th Eur. Conf. Mach. Learn. pp 128–137

[24] http://www.mathworks.com/products/matlab

[25] http://www.cs.waikato.ac.nz/ml/weka

J. Hlaváčová (Ed.): ITAT 2017 Proceedings, pp. 159–166
ISBN 978-1974274741, © 2017 P. Vidnerová, R. Neruda

Evolution Strategies for Deep Neural Network Models Design

Petra Vidnerová, Roman Neruda

Institute of Computer Science, The Czech Academy of Sciences
petra@cs.cas.cz

Abstract: Deep neural networks have become the state-of-art methods in many fields of machine learning recently. Still, there is no easy way how to choose a network architecture which can significantly influence the network performance.

This work is a step towards an automatic architecture design. We propose an algorithm for an optimization of a network architecture based on evolution strategies. The algorithm is inspired by and designed directly for the Keras library [3] which is one of the most common implementations of deep neural networks.

The proposed algorithm is tested on MNIST data set and the prediction of air pollution based on sensor measurements, and it is compared to several fixed architectures and support vector regression.

1 Introduction

Deep neural networks (DNN) have become the state-of-art methods in many fields of machine learning in recent years. They have been applied to various problems, including image recognition, speech recognition, and natural language processing [8, 10].

Deep neural networks are feed-forward neural networks with multiple hidden layers between the input and output layer. The layers typically have different units depending on the task at hand. Among the units, there are traditional perceptrons, where each unit (neuron) realizes a nonlinear function, such as the *sigmoid* function, or the rectified linear unit (*ReLU*).

While the learning of weights of the deep neural network is done by algorithms based on the stochastic gradient descent, the choice of architecture, including a number and sizes of layers, and a type of activation function, is done manually by the user. However, the choice of architecture has an important impact on the performance of the DNN. Some kind of expertise is needed, and usually a trial and error method is used in practice.

In this work we exploit a fully automatic design of deep neural networks. We investigate the use of evolution strategies for evolution of a DNN architecture. There are not many studies on evolution of DNN since such approach has very high computational requirements. To keep the search space as small as possible, we simplify our model focusing on implementation of DNN in the Keras library [3] that is a widely used tool for practical applications of DNNs.

The proposed algorithm is evaluated both on benchmark and real-life data sets. As the benchmark data we use the MNIST data set that is classification of handwritten digits. The real data set is from the area of sensor networks for air pollution monitoring. The data came from De Vito et al [21, 5] and are described in detail in Section 5.1.

The paper is organized as follows. Section 2 brings an overview of related work. Section 3 briefly describes the main ideas of our approach. In Section 4 our algorithm based on evolution strategies is described. Section 5 summarizes the results of our experiments. Finally, Section 6 brings conclusion.

2 Related Work

Neuroevolution techniques have been applied successfully for various machine learning problems [6]. In classical neuroevolution, no gradient descent is involved, both architecture and weights undergo the evolutionary process. However, because of large computational requirements the applications are limited to small networks.

There were quite many attempts on architecture optimization via evolutionary process (e.g. [19, 1]) in previous decades. Successful evolutionary techniques evolving the structure of feed-forward and recurrent neural networks include NEAT [18], HyperNEAT [17] and CoSyNE [7] algorithms.

On the other hand, studies dealing with evolution of deep neural networks and convolutional networks started to emerge only very recently. The training of one DNN usually requires hours or days of computing time, quite often utilizing GPU processors for speedup. Naturally, the evolutionary techniques requiring thousands of training trials were not considered a feasible choice. Nevertheless, there are several approaches to reduce the overall complexity of neuroevolution for DNN. Still due to limited computational resources, the studies usually focus only on parts of network design.

For example, in [12] CMA-ES is used to optimize hyperparameters of DNNs. In [9] the unsupervised convolutional networks for vision-based reinforcement learning are studied, the structure of CNN is held fixed and only a small recurrent controller is evolved. However, the recent paper [16] presents a simple distributed evolutionary strategy that is used to train relatively large recurrent network with competitive results on reinforcement learning tasks.

In [14] automated method for optimizing deep learning architectures through evolution is proposed, extending existing neuroevolution methods. Authors of [4] sketch a genetic approach for evolving a deep autoencoder network enhancing the sparsity of the synapses by means of special operators. Finally, the paper [13] presents two version of an evolutionary and co-evolutionary algorithm for design of DNN with various transfer functions.

3   Our Approach

In our approach we use evolution strategies to search for optimal architecture of DNN, while the weights are learned by gradient based technique.

The main idea of our approach is to keep the search space as small as possible, therefore the architecture specification is simplified. It directly follows the implementation of DNN in Keras library, where networks are defined layer by layer, each layer fully connected with the next layer. A layer is specified by number of neurons, type of an activation function (all neurons in one layer have the same type of an activation function), and type of regularization (such as dropout).

In this paper, we work only with fully connected feedforward neural networks, but the approach can be further modified to include also convolutional layers. Then the architecture specification would also contain type of layer (dense or convolutional) and in case of convolutional layer size of the filter.

4   Evolution Strategies for DNN Design

Evolution strategies (ES) were proposed for work with real-valued vectors representing parameters of complex optimization problems [2]. In the illustration algorithm bellow we can see a simple ES working with n individuals in a population and generating m offspring by means of Gaussian mutation. The environmental selection has two traditional forms for evolution strategies. The so called $(n+m)$-ES generates new generation by deterministically choosing n best individuals from the set of $(n+m)$ parents and offspring. The so called (n,m)-ES generates new generation by selecting from m new offspring (typically, $m > n$). The latter approach is considered more robust against local optima premature convergence.

Currently used evolution strategies may carry more meta-parameters of the problem in the individual than just a vector of mutation variances. A successful version of evolution strategies, the so-called *covariance matrix adaptation ES* (CMA-ES) [12] uses a clever strategy to approximate the full $N \times N$ covariance matrix, thus representing a general N-dimensional normal distribution. Crossover operator is usually used within evolution strategies.

In our implementation (n,m)-ES (see Alg. 1) is used. Offspring are generated using both mutation and crossover operators. Since our individuals are describing network topology, they are not vectors of real numbers. So our operators slightly differ from classical ES. The more detail description follows.

Algorithm 1 (n,m)-Evolution strategy optimizing real-valued vector and utilizing adaptive variance for each parameter

---

procedure (n,m)-ES
  $t \leftarrow 0$
  Initialize population P_t n by randomly generated vectors $\vec{x^t} = (x_1^t, \ldots, x_N^t, \sigma_1^t, \ldots, \sigma_N^t)$
  Evaluate individuals in P_t
  while not *terminating criterion* **do**
    for $i \leftarrow 1, \ldots, m$ **do**
      choose randomly a parent $\vec{x_i}$,
      generate an offspring $\vec{y_i^t}$
      by *Gaussian mutation*:
      for $j \leftarrow 1, \ldots, N$ **do**
        $\sigma_j' \leftarrow \sigma_j \cdot (1 + \alpha \cdot N(0,1))$
        $x_j' \leftarrow x_j + \sigma_j' \cdot N(0,1)$
      end for
      insert $\vec{y_i^t}$ to offspring candidate population P_t'
    end for
    Deterministically choose P_{t+1} as n best individuals from P_t'
    Discard P_t and P_t'
    $t \leftarrow t + 1$
  end while
end procedure

4.1   Individuals

Individuals are coding feed-forward neural networks implemented as Keras model *Sequential*. The model implemented as *Sequential* is built layer by layer, similarly an individual consists of blocks representing individual layers.

$$I = (\quad [size_1, drop_1, act_1, \sigma_1^{size}, \sigma_1^{drop}]_1, \ldots,$$
$$[size_H, drop_H, act_H, \sigma_H^{size}, \sigma_H^{drop}]_H \quad),$$

where H is the number of hidden layers, $size_i$ is the number of neurons in corresponding layer that is dense (fully connected) layer, $drop_i$ is the dropout rate (zero value represents no dropout), $act_i \in \{\texttt{relu}, \texttt{tanh}, \texttt{sigmoid}, \texttt{hardsigmoid}, \texttt{linear}\}$ stands for activation function, and σ_i^{size} and σ_i^{drop} are strategy coefficients corresponding to size and dropout.

So far, we work only with dense layers, but the individual can be further generalized to work with convolutional layers as well. Also other types of regularization can be considered, we are limited to dropout for the first experiments.

4.2   Crossover

The operator *crossover* combines two parent individuals and produces two offspring individuals. It is implemented as one-point crossover, where the cross-point is on the border of a block.

Let two parents be

$$I_{p1} = (B_1^{p1}, B_2^{p1}, \ldots, B_k^{p1})$$

$$I_{p2} = (B_1^{p2}, B_2^{p2}, \ldots, B_l^{p2}),$$

then the crossover produces offspring

$$I_{o1} = (B_1^{p1}, \ldots, B_{cp1}^{p1}, B_{cp2+1}^{p2}, \ldots, B_l^{p2})$$

$$I_{o1} = (B_1^{p2}, \ldots, B_{cp2}^{p2}, B_{cp1+1}^{p1}, \ldots, B_k^{p1}),$$

where $cp_1 \in \{1, \ldots, k-1\}$ and $cp_2 \in \{1, \ldots, l-1\}$.

4.3 Mutation

The operator *mutation* brings random changes to an individual. Each time an individual is mutated, one of the following mutation operators is randomly chosen:

- mutateLayer - introduces random changes to one randomly selected layer. One of the following operators is randomly chosen:

  - changeLayerSize - the number of neurons is changed. Gaussian mutation is used, adapting strategy parameters σ^{size}, the final number is rounded (since size has to be integer).
  - changeDropOut - the dropout rate is changed using Gaussian mutation adapting strategy parameters σ^{drop}.
  - changeActivation - the activation function is changed, randomly chosen from the list of available activations.

- addLayer - one randomly generated block is inserted at random position.

- delLayer - one randomly selected block is deleted.

Note, that the ES like mutation comes in play only when size of layer or dropout parameter is changed. Otherwise the strategy parameters are ignored.

4.4 Fitness

Fitness function should reflect a quality of the network represented by an individual. To assess the generalization ability of the network represented by the individual we use a crossvalidation error. The lower the crossvalidation error, the higher the fitness of the individual.

Classical k-fold crossvalidation is used, i.e. the training set is split into k-folds and each time one fold is used for testing and the rest for training. The mean error on the testing set over k run is evaluated.

The mean squared error is used as an error function:

$$E = 100 \frac{1}{N} \sum_{t=1}^{N} (f(x^t) - y^t)^2,$$

where $T = (x_1, y_1), \ldots, (x_N, y_N)$ is the actual testing set and f is the function represented by the learned network.

4.5 Selection

The tournament selection is used, i.e. each turn of the tournament k individuals are selected at random and the one with the highest fitness, in our case the one with the lowest crossvalidation error, is selected.

Our implementation of the proposed algorithm is available at [20].

5 Experiments

5.1 Data Set

For the first experiment we used real-world data from the application area of sensor networks for air pollution monitoring [21, 5], for the second experiment the well known MNIST data set [11].

The sensor data contain tens of thousands measurements of gas multi-sensor MOX array devices recording concentrations of several gas pollutants collocated with a conventional air pollution monitoring station that provides labels for the data. The data are recorded in 1 hour intervals, and there is quite a large number of gaps due to sensor malfunctions. For our experiments we have chosen data from the interval of March 10, 2004 to April 4, 2005, taking into account each hour where records with missing values were omitted. There are altogether 5 sensors as inputs and 5 target output values representing concentrations of CO, NO_2, NOx, $C6H6$, and $NMHC$.

The whole time period is divided into five intervals. Then, only one interval is used for training, the rest is utilized for testing. We considered five different choices of the training part selection. This task may be quite difficult, since the prediction is performed also in different parts of the year than the learning, e.g. the model trained on data obtained during winter may perform worse during summer (as was suggested by experts in the application area).

Table 1 brings overview of data sets sizes. All tasks have 8 input values (five sensors, temperature, absolute and relative humidity) and 1 output (predicted value). All values are normalized between $\langle 0, 1 \rangle$.

Table 1: Overview of data sets sizes.

Task	train set	test set
CO	1469	5875
NO2	1479	5914
NOx	1480	5916
C6H6	1799	7192
NMHC	178	709

The MNIST data set contains 70 000 images of hand written digits, 28×28 pixel each (see Fig. 1). 60 000 are used for training, 10 000 for testing.

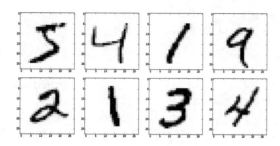

Figure 1: Example of MNIST data set samples.

5.2 Setup

For the sensor data the proposed algorithm was run for 100 generations for each data set, with $n = 10$ and $m = 30$. During fitness function evaluation the network weights are trained by RMSprop (one of the standard algorithms) for 500 epochs. Besides the ES classical GA was implemented and run on sensor data with same fitness function.

For the MNIST data set, the algorithm was run for 30 generations, with $n = 5$ and $m = 10$, for fitness evaluation the RMSprop was run for 20 epochs.

When the best individual is obtained, the corresponding network is built and trained on the whole training set and evaluated on the test set.

5.3 Results

The resulting testing errors obtained by GA and ES in the first experiment are listed in Table 3. There are average, standard deviation, minimum and maximum errors over 10 computations. The performance of ES over GA is slightly better, the ES achieved lower errors in 15 cases, GA in 11 cases.

Table 4 compares ES testing errors to results obtained by support vector regression (SVR) with linear, RBF, polynomial, and sigmoid kernel function. SVR was trained using Scikit-learn library [15], hyperparameters were found using grid search and crossvalidation.

The ES outperforms the SVR, it found best results in 17 cases.

Finally, Table 5 compares the testing error of evolved network to error of three fixed architectures (for example 30-10-1 stands for 2 hidden layers of 30 and 10 neurons, one neuron in output layers, ReLU activation is used and dropout 0.2). The evolved network achieved the most (10) best results.

Since this task does not have much training samples, also the networks evolved are quite small. The typical evolved network had one hidden layer of about 70 neurons, dropout rate 0.3 and ReLU activation function.

The second experiment was the classification of MNIST letters. As a baseline architecture was taken the one from Keras examples, i.e. network with two hidden layers of 512 ReLU units each, both with dropout 0.2. This network has a fairly good performance. It was trained 10 times

Table 2: Test accuracies on the MNIST data set.

model	avg	std	min	max
baseline	98.34	0.13	98.18	98.55
evolved by ES	98.64	0.05	98.55	98.73

and the results are listed in Table 2, together with results obtained by the evolved network.

The evolved network had also two hidden layers, first with 736 ReLU units and dropout parameter 0.09, the second with 471 hard sigmoid units and dropout 0.2. The ES found a competitive result, the evolved network achieved better accuracy than the baseline model.

6 Conclusion

We have proposed an algorithm for automatic design of DNNs based on evolution strategies. The algorithm was tested in experiments on the real-life sensor data set and MNIST dataset of handwritten digits. On sensor data set, the solutions found by our algorithm outperforms SVR and selected fixed architectures. The activation function dominating in solutions is the ReLU function. For the MNIST data set, the network with ReLU and hard sigmoid units was found, outperforming the baseline solution. We have shown that our algorithm is able to found competitive solutions.

The main limitation of the algorithm is the time complexity. One direction of our future work is to try to lower the number of fitness evaluations using surrogate modeling or to use asynchronous evolution.

Also we plan to extend the algorithm to work also with convolutional networks and to include more parameters, such as other types of regularization, the type of optimization algorithm, etc.

The gradient based optimization algorithm depends significantly on the random initialization of weights. One way to overcome this is to combine the evolution of weights and gradient based local search that is another possibility of future work.

Acknowledgment

This work was partially supported by the Czech Grant Agency grant 15-18108S and institutional support of the Institute of Computer Science RVO 67985807.

Access to computing and storage facilities owned by parties and projects contributing to the National Grid Infrastructure MetaCentrum provided under the programme "Projects of Large Research, Development, and Innovations Infrastructures" (CESNET LM2015042), is greatly appreciated.

Table 3: Errors on test set for networks found by GA and ES. The average, standard deviation, minimum and maximum of 10 evaluations of the learning algorithm are listed.

	GA				ES			
	avg	std	min	max	avg	std	min	max
CO part1	**0.209**	0.014	0.188	0.236	0.229	0.026	0.195	0.267
CO part2	0.801	0.135	0.600	1.048	**0.657**	0.024	0.631	0.694
CO part3	0.266	0.029	0.222	0.309	**0.256**	0.045	0.199	0.349
CO part4	**0.404**	0.226	0.186	0.865	0.526	0.108	0.308	0.701
CO part5	0.246	0.024	0.207	0.286	**0.235**	0.025	0.199	0.277
NOx part1	2.201	0.131	1.994	2.506	**2.132**	0.086	2.021	2.284
NOx part2	1.705	0.284	1.239	2.282	**1.599**	0.077	1.444	1.685
NOx part3	**1.238**	0.163	0.982	1.533	1.339	0.242	1.106	1.955
NOx part4	**1.490**	0.173	1.174	1.835	1.610	0.164	1.435	2.041
NOx part5	**0.551**	0.052	0.456	0.642	0.622	0.075	0.521	0.726
NO2 part1	1.697	0.266	1.202	2.210	**1.506**	0.217	1.132	1.823
NO2 part2	2.009	0.415	1.326	2.944	**1.371**	0.048	1.242	1.415
NO2 part3	**0.593**	0.082	0.532	0.815	0.660	0.078	0.599	0.863
NO2 part4	**0.737**	0.023	0.706	0.776	0.782	0.043	0.711	0.856
NO2 part5	1.265	0.158	1.054	1.580	**0.730**	0.111	0.520	0.905
C6H6 part1	**0.013**	0.005	0.006	0.024	**0.013**	0.004	0.007	0.018
C6H6 part2	0.039	0.015	0.025	0.079	**0.034**	0.010	0.020	0.050
C6H6 part3	**0.019**	0.011	0.009	0.041	0.048	0.015	0.016	0.075
C6H6 part4	0.030	0.015	0.014	0.061	**0.020**	0.010	0.010	0.042
C6H6 part5	**0.017**	0.015	0.004	0.051	0.027	0.011	0.014	0.051
NMHC part1	1.719	0.168	1.412	2.000	**1.685**	0.256	1.448	2.378
NMHC part2	**0.623**	0.164	0.446	1.047	0.713	0.097	0.566	0.865
NMHC part3	1.144	0.181	0.912	1.472	**1.097**	0.270	0.775	1.560
NMHC part4	1.220	0.206	0.994	1.563	**1.099**	0.166	0.898	1.443
NMHC part5	1.222	0.126	1.055	1.447	**1.023**	0.050	0.963	1.116
	11				15			
	44%				60%			

Table 4: Test errors for evolved network and SVR with different kernel functions. For the evolved network the average, standard deviation, minimum and maximum of 10 evaluations of learning algorithm are listed.

Task	Evolved network				SVR			
	avg	std	min	max	linear	RBF	Poly.	Sigmoid
CO_part1	**0.229**	0.026	0.195	0.267	0.340	0.280	0.285	1.533
CO_part2	0.657	0.024	0.631	0.694	0.614	**0.412**	0.621	1.753
CO_part3	**0.256**	0.045	0.199	0.349	0.314	0.408	0.377	1.427
CO_part4	**0.526**	0.108	0.308	0.701	1.127	0.692	0.535	1.375
CO_part5	0.235	0.025	0.199	0.277	0.348	0.207	**0.198**	1.568
NOx_part1	2.132	0.086	2.021	2.284	**1.062**	1.447	1.202	2.537
NOx_part2	1.599	0.077	1.444	1.685	2.162	1.838	**1.387**	2.428
NOx_part3	1.339	0.242	1.106	1.955	**0.594**	0.674	0.665	2.705
NOx_part4	1.610	0.164	1.435	2.041	0.864	0.903	**0.778**	2.462
NOx_part5	**0.622**	0.075	0.521	0.726	1.632	0.730	1.446	2.761
NO2_part1	**1.506**	0.217	1.132	1.823	2.464	2.404	2.401	2.636
NO2_part2	**1.371**	0.048	1.242	1.415	2.118	2.250	2.409	2.648
NO2_part3	**0.660**	0.078	0.599	0.863	1.308	1.195	1.213	1.984
NO2_part4	**0.782**	0.043	0.711	0.856	1.978	2.565	1.912	2.531
NO2_part5	**0.730**	0.111	0.520	0.905	1.0773	1.047	0.967	2.129
C6H6_part1	**0.013**	0.004	0.007	0.018	0.300	0.511	0.219	1.398
C6H6_part2	**0.034**	0.010	0.020	0.050	0.378	0.489	0.369	1.478
C6H6_part3	**0.048**	0.015	0.016	0.075	0.520	0.663	0.538	1.317
C6H6_part4	**0.020**	0.010	0.010	0.042	0.217	0.459	0.123	1.279
C6H6_part5	**0.027**	0.011	0.014	0.051	0.215	0.297	0.188	1.526
NMHC_part1	1.685	0.256	1.448	2.378	1.718	1.666	**1.621**	3.861
NMHC_part2	**0.713**	0.097	0.566	0.865	0.934	0.978	0.839	3.651
NMHC_part3	**1.097**	0.270	0.775	1.560	1.580	1.280	1.438	2.830
NMHC_part4	**1.099**	0.166	0.898	1.443	1.720	1.565	1.917	2.715
NMHC_part5	1.023	0.050	0.963	1.116	1.238	**0.944**	1.407	2.960
	17				2	2	4	
	68%				8%	8%	16%	

Table 5: Test errors for evolved network and three selected fixed architectures.

Task	Evolved network		50-1		30-10-1		30-10-30-1	
	avg	std	avg	std	avg	std	avg	std
CO_part1	**0.229**	0.026	0.230	0.032	0.250	0.023	0.377	0.103
CO_part2	**0.657**	0.024	0.861	0.136	0.744	0.142	0.858	0.173
CO_part3	**0.256**	0.045	0.261	0.040	0.305	0.043	0.302	0.046
CO_part4	0.526	0.108	0.621	0.279	0.638	0.213	**0.454**	0.158
CO_part5	**0.235**	0.025	0.283	0.072	0.270	0.032	0.309	0.032
NOx_part1	2.132	0.086	2.158	0.203	**2.095**	0.131	2.307	0.196
NOx_part2	**1.599**	0.077	1.799	0.313	1.891	0.199	2.083	0.172
NOx_part3	1.339	0.242	1.077	0.125	1.092	0.178	**0.806**	0.185
NOx_part4	1.610	0.164	**1.303**	0.208	1.797	0.461	1.600	0.643
NOx_part5	**0.622**	0.075	0.644	0.075	0.677	0.055	0.778	0.054
NO2_part1	1.506	0.217	1.659	0.250	**1.368**	0.135	1.677	0.233
NO2_part2	**1.371**	0.048	1.762	0.237	1.687	0.202	1.827	0.264
NO2_part3	0.660	0.078	0.682	0.148	**0.576**	0.044	0.603	0.069
NO2_part4	0.782	0.043	1.109	0.923	**0.757**	0.059	0.802	0.076
NO2_part5	0.730	0.111	**0.646**	0.064	0.734	0.107	0.748	0.123
C6H6_part1	0.013	0.004	**0.012**	0.006	0.081	0.030	0.190	0.060
C6H6_part2	**0.034**	0.010	0.039	0.012	0.101	0.015	0.211	0.071
C6H6_part3	0.048	0.015	**0.024**	0.007	0.091	0.047	0.115	0.031
C6H6_part4	**0.020**	0.010	0.026	0.010	0.051	0.026	0.096	0.020
C6H6_part5	0.027	0.011	**0.025**	0.008	0.113	0.025	0.176	0.058
NMHC_part1	**1.685**	0.256	1.738	0.144	1.889	0.119	2.378	0.208
NMHC_part2	0.713	0.097	**0.553**	0.045	0.650	0.078	0.799	0.096
NMHC_part3	1.097	0.270	1.128	0.089	0.901	0.124	**0.789**	0.184
NMHC_part4	1.099	0.166	1.116	0.119	0.918	0.119	**0.751**	0.096
NMHC_part5	1.023	0.050	0.970	0.094	0.889	0.085	**0.856**	0.074
	10		6		4		5	
	40%		24%		16%		20%	

References

[1] Jasmina Arifovic and Ramazan Gençay. Using genetic algorithms to select architecture of a feedforward artificial neural network. *Physica A: Statistical Mechanics and its Applications*, 289(3–4):574 – 594, 2001.

[2] H.-G. Beyer and H. P. Schwefel. Evolutionary strategies: A comprehensive introduction. *Natural Computing*, pages 3–52, 2002.

[3] François Chollet. Keras. https://github.com/fchollet/keras, 2015.

[4] Omid E. David and Iddo Greental. Genetic algorithms for evolving deep neural networks. In *Proceedings of the Companion Publication of the 2014 Annual Conference on Genetic and Evolutionary Computation*, GECCO Comp '14, pages 1451–1452, New York, NY, USA, 2014. ACM.

[5] S. De Vito, G. Fattoruso, M. Pardo, F. Tortorella, and G. Di Francia. Semi-supervised learning techniques in artificial olfaction: A novel approach to classification problems and drift counteraction. *Sensors Journal, IEEE*, 12(11):3215–3224, Nov 2012.

[6] Dario Floreano, Peter Dürr, and Claudio Mattiussi. Neuroevolution: from architectures to learning. *Evolutionary Intelligence*, 1(1):47–62, 2008.

[7] Faustino Gomez, Juergen Schmidhuber, and Risto Miikkulainen. Accelerated neural evolution through cooperatively coevolved synapses. *Journal of Machine Learning Research*, pages 937–965, 2008.

[8] Ian Goodfellow, Yoshua Bengio, and Aaron Courville. *Deep Learning*. MIT Press, 2016. http://www.deeplearningbook.org.

[9] Jan Koutník, Juergen Schmidhuber, and Faustino Gomez. Evolving deep unsupervised convolutional networks for vision-based reinforcement learning. In *Proceedings of the 2014 Annual Conference on Genetic and Evolutionary Computation*, GECCO '14, pages 541–548, New York, NY, USA, 2014. ACM.

[10] Yann Lecun, Yoshua Bengio, and Geoffrey Hinton. Deep learning. *Nature*, 521(7553):436–444, 5 2015.

[11] Yann LeCun and Corinna Cortes. The mnist database of handwritten digits, 2012.

[12] Ilya Loshchilov and Frank Hutter. CMA-ES for hyperparameter optimization of deep neural networks. *CoRR*, abs/1604.07269, 2016.

[13] Tomas H. Maul, Andrzej Bargiela, Siang-Yew Chong, and Abdullahi S. Adamu. Towards evolutionary deep neural networks. In Flaminio Squazzoni, Fabio Baronio, Claudia Archetti, and Marco Castellani, editors, *ECMS 2014 Proceedings*. European Council for Modeling and Simulation, 2014.

[14] Risto Miikkulainen, Jason Zhi Liang, Elliot Meyerson, Aditya Rawal, Dan Fink, Olivier Francon, Bala Raju, Hormoz Shahrzad, Arshak Navruzyan, Nigel Duffy, and Babak Hodjat. Evolving deep neural networks. *CoRR*, abs/1703.00548, 2017.

[15] F. Pedregosa et al. Scikit-learn: Machine learning in Python. *Journal of Machine Learning Research*, 12:2825–2830, 2011.

[16] T. Salimans, J. Ho, X. Chen, and I. Sutskever. Evolution Strategies as a Scalable Alternative to Reinforcement Learning. *ArXiv e-prints*, March 2017.

[17] Kenneth O. Stanley, David B. D'Ambrosio, and Jason Gauci. A hypercube-based encoding for evolving large-scale neural networks. *Artif. Life*, 15(2):185–212, April 2009.

[18] Kenneth O. Stanley and Risto Miikkulainen. Evolving neural networks through augmenting topologies. *Evolutionary Computation*, 10(2):99–127, 2002.

[19] B. u. Islam, Z. Baharudin, M. Q. Raza, and P. Nallagownden. Optimization of neural network architecture using genetic algorithm for load forecasting. In *2014 5th International Conference on Intelligent and Advanced Systems (ICIAS)*, pages 1–6, June 2014.

[20] Petra Vidnerová. GAKeras. github.com/PetraVidnerova/GAKeras, 2017.

[21] S. De Vito, E. Massera, M. Piga, L. Martinotto, and G. Di Francia. On field calibration of an electronic nose for benzene estimation in an urban pollution monitoring scenario. *Sensors and Actuators B: Chemical*, 129(2):750 – 757, 2008.

J. Hlaváčová (Ed.): ITAT 2017 Proceedings, pp. 167–173
ISBN 978-1974274741, © 2017 P. Vlašánek, I. Perfilieva

Inpainting Using F-Transform for Cartoon-Like Images

Pavel Vlašánek, Irina Perfilieva

Institute for Research and Applications of Fuzzy Modeling,
University of Ostrava, 30. dubna 22, Ostrava, Czech Republic
`pavel.vlasanek@osu.cz`

Abstract: We propose to modify image inpainting technique based on F-transform for application dedicated to cartoon images. The images have typical features which are taken into consideration. These features make original algorithm ineffective, because of its isotropic nature. Proposed modification changes it to an anisotropic.

1 Introduction

Image restoration, in meaning of object removal or damage recovery, so called image inpainting, is challenging task in image processing. Let us consider input image I which contains unwanted pixels considered as a damage. In the process of image inpainting, the damaged area should be erased and replaced by some proper part of I. The selection of the proper part is crucial. One option is to choose square shaped patch and replace the damaged area by its copy. In that case, we are talking about *patch-based image inpainting*[1, 6, 7, 8]. In this paper, as well as in many others, we use principle of the techniques taking colors of the separated pixels in the close neighborhood of the damaged area to the consideration [2, 3, 4, 5].

Structure of the paper is as follows. Section 2 gives preliminaries including information about F-transform and details about its two types. Section 3 describes basics of the specific type of images used in this paper and Section 4 gives information about mathematical morphology. Detailed description of proposed technique is in Section 5 and conclusion is given in Section 6.

2 Preliminaries

Let us fix the following notation to use throughout the paper. Image I is a 2D vector function such as $I : [0,M] \times [0,N] \to [0,255]^3$, where $[0,255]^3$ stands for pixel intensities in three color channels. We denote $[0,M] = \{0,1,2,\ldots,M\}$, $[0,N] = \{0,1,2,\ldots,N\}$ and $[0,255] = \{0,1,2,\ldots,255\}$. Therefore, $M+1$ is the image width and $N+1$ is the image height. Image I is assumed to be partially defined: it is defined (known) on the area Φ and undefined (unknown, damaged) on the area Ω. The border between these areas is denoted by $\delta\Omega$ and assumed to be unknown. It is assumed that $\Phi \cap \Omega = \emptyset$ and $\Phi \cup \Omega \cup \delta\Omega = [0,M] \times [0,N]$. Mask S is a binary image where white pixels denote unknown area $\Omega + \delta\Omega$. The mask is created by user with respect to areas intended for deletion. The notation is illustrated in Fig. 1.

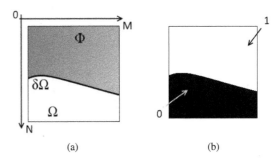

Figure 1: a) Two areas where image I is defined (Φ) and undefined (Ω); b) mask S.

We are focused on image restoration. By this we mean that pixels from $\Omega \cup \delta\Omega$ should be replaced by pixels from Φ. The resulting image should make an impression that damage is not present.

2.1 F^0-Transform

Below, we recall the definition of a fuzzy partition [10]. Fuzzy sets $A_0,\ldots,A_m$ identified with their membership functions (basic functions) $A_0,\ldots,A_m : [0,M] \to [0,1]$, establish a *fuzzy partition* of $[0,M]$ with nodes $0 = x_0 < x_1 < \cdots < x_m = M$ if the following conditions are fulfilled:

1) $A_k : [0,M] \to [0,1]$, $A_k(x_k) = 1$;

2) $A_k(x) = 0$ if $x \notin (x_{k-1}, x_{k+1})$, $k = 0,\ldots,m$;

3) $A_k(x)$ is continuous;

4) $A_k(x)$ strictly increase on $[x_{k-1}, x_k]$, $k = 1,\ldots,m$; and strictly decrease on $[x_k, x_{k+1}]$, $k = 1,\ldots,m$;

5) $\sum_{k=0}^{m} A_k(x) - 1$, $x \subset [0,M]$.

We say that the fuzzy partition given by $A_0,\ldots,A_m$, is an *h-uniform fuzzy partition* if nodes $x_k = hk$, $k = 0,\ldots,m$, are equidistant, $h = M/m$ and two additional properties are met:

6) $A_k(x_k - x) = A_k(x_k + x)$, $x \in [0,h]$, $k = 0,\ldots,m$;

7) $A_k(x) = A_{k-1}(x - h)$, $k = 1,\ldots,m$, $x \in [x_{k-1}, x_{k+1}]$.

Parameter h will be referred to as a radius.

Assume that fuzzy sets $A_0, \ldots, A_m$ establish a fuzzy partition of $[0,M]$. The following vector of real numbers $\mathbf{F}_m[I] = (F_0, \ldots, F_m)$ is the *(direct) discrete F-transform* of I w.r.t. $A_0, \ldots, A_m$ where the k–th component F_k is defined by

$$F_k^0 = \frac{\sum_{x=0}^{M} A_k(x) I(x)}{\sum_{x=0}^{M} A_k(x)}, \ k = 0, \ldots, m. \quad (1)$$

Let us introduce F-transform of a 2D grayscale image I that is considered as a function $I : [0,M] \times [0,N] \to [0,255]$.

Let $A_0, \ldots, A_m$ and $B_0, \ldots, B_n$ be basic functions, $A_0, \ldots, A_m : [0,M] \to [0,1]$ be fuzzy partition of $[0,M]$ and $B_0, \ldots, B_n : [0,N] \to [0,1]$ be fuzzy partition of $[0,N]$.

We say that the $m \times n$-matrix of real numbers $[F_{kl}^0]$ is called *the (discrete) F-transform* of I with respect to $\{A_0, \ldots, A_m\}$ and $\{B_0, \ldots, B_n\}$ if for all $k = 0, \ldots, m$, $l = 0, \ldots, n$,

$$F_{kl}^0 = \frac{\sum_{y=0}^{N} \sum_{x=0}^{M} I(x,y) A_k(x) B_l(y)}{\sum_{y=0}^{N} \sum_{x=0}^{M} A_k(x) B_l(y)}. \quad (2)$$

The coefficients F_{kl}^0 are called *components of the F-transform*.

2.2 F^1-Transform

In this section, we recall the (direct) F^1-transform as it has been presented in [11]. Let $\{A_k \times B_l \mid k = 0, \ldots, m, l = 0, \ldots, n\}$ be a fuzzy partition of $[0,M] \times [0,N]$. $L_2^1(A_k) \subseteq L_2(A_k)$ $(L_2^1(B_l) \subseteq L_2(B_l))^1$ be a linear span of the set consisting of two orthogonal polynomials

$$P_k^0(x) = 1, \quad P_k^1(x) = x - x_k,$$
$$(Q_l^0(y) = 1, \quad Q_l^1(y) = y - y_l),$$

where 1 is a denotation of the respective constant function.

Analogously, let $L_2^1(A_k \times B_l) \subseteq L_2(A_k \times B_l)$ be a linear span of the set consisting of three orthogonal polynomials

$$S_{kl}^{00}(x,y) = 1, \quad S_{kl}^{10}(x,y) = x - x_k, \quad S_{kl}^{01}(x,y) = y - y_l.$$

Let $I \in L_2([0,M] \times [0,N])$, and F_{kl}^1 be the orthogonal projection of $I|_{[x_{k-1},x_{k+1}] \times [y_{l-1},y_{l+1}]}$ on subspace $L_2^1(A_k \times B_l)$, $k = 0, \ldots, m, l = 0, \ldots, n$.

We say that matrix $\mathbf{F}_{mn}^1[I] = (F_{kl}^1)$, $k = 0, \ldots, m$, $l = 0, \ldots, n$, is the F^1-transform of I with respect to $\{A_k \times B_l \mid k = 0, \ldots, m, l = 0, \ldots, n\}$, and F_{kl}^1 is the corresponding F^1-transform component.

$^1 L_2(A_k)$ is a Hilbert space of square-integrable functions $f : [x_{k-1}, x_{k+1}] \to \mathbb{R}$ with the *weighted inner product* $\langle f, g \rangle_k$ given by

$$\langle f, g \rangle_k = \int_{x_{k-1}}^{x_{k+1}} f(x) g(x) A_k(x) dx, \quad (3)$$

where the *weight function* is equal to A_k.

The F^1-transform components of I are linear polynomials in the form

$$F_{kl}^1(x,y) = c_{kl}^{00} + c_{kl}^{10}(x - x_k) + c_{kl}^{01}(y - y_l), \quad (4)$$

where the coefficients are given by

$$
\begin{aligned}
c_{kl}^{00} &= \frac{\sum_{y=0}^{N} \sum_{x=0}^{M} I(x,y) A_k(x) B_l(y)}{\sum_{y=0}^{N} \sum_{x=0}^{M} A_k(x) B_l(y)}, \\
c_{kl}^{10} &= \frac{\sum_{y=0}^{N} \sum_{x=0}^{M} I(x,y)(x-x_k) A_k(x) B_l(y)}{\sum_{y=0}^{N} \sum_{x=0}^{M} (x-x_k)^2 A_k(x) B_l(y)}, \quad (5) \\
c_{kl}^{01} &= \frac{\sum_{y=0}^{N} \sum_{x=0}^{M} I(x,y)(y-y_l) A_k(x) B_l(y)}{\sum_{y=0}^{N} \sum_{x=0}^{M} (y-y_l)^2 A_k(x) B_l(y)}.
\end{aligned}
$$

2.3 F-Transform Image Inpainting

In [12], the technique of F-transforms was proposed for the inpainting. It uses two steps: *direct and inverse* of the 0th-degree F-transform. The direct step is described in the previous section whereas the inverse is as follows

$$O(x,y) = \sum_{k=0}^{m} \sum_{l=0}^{n} F_{kl}^0 A_k(x) B_l(y), \quad (6)$$

where O is the output (reconstructed) image. In fact, the algorithm computes the F-transform components of the input image I and spreads the components afterwards to the size of I. For details see [12].

Let us recall basics of the technique and illustrate its update for the cartoon images. The original technique works with the assumption that damaged pixels of I should not be included in a component value. For that purpose, the binary mask S is used in the computation:

$$F_{kl}^0 = \frac{\sum_{y=0}^{N} \sum_{x=0}^{M} I(x,y) S(x,y) A_k(x) B_l(y)}{\sum_{y=0}^{N} \sum_{x=0}^{M} S(x,y) A_k(x) B_l(y)}.$$

This approach works well for photos as was shown in [13, 15, 12, 9]. For cartoon images, the quality of reconstruction is not sufficient because of the isotropic nature of the algorithm. The problem is that edges are not taken into consideration during the computation.

3 Cartoon Images

In this paper, we suggest inpainting technique aimed to be applied to images with two specific features:

- limited color palette,

- strong and thick uni-color edges.

These features are usually included in simple cartoon images as can be seen in Fig. 2.

For testing purposes, we created a set of artificial images with the same features. The set is in Fig. 3.

(a) Boy (b) Goat

(c) Homer

Figure 2: Test set of cartoon images.

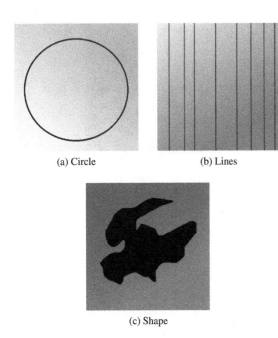

(a) Circle (b) Lines

(c) Shape

Figure 3: Test set of artificial cartoon images.

4 Mathematical Morphology

Application of mathematical morphology [14] is an important step in the proposed method. Let us give a short description of this technique.

In mathematical morphology, a structuring element is selected and applied to the input image. For our method, a binary image is used. We recall three main operations: *erosion*, *dilation* and *closing*.

4.1 Erosion

The erosion is defined as follows

$$I \ominus T = \{z \in [0,M] \times [0,N] \,|\, T_z \subseteq I\},$$

where T is a structuring element and z is a translation vector. Operator of binary erosion is in fact a test whether image I contains areas like T.

4.2 Dilation

The dilation is defined as follows

$$I \oplus T = \bigcup_{t \in T} I_t,$$

where T is a structuring element and I_t is the translation of I by t.

4.3 Closing

Operator of closing is the erosion of dilation defined as follows

$$I \bullet T = (I \oplus T) \ominus T.$$

The effect of binary closing is in filling small holes and imperfections in the image I.

5 Novel Inpainting Technique

If image I contains only few colors and thick edges, reconstruction using original algorithm based on (6) is affected by visible artifacts. Illustration is in Fig. 12. A new proposed algorithm is based on the assumption that similar areas should be reconstructed independently. Main idea is to separate these areas and reconstruct each of them with respect to a particular color. In this paper, we propose to separate edges (pixels with high gradient) from the rest of the image, reconstruct their damaged parts and continue with the other areas afterwards.

For this purpose, another binary image V is taken into consideration. The image V is created automatically during the reconstruction process and it influences the computation of the F^0-transform components as it is shown below

$$F_{kl}^0 = \frac{\sum_{y=0}^N \sum_{x=0}^M I(x,y)S(x,y)V(x,y)A_k(x)B_l(y)}{\sum_{y=0}^N \sum_{x=0}^M S(x,y)V(x,y)A_k(x)B_l(y)}.$$

We can say that image V and mask S overlaps image I. Mask S coincides with the characteristic function of area Φ. Image V designates by 1 the so called *valid pixels*. The latter are used in the reconstruction process. Therefore, the edges are reconstructed from pixels of the known part of edges only and similarly, for pixels from the other non-edge areas. This feature changes isotropic nature of the original inpainting algorithm to anisotropic because pixel colors are not necessarily distributed to the all neighbourhood.

Bellow, the proposed algorithm is illustrated on the input from Fig. 4.

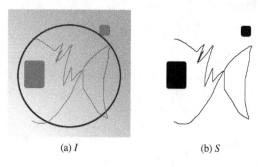

(a) I (b) S

Figure 4: Input image and mask for algorithm description.

1) Compute the F^1-transform.

Comment: At this step, we compute coefficients c^{00}, c^{10}, c^{01} of I F^1-transform components in accordance with (5). The output for the input in Fig. 4 is in Fig. 5.

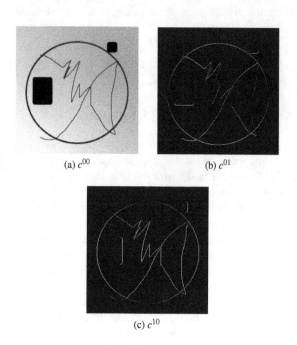

(a) c^{00} (b) c^{01}

(c) c^{10}

Figure 5: Coefficients of F^1-transform. Contrast was enhanced for better visibility.

2) Upscale c^{10} and c^{01} to the size of image I and convert them to gray-scale.

3) Update c^{01} and c^{10} by subtracting mask S from them.

Comment: Performing this update we eliminate false edges. Illustration is in Fig. 6.

4) Make shifted copies of c^{01} and c^{10}.

Comment: Edges are detected in the places with the highest gradient. Because of our assumption about the thick edges in I, we copy and shift c^{01} to the left and c^{10} to the up. Doing this, we restrict horizontal and vertical edges.

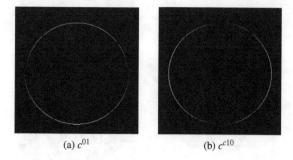

(a) c^{01} (b) c^{c10}

Figure 6: Updated coefficients c^{01} and c^{10}. Contrast was enhanced for better visibility.

5) Create new image V as the union of c^{01}, c^{10} and their shifted copies. Threshold V to obtain the binary image.

Comment: After this step, we obtain binary image V. Its white pixels represent edges whereas black pixels represent areas without significant gradient. Illustration is in Fig. 7.

Figure 7: Image V composed from c^{01}, c^{10} and their shifted copies.

6) Apply morphological closing to V.

Comment: The purpose of this step is to fill in all imperfections of V. In step 3, we subtracted the mask and that created holes in the detected edge area. By closing, we fix these holes and prolong (connect) appropriate parts of image edges. Illustration is in Fig. 8.

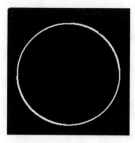

Figure 8: Morphological closing applied on Fig. 7.

7) Use white pixels of V to find edge area of I and by histogram analysis determine a dominant color of it. Further on, the color is called *edge color*.

8) Based on the *edge color* divide I to V_g and V_c and subtract mask from both. Turn V_g and V_c to binary images and apply morphological closing.

Image V_g represents edges of the I whereas V_c the rest. Image V_g contains holes because of the mask subtraction. By closing, we fill the holes. Illustration of this step is in Fig. 9.

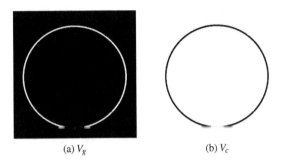

(a) V_g (b) V_c

Figure 9: Binary division of image I to the edge area V_g and the rest V_c followed by a morphological closing.

9) Find intersections of V_g and the mask S.

The intersections determine places on the edge area which are damaged. Let us name this intersection S_g. Illustration is in Fig. 10.

Figure 10: Mask of damaged part of the edges.

10) Use S_g as a mask and V_g as an valid pixels set for edge reconstruction. Use $S - S_g$ as a mask and V_c as a valid pixels set for reconstruction of the rest.

Because we separated edges from the rest, we can reconstruct these two parts independently. Illustration is in Fig. 11.

5.1 Examples and Comparison

Let us illustrate the proposed inpainting algorithm side by side with original technique based on F-transform. The

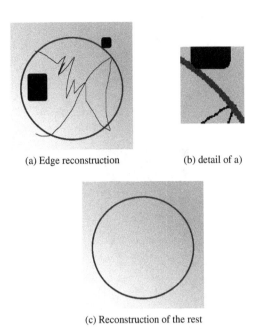

(a) Edge reconstruction   (b) detail of a)

(c) Reconstruction of the rest

Figure 11: a) Reconstruction of the edge; b) detail; c) reconstruction of the rest of the image I.

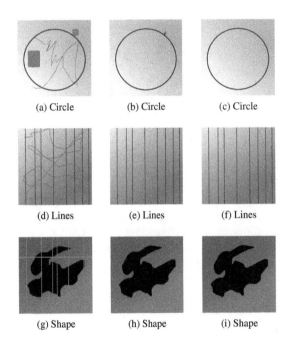

(a) Circle   (b) Circle   (c) Circle

(d) Lines   (e) Lines   (f) Lines

(g) Shape   (h) Shape   (i) Shape

Figure 12: Application of our algorithm to damaged images from Fig. 3. Images a), d), g) are the damaged ones, images b), e) and h) were reconstructed using the original technique and images c), f) and i) were reconstructed using the proposed one.

images from Fig. 3 was damaged and reconstructed afterwards. Results are in Fig. 12.

Let us magnify the details to demonstrate a difference in higher resolution. In Fig. 13, the comparison is given. The original technique blurs the lines, do not follow edges

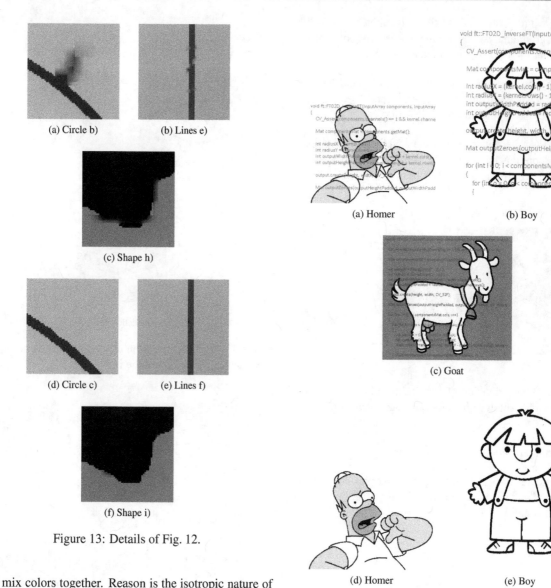

(a) Circle b)   (b) Lines e)

(c) Shape h)

(d) Circle c)   (e) Lines f)

(f) Shape i)

Figure 13: Details of Fig. 12.

(a) Homer   (b) Boy

(c) Goat

(d) Homer   (e) Boy

(f) Goat

Figure 14: The cartoon images from testing set in Fig. 2 damaged and reconstructed.

and mix colors together. Reason is the isotropic nature of the original formula. Thus for cartoon images, we propose to use different approach described in this paper.

In Fig. 14, the novel inpainting technique is illustrated on the set of cartoon images.

6 Conclusion

We propose a novel inpainting technique aimed to specific type of images. Original inpainting technique based on F-transform was applied on photos and introduced in [12].

The main idea of the novel algorithm is in division of input image and independent processing of its parts. In this introduction paper, we suggest to divide the image to two parts: *edges* and *rest*. The edges are separated using coefficients of F^1-transform. Its damaged (missing) parts are connected together using mathematical morphology. Based on that, missing parts of the edges are identified and reconstructed using inpainting technique with updated formulas. The same is applied to the rest of the image.

We illustrated our technique on the two sets of images and compared with original one.

Acknowledgment

This work was supported by the project LQ1602 IT4Innovations excellence in science.

References

[1] M. Ashikhmin. Synthesizing natural textures. In *Proceedings of the 2001 symposium on Interactive 3D graphics*, pages 217–226. ACM, 2001.

[2] C. Ballester, V. Caselles, J. Verdera, M. Bertalmio, and G. Sapiro. A variational model for filling-in gray level and color images. In *Computer Vision, 2001. ICCV 2001. Proceedings. Eighth IEEE International Conference on*, volume 1, pages 10–16. IEEE, 2001.

[3] M. Bertalmio, A. L. Bertozzi, and G. Sapiro. Navier-stokes, fluid dynamics, and image and video inpainting. In *Computer Vision and Pattern Recognition, 2001. CVPR 2001. Proceedings of the 2001 IEEE Computer Society Conference on*, volume 1, pages I–355. IEEE, 2001.

[4] M. Bertalmio, G. Sapiro, V. Caselles, and C. Ballester. Image inpainting. In *Proceedings of the 27th annual conference on Computer graphics and interactive techniques*, pages 417–424. ACM Press/Addison-Wesley Publishing Co., 2000.

[5] T. F. Chan and J. Shen. Nontexture inpainting by curvature-driven diffusions. *Journal of Visual Communication and Image Representation*, 12(4):436–449, 2001.

[6] J. S. De Bonet. Multiresolution sampling procedure for analysis and synthesis of texture images. In *Proceedings of the 24th annual conference on Computer graphics and interactive techniques*, pages 361–368. ACM Press/Addison-Wesley Publishing Co., 1997.

[7] A. A. Efros and W. T. Freeman. Image quilting for texture synthesis and transfer. In *Proceedings of the 28th annual conference on Computer graphics and interactive techniques*, pages 341–346. ACM, 2001.

[8] A. A. Efros and T. K. Leung. Texture synthesis by nonparametric sampling. In *Computer Vision, 1999. The Proceedings of the Seventh IEEE International Conference on*, volume 2, pages 1033–1038. IEEE, 1999.

[9] V. Pavel and P. Irina. Interpolation techniques versus F-transform in application to image reconstruction. In *Fuzzy Systems (FUZZ-IEEE), 2014 IEEE International Conference on*, pages 533–539. IEEE, 2014.

[10] I. Perfilieva. Fuzzy transforms: Theory and applications. *Fuzzy sets and systems*, 157(8):993–1023, 2006.

[11] I. Perfilieva, P. Hodáková, and P. Hurtík. Differentiation by the F-transform and application to edge detection. *Fuzzy Sets and Systems*, 2014.

[12] I. Perfilieva and P. Vlašánek. Image reconstruction by means of F-transform. *Knowledge-Based Systems*, 70:55–63, 2014.

[13] I. Perfilieva, P. Vlašánek, and M. Wrublová. Fuzzy transform for image reconstruction. In *Uncertainty Modeling in Knowledge Engineering and Decision Making*, Singapore, 2012. World Scientific.

[14] J. Serra. *Image analysis and mathematical morphology, v. 1*. Academic press, 1982.

[15] Vlašánek and I. Perfilieva. Image reconstruction with usage of the F-transform. In *International Joint Conference CISIS'12-ICEUTE'12-SOCO'12 Special Sessions*, pages 507–514, Berlin, 2013. Springer.

Slovenskočeský NLP workshop (SloNLP 2017)

SloNLP is a workshop focused on Natural Language Processing (NLP) and Computational Linguistics. Its primary aim is to promote cooperation among NLP researchers in Slovakia and Czech Republic.

The topics of the workshop include automatic speech recognition, automatic natural language analysis and generation (morphology, syntax, semantics, etc.), dialogue systems, machine translation, information retrieval, practical applications of NLP technologies, and other topics of computational linguistics.

Workshop Program Committee

Rudolf Rosa, ÚFAL MFF UK, main organizer
Petra Barančíková, ÚFAL MFF UK, main organizer
Vladimír Benko, JÚĽŠ SAV
Ján Genči, KPI TUKE
Aleš Horák, FI MUNI
Miloslav Konopík, KIV ZČU
Pavel Král, KIV ZČU
Markéta Lopatková, ÚFAL MFF UK
David Mareček, ÚFAL MFF UK
Karel Oliva, freelance linguist

J. Hlaváčová (Ed.): ITAT 2017 Proceedings, pp. 176–180
ISBN 978-1974274741, © 2017 T. Hercig, P. Krejzl, B. Hourová, J. Steinberger, L. Lenc

Detecting Stance in Czech News Commentaries

Tomáš Hercig[1,2], Peter Krejzl[1], Barbora Hourová[1], Josef Steinberger[1], Ladislav Lenc[1,2]

[1] Department of Computer Science and Engineering, Faculty of Applied Sciences,
University of West Bohemia, Univerzitní 8, 306 14 Plzeň, Czech Republic
[2] NTIS—New Technologies for the Information Society, Faculty of Applied Sciences,
University of West Bohemia, Technická 8, 306 14 Plzeň, Czech Republic
nlp.kiv.zcu.cz
{tigi,krejzl,hourova,steinberger,llenc}@kiv.zcu.cz

Abstract: This paper describes our system created to detect stance in online discussions. The goal is to identify whether the author of a comment is in favor of the given target or against. We created an extended corpus of Czech news comments and evaluated a support vector machines classifier, a maximum entropy classifier, and a convolutional neural network.

Keywords: Stance Detection, Opinion Mining, Sentiment Analysis

1 Introduction

Stance detection has been defined as automatically determining from text whether the author is in favor of the given target entity (person, movement, topic, proposition, etc.), against it, or whether neither inference is likely.

Stance detection can be viewed as a subtask of opinion mining, similar to sentiment analysis. In sentiment analysis, systems determine whether a piece of text is positive, negative, or neutral. However, in stance detection, systems predict author's favorability towards a given target, which may not even be explicitly mentioned in the text. Moreover, the text may express positive opinion about an entity contained in the text, but one can also infer that the author is against the defined target (an entity or a topic). It has been found difficult to infer stance towards a target of interest from tweets that express opinion towards another entity[10].

There are many applications which could benefit from the automatic stance detection, including information retrieval, textual entailment, or text summarization, in particular opinion summarization.

We created an extended corpus for stance detection for Czech and evaluate standard top-performing models on this dataset and report the results.

The rest of this paper is organized as follows. We summarise the releated work in Section 2). The creation of the used corpus is covered by Section 3. Our approach is described in Section 4. The convolutional neural network architecture is depicted in Section 5. Evaluation and results discussion is in Section 6 and future work is proposed in Section 7.

2 Related Work

The SemEval-2016 task **Detecting Stance in Tweets**[1] [10] had two subtasks: supervised and weakly supervised stance identification.

The goal of both subtasks was to classify tweets into three classes (*In favor*, *Against*, and *Neither*). The performance was measured by the macro-averaged F1-score of two classes (*In favor* and *Against*). This evaluation measure does not disregard the *Neither* class, because falsely labelling the *Neither* class as *In favor* or *Against* still affects the scores. We use the same evaluation metric ($F1\_2$), accuracy, and the F1-score of all classes ($F1\_3$).

The supervised task (subtask A) tested stance towards five targets: *Atheism*, *Climate Change is a Real Concern*, *Feminist Movement*, *Hillary Clinton*, and *Legalization of Abortion*. Participants were provided with 2814 labeled training tweets for the five targets.

A detailed distribution of stances for each target is given in Table 1. The distribution is not uniform and there is always a preference towards a certain stance (e.g., 63% tweets about *Atheism* are labeled as *Against*). The distribution reflects the real-world scenario, in which a majority of people tend to take a similar stance. It also depends on the source of the data. For example, in the case of *Legalization of Abortion*, we can assume that the distribution will be significantly different in religious communities than in atheistic communities.

For the weakly supervised task (subtask B), there were no labeled training data but participants could use a large number of tweets related to the single target: *Donald Trump*.

The best results for subtask A were achieved by an advanced baseline using SVM classifier with unigrams, bigrams, and trigrams along with character n-grams (2, 3, 4, and 5-gram) as features.

Wei et al. [12] present the best result for subtask B and close second team in subtask A of the SemEval stance detection task. They used a convolutional neural network (CNN) designed according to Kim [4]. It utilizes the same kernel widths and numbers of filters as proposed by Kim. Pre-trained word2vec embeddings are used for initialization of the embedding layer. The main difference from

---
[1]http://alt.qcri.org/semeval2016/task6/

Table 1: Statistics of the SemEval-2016 task corpora in terms of the number of tweets and stance labels.

Target Entity	Total	*In favor*	*Against*	*Neither*
Atheism	733	124 (17%)	464 (63%)	145 (20%)
Climate Change is Concern	564	335 (59%)	26 (5%)	203 (36%)
Feminist Movement	949	268 (28%)	511 (54%)	170 (18%)
Hillary Clinton	934	157 (17%)	533 (57%)	244 (26%)
Legalization of Abortion	883	151 (17%)	523 (59%)	209 (24%)
All	4,063	1,035 (25%)	2,057 (51%)	971 (24%)

Table 2: Statistics of the Czech corpora in terms of the number of news comments and stance labels.

Target Entity	Total	*In favor*	*Against*	*Neither*
"Miloš Zeman" – Czech president	2,638	691 (26%)	1,263 (48%)	684 (26%)
"Smoking Ban in Restaurants" – Gold	1,388	272 (20%)	485 (35%)	631 (45%)
"Smoking Ban in Restaurants" – All	2,785	744 (27%)	1,280 (46%)	761 (27%)

Kim's network is the used voting scheme. During each training epoch, several iterations are selected to predict the test set. At the end of each epoch, the majority voting scheme is applied to determine the label for each sentence. This is done over a specified number of epochs and finally the same voting is applied to the results of each epoch. The train and test data are separated according to the stance targets.

The initial research on Czech data has been done in [7]. They collected 1,460 comments from a Czech news server[2] related to two topics – Czech president – *"Miloš Zeman"* (181 *In favor*, 165 *Against*, and 301 *Neither*) and *"Smoking Ban in Restaurants"* (168 *In favor*, 252 *Against*, and 393 *Neither*).

The results with maximum entropy classifier were *"Miloš Zeman"* $F1\_2^3 = 0.435$, $F1\_3^4 = 0.52$ and *"Smoking Ban in Restaurants"* $F1\_2^3 = 0.456$, $F1\_3^4 = 0.54$.

3 Dataset

We extended the dataset from [7], nearly quadrupling its size. The detailed annotation procedure was described in master thesis [3] in Czech. The whole corpus was annotated by three native speakers. The distribution of stances for each target is given in Table 2.

The target entity "Miloš Zeman" part of the dataset was annotated by one annotator and then 302 comments were also labeled by a second annotator to measure inter-annotator agreement. The target entity "Smoking Ban in Restaurants" part of the dataset was independently annotated by two annotators. To resolve conflicts a third annotator was used and then the majority voting scheme was applied to the gold label selection. The inter-annotator

agreement (Cohen's κ) was calculated between two annotators on 2,203 comments. The final κ is 0.579 for "Miloš Zeman" (2,638 comments) and 0.423 for "Smoking Ban in Restaurants" (2,785 comments).

The inter-annotator agreement for the target "Smoking Ban in Restaurants" was quite low, thus we selected a subset of the "Smoking Ban in Restaurants" part of dataset, where the original two annotators assigned the same label as the gold dataset (1,388 comments).

The corpus is available for research purposes at `http://nlp.kiv.zcu.cz/research/sentiment#stance`.

4 The Approach Overview

We evaluate common supervised classifiers, namely maximum entropy classifier and support vector machines (SVM) classifiers from Brainy[6]. We also experimented with top-performing models for sentiment analysis and stance detection in particular convolutional neural network. The models were trained separately for each target entity.

4.1 Preprocessing

The same preprocessing has been done for all datasets. We use UDPipe [11] with Czech Universal Dependencies 1.2 models for tokenization, POS tagging and lemmatization. Stemming has been done by the HPS stemmer [2]. Preliminary experiments have shown that lower-casing the data achieves slightly better results, thus all the experiments are performed with lower-cased data.

4.2 Features

We selected features commonly used in similar natural language processing tasks e.g. sentiment analysis. The following baseline features were used:

---

[2] `www.idnes.cz`

[3] F1 – (*In favor/Against*)

[4] F1 – (*In favor/Against/Neither*)

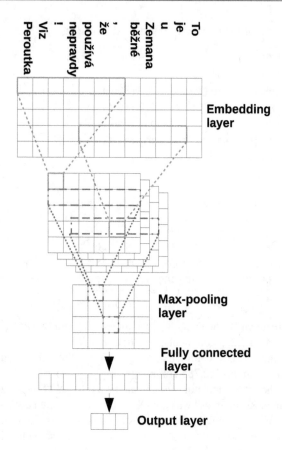

Figure 1: Neural network architecture.

Character n-gram – Separate binary feature for each character n-gram in the text. We do it separately for different orders $n \in \{3, 5, 7\}$.[5]

Bag of words – Word occurrences in the text.

Bag of adverbs – Bag of adverbs from the text.

Bag of adjectives – Bag of adjectives from the text.

Negative emoticons – We used a list of negative emoticons[6] specific to the news commentaries source. The feature captures the presence of an emoticon within the text.

Word shape – We assign words into one of 24 classes[7] similar to the function specified in [1].

We experimented with additional features such as n-grams, text length, etc. but using these features did not lead to better results. Bag of words, adjectives and adverbs use the word lemma or stem. We report results for various feature combinations and perform an ablation study of the best feature set.

---

[5]Note that words e.g. emoticon ":-)" would be separated by spaces during tokenization resulting in ": -)".

[6] ":-(", ";-(", ":-/", "8-o", ";-€", ";-0", "Rv"

[7]We use edu.stanford.nlp.process.WordShapeClassifier [9] with the WORDSHAPECHRIS1 setting.

5 Convolutional Neural Network

The architecture of the proposed CNN is depicted in Figure 1. We use similar architecture to the one proposed in [8]. The input layer of the network receives a sequence of word indices from a dictionary. The input vector must be of a fixed length. We solve this issue by padding the input sequence to the maximum text length occurring in the train data denoted M. A special "PADDING" token is used for this purpose. The embedding layer maps the word indices to the real-valued embedding vectors of length L. The convolutional layer consists of N_C kernels containing $k \times 1$ units and uses rectified linear unit (ReLU) activation function. The convolutional layer is followed by a max-pooling layer and dropout for regularization. The max-pooling layer takes maxima from patches of size $(M - k + 1) \times 1$. The output of the max-pooling layer is fed into a fully-connected layer. Follows the output layer with 3 neurons which corresponds to the number of classes. It has softmax activation function.

In our experimental setup we use the embedding dimensionality $L = 300$ and $N_C = 40$ convolutional kernels with 5×1 units. The penultimate fully-connected layer contains 256 neurons. We train the network using adaptive moment estimation optimization algorithm [5] and cross-entropy is used as the loss function.

6 Results

We used 20-fold cross-validation for models evaluation to compensate the small size of dataset and to prevent overfitting.

For all experiments we report the macro-averaged F1-score of two classes $F1\_2$ (*In favor* and *Against*) – the official metric for the SemEval-2016 stance detection task[10], accuracy, and the macro-averaged F1-score of all three classes ($F1\_3$).

Table 3 shows results for each dataset. CNN-1 is described in Section 5 and CNN-2 is the architecture proposed in [4]. We achieved the best results on average with the maximum entropy classifier with the ***feature set*** consisting of lemma unigrams, word shape, bag of adjectives, bag of adverbs, and character n-grams ($n \in \{3, 5, 7\}$). We further performed ablation study of this combination of features. In Table 3 the bold numbers denote five best results for given column and in the ablation study they denote features with no gain in the given column (i.e. feature sets with no loss).

Both CNNs achieved good results, CNN-2 was slightly better, this is not surprising as it was designed for sentiment analysis while CNN-1 was previously used for document classification. Surprisingly stem worked better than lemma as the word input for both neural networks. The ablation study shows that word shape, bag of adjectives, and bag of adverbs features present little to no information gain for the classifier, thus these features should be discarded or

Table 3: Results on Czech stance detection datasets in %. We report accuracy (*Acc*), the macro-averaged F1-score of two classes (*F*1_2) and the macro-averaged F1-score of all three classes (*F*1_3). *Feature set* consists of lemma unigrams, word shape, bag of adjectives, bag of adverbs, and character *n*-grams ($n \in \{3,5,7\}$). The bold numbers denote five best results for given column and in the ablation study they denote features with no gain in the given column (i.e. feature sets with no loss).

Classifier	Features	Zeman			Smoking All			Smoking Gold		
		*F*1_3	*F*1_2	*Acc*	*F*1_3	*F*1_2	*Acc*	*F*1_3	*F*1_2	*Acc*
SVM	Random Class	32.7	34.6	33.4	32.4	34.4	33.0	31.2	27.2	32.2
SVM	Majority Class	21.6	32.4	47.9	21.0	31.5	46.0	20.8	0.0	45.5
CNN-1	lemma	48.6	52.1	51.9	51.4	54.2	54.2	61.2	55.6	**65.1**
CNN-1	stemm	**50.7**	55.3	**54.5**	51.7	54.6	54.5	60.6	54.8	64.8
CNN-2	lemma	48.3	51.7	51.3	51.8	54.9	54.5	61.2	55.9	64.8
CNN-2	stemm	**51.3**	**55.7**	**54.9**	**52.1**	54.9	54.6	**61.7**	56.4	**65.5**
MaxEnt	lemma	47.7	51.8	50.2	48.8	52.3	50.9	58.1	52.2	61.6
SVM	lemma	46.7	52.0	50.7	50.4	55.3	53.8	60.1	54.5	63.5
MaxEnt	stem	47.2	50.9	49.5	49.5	52.5	51.8	58.3	52.2	62.2
SVM	stem	48.3	52.8	51.8	51.5	55.3	54.2	57.3	52.4	60.6
MaxEnt	char. *n*-gram 3,5,7	50.4	**55.7**	53.7	50.3	54.9	53.1	**61.6**	**56.8**	65.0
SVM	char. *n*-gram 3,5,7	47.4	53.4	52.2	51.3	**57.2**	**54.9**	57.6	53.2	60.8
MaxEnt	shape	45.0	50.2	48.4	45.7	50.2	47.9	53.9	48.6	57.0
SVM	shape	45.5	50.3	49.7	48.1	52.0	50.6	56.5	50.8	60.7
MaxEnt	feature set	**50.6**	**56.0**	**53.9**	**51.9**	55.8	54.7	62.6	57.5	66.5
SVM	feature set	47.9	54.3	52.7	**52.6**	**58.2**	**56.0**	59.8	55.3	62.9
MaxEnt	feature set + emoticons	**50.5**	**56.0**	**53.9**	51.6	55.7	54.2	**62.7**	**57.7**	**66.4**
SVM	feature set + emoticons	47.3	53.3	51.9	**52.3**	**58.1**	**55.6**	61.0	**56.8**	63.5
MaxEnt	feature set + emoticons + stem	**50.7**	**56.0**	**53.9**	**51.9**	55.5	54.5	62.6	**57.6**	66.3
SVM	feature set + emoticons + stem	47.7	53.5	52.2	51.6	**57.4**	**55.0**	60.6	55.6	64.1
MaxEnt	feature set - shape	**50.8**	**56.0**	**54.0**	51.6	**56.1**	54.4	**63.0**	**58.3**	**66.5**
MaxEnt	feature set - bag of adj.	**50.7**	**56.1**	**54.0**	51.8	55.4	54.4	**62.7**	**57.7**	66.4
MaxEnt	feature set - bag of adv.	**50.9**	**56.4**	**54.3**	51.8	55.4	54.6	62.6	57.4	**66.5**
MaxEnt	feature set - lemma	50.2	55.6	53.6	50.8	55.1	53.6	62.4	57.3	66.2
MaxEnt	feature set - char. *n*-gram 3,5,7	46.9	51.7	49.9	48.6	52.3	50.9	58.1	52.3	61.8

readjusted to better capture the stance in comments. However, the selected feature combination still performed reasonably well.

The best results for the target "Miloš Zeman" were achieved by CNN-2 in terms of accuracy and *F*1_3, *F*1_2 was the highest for maximum entropy classifier with lemma unigrams, word shape, bag of adjectives, and character *n*-grams. The entity "Smoking Ban in Restaurants" was best assessed by SVM with the selected feature set for all data and by maximum entropy classifier with the same feature set for the gold dataset.

Character *n*-grams alone present a strong baseline for this task.

7 Conclusion

The paper describes our system created to detect stance in online discussions. We evaluated top-performing models used for sentiment analysis and stance detection. We conducted feature ablation and concluded that more features still need to be readjusted for this task.

The used features are very common in natural language processing, however even in the SemEval-2016 stance detection task, the best results were achieved by commonly used features. This suggests that stance detection is still in its infancy and more gain can be expected in the future as researchers better understand this new task.

In future work, we plan to extend the dataset to other domains, include more target entities and comments, which will let us draw stronger conclusions and move the task closer to the industrial expectations. Given that there are vast amounts of news comments related to highly discussed topics, we will study stance summarization which should aim at identifying the most important arguments. Another interesting experiment would be supplementing the dataset with sentiment annotation.

Acknowledgments

This publication was supported by the project LO1506 of the Czech Ministry of Education, Youth and Sports under the program NPU I., by Grant No. SGS-2016-018 Data and Software Engineering for Advanced Applications and by project MediaGist, EU's FP7 People Programme (Marie Curie Actions), no. 630786.

References

[1] Daniel M. Bikel, Scott Miller, Richard Schwartz, and Ralph Weischedel. Nymble: a high-performance learning name-finder. In *Proceedings of the fifth conference on Applied natural language processing*, pages 194–201. Association for Computational Linguistics, 1997.

[2] Tomáš Brychcín and Miloslav Konopík. Hps: High precision stemmer. *Information Processing & Management*, 51(1):68–91, 2015.

[3] Barbora Hourová. Automatic detection of argumentation. Master's thesis, University of West Bohemia, Faculty of Applied Sciences, 2017.

[4] Yoon Kim. Convolutional neural networks for sentence classification. In *Proceedings of the 2014 Conference on Empirical Methods in Natural Language Processing (EMNLP)*, pages 1746–1751, Doha, Qatar, October 2014. Association for Computational Linguistics. URL http://www.aclweb.org/anthology/D14-1181.

[5] Diederik Kingma and Jimmy Ba. Adam: A method for stochastic optimization. *arXiv preprint arXiv:1412.6980*, 2014.

[6] Michal Konkol. Brainy: A machine learning library. In Leszek Rutkowski, Marcin Korytkowski, Rafal Scherer, Ryszard Tadeusiewicz, Lotfi Zadeh, and Jacek Zurada, editors, *Artificial Intelligence and Soft Computing*, volume 8468 of *Lecture Notes in Computer Science*, pages 490–499. Springer International Publishing, 2014. ISBN 978-3-319-07175-6.

[7] Peter Krejzl, Barbora Hourová, and Josef Steinberger. Stance detection in online discussions. In Mária Bieliková and Ivan Srba, editors, *WIKT & DaZ 2016 11th Workshop on Intelligent and Knowledge Oriented Technologies 35th Conference on Data and Knowledge*, pages 211–214. Vydateľstvo STU, Vazovova 5, Bratislava, Slovakia, November 2016. ISBN 978-80-227-4619-9.

[8] Ladislav Lenc and Pavel Král. Deep neural networks for czech multi-label document classification. *CoRR*, abs/1701.03849, 2017. URL http://arxiv.org/abs/1701.03849.

[9] Christopher D. Manning, Mihai Surdeanu, John Bauer, Jenny Finkel, Steven J. Bethard, and David McClosky. The Stanford CoreNLP natural language processing toolkit. In *Association for Computational Linguistics (ACL) System Demonstrations*, pages 55–60, 2014. URL http://www.aclweb.org/anthology/P/P14/P14-5010.

[10] Saif Mohammad, Svetlana Kiritchenko, Parinaz Sobhani, Xiaodan Zhu, and Colin Cherry. Semeval-2016 task 6: Detecting stance in tweets. In *Proceedings of the 10th International Workshop on Semantic Evaluation (SemEval-2016)*, pages 31–41, San Diego, California, June 2016. Association for Computational Linguistics. URL http://www.aclweb.org/anthology/S16-1003.

[11] Milan Straka, Jan Hajič, and Jana Straková. UD-Pipe: trainable pipeline for processing CoNLL-U files performing tokenization, morphological analysis, pos tagging and parsing. In *Proceedings of the Tenth International Conference on Language Resources and Evaluation (LREC'16)*, Paris, France, May 2016. European Language Resources Association (ELRA). ISBN 978-2-9517408-9-1.

[12] Wan Wei, Xiao Zhang, Xuqin Liu, Wei Chen, and Tengjiao Wang. pkudblab at semeval-2016 task 6 : A specific convolutional neural network system for effective stance detection. In *Proceedings of the 10th International Workshop on Semantic Evaluation (SemEval-2016)*, pages 384–388, San Diego, California, June 2016. Association for Computational Linguistics. URL http://www.aclweb.org/anthology/S16-1062.

J. Hlaváčová (Ed.): ITAT 2017 Proceedings, pp. 181–185
ISBN 978-1974274741, © 2017 T. Jelínek

FicTree: a Manually Annotated Treebank of Czech Fiction

Tomáš Jelínek

Charles Univeristy, Faculty of Arts,
Prague, Czech Republic
Tomas.Jelinek@ff.cuni.cz

Abstract: We present a manually annotated treebank of Czech fiction, intended to serve as an addendum to the Prague Dependency Treebank. The treebank has only 166,000 tokens, so it does not serve as a good basis for training of NLP tools, but added to the PDT training data, it can help improve the annotation of texts of fiction. We describe the composition of the corpus, the annotation process including inter-annotator agreement. On the newly created data and the data of the PDT, we performed a number of experiments with parsers (TurboParser, Parsito, MSTParser and MaltParser). We observe that the extension of PDT training data by a part of the new treebank actually does improve the results of the parsing of literary texts. We investigate cases where parsers agree on a different annotation than the manual one.

1 Introduction

The Czech National Corpus (CNC) has decided to enrich the annotation of some of its large synchronous corpora by syntactic annotation, using the formalism of the Prague Dependency Treebank (PDT) [4]. The parsers used for syntactic annotation must be trained on manually annotated data, with only PDT data available now. To achieve a reliable parsing, it is necessary to ensure the training data to be as close as possible to the target text, but in PDT, the texts are only journalistic, while one third of the texts in representative corpora of synchronous written Czech of the CNC belongs to the fiction genre. In many ways, fiction differs considerably from the characteristics of journalistic texts, for example by a significantly lower proportion of nouns versus verbs: in the journalistic genre, 33.8% tokens are nouns and 16.0% are verbs; in fiction, the ratio of nouns and verbs is almost equal, 24.3% tokens are nouns, and 21.2% verbs (based on statistics [1] from the SYN2005 corpus [3]).

Therefore, a new manually annotated treebank of fiction texts was created; it was annotated according to the PDT a-layer guidelines. The scope of the new treebank is only about 11% of the PDT data, due to the difficulties of manual syntactic annotation, but even so, using this new resource does improve the parsing of fiction texts.

In this article we present this new treebank, named FicTree (*Tree*bank of Czech *ficti*on), its composition, and the annotation process. We describe the first experiments with parsers based on the data of FicTree and PDT. In the data of the FicTree treebank parsed by four parsers, we investi-

gate cases where all parsers agree on a syntactic annotation of one token which differs from the manual annotation.

2 Composition of the Treebank

The manually annotated treebank FicTree is composed of eight texts and longer fragments of texts from the genre of fiction published in Czech from 1991 to 2007, with a total of 166,437 tokens, 12,860 sentences. It is annotated according to the PDT a-layer annotation guidelines [5]. The PDT data annotated on the analytical layer comprise, for comparison, 1,503,739 tokens, 87,913 sentences. Seven of the eight texts which compose the FicTree treebank, were included in the CNC corpus SYN2010 [7] (the eigth one was originally intended to be included in the SYN2010 corpus too, but was removed in the balancing process). The size of the eight texts ranges from 4,000 to 32,000 tokens, the average is 20,800 tokens. Most of the texts are written in original Czech (80%), the remaining 20% are translations (from German and Slovak). Most of the texts belong to the fiction genre without any subgenre (according to the classification of the CNC), one large text (18.2% of all tokens) belongs to the subclass of memoirs, 5.9% tokens come from texts for children and youth.

The language data included in the PDT and in FicTree differ in many characteristics in a similar way to the differences between the whole genres of journalism and fiction described above. In FicTree, there are significantly shorter sentences with an average of 12.9 tokens per sentence compared to an average of 17.1 tokens per sentence in PDT. The part-of-speech ratio is also significantly different, as shown in Table 1.

It is evident from the table that there is a significantly lower proportion of nouns, adjectives and numerals in FicTree, and a higher proportion of verbs, pronouns and adverbs, which corresponds to the assumption that in fiction, verbal expressions are preferred, whereas journalism tends to use more nominal expressions.

3 Annotation Procedure

The FicTree treebank was syntactically annotated according to the formalism of the analytical layer of the Prague Dependency Treebank. The texts were lemmatized and morphologically annotated using a hybrid system of rule-based desambiguation [6] and stochastic tagger Featu-

Table 1: POS proportion in PDT and FicTree

	PDT	FicTree
Nouns	35.60	22.31
Adjectives	13.72	7.73
Pronouns	7.68	16.42
Numerals	3.83	1.53
Verbs	14.34	23.16
Adverbs	6.18	9.19
Prepositions	11.39	9.14
Conjunctions	6.61	9.39
Particles	0.64	1.05
Interjections	0.01	0.07
Total	100	100

rama[1]. The texts were then doubly parsed using two parsers: MSTParser [9] and MaltParser [10] (the parsing took place several years ago when better parsers such as TurboParser [8] were not available) trained on the PDT a-layer training data. The difference in the algorithms of both parsers ensured that the errors in the texts were distributed differently, it can be assumed that errors in the subsequent manual corrections will not be identical. According to Berzak [2] there are likely some deviations common for both parsers, which will also manifest in the final (manual) annotation, but this distortion of the data could not be avoided.

3.1 Manual Correction of Parsing Results

The automatically annotated data was then distributed to three annotators that checked one sentence after using the TrEd software for manual treebank editing and corrected the data. The two versions of the parsed text (parsed by the MSTParser and by the MaltParser) were always assigned to two different annotators, we ensured that the combinations of parsers and annotators were varied. The data were divided into 163 text parts of approx. 1000 tokens, every combination of parsers and annotators has occurred in at least 10 text parts (the proportion of texts corrected by indivudual annotators was 26%, 35% and 39%).

The task of the manual annotators was to correct syntactic structure and syntactic labels, but they also had the possibility to suggest corrections of segmentation, tokenization or morphological annotation and lemmatization.

3.2 Adjudication

The two corrected versions of syntactic annotation from each text were merged, the resulting doubly annotated texts were examined by an experienced annotator (adjudicator) who decided which of the proposed annotations

[1] See http://sourceforge.net/projects/featurama.

to accept. The adjudicator was not limited to the two manually corrected versions, she was allowed to choose another solution consistent with the PDT annotation manual and data. Some changes in tokenization and segmentation were also performed (159 cases, mainly sentence split or merge). The adjudication took approximately five years of work due to the difficulty of the task, the effort to maximize the consistency of the same phenomenon across the treebank (and in accordance with PDT data), and other workload with a higher priority.

3.3 Accuracy of the Parsing and of the Manual Corrections

In the following two tables, we will present the accuracy of each step of annotation and the inter-annotator agreement. Table 2 shows to what extent the automatically parsed and the manually corrected versions of the text agree with the final syntactic annotation, first for the texts annotated with the MSTParser, then for the ones annotated with the Malt-Parser. Two measures of agreement with the final annotation are shown: UAS (unlabeled attachment score, i.e. the proportion of tokens with a correct head) and LAS (labeled attachment score, i.e. the proportion of tokens with a correct head and dependency label).

Table 2: Accuracy of annotated versions

	UAS:auto.	UAS:man.	LAS:auto.	LAS:man.
MST	83.37	96.92	75.31	95.03
Malt	86.08	96.40	79.39	94.42

It is clear from the table that due to the relatively low input parsing quality, the annotators had to carry out a large number of manual interventions in the parsing correction process. The dependencies or labels were modified for 15–20% of tokens. The manually corrected versions differ much less from the final annotation, the disagreement is approx. 5% of the tokens.

Table 3 presents the agreement between the two automatically parsed versions and the inter-annotator agreement (the agreement between the two manually corrected versions). As in the previous table, we use the measures UAS and LAS.

Table 3: Agreement between parsers and inter-annotator agreement

	UAS	LAS
Parsers	83.48	75.66
Annotators	93.89	90.26

The table shows that the agreement between the automatically annotated versions is very similar to the agreement between the final annotation and the worse of the two parsing results. After the manual corrections, the agreement between the two versions of texts has increased considerably, but the difference is approximately twice the difference between each of the manually corrected versions of texts and final syntactic markings. This fact shows that the final annotation alternately used the solutions from both versions of the texts.

4 Parsing Experiments

We conducted a series of experiments on PDT and FicTree data. All data was automatically lemmatized and morphologically tagged using the MorphoDiTa tagger [12].[2] We used four parsers, two parsers of older generation, which were used for the automatic annotation of FicTree data (before manual corrections, with a different morphological annotation and with other settings providing a better parsing accuracy): MSTParser [9][3] and MaltParser [10];[4] and two newer parsers: TurboParser [8][5] and Parsito [11].[6] We use three measures: UAS (unlabeled attachment score), LAS (labeled attachment score) and SENT (labeled attachment score for whole sentences, i. e. the proportion of sentences in which all tokens have correct heads and syntactic labels).

4.1 Training on the PDT Data

The first experiment was to compare the parsing of the PDT test data (journalism) and the whole FicTree data (fiction) using parsers trained on PDT training data (journalism). The results of the experiment are shown in Table 4. Two following columns compare the results on the PDT etest and on the whole FicTree data.

Table 4: Accuracy of parsers trained on PDT train data

| | UAS | UAS | LAS | LAS | SENT | SENT |
	etest	FicTree	etest	FicTree	etest	FicTree
MST	85.93	84.91	78.85	76.82	23.79	26.94
Malt	86.32	85.01	80.74	77.94	31.32	31.86
Parsito	86.30	84.62	80.78	77.65	31.17	31.32
Turbo	88.27	86.66	81.79	79.06	27.74	29.61

[2]Available on http://ufal.mff.cuni.cz/morphodita.

[3]Available on https://sourceforge.net/projects/mstparser/. Used with the parameters: decode-type:non-proj order:2.

[4]Available on http://www.maltparser.org/. Used with the stacklazy algorithm, libsvm learner and a set of optimized features obtained with MaltOptimizer.

[5]Available on http://www.cs.cmu.edu/~ark/TurboParser/. Used with default options.

[6]Available on https://ufal.mff.cuni.cz/parsito. Used with hidden_layer= 400, sgd= 0.01,0.001, transition_system= link2, transition_oracle= static.

The results of the experiment with the UAS and LAS scores for all parsers are approximately 2% worse for Fic-Tree than for PDT, probably due to the genre differences of FicTree versus PDT data. In the case of SENT, the FicTree scores are comparable or better than the PDT etest, probably because the sentence length in FicTree is significantly lower, so there is a higher percentage of well-parsed sentences.

4.2 Training on PDT Data Combined with FicTree

In the second experiment, we split FicTree data into training data (90%) and test data (10%) and combined the Fic-Tree training data with the PDT training data. This experiment was repeated three times with different distribution of the FicTree data, in order to achieve a more reliable result (10% of FicTree is only 16,000 tokens). In that way, 30% of FicTree has effectively been used as test data, the parsers beeing trained on PDT training data plus each time 90% of FicTree. It would have been better to use the whole FicTree data in a 10-fold cross-validation experiment (always adding 90% of data to train PDT and testing the remaining 10%), but we lacked the time and computational resources to do so. Table 5 compares the results of parsers trained on the PDT training data itself and on these merged data (train+ in the table), using PDT etest data and FicTree test data. For each of the measures (UAS, LAS, SENT), the accuracy of the parser trained on the PDT training data is always in one table column, in the following column, there is the accuracy measured for the parser trained on the combined training data (PDT and FicTree, train+). The average for the three experiments is shown.

Table 5: Accuracy of parsers trained on PDT train data (train) and PDT&FicTree train data (train+)

	UAS	UAS	LAS	LAS	SENT	SENT
Etest	train	train+	train	train+	train	train+
MST	85.93	85.98	78.85	78.90	23.79	23.23
Malt	86.32	86.41	80.74	80.87	31.32	31.62
Parsito	86.30	86.48	80.78	81.02	31.17	31.53
Turbo	88.27	88.34	81.79	81.89	27.74	27.93
	UAS	UAS	LAS	LAS	SENT	SENT
FicTree	train	train+	train	train+	train	train+
MST	85.03	85.49	77.24	77.68	26.78	27.18
Malt	85.10	87.14	78.25	81.39	28.92	36.14
Parsito	84.81	86.42	77.99	80.53	31.01	36.52
Turbo	87.00	88.35	79.69	81.69	29.12	34.92

It is clear from the table that extending the training data by a part of the FicTree treebank is beneficial both for parsing the PDT test data and for parsing FicTree data. The improvement in the parsing of the PDT etest is not statistically significant (approximately 0.05% for UAS), but it is consistent for all parsers and measures except for the measure SENT for the MSTParser.

For the FicTree test data, we note a significant improvement in parsing, the increase in the measures is between 0.4% and 2.5%. It is therefore clear that for the syntactic annotation of texts of fiction, the extension of the training data by the FicTree training data is definitely beneficial.

5 The Agreement of Parsers versus the Manual Annotation

We also attempted to use the results of the parsing to assess the quality of the manual annotation and adjudication of the FicTree treebank. The whole FicTree data was annotated by four parsers trained on the PDT training data. From these parsed data, we chose those cases where all four parsers agree on one dependency relation and / or syntactic function of a token, whereas the manual syntactic annotation is different. In total, parsers agreed for 70.04% of tokens in the FicTree data (78.12% if we only count dependencies without syntactic labels). 5.17% of all tokens do not match manual annotation (3.43% of tokens without syntactic labels). Table 6 shows 10 syntactic functions which occur most frequently in such cases of agreement between four parsers and disagreement with manual annotation. In the first column, the syntactic label from the manual annotation is shown. In the second column, we present the proportion of disagreement in the tokens with this syntactic label, in the third column, there is the absolute number of occurrences.

Table 6: Syntactic labels where parsers agree with each other but disagree with manual annotation

Synt. label	Ratio	Number
Adv	5.49	1135
Obj	6.20	1065
AuxX	6.08	618
Sb	5.64	561
ExD	13.96	543
AuxC	11.65	536
AuxP	4.05	501
Atr	1.76	339
AuxV	8.08	302
AuxY	15.85	271

The data in the table shows that differences between parsers and manual markup often occur with the Adv and Obj syntactic labels (adverbial and object), since the annotation performed by parsers often differs from the manual annotation due to the difficulty of linguistic phenomena. Frequent differences between parsing results and manual annotations are discussed in more detail later, we will first give two examples of such differences and their supposed reason.

5.1 Examples of Differences between Manual Annotation and Parsing Results

The first example, a sentence fragment *pohledy plné bezměrné důvěry*, 'regards full of unbounded trust' displayed below, shows a typical example of wrong parsing result due to incorrect morphological annotation. The parsers agree on an erroneous interpretation of the syntactic structure. After the tokens where dependencies or syntactic labels differ, we show the annotation (numbers indicate relative differences, –1 means that the governing node is positioned 1 to the left, +2 governing node is 2 to the right; syntactic labels are shown if they differ).

Pohledy plné/–1/+2 bezměrné důvěry/Obj/-2/Atr/–3
Regards full of unbounded trust

Incorrect morphological tagging of the ambiguous form *plné* 'full' (which can formally agree both with the preceding noun *pohledy* 'regards' and with the following noun *důvěry* 'trust' in number, gender and case) led the parsers to ignore the valency characteristics of the adjective *plný* 'full', they consider it to be the attribute of the following noun *důvěry* 'trust', which they interpret as a nominal attribute of the preceding noun *pohledy* 'regards'. The manual annotation is correct, the adjective *plný* 'full' is dependent on the preceding noun *pohledy* 'regards', the following noun *důvěry* 'trust' is an object of the adjective. Similar differences in the attribution of the Adv and Obj syntactic labels and their dependency relations are common, the manual annotation is in most cases correct (the parsers agree on an erroneous syntactic structure).

In some cases, it is unclear whether the manual annotation or the parsing results are correct, as in the following sentence:

Doktorka/+6/+1 vychutnávala chvíli efekt svých slov a pak pokračovala:
The doctor enjoyed for a while the effect of her words, and then went on:

The head of the subject *Doktorka* 'doctor' in manual annotation is the coordinating conjunction *a* 'and' which coordinates two verbs representing two clauses: *vychutnávala* 'enjoyed' and *pokračovala* 'went on/continued'. The subject is considered as a sentence member modifying the whole coordination (i. e. both verbs). However, all parsers agree on a different head: the verb *vychutnávala* 'enjoyed' closest to the subject. In this interpretation, the second verb has a null subject (pro-drop). Both interpretations are possible in the formalism of PDT, there is no strict rule indicating when the subject should modify coordinated verbs and when it should depend on the closest verb only. In the PDT data, both solutions are used. (The more the structures in the coordinated sentences are similar and simple, the more likely it is that the subject will be common.).

5.2 Most Frequent Discrepancies between Parsing Results and Manual Annotation

In cases where dependencies between the manually assigned one and the one on which the parsers agree are different, the syntactic labels are usually the same. These functions are mostly auxiliary functions: AuxV (auxiliary verbs), AuxP (prepositions) and AuxC (conjunctions) or are related to punctuation (AuxX, AuxK, AuxG). When the syntactic labels differ, the most frequent mismatches are Obj and Adv, Sb and Obj, Adv and Atr.

The highest proportion of discrepancies between the manually and automatically assigned functions is related to the following functions: AuxO (46.5%), AuxR (21.9%), AuxY (15.9%), ExD (14.0%) and Atv (13.5%). AuxO and AuxR refer to two possible syntactic functions of the reflexive particles *se/si* 'myself, yourself, herself...' depending on context, for correct parsing, understanding of semantics and use of lexicon would be necessary. The AuxY function covers particles and other auxiliary functions, ExD is a function which covers several different phenomena in the PDT formalism and is difficult to parse automatically. None of these functions occur frequently in the training data.

5.3 Manual Analysis

When we analyzed manually a sample of sentences in which four parsers agree on a dependency or syntactic label different from the one chosen manually, we found out that in 75% of cases, the manual annotation was certainly correct, about 20% of the occurrencies could not be decided quickly due to the complexity of the construction, in less than 5% of such occurrences the manual annotation was incorrect. It would certainly be useful to carefully check all cases of such discrepancy, it may reduce the error rate in FicTree data by about 0.2–0.5%, but for now we lack the resources to do so.

6 Conclusion

The new manually annotated treebank of Czech fiction FicTree will allow for a better syntactic annotation of texts of fiction when we add it to the PDT training data. Given that larger training data were shown to be beneficial in parsing journalistic texts as well, its use may be broader. We plan to publish the FicTree trebank in the Lindat / CLARIN repository in the near future (after additional checks of selected phenomena) and we would like to publish it later in the Universal Dependencies[7] format, too, using publicly available conversion and verification tools.

Acknowledgement

This paper, the creation of the data and the experiments on which the paper is based have been supported by the Ministry of Education of the Czech Republic, through the project Czech National Corpus, no. LM2015044.

References

[1] T. Bartoň, V. Cvrček, F. Čermák, T. Jelínek, V. Petkevič: "Statistiky češtiny /Statistics of Czech". NLN, Prague, 2009.

[2] Y. Berzak, Y. Huang, A. Barbu, A. Korhonen, B. Katz: "Bias and Agreement in Syntactic Annotations", in Computing Research Repository, 1605.04481, 2016.

[3] F. Čermák, D. Doležalová-Spoustová, J. Hlaváčová, M. Hnátková, T. Jelínek, J. Kocek, M. Kopřivová, M. Křen, R. Novotná, V. Petkevič, V. Schmiedtová, H. Skoumalová, M. Šulc, Z. Velíšek: "SYN2005: a balanced corpus of written Czech". Institute of the Czech National Corpus, Prague, 2005. Available on-line: http://www.korpus.cz.

[4] J. Hajič: "Complex Corpus Annotation: The Prague Dependency Treebank," in Šimková M. (ed.): Insight into the Slovak and Czech Corpus Linguistics, pp. 54–73. Veda, Bratislava, Slovakia, 2006.

[5] J. Hajič, J. Panevová, E. Buráňová, Z. Urešová, A. Bémová, J. Štěpánek, P. Pajas, J. Kárník: "A manual for analytic layer tagging of the prague dependency treebank." ÚFAL Internal Report, Prague, 2001.

[6] T. Jelínek, V. Petkevič: "Systém jazykového značkování současné psané češtiny," in Čermák F. (ed.): Korpusová lingvistika Praha 2011, vol. 3: Gramatika a značkování korpusů, pp. 154-170. NLN, Prague, 2011.

[7] M. Křen, T. Bartoň, V. Cvrček, M. Hnátková, T. Jelínek, J. Kocek, R. Novotná, V. Petkevič, P. Procházka, V. Schmiedtová, H. Skoumalová: "SYN2010: a balanced corpus of written Czech". Institute of the Czech National Corpus, Prague, 2010. Available on-line: http://www.korpus.cz.

[8] A.F.T. Martins, M.B. Almeida, N.A. Smith: "Turning on the Turbo: Fast Third-Order Non-Projective Turbo Parsers," in Proceedings of ACL 2013, 2013.

[9] R. McDonald, F. Pereira, K. Ribarov, J. Hajič: "Non-projective Dependency Parsing using Spanning Tree Algorithms," in Proceedings of EMNLP 2005, 2005.

[10] J. Nivre, J. Hall, J. Nilsson: "MaltParser: A Data-Driven Parser-Generator for Dependency Parsing," in Proceedings of LREC 2006, 2006.

[11] M. Straka, J. Hajič, J. Straková, J. Hajič jr.: "Parsing Universal Dependency Treebanks using Neural Networks and Search-Based Oracle," in Proceedings of TLT 2015, 2015.

[12] J. Straková, M. Straka, J. Hajič: "Open-Source Tools for Morphology, Lemmatization, POS Tagging and Named Entity Recognition," in Proceedings of ACL 2014, 2014.

---

[7]See universaldependencies.org.

J. Hlaváčová (Ed.): ITAT 2017 Proceedings, pp. 186–192
ISBN 978-1974274741, © 2017 L. Lenc, P. Král

Ensemble of Neural Networks for Multi-label Document Classification

Ladislav Lenc[1,2] and Pavel Král[1,2]

[1] Department of Computer Science and Engineering, Faculty of Applied Sciences,
University of West Bohemia, Univerzitní 8, 306 14 Plzeň, Czech Republic
[2] NTIS—New Technologies for the Information Society, Faculty of Applied Sciences,
University of West Bohemia, Technická 8, 306 14 Plzeň, Czech Republic
nlp.kiv.zcu.cz
{llenc,pkral}@kiv.zcu.cz

Abstract: This paper deals with multi-label document classification using an ensemble of neural networks. The assumption is that different network types can keep complementary information and that the combination of more neural classifiers will bring higher accuracy. We verify this hypothesis by an error analysis of the individual networks. One contribution of this work is thus evaluation of several network combinations that improve performance over one single network. Another contribution is a detailed analysis of the achieved results and a proposition of possible directions of further improvement. We evaluate the approaches on a Czech ČTK corpus and also compare the results with state-of-the-art approaches on the English Reuters-21578 dataset. We show that the ensemble of neural classifiers achieves competitive results using only very simple features.

Keywords: Czech, deep neural networks, document classification, multi-label

1 Introduction

This paper deals with multi-label document classification by neural networks. Formally, this task can be seen as the problem of finding a model M which assigns a document $d \in D$ a set of appropriate labels (categories) $c \in C$ as follows $M : d \rightarrow c$ where D is the set of all documents and C is the set of all possible document labels. The multi-label classification using neural networks is often done by thresholding of the output layer [1, 2]. It has been shown that both standard feed-forward networks (FNNs) and convolutional neural networks (CNNs) achieve state-of-the-art results on the standard corpora [1, 2].

However, we believe that there is still some room for further improvement. A combination of classifiers is a natural step forward. Therefore, we combine a CNN and an FNN in this work to gain further improvement in the terms of precision and recall. We support the claim that combination may bring better results by studying the errors of the individual networks. The main contribution of this paper thus consists in the analysis of errors in the prediction results of the individual networks. Then we present the results of several combination methods and illustrate that the ensemble of neural networks brings significant improvement over the individual networks.

The methods are evaluated on documents in the Czech language, being a representative of highly inflectional Slavic language with a free word order. These properties decrease the performance of usual methods. We further compare the results of our methods with other state-of-the-art approaches on English Reuters-21578[1] dataset in order to show its robustness across languages. Additionally we analyze the final F-measure on document sets divided according to the number of assigned labels in order to improve the accuracy of the presented approach.

The rest of the paper is organized as follows. Section 2 is a short review of document classification methods with a particular focus on neural networks. Section 3 describes our neural network models and the combination methods. Section 4 deals with experiments realized on the ČTK and Reuters corpora and then analyzes and discusses the obtained results. In the last section, we conclude the experimental results and propose some future research directions.

2 Related Work

Document classification is usually based on a supervised machine learning. A classifier is trained on an annotated corpus and it then assigns class labels to unlabelled documents. Most works use vector space model (VSM), which generally represents each document as a vector of all word occurrences usually weighted by their tf-idf.

Several classification methods have been successfully used [3], as for instance Bayesian classifiers, maximum entropy, support vector machines, etc. However, the main issue of this task is that the feature space is highly dimensional which decreases the classification results. Feature selection/reduction [4] or better document representation [5] can be used to solve this problem.

Nowadays, "deep" neural nets outperform majority of the state-of-the-art natural language processing (NLP) methods on several tasks with only very simple features. These include for instance POS tagging, chunking, named entity recognition and semantic role labelling [6]. Several different topologies and learning algorithms were proposed. For instance, Zhang et al. [7] propose two convolutional neural nets (CNN) for ontology classification, sen-

---

[1]http://www.daviddlewis.com/resources/testcollections/reuters21578/

timent analysis and single-label document classification. They show that the proposed method significantly outperforms the baseline approach (bag of words) on English and Chinese corpora. Another interesting work [8] uses in the first layer pre-trained vectors from word2vec [9]. The authors show that the proposed models outperform the state of the art on 4 out of 7 tasks, including sentiment analysis and question classification. Recurrent convolutional neural nets are used for text classification in [10]. The authors demonstrated that their approach outperforms the standard convolutional networks on four corpora in single-label document classification task.

On the other hand, traditional feed-forward neural net architectures are used for multi-label document classification rather rarely. These models were more popular before as shown for instance in [11]. They build a simple multi-layer perceptron with three layers (20 inputs, 6 neurons in hidden layer and 10 neurons in the output layer, i.e. number of classes) which gives F-measure about 78% on the standard Reuters dataset. The feed-forward neural networks were used for multi-label document classification in [12]. The authors have modified standard backpropagation algorithm for multi-label learning (BP-MLL) which employs a novel error function. This approach is evaluated on functional genomics and text categorization.

A recent study on multi-label text classification was proposed by Nam et al. in [1]. The authors build on the assumption that neural networks can model label dependencies in the output layer. They investigate limitations of multi-label learning and propose a simple neural network approach. The authors use cross-entropy algorithm instead of ranking loss for training and they also further employ recent advances in deep learning field, e.g. rectified linear units activation, AdaGrad learning with dropout [13, 14]. TF-IDF representation of documents is used as network input. The multi-label classification is handled by performing thresholding on the output layer. Each possible label has its own output node and based the final value of the node a final decision is made. The approach is evaluated on several multi-label datasets and reaches results comparable to the state of the art.

Another method [15] based on neural networks leverages the co-occurrence of labels in the multi-label classification. Some neurons in the output layer capture the patterns of label co-occurrences, which improves the classification accuracy. The architecture is basically a convolutional network and utilizes word embeddings for initialization of the embedding layer. The method is evaluated on the natural language query classification in a document retrieval system.

An alternative approach to handling the multi-label classification is proposed by Yang and Gopal in [16]. The conventional representations of texts and categories are transformed into meta-level features. These features are then utilized in a learning-to-rank algorithm. Experiments on six benchmark datasets show the abilities of this approach in comparison with other methods.

Another recent work proposes novel features based on the unsupervised machine learning [17].

A significant amount of work about combination of classifiers was done previously. Our approaches are motivated by the review of Tulyakov et al. [18].

3 Neural Networks and Combination

3.1 Individual Nets

We use two individual neural nets with different activation functions (*sigmoid* and *softmax*) in the output layer. Their topologies are briefly presented in the following two sections.

Feed-forward Deep Neural Network (FDNN) We use a Multi-Layer Perceptron (MLP) with two hidden layers[2]. As the input of our network we use the simple bag of words (BoW) which is a binary vector where value 1 means that the word with a given index is present in the document. The size of this vector depends on the size of the dictionary which is limited by N most frequent words which defines the size of the input layer. The first hidden layer has 1024 while the second one has 512 nodes. This configuration was set based on the experimental results. The output layer has the size equal to the number of categories $|C|$. To handle the multi-label classification, we threshold the values of nodes in the output layer. Only the labels with values larger than a given threshold are assigned to the document.

Convolutional Neural Network (CNN) The input is a sequence of words in the document. We use the same dictionary as in the previous approach. The words are then represented by the indexes into the dictionary. The architecture of our network (see Figure 1) is motivated by Kim in [8]. However, based on our preliminary experiments, we used only one-dimensional (1D) convolutional kernels instead of the combination of several sizes of 2D kernels. The input of our network is a vector of word indexes of the length L where L is the number of words used for document representation. The issue of the variable document size is solved by setting a fixed value (longer documents are shortened and the shorter ones padded). The second layer is an embedding layer which represents each input word as a vector of a given length. The document is thus represented as a matrix with L rows and EMB columns where EMB is the length of the embedding vectors. The third layer is the convolutional one. We use N_C convolution kernels of the size $K \times 1$ which means we do 1D convolution over one position in the embedding vector over K input words. The following layer performs max-pooling over the length $L - K + 1$ resulting in N_C $1 \times EMB$ vectors.

---

[2]We have also experimented with an MLP with one hidden layer with lower accuracy.

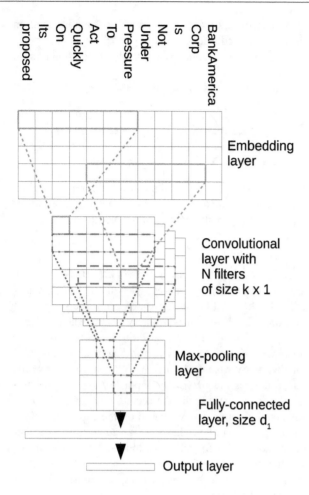

Figure 1: CNN architecture

The output of this layer is then flattened and connected with the output layer containing $|C|$ nodes. The final result is, as in the previous case, obtained by the thresholding of the network outputs.

3.2 Combination

We consider that the different nets keep some complementary information which can compensate recognition errors. We also assume that similar network topology with different activation functions can bring some different information and thus that all nets should have its particular impact for the final classification. Therefore, we consider all the nets as the different classifiers which will be further combined.

Two types of combination will be evaluated and compared. The first group does not need any training phase, while the second one learns a classifier.

Unsupervised Combination The first combination method compensates the errors of individual classifiers by computing the average value from the inputs. This value is thresholded subsequently to obtain the final classification

result. This method is called hereafter *Averaged thresholding*.

The second combination approach first thresholds the scores of all individual classifiers. Then, the final classification output is given as an agreement of the majority of the classifiers. We call this method as *Majority voting with thresholding*

Supervised Combination We use another neural network of type multi-layer perceptron to combine the results. This network has three layers: $n \times |C|$ inputs, hidden layer with 512 nodes and the output layer composed of $|C|$ neurons (number of categories to classify). n value is the number of the nets to combine. This configuration was set experimentally. We also evaluate and compare, as in the case of the individual classifiers, two different activation functions: *sigmoid* and *softmax*. These combination approaches are hereafter called *FNN with sigmoid* and *FNN with softmax*. According to the previous experiments with neural nets on multi-label classification, we assume better results of this net with sigmoid activation (see first part of Table 1).

4 Experiments

In this section we first describe the corpora that we used for evaluation of our methods. Then, we describe the performed experiments and the final results.

4.1 Tools and Corpora

For implementation of all neural nets we used Keras toolkit [19] which is based on the Theano deep learning library [20]. It has been chosen mainly because of good performance and our previous experience with this tool. All experiments were computed on GPU to achieve reasonable computation times.

4.2 Czech ČTK Corpus

For the following experiments we used first the Czech ČTK corpus. This corpus contains 2,974,040 words belonging to 11,955 documents. The documents are annotated from a set of 60 categories as for instance agriculture, weather, politics or sport out of which we used 37 most frequent ones. The category reduction was done to allow comparison with previously reported results on this corpus where the same set of 37 categories was used. We have further created a development set which is composed of 500 randomly chosen samples removed from the entire corpus. Figure 2 illustrates the distribution of the documents depending on the number of labels. Figure 3 shows the distribution of the document lengths (in word tokens). This corpus is freely available for research purposes at http://home.zcu.cz/~pkral/sw/.

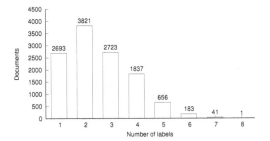

Figure 2: Distribution of documents depending on the number of labels assigned to the documents

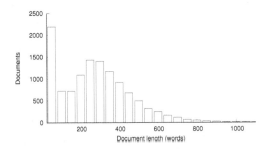

Figure 3: Distribution of the document lengths

We use the five-folds cross validation procedure for all experiments on this corpus. The optimal value of the threshold is determined on the development set. For evaluation of the multi-label document classification results, we use the standard recall, precision and F-measure (*F1*) metrics [21]. The values are micro-averaged.

Reuters-21578 English Corpus The Reuters-21578[3] corpus is a collection of 21,578 documents. This corpus is used to compare our approaches with the state of the art. As suggested by many authors, the training part is composed of 7769 documents, while 3019 documents are reserved for testing. The number of possible categories is 90 and average label/document number is 1.23.

4.3 Results of the Individual Nets

The first experiment (see Table 1) shows the results of the individual neural nets with sigmoid and softmax activation functions against the baseline approach proposed by Drychcín et al. [17]. These nets will be further referenced by the method number.

This table demonstrates very good classification performance of both individual nets and that the classification results are very close to each other and comparable. This table also shows that softmax activation function is slightly better for FDNN, while sigmoid activation function gives significantly better results for CNN.

Another interesting fact regarding to these results is that the approaches no. 1 - 3 have comparable precision and

[3]http://www.daviddlewis.com/resources/testcollections/reuters21578/

Table 1: Results of the individual nets with sigmoid and softmax activation functions against the baseline approach

No.	Network/activation		Prec.	Recall	F1 [%]
1.	FDNN	softmax	84.4	82.1	83.3
2.		sigmoid	83.0	81.2	82.1
3.	CNN	softmax	80.6	80.8	80.7
4.		sigmoid	86.3	81.9	**84.1**
	Baseline [17]		89.0	75.6	81.7

recall, while the best performing method no. 4 has significantly better precision than recall ($\Delta \sim 4\%$).

This table further shows that three individual neural networks outperform the baseline approach.

Error Analysis To confirm the potential benefits of the combination we analyze the errors of the individual nets. As already stated, we assume that different classifiers retain different information and thus they should bring different types of errors which could be compensated by a combination. Following analysis shows the numbers of incorrectly identified documents for two categories. We present the numbers of errors for all individual classifiers and compare it with the combination of all classifiers.

The upper part of Figure 4 is focused on the most frequent class - *politics*. The graph shows that the numbers of errors produced by the individual nets are comparable. However, the networks make errors on different documents and only few ones (384 from 2221 are common for all the nets.

The lower part of Figure 4 is concentrated on the less frequent class - *chemical industry*. This analysis demonstrates that the performances of the different nets significantly differ, the sigmoid activation function is substantially better than the softmax and the different nets provide also different types of errors. The number of the common errors is 49 (from 232 in total).

To conclude, both analysis clearly confirm our assumption that the combination should be beneficial for improvement of the results of the individual nets.

4.4 Results of Unsupervised Combinations

The second experiment shows (see Table 2) the results of *Averaged thresholding* method. These results confirm our assumption that the different nets keep complementary information and that it is useful to combine them. This experiment further shows that the combination of the nets with lower scores (particularly with net no. 2) can degrade the final classification score (e.g. combination 1 & 2 vs. individual net no. 1).

Another interesting, somewhat surprising, observation is that the CNN with the lowest classification accuracy can have some positive impact to the final classification

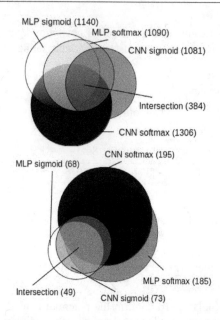

MLP sigmoid (1140)
MLP softmax (1090)
CNN sigmoid (1081)
Intersection (384)
CNN softmax (1306)

CNN softmax (195)
MLP sigmoid (68)
MLP softmax (185)
Intersection (49)
CNN sigmoid (73)

Figure 4: Error analysis of the individual nets for the most frequent (top, *politics*) and for the less frequent (bottom, *chemical industry*) classes, numbers of incorrectly identified documents in brackets

Table 2: Combinations of nets by *Averaged thresholding*

Net combi.	Precision	Recall	F1 [%]
1 & 2	83.0	82.4	82.7
1 & 3	83.2	84.6	83.9
1 & 4	85.7	84.3	85.0
2 & 3	86.2	79.6	82.8
2 & 4	84.9	83.5	84.2
3 & 4	87.3	81.7	84.4
1 & 2 & 3	84.8	81.9	83.3
1 & 2 & 4	90.1	79.6	84.5
1 & 3 & 4	86.7	83.5	**85.1**
2 & 3 & 4	89.3	80.5	84.6
1 & 2 & 3 & 4	89.7	80.5	84.9

(e.g. combination 1 & 3). However, the FDNN no. 2 (with significantly better results) brings only very small positive impact to any combination.

The next experiment which is depicted in Table 3 deals with the results of the second unsupervised combination method, *Majority voting with thresholding*. Note, that we consider an agreement of at least one half of the classifiers to obtain unambiguous results. Therefore, we evaluated the combinations of at least three networks.

This table shows that this combination approach brings also positive impact to document classification and the results of both methods are comparable. However, from the point of view of the contribution of the individual nets, the net no. 2 contributes better for the final results as in the previous case.

Table 3: Combinations of the nets by *Majority voting with thresholding*

Net combi.	Precision	Recall	F1 [%]
1 & 2 & 3	86.1	82.9	84.6
1 & 2 & 4	87.5	82.6	**85.0**
1 & 3 & 4	86.5	82.9	84.6
2 & 3 & 4	86.9	82.7	84.8
1 & 2 & 3 & 4	84.1	85.7	84.9

4.5 Results of Supervised Combinations

The following experiments show the results of the supervised combination method with an FNN (see Sec 3.2). We have evaluated and compared the nets with both sigmoid (see Table 4) and softmax (see Table 5) activation functions.

These tables show that these combinations have also positive impact on the classification and that sigmoid activation function brings better results than softmax. This

Table 4: Combinations of the nets by *FNN with sigmoid*

Net combi.	Precision	Recall	F1 [%]
1 & 2	86.1	82.1	84.1
1 & 3	87.1	81.5	84.2
1 & 4	88.4	81.9	85.0
2 & 3	86.6	81.4	83.9
2 & 4	87.7	82.0	84.7
3 & 4	89.3	80.0	84.4
1 & 2 & 3	86.9	82.4	84.6
1 & 2 & 4	87.9	82.8	85.3
1 & 3 & 4	88.2	82.5	85.2
2 & 3 & 4	87.9	82.2	85.0
1 & 2 & 3 & 4	88.0	82.8	**85.3**

Table 5: Combinations of the nets by *FNN with softmax*

Net combi.	Precision	Recall	F1 [%]
1 & 2	85.3	81.6	83.4
1 & 3	85.4	81.8	83.6
1 & 4	86.3	82.6	84.4
2 & 3	85.4	80.9	83.1
2 & 4	86.1	82.0	84.0
3 & 4	86.7	81.3	83.9
1 & 2 & 3	85.0	82.7	83.9
1 & 2 & 4	85.7	83.2	84.4
1 & 3 & 4	85.8	83.3	84.5
2 & 3 & 4	85.6	82.9	84.3
1 & 2 & 3 & 4	85.7	83.6	**84.6**

is a similar behaviour as in the case of the individual nets. Moreover, as supposed, this supervised combination slightly outperforms both previously described unsupervised methods.

4.6 Final Results Analysis

Finally, we analyze the results for the different document types. The main criterion was the number of the document labels. We assume that this number will play an important role for classification and intuitively, the documents with less labels will be easier to classify. We thus divided the documents into five distinct classes according to the number of labels (i.e. the documents with one, two, three and four labels and the remaining documents). Then, we tried to determine an optimal threshold for every class and report the F-measure. This value is compared to the results obtained with *global* threshold identified previously (one threshold for all documents).

The results of this analysis are shown in Figure 5. We have chosen two representative cases to analyze, the individual *FDNN with softmax* (left side) and the combination by *Averaged thresholding* method (right side). The adaptive threshold means that the threshold is optimized for each group of documents separately. The fixed threshold is the one that was optimized on the development set. This figure confirms our assumption. The best classification results are for the documents with one label and then they decrease. Moreover, this analysis shows that this number plays a crucial role for document classification for all cases. Hypothetically, if we could determine the number of labels for a particular document before the thresholding, we could improve the final F-measure by 1.5%.

4.7 Results on English Corpus

This experiment shows results of our methods on the frequently used Reuters-21578 corpus. We present the results on English dataset mainly for comparison with other state-of-the-art methods while we cannot provide such comparison on Czech data. Table 6 shows the performance of proposed models on the benchmark Reuters-21578 dataset. The bottom part of the table provides comparison with other state-of-the-art methods.

5 Conclusions and Future Work

In this paper, we have used several combination methods to improve the results of individual neural nets for multi-label document classification of Czech text documents. We have also presented the results of our methods on a standard English corpus. We have compared several popular (unsupervised and also supervised) combination methods.

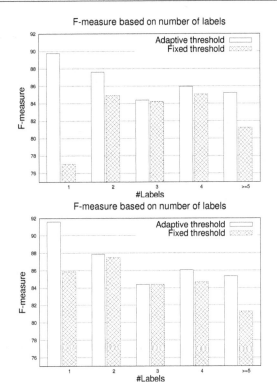

Figure 5: F-measure according to the number of labels for adaptive and fixed thresholds, the upper graph shows the results for MLP with softmax while the lower one is for the combination of all nets

Table 6: Results on the Reuters-21578 dataset

Method	Precision	Recall	F1 [%]
MLP/softmax	89.08	80.6	85.0
MLP/sigmoid	89.6	82.7	86.0
CNN/softmax	87.8	84.1	85.9
CNN/sigmoid	89.4	81.3	85.2
Supervised combi	91.4	84.1	87.6
NN_{AD} [1]	90.4	83.4	86.8
$BP-MLL_{TAD}$ [1]	84.2	84.2	84.2
BR_R [22]	89.8	86.0	87.9

The experimental results have confirmed our assumption that the different nets keep different information. Therefore, it is useful to combine them to improve the classification score of the individual nets. We have also proved that the thresholding is a good method to assign the document labels of multi-label classification. We have further shown that the results of all the approaches are comparable. However, the best combination method is the supervised one which uses an FNN with sigmoid activation function. The F-measure on Czech is 85.3% while the best result for English is 87.6%. Results on both languages are thus at least comparable with the state of the art.

One perspective for further work is to improve the com-

---

[1] Approach proposed by Zhang et al. [12] and used with ReLU activation, AdaGrad and dropout.

bination methods while the error analysis has shown that there is still some room for improvement. We have also shown that knowing the number of classes could improve the result. Another perspective is thus to build a classifier with thresholds dependent on the number of labels.

Acknowledgements

This work has been supported by the project LO1506 of the Czech Ministry of Education, Youth and Sports. We also would like to thank the Czech New Agency (ČTK) for support and for providing the data.

References

[1] Nam, J., Kim, J., Mencía, E.L., Gurevych, I., Fürnkranz, J.: Large-scale multi-label text classification—revisiting neural networks. In: Joint European Conference on Machine Learning and Knowledge Discovery in Databases, Springer (2014) 437–452

[2] Lenc, L., Král, P.: Deep neural networks for czech multi-label document classification. CoRR abs/1701.03849 (2017)

[3] Della Pietra, S., Della Pietra, V., Lafferty, J.: Inducing features of random fields. IEEE Transactions on Pattern Analysis and Machine Intelligence 19(4) (1997) 380–393

[4] Yang, Y., Pedersen, J.O.: A comparative study on feature selection in text categorization. In: Proceedings of the Fourteenth International Conference on Machine Learning. ICML '97, San Francisco, CA, USA, Morgan Kaufmann Publishers Inc. (1997) 412–420

[5] Ramage, D., Hall, D., Nallapati, R., Manning, C.D.: Labeled lda: A supervised topic model for credit attribution in multi-labeled corpora. In: Proceedings of the 2009 Conference on Empirical Methods in Natural Language Processing: Volume 1 - Volume 1. EMNLP '09, Stroudsburg, PA, USA, Association for Computational Linguistics (2009) 248–256

[6] Collobert, R., Weston, J., Bottou, L., Karlen, M., Kavukcuoglu, K., Kuksa, P.: Natural language processing (almost) from scratch. The Journal of Machine Learning Research 12 (2011) 2493–2537

[7] Zhang, X., LeCun, Y.: Text understanding from scratch. arXiv preprint arXiv:1502.01710 (2015)

[8] Kim, Y.: Convolutional neural networks for sentence classification. arXiv preprint arXiv:1408.5882 (2014)

[9] Mikolov, T., Chen, K., Corrado, G., Dean, J.: Efficient estimation of word representations in vector space. In: Proceedings of Workshop at ICLR. (2013)

[10] Lai, S., Xu, L., Liu, K., Zhao, J.: Recurrent convolutional neural networks for text classification. (2015)

[11] Manevitz, L., Yousef, M.: One-class document classification via neural networks. Neurocomputing 70(7-9) (2007) 1466–1481

[12] Zhang, M.L., Zhou, Z.H.: Multilabel neural networks with applications to functional genomics and text categorization. Knowledge and Data Engineering, IEEE Transactions on 18(10) (2006) 1338–1351

[13] Nair, V., Hinton, G.E.: Rectified linear units improve restricted boltzmann machines. In: Proceedings of the 27th international conference on machine learning (ICML-10). (2010) 807–814

[14] Srivastava, N., Hinton, G.E., Krizhevsky, A., Sutskever, I., Salakhutdinov, R.: Dropout: a simple way to prevent neural networks from overfitting. Journal of Machine Learning Research 15(1) (2014) 1929–1958

[15] Kurata, G., Xiang, B., Zhou, B.: Improved neural network-based multi-label classification with better initialization leveraging label co-occurrence. In: Proceedings of NAACL-HLT. (2016) 521–526

[16] Yang, Y., Gopal, S.: Multilabel classification with meta-level features in a learning-to-rank framework. Machine Learning 88(1-2) (2012) 47–68

[17] Brychcín, T., Král, P.: Novel unsupervised features for Czech multi-label document classification. In: 13th Mexican International Conference on Artificial Intelligence (MICAI 2014), Tuxtla Gutierrez, Chiapas, Mexic, Springer (16-22 November 2014) 70–79

[18] Tulyakov, S., Jaeger, S., Govindaraju, V., Doermann, D.: Review of classifier combination methods. In: Machine Learning in Document Analysis and Recognition. Springer (2008) 361–386

[19] Chollet, F.: keras. https://github.com/fchollet/keras (2015)

[20] Bergstra, J., Breuleux, O., Bastien, F., Lamblin, P., Pascanu, R., Desjardins, G., Turian, J., Warde-Farley, D., Bengio, Y.: Theano: a cpu and gpu math expression compiler. In: Proceedings of the Python for scientific computing conference (SciPy). Volume 4., Austin, TX (2010) 3

[21] Powers, D.: Evaluation: From precision, recall and f-measure to roc., informedness, markedness & correlation. Journal of Machine Learning Technologies 2(1) (2011) 37–63

[22] Rubin, T.N., Chambers, A., Smyth, P., Steyvers, M.: Statistical topic models for multi-label document classification. Machine learning 88(1-2) (2012) 157–208

J. Hlaváčová (Ed.): ITAT 2017 Proceedings, pp. 193–200
ISBN 978-1974274741, © 2017 M. Novák

Coreference Resolution System Not Only for Czech

Michal Novák

Charles University, Faculty of Mathematics and Physics
Institute of Formal and Applied Linguistics
Malostranské náměstí 25, CZ-11800 Prague 1
mnovak@ufal.mff.cuni.cz

Abstract: The paper introduces Treex CR, a coreference resolution (CR) system not only for Czech. As its name suggests, it has been implemented as an integral part of the Treex NLP framework. The main feature that distinguishes it from other CR systems is that it operates on the tectogrammatical layer, a representation of deep syntax. This feature allows for natural handling of elided expressions, e.g. unexpressed subjects in Czech as well as generally ignored English anaphoric expression – relative pronouns and zeros. The system implements a sequence of mention ranking models specialized at particular types of coreferential expressions (relative, reflexive, personal pronouns etc.). It takes advantage of rich feature set extracted from the data linguistically preprocessed with Treex. We evaluated Treex CR on Czech and English datasets and compared it with other systems as well as with modules used in Treex so far.

1 Introduction

Coreference Resolution (CR) is a task of discovering coreference relations in a text. Coreference connects *mentions* of the same real-world entity. Knowing coreference relations may help in understanding the text better, and thus it can be used in various natural language processing applications including question answering, text summarization, and machine translation.

Most of the works on CR have focused on English. In English, a mention almost always corresponds to a chunk of actual text, i.e. it is expressed on the surface. But Czech, for instance, is a different story. Czech is a typical example of pro-drop languages. In other words, a pronoun in the subject position is usually dropped as it is in the following example: *"Honza miluje Márii. Taky <ZERO-on> miluje pivo."* (*"John loves Mary. He also loves beer."*) If we ignored Czech *subject zeros*, we would not be able to extract a lot of information encoded in the text.

But subject zeros are not the only coreferential expression that may be dropped from the surface. Indeed, such zero mentions may appear even in the language where one would not expect them. For instance, the following English sentence does not express the relative pronoun: *"John wants the beer <ZERO-that> Mary drinks."*

This paper presents the *Treex Coreference Resolver (Treex CR)*.[1] It has been primarily designed with focus on

resolution in Czech texts. Therefore, Treex CR naturally supports coreference resolution of zero mentions.

The platform that ensures this and that our system operates on is called *tectogrammatical layer*, a deep syntax representation of the text. It has been proposed in the theory of Prague tectogrammatics [32]. The tectogrammatical layer represents a sentence as a dependency tree, whose nodes are formed by content words only. All the function and auxiliary words are hidden in a corresponding content node. On the other hand, the tectogrammatical tree can represent a content word that is unexpressed on the surface as a full-fledged node.

T-layer is also the place where coreference is represented. A generally used style of representing coreference is by co-indexing continuous chunks of surface text. Tectogrammatics adopts a different style. A coreference link always connects two tectogrammatical nodes that represent mentions' heads. Unlike the surface style, tectogrammatics does not specify a span of the mention, though. Such representation should be easier for a resolver to handle as the errors introduced by wrong identification of mention boundaries are eliminated. On the other hand, for some mentions it may be unclear what its head is.[2]

At this point, let us introduce the linguistic terminology that we use in the rest of the paper. Multiple coreferential mentions form a chain. Splitting the chain into pairs of mentions, we can adopt the terminology used for a related phenomena – *anaphoric relations*. The anaphoric relation connects the mention which depends upon another mention used in the earlier context.[3] The later mention is denoted as the *anaphor* while the earlier mention is called the *antecedent*.

This work is motivated by cross-lingual studies of coreferential relations. We thus concentrate mostly on pronouns and zeros, which behave differently in distant languages, such as Czech and English.[4] Coreference of nominal groups is not in the scope of this work because it is less interesting from this perspective.

However, Treex CR is still supposed to be a standard coreference resolver. We thus compare its performance with three coreference resolvers from the Stanford Core

---

[1]It is freely available at https://github.com/ufal/treex

as the module `Treex::Scen::Coref` in the Treex framework.

[2]As we demonstrate in Section 5.

[3]As opposed to *cataphoric relations*, where the dependence is oriented to the future context.

[4]A thorough analysis of correspondences between Czech and English coreferential expressions has been conducted in [26].

NLP toolkit, which are the current and former state-of-the-art systems for English. Since we evaluate all the systems on two datasets using the measure that may focus on specific anaphor types, this work also offers a non-traditional comparison of established systems for English.

2 Related Work

Coreference resolution has experienced evolution typical for most of the problems in natural language processing. Starting with rule-based approaches (summarized in [20]), the period of supervised (summarized in [23]) and unsupervised learning methods (e.g. [6] and [15]) followed. This period has been particularly colorful, having defined three standard models for CR and introduced multiple adjustments of system design. For instance, our Treex CR system implements some of them: mention-ranking model [10], joint anaphoricity detection and antecedent selection, and specialized models [11]. A recent tsunami of deep neural network appears to be a small wave in the field of research on coreference. Neural Stanford system [8] set a new state of the art, yet the change of direction has not been as rapid and massive as for the other, more popular, topics, e.g. machine translation.

The evolution of CR for Czech proceeded in a similar way. It started during the annotation work on Prague Dependency Treebank 2.0 [16, PDT 2.0] and a set of deterministic filters for personal pronouns proposed by [17], followed by a rule-based system for all coreferential relations annotated in PDT 2.0 [24]. Release of the first coreference-annotated treebank opened the door for supervised methods. A supervised resolver for personal pronouns and subject zeros [25] is the biggest inspiration for the present work. We use a similar architecture implementing multiple mention-ranking models [10] specialized on individual anaphor types [11]. Unlike [25], we use a richer feature set and extend the resolver also to other anaphor types.

Moreover, we rectify a fundamental shortcoming of all these coreference resolvers for Czech – the experiments with them were conducted on the manual annotation of tectogrammatical layer. In this way, the systems could take advantage of gold syntax or disambiguated genders and numbers. While the rule-based system [24] reports around 99% F-score on relative pronouns, fair evaluation of a similar method but run on automatic tectogrammatical annotation reports only 57% F-score (see Table 2). If the system uses linguistically pre-processed data, the pre-processing must always be performed automatically.

3 System Architecture

Treex Coreference Resolver has been developed as an integral part of the Treex framework for natural language processing [29]. Treex CR is a unified solution for finding coreferential relations on the t-layer. For that reason, it requires the input texts to be automatically pre-processed up to this level of linguistic annotation. The system is based on machine learning, thus making all the components fully trainable if the appropriate training data is available. Up to now, the system has been build for Czech, English, Russian and German.[5] In this paper, we focus only on its implementation for Czech and English.

3.1 Preprocessing to a Tectogrammatical Representation

Before coreference resolution is carried out, the input text must undergo a thorough analysis producing a tectogrammatical representation of its sentences. Treex CR cannot process a text that has not been analyzed this way. Input data must comply with at least basics of this annotation style. The text should be tokenized and labeled with part-of-speech tags in order for the resolver to focus on nouns and pronouns as mention candidates. However, the real power of the system lies in exploiting rich linguistic annotation that can be represented by tectogramatics.

Czech and English analysis. We make use of rich pipelines for Czech and English available in the Treex framework, previously applied for building the Czech-English parallel treebank CzEng 1.6 [4].

Sentences are first split into tokens, which is ensured by rule-based modules. Subsequently, the tokens are enriched with morphological information including part-of-speech tag, morphological features as well as lemmas. Whereas in English, the Morče tool [33] is used to collect part-of-speech tags, followed by a rule-based lemmatizer, the Czech pipeline utilizes the MorphoDiTa tool [34] to obtain all.

A dependency tree is build on top of this annotation, using MST parser [19] and its adapted version [28] for English and Czech, respectively. Named entity recognition is carried out by the NameTag [35] tool in both languages.

The NADA tool [3] is applied to help distinguish referential and non-referential occurrences of the English pronoun "it". Every occurrence is assigned a probability estimate based on n-gram features.

Transition from a surface dependency tree to the tectogrammatical one consists of the following steps. As tectogrammatical nodes correspond to content words only, function words such as prepositions, auxiliary verbs, particles, punctuation must be hidden. Morpho-syntactic information is transferred to tectogrammatical layer by two channels: (i) morpho-syntactic tags called *formemes* [13] and (ii) features of deep grammar called *grammatemes*. All nodes are then subject to semantic role labeling assigning them roles such as Actor and Patient, and linking of verbs to items in Czech valency dictionary [12].

---

[5]Russian and German version has been trained on automatic English coreference labeling projected to these languages through a parallel corpus. See [27] for more details.

Reconstructing zeros. To mimic the style of tectogrammatical annotation in automatic analysis, some nodes that are not present on the surface must be reconstructed. We focus on cases that directly relate to coreference. Such nodes are added by heuristics based on syntactic structures.

Subject zeros are the most prominent anaphoric zeros in Czech. A subject is generated as a child of a finite verb if it has no children in subject position or in nominative case. Grammatical person, number and gender are inferred from a form of the verb.

Perhaps surprisingly, English uses zeros as well. The coreferential ones can be found in *relative clauses* (see the example in Section 1) and *non-finite verbal constructions*, e.g. in participles and infinitives. We seek for such constructions and add a zero child with a semantic role corresponding to the type of the construction. This work extends the original Treex module for English zeros' generation, which addressed only infinitives.

3.2 Model design

Treex CR models coreference in a way to be easily optimized by supervised learning. Particularly, we use logistic regression with stochastic gradient descend optimization implemented in the Vowpal Wabbit toolkit.[6] Design of the model employs multiple concepts that have proved to be useful and simple at the same time.

Mention-ranking model. Given an anaphor and a set of antecedent candidates, *mention-ranking* models [10] are trained to score all the candidates at once. Competition between the candidates is captured in the model. Every antecedent candidate describes solely the actual mention. It does not represent a possible cluster of coreferential mentions built up to the moment.

Antecedent candidates for an anaphor are selected from the context window of a predefined size. This is done only for the nodes satisfying simple morphological criteria (e.g. nouns and pronouns). Both the window size and the filtering criteria can be altered as hyperparameters.

Joint anaphoricity detection and antecedent selection. What we denote as an anaphor in the model is, in fact, an anaphor candidate. There is no preprocessing that would filter out non-referential anaphor candidates. Instead, both decisions, i.e. (i) to determine if the anaphor candidate is referential and (ii) to find the antecedent of the anaphor, are performed in a single step. This is ensured by adding a fake "antecedent" candidate representing solely the anaphor candidate itself. By selecting this candidate, the model labels the anaphor candidate as non-referential.

A cascade of specialized models. Properties of coreferential relations are so diverse that it is worth modeling individual anaphor types rather separately than jointly as shown in [11]. For instance, while personal pronouns may refer to one of the previous sentences, the antecedent of relative and reflexive pronouns always lies in the same sentence. By representing coreference of these expressions separately in multiple specialized models, the abovementioned hyperparameters can be adjusted to suit the particular anaphor type. Processing of these anaphor types may be sorted in a cascade so that the output of one model might be taken into account in the following models. Currently, we do not take advantage of this feature, though. Models are thus independent on each other and can be run in any ordering.

3.3 Feature extraction

The preprocessing stage (see Section 3.1) enriches a raw text with substantial amount of linguistic material. Feature extraction stage then uses this material to yield *features* consumable by the learning method. In addition, Vowpal Wabbit, the learning tool we use, supports grouping features into namespaces. The tool may introduce combinations of features as a Cartesian product of selected namespaces and thus massively extend the space of features. This can be controlled by hyperparameters to Vowpal Wabbit.

Features used in Treex CR can be categorized by their form. The categories differ in the number of input arguments they require. *Unary features* describe only a single node, either anaphor or antecedent candidate. Such features start with prefixes `anaph` and `cand`, respectively. *Binary features* require both the anaphor and the antecedent candidate for their construction. Specifically, they can be formed by agreement or concatenation of respective unary features, but they can generally describe any relation between the two arguments. Finally, *ranking features* need all the antecedent candidates along with the anaphor candidate to be yielded. Their purpose is to rank antecedent candidates with respect to a particular relation to an anaphor candidate.

Our features also differ by their content. They can be divided into three categories: (i) location and distance features, (ii) (deep) morpho-syntactic features, and (iii) lexical features. The core of the feature set was formed by adapting features introduced in [25].

Location and distance features Positions of anaphor and an antecedent in a sentence were inspired by [6]. Position of the antecedent is measured backward from the anaphor if they lie in the same sentence, otherwise it is measured forward from the start of the sentence. As for distance features, we use various granularity to measure distance between an anaphor and an antecedent candidate: number of sentences, clauses and words. In addition, an ordinal number of the current candidate antecedent among the others is

---

[6]https://github.com/JohnLangford/vowpal_wabbit/wiki

included. All location and distance features are bucketed into predefined bins.

(Deep) morpho-syntactic features. They utilize the annotation provided by part-of-speech taggers, parsers and tectogrammatical annotation. Their unary variants capture the mention head's part-of-speech tag and morphological features, e.g. gender, number, person, case. As gender and number are considered important for resolution of pronouns, we do not rely on their disambiguation and work with all possible hypotheses. We do the same for some Czech words that are in nominative case but disambiguation labeled them with the accusative case. Such case is a typical source of errors in generating a subject zero as it fills a missing nominative slot in the governing verb's valency frame. To discover potentially spurious subject zeros, we also inspect if the verb has multiple arguments in accusative and if the argument in nominative is refused by the valency, as it is in the phrase "*Zdá se mi, že...*" ("*It seems to me that...*"). Furthermore, the unary features contain (deep) syntax features including its dependency relation, semantic role, and formeme. We exploit the structure of the syntactic tree as well, extracting some features from the mention head's parent.

Many of these features are combined to binary variants by agreement and concatenation. Heuristics used in original Treex modules for some anaphor types gave birth to another pack of binary features. For instance, the feature indicating if a candidate is the subject of the anaphor's clause should target coreference of reflexive pronouns. Similarly, signaling whether a candidate governs the anaphor's clause should help with resolution of relative pronouns.

Lexical features Lemmas of the mentions' heads and their parents are directly used as features. Such features may have an effect only if built from frequent words, though. By using them with an external lexical resource, this data sparsity problem can be reduced.

Firstly, we used a long list of noun-verb collocations collected by [25] on Czech National Corpus [9]. Having this statistics, we can estimate how probable is that the anaphor's governing verb collocates with an antecedent candidate.

Another approach to fight data sparsity is to employ an ontology. Apart from an actual word, we can include all its hypernymous concepts from the hierarchy as features. We exploit WordNet [14] and EuroWordNet [38] for English and Czech, respectively.

To target proper nouns, we also extract features from tags assigned by named entity recognizers run during the preprocessing stage.

4   Datasets

We exploited two treebanks for training and testing purposes: Prague Dependency Treebank 3.0 [2, PDT] and

	Czech		English		
	Train	Eval test	Train	Eval test	CoNLL 2012
sents	38k	5k	39k	5k	9.5k
words	652k	92k	912k	130k	170k
t-nodes	528k	75k	652k	91k	116k
anaph	92k	14k	103k	15k	15k
Relative	7.2k	1k	6.4k	0.8k	–
Reflexive	3.4k	0.6k	0.4k	0.05k	0.1k
PP3	–	–	19k	2.4k	4.5k
SzPP3	12k	2k	–	–	–
Zero	–	–	23k	3.2k	–
Other	70k	10k	54k	8.0k	10.4k

Table 1: Basic statistics of used datasets. The class *SzPP3* stands for 3rd person subject zeros, personal and possessive pronouns, while the class *PP3* excludes subject zeros.

Prague Czech-English Dependency Treebank 2.0 Coref [22, PCEDT] for Czech and English, respectively. Although PCEDT is a Czech-English parallel treebank, we used only its English side. Both treebanks are collections of newspaper and journal articles. In addition, they both follow the annotation principles of the theory of Prague tectogrammatics [32]. They also comprise a full-fledged manual annotation of coreferential relations.[7]

Training and *evaluation test* dataset for Czech are formed by PDT sections `train-*` and `etest`, respectively. As for English, these two datasets are collected from PCEDT sections `00-18` and `22-24`, respectively.[8]

In addition, we used the official testset for CoNLL 2012 Shared Task to evaluate English systems [31]. This dataset has been sampled from the OntoNotes 5.0 [30] corpus. OntoNotes, and thus CoNLL 2012 testset as well, differ from the two treebanks in the following main aspects: (i) coreference is annotated on the surface, where mentions of the same entity are co-indexed spans of consecutive words, (ii) it contains no zeros and relative pronouns are not annotated for coreference.[9] These differences must be reflected when evaluating on this dataset (see Section 5).

A basic statistics collected on these datasets is shown in Table 1. The anaphor types treated by Treex CR cover around 50% and 25-30% of all anaphors in English and Czech tectogrammatical treebanks, respectively. The main reason of the disproportion is that we did not include Czech non-subject zeros to the collection (class *Zero*). Czech subject zeros are merged to a common class with personal and possessive pronouns in 3rd person (class *SzPP3*), as they are trained in a joint model (see Section 5). Due the same reason, English personal and possessive pronouns in 3rd person form a common class *PP3*. As the CoNLL 2012 testset has no annotation of relative pronouns and zeros, Treex CR covers 30% of all the anaphors.

---

[7]See [21] for more information on coreference annotation.

[8]During development of our system, we employed the rest of the treebanks' data as *development test* dataset for intermediate testing.

[9]Reasons for ignoring relative pronouns in OntoNotes are unclear. They might be seen as so tied up with rules of grammar and syntax that annotation of such cases is too unattractive to deal with.

5   Experiments and Evaluation

Our system uses two specialized models for relative and reflexive pronouns in both languages. The Czech system in addition contains a joint model for subject zeros, personal and possessive pronouns in 3rd person (denoted as *SzPP3*). The English system contains two more models: one for personal and possessive pronouns in 3rd person (denoted as *PP3*) and another one for zeros.

Systems to compare. To show performance of Treex CR in a context, we evaluated multiple other systems on the same data. Since currently there is no other publicly available system for Czech to our knowledge, we compare it with the original Treex set of modules for coreference. The set consists of rule-based modules for relative and reflexive pronouns, and a supervised model for SzPP3 mentions. It has been previously used for building a Czech-English parallel treebank CzEng 1.0 [5].

We also report performance of the English predecessor of Treex CR used to build CzEng 1.0. It comprises a rule-based module for relative pronouns and zeros, and a joint supervised model for reflexives and PP3 mentions. In addition, we include the Stanford Core NLP toolkit to the evaluation. It contains three approaches to full-fledged CR that all claimed to improve over the state of the art at the time of their release: deterministic [18], statistical [7], and neural [8]. In fact, the neural system has not been outperformed, yet.

Stanford Core NLP predicts surface mentions, which is not compatible with the evaluation schema designed for tectogrammatical trees. The surface mentions thus must be transformed to the tectogrammatical style of coreference annotation, i.e. the mention heads must be connected with links. We may use the information on mention heads provided by the Stanford system itself. However, by using this approach results we observed completely contradictory results on different datasets. Manual investigation on a sample of the data revealed that often the Stanford system in fact identified a correct antecedent mention, but selected a head different to the one in the data. Most of these cases, e.g. company names like "McDonald's Corp." or "Walt Disney Co.", have no clear head, though. Therefore, we decided to use the gold tectogrammatical tree to identify the head of the mention labeled by the Stanford system. Even though employing gold information for system's decision is a bad practice, here it should not affect the result so much and we use it only for the third-party systems, not for our Treex CR.

Evaluation measure. Standard evaluation metrics (e.g. MUC [37], B^3 [1]) are not suitable for our purposes as they do not allow for scoring only a subset of mentions. Instead, we use a measure similar to scores proposed by [36]. For an anaphor candidate a_i, we increment the three following counts:

- *true*(a_i) if a_i is anaphoric in the gold annotation,

	Relative	Reflexive	SzPP3	All
Count	1,075	579	1,950	3,604
Treex				
CzEng 1.0	57.14	67.57	50.52	55.20
Treex CR	78.40	76.19	61.31	**68.46**

Table 2: F-scores of Czech coreference resolvers measured on all anaphor types both separately and altogether. The type *SzPP3* denotes 3rd person subject zeros, personal and possessive pronouns.

- *pred*(a_i) if the CR system claims a_i is anaphoric,

- *both*(a_i) if both the system and gold annotation claim a_i is anaphoric and the antecedent found by the system belongs to the transitive closure of all mentions coreferential with a_i in the gold annotation.

After aggregating these counts over all anaphor candidates, we compute the final Precision, Recall and F-score as follows:

$$P = \sum_{a_i} \frac{both(a_i)}{pred(a_i)} \quad R = \sum_{a_i} \frac{both(a_i)}{true(a_i)} \quad F = \frac{2PR}{P+R}$$

To evaluate only a particular anaphor type, the aggregation runs over all anaphor candidates of the given type.

The presented evaluation schema, however, needs to be adjusted for the CoNLL 2012 dataset. As mentioned in Section 4, in this dataset relative pronouns are not considered coreferential and zeros are missing at all. As a result, a system that marks such expressions as antecedents would be penalized. We thus apply the following patch specifically for the CoNLL 2012 dataset to rectify this issue. If the predicted antecedent is a zero or a relative pronoun, instead of using it directly we follow the predicted coreferential chain until the expression outside of these two categories is met. The found expression is then used to calculate the counts, as described above. If no such expression is found, the direct antecedent is used, even if it is a zero or a relative pronoun.

All the scores presented in the rest of the paper are F-scores.

Results and their analysis. Table 2 shows results of evaluation on the Czech data. The Czech version of Treex CR succeeded in its ambition to replace the modules used in Treex until now. It significantly[10] outperformed the baseline for each of the anaphor type, with the overall score by 13 percentage points higher. The jump for relative pronouns was particularly high.

The analysis of improved examples for this category shows that apart from the syntactic principles used in the rule-based module, it also exploits other symptoms of

---

[10]Significance has been calculated by bootstrap resampling with a confidence level 95%.

	PCEDT Eval					CoNLL 2012 test set		
	Relative	Reflexive	PP3	Zeros	All	Reflexive	PP3	All
Count	842	49	2,494	3,260	6,645	111	4,583	4,710
Stanford								
deterministic	1.16	55.67	63.65	0.00	34.96	71.11	60.55	60.79
statistical	0.00	63.74	72.71	0.00	39.09	80.56	*71.07*	**71.29**
neural	0.00	70.97	*76.36*	0.00	41.56	*80.73*	70.45	70.70
Treex								
CzEng 1.0	70.64	65.93	73.52	28.48	55.34	76.02	67.93	68.13
Treex CR	*75.99*	*81.63*	74.11	*45.37*	**60.87**	79.65	66.64	66.96

Table 3: F-scores of English coreference resolvers measured on all anaphor types both separately and altogether. The type *PP3* denotes personal and possessive pronouns in 3rd person.

coreference. The most prominent are agreement of the anaphor and the antecedent in gender and number as well as the distance between the two. It also succeeds in identifying non-anaphoric examples, for instance interrogative pronouns, which use the same forms.

Results of evaluation on the English data are highlighted in Table 3. Similarly to the Czech system, the English version of Treex CR outperforms its predecessor in Treex by a large margin of 15 percentage points on the PCEDT Eval testset. Most of it stems from a large improvement on the biggest class of anaphors, zeros. Unlike for Czech relative pronouns, the supervised CR is not the only reason for this leap. It largely results from the extension that we made to the method for adding zero arguments of non-finite clauses (see Section 3.1). Consequently, the coverage of these nodes compared to their gold annotation rose from 34% to 80%. Comparing these two versions of the Treex system on the CoNLL 2012 testset, we see a different picture. The systems' performances are more similar, the baseline system for PP3 even slightly outperforms the new Treex CR.

As for the comparison with the Stanford systems, we should not look at the scores aggregated over all the anaphor types under scrutiny, because Stanford systems apparently do not address zeros and relative pronouns.[11] In fact, the Stanford systems try to reconstruct coreference as it is annotated in OntoNotes 5.0.

The classes of reflexive and PP3 pronouns are the only ones within the scope of all the resolvers. The Stanford deterministic system seems to be consistently outperformed by all the other approaches. Performance rankings on reflexive pronouns differ for the two datasets, which is probably the consequence of low frequency of reflexives in the datasets. Regarding the PP3 pronouns, Treex CR does not achieve the performance of the state-of-the-art Stanford neural system. On the CoNLL 2012 testset it is outperformed even by the Stanford statistical system. Neverthe-

less, in all the cases the performance gaps are not so big and thus it is reasonable using Treex CR for further experiments in the future.

To best of our knowledge, no analysis of how Stanford systems perform for individual anaphor types has been published, yet. Interestingly, our result show that even though the overall performance of the neural system on the CoNLL 2012 testset is reported to be higher [8], for personal and possessive pronouns in third person it is slightly outperformed by the statistical system. However, as the evaluation on the PCEDT Eval testset shows completely the opposite, we cannot arrive at any conclusion on their mutual performance comparison on this anaphor type.

6   Conclusion

We described Treex CR, a coreference resolver not only for Czech. The main feature of the system is that it operates on the tectogrammatical layer, which allows it to address also coreference of zeros. The system uses a supervised model, supported by a very rich set of linguistic features. We presented modules for processing Czech and English and evaluated them on several datasets. For comparison, we conducted the evaluation with the predecessors of Treex CR and three versions of the Stanford system, one of which was a state-of-the-art neural resolver for English. Our system seems to have outperformed the baseline system on Czech. On English, although it could not outperform the best approaches in the Stanford system, its performance is high enough to be used in future experiments. Furthermore, it may be used for resolution of anaphor types that are ignored by most of the coreference resolvers for English, i.e. relative pronouns and zeros.

In the future work, we would like to use Treex CR in cross-lingual coreference resolution, where the system is applied on parallel corpus and thus it may take advantage of both languages.

---

[11] On the other hand, they address coreference of nominal groups and pronouns in first and second person. Treex CR does not provide Czech or English models for these classes, so far. Nevertheless, experimental projection-based models already exist for German and Russian [27].

Acknowledgments

This project has been funded by the GAUK grant 338915 and the Czech Science Foundation grant GA-16-05394S. This work has been also supported and has been using language resources developed and/or stored and/or distributed by the LINDAT/CLARIN project No. LM2015071 of the Ministry of Education, Youth and Sports of the Czech Republic.

References

[1] Amit Bagga and Breck Baldwin. Algorithms for Scoring Coreference Chains. In *In The First International Conference on Language Resources and Evaluation Workshop on Linguistics Coreference*, pages 563–566, 1998.

[2] Eduard Bejček, Eva Hajičová, Jan Hajič, Pavlína Jínová, Václava Kettnerová, Veronika Kolářová, Marie Mikulová, Jiří Mírovský, Anna Nedoluzhko, Jarmila Panevová, Lucie Poláková, Magda Ševčíková, Jan Štěpánek, and Šárka Zikánová. Prague Dependency Treebank 3.0, 2013.

[3] Shane Bergsma and David Yarowsky. NADA: A Robust System for Non-referential Pronoun Detection. In *Proceedings of the 8th International Conference on Anaphora Processing and Applications*, pages 12–23, Berlin, Heidelberg, 2011. Springer-Verlag.

[4] Ondřej Bojar, Ondřej Dušek, Tom Kocmi, Jindřich Libovický, Michal Novák, Martin Popel, Roman Sudarikov, and Dušan Variš. CzEng 1.6: Enlarged Czech-English Parallel Corpus with Processing Tools Dockered. In *Text, Speech, and Dialogue: 19th International Conference, TSD 2016*, number 9924 in Lecture Notes in Artificial Intelligence, pages 231–238, Heidelberg, Germany, 2016. Springer International Publishing.

[5] Ondřej Bojar, Zdeněk Žabokrtský, Ondřej Dušek, Petra Galuščáková, Martin Majliš, David Mareček, Jiří Maršík, Michal Novák, Martin Popel, and Aleš Tamchyna. The Joy of Parallelism with CzEng 1.0. In *Proceedings of the 8th International Conference on Language Resources and Evaluation (LREC 2012)*, pages 3921–3928, Istanbul, Turkey, 2012. European Language Resources Association.

[6] Eugene Charniak and Micha Elsner. EM Works for Pronoun Anaphora Resolution. In *Proceedings of the 12th Conference of the European Chapter of the Association for Computational Linguistics*, pages 148–156, Stroudsburg, PA, USA, 2009. Association for Computational Linguistics.

[7] Kevin Clark and Christopher D. Manning. Entity-Centric Coreference Resolution with Model Stacking. In *Proceedings of the 53rd Annual Meeting of the Association for Computational Linguistics and the 7th International Joint Conference on Natural Language Processing (Volume 1: Long Papers)*, pages 1405–1415, Beijing, China, 2015. Association for Computational Linguistics.

[8] Kevin Clark and Christopher D. Manning. Improving Coreference Resolution by Learning Entity-Level Distributed Representations. In *Proceedings of the 54th Annual Meeting of the Association for Computational Linguistics (Volume 1: Long Papers)*, pages 643–653, Berlin, Germany, 2016. Association for Computational Linguistics.

[9] CNC. Czech national corpus – SYN2005, 2005.

[10] Pascal Denis and Jason Baldridge. A Ranking Approach to Pronoun Resolution. In *Proceedings of the 20th International Joint Conference on Artifical Intelligence*, pages 1588–1593, San Francisco, CA, USA, 2007. Morgan Kaufmann Publishers Inc.

[11] Pascal Denis and Jason Baldridge. Specialized Models and Ranking for Coreference Resolution. In *Proceedings of the Conference on Empirical Methods in Natural Language Processing*, pages 660–669, Stroudsburg, PA, USA, 2008. Association for Computational Linguistics.

[12] Ondřej Dušek, Jan Hajič, and Zdeňka Urešová. Verbal Valency Frame Detection and Selection in Czech and English. In *The 2nd Workshop on EVENTS: Definition, Detection, Coreference, and Representation*, pages 6–11, Stroudsburg, PA, USA, 2014. Association for Computational Linguistics.

[13] Ondřej Dušek, Zdeněk Žabokrtský, Martin Popel, Martin Majliš, Michal Novák, and David Mareček. Formemes in English-Czech Deep Syntactic MT. In *Proceedings of the Seventh Workshop on Statistical Machine Translation*, pages 267–274, Montréal, Canada, 2012. Association for Computational Linguistics.

[14] Christiane Fellbaum. *WordNet: An Electronic Lexical Database (Language, Speech, and Communication)*. The MIT Press, 1998.

[15] Aria Haghighi and Dan Klein. Coreference Resolution in a Modular, Entity-centered Model. In *Human Language Technologies: The 2010 Annual Conference of the North American Chapter of the Association for Computational Linguistics*, pages 385–393, Stroudsburg, PA, USA, 2010. Association for Computational Linguistics.

[16] Jan Hajič et al. Prague Dependency Treebank 2.0. CD-ROM, Linguistic Data Consortium, LDC Catalog No.: LDC2006T01, Philadelphia, 2006.

[17] Lucie Kučová and Zdeněk Žabokrtský. Anaphora in Czech: Large Data and Experiments with Automatic Anaphora. In *Lecture Notes in Artificial Intelligence, Proceedings of the 8th International Conference, TSD 2005*, volume 3658 of *Lecture Notes in Computer Science*, pages 93–98, Berlin / Heidelberg, 2005. Springer.

[18] Heeyoung Lee, Yves Peirsman, Angel Chang, Nathanael Chambers, Mihai Surdeanu, and Dan Jurafsky. Stanford's Multi-Pass Sieve Coreference Resolution System at the CoNLL-2011 Shared Task. In *Proceedings of the Fifteenth Conference on Computational Natural Language Learning: Shared Task*, pages 28–34, Portland, Oregon, USA, 2011. Association for Computational Linguistics.

[19] Ryan McDonald, Fernando Pereira, Kiril Ribarov, and Jan Hajič. Non-projective Dependency Parsing Using Spanning Tree Algorithms. In *Proceedings of the Conference on Human Language Technology and Empirical Methods in Natural Language Processing*, pages 523–530, Stroudsburg, PA, USA, 2005. Association for Computational Linguistics.

[20] Ruslan Mitkov. *Anaphora Resolution*. Longman, London, 2002.

[21] Anna Nedoluzhko, Michal Novák, Silvie Cinková, Marie Mikulová, and Jiří Mírovský. Coreference in Prague Czech-English Dependency Treebank. In *Proceedings of the 10th International Conference on Language Resources and Evaluation (LREC 2016)*, pages 169–176, Paris, France, 2016. European Language Resources Association.

[22] Anna Nedoluzhko, Michal Novák, Silvie Cinková, Marie Mikulová, and Jiří Mírovský. Prague czech-english dependency treebank 2.0 coref, 2016.

[23] Vincent Ng. Supervised Noun Phrase Coreference Research: The First Fifteen Years. In *Proceedings of the 48th Annual Meeting of the Association for Computational Linguistics*, pages 1396–1411, Stroudsburg, PA, USA, 2010. Association for Computational Linguistics.

[24] Giang Linh Nguy. Návrh souboru pravidel pro analýzu anafor v českém jazyce. Master's thesis, MFF UK, Prague, Czech Republic, 2006. In Czech.

[25] Giang Linh Nguy, Václav Novák, and Zdeněk Žabokrtský. Comparison of Classification and Ranking Approaches to Pronominal Anaphora Resolution in Czech. In *Proceedings of the SIGDIAL 2009 Conference*, pages 276–285, London, UK, 2009. The Association for Computational Linguistics.

[26] Michal Novák and Anna Nedoluzhko. Correspondences between Czech and English Coreferential Expressions. *Discours: Revue de linguistique, psycholinguistique et informatique.*, 16:1–41, 2015.

[27] Michal Novák, Anna Nedoluzhko, and Zdeněk Žabokrtský. Projection-based Coreference Resolution Using Deep Syntax. In *Proceedings of the 2nd Workshop on Coreference Resolution Beyond OntoNotes (CORBON 2017)*, pages 56–64, Valencia, Spain, 2017. Association for Computational Linguistics.

[28] Václav Novák and Zdeněk Žabokrtský. Feature engineering in maximum spanning tree dependency parser. volume 4629, pages 92–98, Berlin / Heidelberg, 2007. Springer.

[29] Martin Popel and Zdeněk Žabokrtský. TectoMT: Modular NLP Framework. In *Proceedings of the 7th International Conference on Advances in Natural Language Processing*, pages 293–304, Berlin, Heidelberg, 2010. Springer-Verlag.

[30] Sameer Pradhan, Alessandro Moschitti, Nianwen Xue, Hwee Tou Ng, Anders Björkelund, Olga Uryupina, Yuchen Zhang, and Zhi Zhong. Towards Robust Linguistic Analysis using OntoNotes. In *Proceedings of the Seventeenth Conference on Computational Natural Language Learning*, pages 143–152, Sofia, Bulgaria, 2013. Association for Computational Linguistics.

[31] Sameer Pradhan, Alessandro Moschitti, Nianwen Xue, Olga Uryupina, and Yuchen Zhang. CoNLL-2012 Shared Task: Modeling Multilingual Unrestricted Coreference in OntoNotes. In *Joint Conference on Empirical Methods in Natural Language Processing and Computational Natural Language Learning - Proceedings of the Shared Task: Modeling Multilingual Unrestricted Coreference in OntoNotes, EMNLP-CoNLL 2012*, pages 1–40, Jeju, Korea, 2012. Association for Computational Linguistics.

[32] Petr Sgall, Eva Hajičová, Jarmila Panevová, and Jacob Mey. *The meaning of the sentence in its semantic and pragmatic aspects.* Springer, 1986.

[33] Drahomíra Spoustová, Jan Hajič, Jan Votrubec, Pavel Krbec, and Pavel Květoň. The Best of Two Worlds: Cooperation of Statistical and Rule-based Taggers for Czech. In *Proceedings of the Workshop on Balto-Slavonic Natural Language Processing: Information Extraction and Enabling Technologies*, pages 67–74, Stroudsburg, PA, USA, 2007. Association for Computational Linguistics.

[34] Jana Straková, Milan Straka, and Jan Hajič. Open-Source Tools for Morphology, Lemmatization, POS Tagging and Named Entity Recognition. In *Proceedings of 52nd Annual Meeting of the Association for Computational Linguistics: System Demonstrations*, pages 13–18, Baltimore, Maryland, 2014. Association for Computational Linguistics.

[35] Jana Straková, Milan Straka, and Jan Hajič. Open-Source Tools for Morphology, Lemmatization, POS Tagging and Named Entity Recognition. In *Proceedings of 52nd Annual Meeting of the Association for Computational Linguistics: System Demonstrations*, pages 13–18, Baltimore, Maryland, 2014. Association for Computational Linguistics.

[36] Don Tuggener. Coreference Resolution Evaluation for Higher Level Applications. In Gosse Bouma and Yannick Parmentier, editors, *Proceedings of the 14th Conference of the European Chapter of the Association for Computational Linguistics, EACL 2014, April 26-30, 2014, Gothenburg, Sweden*, pages 231–235. The Association for Computer Linguistics, 2014.

[37] Marc Vilain, John Burger, John Aberdeen, Dennis Connolly, and Lynette Hirschman. A Model-theoretic Coreference Scoring Scheme. In *Proceedings of the 6th Conference on Message Understanding*, pages 45–52, Stroudsburg, PA, USA, 1995. Association for Computational Linguistics.

[38] Piek Vossen. Introduction to EuroWordNet. *Computers and the Humanities, Special Issue on EuroWordNet*, 32(2–3), 1998.

J. Hlaváčová (Ed.): ITAT 2017 Proceedings, pp. 201–208
ISBN 978-1974274741, © 2017 R. Rosa

MonoTrans: Statistical Machine Translation from Monolingual Data

Rudolf Rosa

Charles University, Faculty of Mathematics and Physics,
Institute of Formal and Applied Linguistics,
Malostranské náměstí 25, 118 00 Prague, Czech Republic
rosa@ufal.mff.cuni.cz

Abstract: We present MonoTrans, a statistical machine translation system which only uses monolingual source language and target language data, without using any parallel corpora or language-specific rules. It translates each source word by the most similar target word, according to a combination of a string similarity measure and a word frequency similarity measure. It is designed for translation between very close languages, such as Czech and Slovak or Danish and Norwegian. It provides a low-quality translation in resource-poor scenarios where parallel data, required for training a high-quality translation system, may be scarce or unavailable. This is useful e.g. for cross-lingual NLP, where a trained model may be transferred from a resource-rich source language to a resource-poor target language via machine translation. We evaluate MonoTrans both intrinsically, using BLEU, and extrinsically, applying it to cross-lingual tagger and parser transfer. Although it achieves low scores, it does surpass the baselines by respectable margins.

1 Introduction

In machine translation (MT), the most common and most successful approach is to train a translation model from parallel text corpora, i.e. from a set of bilingual sentence pairs with corresponding meanings. This approach was pioneered by the IBM models [2], which led to the development of many phrase-based MT systems, with Moses [8] being the most well-known and wide-spread one. In recent years, Neural MT [1] is taking the lead, with one of the main representants being Nematus [15]. Still, all of these systems rely on parallel corpora as the key resource.

Fortunately, parallel text corpora are a naturally occurring resource. They can be mined from film subtitles, book translations, documents published by international institutions, software localization data, etc. Probably the largest freely available collection of parallel data is Opus [18], providing parallel corpora for roughly 100 languages for download,[1] comprising many smaller preexisting collections. However, rough estimates of the number of world's languages are in thousands, which means that for the vast majority of existing languages, parallel data are not available easily, or not available at all.

A common feature of language that is not usually exploited in main-stream MT, is interlingual word similarity. Typically, the systems treat the source language words and the target language words completely independently, usually by representing each word with a unique identifier, with source word identifiers and target word identifiers belonging to different domains. Only in case of out-of-vocabulary source words (OOVs), which are not part of the available source language vocabulary and therefore cannot be translated by the system, approaches that do acknowledge potential interlingual word similarity are sometimes applied, such as transliteration by a character-based translation model [4]; although, in most cases, OOVs are simply left untranslated.[2]

In our work, we create a data-driven MT system for very close languages, based on utilizing only monolingual corpora and a set of heuristics with a high level of language independence. In this way, we target languages which are very low on available resources: the only resource we require for both the source and the target language is a plain-text monolingual corpus, i.e. any text written in that language (even a short one). Arguably, this is the lowest possible requirement to perform any text-based processing of a language: at least a textual input must be available, otherwise there is nothing to process. The key assumption behind our approach is that corresponding words often have the following two properties:

- They are similar on the character level, i.e. the string similarity of the source word and the corresponding target word is often high.

- They appear in the language with a similar frequency, i.e. the frequency of the source word in a source language corpus and the frequency of the target word in a target language corpus is usually similar.

While these assumptions obviously do not hold in general, we believe that they are mostly valid in case of very close languages (such as Czech and Slovak or Danish and Norwegian, which we use in our evaluation).

Our general approach to translating a given source language word is to look through all of the target words present in our corpus, and to return the most similar one

---

[1] http://opus.lingfil.uu.se/

[2] This can also be understood as a very rough way of acknowledging interlingual word similarity, in the sense that it is implicitly assumed that the unknown source word may happen to be also used in the target language in an identical form. This assumption may often be true, especially in case of named entities, which constitute a major share of OOVs. Still, even in such cases, transliteration or similar transformations may be necessary to obtain the correct target word form.

as the most probable translation, based on the two dimensions of similarity noted above and described in detail in Section 3.

In practice, an exhaustive search over the full target vocabulary is not viable. Therefore, we introduce a number of heuristics to speed up the search, and describe the whole translation process, in Section 4.

In Section 5.1, we evaluate MonoTrans instrinsically with BLEU [12]. As could be expected, our method delivers a very low quality translation, far beyond the best reported translation scores for the evaluated language pairs. However, our focus is on scenarios where none of the better-performing approaches are applicable, as neither parallel data nor a rule-based translation system are available. In that regard, the only baseline for us is to leave the text untranslated, which we surpass by large margins.

The quality of MonoTrans translation is too low to be useful when targeting humans; moreover, for a speaker of the target language, a similar close language is typically partially intelligible even without translation. In fact, it is exactly this partial cross-lingual intelligibility of similar languages, common with humans but generally inaccessible to machines, that we want to simulate with Mono-Trans. We focus on the task of cross-lingual transfer of trained NLP tools, namely part-of-speech (POS) taggers and dependency parsers, where even a low-quality translation can provide the tools with a partial understanding of an unknown language and allow them to be applied to that language, even if their performance will inevitably be low. We evaluate MonoTrans extrinsically in this setup in Section 5.2.

2 Related Work

While being a stranger in data-driven machine translation, interlingual word similarity has often been utilized in rule-based MT, in particular when translating between similar languages. While rule-based MT has generally been superseded by statistical MT, a number of fully rule-based or hybrid[3] machine translation systems do exist, such as Apertium [5]; for an overview of MT systems for related languages, see e.g. [20]. Moreover, when focusing on special classes of words, such as technical terminology, systematic interlingual word similarity can be exploited even across very distant languages, such as Czech and English, as investigated already in [7]. However, these systems still require sets of language-specific rules, large bilingual dictionaries, and/or parallel corpora, to perform the end-to-end translation. To the best of our knowledge, devising a machine translation system for such a low-resource setting is rather unique.

The somewhat solitary work of Irvine and Callison-Burch [6] does go extraordinarily far in a similar direction to ours, estimating the correspondence of words based on

a large number of predictors, including both orographic similarity and frequency similarity as we do,[4] and also using contextual similarity, temporal similarity, topic similarity, etc. However, most of these predictors rely on at least small amounts of bilingual data, in the form of parallel corpora, bilingual dictionaries, and/or comparable corpora; some also require other meta data, such as segmentation of the data into documents, or a time stamp marking the date of creation of the text. In our work, we omit the predictors which require such additional data, and focus on fine-tuning the two most resource-light predictors instead – the string similarity and the frequency similarity.

There is also a handful of older work attempting to construct a bilingual lexicon and/or to perform machine translation without parallel corpora, most notably by Koehn and Knight [9], Persman and Padó [13], Ravi and Knight [14], and Vulić and Moens [21].

3 Interlingual Word Similarity

The key component of MonoTrans is a word similarity measure, composed of a string similarity sim_{str} and a frequency similarity sim_f; the string similarity is itself composed of a Jaro-Winkler-based similarity sim_{jw*} and a length-based similarity sim_l:

$$sim(w_{src}, w_{tgt}) = sim_{str}(w_{src}, w_{tgt}) \cdot sim_f(w_{src}, w_{tgt})$$
$$sim_{str}(w_{src}, w_{tgt}) = sim_{jw*}(w_{src}, w_{tgt}) \cdot sim_l(w_{src}, w_{tgt})$$

(1)

where w_{src} and w_{tgt} are the source and target word, respectively. The following subsections provide detailed descriptions of each of these components.

3.1 Jaro-Winkler-Based Similarity

Our string similarity measure is based on the Jaro-Winkler (JW) similarity [22], which has an interesting property of giving more importance to the beginnings of the strings than to their ends. This nicely suits our setting, as in flective languages, most of the inflection usually happens at the end of the word, while the beginning of the word tends to carry more of the lexical meaning. Thus, we expect the JW similarity to give more weight to the similarity of the meanings of the words than to the particular inflected forms in which they appear.[5]

However, JW similarity does not account for a number phenomena that are common in interlingual word similarity. We believe the following two to be of the highest importance:

---

[3] A hybrid MT system is a system which combines rule-based and statistical components.

[4] Interestingly, the authors seem to use a measure of frequency similarity very close to ours, although the provided formula (4) seems to be inverted by mistake, measuring frequency *dissimilarity* instead.

[5] From another perspective, we could say that JW similarity implicitly performs a simple soft stemming of its arguments.

- diacritical marks tend to be cross-lingually inconsistent, and languages are usually intelligible even when diacritics are stripped from the text,

- consonants tend to carry more meaning than vowels and tend to be more cross-lingually consistent.

Therefore, we introduce two preprocessing steps that can be employed to simplify the word forms before the computation of the JW similarity: transliteration to ASCII, and devowelling.

The **transliteration to ASCII**, provided by the `unidecode` Python module,[6] maps all characters into ASCII, trying to replace each non-ASCII character by one "near what a human with a US keyboard would choose". However, it does not handle non-alphabetic scripts, such as Chinese or Japanese. We denote transliteration of a word w by $T(w)$.

The **devowelling** strips all vowel characters, i.e. all characters that, after transliteration to ASCII, belong to the following group: a, e, i, o, u, y. We denote devowelling of a word w by $D(w)$.

The JW-based similarity sim_{jw*} is then computed as a multiplication of several components:

$$sim_{jw*}(w_{src}, w_{tgt}) = \prod_{J \in \{jw, jwT, jwD, jwDT\}} sim_J(w_{src}, w_{tgt}) \quad (2)$$

The first component, sim_{jw}, is the JW similarity without any preprocessing. However, as it is undefined for empty words (ε), we modify it slightly:

$$sim_{jw}(w_{src}, w_{tgt}) = \begin{cases} \frac{1}{1+len(w_{src})} & \text{if } w_{tgt} = \varepsilon \\ \frac{1}{1+len(w_{tgt})} & \text{if } w_{src} = \varepsilon \quad (3) \\ sim'_{jw}(w_{src}, w_{tgt}) & \text{otherwise} \end{cases}$$

where $len(w)$ is the number of characters in word w, and sim'_{jw} is the Jaro-Winkler similarity provided by the `pyjarowinkler` Python module.[7][8]

The following components are the JW similarity of transliterated words (sim_{jwT}), the JW similarity of devowelled words (sim_{jwD}), and the JW similarity of transliterated and devowelled words (sim_{jwDT}):

$$sim_{jwT}(w_{src}, w_{tgt}) = sim_{jw}(T(w_{src}), T(w_{tgt}))$$
$$sim_{jwD}(w_{src}, w_{tgt}) = sim_{jw}(D(w_{src}), D(w_{tgt}))$$
$$sim_{jwDT}(w_{src}, w_{tgt}) = sim_{jw}(D(T(w_{src})), D(T(w_{tgt})))$$
$$(4)$$

3.2 Length-Based Similarity

A target word that is significantly shorter or longer than a given source word is unlikely to be its translation; however, we found that the Jaro-Winkler similarity for such a

---

[6] https://pypi.python.org/pypi/Unidecode

[7] https://pypi.python.org/pypi/pyjarowinkler

[8] Interestingly, the module method `get_jaro_distance` does *not* provide the Jaro-Winkler *distance* d_{jw}, but the Jaro-Winkler *similarity* $1 - d_{jw}$; i.e., a value of 1 corresponds to identical strings, and the value of 0 to completely dissimilar strings.

pair of words is often too high. Therefore, we introduce an additional penalty for words that differ in length:

$$sim'_l(w_{src}, w_{tgt}) = \frac{1}{1 + L \cdot |len(w_{src}) - len(w_{tgt})|} \quad (5)$$

where $len(w)$ is the length of word w. The length importance L is used to put less weight on length similarity than on the other string similarity components; we use $L = 0.2$.

The length similarity is computed both on the original words as well as on their devowelled variants:

$$sim_l = sim'_l(w_{src}, w_{tgt}) \cdot sim'_l(D(w_{src}), D(w_{tgt})) \quad (6)$$

3.3 Frequency Similarity

We expect corresponding words to appear with a similar frequency in the monolingual corpora. Of course, one of them may be several times more frequent than the other, but their frequencies should be similar at least in orders of magnitude. Thus, we compare the logarithms of the frequencies to calculate the similarity:

$$sim'_f(w_{src}, w_{tgt}) = \frac{1}{1 + |log(f_{w_{src}}) - log(f_{w_{tgt}})|} \quad (7)$$

The occurrence frequencies are computed from the monolingual corpora:

$$f_{w_{corpus}} = \frac{count_{corpus}(w) + S}{size_{corpus}} \quad (8)$$

using a smoothing factor S that allows us to output, with a low probability, even unknown words; we use $S = 0.1$.

Such a measure seems to be appropriate for corpora of similar sizes. However, if one of the corpora is significantly smaller than the other, the frequencies of words in the smaller corpus are somewhat boosted due to the smaller number of word types appearing in the corpus among which the total mass is distributed. Therefore, we downscale the frequencies computed on the smaller corpus by upscaling its size used in (8):

$$size_A = \begin{cases} |A| \cdot \sqrt{\frac{|B|}{|A|}} & \text{if } |A| < |B| \\ |A| & \text{otherwise} \end{cases} \quad (9)$$

where $|X|$ denotes the number of words in the corpus X.

We found that the definition of frequency similarity in (7) does a good job in removing many bad target language candidates; usually these are very infrequent words that are by chance string-wise similar to the source word. However, we also found that it inappropriately boosts target words with a low similarity to the source word that by chance have an extremely similar frequency. Thus, we need to keep the similarity harsh for low values, but soften it for high values. Therefore, if the value of sim'_f is higher than a threshold T_f, we push the part of it which is above the threshold down, by multiplying it by a decay factor D_f:

$$sim_f = \begin{cases} T_f + D_f \cdot (sim'_f - T_f) & \text{if } sim'_f > T_f \\ sim'_f & \text{otherwise} \end{cases} \quad (10)$$

We use $T_f = 0.5$ and $D_f = 0.1$.

3.4 Discussion

While the similarity measure we use is intended to be language-independent, we do acknowledge that it was hand-tuned particularly on the Czech-Slovak language pair, as the authors have a strong knowledge of both of these languages, and may not be fully adequate for all language pairs. In particular, we expect it to work best for flective languages with a preference for word-final inflection. For an optimal performance, it should be hand-tuned or machine-tuned on a more diverse set of languages.

The transliteration component is useless for languages that only use ASCII characters. Moreover, due to its implementation, it cannot handle non-alphabetic languages, such as Chinese or Japanese.

Also, we fail to identify systematic differences in the languages, such as "w" in Polish consistently corresponding to "v" in Czech or Slovak. We believe that the method would highly benefit from being able to find such correspondences automatically in the monolingual data, e.g. by exploring the distributions of character unigrams or n-grams, and/or by employing an EM-like approach to find a likely mapping.

Finally, the measure completely ignores the fact that words with similar meanings can be expected to appear in similar contexts. While reflecting on that fact would most probably make the computation of the similarity much more complicated and slower, it could allow the method to detect even corresponding words that are dissimilar according to the string similarity measures. A more viable approach could be to at least account for the fact that a given target word is likely to appear in similar target contexts, as mediated e.g. by a language model.

4 The Translation System

The MonoTrans translation system consists of two components: a training component, and a translation component.

The **training component** creates a pair of word frequency lists, based on source and target monolingual corpora. Any monolingual corpora can be used for the training, with larger corpora leading to better results. The frequency similarity measure works more reliably when the source and target corpora are of similar sizes, at least in orders of magnitude. However, if the source language is very low on available resources, the input text to be translated can by itself also serve as the only source corpus.

The **translation component** then performs a word-based 1:1 monotone translation, trying to translate each source word by the most similar target word from the target word list, based on the similarity measure described in the previous section. The translation of each word is performed independently.

4.1 Computational Efficiency

In theory, for each input source word, the translation component could always go through all target words in the target language word list, measure the similarity of the source word and each candidate target word, and then emit the most similar target word as the translation.

However, this is only feasible in cases where the target word list is very small, containing hundreds or at most thousands of words, allowing us to translate each source word in a matter of seconds at most. Once the target word list goes into tens of thousands of words and beyond (which it usually does in our experiments), the translation times become far too long for an exhaustive search to be practical.

Therefore, we introduce a range of heuristics and technical measures, both lossless and lossy, to sufficiently speed up the translation process while trying to keep the translation quality as high as possible. We describe the most important two of them in the following subsections; we also use other less interesting measures, such as caching of method calls.

4.2 Word List Partitioning

The main speedup comes from a hard partitioning of the word lists, which is the only lossy procedure we employ. Following our observations in Section 3, we assume that for a pair of corresponding source and target words:

- the lengths of the devowelled transliterated words differ by at most 1,

- the first two characters of the devowelled transliterated words are identical.

None of these assumptions hold universally, but we believe that they do hold for a vast majority of words that can be translated by our system (i.e. words that are sufficiently similar to their target counterparts). Most importantly, they let us only go through a tiny part of the target word list when translating a source word, bringing a key speedup to the translation system.

Thus, instead of using a flat word list, the training component stores each word in a specific partition, addressed by a compound key, consisting of the first two transliterated consonants of the word and the length of the transliterated devowelled word. The translation component then only traverses three of these partitions, corresponding to the first two transliterated consonants of the source word and the length of the transliterated devowelled source word, increased by +1, 0, and -1.

4.3 Frequency-Based Early Stopping

Even after the partitioning, many of the partitions are too large to be traversed exhaustively for each matching source word. We can deal with that issue thanks to the following two observations:

- word frequency similarity is a powerful component of our similarity measure,

- words in a language have a Zipf-like distribution, with a small number of frequent words and a high number of rare words.

Therefore, we can achieve a significant speedup by ordering the words in each partition descendingly by frequency, and introducing the following early-stopping criterion: once we reach a target word so infrequent that its frequency-based similarity to the source word alone is lower than the total similarity of the most similar target word found so far, we can stop processing the current partition, as none of the remaining target words would be able to surpass the currently best candidate; i.e., we stop once:

$$f_{w'_{tgt}} < f_{w_{src}} \wedge sim_f(w_{src}, w'_{tgt}) < sim(w_{src}, w^*_{tgt}) \quad (11)$$

where w'_{tgt} is the current target word candidate, and w^*_{tgt} is the best target word found so far.

As we, by definition, encounter frequent words more frequently than rare words, this allows us to often skip the processing of the long tail of infrequent words; it only gets processed if the source word is a rare one, or if it is not sufficiently similar to any of the frequent target words.

5 Evaluation

In this section, we evaluate MonoTrans both intrinsically and extrinsically. However, for the real under-resourced languages with no parallel data and no annotated corpora available, there is no way for us to perform an automatic evaluation, and a manual evaluation would be difficult to obtain for us. Therefore, as is usual in these scenarios, we simulate the under-resourced setting by evaluating on pairs of similar but resource-rich languages, allowing us to use standard automatic evaluation measures. Specifically, we use the following language groups in our experiments:

- Czech (cs) and Slovak (sk),
- Danish (da), Norwegian (no) and Swedish (sv),
- Catalan (ca) and Spanish (es).

Please note that we hand-tuned our method partially based on brief manual inspections of the results on the sk-cs pair.

5.1 Instrinsic Evaluation

We first evaluate the quality of the MonoTrans translation itself with BLEU [12]. We use the OpenSubtitles2016 subcorpus of the Opus collection [10], which contains translated movie subtitles from the OpenSubtitles website.[9] We

---

[9]http://www.opensubtitles.org/

Table 1: Evaluation of MonoTrans with BLEU.

Langs	SrcLex	MonoTrans	Rel.diff.
cs-sk	10.1	13.1	30%
sk-cs	10.1	14.8	46%
da-no	16.8	18.3	8%
sv-no	7.7	14.7	90%
no-da	16.6	17.7	7%
no-sv	7.7	12.5	63%
ca-es	5.5	8.3	51%
es-ca	5.4	7.9	46%
AVG	**10.0**	**13.4**	**43%**

Table 2: Evaluation of MonoTrans with BLEU, using large monolingual corpora for training.

Langs	SrcLex	MonoTrans	Rel.diff.
cs-sk	10.1	15.6	55%
sk-cs	10.1	17.1	70%
AVG	**10.1**	**16.4**	**62%**

use the first 10,000 target sentences and the last 10,000 source sentences for training, and then evaluate the source-to-target translation quality on the last 10,000 sentences; i.e. the source side of the evaluation data is used for training, but the target side, which serves as the reference translation, is not.

Table 1 shows the BLEU scores achieved by MonoTrans, compared to the SrcLex baseline, i.e. to performing no translation at all; thanks to the high similarity of the languages, even the baseline achieves a non-trivial translation score. The BLEU scores are rather low, reaching 13.4 on average, whereas a state-of-the-art MT system trained on large amounts of parallel data could easily reach scores around 30 BLEU points (or probably even more, provided that the source and target languages are very similar). However, we can see a large and consistent improvement over the baseline of 3.4 BLEU points in average. We also report the relative improvement over the baseline which, thanks to the very low scores achieved by the baseline, is very high, reaching up to 90% (for sv-no) and 43% on average.

Generally, we do not expect very large corpora to be available for under-resourced languages. Still, to measure the scaling potential of our method, we also evaluated MonoTrans trained on significantly larger Czech and Slovak monolingual corpora. For this experiment, we used large web corpora, namely CWC for Czech [16] and sk-TenTen for Slovak [3]. We used the first 100 millions of words from each of the corpora for training, i.e. roughly a thousand times larger datasets, and then evaluated the translation system on the same OpenSubtitles data as in the previous experiments.

The results in Table 2 show that increasing the data size improves the translation quality, with the improvement over the SrcLex baseline being nearly doubled. However, considering the factor by which we increased the training data size, we find the improvement to be rather moderate.

Table 3: Evaluation of MonoTrans with BLEU, using smaller corpora for training; "0" corresponds to SrcLex, "10,000" is identical to Table 1.

Training sentences	cs-sk	sk-cs
0	10.1	10.1
10	10.0	10.0
100	11.3	11.4
1,000	12.4	12.3
10,000	13.1	14.8

Table 4: Examples of outputs of the Czech–Slovak and Slovak–Czech translation.

Language	Text
sk source	Mal ho len vystrašiť aby ho udržal mlčať.
cs transl.	Měl ho loni vystrašit aby ho udržel mlčet.
cs correct	Měl ho **jen** vystrašit aby ho udržel mlčet.
sk source	Počúvaj, nemám rád prípady, ako je tento, ale som vďačný za to, že ste ho chytili.
cs transl.	**Počkají**, nemám rád případy, **ako** je tento, ale **sám** vděčný za to, že **set** ho chytili.
cs correct	**Poslouchej**, nemám rád případy, **jako** je tento, ale **jsem** vděčný za to, že **jste** ho chytili.
cs source	Když zemřela, neměla jsem chuť o tom mluvit.
sk transl.	**Kde** zomrela, nemala **jsem** chuť o tom **milovať'**.
sk correct	**Keď** zomrela, nemala **som** chuť o tom **hovoriť'**.

Table 5: Evaluation of MonoTrans in cross-lingual POS tagger transfer, using tagging accuracy.

Langs	SrcLex	MonoTrans	Supervised	Err.red.
cs-sk	78.0	82.7	94.1	29%
sk-cs	70.9	76.7	98.3	21%
da-no	76.8	78.3	97.0	8%
sv-no	64.7	72.8	97.0	25%
no-da	78.7	80.4	95.5	10%
no-sv	56.0	72.6	95.1	42%
ca-es	76.7	78.1	96.2	7%
es-ca	69.9	81.1	98.0	40%
AVG	**71.5**	**77.8**	**96.4**	**23%**

Table 6: Evaluation of MonoTrans in cross-lingual parser transfer, using LAS.

Langs	SrcLex	MonoTrans	Supervised	Err.red.
cs-sk	46.6	56.3	68.7	44%
sk-cs	35.9	42.9	73.1	19%
da-no	45.8	49.0	79.4	9%
sv-no	30.2	40.0	79.4	20%
no-da	46.3	48.7	71.4	10%
no-sv	24.0	41.7	69.4	39%
ca-es	44.4	48.2	77.4	11%
es-ca	39.5	51.3	80.3	29%
AVG	**39.1**	**47.3**	**74.9**	**23%**

Next, we tried to downscale the training data instead, training and evaluating the system identically to Table 1 but using only a part of the training data. Table 3 shows that already with 100 monolingual non-corresponding sentences for each of the languages, i.e. very modest data, improvements of over +1 BLEU over the non-translation baseline can be achieved.

Finally, in Table 4, we show several examples of the inputs and outputs of the MonoTrans system, taken from the evaluation datasets translated by the systems trained on the large datasets; the "correct" translation is not the reference translation, but a corrected version of the MonoTrans output, and errors are highlighted. We can see many correctly translated words in the outputs, as well as many words correctly left untranslated. Moreover, many of the errors can be easily accounted to the word list partitioning that we employ, making it impossible for MonoTrans to perform translations such as "len–jen", "som–jsem", or "počúvaj–poslouchej". This suggests that many of the errors are actually search errors, not scoring errors, and could be eliminated if we had a better way of efficiently searching for candidate target translations.

5.2 Extrinsic Evaluation

We also evaluated MonoTrans extrinsically, in the task of cross-lingual transfer of trained NLP models across closely related languages, inspired by the cross-lingual parsing shared task of the VarDial 2017 workshop [23].

The task constitutes of using an annotated corpus of a resource-rich source language to train an NLP model in such a way that it can be applied to analyzing a different but very similar resource-poor target language.

We loosely follow the approach of Tiedemann et al. [19], proceeding in the following steps:

- Translate the words in an annotated source corpus into the target language by an MT system.

- Train a lexicalized model on the resulting corpus.

- Apply the model to target language data.

Specifically, we employ the Universal Dependencies (UD) v1.4 treebanks [11] as the annotated data, MonoTrans as the translation tool, and the UDPipe tagger and parser [17] as the models to be trained.

The MonoTrans system is trained using the word forms from the training part of the source treebank and the development part of the target treebank, and applied to translate the training part of the source treebank into the target language. Then, the UDPipe tagger and parser are trained on the resulting corpus; the tagger is trained to predict the Universal POS tag (UPOS) based on the word form, and the parser is trained to predict the labelled dependency tree based on the word form and the UPOS tag predicted by the tagger. Finally, both the tagger and the parser are applied to the development part of the target language treebank, and evaluated against its gold-standard annotation.

We report the tagger accuracy in Table 5, and the parser LAS[10] in Table 6. As a baseline, we also include SrcLex, i.e. using a tagger and parser trained on an untranslated source treebank, and as an upper bound, we include a supervised tagger and parser, trained on the training part of the target treebank; as the languages are very similar, the baselines are quite strong. This allows us to also compute the error reduction, i.e. the proportion of the gap between the baseline and the upper bound filled by our method.

The taggers reach an average accuracy of 77.8% and the parsers an average LAS of 47.3%, which is not much in absolute terms – when large parallel data are available, LAS scores around 60% can be reached. However, in relative terms, the scores are rather impressive, obtaining an average 23% error reduction in both the tagging and the parsing, and reaching average absolute improvements of +6.3 in tagging accuracy and +8.2 in parsing LAS. Given our setting, we find the results to be wonderful, provided that we only used small monolingual corpora to train the MT system; in fact, in the target language, we only used the evaluation input data, which is probably the lowest imaginable data requirement.

6 Further Possible Improvements

6.1 Language Model Scoring

As we mentioned in Section 3.4, a clear shortcoming of our method is the fact that the translation is performed in a context-independent way. Employing an n-gram language model is a standard way of getting better machine translation outputs, only plaintext target-language data are needed to create one, and there already exists a plethora of state-of-the-art ready-to-use language modelling tools. Therefore, it may seem straightforward to employ a language model in MonoTrans as well.

However, there is a range of technical issues that need to be overcome. If we were able to generate a translation lexicon, we could then even easily plug it into a full-fledged MT system, such as Moses, easily combining it with a language model; however, generating the lexicon would be computationally prohibitive in our case, for reasons mentioned in Section 4.1. At best, we could potentially try to generate a translation lexicon only for the words that appear in the test data. Moreover, even using a beam search in MonoTrans decoding is too costly for us, as it prohibits the employment of the early stopping mechanisms.

So far, we have only managed to perform a set of preliminary experiments, adding a simple trigram language model and using its score as an additional scoring component; as we found that using the score directly had a too strong and negative effect on the translations, we weaken it by taking its fourth root. When evaluated on the large Czech and Slovak corpora in both directions, we observed

only negligible improvements around +0.1 BLEU. We believe that this is mainly due to the fact that our approach in these preliminary experiments was too rough and simplistic, and that with proper tuning and a more sophisticated implementation, clear improvements may be gained.

6.2 Better Searching for Candidate Translations

Based on inspection of the translation outputs, as well as from the examples in Table 4, it is clear that the word list partitioning is way too crude, preventing the system from generating the correct translation in many cases, even though its similarity to the source word is sufficiently high. On the other hand, it is completely impossible for the system to search through all possible translations, and some kind of harsh pruning of the search space is vital.

As a quick remedy, we tried to use the trigram language model to generate additional translation candidates. Specifically, for each source word we also investigated N candidate translations taken from N words that are, according to the language model, the most likely to follow the words selected as translations of the previous words. With $N = 20$, we observed a promising improvement of +0.6 BLEU for cs-sk, while the translation times remained competitive (they doubled). With $N = 1000$, the improvement for sk-cs further jumped to +1.3 BLEU; however, at this point, the translation became about 50 times slower (taking 10 hours to translate 10,000 sentences), showing that this approach is somewhat promising in terms of translation quality but too computationally demanding. For sk-cs, negligible or no improvements were observed.

An interesting possibility of clustering the search space which was suggested to us is to use a standard clustering algorithm, such as k-means or hierarchical k-means, with the word similarity used as the distance of the target words. This is expected to be permissibly fast to compute as well as to allow a sufficiently fast search for translation candidates; however, due to time constraints, we have not been able to design an experiment to test that.

7 Conclusion

We presented MonoTrans, a data-driven translation system trained only on plaintext monolingual corpora, intended for low-quality machine translation between very similar languages in a low-resource scenario.

We showed that even with very small training corpora available, the system shows respectable performance according to both intrinsic and extrinsic evaluation, consistently surpassing the no-translation baseline by large margins. Moreover, we showed that the system performance scales with larger training data, even though rather slowly.

In particular, when evaluated extrinsically as a component of cross-lingual tagger and parser transfer, employing MonoTrans leads to high improvements in both tagging accuracy and parser LAS with respect to the baselines, achieving an average 23% error reduction in both of

---

[10]Labelled Attachment Score, i.e. the number of correctly predicted labelled dependency relations in the output tree.

the tasks when supervised models are taken as the upper bounds.

Acknowledgments

This work has been supported by the grant No. DG16P02B048 of the Ministry of Culture of the Czech Republic, the grant No. CZ.02.1.01/0.0/0.0/16_013/0001781 of the Ministry of Education, Youth and Sports of the Czech Republic, and the SVV 260 453 grant. This work has been using language resources and tools developed, stored and distributed by the LINDAT/CLARIN project of the Ministry of Education, Youth and Sports of the Czech Republic (project LM2015071). We would also like to thank the anonymous reviewers and our colleagues from the ÚFAL MT group (especially Jindřich Libovický) for helpful comments and suggestions for improvement.

References

[1] Dzmitry Bahdanau, Kyunghyun Cho, and Yoshua Bengio. Neural machine translation by jointly learning to align and translate. *arXiv preprint arXiv:1409.0473*, 2014.

[2] Peter Brown, John Cocke, S Della Pietra, V Della Pietra, Frederick Jelinek, Robert Mercer, and Paul Roossin. A statistical approach to language translation. In *COLING*, pages 71–76. Association for Computational Linguistics, 1988.

[3] Masaryk University NLP Centre. skTenTen, 2011. LINDAT/CLARIN digital library at the Institute of Formal and Applied Linguistics, Charles University.

[4] Nadir Durrani, Hassan Sajjad, Hieu Hoang, and Philipp Koehn. Integrating an unsupervised transliteration model into statistical machine translation. In *EACL*, volume 14, pages 148–153, 2014.

[5] Mikel L Forcada, Mireia Ginestí-Rosell, Jacob Nordfalk, Jim O'Regan, Sergio Ortiz-Rojas, Juan Antonio Pérez-Ortiz, Felipe Sánchez-Martínez, Gema Ramírez-Sánchez, and Francis M Tyers. Apertium: a free/open-source platform for rule-based machine translation. *Machine translation*, 25(2):127–144, 2011.

[6] Ann Irvine and Chris Callison-Burch. End-to-end statistical machine translation with zero or small parallel texts. *Journal of Natural Language Engineering*, 22:517–548, 2016.

[7] Zdeněk Kirschner. On a device in dictionary operations in machine translation. In *COLING*, COLING '82, pages 157–160, Czechoslovakia, 1982. Academia Praha.

[8] Philipp Koehn, Hieu Hoang, Alexandra Birch, Chris Callison-Burch, Marcello Federico, Nicola Bertoldi, Brooke Cowan, Wade Shen, Christine Moran, Richard Zens, et al. Moses: Open source toolkit for statistical machine translation. In *ACL*, pages 177–180. Association for Computational Linguistics, 2007.

[9] Philipp Koehn and Kevin Knight. Learning a translation lexicon from monolingual corpora. In *ULA*, ULA '02, pages 9–16, Stroudsburg, PA, USA, 2002. Association for Computational Linguistics.

[10] Pierre Lison and Jörg Tiedemann. Opensubtitles2016: Extracting large parallel corpora from movie and tv subtitles. In *LREC*, 2016.

[11] Joakim Nivre et al. Universal dependencies 1.4, 2016. LINDAT/CLARIN digital library at the Institute of Formal and Applied Linguistics, Charles University.

[12] Kishore Papineni, Salim Roukos, Todd Ward, and Wei-Jing Zhu. Bleu: a method for automatic evaluation of machine translation. In *ACL*, pages 311–318. Association for Computational Linguistics, 2002.

[13] Yves Peirsman and Sebastian Padó. Cross-lingual induction of selectional preferences with bilingual vector spaces. In *HLT-NAACL*, HLT '10, pages 921–929, Stroudsburg, PA, USA, 2010. Association for Computational Linguistics.

[14] Sujith Ravi and Kevin Knight. Deciphering foreign language. In *ACL-HLT*, HLT '11, pages 12–21, Stroudsburg, PA, USA, 2011. Association for Computational Linguistics.

[15] Rico Sennrich, Orhan Firat, Kyunghyun Cho, Alexandra Birch, Barry Haddow, Julian Hitschler, Marcin Junczys-Dowmunt, Samuel Läubli, Antonio Valerio Miceli Barone, Jozef Mokry, et al. Nematus: A toolkit for neural machine translation. *EACL 2017*, page 65, 2017.

[16] Johanka Spoustová and Miroslav Spousta. A high-quality web corpus of Czech. In Nicoletta Calzolari (Conference Chair), Khalid Choukri, Thierry Declerck, Mehmet Uğur Doğan, Bente Maegaard, Joseph Mariani, Asuncion Moreno, Jan Odijk, and Stelios Piperidis, editors, *LREC*, Istanbul, Turkey, may 2012. European Language Resources Association (ELRA).

[17] Milan Straka, Jan Hajič, and Jana Straková. UDPipe: trainable pipeline for processing CoNLL-U files performing tokenization, morphological analysis, pos tagging and parsing. In *LREC*, Paris, France, May 2016. European Language Resources Association (ELRA).

[18] Jörg Tiedemann. Parallel data, tools and interfaces in OPUS. In *LREC*, volume 2012, pages 2214–2218, 2012.

[19] Jörg Tiedemann, Željko Agić, and Joakim Nivre. Treebank translation for cross-lingual parser induction. In *CoNLL*, 2014.

[20] Jernej Vičič, Vladislav Kuboň, and Petr Homola. Česílko goes open-source. *The Prague Bulletin of Mathematical Linguistics*, 107(1):57–66, 2017.

[21] Ivan Vulic and Marie-Francine Moens. A study on bootstrapping bilingual vector spaces from non-parallel data (and nothing else). In *EMNLP*, pages 1613–1624. ACL, 2013.

[22] William E. Winkler. String comparator metrics and enhanced decision rules in the fellegi-sunter model of record linkage. In *Proceedings of the Section on Survey Research Methods (American Statistical Association)*, pages 354–359, 1990.

[23] Marcos Zampieri, Shervin Malmasi, Nikola Ljubešić, Preslav Nakov, Ahmed Ali, Jörg Tiedemann, Yves Scherrer, and Noëmi Aepli. Findings of the VarDial evaluation campaign 2017. In *VarDial*, Valencia, Spain, 2017.

"W3-ChaT" — WWW — Challenges and Trends (W3-ChaT 2017)

The W3-ChaT workshop is focused on addressing existing challenges we are facing today on the Web (and in general on Internet). Solution of such challenges are crucial to support/improve smooth experience of users with the Web as well their decision making. Web challenges are strongly associated with intelligent algorithms of various kind and purpose acting as clever solutions simplifying many tasks such that mining users' data and relevant data sources with associated semantics, extracting users' contexts and predicting their interests leading to improved data providers, user experience and semantics as proper knowledge representations.

Workshop Program Committee

Milan Dojchinovski, ČVUT Praha
László Grad-Gyenge, Creo Group, Budapest
Tomáš Horváth, ELTE Budapest
Tomáš Kliegr, VŠE Praha
Jaroslav Kuchař, ČVUT Praha
András Micsik, MTA SZTAKI, Budapest
Ladislav Peska, UK Praha
Tomáš Vitvar, CVUT Praha
Peter Vojtáš, UK Praha

J. Hlaváčová (Ed.): ITAT 2017 Proceedings, pp. 210–217
ISBN 978-1974274741, © 2017 L. Grad-Gyenge

On the Optimal Setting of Spreading Activation Parameters to Calculate Recommendations on the Knowledge Graph

László Grad-Gyenge

Eötvös Loránd University, Budapest, Hungary
laszlo.grad-gyenge@inf.elte.hu,
WWW home page: http://laszlo.grad-gyenge.com

Abstract: This paper presents the analysis on the optimal settings of the spreading parameters of the spreading activation technique. The method is applied on the knowledge graph, an information representation technique that combines collaborative and content-based information. The evaluation of the recommendation technique is based on recommendation lists. The involved measures are precision, recall and normalized discounted cumulative gain. The numerical experiments are conducted on the MovieLens 1M dataset. The evaluation results show that spreading activation delivers a stable performance regarding to the evaluation measures over different parameter settings. The quality of the recommendations degrade in the case, the method parameters are set to extreme values.

1 Introduction

As discussed in detail by Grad-Gyenge et al. [1], in contrast to the paradigm of user preference, the paradigm of relatedness provides a more general and effective approach to the design and development of the recommendation algorithms. The essence of the paradigm is to focus on the relations between the entities of the recommendation scenario instead of involving models emphasizing the user item interactions. The primary outcome of the application of the paradigm is the potential to involve transitivity into the recommendation techniques. Transitivity is one possibility to define the relation between the users and the recommended items in a more general way.

The application of spreading activation in the field of recommender systems is an illustrative example of the utilization of the paradigm. The method is applied on the knowledge graph [2], which is a general information representation technique. The entities of the recommendation scenario and also the relatations between them are generalized. The users, items and their attribute values are represented with nodes. User preferences on items and content based information are represented with edges. The transitive relation in this case means the possibilty to involve paths of heterogeneous types between two nodes. The advantage of the paradigm is that it does not restrict the type of the individual edges on the path between two nodes, thus the relations between the entities can be treated as generalized and transitive.

The past research on the evaluation of spreading activation to generate recommendations showed its potential.

Although the optimal parameter settings of the method should have been further investigated. In order to fill this gap, this paper presents the results of our numerical experiments conducted to identify the optimal values for the relax parameters of the technique. Our results show that the method delivers a stable performance regarding the different parameter settings. The quality of the recommendations calculated by the method become low if the relax parameters are set to extreme values.

The rest of the paper is organized as follows. Section 2 discusses the work related to graph based information representation and the application of spreading activation as a recommendation technique. Section 3 presents the representation technique and the dataset the method is evaluated on. Section 4 describes the recommendation technique. Section 5 discusses the evaluation technique and presents the evaluation results. Section 6 concludes the paper and gives insight into our plans for the future.

2 Related Work

Next to matrix factorization methods [3][4][5], the graph based information representation technique has proven its effectiveness. Several research projects utilize the general information representation capability of heterogeneous graphs.

As the state of the art results of the research on recommender systems illustrate, the application of graph based information representation techniques gaining attention nowadays. Graphs are powerful tools of knowledge representation. An example of the involvement of a hybridization technique at the information representation level, Lee at al. [6] introcude a heterogeneous graph based technique to combine collaborative and content based information. Further investigating the topic, Lee et al. [7] analyse the correlations of the entities found in the graph. As the work presented by Tiroshi et al. [8] illustrate, the graph based representation is straightforward technique in the case of modeling social relations.

In addition to ontologies, the involvement of social networks into the recommendation process is an intensively researched field. Typically, there are two classes of the approaches modeling social networks, the asymmetric and the symmetric case. The asymmetric case can be described as the follow and the trust relationships. The symmetric case can be described as the friendship relationship. Influencing results conducted on trust networks are published by Guha et al. [9], Massa et al. [10], Ziegler et al. [11], and Jøsang et al. [12]. Important works calculating recommendations with the help of the social network are published by Guy et al. [13], Konstas et al. [14], and He et al. [15]. The layered graph technique is a typical representation method found in the early works in this field. Kazienko et al. [16] also derive recommendations with the help of this technique. Cantador et al. [17] present a clustering technique based method on the layered graph based representation.

An important feature of the knowledge graph is its capability to represent heterogeneous information. Probably, this is the reason why the technique is intensively researched as the more the involved information sources are, the less the cold start cases occur. Hu et al. [18] generate leads with a label propagation technique. Catherine et al. [19] introduce a probabilistic logic method to calculate recommendations with the help of the knowledge graph. Yu et al. [20] investigate the observed and the potential paths of the knowledge graph. To have a numerical measure, they involve the PathSim measure for path comparison. Kouki et al. [21] describe a hybridization technique with the help of a probabilistic framework. Burke et al. [22] present a recommendation technique based on the k-Nearest Neighbours method applied to various matrices as the user-tag matrix, user-resource matrix, resource-tag matrix and the resource-user matrix.

The spreading activation technique was originally applied to ontologies and is recently involved in different domains to derive recommendations. The primary goal of Hussein et al. is to close the gap between context-awareness and self-adaptation [23]. To perform this task, SPREADR, a spreading activation based recommendation method is defined. Gao et al. [24] propose an ontology based approach to model both user interests and items in the same knowledge base. Jiang et al. [25] define a user model with the help of an ontology and calculate recommendations with the help of the spreading activation. Blanco-Fernandez et al. [26] argue that spreading activation is to be involved to avoid overspecialisation. They present a semantic model of the preferences of the users and apply spreading activation to proceed content based reasoning. Codina et al. [27] define an item score based on the weighted average of concepts related to each other in their model. In their work, they estimate user ratings with a semantic recommendation technique treating it a reasoning method. Troussov et al. [28] investigate decay configurations over a tag aware representation. Alvarez et al. [29] introduce ONTOSPREAD in the field of medical systems.

3 Dataset

3.1 Representation Technique

To represent the data, a graph based technique described by Grad-Gyenge et al [2] is involved. The advantage of this method is its ability to represent various information sources by alloying both collaborative and content based information. The essence of the method is to represent the information in a labeled, heterogeneous graph. Each user and each item is represented with a dedicated node. The explicit or implicit interaction between the users and the items are modeled with relations annotated by the specific type of the interaction. In addition, the content-based information, namely the user and the item attributes are represented with the so-called attribute value nodes. In this case, a dedicated node is created for each attribute value. The node representing the user or item is bound to the specific attribute value node indicating then the particular attribute value. This representation technique leads to a knowledge graph containing heterogeneous information at the informaiton representation level.

The information is represented in a labeled, undirected, weighted graph. The definition of the graph is extended with labels, thus types can be assigned to the nodes and edges of the graph. Although parallel edges are allowed, in practical applications it is recommended to add only one edge per type between two specific nodes in order to reduce the computational complexity. Equation 1 presents the definition of the knowledge graph.

$$\mathscr{K} = (T_n, T_e, N, E, t_n, t_e, r_e), \qquad (1)$$

where T_n stands for the node types, T_e stands for the edge types. N stands for the nodes of the graph. $E \subseteq \{\{u,v\} | u \in N \wedge v \in N \wedge u \neq v\}$ stands for the set of edges, thus the graph is undirected. The function $t_n \subset N \times T_n$ specifies the type of the nodes. The function $t_e \subset E \times T_e$ specifies the type of the edges. The function $r_e \subset E_u \times \mathbb{R}$ specific the rating value of the appropriate edges. The function r_e does not assign rating to all edges of the graph, thus r_e is partial.

3.2 MovieLens

To analyse the performance of the various method configurations, the MovieLens 1M dataset is involved [30]. The advantage of the MovieLens 1M dataset over the other published MovieLens dataset is that in addition to user preferences on items it also contains user and item attributes. This allows us to utilize both the collaborative and content-based information to come to a lower cold start rate than the pure collaborative filtering technique has.

To give an insight into the information representation technique, Figure 1 presents a detailed part of the knowledge graph in the case of the MovieLens 1M dataset. To illustrate the different information source types, the nodes

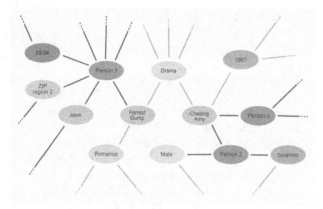

Figure 1: A detailed view of the MovieLens dataset represented in the knowledge graph.

and the relations are coloured to show the type of information they represent.

Colour light blue annotates the items to recommend, i.e., `Jaws`, `Forrest Gump` and `Chasing Amy`. Colour light brown annotates the movie genres, i.e., `Romance` and `Drama`. Colour orange annotates the release year of a movie, i.e., `1997`. Colour lilac annotates the users, i.e., `Person 1`, `Person 2` and `Person 3`. Colour grey annotates the gender of a person, i.e., `Male`. Colour blue annotates the occupation of a person, i.e., `Scientist`. Colour green annotates the ZIP region of a person, i.e., `ZIP region 2`. Colour red annotates the age category, i.e., `25-34`.

In order to represent the users of the recommendation scenario, a node with the appropriate type (`User`) is created in the knowledge graph. The user attribute values are represented with the attribute node technique. For each attribute value, a node of the appropriate type is created and bound to the user with a corresponding edge. The node types introduced in this expriment are as follows.

- Type `Gender` annotates the genders of the users.

- Type `AgeCategory` annotates the age categories.

- Type `Occupation` annotates the occupations.

- Type `ZipCodeRegion` annotates the ZIP code regions. The ZIP code region is derived from the ZIP code by using only its first digit representing the U.S. region.

The user attribute values are bound to the users with edges of the corresponding type. The edge types defined are `PersonGender`, `PersonAgeCategory`, `PersonOccupation` and `PersonZipCodeRegion`, respectively.

Analogously to the user attribute values, the items are represented with a dedicated node of the appropriate type (`Item`) is created in the knowledge graph. The item attribute values are also represented with the attribute node

technique. For each attribute value, a node of the appropriate type is created and bound to the item with a corresponding edge. The node types introduced in this expriment are as follows.

- Type `YearOfRelease` annotates the years of release.

- Type `Genre` annotates the genres. In the case of the MovieLens 1M dataset, multiple genres can be assigned to a movie. It means the a node representing an item can be connected to multiple nodes representing a genre.

The item attribute values are bound to the items with edges of the corresponding type. The edge types defined are `ItemGenre` and `ItemYearOfRelease`, respectively.

The advantage of the MovieLens 1M dataset is that it contains both collaborative and content-based information. The content-based information is described above. The collaborative information in this case is basically the 1 000 209 known user rating events contained in the dataset. Each rating event consists of a user, an item, a preference value and a time-stamp. The preference values are in the $[1,5]$ interval. In the current experiment, a linear normalization is conducted on this value to the $[0.2,1]$ interval.

In order to represent the known rating in the dataset, the edge type `ItemRating` is introduced. Adding a known rating to the knowledge graph means the creation of the edge of the appropriate type (`ItemRating`) between the particular user and item. The concrete value of the rating is assigned to the particular edge by the r_e partial function.

Table 1 presents the amount of information contained in the knowledge graph in two subtables. Table 1a and Table 1b contain the amount of nodes and edges per type, respectively. The knowledge graph contains 10 062 nodes in total. Not counting the edges of type `ItemRating`, the knowledge graph contains 34 451 edges in total.

4   Recommendation Technique

According to Grad-Gyenge et al. [1], the application of spreading activation on the knowledge graph described in Section 3.1 to estimate user preferences on items leads to high quality recommendations. As described in several works in the past [29, 28, 24, 26, 25, 23, 27], spreading activation is an iterative technique to calculate a similarity between a source node and the other nodes of a particular graph. As already discussed by Grad-Gyenge et. al [1], the advantage of the method is that the similarity value incorporates both the distance between two nodes and the parallel paths in between.

As already mentioned, spreading activation is an iterative method. In this experiment, similarly to Grad-Gyenge et al. [1], the iteration is conducted until a pre-specified iteration step (c) limit is reached. The method assigns

Table 1: Count of node and edge types in the MovieLens dataset.

(a) Count of node types.

Node type	Count
Person	6 040
AgeCategory	7
Gender	2
Occupation	21
ZipCodeRegion	10
Item	3 883
Genre	18
YearOfRelease	81

(b) Count of edge types.

Edge type	Count
PersonAgeCategory	6 040
PersonGender	6 040
PersonOccupation	6 040
PersonZipCodeRegion	6 040
ItemGenre	6 408
ItemYearOfRelease	3 883
ItemRating	1 000 209

activation values to the nodes of the graph as defined in Equation 2.

$$a_{(i)} \subset N \times \mathbf{R}, \qquad (2)$$

where a denotes the activation function.

In the initial step of the iteration, the activation of the source node is set to 1 ($a_{(0)}(n_s) = 1$). The source node (n_s) represents the user the recommendations are generated for. The activation of all the other nodes are set to 0 ($a_{(0)}(n) = 0, n \in N, n \neq n_s$).

In each iteration step, the activation of the nodes is maintained. A part of the activation of each node is propagated to its neighbour nodes and a part of the activation of each node is being kept at the node. The distribution of the propagated activation values is conducted based on the weight of the edges. In our case the graph is not weighted, in other words, the edges are weighted basically equally. In order to control the propagation process, two parameters are introduced. The parameter spreading relax (r_s) controls the amount of the distributed activation. The parameter activation relax (r_a) controls the amount of activation kept at each node. The function to maintain the activation of the nodes is defined in Equation (3).

$$a_{(i+1)}(n) = r_a a_{(i)}(n) + r_s \sum_{m \in M_n} \frac{a_{(i)}(m)}{|M_n|}, \qquad (3)$$

where $n \in N$, $i \geq 0$. M_n stands for the neighbour nodes of n. $M_n = \{m | \{m, n\} \in E\}$.

Having the iteration step count (c) reached, the preference value of each node regarding the source node is defined as the value of the activation function.

5 Evaluation

5.1 Evaluation Technique

The methods are evaluated with an iterative process as also described by Grad-Gyenge et al. [2]. Before starting the iteration, all the user preference information is removed from the knowledge graph, thus it contains no edges representing ratings. In the initial step, the knowledge graph is filled with content-based information, meaning that it contains the nodes representing the users, items and their attribute values. The relations between users and user attribute values, items and item attributes values are also present in the knowledge base.

Having the knowledge base initialized, the evaluation process is basically an iteration over the known rating values. This iteration is conducted in an ascending order by the timestamp of the known rating. It also means that the knowledge graph is filled with collaborative information during the evaluation process. Each iteration step consist of the following operations.

1. Generate recommendations with the evaluated method.

2. Record the evaluation measures.

3. Add the known rating to the knowledge graph.

The advantage of this evaluation method is that in the beginning the methods are analysed in a cold start environment. As the knowledge based is being filled with collaborative information, the analsys tends to be conducted in an information dense environment. According to our past experiments [1, 2], in order to represent the problem, the experiments are to be conducted on the first 10 000 known ratings. This is the amount of information, the performance indicators of the methods typically stabilize, thus the methods can be interpreted.

The analysis of the spreading parameters is basically a greedy search method. All the combinations of the r_s and the r_a parameters are evaluated in the interval $[0, 1]$. The fidelity of the analysis is 0.1. The experiment covers all possible combinations of the parameter values and does not restrict to the $r_s + r_a = 1$ cases.

To evaluate the methods, the precision, recall and the nDCG measure is recorded at each evaluation step for a concrete method configuration. The recorded measure values are then averaged and are presented. The measures are calculated on the first 10 items of the list of recommended items. The relevance of an item is defined as follows. If the known rating value of a specific item is 4 or 5 then the item is treated relevant. In other words, relevance is defined as the threshold 0.8 on the normalized rating value.

5.2 Evaluation Results

Figure 2 contains the results of the evaulation in three subfigures. Subfigure 2a, 2b and 2c presents the precision, recall and nDCG of the methods, respectively. On each figure, the horizontal axis represents the setting of the activation relax (r_a) parameter, the vertical axis represents the setting of the spreading relax (r_s) parameter. The color of each cell represents the average value of the respective evaluation measure as also indicated in the legend of the figure.

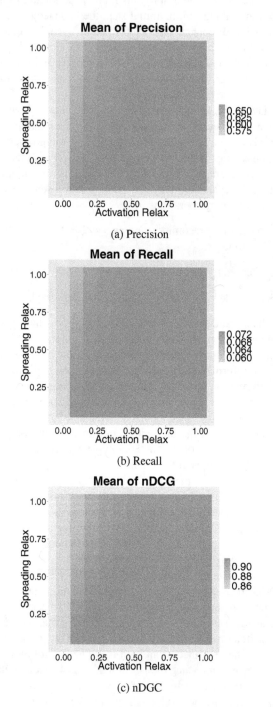

(a) Precision

(b) Recall

(c) nDGC

Figure 2. Evaluation measures at different spreading parameter settings.

In order to easier interpret the results visually, the figures do not present the evaluation measures resulted in the $r_s = 0$ case. This is the case when no recommendation can

be generated as due to the setting of the parameter the activation can not spread from the source node to neighbouring nodes, thus the evaluation measures of these cases are 0. This presentation allows us to investigate the evaluation measures more refined.

The figures show that the low values of r_a lead to a decrease in the recommendation quality. Especially if the setting of r_s is high. Taking a closer look, it can be read from the figures that the difference in the quality occurs from the second or the third digit depending on the concrete evaluation measure. It means that although the quality of the recommendations may decrease in some cases but the method shows a quite stable performance on this dataset. The reason behind this stabily can be found in its network science background. We assume that the fact that the method operates on the network is more important than its actual configuration.

Table 2 presents the result of the evaluation in numbers in its subtables. Subtable 2a, 2b and 2c presents the precision, recall and nDCG values respectively. The columns of the table represent different activation relax (r_a) parameter settings. The rows of the table represent different spreading relax (r_s) parameter settings. The value of each table cell contain the actual value of the appropriate evaluation measure.

The results give a deeper insight into the performance of the methods than the figure based presentation. The table shows that setting the r_s to zero leads to unproducible recommendation lists. Regarding precision and recall, the highest recommendation quality can be achieved by setting r_s to 0.1 and setting r_a to higher than 0.5. It means that in the case of precision and recall, low spreading and high activation values lead to higher performance. Looking at nDCG, the configurations leading to the highets quality for (r_s, r_a) are $(0.4, 0.3)$ and $(0.5, 0.4)$. In this case a less extreme and a more common setting of the parameters can be adequate.

At the macro level, the numerical presentation of the values shows a consistent view to the figure based representation. The results show that the extreme setting of the method configuration parameters (r_s=0) leads to a significant decrease in the recommendation quality. In addition, setting r_a to a low value while setting r_s to a high value is not recommended.

To summarize the results, in the case there is no research capacity available to analyise the optimal setting of the spreading parameters, a good practice can be to set these parameters to a moderate value, e.g., to the mean of the value interval.

6   Conclusion

The paper discusses the analysis of the configuration of the spreading activation method. The technique is applied on the knowledge graph to generate recommendations. Parameters spreading and activation relax are investigated

Table 2. The evaluation measures of the method configuration over various spreading parameter settings.

(a) Precision.

S / A	0.0	0.1	0.2	0.3	0.4	0.5	0.6	0.7	0.8	0.9	1
1.0	0.5592	0.5922	0.6326	0.6495	0.6568	0.6616	0.6655	0.6669	0.6697	0.6716	0.6718
0.9	0.5592	0.5981	0.6370	0.6530	0.6594	0.6642	0.6664	0.6693	0.6715	0.6718	0.6719
0.8	0.5592	0.6042	0.6426	0.6558	0.6616	0.6661	0.6685	0.6714	0.6718	0.6719	0.6723
0.7	0.5592	0.6117	0.6476	0.6585	0.6647	0.6673	0.6710	0.6718	0.6720	0.6723	0.6726
0.6	0.5592	0.6210	0.6530	0.6616	0.6664	0.6706	0.6718	0.6721	0.6725	0.6726	0.6728
0.5	0.5592	0.6326	0.6568	0.6655	0.6697	0.6718	0.6722	0.6726	0.6727	0.6729	0.6732
0.4	0.5592	0.6426	0.6616	0.6685	0.6718	0.6723	0.6726	0.6729	0.6732	0.6734	0.6734
0.3	0.5592	0.6530	0.6664	0.6718	0.6725	0.6728	0.6732	0.6733	0.6733	0.6734	0.6735
0.2	0.5592	0.6616	0.6718	0.6726	0.6732	0.6734	0.6734	0.6735	0.6735	0.6736	0.6736
0.1	0.5592	0.6718	0.6732	0.6734	0.6735	0.6736	**0.6737**	**0.6737**	**0.6737**	**0.6737**	**0.6737**
0.0	0.0000	0.0000	0.0000	0.0000	0.0000	0.0000	0.0000	0.0000	0.0000	0.0000	0.0000

(b) Recall.

S / A	0.0	0.1	0.2	0.3	0.4	0.5	0.6	0.7	0.8	0.9	1
1.0	0.0574	0.0632	0.0693	0.0712	0.0719	0.0723	0.0726	0.0727	0.0729	0.0730	0.0730
0.9	0.0574	0.0641	0.0698	0.0716	0.0721	0.0725	0.0727	0.0728	0.0730	0.0730	0.0730
0.8	0.0574	0.0650	0.0705	0.0718	0.0723	0.0726	0.0728	0.0730	0.0730	0.0730	0.0730
0.7	0.0574	0.0663	0.0710	0.0721	0.0725	0.0727	0.0729	0.0730	0.0730	0.0731	0.0731
0.6	0.0574	0.0678	0.0716	0.0723	0.0727	0.0729	0.0730	0.0730	0.0731	0.0731	0.0731
0.5	0.0574	0.0693	0.0719	0.0726	0.0729	0.0730	0.0730	0.0731	0.0731	0.0731	0.0731
0.4	0.0574	0.0705	0.0723	0.0728	0.0730	0.0730	0.0731	0.0731	0.0731	0.0731	0.0731
0.3	0.0574	0.0716	0.0727	0.0730	0.0731	0.0731	0.0731	0.0731	0.0731	0.0731	0.0731
0.2	0.0574	0.0723	0.0730	0.0731	0.0731	0.0731	0.0731	0.0731	0.0731	0.0731	0.0731
0.1	0.0574	0.0730	0.0731	0.0731	0.0731	0.0731	**0.0732**	**0.0732**	**0.0732**	**0.0732**	**0.0732**
0.0	0.0000	0.0000	0.0000	0.0000	0.0000	0.0000	0.0000	0.0000	0.0000	0.0000	0.0000

(c) nDCG.

S / A	0.0	0.1	0.2	0.3	0.4	0.5	0.6	0.7	0.8	0.9	1
1.0	0.8508	0.8694	0.8897	0.9008	0.9075	0.9124	0.9145	0.9166	0.9168	0.9166	0.9165
0.9	0.8508	0.8717	0.8927	0.9040	0.9099	0.9134	0.9162	0.9169	0.9166	0.9165	0.9165
0.8	0.8508	0.8743	0.8960	0.9065	0.9124	0.9154	0.9168	0.9167	0.9165	0.9165	0.9163
0.7	0.8508	0.8785	0.9003	0.9087	0.9140	0.9165	0.9167	0.9165	0.9164	0.9163	0.9163
0.6	0.8508	0.8843	0.9040	0.9124	0.9162	0.9167	0.9165	0.9164	0.9163	0.9163	0.9162
0.5	0.8508	0.8897	0.9075	0.9145	**0.9168**	0.9165	0.9164	0.9163	0.9162	0.9162	0.9161
0.4	0.8508	0.8960	0.9124	**0.9168**	0.9165	0.9163	0.9163	0.9162	0.9161	0.9161	0.9161
0.3	0.8508	0.9040	0.9162	0.9165	0.9163	0.9162	0.9161	0.9160	0.9161	0.9161	0.9160
0.2	0.8508	0.9124	0.9165	0.9163	0.9161	0.9161	0.9161	0.9160	0.9160	0.9160	0.9160
0.1	0.8508	0.9165	0.9161	0.9161	0.9160	0.9160	0.9160	0.9159	0.9159	0.9159	0.9159
0.0	0.0000	0.0000	0.0000	0.0000	0.0000	0.0000	0.0000	0.0000	0.0000	0.0000	0.0000

via an exhaustive search over the parameter space with the fidelity of 0.1 in the interval $[0,1] \times [0,1]$. Evaluation measures precision, recall and nDCG are recorded during the evaluation on the first 10 000 known ratings values. The results are presented both graphically and numerically.

The primary finding of the numerical experiments is that the quality of the recommendations decreases in the case of setting the activation relax (r_a) parameter to a low value (close to 0). The quality stays low especially if the setting of the spreading relax (r_s) is set to a high value (close to 1). In addition, the method is not able to calculate recommendations if the spreading relax (r_s) parameter is set to 0.

To be more exact, not counting the $r_s = 0$ case, spreading activation shows a stable performance. Depending on the evaluation measure, the quality of the recommendations changes numerically only from the second or the third digit. We assume that the reason behind this issue can be found in the theoretical foundations of the technique. Spreading activation is a typical example of the paradigm of relatedness, which paradigm generalizes the connections between the entities and emphasizes the network like behaviour of the graph. It also means that the method strongly relies on the structure of the graph, thus it involves also network science. We would conculde that the presence or involvement of the network leads to a stable calculation mechanism which is less sensitive to the actual setting of the parameters.

Our plans for the future is to analyse the stability of recommendation spreading as introduced by Grad-Gyenge et al. [2]. Another important direction is the temporal influence as a still open question in the case of the graph based techniques as also investigated by Dojchinovski et al. [31].

References

[1] L. Grad-Gyenge and P. Filzmoser, "The Paradigm of Relatedness," in *AKTB 2016 : 8th Workshop on Applications of Knowledge-Based Technologies in Business*. Springer International Publishing AG, 2017, pp. 57–68.

[2] L. Grad-Gyenge, P. Filzmoser, and H. Werthner, "Recommendations on a Knowledge Graph," in *MLRec 2015 : 1st International Workshop on Machine Learning Methods for Recommender Systems*, 2015, pp. 13–20. [Online]. Available: http: //mlrec.org/2015/papers/grad2015recommendation.pdf

[3] Y. Koren, R. Bell, and C. Volinsky, "Matrix Factorization Techniques for Recommender Systems," *Computer*, vol. 42, no. 8, pp. 30–37, Aug. 2009. [Online]. Available: http://dx.doi.org/10.1109/MC.2009.263

[4] S. Zhang, W. Wang, J. Ford, and F. Makedon, "Learning from incomplete ratings using non-negative matrix factorization," in *In Proc. of the 6th SIAM Conference on Data Mining (SDM*, 1996, pp. 549–553.

[5] S. Purushotham and Y. Liu, "Collaborative Topic Regression with Social Matrix Factorization for Recommendation Systems." in *ICML*. icml.cc / Omnipress, 2012. [Online]. Available: http://dblp.uni-trier.de/db/conf/icml/icml2012. html#PurushothamL12

[6] S. Lee, S. Park, M. Kahng, and S. goo Lee, "PathRank: Ranking nodes on a heterogeneous graph for flexible hybrid recommender systems." *Expert Syst. Appl.*, no. 2, pp. 684–697.

[7] K. Lee and K. Lee, "Escaping your comfort zone: A graph-based recommender system for finding novel recommendations among relevant items." *Expert Syst. Appl.*, no. 10, pp. 4851–4858.

[8] A. Tiroshi, S. Berkovsky, M. A. Kâafar, D. Vallet, and T. Kuflik, "Graph-Based Recommendations: Make the Most Out of Social Data." in *UMAP*, ser. Lecture Notes in Computer Science, V. Dimitrova, T. Kuflik, D. Chin, F. Ricci, P. Dolog, and G.-J. Houben, Eds. Springer, pp. 447–458.

[9] R. Guha, R. Kumar, P. Raghavan, and A. Tomkins, "Propagation of trust and distrust," in *WWW '04: Proceedings of the 13th international conference on World Wide Web*. New York, NY, USA: ACM, 2004, pp. 403–412.

[10] P. Massa and P. Avesani, "Trust-Aware Collaborative Filtering for Recommender Systems." in *CoopIS/DOA/ODBASE (1)*, ser. Lecture Notes in Computer Science, R. Meersman and Z. Tari, Eds., vol. 3290. Springer, 2004, pp. 492–508.

[11] C.-N. Ziegler and G. Lausen, "Propagation Models for Trust and Distrust in Social Networks," *Information Systems Frontiers*, vol. 7, no. 4-5, pp. 337–358, Dec. 2005.

[12] A. Jøsang, S. Marsh, and S. Pope, "Exploring Different Types of Trust Propagation." in *iTrust*, ser. Lecture Notes in Computer Science, K. Stølen, W. H. Winsborough, F. Martinelli, and F. Massacci, Eds., vol. 3986. Springer, 2006, pp. 179–192.

[13] I. Guy *et al.*, "Personalized recommendation of social software items based on social relations." in *RecSys*, L. D. Bergman, A. Tuzhilin, R. D. Burke, A. Felfernig, and L. Schmidt-Thieme, Eds. ACM, pp. 53–60.

[14] I. Konstas, V. Stathopoulos, and J. M. Jose, "On Social Networks and Collaborative Recommendation," in *Proceedings of the 32Nd International ACM SIGIR Conference on Research and Development in Information Retrieval*, ser. SIGIR '09. New York, NY, USA: ACM, 2009, pp. 195–202.

[15] J. He, "A Social Network-based Recommender System," Ph.D. dissertation, Los Angeles, CA, USA, 2010, aAI3437557.

[16] P. Kazienko, K. Musial, and T. Kajdanowicz, "Multidimensional Social Network in the Social Recommender System," *Trans. Sys. Man Cyber. Part A*, vol. 41, no. 4, pp. 746–759, Jul. 2011.

[17] I. Cantador and P. Castells, *Multilayered Semantic Social Network Modeling by Ontology-Based User Profiles Clustering: Application to Collaborative Filtering*. Berlin, Heidelberg: Springer Berlin Heidelberg, pp. 334–349.

[18] Q. Hu *et al.*, "HeteroSales: Utilizing Heterogeneous Social Networks to Identify the Next Enterprise Customer," in *Proceedings of the 25th International Conference on World Wide Web*, ser. WWW '16. Republic and Canton of Geneva, Switzerland: International World Wide Web Conferences Steering Committee, pp. 41–50.

[19] R. Catherine and W. Cohen, "Personalized Recommendations Using Knowledge Graphs: A Probabilistic Logic Pro-

gramming Approach," in *Proceedings of the 10th ACM Conference on Recommender Systems*, ser. RecSys '16. New York, NY, USA: ACM, pp. 325–332.

[20] X. Yu *et al.*, "Personalized Entity Recommendation: A Heterogeneous Information Network Approach," in *Proceedings of the 7th ACM International Conference on Web Search and Data Mining*, ser. WSDM '14. New York, NY, USA: ACM, pp. 283–292.

[21] P. Kouki, S. Fakhraei, J. Foulds, M. Eirinaki, and L. Getoor, "HyPER: A Flexible and Extensible Probabilistic Framework for Hybrid Recommender Systems," in *Proceedings of the 9th ACM Conference on Recommender Systems*, ser. RecSys '15. New York, NY, USA: ACM, pp. 99–106.

[22] R. Burke, "The Adaptive Web," P. Brusilovsky, A. Kobsa, and W. Nejdl, Eds. Berlin, Heidelberg: Springer-Verlag, ch. Hybrid Web Recommender Systems, pp. 377–408.

[23] T. Hussein, D. Westheide, and J. Ziegler, "Context-adaptation based on Ontologies and Spreading Activation," in *LWA 2007: Lernen - Wissen - Adaption, Halle, September 2007, Workshop Proceedings*, 2007, pp. 361–366.

[24] Q. Gao, J. Yan, and M. Liu, "A Semantic Approach to Recommendation System Based on User Ontology and Spreading Activation Model." in *NPC Workshops*, J. Cao, M. Li, C. Weng, Y. Xiang, X. Wang, H. Tang, F. Hong, H. Liu, and Y. Wang, Eds. IEEE Computer Society, 2008, pp. 488–492.

[25] X. Jiang and A.-H. Tan, "Learning and inferencing in user ontology for personalized Semantic Web search." *Inf. Sci.*, vol. 179, no. 16, pp. 2794–2808, 2009.

[26] Y. Blanco-Fernández, M. L. Nores, A. Gil-Solla, M. R. Cabrer, and J. J. P. Arias, "Exploring synergies between content-based filtering and Spreading Activation techniques in knowledge-based recommender systems." *Inf. Sci.*, vol. 181, no. 21, pp. 4823–4846, 2011.

[27] V. Codina and L. Ceccaroni, "Taking Advantage of Semantics in Recommendation Systems." in *CCIA*, ser. Frontiers in Artificial Intelligence and Applications, R. Alquézar, A. Moreno, and J. Aguilar-Martin, Eds., vol. 210. IOS Press, 2010, pp. 163–172.

[28] A. Troussov, D. Parra, and P. Brusilovsky, "Spreading Activation Approach to Tag-aware Recommenders: Modeling Similarity on Multidimensional Networks," D. Jannach, W. Geyer, J. Freyne, S. S. Anand, C. Dugan, B. Mobasher, and A. Kobsa, Eds., 2009, pp. 57–62.

[29] J. M. Alvarez, L. Polo, P. Abella, W. Jimenez, and J. E. Labra, "Application of the Spreading Activation Technique for Recommending Concepts of well-known ontologies in Medical Systems," 2011.

[30] P. Resnick, N. Iacovou, M. Suchak, P. Bergstorm, and J. Riedl, "GroupLens: An Open Architecture for Collaborative Filtering of Netnews," in *Proc. of ACM 1994 Conference on Computer Supported Cooperative Work*. Chapel Hill, North Carolina: ACM, 1994, pp. 175–186.

[31] M. Dojchinovski, J. Kuchar, T. Vitvar, and M. Zaremba, *Personalised Graph-Based Selection of Web APIs*. Berlin, Heidelberg: Springer Berlin Heidelberg, 2012, pp. 34–48. [Online]. Available: https://doi.org/10.1007/978-3-642-35176-1_3

J. Hlaváčová (Ed.): ITAT 2017 Proceedings, pp. 218–222
ISBN 978-1974274741, © 2017 B. Horváth, T. Horváth

Evaluating Data Sources for Crawling Events from the Web

Balázs Horváth and Tomáš Horváth

ELTE – Eötvös Loránd University, Budapest, Hungary
Faculty of Informatics, Department of Data Science and Engineering
horvath.balazs221@gmail.com, tomas.horvath@inf.elte.hu
http://t-labs.elte.hu

Abstract: The bottleneck of event recommender systems is the availability of actual, up-to-date information on events. Usually, there is no single data feed, thus information on events must be crawled from numerous sources. Ranking these sources helps the system to decide which sources to crawl and how often. In this paper, a model for event source evaluation and ranking is proposed based on well-known centrality measures from social network analysis. Experiments made on real data, crawled from Budapest event sources, shows interesting results for further research.

1 Introduction

Tourist event recommender systems need a big amount of data, preferably all events around a particular location. In order to get that data we need the organizers to upload every new event what they organize/create/host to the application which handles the data. It can be the recommender application or just a backed application where the organizers would want to be shown. If the previous solution is not acceptable or the organizers would not put enough effort to do it, then the recommender system lacks of information and cannot work as good as expected.

The other solution would be to find a feed which contains the upcoming events from each location. Unfortunately there are no feeds like that, feeds can be found about one particular topic or location's events that can be crawled as well, but do not satisfies the tourist event recommender systems need. There are almost good sources for one or two big cities in the USA, but that is not scalable if the system would expect every city or town to have their own feed like those.

The only solution for the current situation is to collect the information about the events semi-automatically from numerous sources through a data crawler engine. These event sources (denoted "sources" in the rest of the paper) can be on a different level in usefulness, some of them can be completely redundant for the system, because the same information about its events is already crawled. Others can upload informations or new events very rarely, so it is not worth to check them often. Quality differences can be discovered through the observation of the different sources. In order to save computational resources, or when a system reaches its limit, the import method have to rank sources in the queue, but how could it decide which one to rank

higher? What happens if it ranks a source which played a very important role in the system very low? These sources have to be evaluated and indexed according to their importance related to our purposes.

As it is mentioned in [14], WIEN [7], XWRAP [9], STALKER [5], NoDoSe [1] and BYU [4] is a selection of the well-known often-quoted solutions for Web Data Extraction (WDE). In the past few years new approaches were published like FiVaTech [6], FiVaTech2 [2], NEXIR [12], AutoRM [13] and OXPath [15]. The last one is a wrapper language which has an optimized syntax for making the description of the WDE task easier. It also supports Javascript or CSS3 transitions, most of the modern Document Object Model (DOM) modification triggers and it can recognize Drag-and-Drop features as well. Pagination is a problem from the dynamic web pages, for that, link extraction is needed. OXPath and other solutions can handle that problem already. Unfortunately to write OXPath expressions and maintain them is costly, and involves much effort, thus it is not scaling well. DIADEM [16] utilized OXPath to give wrapper generators, which is a step closer to the right solution but they do not provider deep insight into it. An other wrapper language called NEXIR has been created for covering the whole WDE process, with pagination, data extraction and integration. The problem of scaling is not solved with wrapper languages either. FiVaTech and its improved version FiVaTech2 provide a page-level extraction approach which utilizes different DOM-based information to build up a wrapper. FiVaTech therefore utilizes tree matching, tree alignment and mining techniques to identify a template from a set of pages. FiVaTech2 improves the node recognition by including node specific features, such as visual information, DOM tree information, HTML tag contents, id-s and classes. It is clearly visible, that a ranking system is needed to be able to differentiate between solutions, ARIEX [10] is a defined framework for ranking data and information extractors and solves a specific problem, with comparing different approaches. Other missing approach is to make ranking between data sources, not the approaches. When we talk about scalability, until we do not have a general solution for the problem, we can limit the scaling by finding the way of ranking the sources and leave out the unnecessary ones. There is no such publication or solution available for the public, so we take this approach in this research. For reaching the results, a bipartite graph can be used and social network analysis methods on it. The importance of centrality measures and social network analysis methods are discussed in [11].

An approach to event data source evaluation and ranking, using network centrality measures, is presented in the following section, followed by the description of a small proof-of-concept preliminary experiment.

2 The Proposed Model

For evaluation of sources we are considering the following attributes:

- Uniqueness of events contained in the source

- Number of events the source contains

- The importance of the source w.r.t. the other sources

- Freshness of events in the source

- Location of events contained in the source

The decision was to represent sources and events in a bipartite graph, where events and sources are both vertices and their connection is represented with edges. Thus, well-known centrality measures from social network analysis [8] can be utilized to compute the above mentioned attributes of sources.

2.1 Uniqueness

To get an indicator like uniqueness, different approaches could be considered. The first point is to find those sources, which has at least one unique event. If a source has a unique event, it is important information for the model, because it means, that if we lose that source, than we cannot get those unique events from other sources. For the purpose of finding those sources, the algorithm should go through and check the **cardinality** of each event and source as well.

For the unique event calculation, the cardinality of sources are less important than the cardinality of events. If an event can be found just in one source, that means that source is irreplaceable. Of course we cannot ignore the fact that probably the system should be able to make difference between sources which do not have unique events: It is because if one of the sources which has a lot of events, both unique and not, becomes unreachable or stops working than it is predictable that it will cause uniqueness changes in the graph.

The way of computing the uniqueness, illustrated in the algorithm 1, works as follows:

It creates a copy of the whole graph and checks for the lowest cardinality event (if there are more, then it picks a random one). It chooses one of its sources and increasing that source's uniqueness index. Then, it is going though all of the events of that source and deleting them one by one. When this step finished the source with no cardinality becomes deleted as well. These steps from picking

the lowest cardinality event repeating until all the event vertices disappear from the copied graph. Then the whole loop is repeated 100 times to make the result smoother and the indicators to converge to the correct value (this step is necessary because of the random pick). In the end, to get the indicators between 0 and 1, we have to divide them with one hundred. The repetition time can be increased or decreased to make the result even smoother or make the algorithm run faster.

With this approach there will be differences between the sources which does not have any unique event, so the issue is solved with this solution.

An other issue is that sometimes to download often all the unique event holder sources the resources are not enough, that is why we need to distinguish between sources which has unique events to be able to choose the most valuable of them.

The other reason why is it needed to make a difference between unique event holder sources is, that if the sources would know the algorithm they could just try to avoid to be left out or get low ranking and they would trick the system with fake unique events. This happened with Google indexing, called black hat search engine optimization, where fake back links and meta keywords were embedded in sites to increase their position in the search results.

An approach for handling these issues is to make an additional variable, the **distinguisher**, added to the previously calculated indicators, defined as

$$distinguisher(s) = \frac{u}{uall} * \frac{1}{1 + e^{-(u-\bar{u})}} \qquad (1)$$

where s denotes the source, $uall$ is the sum of all unique events in the graph, u is the sum of all unique events of the source and $\bar{u}$ is the average unique events for sources in the whole graph.

The sigmoid function in the second part of the equation handles outliers such that this step just have to distinguish between unique event holders, while not making big differences, just make a ranking. Using a sigmoid function, the differences between unique event holders are smoothed out while keeping the ranking.

2.2 Degree and Betweenness

To compute the number of events contained in the source a simple centrality measure, the degree, of the source (as a vertex in the graph) is used. Basically, the degree of the source is the number of events it contains.

An other, important, property of the source is its betweenness. It is a measure, which shows how important is the position of that particular vertex (source) in the whole network, and is computed as

$$betweenness(v) = \sum_{u \neq v \neq t} \frac{nsp_v(u,t)}{nsp(u,t)} \qquad (2)$$

where u and t are vertices not equal with v and $nsp(u,t)$ is the number of the shortest paths form u to t and the

Algorithm 1 Uniqueness

```
1:  procedure UNIQUENESS(copy of graph)
2:      while size of events > 0 do
3:          e ← minCardinalityEvent(events)
4:          s ← randomPick(sources containing e)
5:          increaseIndicator(originalDatasource(s))
6:          for all a ∈ getevents(s) do
7:              delete(a)
8:          end for
9:          delete(s)
10:     end while
11:     indicators = {indicator(s_1), indicator(s_2), ...
12:                  ..., indicator(s_n)}
13:     for all i ∈ indicators do
14:         i = i + distinguisher(s)
15:     end for
16:     return indicators
17: end procedure
```

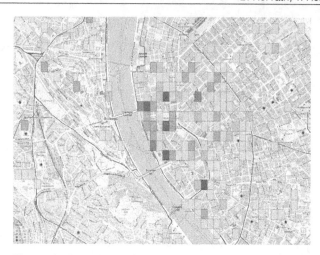

Figure 1: Locational data aggregated into hash areas in Budapest

$nsp_v(u,t)$ is the number of shortest paths between the nodes, which goes through v vertex [17]. In our case it is used for showing how important is a source for events and find events which has high betweenness. That means that an event is connecting sources and we can observe if that is the only event which makes the source less unique or there are more of these high betweenness events in its list of events. If there is more than one of those, then we should observe if the events are connected between only the same sources, or they are distributed: it means that the source can be the connection between more sources and it can be a feed as well, which provides important information even if it does not have any unique events.

It is important to know for us which are the nodes within betweenness centrality. It is because it shows those nodes which can be concert halls, clubs or concert venues, forums, etc., collecting events of different artists. If a source is such an event collector, it can leads us to the decision, that even if it does not have unique events, it is very important for the model, because it can post new events from a new artist whose website is not crawled yet by us.

2.3 Location

From the previous properties, we can already make good measurements and propose an ranking, but there are other relevant informations, which can be important in some cases, such as keeping the data up to date or focusing on different areas or performance optimization. Location is not focusing on exact locations in this measure, just trying to decide what distance is worth to travel for the tourists.

In the preliminary experiment, using the Budapest events dataset, big part of the events are inside the smaller ring road (tram line 4–6) as illustrated in the Figure 1. For this measure we need to observe if the source is having events on the same location most of the time, or its events are at different locations, usually. If events are at the same

location then the task is easy, i.e. find the relevance borders for the recommender and divide the area into circles and give points according to that. The other case is when most of the events have different locations, then the algorithm should calculate the center of the locations (carefully with the outliers) and give the score according to that.

2.4 Actuality

Freshness is a binary function [3] that measures whether the downloaded local copy is accurate according to the live page. The freshness of a page p in the repository at time t is defined as $F_p(t) = 1$ if p is equal to the local copy at time t, and, $F_p(t) = 0$, otherwise.

Age is a measure, which indicates how outdated the downloaded copy is. The age of a page p in the repository, at time t is defined as $A_p(t) = 0$ if p is not modified at time t, and, $A_p(t) = t - mt(p)$, otherwise, where $mt(p)$ is the last modification time of p.

With the help of these functions, the scheduler can calculate how often a page is usually updating the content, or in other words, how ofter is the downloaded copy gets outdated. The frequency information can tell us from different sources for the same event, which one of them posted it earlier or which one is posting more frequently. That information can influence the importance result. As an example it can be important to know if an event is canceled or changed its information like the location or the starting time. For applications where to be up to date with event informations is crucial the freshness property can be weighted more.

2.5 The Evaluation Model

This different attributes introduced in the previous chapters are aggregated to a final evaluation or ranking model of sources as follows:

$$Rank(s) = w_1 U(s) + w_2 D(s) + w_3 \frac{1}{B(s)} + w_4 A(s) + w_5 L(s)$$

$$(3)$$

where $w = \{w_1, w_2, w_3, w_4, w_5\}$ are the weights which will change according to the application's needs, and s is the current source what the algorithm is evaluating/ranking while U, D, B, A and L refer to the uniqueness, degree, betweenness, actuality and location of the source, respectively. The weighting is important, because there can be application which has a goal of getting all the events or as much as possible. Others can focus on performance to be able to offer trust worth fast running applications on the crawled data, and that is not harming it, if it cost some percent of the events.

3 Preliminary Experiments

251 event sources were crawled from the Web and Facebook event pages (using the Facebook Graph API), resulting in more than 1500 events (after the unification of the duplicate events). All the events crawled were from Budapest including concerts, museums, galleries, etc. The events were located mainly in the city center as can be seen in the figure 1.

The final experiments on the uniqueness part of the model were made on a dataset, where data were crawled from Facebook pages' events and clubs and museums websites. We had to consider all the possible future cases, so we made test sources as well like a complete copy of a website data, or partial copies, copies which are more important than some Facebook pages and vice versa, etc. The distinguisher is not rounded because it still should be able to make difference between sources even if the difference is smaller. In opposite of the other case where we calculate the uniqueness function on the sources, it is better to round that number, because we do not have to make too much loops to make it smoother.

A part of the result on uniqueness is illustrated on the figure 2. As can be seen, the "bjc.hu" and its copy "copy-ofbjc" do not have a distinguisher number, because they do not hold any unique event, obviously because they are copies of each other. So the highest number of non unique event holders is 0.5. If their event can be found in more than one other sources, then the number decreases.

Figure 3 shows an example, from of our experiments, with seven sources and their events. It is obvious that events' distances are very different from their sources. Despite these distances are not connected to the similarity of the source and the event, they represent how similar the events are. As we see in the middle, couple of the events of the big source in the middle are very far away from the others, but they are also connected to the other two sources. Those events are Jazz lessons with a famous artist and all the other events are Jazz concerts with different artists.

4 Conclusions

A work-in-progress research was introduced in the paper focusing on ranking and evaluation of event data sources.

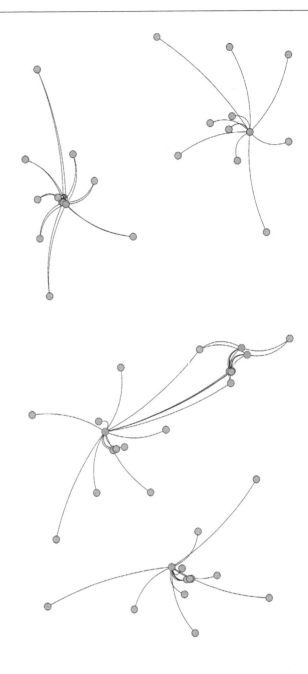

Figure 3: Visualization on 7 sources

The approach utilized well-known centrality measures from social network analysis what is, according to the best knowledge of the authors, the first attempt for event source evaluation.

The proposed model is quite general and can be easily modified to specific use-cases and domains. Experiments on real-world data crawled from Budapest event websites as well as Facebook pages show interesting results and promising future research directions.

```
DataSource{name='Facebook/Booty Call Thursdays'} = 1.0 + 1.950034933242048E-3
DataSource{name='Facebook/Újszínház Budapest'} = 1.0 + 0.010709504630320549
DataSource{name='Facebook/Zrínyi Miklós Gimnázium, Budapest X.'} = 1.0 + 0.010040160260964218
DataSource{name='copyofbjc'} = 0.5 + 0.0
DataSource{name='bjc.hu'} = 0.5 + 0.0
DataSource{name='budapestbylocals.com'} = 1.0 + 0.025435073627844713
DataSource{name='eventbrite.com'} = 1.0 + 0.048862115127175365
```

Figure 2: Partial result of running the uniqueness method

Acknowledgement

Authors would like to thank T-Labs for the support and environment provided for this research. The research was conducted within the industrial project "Telekom Open City Services" supported by Magyar Telekom Nyrt.

References

[1] B. Adelberg. Nodosea tool for semi-automatically extracting structured and semistructured data from text documents. *ACM Sigmod Record vol. 27, no. 2.*, pages 283–294, 1998.

[2] C.-H. Chang C.-H. Chang and M. Kayed. Fivatech: Page-level web data extraction from template pages. *Knowledge and Data Engineering, IEEE Transactions on, vol. 22, no. 2*, pages 249–263, 2010.

[3] Carlos Castillo. *Effective Web Crawling*. PhD thesis, University of Chile, 11 2004.

[4] Y. S. Jiang S. W. Liddle D. W. Lonsdale Y.-K. Ng D. W. Embley, D. M. Campbell and R. D. Smith. Conceptual-model-based data extraction from multiple-record web pages. *Data & Knowledge Engineering, vol. 31, no. 3*, pages 227–251, 1999.

[5] Steve Minton Ion Muslea and Craig Knoblock. Stalker: Learning extraction rules for semistructured, web-based information sources. *Proceedings of AAAI-98 Workshop on AI and Information Integration*, pages 74–81, 1998.

[6] M. Kayed and C.-H. Chang. Fivatech2: A supervised approach to role differentiation for web data extraction from template pages. *Proceedings of the 26th annual conference of the Japanese Society for Artifical Intelligence, Special Session on Web Intelligence & Data Mining, vol. 26*, pages 1–9, 2012.

[7] N. Kushmerick. *Wrapper induction for information extraction*. PhD thesis, University of Washington, 1997.

[8] Frederic Lee and Bruce Cronin. *Handbook of Research Methods and Applications in Heterodox Economics*. Edward Elgar Publishing, 2016.

[9] L. Liu, C. Pu, and W. Han. Xwrap: an xml-enabled wrapper construction system for web information sources. In *Proceedings of 16th International Conference on Data Engineering (Cat. No.00CB37073)*. IEEE Comput. Soc.

[10] R. Corchuelo P. Jimenez and H. A. Sleiman. Ariex: Automated ranking of information extractors. *Knowledge-Based Systems, vol. 93*, pages 84–108, 2016.

[11] Sebastiano Vigna Paolo Boldi. Axioms for Centrality, 2013.

[12] Y. Liu H. Wang L. Luo C. Yuan S. Shi, W. Wei and Y. Huang. Nexir: A novel web extraction rule language toward a three-stage web data extraction model. *Web Information Systems Engineering–WISE 2013. Springer*, pages 29–42, 2013.

[13] Y. Shen C. Yuan S. Shi, C. Liu and Y. Huang. Autorm: An effective approach for automatic web data record mining. *Knowledge-Based Systems, vol. 89*, pages 314–331, 2015.

[14] Andreas Schulz, Jorg Lassig, and Martin Gaedke. Practical web data extraction: Are we there yet? - a short survey. In *2016 IEEE/WIC/ACM International Conference on Web Intelligence (WI)*. IEEE, oct 2016.

[15] G. Grasso C. Schallhart T. Furche, G. Gottlob and A. Sellers. Oxpath: A language for scalable, memory-efficient data extraction from web applications. *Proceedings of the VLDB Endowment, vol. 4, no. 11*, pages 1016–1027, 2011.

[16] G. Grasso O. Gunes X. Guo A. Kravchenko G. Orsi C. Schallhart-A. Sellers T. Furche, G. Gottlob and C. Wang. Diadem: domain-centric, intelligent, automated data extraction methodology. *Proceedings of the 21st international conference companion on World Wide Web. ACM*, pages 267–270, 2012.

[17] Pang-Ning Tan, Michael Steinbach, and Vipin Kumar. *Introduction to Data Mining*. Addison Wesley, us ed edition, May 2005.

J. Hlaváčová (Ed.): ITAT 2017 Proceedings, pp. 223–227
ISBN 978-1974274741, © 2017 J. Hradil

Identification and Origin of User Interfaces

Jiří Hradil

University of Economics, Prague
Department of Information and Knowledge Engineering
W. Churchill Sq. 4, 130 67 Prague, Czech Republic
jiri.hradil@vse.cz

Abstract. This paper identifies typical patterns of user interfaces in software applications and try to conclude their origin based on association with phenomena of the surrounding world. First, four basic phenomena are chosen (Time, Gravity, Space and Similarity) and then related user interfaces are assigned under them. Each user interface is described, explained and put into the right usability context. Author believes that when we identify and understand these connections between phenomena and user interfaces, and follow the concept of inspiration from the outside world, we will be able to create more usable software which will serve people better. The user interface patterns research is just a part of author's broader research in software ergonomics field.

1 Introduction

Software ergonomics is a domain of research which looks at software from the user's point of view. Its main goal is to harmonize the communication between a man and machine. People play a dominant role in software, and software design considers people from its very first design.

Software ergonomics covers all the parts in software which are related or dedicated to human being. Author's PhD dissertation (currently in progress) splits the ergonomics into four parts: Speed, Psychology of Colors, Psychology of Shapes, and External and Environmental Influences.

This article is related to the Psychology of Shapes part. Identification and origin of user interfaces and their archetypes is also related to Psychology, Physics or Sociology. All the interfaces described should be considered as "soft systems". Even the interfaces are just a reflection of the outside world and they are interpreted and used from human being perspective, their interpretation could be still subjective. Nevertheless, author tries to identify, categorize and describe these interfaces and link them with phenomena of the outside world to help to be used in the right context.

Current scientific research and publications look at software ergonomics vicariously or indirectly. For example, fragments of Psychology of Colors are mentioned in [1] and [2]. Human factors and Psychology of Shapes is partly described in [3]. Design patters related to software are mentioned in [4] and [5]. There are also general guidelines for software developers [6], [7], [8]. However, neither all the described interfaces nor single components miss a connection to their origin and association with the outside world. This way, it's hard to predict their behavior.

The author assumes the following:

1. Involving outside world phenomena, general user interface boundaries are set. Software user interfaces could be designed and developed inside these boundaries of the known world so its control and behavior will be more predictable.
2. User interfaces will be used in the right context.
3. Software will be consequently simpler for its users.

2 Phenomena

Based on observation of the surrounding world, four generally known phenomena have been chosen as a basis for user interface identification and classification.

2.1 Time

Time represents change, growth and perpetual moving, expresses a dependency of human being on surrounding environment, reflects interaction and links an action with a reaction. While perceiving time, we can refer basic time frames – past, present and future. On the mental timeline (how we perceive time in surrounding space), past is understood on the left and the future on the right [9].

User interfaces take time into account with horizontal layouts, unfolding information from left-to-right, and with determining components priority (on the right is the newest and so more important).

The following user interfaces have been categorized under *Time* phenomenon:

2.1.1 2-Column Horizontal Layout

The screen is split into 2 parts which are positioned next to each other. The left side displays older/less important data and the right side newest/more important data, or both sides show equally important data. This could be used for a comparison or for displaying duplicates.

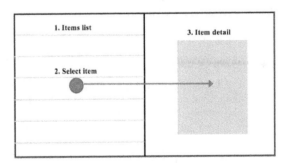

Figure 1: 2-Column Horizontal Layout user interface

2.1.2 3-Column Horizontal Layout

This interface is an extension of 2-column Horizontal Layout and adds another layer of detail or granularity. Displaying is in the form of 3 columns horizontally positioned next to each other. The left side could display Past, the middle one Present, and the right side Future. The interface could also follow granularity principle where coarse-grained data is on the left, data in normal resolution in the middle and fine-grained data on the right.

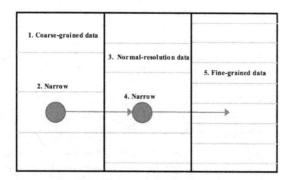

Figure 2: 3-Column Horizontal Layout user interface

2.1.3 Menu on the Left

This interface is a special variant of the *2-Column Horizontal Layout*. Application menu is positioned on the left. Therefore, the menu is the main control interface and could be used earlier than the middle (working) part of the application. For example, one needs to choose a file which he would like to work with.

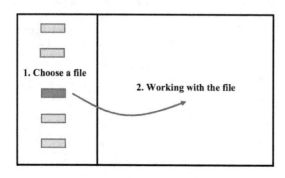

Figure 3: Menu on the Right user interface

2.1.4 Menu on the Right

The application menu in this interface is just an additional (second class) component. Due to mental timeline perception, the right part of the screen is recognized later than the left one. Hence menu contains control elements which are used less frequently compared to *Menu on the Left* interface. For example, one works with a photography and they decide to apply a filter on the photography.

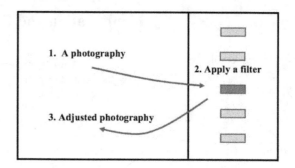

Figure 4: Menu on the Right user interface

2.2 Gravity

Perception of gravity as a law of nature and its influence on human being reflects user interfaces in top-to-bottom design. More important is on the top and less important on the bottom. We can understand gravity as a vertical timeline. Designing future is very difficult, maybe impossible here. In the vertical space, we can express future on the top but user interfaces are positioned just ahead of us which connotes present, not future. Therefore, it's reasonable to reduce time-frames under this phenomenon only to past and present.

The following user-interface type has been identified under *Gravity* phenomenon:

2.2.1 List

This user interface is represented by a vertical list of items, typically sorted by their priority. The most important or newest item is on the top and less important or oldest is on the bottom. One item represents one encapsulated information or entity (a task, email, document etc.). In case of many items it's advisable to split the list by a blank space or horizontal line into smaller groups (3-5 items in groups, for example).

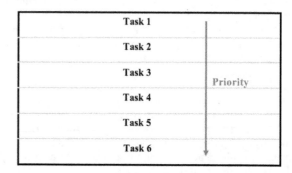

Figure 5: List user interface

2.3 Space

Space phenomenon is derived from perception of the world by human being. Assume that one perceives space around him, realizes the boundaries (and so the size of the space), recognizes objects inside it and knows his position. Then we can say that space perception is dependent on the size of the space and, objects perception is related to the distance of each object from the others. Objects placed close to each other are recognized as a group and we think about them as the whole. If there are some groups and the object doesn't belong to any of them, it's independent and has an exclusivity. It differs from the others, grouped objects. This object has probably other, special attributes and so it is more important.

Space perception establishes relations among distance, size and importance in user interfaces. In general, when we strive for simpler interfaces we could have as few elements as possible. Each element occupies a part of user's field of vision, demands an attention and increases a possibility of interactions among elements, or between an element and user.

These user interfaces have been categorized under *Space* phenomena:

2.3.1 Workbench

Workbench is a composite interface derived from phenomena *Space* and *Similarity* (see *Similarity* below). A typical representation of the interface is a maximized window where the middle part is dominant and used as the main working area. Displaying is not split into more parts and the focus is in the middle of the window. The middle is the safest area because it has the biggest distance from borders (objects in the middle can't be lost because they can't fall off the borders). The similarity with a real workbench is obvious but the interface has been classified under Space phenomena because its attributes are more about distance and size.

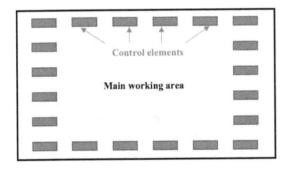

Figure 6: Workbench user interface

2.3.2 Bigger is more important

Importance can be expressed by size. Bigger objects grab more attention because they occupy larger area of the user 's field of vision which is limited. We can express superiority with larger cover of the field of vision. This interface can be combined with *Workbench* interface to highlight control elements which are used more often than the others.

By increasing elements visibility, cognitive load and knowledge activation are both increased [10]. Therefore, bigger control elements are becoming more important.

Importance can be also expressed by colors. White and lighter objects seem to be bigger than they really are and dark-colored objects are smaller [1]. This way, if there are more objects with the same size, colors can highlight their importance. Colors perception is also a subject of social, religious or geographical context [2].

2.3.3 Group

A group of items contains elements with similar or unique features. Elements can be grouped by their attributes, importance or frequency of use. A group encapsulates its members from the others. The importance is redeemed by space around the group which can't be used otherwise.

A group can be also split into subgroups. For example, in the *List* user interface we can optically shrink the number of elements by adding a space after every fifth element. The space makes the list lighter and the look will be simpler. One can recall and repeat about seven items from memory at once [11]. Hence the individual group size shouldn't exceed this limit.

2.4 Similarity

Similarity phenomenon means an association of user interface and its components with objects and their attributes from the real world. The advantage is an existing mental association followed by identification of the component with a pattern from the outside world and prediction of its function without a need of learning. The association decreases entropy. The similarity is only an approximation based on conformity of attributes and expressions of the original object (shape, color, behavior) with the component. In most cases, these attributes can be captured by eyesight or hearing.

The principle of the phenomenon can be described as follows:

1. A user has a pre-existing association from the outside world based on previous knowledge.

2. The user sees a component in user interface for the first time (he hasn't known it yet).

3. The user likens the new component with an object from outside world which is known already. A new association is created.

4. From now on, the component is recognized automatically.

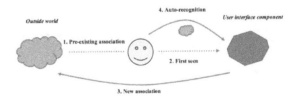

Figure 7: Similarity phenomenon principle

Following this principle, this user interface has been categorized under *Similarity* phenomenon:

2.4.1 Tiles

Tiles user interface puts components into a grid. The name evokes similarity with tiles on a pavement. The grid acts orderly if there is the same spacing among components in horizontal or vertical direction.

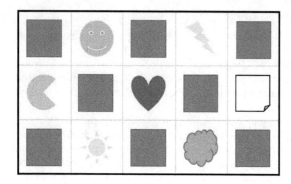

Figure 8: Tiles user interface

3   Relationships among Phenomena

Relationships among phenomena *Time*, *Gravity*, *Space* and *Similarity* can be visualized as Figure 9. As it is evident, phenomena co-exist as well as their patterns in the real world. *Gravity* relates to *Time* and *Space*, and *Similarity* occurs in *Space*. Phenomena interact with each other. Therefore, when mapping user interfaces to phenomena, it's possible to categorize one interface to more phenomena at once. Then, the interface is a composite type.

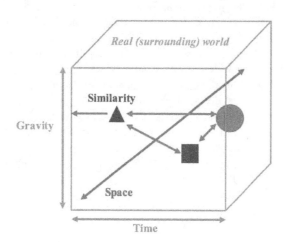

Figure 9: Relationships among phenomena

4   Conclusions

In summary, four basic phenomena with nine user interface types have been identified and described.

The purpose of this article is to show a connection between software and real world through user interfaces which are inspired by world's phenomena. People know described phenomena very well and understand their basic connections. If we apply this pre-learned experience to software user interfaces, we can shorten adaptation time on new software. Software control will be simpler and in the end, software would serve better.

The list of phenomena and user interfaces shouldn't be considered as final. It's just an introduction and inspiration designed to be extended. Level of their abstraction can be adjusted anytime based on current needs and research.

However, when software creators learn how to create and improve user interfaces according to patterns of the real world, interfaces will be designed better because the borders have been already defined and are generally known.

As a continuing research goal, described phenomena needs to be tested in a real, production environment. A search for other phenomena will continue. When found, more existing interfaces will be categorized under phenomena. As a final goal, this research will help to build ergonomic software which will be user-friendly, straight to use and allows people to achieve their goals through natural user interfaces.

References

[1] Birren, Faber. *Color Psychology and Color Therapy*. Martino Fine Books (November 4, 2013). [cit. 2017-01-12]. ISBN 978-1-61427-513-8.

[2] Löffler, Diana, 2014. Happy is pink: designing for intuitive use with color-to-abstract mappings. In: *CHI '14 Extended Abstracts on Human Factors in Computing Systems (CHI EA '14)*. ACM, New York, NY, USA, s. 323-326. [cit. 2017-01-05]. DOI: http://doi.acm.org/10.1145/2559206.2559959

[3] Chapanis, Alphonse, 1999. *The Chapanis Chronicles: 50 Years of Human Factors Research, Education, and Design*. Aegean Pub Co. 1999. ISBN: 978-0963617897.

[4] Freeman, Eric, Elisabeth ROBSON, Bert BATES, Kathy SIERRA, 2004. *Head First Design Patterns*. O'Reilly Media. 2004. ISBN 978-0-596-00712-6.

[5] Krug, Steve, 2014. *Don't Make Me Think, Revisited: A Common-Sense Approach to Web Usability (3rd Edition) (Voices That Matter)*. New Riders. 3rd edition. 2014. ISBN 978-0321965516.

[6] APPLE, 2017a. *iOS Human Interface Guideline* [online]. [cit. 2017-01-12]. Available from: https://developer.apple.com/ios/human-interface-guidelines/overview/design-principles/

[7] GOOGLE, 2017a. *Google Design* [online]. [cit. 2017-01-12]. Available from: https://design.google.com

[8] MICROSOFT, 2017a. *Microsoft Design Language* [software]. [cit. 2017-01-12]. Available from: https://developer.microsoft.com/en-us/windows/apps/design

[9] Thomson, Helena, 2014, *Past is a blur if the right side of your brain is faulty*, New Scientist, 221, 2950, s. 13, Academic Search Complete, EBSCOhost, [cit. 2017-01-09]. ISSN 0262-4079.

[10] Javadi, Elahe, Judith Gebauer a Joseph Mahoney. The Impact of User Interface Design on Idea Integration in Electronic Brainstorming: An Attention-Based View. Journal of the Association for Information Systems [online]. 2013, vol. 14, no. 1, s. 1-21. ISSN 15369323.

[11] Anderson, J.R, 2005. *Cognitive psychology and its implications*. New York, NY: W. H. Freeman. 6th edition. ISBN 978-1429219488.

About the author

The author is a professional programmer and web-application developer since 1998. In 2004, he founded a software company Kyberie in the Czech Republic which had been developing a software platform for insurance brokers for 8 years. In 2012, he sold the company including the technology platform and co-founded another company Wikilane in the United States which offers an invoicing software platform Invoice Home. Currently, the system has more than 900,000 active users and it's offered in about 150 countries around the world. The author also teaches Web Technologies and Web Application Development at the University of Economics, Prague and his is involved in software ergonomics and financial systems.

The author is currently in 3rd year of Applied Informatics PhD program at the University of Economics, Prague. In past, he graduated from the same university in Applied Informatics Bachelor's program and Master's program Cognitive Informatics, with Philosophy as a second specialization.

Author's PhD dissertation title is Software Ergonomics and Long-Term Sustainability Trends of User Interfaces and it is going to be completed till the end of 2017.

Author's supervisor in his PhD program is Vilém Sklenák, the chief of the Department of Information and Knowledge Engineering at the Faculty of Informatics and Statistics of University of Economics, Prague.

J. Hlaváčová (Ed.): ITAT 2017 Proceedings, pp. 228–234
ISBN 978-1974274741, © 2017 M. Kopecky, M. Vomlelova, P. Vojtas

Repeatable Web Data Extraction and Interlinking

M. Kopecky[1], M. Vomlelova[2], P. Vojtas[1]

Faculty of Mathematics and Physics
Charles University
Malostranske namesti 25,
Prague, Czech Republic

[1]{kopecky|vojtas}@ksi.mff.cuni.cz, [2]marta@ktiml.mff.cuni.cz

Abstract. We would like to make all the web content usable in the same way as it is in 5 star Linked (Open) Data. We face several challenges. Either there are no LODs in the domain of interest or the data project is no longer maintained or even something is broken (links, SPARQL endpoint etc.).

We propose a dynamic logic extension of the semantic model. Data could bear also information about their creation process. We calculate this on several movie datasets.

In this work in progress we provide some preference learning experiments over extracted and integrated data.

Keywords

Repeatable experiments; web data extraction, annotation, linking; dynamic logic; preference learning

1 Introduction, Motivation, Recent Work

For our decisions we often need automated processing of integrated web data. Linked (open) data are one possibility to achieve this vision. Still, there are some challenges.

Production URLs are sometimes subjects of change ([A]). Data migrate, data project run out of contracted sustainability period and so on.

SPARQL endpoints are expensive for the server, and not always available for all datasets. Downloadable dumps are expensive for clients, and do not allow live querying on the Web ([V+]).

In some areas there are no corresponding Linked data projects available at all. Imagine e.g. a customer looking for a car. He or she would like to aggregate all web data. Our idea is to remember previous successful extractions in given domain and use this in the current situation. For evaluation of previous extractions can help also social networks. We have presented this idea first in [PLEDVF]. We concentrated on one specific purpose – extract object attributes and use of these data in recommender systems. In this research we have tried to contribute to increase the degree of automation of web content processing. We presented several methods for mining web information and assisted annotations.

1.1 Semantic Annotator for (X)HTML

A tool for assisted annotation is available in [F2]. *Semantic Annotator* allows both manual and assisted annotation of web pages directly in Google Chrome. It requires no complicated installation and is available on all platforms and devices where it is possible to install Google Chrome. Semantic annotation is available to all current users of the Internet not only to authors' site. Browser extension *Semantic Annotator* began as a prototype implementation in the Thesis [F1].

Google Chrome extension *Semantic Annotator* is used for manual semantic annotation of Web sites. The goal of semantic annotation is to assign meaning to each part of the page. The significance of real-world objects and their properties and relationships are described in dictionaries – either self-created or imported. Then the annotation process consists of selecting parts of the site and the assignment of meaning from the dictionary.

Figure 1: Illustrative figure for Semantic annotator, more in [F1], [F2]

In Figure 1 we show an example of annotation of product pages in e-shop. The user selects a web page and product name from the dictionary describing products that assigns a name meaning "product name". Then on the same page the user selects a product price and gives it the meaning of "price". Because of similarity of pages and usage of templates, annotating few pages enables to train an annotator for the whole site. Consequently, search of annotated website is then much more accurate.

1.2 Semantic Annotations for Texts

In previous section we have described a tool for annotation of (X)HTML pages. These are useful for extraction of attributes of products on pages created by the same template even if texts are a little bit different. Even if there are no templates, in a fixed domain like reports on traffic accidents, there are still repetitions.

A tool for annotation of text was developed in our group in PhD thesis [D1]. The tool is available under [D2]. It is built on GATE [BTMC], using UFAL dependency parsing [UFAL] and Inductive Logic Programming extension. It represents a tool for information extraction and consequent annotation.

In the thesis [D1] are presented four relatively separate topics. Each topic represents one particular aspect of the information extraction discipline. The first two topics are focused on new information extraction methods based on deep language parsing in combination with manually designed extraction rules. The second topic deals with a method for automated induction of extraction rules using inductive logic programming. The third topic of the thesis combines information extraction with rule based reasoning. The core extraction method was experimentally reimplemented using semantic web technologies, which allows saving the extraction rules in so called shareable extraction ontologies that are not dependent on the original extraction tool. See Fig.2. on traffic accident data.

The last topic of the thesis deals with document classification and fuzzy logic. The possibility of using information obtained by information extraction techniques to document classification is examined. For more see also [PLEDVF].

In this research proposal we concentrate on synergy effect of annotation and integration of data for user preference learning, and consequently for recommendation.

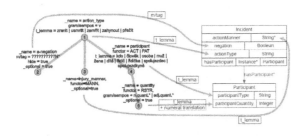

Figure 2: Illustrative figure of an extraction pattern for dependency tree, more in [D1], [D2].

It turns out that similarity and dynamic aspects of web data play a role here as well. We propose an appropriate *dynamic logic model* of web data dynamics and provide some experiments. We hope this can serve as preliminary experiments for a more extended research proposal.

2   Extraction Experiments

Our main goal is: Try to remember information about the context of data creation in order to enable repetition of extraction. In general we can remember algorithms, training data and metrics of success.

In this chapter we try to describe some extraction algorithms and process of data integration in movie domain. These data will be used in preference learning. By this we would like to illustrate our main goal.

2.1   Integration

We use *Flix* data (enriched *Netflix* competition data), *RecSys 2014 challenge* data [T] and *RuleML Challenge* data [K].

The datasets are quite different but they still have few things in common. Movies have their title and usually also the year of their production. Ratings are equipped by timestamp that allows us to order ratings from individual users chronologically.

One of problems was that different datasets use different MOVIEID's, so the movies cannot be straightforwardly mapped across datasets. To achieve this goal we wanted to enhance every movie by the corresponding IMDb identifier.

We observed that the *Twitter datasets* use as their internal **MOVIEID** the numeric part of the IMDb identifier. So the movie "Midnight Cowboy" with Twitter **MOVIEID** = 64665 corresponds to the IMDb record with ID equal to 'tt0064665'. Therefore, we construct the algorithm

τ_1: Twitter-**MOVIEID** → IMDbId

which simply concatenated prefix 'tt' with the **MOVIEID** left-padded by zeroes to seven positions. The successfulness of this algorithm is shown in Table 1.

Table 1: Simple identifier transformation

Algorithm	MovieLens	Flix	Twitter
$\tau_1()$	0%	0%	100%

To be able to assign IMDb identifiers to movies from other datasets, we had to use the search capabilities of the IMDb database. We used an HTTP interface for searching movies according to their name. The request is send by HTTP request in form `http://www.imdb.com/find?q=movie+title&s=tt`.

The other versions of algorithm for assigning IMDb identifiers to movies can be in general formally described as

$\tau_2^{i,j}$: **TITLE** × **YEAR** → **TT**

that is implemented by two independent steps

$\tau_2^{i,j}(\textbf{TITLE},\textbf{YEAR}) = \sigma_j(\eta_i(\textbf{TITLE}),\textbf{TITLE},\textbf{YEAR})$

where the algorithm η_i transforms movie title to query string needed for IMDb search, while the σ_j algorithm then looks for the correct record in returned table. The simplest implementation of algorithms can be denoted as follows:

η_1: **TITLE** → **TABLE**

σ_1: **TABLE** × **TITLE** × **YEAR** → **TT**

where η_1 algorithm concatenates all words of the title by the plus sign and σ_1 algorithm returns TT in case the resulting table contains exactly one record. The results of this combination of algorithm are shown in Table 2 (ratio of correct answers).

Table 2: The simplest version of IMDb search by title name

Algorithm	MovieLens	Flix	Twitter
$\sigma_1(\eta_1())$	42,7%	51,2%	Not needed

To illustrate different algorithms for same extraction task we describe another version. Here the algorithm is not learned, but it is hand crafted. One of reasons for relatively low effectiveness of $\sigma_1(\eta_1())$ algorithm was the sub-optimal query string used for IMDb search due to quite different naming conventions of movie titles in different datasets. To improve the results we enhanced the movie title transformation incrementally and produced its new versions. Every new version added new step of transformation of the movie title:

η_2: Convert all letters in movie title to lower case.

η_3: If the movie title contains year of production at its end in brackets remove it.

η_4: If the movie title still contains text in brackets at its end, remove it. This text usually contained original name of movie in original language.

η_5: Move word "the", respectively "a"/ "an" from the end of the title to the beginning.

η_6: Translate characters "_", ".", "?" and "," to spaces

η_7: Translate "&" and "&" in titles to word "and"

For example, the η_7 transformation changes title **"Official Story, The (La Historia Oficial) (1985)"** to its canonical form **"the official story"**.

This version of transformation then constructs the IMDb query in form http://www.imdb.com/find?q=the+official+story&s=tt&… and then looks up the resulting table to find identifier "tt0089276".

The results of this combination of algorithm were:

Table 3: The more complex version of IMDb search by title name

Algorithm	MovieLens	Flix	Twitter
$\sigma_1(\eta_7())$	45,4%	70,9%	Not needed

In optimal case, the table returning from the IMDb search contains exactly one row with the requested record. For this situation the algorithm σ_1 behaves well and is able to retrieve the correct IMDb identifier. In many other cases the result contains more rows and the correct one or the best possible one has to be identified. For this purpose we constructed more versions of the σ_j algorithm as well:

σ_2: The correct record should be from the requested year, so search only for records from this year and ignore other records

σ_3: The IMDb search provides more levels of tolerance in title matching. Try to use thee of them from the most exact one to the most general. If the matching record from requested year cannot be found using stricter search, the other search level is used.

Currently, we have 13 081 out of all 17 770 *Flix* movies mapped onto the IMDb database. Even all 27 278 movies from the *MovieLens* set are mapped to the equivalent IMDb record. So the current results provided by the combination of most advanced versions of algorithms are:

Table 4: The most complex version of IMDb search by title name

Algorithm	MovieLens	Flix	Twitter
$\sigma_3(\eta_7())$	100.0%	73.6%	Not needed

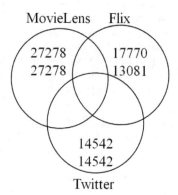

Figure 3: Numbers of movies mapped onto IMDb database

The diagram in the Figure 3 shows the number of movies in individual datasets and number of movies assigned to their corresponding IMDb record. Amount of movies associated to the IMDb record in different intersections after the integration is different. For example, the *MovieLens* dataset contains in total 27 278 movies. From these are 13 134 unique associated movies and also contain 3 759 associated movies common with the *Flix* dataset not existing in the *Twitter* dataset. The number of movies common for all three datasets is equal to 4 075. By summing of 3 759 and 4 075 we get the total number of 7 654 associated movies belonging to both *MovieLens* and *Flix* datasets, etc.

2.2   Extraction of attributes

For each movie registered in the IMDb database we then retrieved XML data from the URL address

```
http://www.omdbapi.com/?i=ttNNNNNNN&plot
=full&r=xml
```

and then from the XML data retrieve following movie attributes:

IMDb title	(/root/movie/@title),
IMDb rating	(/root/movie/@imdbRating),
IMDb rated	(/root/movie/@rated),
IMDb awards	(/root/movie/@awards),
IMDb metascore	(/root/movie/@metascore),
IMDb year	(/root/movie/@year),
IMDb country	(/root/movie/@country),
IMDb language	(/root/movie/@language),
IMDb genres	(/root/movie/@genre),
IMDb director	(/root/movie/@director),
IMDb actors	(/root/movie/@actors)

The similar way the movies from datasets are mapped onto IMDb movies, we implemented the mapping technique described in [K] and assigned *DbPedia*[1] identifiers and semantic data to IMDb movies.

The *DbPedia* identifier of movie is a string, for example "The_Official_Story" or "The_Seventh_Seal". This identifier can then be used to access directly the *DbPedia* graph database or retrieve data in an XML format through the URL address in form `http://dbpedia.org/page/DbPediaIdentifier`. From the data available on the *DbPedia* page can be directly or indirectly extracted movie attributes GENRE, GENRE1, ACTION, ADVENTURE, ANIMATION, CHILDRENS, COMEDY, CRIME, DOCUMENTARY, DRAMA, FANTASY, FILM_NOIR, HORROR, MYSTERY, MUSICAL, ROMANCE, SCI_FI, THRILLER, WAR, WESTERN or attributes CALIF, LA, NY, CAMERON, VISUAL, SEDIT, NOVELS, SMIX, SPIELBERG, MAKEUP, WILLIAMS and many others.

3   A Dynamic Logic Model for Web Annotation

For effective using of changing and/or increasing information we have to evolve tools (e.g. inductive methods) used for creation of specific web service (here recommendation of movies). Our goal is to extend the semantic web foundations to enable describing creation, dynamics and similarities on data. To describe the reliability of extraction algorithms we propose a "half-a-way" extension of dynamic logic.

Our reference for dynamic logic is the book of D. Harel, D. Kozen, J. Tiuryn [HKT].

Dynamic logic has two types of symbols: propositions/formulas $\varphi, \psi \in \Pi$ and programs $\alpha, \beta \in \Phi$. One can construct a program also from a formula by test $\varphi?$ and formulas also by generalized modality operations $[\alpha]$, $<\alpha>$. The expression $<\alpha>\varphi$ says that it is possible to execute α and halt in a state satisfying φ; the expression $[\alpha]\varphi$ says that whenever α halts, it does so in a state satisfying φ.

Main goal of dynamic logic is reasoning about programs, e.g. in program verification. In our case programs will be extractor/annotators and can be kept propositional, as for now we are not interested in procedural details of extractors. Formulas will be more expressible in order to be able to describe the context of extraction.

Using the example above, let

φ be the statement that a Twitter data entry has title "Midnight Cowboy" and **MOVIEID** = 64665;

α be the algorithm concatenating prefix 'tt' with the **MOVIEID** left-padded by zeroes to seven positions; and

ψ says movie "Midnight Cowboy" corresponds to the IMDb record with ID equal to 'tt0064665'.

The corresponding dynamic logic expression is

$$\forall x(\varphi(x) \rightarrow [\alpha]\psi(x))$$

saying that whenever α starts in a state satisfying $\varphi(m_1)$ then whenever α halts, it does so in a state satisfying $\psi(m_1)$ - see illustration in Fig.4.

Programs (extractors) remain propositional, states correspond to different representation of content on the web. On each of states the respective semantics is defined using appropriate query language.

Our logic has expressions of two sorts and each sort is, respectively can be typed:

Statements about web data: can be either atomic, e.g. Φ_0^{RDF}, Φ_0^{FOL}, Φ_0^{RDB}, Φ_0^{XML}, Φ_0^{DOM}, Φ_0^{BoW}, Φ_0^{PoS}, $\Phi_0^{DepTree}$, etc. or more complex, e.g. φ^{RDF}, ψ^{FOL}, etc. With the corresponding data model and query language based semantics. All can be subject of uncertainty, probability extensions.

Programs (propositional): atomic Π_0^{σ} for subject extraction, Π_0^{π} for property extraction or Π_0^{ω} for object value extraction in case of HTML, XHTML, or XML data; Π_0^{ner} for named entity extraction in case of text data, etc. and more complex $\alpha^{\sigma\pi\omega}$, $\beta^{\sigma\pi\omega}$, $\gamma^{\sigma\pi\omega}$, etc. In this logic we do not prove any statements about program depending on their code, so program names point to code one would reuse.

Statements are typically accompanied by information about program creation like data mining tool, training data, metrics (e.g. precision, recall), etc. There is also a lot of reification describing the training and testing data and the metrics of learning. Our model is based on dynamic logic, calculates similarity of states and describes uncertain/stochastic character of our knowledge.

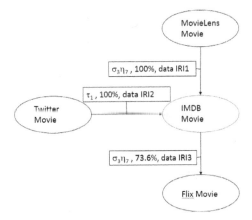

Figure 4: Extraction data enriched

[1] http://wiki.dbpedia.org/

Hence we are able to express our extraction experience in statements like

$$\varphi \rightarrow [\alpha]_x \psi$$

where φ is a statement about data D_1 before extraction (preconditions), ψ is a statement about data/knowledge D_2, K_2 after extraction (postconditions), α is the program used for extraction. Modality $[\alpha]_x$ can be weighted, describing uncertainty aspects of learning.

Lot of additional reification about learning can be helpful.

The main idea of this paper is that if there are some data D_1' similar to D_1 and φ is true in some degree – e.g. because both resources were created using same template - then after using α we can conclude with high certainty/probability that the statement ψ will be true on data D_2' (knowledge K_2').

For instance the formula

"MyData are similar to IRI3" $\rightarrow [\sigma_3\eta_7]_{0.736}$ "IMDBId is correct"

Experiments with extraction and integration of movie data can serve as an example of this. In the next chapter we would like illustrate how this influences recommendation.

4 Preference Learning Experiments

To show usability of extracted and annotated data, we provide experiments in area of recommender systems.

4.1 Data Preprocessing

We selected all *Twitter* users with ratings less or equal to 10, random 3000 *MovieLens* users and random 3000 *Flix* users.

For these, we split the **RATING** data by assigning last (according to time stamp) 5 records from each user as a test data, the remaining data was used as train data.

Based on train data, we calculated aggregated variables:

Table 5: Computed variables for each movie

Variable	Description
α_1 CNT	Number of ratings for a movie
α_2 MAVG	Average rating for a movie
α_3 BAYESAVG	(GLOBAL.AVERAGE*50 +MAVG*CNT) / (CNT+50)

Table 6: Computed variables for each user

Variable	Description
α_4 USERSHIFT	The average over rated movies (user.rating-BAYESAVG)

Table 7: Computed variables for each pair of user and movie

Variable	Description
α_5 GENREMATCH	Equality of the most frequent user's genre and the movie's genre

4.2 Results

Based on these attributes, we learned a linear model of RATING as a function of (CNT+BAYESAVG+MAVG+USERSHIFT+GENREMATCH).

Table 8 summarizes the train mean square error, test mean square error and for comparison the mean square error of the 'zero' model predicting always the overall average of training data. These are the uncertainty part of our dynamic logic.

Table 8: Result summarization

Dataset	MRSS train	MRSS test	MTSS train
Flix	0.690	0.714	1.100
Twitter	1.420	1.660	2.890
MovieLens	0.607	0.633	1.070

We can see that in all datasets, the difference between train and test error is very small compared with the results of the zero model. This means the model is not overfitted.

Since the *Twitter* dataset uses scale 0 to 10 compared to the scale 0 to 5 for *Flix* and *MovieLens*, the error differences cannot be compared directly.

The models may be compared by the R^2 statistics, the amount of variance explained by the model
$$R^2 = 1 - Sum(R[i]^2) / Sum((y[i]- y^*)^2)$$
Here $R[i]$ is the ith residual, $y[i]$ is the rating of ith record, y^* is average rating over all train records in dataset. Its range is from 0 (useless model) to 1 (prefect prediction).

In table 9 we can see significant differences between datasets, ranging from 0.506 for Twitter (best improvement) compared to 0.356 for *MovieLens* and 0.262 for *Flix*.

Table 9: R^2 statistics

Dataset	R^2
Flix	0.262
Twitter	0.506
MovieLens	0.356

In Table 10 we show preliminary results on testing repeatability. We trained the model on the data set in the row and tested on the test data in column. No surprise that in each column the best result is on the diagonal.

Table 10: Repeatability tests

Dataset	Flix test	Twitter test	MovieLens test
Flix train	**0.714**	1.731	0.635
Twitter train	0.723	**1.658**	0.639
MovieLens train	0.715	1.679	**0.633**
Zero model	1.100	2.890	**1.070**

As the zero model we use movie rating average MAVG.

In this research proposal, we do not evaluate role of similarity, we just illustrate similarity of our datasets.

In Figure 5 we show MAVG function on a sample of movies (with IMDB ID#s). Table 11 show MAVG distances below diagonal. So far it is not clear to us which metrics to use to compute similarity – Euclidean or cosine? Further experiments are required as this can depend on domain.

MAVG Function Comparison

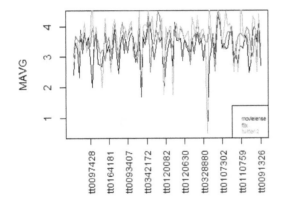

Figure 5: Towards calculating similarity – which vectors, which metrics? Here MAVG.

Maybe the right idea to calculate similarity is content based. We illustrate this by Fig. 6 with behavior of statistics on genres. Table 11 show genre based distance in cells above diagonal.

5 Proposal, Conclusions, Future Work

We have provided preliminary experiments with reusability of our algorithms. Results are promising, but still we need more extensive testing.

5.1 Proposal of Reusability Quality

Similarly, as in Linked data quality assessment, we can imagine similar assessment for reusability.

The main idea is, that this will be less sensitive to URL change, migration and "end-of-project-phenomenon". One can imagine, that these information are published at https://sourceforge.net/ or similar service. What follows is a vision, we would like to discuss:

Average MAVG for Movie Genres

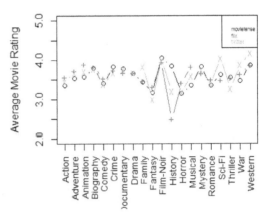

Figure 6: Maybe genres play a role?

Table 11: Distance of datasets. Below diagonal by MAVG, above diagonal with Genres

	Flix	Twitter	Movie Lens
Flix	0.00	0.10	0.14
Twitter	0.51	0.00	**0.06**
MovieLens	**0.42**	0.54	0.00

6★ Reusability extraction describes the algorithm, training data, metrics and results.

7★ Reusability extraction extends a 6★ one by additional similarity measures and thresholds for successful reuse. A corresponding formula can look like

"Data $\approx_{0.2}$ IRI3" → $[\sigma_3\eta_7]_{0.654}$ "IMDBId is correct"

8★ Reusability extraction describes a 7★ one in a more extensive way with several different data examples and similarities. This can increase the chance that for a given domain you find solution which fits your data.

9★ Reusability extraction assumes a 8★ one in a server/cloud implementation. You do not have to solve problems that the extractor does not run in your environment properly.

10★ Reusability extraction assumes a 9★ one in a more user friendly way, you just upload your data (or their URL) and the system finds solution and you can download result. It is also possible to imagine this enhanced with some social network interaction.

5.2   Conclusions

We have presented a research proposal for improving degree of automation of web information extraction and annotation. We propose a formal dynamic logic model for automated web annotation with similarity and reliability.

We illustrated our approach by an initial prototype and experiments on recommendation on movie data (annotated and integrated).

5.3   Future work

The challenge is twofold:
- extend this to other domains
- provide deeper analysis of data mining and possible similarities

We can consider some more complex algorithms for preference learning, e.g., based on the spreading activation [GG].

Acknowledgement

Research was supported by Czech project Progres Q48.

References

[A] [IBM] John Arwe. Coping with Un-Cool URIs in the Web of Linked Data, LEDP-Linked Enterprise Data Patterns workshop. Data-driven Applications on the Web. 6-7 December 2011, Cambridge, MA Hosted by W3C/MIT

[BTMC] K. Bontcheva, V. Tablan, D. Maynard, and H. Cunningham (2004), Evolving GATE to Meet New Challenges in Language Engineering, Natural Language Engineering, 10(3/4):349—373.

[D1] J. Dedek, Semantic Annotations 2012, http://www.ksi.mff.cuni.cz/~dedek/publications/Dedek_Ph D_Semantic_Annotations.pdf

[D2] J. Dedek. Semantic Czech, http://czsem.sourceforge.net/

[F1] D. Fiser. Semantic annotation of domain dependent data (in Czech). Master thesis, Charles University, Prague 2011

[F2] D. Fiser. Semantic annotator. https://chrome.google.com/webstore/detail/semantic-annotator/gbphidobolopkilhnpkbagodhalimojj   , http://www.doser.cz/projects/semantic-annotator/ (User Guide and Installation Guide (server part) in Czech),

[GG] L. Grad-Gyenge, Recommendations on a knowledge graph, 2015

[HKT] D. Harel, D. Kozen, J. Tiuryn. Dynamic Logic (Foundations of Computing) The MIT Press 2000

[K]   Kuchar J.: Augmenting a Feature Set of Movies Using Linked Open Data, Proceedings of the RuleML 2015

Challenge, Berlin, Germany. Published by CEUR Workshop Proceedings, 2015

[PLEDVF] L. Peska, I. Lasek, A. Eckhardt, J. Dedek, P. Vojtas, D. Fiser: Towards web semantization and user understanding. In EJC 2012, Y. Kiyoki et al Eds. Frontiers in Artificial Intelligence and Applications 251, IOS Press 2013, pp 63-81

[T] Twitter data from RecSys 2014 challenge http://2014.recsyschallenge.com/

[UFAL] S. Cinková, J. Hajič, M. Mikulová, L. Mladová, A. Nedolužko, P. Pajas, J. Panevová, J. Semecký, J. Šindlerová, J. Toman, Z. Urešová, Z. Žabokrtský (2006), Annotation of English on the tectogrammatical level, Technical Report 35, UFAL MFF UK, URL http://ufal.mff.cuni.cz/pedt/papers/TR_En.pdf.

[V+] Verborgh R. et al. (2014) Querying Datasets on the Web with High Availability. In: Mika P. et al. (eds) The Semantic Web – ISWC 2014. ISWC 2014. Lecture Notes in Computer Science, vol 8796. Springer, Cham

J. Hlaváčová (Ed.): ITAT 2017 Proceedings, pp. 235–239
ISBN 978-1974274741, © 2017 T. Kliegr, J. Kuchař, S. Vojíř, V. Zeman

EasyMiner – Short History of Research and Current Development

Tomáš Kliegr[1], Jaroslav Kuchař[2], Stanislav Vojíř[1], and Václav Zeman[1]

[1] Department of Information and Knowledge Engineering, Faculty of Informatics and Statistics, University of Economics, Prague,
W. Churchill Sq. 4, Prague 3, Czech Republic
[2] Web Intelligence Research Group, Faculty of Information Technology, Czech Technical University, Thákurova 9, 160 00, Prague 6,
Czech Republic
`first.last@{vse|fit.cvut}.cz`

Abstract: EasyMiner (`easyminer.eu`) is an academic data mining project providing data mining of association rules, building of classification models based on association rules and outlier detection based on frequent pattern mining. It differs from other data mining systems by adapting the "web search" paradigm. It is web-based, providing both a REST API and a user interface, and puts emphasis on interactivity, simplicity of user interface and immediate response. This paper will give an overview of research related to the EasyMiner project.

1 Introduction

In this paper, we present the history of research and development of the EasyMiner project `http://easyminer.eu`. EasyMiner is an academic data mining project providing data mining of association rules, building of classification models based on association rules and outlier detection based on frequent pattern mining.

EasyMiner was to our knowledge the first interactive web-based data mining system that supported the complete machine learning process. While today there are several web-based machine learning systems on the market[1], owing to continuous development EasyMiner provides distinct user experience. While most existing machine learning systems offer versatile user interfaces, where the user has to in some way for each task compose a new machine learning workflow, in EasyMiner the user interface is crafted to provide the "web search" experience. The user visually constructs a query against the data, and the system responds with a set of interesting patterns (presented as rules) or a classifier (Figure 1).

Over the years of development, EasyMiner served as a testbed for a number of new technologies and research ideas. The purpose of this paper is to give a brief overview of this research.

This paper is organized as follows. Section 2 is focused on SEWEBAR-CMS, the predecessor of EasyMiner, used in research on the use of domain knowledge in data mining. Section 3 focuses on association rule discovery. Section 4 presents the adaptation of EasyMiner for learning business rules and Section 5 consequently for association rule classification. Section 6 presents the current focus on

outlier detection. The architecture of the system is presented in Section 7. Since the beginnings, the research was accompanied with standardization efforts, which are presented in Section 8. The current development efforts focus also on distributed computation platforms – this is covered in Section 9. Section 10 provides an overview of the features that were at some point in time developed as well as of those that are supported by the current version of EasyMiner. Finally, the conclusions present a case for using EasyMiner as a component in new project requiring data mining functionality and refers the interested reader to other publications regarding comparison with other machine learning as a service (MLaaS) systems.

2 Handling of Domain Knowledge

EasyMiner evolved from the SEWEBAR (SEmantic-WEB Analytical Reports) project, which focused on semantically readable machine learning. In [9], we presented SEWEBAR-CMS as a set of extensions for the Joomla! content management system (CMS) that extends it with functionality required to serve as a communication platform between the data analyst, domain expert and the report user. The system later supported elicitation of domain knowledge from the analyst [12]. Association rules discovered from data with the LISp-Miner system (`http://lispminer.vse.cz`) were stored in a semantic form in the SEWEBAR-CMS system. The background knowledge was used to help answer user search queries, for example, to find rules that are contradicting existing domain knowledge [6]. Another novel element in the system was the use of ontology for representation of the data mining domain.

Related research focused on improving semantic capabilities of content management systems [3] and on designing ontologies and schemata for representation of background knowledge [8, 11].

3 Association Rule Discovery

In its first release, EasyMiner provided a web-based interface for the LISp-Miner system, which was used for association rule mining [23]. EasyMiner interacted with LISp-Miner using its LM-Connect component, which is a web application providing the functionality of LISp-Miner through REST API.

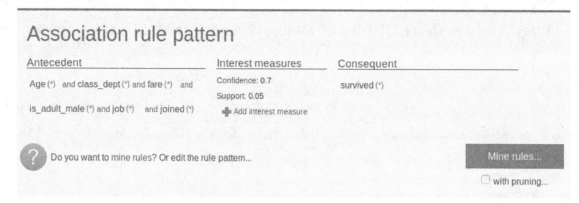

Figure 1: Visual query designer in EasyMiner.

Table 1: Features supported in EasyMiner 2.4. Year - when was the paper describing the feature published, API - feature available in the REST API, UI - feature available in the user interface.

Feature	Year	API	UI
Content Management System [9]	2009	No	No
Semantic search over discovered rules [3]	2010	No	No
Support for GUHA extension of PMML [10]	2010	Yes	Yes
Query for related (confirming, contradicting) rules to the selected rule [6]	2011	No	No
Editor of background knowledge [12]	2011	No	No
LISp-Miner interface (disjunctions, negations, partial cedents, quantifiers, cuts, coefficients) [23]	2012	No	No
Export of business rules to Drools [21]	2013	No	No
Rule pruning with CBA [5]	2014	Yes	Yes
Evaluation of quality of classification models [20]	2014	Yes	No
Rule selection and editing for classification model building [20]	2014	Yes	No
R interface (arules package) [22]	2015	Yes	Yes
Spark backend [25]	2016	Yes	Yes
Discretization algorithms [25]	2016	Yes	No
Support for the input RDF data format	2017	Yes	No
Outlier detection [19]	2017	Yes	No

EasyMiner with LISp-Miner backend offered several unique features: 1. negation on attributes, 2. disjunction between attributes, 3. subpatterns allowing for scoping logical connectives, 4. multiple interest measures (called quantifiers in GUHA), 5. mines directly on multivalued attributes, no need to create "items", 6. dynamic binning operators (called coefficients in GUHA), 7. PMML-based import and export, 8. grid support.

Since LM-Connect component is no longer developed and maintained, the integration of the current version of EasyMiner and LISp-Miner is thus currently not working.[2]

The current version of EasyMiner primarily relies on the R arules package [2], which wraps a C implementation of the apriori association rule mining algorithm [1].

4   Learning Business Rules

One of the first use cases for EasyMiner was learning business rules. In [21] we presented a software module for EasyMiner, which allows to export selected rules to Business Rules Management System (BRMS) Drools, transforming the output of association rule learning into the DRL format supported by Drools. We found that the main obstacles for a straightforward use of association rules as candidate business rules are the excessive number of rules discovered even on small datasets, and the fact that contradicting rules are generated. In [5] we propose that a potential solution to these problems is provided by the seminal association rule classification algorithm CBA [16]. In [20] we presented a software module for EasyMiner, which allows the domain expert to edit the discovered rules.

5   Association Rule Based Classification

In [5] we started to use the CBA algorithm for postprocessing association rule learning results into a classifier. In [22] we presented an extension for EasyMiner for building of classification models. A benchmark against standard symbolic classification algorithms on a news recommender task was presented in [7].

---

[2]It should be noted that all the features list above can be used directly from the LISp-Miner system.

6   Outlier Detection

The most recent addition of new tasks supported by EasyMiner is frequent pattern-based anomaly (outlier) detection. The main idea of the approach is that if an instance contains more frequent patterns, it is unlikely to be an anomaly. The presence or absence of the frequent patterns is then used to assign the deviation level [4]. In [19] we present extension of EasyMiner REST API with our innovated outlier detection algorithm called *Frequent Pattern Isolation* (FPI)[15] that is inspired by an existing algorithm called Isolation Forests (IF) [17, 18]. Since PMML does not yet support outlier (anomaly) detection, in [14] we present our proposal for a new PMML outlier model. The goal of our work was to design modular solution that would support broader range of anomaly detection algorithms including our FPI method.

7   EasyMiner Architecture

During the development of EasyMiner system, its architecture was transformed to multiple reusable web services. A schema of the architecture is shown in Figure 2. All the services are fully documented in Swagger.

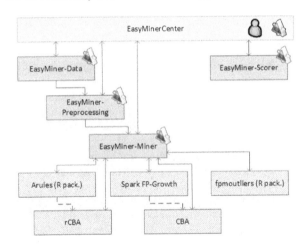

Figure 2: Architecture of the system EasyMiner

The central component (service) is **EasyMinerCenter**. This component integrates the functionality of other services and provides the main graphical web interface and REST API for end users. Internally, this component provides user account and task management, stores discovered association rules and works as authentication service for other components.

For storing and preparing data before mining, the system uses services EasyMiner-Data and EasyMiner-Preprocessing. **EasyMiner-Data** is a web services for management of data sources. It supports upload of data files in CSV and RDF and stores them into databases as the set of transactions. **EasyMiner-Preprocessing** service supports creation of datasets from data sources stored

using EasyMiner-Data using user-defined preprocessing methods. The attributes for data mining are created from uploaded data fields using one of these preprocessing algorithms: each value-one bin, enumeration of intervals, enumeration of nominal values, equidistant intervals, equifrequent intervals, equisized intervals (by minimal support of every interval). The preprocessing algorithms as well as data storage are independent of the selected data mining algorithm. The implemented web services support hashing functionality to avoid potentially problems with special characters in attribute names and its values. The mining following services work on the "safe" datasets with hashed values.

The main data mining functionality is provided by the service **EasyMiner-Miner**. This web service provides association rule learning, prunning of discovered association rule sets and building of classification models and outlier detection. EasyMiner-Miner initializes execution of used R packages and another algorithms.

EasyMiner-Scorer is a web service for testing of classification models based on association rules.

8   Distributed Backend: Spark/Hadoop

As laid out in the previous section, EasyMiner is modular in terms of mining backends. In addition to the default mining backend provided by the arules and rCBA packages, EasyMiner supports an alternate one built on top of Apache Spark/Hadoop introduced in [25].

The Spark backend is suitable for larger datasets, which can benefit from parallel computation distributed over multiple machines. The Spark backend also uses FP-Growth frequent pattern mining algorithm instead of apriori. FP-Growth is generally considered as faster than apriori. However, for smaller datasets using apriori with the R backend is recommended as it provides faster response times, due to the ability of the implementation to provide intermediate results as the mining progresses.

9   Standardization Efforts (PMML)

Already the earliest research related to EasyMiner was linked to work on standardization efforts. While association rules were supported already in the early versions of PMML, the industry standard format for exchange of data mining models, the GUHA method that was initially used did not comply to this standard, since it produced rules containing number of constructs not supported by PMML. Since our research involved background knowledge elicited from domain experts, definition of data format supporting this type of knowledge was also required.

In [8] we proposed a topic map-based ontology for association rule learning, which was based on the GUHA method and in [11] an extension of this approach that dealt with domain knowledge. An extension of PMML for

GUHA-based models was presented in [10] and for handling of background knowledge [13]. Neither of these efforts was successful – the ISO Topic Maps standard waded in favour of the W3C RDF/OWL stack. The industry was not concerned with exchange of background knowledge at the time, and support of GUHA method, implemented essentially only by the LISp-Miner system, increased complexity of the models as opposed to the existing PMML association rule models.[3] Our latest standardization effort is related to outlier detection [14] and targets PMML. This proposal is closes industry adoption as it was included into a roadmap for the next release of PMML.

10 Features in the EasyMiner Version 2.4

Table 1 presents an overview of the most salient features that were in some for published between 2009, when the first paper on EasyMiner's predecessor SEWEBAR-CMS appeared, and 2017, when the current version of EasyMiner was released. As follows from the table, a number of features is not supported in the current release.

11 Using EasyMiner in Your Project

During the years of development, EasyMiner was extensively used by over thousand of students at the Faculty of Informatics and Statistics to complete their assignments in association rule learning. The software has also been used in several applied research projects. For example, within the linkedtv.eu project EasyMiner was used to analyze user preferences and within the openbudgets.eu project to analyze budgetary data.

The full project is based on composition of components and services with fully documented REST APIs. Most of the components and services[4] are available under open source Apache License, Version 2.0. This is an important factor which differentiates EasyMiner from the commercial MLaaS offerings. For a more detailed comparison with other machine learning systems refer to [24].

In addition to the visual web-based interface, the project exposes a REST API. This API provides full functionality of EasyMiner, including also functions, which are not yet available in the GUI. It is possible to use this API to extend your own project by data mining functionality. It is suitable for building of mashup applications or data processing using script languages. An example of data mining using API is available at http://www.easyminer.eu/api-tutorial.

EasyMiner can also be extended with new algorithms - rule mining, outlier detection or scorer service. For this purpose, the integration component EasyMinerCenter provides documented interfaces in PHP.

---

[3]Currently, EasyMiner supports export of association rule models in formats GUHA PMML also as in standard form PMML 4.3 Association Rules.

[4]The main services were presented in section 7.

Acknowledgment

This paper was supported by IGA grant 29/2016 of the University of Economics, Prague.

References

[1] Rakesh Agrawal, Tomasz Imielinski, and Arun N. Swami. Mining association rules between sets of items in large databases. In *SIGMOD*, pages 207–216. ACM Press, 1993.

[2] Michael Hahsler, Sudheer Chelluboina, Kurt Hornik, and Christian Buchta. The arules r-package ecosystem: analyzing interesting patterns from large transaction data sets. *Journal of Machine Learning Research*, 12(Jun):2021–2025, 2011.

[3] Andrej Hazucha, Jakub Balhar, and Tomáš Kliegr. A PHP library for Ontopia-CMS integration. In *TMRA 2010*. University of Leipzig, 2010.

[4] Z. He, X. Xu, Z. Huang, and S. Deng. FP-outlier: Frequent pattern based outlier detection. *Computer Science and Information Systems/ComSIS*, 2(1):103–118, 2005.

[5] Tomáš Kliegr, Jaroslav Kuchař, Davide Sottara, and Stanislav Vojíř. Learning business rules with association rule classifiers. In Antonis Bikakis, Paul Fodor, and Dumitru Roman, editors, *Rules on the Web. From Theory to Applications: 8th International Symposium, RuleML 2014, Co-located with the 21st European Conference on Artificial Intelligence, ECAI 2014, Prague, Czech Republic, August 18-20, 2014. Proceedings*, pages 236–250, Cham, 2014. Springer International Publishing.

[6] Tomáš Kliegr, Andrej Hazucha, and Tomáš Marek. Instant feedback on discovered association rules with PMML-based query-by-example. In *Web Reasoning and Rule Systems*. Springer, 2011.

[7] Tomáš Kliegr and Jaroslav Kuchař. Benchmark of rule-based classifiers in the news recommendation task. In Josiane Mothe, Jacques Savoy, Jaap Kamps, Karen Pinel-Sauvagnat, Gareth J. F. Jones, Eric SanJuan, Linda Cappellato, and Nicola Ferro, editors, *Experimental IR Meets Multilinguality, Multimodality, and Interaction - 6th International Conference of the CLEF Association, CLEF 2015, Toulouse, France, September 8-11, 2015, Proceedings*, volume 9283 of *Lecture Notes in Computer Science*, pages 130–141. Springer, 2015.

[8] Tomáš Kliegr, Marek Ovečka, and Jan Zemánek. Topic maps for association rule mining. In *Proceedings of TMRA 2009*. University of Leipzig, 2009.

[9] Tomáš Kliegr, Martin Ralbovský, Vojtěch Svátek, Milan Šimunek, Vojtěch Jirkovský, Jan Nemrava, and Jan Zemánek. Semantic analytical reports: A framework for post-processing data mining results. In *ISMIS'09: 18th International Symposium on Methodologies for Intelligent Systems*, pages 453–458. Springer, 2009.

[10] Tomáš Kliegr and Jan Rauch. An XML format for association rule models based on the GUHA method. In *Proceedings of the 2010 International Conference on Semantic Web Rules*, RuleML'10, pages 273–288, Berlin, Heidelberg, 2010. Springer-Verlag.

[11] Tomáš Kliegr, Vojtěch Svátek, Milan Šimůnek, Daniel Štastný, and Andrej Hazucha. An XML schema and a topic map ontology for formalization of background knowledge in data mining. In *IRMLeS-2010, 2nd ESWC Workshop on Inductive Reasoning and Machine Learning for the Semantic Web, Heraklion, Crete, Greece*, 2010.

[12] Tomáš Kliegr, Vojtěch Svátek, Milan Šimůnek, and Martin Ralbovský. Semantic analytical reports: A framework for post-processing of data mining results. *Journal of Intelligent Information Systems*, 37(3):371–395, 2011.

[13] Tomáš Kliegr, Stanislav Vojíř, and Jan Rauch. Background knowledge and PMML: first considerations. In *Proceedings of the 2011 workshop on Predictive markup language modeling*, PMML '11, pages 54–62, New York, NY, USA, 2011. ACM.

[14] Jaroslav Kuchař, Adam Ashenfelter, and Tomáš Kliegr. Outlier (anomaly) detection modelling in PMML. In *RuleML 2017 Poster and Challenge Proceedings*. CEUR-WS, 2017.

[15] Jaroslav Kuchař and Vojtěch Svátek. Spotlighting anomalies using frequent patterns. In *KDD 2017 Workshop on Anomaly Detection in Finance, Halifax, Nova Scotia, Canada*, 2017.

[16] Bing Liu, Wynne Hsu, and Yiming Ma. Integrating classification and association rule mining. In *Proceedings of the Fourth International Conference on Knowledge Discovery and Data Mining*, KDD'98, pages 80–86. AAAI Press, 1998.

[17] F. T. Liu, K. M. Ting, and Z. H. Zhou. Isolation forest. In *Proceedings of the 8th IEEE International Conference on Data Mining (ICDM'08)*, pages 413–422, 2008.

[18] Fei Tony Liu, Kai Ming Ting, and Zhi-Hua Zhou. Isolation-based anomaly detection. *ACM Trans. Knowl. Discov. Data*, 6(1):3:1–3:39, March 2012.

[19] Stanislav Vojíř, Jaroslav Kuchař, Václav Zeman, and Tomáš Kliegr. Using easyminer API for financial data analysis in project openbudgets.eu. In *RuleML 2017 Poster and Challenge Proceedings*. CEUR-WS, 2017. To appear.

[20] Stanislav Vojíř, Přemysl Václav Duben, and Tomáš Kliegr. Business rule learning with interactive selection of association rules. *RuleML Challenge, 2014*, 2014.

[21] Stanislav Vojíř, Tomáš Kliegr, Andrej Hazucha, Radek Skrabal, and Milan Šimůnek. Transforming association rules to business rules: EasyMiner meets Drools. In Paul Fodor, Dumitru Roman, Darko Anicic, Adam Wyner, Monica Palmirani, Davide Sottara, and Francois Lévy, editors, *RuleML-2013 Challenge*, volume 1004 of *CEUR Workshop Proceedings*. CEUR-WS.org, 2013.

[22] Stanislav Vojíř, Václav Zeman, Jaroslav Kuchař, and Tomáš Kliegr. Easyminer/R preview: Towards a web interface for association rule learning and classification in R. In *Challenge+ DC@ RuleML*, 2015.

[23] Radek Škrabal, Milan Šimůnek, Stanislav Vojíř, Andrej Hazucha, Tomáš Marek, David Chudán, and Tomáš Kliegr. Association rule mining following the web search paradigm. In Peter A. Flach, Tijl Bie, and Nello Cristianini, editors, *Machine Learning and Knowledge Discovery in Databases*, volume 7524 of *Lecture Notes in Computer Science*, pages 808–811. Springer Berlin Heidelberg, 2012.

[24] Václav Zeman. Analýza cloudového řešení akademického nástroje pro dolování pravidel z databází. *Systémová Integrace*, 23, 2016.

[25] Václav Zeman, Stanislav Vojíř, Jaroslav Kuchař, and Tomáš Kliegr. Využití cloudu pro dolování asociačních pravidel z velkých dat přes webové rozhraní. In *WIKT/DaZ 2016*, 2016.

J. Hlaváčová (Ed.): ITAT 2017 Proceedings, pp. 240–245
ISBN 978-1974274741, © 2017 L. Peska

Multimodal Implicit Feedback for Recommender Systems

Ladislav Peska

Department of Software Engineering, Faculty of Mathematics and Physics
Charles University, Prague, Czech Republic

Abstract. *In this paper, we present an overview of our work towards utilization of multimodal implicit feedback in recommender systems for small e-commerce enterprises. We focus on deeper understanding of implicit user feedback as a rich source of heterogeneous information. We present a model of implicit feedback for e-commerce, discuss important contextual features affecting its values and describe ways to utilize it in the process of user preference learning and recommendation. We also briefly report on our previous experiments within this scope and describe a publicly available dataset containing such multimodal implicit feedback.*

1 Introduction

Recommender systems belong to the class of automated content-processing tools, aiming to provide users with unknown, surprising, yet relevant objects without the necessity of explicitly query for them. The core of recommender systems are machine learning algorithms applied on the matrix of user to object preferences. In large enterprises, user preference is primarily derived from explicit user rating (also referred as *explicit feedback*) and collaborative-filtering algorithms [11] usually outperforms other approaches [3].

In our research, however, we foucus on small or medium-sized e-commerce enterprises. This domain introduce several specific problems and obstacles making the deployment of recommender systems more challenging. Let us briefly list the key challenges:

- High concurrency has a negative impact on user loyalty. Typical sessions are very short, users quickly leave to other vendors, if their early experience is not satisfactory enough. Only a fraction of users ever returns.

- For those single-time visitors, it is not sensible to provide any unnecessary information (e.g., ratings, reviews, registration details).

- Consumption rate is low, users often visit only a handful (0-5) of objects.

All the mentioned factors contribute to the data sparsity problem. Although the total number of users may be relatively large (hundreds or thousands per day), explicit feedback is very scarce. Also the volume of visited objects per user is limited and utilizing popularity-based approaches w.r.t. purchases is questionable at best. Furthermore the identification of unique user is quite challenging.

Despite these obstacles, the potential benefit of recommender systems is considerable, it can contribute towards better user experience, increase user loyalty and consumption and thus also improve vendor's key success metrics.

Our work within this framework aims to bridge the data sparsity problem and the lack of relevant feedback by modelling, combining and utilizing novel/enhanced sources of information, foremost various *implicit feedback* features, i.e., features based on the observed user behavior.

Contrary to the explicit feedback, usage of implicit feedback [5], [17], [18], [28] requires no additional effort from the users. Monitoring implicit feedback in general varies from simple features like user visits or play counts to more sophisticated ones like scrolling or mouse movement tracking [12], [29]. Due to its effortlessness, data are obtained in much larger quantities for each user. On the other hand, data are inherently noisy, messy and harder to interpret [10]. **Figure 1** depicts a simplified view of human-computer interaction on small e-commerce enterprises with accent on the implicit feedback provided by the user.

Our work lies a bit further from the mainstream of the implicit feedback research. To our best knowledge, the vast majority of researchers focus on interpreting single type of implicit feedback [6], proposing various latent factor models [10], [26], its adjustments [9], [19] or focusing on other aspects of recommendations using implicit feedback based datasets [2], [25]. Also papers using binary implicit feedback derived from explicit user rating are quite common [16], [19].

In contrast to the majority of research trends, we consider implicit feedback as multimodal and context-dependent. As our aim in this direction is a long-term one, we already published some of our findings [17], [18], [20], [22], [23]. In our aim towards improving recommender systems on small e-commerce enterprises, we focused on following aspects of implicit feedback:

- Cover the *multimodality of implicit feedback*.
- Propose relevant *context of collected feedback*.
- Derive models of *negative preference* based on implicit feedback

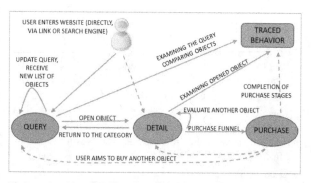

Figure 1: Simplified state diagram of human-computer interaction in e-commerce: User enters the site via *query* or object's *detail*. He/she can navigate through category or search result pages implicitly updating his/her query, or proceed to evaluate *details* of selected objects and eventually execute steps to buy them.

We reserve Section 2.1 to the description of multimodal implicit feedback, Section 2.2 to the contextualization of user feedback and Section 2.3 to the problem of learning negative preference. For each problem, we describe relevant state of the art, current challenges as well as our proposed methods and models. Finally, we remark on the evaluation of proposed methods in Section 3 and conclude in Section 4.

2   Materials and Methods

2.1   Multimodal Implicit Feedback

Despite the large volume of research based on a single implicit feedback feature, we consider implicit feedback to be inherently multimodal. Users utilize various I/O devices (mouse, keybord) to interact with different webpage's GUI controls, so there is an abundant amount of potentially interesting user actions.   As the complexity of such environment is overwhelming, we imposed some restrictions:

- Limit to the feedback related directly to some specific object, i.e., collect the feedback only from the object's detail page.
- Aggregate the same types of user actions on per session and per object basis.
- Focus only on user actions which can be numerically aggregated, i.e., the desired feedback features have numerical domain.

See **Figure 2** for an example of feedback features derived from user actions. In the following experiments, we consider these implicit feedback features[1]:

- Number of *views* of the page
- *Dwell Time* (i.e., the time spent on the object)
- Total *distance* travelled by the *mouse* cursor.
- Total m*ouse* in motion *time*.
- Total *scrolled distance*.
- *Scroll Time* (i.e., the time spent by scrolling)
- *Clicks count* (i.e., the volume of mouse clicks)
- *Purchase* (i.e., binary information whether user bought this object).

Although multimodal implicit feedback is not a mainstream research topic, we were able to trace some research papers. One of the first paper mentioning implicit feedback was Claypool et al. [5], which compared three implicit preference indicators against explicit user rating. More recently Yang et al. [29] analyzed several types of user behavior on YouTube. Authors described both positive and negative implicit indicators of preference and proposed linear model to combine them. Also Lai et al. [12] work on RSS feed recommender utilizing multiple reading-related user actions.

However, the lack of publicly available datasets containing multimodal implicit feedback significantly hinders advance of the area. Some work towards bridging

---

[1] Please note that the dataset used for the experiments contains also other feedback features such as number of page prints, followed links count, several non-numeric feedback features etc. These features seemed not relevant for the current task, however they may be utilized in the future.

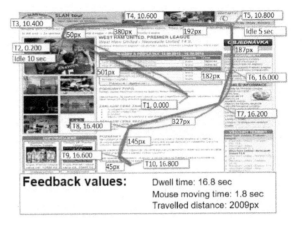

Figure 2: An example of mouse movement-based feedback collection on an e-commerce product detail page. Cursor positions (red line) are sampled periodically. Based on the samples, approximated mouse in-motion time (green boxes) and travelled distance (blue line) are calculated. Cursor motion log is also stored for later reasoning.

this data gap was done quite recently in RecSys Challenges 2016 and 2017[2]. Both challenges' datasets focused on job recommendation and contained several types of positive and negative user feedback. Although the dataset was not made publicly available, some approaches proposed relevant methods to deal with multimodal implicit feedback, e.g., fixed weighting scheme [31], hierarchical model of features [15] or utilizing features separately [28]. Some authors also mention the probability of re-interaction with objects on some domains [4], [33].

2.1.1   Methods Utilizing Multimodal Feedback

Vast majority of the state-of-the-art approaches transforms multimodal implicit feedback into a single numeric output $\bar{r}$, which can be viewed as a proxy towards user rating. However, these methods mostly use some fixed model of implicit feedback (i.e., predefined weights or hierarchy of feedback features), or perform predictions based on each feedback feature separately [28].

In contrast to the other approaches, we aim on estimating $\bar{r}$ via machine learning methods applied on a purchase prediction task. Our approach is based on the fact that the only measurable implicit feedback with direct interpretation of preference is buying an object. Such events are however too scarce to be used as a sole user preference indicator. However, we can define a classification task to determine, based on the values of other feedback types, whether the object will be purchased by the user. The estimated rating $\bar{r}$ is defined as the probability of the *purchased* class.

We evaluated several machine learning methods, such as decision trees, random forests, boosting, lasso regression and linear regressions. We also evaluated approaches based on *the more feedback the better* heuristics, i.e., the higher value of particular feedback feature implies higher user preference. In order to make the domains of all feedback features comparable, we utilized either standardization of

---

[2] [2016|2017].recsyschallenge.com

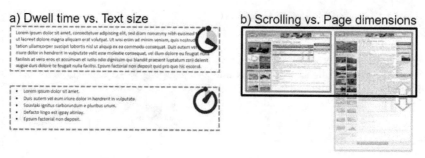

Figure 4: Two examples of relevant presentation context. A: overall length of text (and possibly also amount of other objects, e.g., images) affects the necessary reading time accessed through the *dwell time* feedback feature. B: the difference between page dimensions and device displaying size affects the necessity to scroll the content and thus, e.g., *scrolled distance* feature.

feedback values (denoted as *Heuristical with STD* in results), or used empirical cumulative distribution instead of raw feedback values (*Heuristical with CDF*). The estimated rating $\bar{r}$ is defined as the mean of *STD* or *CDF* values of all feedback features for the respective user and object. For more details on heuristical approaches please refer to [23], for more details on machine learning approaches please refer to [18].

2.2 Context of User Feedback

Although the user feedback may be processed directly, the perceived feedback values are significantly affected by the presentation of the page (i.e., device parameters) and also by the amount of contained information. Both the displaying device and the page's complexity can be described by several numeric parameters, which we generally denote as the *presentation context*. See **Figure 4** for some examples of relevant presentation context.

We can trace some notions of presentation context in the literature. Yi et al. [30], proposed to use dwell time as an indicator of user engagement. Authors discussed the usage of several contextual features, e.g., content type, device type or article length as a baseline dwell time estimators. Furthermore, Radlinski et al. [24] and Fang et al. [8] considered object position as a relevant context for clickstream events.

The *presentation context* differs significantly from more commonly used *user context* [1] in both its definition, methods for feature collection as well as ways to incorporate it into the recommending pipeline. While the nature of *user context* is rather restrictive [32], we interpret *presentation context* as a baseline predictor or an input feature for machine learning process.

In our work, we considered following *presentation context* features:

- *Volumes of text*, *images* and *links* on the page.
- *Page dimensions* (width, height).
- *Browser's visible area* dimensions (width, height).
- *Visible area ratio*.
- *Hand-held device* indicator.

We evaluated several approaches utilizing biases for feedback feature values based on the current presentation context. Such approaches, however, were not very successful and in particular often did not improve over the baselines without any context at all. On the other hand, we

signifficantly improve over the baseline methods while using presentation context features as additional input of the machine learning methods described in Section 2.1.1.

2.3 Negative Implicit Feedback and Preferential Relations

One of the open problems in implicit feedback utilization is learning negative preference from implicit feedback. Several approaches were proposed for this task including uniform negative preference of all unvisited objects [10], considering low volume of feedback as negative preference [20] or defining special negative feedback feature [13], [29], [31].

We propose to utilize negative preference as relations among less and more preferred objects, i.e. to model a partial ordering $o_1 <_p o_2$. This model is based on the

Figure 3: An example of preference relations based on the feedback on a category page. Initially, objects $o_1 - o_4$ are visible. After some time, user scrolls and also object o_5 gets to the visible window. However, objects o_6 and o_7 remains outside of the visible area. If user clicks on object o_3, his/her behavior induces negative feedback on objects $o_{1,2,4,5}$ and we collect relations $o_{1,2,4,5} <_p o_3$. However, the intensity of $o_5 <_p o_3$ is smaller than for the other objects, because o_5 was visible only for a short period of time and thus it is more probable that user did not notice it.

work of Eckhardt et al. [7] proposing to consider user ratings (implicit feedback in our scenario) in the context of other objects available on the current page. Implicit preferential relations can be naturally obtained from implicit feedback collected on category pages, search results or similar pages. In such cases, user usually selects one (or more) objects out of the list of available objects for further inspection. By this behavior, user also implicitly provides negative feedback on the ignored choices and thus induce a preferential relation *ignored* $<_p$ *selected*. However, we need to approach to such negative feedback with caution as some of the options might not be visible for the user at all, or only for a very short time. This is quite serious problem, because, in average, only 47% of the catalogue page content was visible in the browser window in our dataset. Thus, we also introduce intensity of the relation $<_p$ based on the visibility of the ignored object. **Figure 3** illustrates this.

We incorporate preferential relations into the recommendation pipeline by extending collected relations along the content-based similarity of both *ignored* and *selected* objects (decreasing level of similarity effectively decreases also the intensity of the relation). Afterwards, we apply re-ranking approach taking output of some baseline recommender and re-order the objects so that the relations with higher intensity holds. Re-ranking algorithm considers the relations according to the increasing intensity and corrects the ordering induced by the relation. Thus, more intense relations should be preferred in case of conflicts. Details of the re-ranking algorithm can be found in [22].

3   Evaluation

In this section, we would like to report on the experiments conducted to evaluate models and methods utilizing multimodal implicit feedback. However, let us first briefly describe the dataset and evaluation procedures.

3.1   Evaluation Procedure

The dataset of multimodal user feedback (including presentation context) was collected by observing real visitors of a mid-sized Czech travel agency. The dataset was collected by the IPIget tool [17] over the period of more than one year, contains over 560K records and is available for research purposes[3]. In addition to the feedback features, the dataset also contains several content-based attributes of objects and thus enables usage of content-based recommender systems as well.

In evaluation of the methods, we considered following tasks:

- *Purchase prediction* based on the other feedback available for particular user-object pair. This scenario provides preliminary results for the methods aiming to estimate user rating $\bar{r}$.
- *Recommending purchased objects*. In this scenario, we employ leave-one-out cross-validation protocol on purchased objects (i.e., for each purchased object, all other feedback is used as a train set and we aim to recommend object, which was actually purchased by the user).
- *Recommending "future" user actions*. In this scenario, we use older user feedback (usually 2/3 of available feedback per user) as a train set. During the recommendation phase, we recommend top-k objects to each user, while the objects from the test set visited by the user should appear on top of the list.

In several of our previous works (see, e.g., [21] or the results of Matrix Factorization [11] in Table 3) we have shown that purely collaborative methods are not very suitable for small e-commerce enterprises due to the ongoing cold-start problem. Thus, we mostly focus on the content-based and hybrid recommending techniques. More specifically, we utilized Vector Space Model (VSM) [14],

Table 1: Results (nDCG) of *purchase prediction task* based on multimodal implicit feedback and presentation context. The task was considered as ranking (i.e., purchased objects should appear on top of the list of all visited objects).

Method	Dwell Time	Multimodal feedback	Feedback + Context	Feedback + aggregated BP	Feedback + individual BP
Heuristical with CDF	0.663	0.712	0.780	0.696	0.690
Heuristical with STD	0.747	0.703	0.856	0.695	0.704
Linear Regression	0.747	0.789	0.917	0.804	**0.925**
J48 decision tree	0.663	0.722	0.908	0.839	0.876

Table 2: Results (nDCG) of *recommending purchased objects* task. Combination of most-popular and VSM recommender was used to derive the list of objects. *Aggregated BP* denotes baseline predictors aggregated for a particular feedback feature over all available context, *individual BP* introduces a baseline predictor for each pair of contextual and feedback feature, *Feedback + Context* treats contextual features as additional input oft he methods estimating $\bar{r}$.

Method	Binary Feedback	Dwell Time	Multimodal feedback	Feedback + Context	Feedback + aggregated BP	Feedback + individual BP
Heuristics with CDF		0.255	0.257	0.253	0.258	0.257
Heuristics with STD	0.255	0.208	0.174	0.196	0.161	0.158
Linear Regression		0.256	0.254	0.176	0.252	0.251
J48 decision tree		0.238	0.256	**0.273**	0.240	0.248

---

[3]http://bit.ly/2tWtRg2

Table 3: Results (nDCG) of *recommending future interactions* task with re-ranking based on the preferencial relations.

Method	nDCG
VSM + Preferential Relations	**0.4381**
VSM	0.4376
Popular SimCat + Preferential Relations	0.3982
Popular SimCat	0.3962
Matrix Factorization + Preferential Relations	0.220
Matrix Factorization	0.138

its combination with the most popular recommendations and a hybrid algorithm proposing most popular objects from the categories similar (based on collaborative filtering) to the visited ones [22]. As we consider recommending problem as a ranking optimization, all methods were evaluated w.r.t. normalized discounted cumulative gain (nDCG).

3.2 Results and Discussion

Results of several methods aiming to learn estimated rating $\bar{r}$ based on various feature sets are displayed in Table 1 (purchase prediction task) and Table 2 (recommending purchased objects task). As we can see in Table 1, multimodal feedback significantly improves purchase prediction capability across all methods. Usage of presentation context can further improve the results, if used as additional input feature (*Feedback + Context*). However, if the contextual features are used as baseline predictors, the results across all methods are inferior to the results of *Feedback + Context* with just one exception. In several cases, the results are worse than using multimodal feedback alone. This observation indicates that some more complex dependence exists between implicit feedback, presentation context and user preference. Although it seems that the examined machine learning methods can partially discover this relation, another option to try is to hand-pick only several relevant contextual scenarios instead of the global model applied so far. Results of recommendation task also revealed a potential problem of overfitting on the purchase prediction task. *Linear regression*, although it performed the best in purchase prediction scenario, did not improve over binary feedback baseline. On the other hand, we can conclude that if a suitable rating prediction is selected, multimodal implicit feedback together with presentation context can improve the list of recommended objects.

Results of re-ranking approach based on preferential relations are depict in **Table 3**. Re-ranking based on preferential relations improved results of all evaluated recommending algorithms, although the improvement was rather modest in case of VSM. During evaluation, we observed that in case of VSM, only the relations with highest intensity should be applied to improve the results. For matrix factorization approach, on the other hand, also relations with very low intensities should be incorporated. Another point is that the offline evaluation is naturally focused on mere learning past user behavior and both VSM and Popular SimCat are largely biased towards exploitation in exploration vs. exploitation problem [27]. Hence, there

may be further benefits of using preferential relations in online scenarios.

4 Conclusions

In this paper, we describe our work in progress towards utilizing multimodal implicit feedback in small e-commerce enterprises. Specifically, we focused on three related tasks. Integrate multiple types of feedback collected on the detail of an object into an estimated user rating $\bar{r}$, incorporate presentation context into the previous model and utilize negative implicit feedback collected on category pages. We propose models and methods for each of the task and also provide evaluation w.r.t. top-k ranking.

Although the proposed methods statistically significantly improved over the baselines, the relative improvement is not too large, so our work is not finished yet. One of the important future tasks is to perform online evaluation as the offline evaluation was focused on the exploitation only. Further tasks are to propose context incorporation models specific for some context-feedback feature pairs, explore other possibilities to incorporate negative feedback and also to evaluate unified approach integrating all presented methods.

Acknowledgment

The work on this project was supported by Czech grant P46. Source codes and datasets for incorporation of presentation context can be obtained from http://bit.ly/2rJZzg3, source codes of preferential relations approach can be obtained from http://bit.ly/2symm17 and raw dataset can be obtained from http://bit.ly/2tWtRg2.

References

[1] Adomavicius, G. & Tuzhilin, A. Context-Aware Recommender Systems. *Recommender Systems Handbook, Springer US*, **2015**, 191-226

[2] Baltrunas, L. & Amatriain, X.: Towards time-dependant recommendation based on implicit feedback. *In CARS 2009 (RecSys)*.

[3] de Campos, L. M.; Fernandez-Luna, J. M.; Huete, J. F. & Rueda-Morales, M. A. Combining content-based and collaborative recommendations: A hybrid approach based on Bayesian networks. *International Journal of Approximate Reasoning*, **2010**, *51*, 785 – 799

[4] Carpi, T.; Edemanti, M.; Kamberoski, E.; Sacchi, E.; Cremonesi, P.; Pagano, R. & Quadrana, M. Multi-stack Ensemble for Job Recommendation. *In proceedings of the Recommender Systems Challenge, ACM*, **2016**, 8:1-8:4

[5] Claypool, M,; Le, P.; Wased, M. & Brown, D.: Implicit interest indicators. *In IUI '01, ACM*, **2001**, 33-40.

[6] Cremonesi, P.; Garzotto, F.; Turrin, R.: User-Centric vs. System-Centric Evaluation of Recommender Systems. *In INTERACT 2013, Springer LNCS 8119*, **2013**, 334-351

[7] Eckhardt, A.; Horvath, T. & Vojtas, P. PHASES: A User Profile Learning Approach for Web Search. *In WI-IAT '07, IEEE Computer Society*, **2007**, 780-783

[8] Fang, Y. & Si, L. A Latent Pairwise Preference Learning Approach for Recommendation from Implicit Feedback. *In CIKM 2012, ACM*, **2012**, 2567-2570

[9] Hidasi, B. & Tikk, D.: Initializing Matrix Factorization Methods on Implicit Feedback Databases. *J. UCS*, **2013**, *19*, 1834-1853

[10] Hu, Y.; Koren, Y. & Volinsky, C.: Collaborative Filtering for Implicit Feedback Datasets. *In ICDM 2008, IEEE* **2008**, 263-272

[11] Koren, Y.; Bell, R. & Volinsky, C. Matrix Factorization Techniques for Recommender Systems. *Computer, IEEE Computer Society Press*, **2009**, *42*, 30-37

[12] Lai, Y., Xu, X., Yang, Z., Liu, Z. User interest prediction based on behaviors analysis. *Int. Journal of Digital Content Technology and its Applications*, 6 (13), **2012**, 192-204

[13] Lee, D. H. and Brusilovsky, P.: Reinforcing Recommendation Using Implicit Negative Feedback. *In UMAP 2009*, Springer, LNCS, **2009**, *5535*, 422-427

[14] Lops, P.; de Gemmis, M. & Semeraro, G. Content-based Recommender Systems: State of the Art and Trends. Recommender Systems Handbook, Springer, **2011**, 73-105

[15] Mishra, S. K. & Reddy, M. A Bottom-up Approach to Job Recommendation System. *In proceedings of the Recommender Systems Challenge, ACM*, **2016**, 4:1-4:4

[16] Ostuni, V. C.; Di Noia, T.; Di Sciascio, E. & Mirizzi, R.: Top N recommendations from implicit feedback leveraging linked open data. *In RecSys 2013, ACM*, **2013**, 85-92.

[17] Peska, L.: IPIget – The Component for Collecting Implicit User Preference Indicators. In ITAT 2014, Ustav informatiky AV CR, **2014**, 22-26, http://itat.ics.upjs.sk/workshops.pdf

[18] Peska, L.: Using the Context of User Feedback in Recommender Systems. *MEMICS 2016*, EPTSC 233, **2016**, 1-12.

[19] Peska, L.: Linking Content Information with Bayesian Personalized Ranking via Multiple Content Alignments. *To appear in HT 2017, ACM*, **2017**

[20] Peska, L. & Vojtas, P.: Negative implicit feedback in e-commerce recommender systems *In WIMS 2013, ACM*, **2013**, 45:1-45:4

[21] Peska, L. & Vojtas, P.: Recommending for Disloyal Customers with Low Consumption Rate. *In SOFSEM 2014, Springer, LNCS 8327*, **2014**, 455-465

[22] Peska, L. & Vojtas, P. Using Implicit Preference Relations to Improve Recommender System. *J Data Semant*, 6(1), **2017**, 15-30.

[23] Peska, L. & Vojtas, P. Towards Complex User Feedback and Presentation Context in Recommender Systems. *BTW 2017 Workshops, GI-Edition, LNI, P-266*, **2017**, 203-207

[24] Radlinski, F. & Joachims, T. Query chains: learning to rank from implicit feedback. *In ACM SIGKDD 2005, ACM*, **2005**, 239-248

[25] Raman, K.; Shivaswamy, P. & Joachims, T.: Online Learning to Diversify from Implicit Feedback. *In KDD 2012, ACM*, **2012**, 705-713

[26] Rendle, S.; Freudenthaler, C.; Gantner, Z. & Schmidt-Thieme, L. BPR: Bayesian Personalized Ranking from Implicit Feedback. *In UAI 2009, AUAI Press*, **2009**, 452-461.

[27] Rubens, N.; Kaplan, D. & Sugiyama, M. Active Learning in Recommender Systems. *In Recommender Systems Handbook, Springer US*, **2011**, 735-767

[28] Xiao, W.; Xu, X.; Liang, K.; Mao, J. & Wang, J. Job Recommendation with Hawkes Process: An Effective Solution for RecSys Challenge 2016. *In proceedings of the Recommender Systems Challenge, ACM*, **2016**, 11:1-11:4

[29] Yang, B.; Lee, S.; Park, S. & Lee, S.: Exploiting Various Implicit Feedback for Collaborative Filtering. *In WWW 2012, ACM*, **2012**, 639-640.

[30] Yi, X.; Hong, L.; Zhong, E.; Liu, N. N. & Rajan, S. Beyond Clicks: Dwell Time for Personalization. *In RecSys 2014, ACM*, **2014**, 113-120.

[31] Zhang, C. & Cheng, X. An Ensemble Method for Job Recommender Systems. *In proceedings of the Recommender Systems Challenge, ACM*, **2016**, 2:1-2:4

[32] Zheng, Y.; Burke, R. & Mobasher, B. Recommendation with Differential Context Weighting. *In UMAP 2013, Springer*, **2013**, 152-164

[33] Zibriczky, D. A Combination of Simple Models by Forward Predictor Selection for Job Recommendation. *In proceedings of the Recommender Systems Challenge, ACM*, **2016**, 9:1-9:4

Index

Bajer, L., 120, 136
Bayer, J., 65
Borovička, T., 144
Brejová, B., 27, 48
Brunetto, R., 57
Buk, Z., 153

Cinková, S., 5
Čížek, P., 65

Danel, M., 71

Faigl, J., 65

Grad-Gyenge, L., 210
Gurský, P., 23, 35

Hana, J., 1
Hercig, T., 176
Holeňa, M., 93, 120, 129, 136, 144
Horváth, B., 218
Horváth, T., 218
Hourová, B., 176
Hradil, J., 223

Ibrova, A., 153

Jelínek, T., 181

Kalina, J., 78
Kettnerová, V., 15
Kliegr, T., 235
Knöll, F., 86
Kopecky, M., 228
Kopp, M., 93
Kordík, P., 106
Král, P., 186
Krejzl, P., 176
Kuchař, J., 235
Kůrková, V., 100

Lenc, L., 176, 186
Ligęza, A., 2
Linková, M., 23
Lipovský, M., 27
Lopatková, M., 15

Motl, J., 106
Mráz, F., 40

Navara, M., 112
Neruda, R., 159
Nikl, M., 93
Novák, M., 193

Okhrin, O., 3
Otto, F., 40

Pavel, R., 35
Peštová, B., 78
Perfilieva, I., 167
Peska, L., 240
Pitra, Z., 120, 136
Plátek, M., 40
Puchýř, J., 129

Rabatin, R., 48
Repický, J., 120, 136
Rosa, R., 201

Šabata, T., 144
Simko, V., 86
Šindelář, J., 112
Skrbek, M., 71
Soukup, L., 4
Steinberger, J., 176
Stepanovsky, M., 153

Trunda, O., 57

Veleminska, J., 153

Vernerová, A., 5
Vidnerová, P., 159
Vinař, T., 27, 48
Vlašánek, P., 167
Vojíř, S., 235
Vojtas, P., 228
Vomlelova, M., 228

Zeman, V., 235

www.ingramcontent.com/pod-product-compliance
Lightning Source LLC
LaVergne TN
LVHW060138070326
832902LV00018B/2848